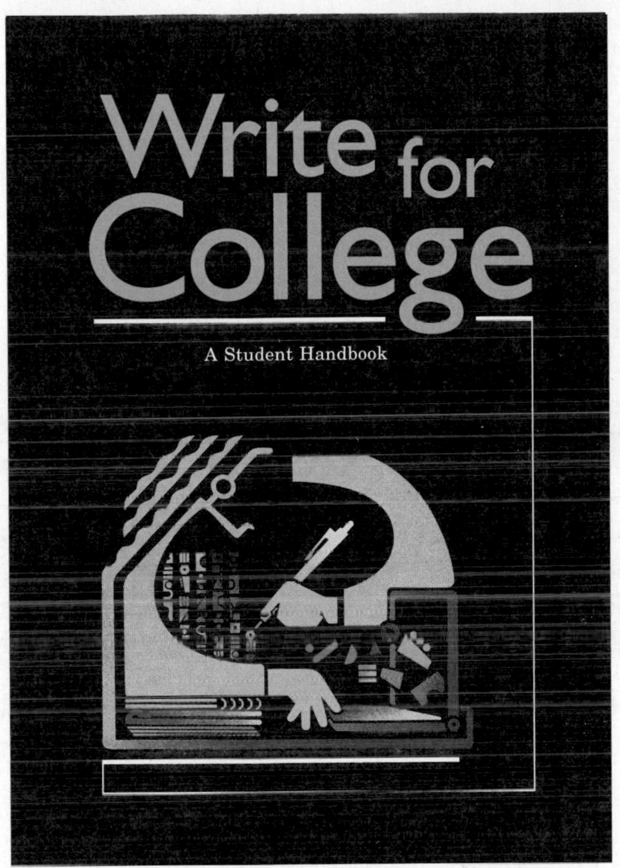

Written and Compiled by
Patrick Sebranek, Verne Meyer, and Dave Kemper

Illustrated by
Chris Krenzke

WRITE SOURCE®

GREAT SOURCE EDUCATION GROUP
a division of Houghton Mifflin Company
Wilmington, Massachusetts

Reviewers

Mark Bazata
Oshkosh West High School
Oshkosh, Wisconsin

Randolph Bernard
Lafayette Parish School System
Lafayette, Louisiana

MarlaKay Dandrea
Gahanna–Jefferson Public Schools
Gahanna, Ohio

Raymond F. Klejmont
School District of DeSoto County
Arcadia, Florida

Lenora Laverpool
Alief Independent School District
Houston, Texas

Scott McLaughlin
Huntington Beach Union High School District
Huntington Beach, California

Christine Neuner
Iberia Parish School System
New Iberia, Louisiana

Ms. Marie Raduazzo
Arlington Public Schools
Arlington, Massachusetts

Elizabeth Rehberger
Huntington Beach High School
Huntington Beach, California

Sean Rochester
Parkway Central School District
St. Louis, Missouri

Stephanie Saltikov-Izabal
Huntington Beach High School
Huntington Beach, California

Catherine Wrenn
Carl Schurz High School
Chicago, Illinois

Technology Connection for *Write for College*

Visit our Web site for additional student models, writing prompts, multimedia reports, information about submitting your writing, and more.

The Write Source Web site . . . . **www.thewritesource.com**

Printed in the United States of America

International Standard Book Number: 978-0-669-00044-3 (hardcover)

4 5 6 7 8 9 10 –1083– 12 11 10

International Standard Book Number: 978-0-669-00031-3 (softcover)

7 8 9 10 –1083– 12

4500361420

Using the Handbook

Write for College emphasizes the kinds of writing that will prepare you for college course work. However, the handbook covers much more than writing. It also provides information and guidelines for speaking, thinking, critical reading, note taking, test taking, researching, and nearly every other topic essential to success.

The **Table of Contents** gives you a list of the major sections in the handbook and the chapters found in each. The **Index** includes every topic discussed in the handbook. The numbers found there are page numbers. The **Cross-References** throughout the handbook tell you where to turn for more information about a topic.

As you page through the **Body** of your handbook, notice the wide variety of information. Pay special attention to "The Forms of Writing" (pages 143–315), "The Research Center" (pages 317–399), and "The Testing Center" (pages 465–507). Within these sections, you should find almost everything you need to handle assigned writing tasks and exams. Continue to search for other helpful material—and then make sure to use it.

> "Knowledge is of two kinds. We know a subject ourselves, or we know where we can find information upon it."
>
> —Samuel Johnson

Contents

THE WRITING PROCESS

THE BASIC ELEMENTS OF WRITING

WRITER'S RESOURCE

The Forms of Writing

The Research Center

The Tools of Learning

The Testing Center

Proofreader's Guide

Almanac

Why Write?

Writing is important (1) because it helps you derive meaning from your experiences, (2) because it helps you think more clearly, which in turn helps you learn more effectively, and (3) because it helps you form new understandings or make new connections.

All three of these points are important reasons to write, and will, most assuredly, be seconded by your writing instructors. Rather than have us (or your instructors) tell you why writing is so valuable, read what the following writers have to say about the power of putting pen to paper or fingers to the keyboard. Their thoughts eloquently echo these same three reasons.

Deriving Meaning from Experiences

"Writing is a long process of self-understanding."
—Edwidge Danticat

"To write is to sit in judgment on oneself."
—Henrik Ibsen

Thinking More Clearly

"I see only one rule: to be clear. If I am not clear, then my entire world crumbles into nothing."
—Stendhal

"Writing and rewriting is a constant search for what one is trying to say."
—John Updike

Forming New Understandings

"I learn by going where I have to go."
—Theodore Roethke

"I have never written a book that was not born out of a question that I needed to answer for myself."
—May Sarton

"In search of my mother's garden I found my own."
—Alice Walker

Experiencing the Power of Writing

Write for College is designed to facilitate your academic writing. The handbook contains guidelines and models for essays, reports, research papers, and so on. As you page through the text, you will begin to appreciate how extensively we cover a variety of academic forms.

In addition to your assigned writing tasks, we urge you to practice "personal writing" and "writing to learn." The true power of the pen manifests itself as you write for yourself as well as for your instructors and your peers.

Personal Writing

What makes personal writing (in a notebook or journal) so attractive is the freedom that it offers you to write when you want, where you want, and about what you want. (Any thought, feeling, or experience can be a starting point.) Naturally, it is most helpful when you write on a regular basis. Don't worry about how your writing sounds or looks; you are writing for no one except yourself. New insights will emerge as you make an honest effort; and, in time, personal writing will make you feel a little sharper, as if your senses have been fine-tuned.

"Regular notebook writing acts as a wake-up call, a daily reminder to keep all your senses alert."

—Ralph Fletcher

Writing to Learn

You should also write in a classroom notebook about new concepts covered in your classes. Again, this type of writing is completely under your control. You can react to lectures or readings, describe processes, analyze new concepts, and make thoughtful connections. The linearity of writing—recording one word after another—leads to coherent and sustained thought. It personalizes learning so you understand new ideas more effectively. Writing in this way serves as the ultimate learning tool. (See pages 422–423 for more information.)

"How do I know what I think until I see what I say?"

—E. M. Forster

BOTTOM LINE

Your ability to write well is your key to academic success. In most of your classes, you will have to show your mastery of new concepts in assigned writings. Also remember that writing for yourself—free from the gravitational pull of grades and expectations—will help you think clearly about your experiences and your course work and increase your confidence in your writing ability. (Real improvement in writing comes through regular practice.) Approach all writing, then, as a special opportunity to learn and to grow, and you will soon appreciate its value in the classroom and beyond.

The Writing Process

One Writer's Process

How do you get from the start ("My sociology instructor gave me this writing assignment.") to the finish ("This may be my best essay yet.")? You may know the answer already: You use the writing process. This important process can help you . . .

- collect and focus your thoughts (*prewriting*),
- generate an initial version of your writing *(drafting)*,
- improve upon your writing *(revising)*, and
- prepare it for submission *(editing/proofreading)*.

You should also remember that (1) the writing process is personal—different writers follow different routes; (2) it's reciprocal—you may, for example, go from *revising* back to *prewriting* and then to *revising* again; and (3) it's adaptable to any writing task—from research papers to responding to prompts.

WHAT'S AHEAD

In this chapter, you will see firsthand how a writer uses the writing process to shape an initial writing idea into an effective personal essay.

Prewriting and Planning

Student writer Mark Klompien received the following assignment in his composition class:

> **Write a two- or three-page essay relating a personal experience to a current cultural, social, or political issue.**

As you follow his work on the next four pages, you'll see how he collected and focused his thoughts for writing. During this initial step in the process, he carried out a number of effective prewriting strategies, including clustering and freewriting.

Selecting a Subject

Choosing a subject was no problem. Mark decided to write about the time he traveled to Valle Verde, Mexico, with his youth group. The people he met, and their living conditions, made him think about many issues, including the current debate about illegal immigration.

Collecting Ideas

As part of his initial thinking on his subject, Mark listed these three questions: *What was at the core of this experience? What should be the specific focus of my writing? What details should be included?* To explore possible answers, Mark began his prewriting with a cluster.

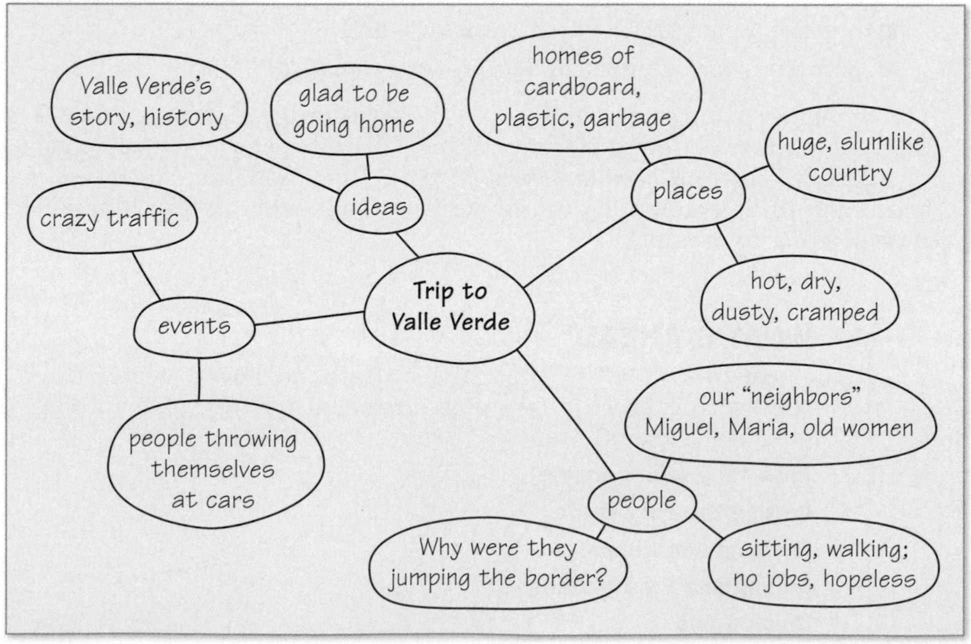

Freewriting for Ideas

To continue gathering and focusing his thoughts, Mark wrote freely about three dominant ideas in his cluster.

Huge, slumlike country . . .

Everything around seemed hopeless. Mothers were often alone as their husbands left for jobs elsewhere because they couldn't support the family. But what about the mothers?

Visions of heat waves, dust devils, dry wind constantly beating down. Many buildings are empty outside of Tijuana. Graffiti. Men walking around the city when it seems they should be at work. Many kids aren't in school. Cars on blocks, half-finished buildings, stacks of bricks salvaged from buildings, shacks of tin and plywood, packed together like sardines.

People there are like me. They are desperate to cross the border.

Why are these people jumping the border?

Never mind facts, figures, and rational arguments, remember REAL LIVES! Remember the lady whose husband took off under pressures of the family . . . lost his job and fled because of the debt he'd run up.

One guy we met had fled north because of the violence and civil wars in the South of the country. His brother was shot. He feared for his own life . . . This is one reason refugees fled to "Valle Verde" (the green valley?).

The city was established because of a large flood . . . these hopeless folks needed some hope and a place to live.

The immigration issue is often about facts and figures and how much it costs Americans. We look at immigrants as criminals who cost us money. But what about Miguel and Maria living hopelessly in Mexico—a lost brother, a lost husband. You see it in their homes, their faces, and especially their EYES.

Glad to be going home . . .

We jumped back in the station wagon and headed home. We could return to our prosperity. I thought about a good dinner and clean water that didn't need to be delivered by truck. I wished I could take the friends we met home.

What changed? Did this experience affect my return home? Should we get involved in fixing these problems? What should I do with my life?

Others in the group? Will this experience affect them when they decide what clothes to buy, when they vote in the next election, and when they choose a major in college? We must remember this trip and encourage each other.

Carrying Out Additional Research

Mark knew that he needed to connect his personal experience with an important issue currently in the news. His issue—illegal immigration—was hotly debated at both the state and federal levels. He needed to know more about the immigration problem, so he consulted current sources addressing this issue. (His notes from two magazine articles are listed below.)

Notes on Illegal Immigration

Ramos, Jorge. Dying to Cross: The Worst Immigrant Tragedy in the History of the United States. New York: HarperCollins, 2005.

- the death of 19 people: a symbol of people "willing to assume whatever risks they must" (166)
- Coyotes (traffickers in human labor) and migrants: small parts of grand governmental failures—Mexican poverty and U.S. reliance on cheap, often undocumented labor
- In 2003, 80 abandoned Mexicans and Central Americans in locked trailer near Houston > sweltering heat kills 19 of these illegal immigrants
- a complicated issue: "not just a humanitarian question," also "a question of economics and national security" (XVI)

Marek, Angie. "Back at Home, but Nowhere to Hide." U.S. News and World Report (May 1, 2006) 35.

- Pro-immigration, traffic-blocking rally near the federal courthouse in Kansas City—two weeks later, a counter rally of 500 people for tougher immigration policies
- The congressional compromise hammered out one day, dropped the next > no escape for members of Congress on recess—immigration a hot issue
- Judiciary committee member, John Cornyn of Texas, claims loopholes in the compromise plan: criminals can get green cards
- The Senate Judiciary Committee to study the economic impact of immigrant labor

Establishing a Focus

Mark next considered a focus for his writing. After reviewing all of his prewriting and collecting notes, he decided to concentrate on the living conditions of the people he met in Mexico and how these conditions result in illegal immigration. He then wrote this working thesis statement to serve as a general guide for his planning and drafting:

Working Thesis Statement: Illegal immigration is about real people with real problems.

NOTE: A thesis statement usually contains two main elements: a manageable or limited subject *(illegal immigration)* plus a specific feeling or idea about it *(the real people and problems behind it).*

Designing a Writing Plan

Mark's thesis statement establishes a basic direction and focus for his writing. At this point, Mark was ready to sketch out a basic writing plan. He decided to share significant aspects of his trip before making a connection to the reality of illegal immigration.

Basic Plan

- Entry into Mexico
- Description of Tijuana
- Description of Valle Verde
- People in Valle Verde
- Reality of Immigration Problem

Getting Ready to Write

Mark read through his freewriting one last time for ideas to help him get started on his first draft. As you can see below, he noted important points or feelings to include in his writing:

→ Remember Maria!

Everything around seemed hopeless. Mothers were often alone as their husbands left for jobs elsewhere because they couldn't support the family. But what about the mothers?

broken windows

Visions of heat waves, dust devils, dry wind constantly beating down whatever is around. Many buildings are empty outside of Tijuana. Most concrete is covered with graffiti. Many men walk around the city when it seems they should be at work. Many kids aren't in school. Remember cars on blocks, half-finished buildings, stacks of bricks saved/salvaged from past buildings, shacks made of tin and plywood, packed together like sardines.

← How old was Miguel—16? 17?

People there are just like you and me. What do they think about the situation? They obviously are desperate to cross the border.

Writing the First Draft

In his first draft, Mark pulls together ideas, images, and questions that address his thesis. He completed this draft in one sitting, using his basic plan as a general guide for his writing. He also referred to his collecting ideas and notes as needed during his drafting.

The writer identifies the thesis of his writing.

Though the illegal immigration problem is often about facts and figures, the issue is much bigger. Illegal immigration is about real people with real problems.

Last year our youth group traveled to Mexico on a service trip. We didn't know what to expect. What would the mission outside of Tijuana look like and how would we be accepted?

He uses details from his freewriting to help the reader visualize the setting and the people.

As we traveled the riddled road through Tijuana we saw grim poverty all around. In the shantytown on the outskirts the dusty road at times was lined with cars on blocks. Men who should be at work stand around. Children aren't in school.

On daily trips around the city I met a few of the inhabitants. Miguel scowled at us from his seat—a five-gallon bucket. He recalled the story of his brother's murder in the civil war of the south and how after that he fled here, to Valle Verde.

The writer focuses on getting his ideas on paper rather than on producing correct copy.

Maria was another refugee, speaking in broken English. With a baby hanging from her side, she told me about her husband. After losing his job, the household bills kept rising, so he left.

I'm still haunted by Miguel's and maria's eyes. Nobody's eyes should have that look.

General background information is shared.

Why did they (and so many others) come here? The city was built as a refugee camp by citizens washed out of Tijuana by a flood. With the rains, the hope the city had for its future was washed away as well.

A small town started on a dry dusty plain outside of Tijuana. The people took cardboard, plastic, tin, and plywood to build homes close together like sardines. When the wind blows through them, they make a depressing moan. Though they squatted on land owned by the government there was little the government could do but let them stay.

Mostly the front yards are bare except for the litter—plastic wrappers and rusting soup cans. Latrines are dug into the tough dirt by the women. Every household has at least one bone-skinny dog guarding the homes filled with nothing.

In closing, the writer reconnects with his thesis—the issue of immigration.

Whatever one thinks about the immigration problem, this place and these people can't be forgotten. Can we neglect real people and their situations when we deal with the immigration issue?

Link to the Traits

As Mark developed his first draft, he focused on three key traits: *ideas, organization,* and *voice.*

Ideas Mark connected his initial ideas about the topic and entertained new ideas as they came to mind.

Organization He included beginning, middle, and ending parts.

Voice He let his words flow freely, as if he were in a conversation with the reader.

Revising and Refining

Mark took a break before he reviewed his first draft. When he was ready to review his work, he made a printed copy of his draft and looked carefully at the developing ideas. He wrote brief notes in the margin, indicating parts that needed to be reworked, expanded, or cut. In the copy below, you can see some of the changes he made.

First Revision

Writer's Comments:

Need to expand opening.

Though the illegal immigration problem is often
This political and social problem goes way beyond border
about facts and figures, the issue is much bigger.^ Illegal
crossings.
immigration is about real people with real problems.

Focus more on trip . . . border guards and vendors.

Last year our youth group traveled to Mexico on a service
Two adult supervisers drove us in vans to a mission where we
trip.^ ~~We didn't know what to expect. What would the mission~~
planned to help residents improve there housing and promote
~~outside of Tijuana look like and how would we be accepted?~~
the work of the mission. As we approached the boarder . . .

Add more detail here.

As we traveled the riddled road through Tijuana we saw
dilapidated buildings and graffiti-covered walls
^ ~~grim poverty all around~~. In the shantytown on the outskirts
junker beside shacks
the dusty road at times was lined with^ cars on blocks^. ~~Men~~

Drop this idea for now.

Bone-skinny dogs and spindly chickens . . .
^ ~~who should be at work stand around. Children aren't in~~
~~school~~

Tell more about Miguel—how he cried!

On daily trips around the city I met a few of the
sitting on
inhabitants. Miguel^ ~~scowled at us from his seat~~ a five-gallon
asked me about my home. After answering, I returned
bucket,^ He recalled the story of his brother's murder in the
the question. Miguel's head sank and he clenched a first to hold
civil war of the south and how after that he fled here, to
back tears.
Valle Verde.

Maria was another refugee, speaking in broken English. With a baby hanging from her side, she told me about her husband. After losing his job, the household bills kept rising, so he left.

Too subjective?

~~I'm still haunted by Miguel's and maria's eyes. Nobody's eyes should have that look.~~

Why did they (and so many others) come here? The city was built as a refugee camp by citizens washed out of Tijuana by a flood. With the rains, the hope the city had for its future was washed away as well.

A small town started on a dry dusty plain outside of Tijuana. The people took cardboard, plastic, tin, and plywood to build shacks. ~~homes close together like sardines.~~ When the wind blows through them, they make a depressing moan. Though the people ~~they~~ squatted on land owned by the government there was little the government could do but let them stay.

Mostly the front yards are bare except for the litter—plastic wrappers and rusting soup cans. Latrines are dug into the tough dirt by the women. Every household has at least one bone-skinny dog guarding the homes filled with nothing.

Include many of these underlined details earlier, in the second middle paragraph.

Whatever one thinks about the immigration problem, this place and these people can't be forgotten. Can we neglect real people and their situations when we deal with the immigration issue?

Need more facts here about the causes of illegal immigration. Review my research.

The causes of illegal immigration are clear: The government has failed to deal with poverty in Mexico, and we came to rely on cheap undocumented labor (Ramos, 2005). On a more personal level, thousands like Miguel and Maria have simply lost hope. To these people, finding jobs in the U.S. and having access to basic services . . .

Peer Reviewing

After revising his first draft, Mark asked a writing peer to review his work. Her comments are in the margin. Mark noted her concerns and made additional changes in his essay, some of which you can see below.

Second Revision

Peer Reviewer's Comments:

What facts and figures? What does the news say about the problem?

In recent months, TV news and other media have carried two
~~Though the illegal immigration problem is often about~~
types of stories about Mexicans entering the United States
~~facts and figures, the issue is much bigger.~~ This political
illegally. In the first type . . .
and social problem goes way beyond border crossings. Illegal
immigration is about real people with real problems.

I was a part of a 10 day
Last year, ~~our~~ youth group ~~traveled to Mexico~~ on a service
project in Mexico.
~~trip.~~ Two adult supervisers drove us in vans to a mission
where we planned to help residents improve there housing
and promote the work of the mission. As we approached the

What questions did they ask?

where we were going and how long we would stay,
boarder, three armed guards stopped us and asked ~~questions,~~
questions
~~which~~ we expected, but not what happened next. Less than
50 feet from the checkpoint, dozens of street vendors mobbed
our moving vehicles—risking broken limbs for precious U.S.
dollars.

From there, we followed a past the
~~As we traveled the~~ riddled road ~~through Tijuana we~~
of Tijuana. Beyond its
~~saw~~ dilapidated buildings and graffiti-covered walls. ~~In the~~

Does this shantytown have a name?

outskirts lay Valle Verde, a town whose name means Green Valley.
~~shanty town on the outskirts the dusty road at times was~~
There, sat
~~lined with~~ junker cars on blocks beside shacks. Bone-skinny
dogs and spindly chickens guarded front-yard latrines.
Rusting soup cans and plastic food wrappers littered yards.
Hot breezes played rickety buildings like wind chimes.

People fill Valle Verde, but don't want to be there. One individual,
~~On daily trips around the city I met a few of the~~

These details about Miguel are important and tie in with your thesis.

~~inhabitants.~~ Miguel, sitting on a five-gallon bucket, asked
me about my home. After answering, I returned the question.
Miguel's head sank and he clenched a fist to hold back tears.
had fled from the south after his only brother was shot dead
He ~~recalled the story of his brother's murder in the civil war~~
in the civil war there.
~~of the south and how after that he fled here, to Valle Verde.~~

Tell more about Maria.

Another English-speaking named Maria offered her story.

~~Maria was another~~ refugee, ~~speaking in broken English~~ grimy infant on her hip, and three more running around, With a ~~baby~~ hanging ~~from her side, she told me about her~~ she told me how she once lived in a three-bedroom house . . . ~~husband. After losing his job, the household bills kept rising so he left.~~

History is interesting, but is it necessary to your focus?

~~Why did they (and so many others) come here? The city was built as a refugee camp by citizens washed out of Tijuana by a flood. With the rains, the hope the city had for its future was washed away as well. A small town started on a dry dusty plain outside of Tijuana. Though the people squatted on land owned by the government there was little the government could do but let them stay.~~

Which government, and who do you mean by "we"?

The causes of illegal immigration are clear: The Mexican government has failed to deal with poverty in Mexico, and ~~we~~ the U.S. came to rely on cheap undocumented labor (Ramos, 2005).

However, ~~O~~on a more personal level, thousands like Miguel and Maria have simply lost hope. They see crossing the border as the only option. To these people, finding jobs in the United States and having access to basic services are matters of survival.

What were the angry responses?

Labeling immigrants as "criminal" could be misconstrued.

Many U.S. citizens, quite understandably, respond angrily. "Illegals are breaking the law, taking our jobs, raising our taxes. They should apply legally and walk in the front door." According to one article, the economic impact of cheap labor and the concern that some ~~criminal~~ immigrants with criminal intent are getting green cards are two anger raising factors (Marek, 2006). The recent immigration rallies in the United States have only magnified concern over this issue, prompting emotional responses from people on all sides of the issue.

Ending shows you care. What are their choices with this issue?

~~Whatever one thinks about the illegal immigration problem, this place and these people can't be forgotten.~~ Do we send illegal immigrants back because we don't want to share our prosperity? Or do we . . . Can we neglect real people and their situations when we deal with the immigration issue? Before we answer . . .

Editing and Proofreading

After a peer review, Mark completed one more revision. Then he edited his writing for accuracy, using the computer spell-checker, his dictionary, and his writing handbook. Mark also asked a peer to check his paper for errors. After making corrections (see below) and adding a title, he printed out a final copy of the essay, carefully proofread it, and turned it in.

Escaping the "Green Valley"

In recent months, TV news and other media have carried two types of stories about Mexicans entering the United States illegally. In the first type, news cameras catch illegals sneaking across the Mexican-U.S. border. In the second type, reports show U.S. citizens angry about illegal ~~immigrant's~~ immigrants' access to jobs, education, and health care. This political and social problem goes way beyond border crossings. Illegal immigration is about real people with real problems.

A possessive form is corrected.

Last year, I was part of a youth group on a 10-day service project in Mexico. Two adult supervisers (supervisors) drove us in vans to a mission where we planned to help residents improve ~~there~~ their housing and promote the work of the mission. As we approached the ~~boarder~~ border, three armed guards stopped us and asked where we were going and how long we would stay, we (. We) expected questions but not what happened next. ~~Less~~ Fewer than 50 feet from the checkpoint, dozens of street vendors mobbed our moving vehicles—risking broken limbs for precious U.S. dollars.

Punctuation, spelling, and usage errors are addressed.

A comma splice is corrected.

From there, we followed a riddled road past the dilapidated buildings and graffiti-covered walls of Tijuana. Beyond its outskirts lay Valle Verde, a town whose name means "Green Valley." There, junker cars sat on blocks beside shacks. Bone-skinny dogs and spindly chickens guarded

Quotation marks are added to distinguish a word.

An added word corrects and clarifies the thought.

The present tense lends immediacy to the message.

A shift in verb tense is corrected.

One word reconnects to the thesis.

front-yard latrines. Rusting soup cans and plastic food wrappers littered yards, and hot breezes played rickety buildings like wind chimes. . . .

Another English-speaking refugee named Maria offered her story. With a grimy infant hanging on her hip, and three more children running around, she told me how she once lived in a three-bedroom house with her husband, who brought home a check every week. Later, he lost his job, ran up bills, and finally just left. Now Maria and the kids barely survive ~~survived~~ in a makeshift shack.

The causes of illegal immigration are clear: The Mexican government has failed to deal with poverty in Mexico, and the United States has come ~~came~~ to rely on cheap, undocumented labor (Ramos, 2005). However, on a more personal level, thousands like Miguel and Maria have simply lost hope. They see crossing the border as the only option. . . .

Many U.S. citizens, quite understandably, respond angrily: "Illegals are breaking the law, taking our jobs, raising our taxes. They should apply legally and walk in the front door." According to one article, the economic impact of cheap labor and the concern that some immigrants with criminal intent are getting green cards are two anger-raising factors (Marek, 2006). The recent immigration rallies in the United States have only magnified concern over this matter ~~issue~~, prompting emotional responses from people on all sides of the issue.

Do we send illegal immigrants back because we don't want to share our prosperity? Or do we make room for real people like Miguel and Maria? Before we answer, let's look beyond our own interests. Surely some empathy remains for desperate individuals who are simply trying to survive.

The Writing Process

QUICK GUIDE

The writing process is based on the following premise: An effective paper is almost always the result of a great deal of planning, writing, and rewriting (as demonstrated in Mark's essay). For the sake of discussion and analysis, the writing process is divided into the five steps listed below.

PREWRITING

1. Find a worthwhile idea to write about.
2. Learn as much as you can about the subject. (See page 25.)
3. Form a thesis and plan your writing.

WRITING THE FIRST DRAFT

1. Write the first draft while your prewriting is fresh in your mind.
2. Write as freely as you can, using your planning as a guide.
3. Keep writing until you come to a natural stopping point.

REVISING

1. Review your first draft, keeping in mind the purpose of the assignment, your thesis, and your audience.
2. Also have your instructor or a writing peer review your work.
3. Add, cut, rework, or rearrange ideas as necessary.

EDITING AND PROOFREADING

1. Read your final draft aloud to test it for sense and sound.
2. Check for errors in usage, punctuation, capitalization, spelling, and grammar. (Have a peer editor check your work as well.)
3. Prepare a neat final copy of your writing.
4. Proofread the final draft for errors before submitting it.

PUBLISHING

1. Submit your work in class or for publication.
2. Collect your best writing in a portfolio.

Insights into Writing

Remember that writing seldom follows a straight path. Writing is a backward as well as a forward activity, so don't expect to move neatly through the writing process. Writing by its very nature includes detours, wrong turns, and repeat visits.

Traits of Writing

Novelist Mary Gordon may be right: "No marks on paper can ever measure up to the word's music in the mind." But surely Shakespeare's rhythmic sonnets come close: "When to the sessions of sweet silent thought/I summon up remembrance of things past,/I sigh the lack of many a thing I sought, . . . " And certainly Gloria Naylor's stories snap with an intended beat: "That Butch Fuller is a no-'count ditch hound, and no decent woman would be seen talkin' to him."

Will your own writing ever "measure up"? There's only one way to ensure that it will, and that's by practicing the craft. That means you must write on a regular basis, as in every day. Nothing will help more. Second, you must read anything and everything—novels, nonfiction, poetry—internalizing the special rhythms of other writers. Third, you must acquire a working knowledge of the traits of effective writing. This chapter serves as an introduction to these traits.

WHAT'S AHEAD

The chapter presents the traits of writing—*ideas, organization, voice, word choice, sentence fluency,* and *conventions*—in action. A valuable traits-based checklist of effective writing is also included.

QUICK GUIDE

The six traits listed below identify the main features found in effective essays, stories, and articles. If you write with these traits in mind, you will most likely be pleased with the results.

IDEAS: Effective writing presents interesting and vital information about a specific topic. It has a clear purpose or focus, or as writer Donald Murray states, "It has a controlling vision, which orders what is being said." The ideas are thoroughly elaborated and analyzed and hold the reader's attention from start to finish.

ORGANIZATION: In terms of basic structure, good writing has a clearly developed beginning, middle, and ending. Within the text, transitions are used to show relationships between ideas. The overall arrangement of ideas unifies the writing and makes the writer's purpose clear.

VOICE: In the best writing, you can hear the writer's voice—his or her special way of expressing ideas and emotions. Voice gives writing personality: it shows that the writer sincerely cares about the topic and about the reader.

WORD CHOICE: In memorable writing, the nouns and verbs are specific. The modifiers are colorful (and used sparingly). The overall level of language helps to communicate the message and set an appropriate tone. In short, all the right words are in all the right places.

SENTENCE FLUENCY: Effective writing flows from sentence to sentence. But it isn't, by any means, predictable. Sentences vary in length, and they don't all begin in the same way. Sentence fluency gives rhythm to writing, which makes the writing enjoyable to read.

CONVENTIONS: Good writing follows the accepted standards of punctuation, mechanics, usage, and spelling. It is edited with care to ensure that the work is accurate and easy to follow.

(One additional trait to consider is the **presentation** of your writing. Effective writing looks inviting and follows guidelines for margins, spacing, indenting, and so on. See pages 125–132 and 352–353.)

The Traits in Action

On the next three pages, writing samples exhibit effective use of the traits of writing. Pay special attention to the note following each sample.

Ideas

The following paragraph focuses on a timely topic that is well developed with important details.

A number of scientific studies have found a connection between anorexia and excessive exercise. Researchers David Pierce and Frank Epling from the University of Alberta did one of the studies, and they used rats to explore the topic. Pierce and Epling placed rats in two cages. The rats in the first cage were given a functional running wheel, along with a reduced diet of one meal per day. The rats in the second cage were given a nonfunctional running wheel, but they also received a reduced diet of one meal per day. According to the two scientists, the rats with unlimited access to the functional running wheel ran each day, and gradually increased the amount of running; in addition, they started to eat less. At the end of one week, some rats in the first group stopped eating altogether and ran themselves to death. Rats in the second group had a happier ending. Because their running wheel did not function, these rats did not run, soon adapted to their reduced diet, and stayed healthy. Pierce and Epling concluded that given the opportunity to run, rats on a reduced diet would exercise to the point of hurting their health (McGovern 1–2).

- Details such as *explanations* and *descriptions* provide the reader with a clear picture of the study.

Organization

In this paragraph, a student writer classifies the medieval theory of temperament.

Medieval doctors believed that "four temperaments rule mankind wholly." According to this theory, each person has a distinctive temperament or personality (sanguine, phlegmatic, melancholic, or choleric) based on the balance of four elements in the body. The theory was built on Galen's and Hippocrates' notion of "humors," that the body contains blood, phlegm, black bile, and yellow bile that maintain the balance within the body. The sanguine person was dominated by blood: Blood was hot and moist, and the person was courageous and prone to laughter. The phlegmatic person was dominated by phlegm (mucous): Phlegm was cold and moist, and the person was calm and unemotional. The melancholic person was dominated by cold, dry black bile and was pensive, peevish, and solitary. The choleric person was dominated by hot, dry yellow bile and was inclined to be angry.

- The four temperaments are discussed according to the body's four "humors." This order makes the ideas easy to follow.

Voice

In the following passage, the writer takes a whimsical approach to defining the word *eclectic.*

Go-carting, Handel's *Messiah,* a blue bike, pump organs, box cities, tenth grade . . . "But what do these have to do with each other?" you wonder. Nothing. My memories, like the things I enjoy, can only be described in one way: *eclectic,* a word I find endlessly fascinating. *Ec-lec-tic.* Say it out loud, savoring each syllable—*ec . . . lec . . . tic.* Notice the different positions of your tongue. Odd how a word made of nothing more than clicking noises conveys meaning. I love to say the word. The lips do absolutely no work. Now try saying it with your lips separated as little as possible. It still works. All the action is done on the inside, a dance of the muscular tongue on the roof of your mouth. If I were a ventriloquist, I would use the word as often as possible. Notice how the sound emerges as you form the letters. *E*—here it comes right down the center, *cl*—out from either side, *e*—an open corridor, *c*—the sound cut off, *ti*—the sound exploding past the tongue and over the teeth until it's finally pinched off—*c*.

- From sentence to sentence, the writer's engaging voice comes through, exhibiting a strong personal attachment to the topic.

Word Choice

In this passage, the writer shares information about the people that Christopher Columbus first met in the Americas. The writer chooses his words very carefully to help the reader appreciate these people.

The word *Taino* means "men of the good," and from most indications, the Taino were very good. Living on tropical islands in the Caribbean, the indigenous people of "La Taina" developed gentle personalities. By all accounts, generosity and kindness directed daily life at the time of Taino contact with the Spanish. To understand the Taino world, picture South Pacific islands, lush and inviting. The people dwelled in small, spotless villages of neatly appointed thatch huts along inland rivers and coastal waters. These handsome people had no need of clothing for warmth. They bathed often, which prompted a curious royal law forbidding the practice. The Spanish obviously did not appreciate the benefits of regular bathing.

- Notice the specific verbs *(directed, picture, bathed, prompted)* and the colorful adjectives *(tropical, gentle, indigenous, lush, inviting, spotless).* These words create the image of an untroubled, idyllic lifestyle.

Sentence Fluency

This paragraph compares writing for the stage with screenwriting and emphasizes the differences between the two forms. To create a pleasing flow, the student writer varies the length and structure of her sentences.

Though playwriting and screenwriting seem similar, they are very different art forms. Since the time of Sophocles and Aeschylus 2,500 years ago, stage plays have had to work within the limits of sets, lighting, costumes, and a handful of special effects. As a result, stage plays have always focused on dialogue to tell their stories. Screenwriting, a much younger art form, has always deemphasized dialogue. For the first three decades of filmmaking, films were silent, and the only dialogue appeared on "cards" to be read between shots. Screenwriters, therefore, focused on action, quick cuts, and special effects to tell their stories. This difference remains true today. A successful film such as *The Lion King* has to be completely rewritten to work on stage, while the masterworks of Shakespeare are often reworked for the screen. These two unique art forms have served storytellers well throughout the years and will continue to do so.

- Note that the sentences vary in length from 5 words to 29 words and no two sentences begin in the same way. This variety creates a smooth flow of ideas.

Conventions

In the paragraph below, the writer explores a particular style in art and literature.

First of all, what is the grotesque—in visual art and in literature? A term originally applied to Roman cave art that distorted the normal, the grotesque presents the body and mind so that they appear abnormal—different from the bodies and minds that we think belong in our world. Both spiritual and physical, bizarre and familiar, ugly and alluring, the grotesque shocks us, and we respond with laughter and fear. We laugh because the grotesque seems bizarre enough to belong only outside of our world; we fear because it feels familiar enough to be part of our world. Seeing the grotesque version of life as it is portrayed in art stretches our vision of reality. As Bernard McElroy argues, "The grotesque transforms the world from what we 'know' it to be to what we fear it might be. It distorts and exaggerates the surface of reality in order to tell a qualitative truth about it."

- Notice how the commas and semicolons direct the progression of ideas in this writing and how the dashes emphasize important points. Attention to proper punctuation establishes an effective, smooth rhythm and clarity in the passage.

Checklist for Effective Writing

If a piece of writing meets the following standards, it exhibits the traits of effective writing. Check your work using these standards.

Ideas

The writing . . .

_____ maintains a clear, specific focus or purpose.

_____ presents information that elaborates on the focus.

_____ holds the reader's attention and answers questions about the topic.

Organization

_____ includes a clear beginning, middle, and ending.

_____ contains specific details—arranged in the best order—to support the main ideas.

Voice

_____ speaks to the intended audience.

_____ shows that the writer cares about the topic.

Word Choice

_____ contains specific nouns, active verbs, and colorful modifiers.

_____ presents an appropriate level of formality or informality.

Sentence Fluency

_____ flows smoothly from sentence to sentence.

_____ displays varied sentence beginnings and lengths.

Conventions and Presentation

_____ adheres to the rules of grammar, capitalization, spelling, and punctuation.

_____ follows established guidelines for presentation.

A Guide to Prewriting

Writer Joyce Carol Oates made the following observation in reference to the writing process: " . . . as soon as you connect with your true subject, you will write." Her comment refers to fiction writing, but it really holds true for all writing, including your academic essays. Writing, in the early stages, is the process of "connecting with your true subject."

How you make this connection depends on the writing task. If you are developing a personal narrative, you may easily identify your true subject by considering your own experience. On the other hand, if you are writing a research paper or an essay of argumentation, you may need to do some careful prewriting (researching, reflecting, and so on) to connect with a worthy writing idea.

WHAT'S AHEAD

Prewriting refers to various strategies that help you select and shape a subject for writing. This chapter explains a number of these strategies. Experiment with them to determine which ones can best help you plan your papers.

Selecting a Topic

The following strategies will help you find a worthy topic for your writing, or a compelling angle for a topic already assigned to you. Read through the entire list before you choose a strategy to begin your search.

Journal Writing

Write in a journal (notebook) on a regular basis. Explore your personal feelings, develop your innermost thoughts, and record the happenings of each day. Periodically go back and underline ideas that you would like to explore in writing assignments.

Freewriting

Write nonstop for 10 minutes or more to discover possible writing ideas or angles. Begin writing with or without a particular focus in mind; either way, you'll soon be discovering and exploring ideas that may otherwise not have occurred to you. (See pages 24–25 for more information about freewriting.)

Clustering

Begin a cluster with a nucleus word or phrase (like *weight lifting*) that is related to your writing topic or assignment. Then record or cluster ideas around it. Circle each idea as you write it, and draw a line connecting it to the closest related idea.

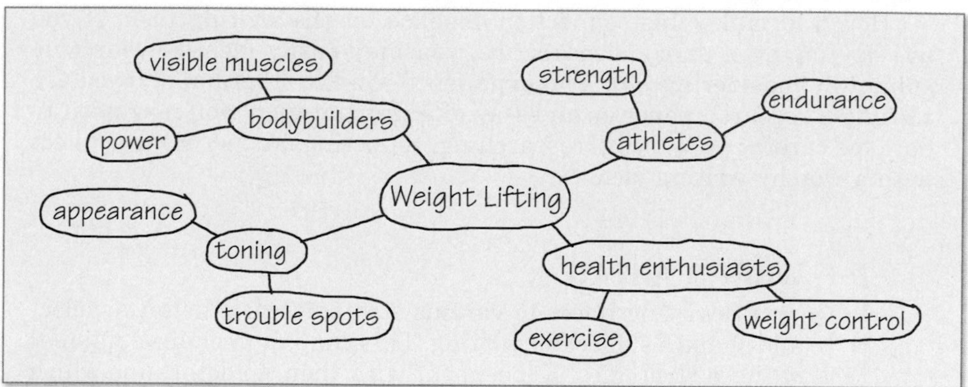

NOTE: After a few minutes of clustering, scan your notes for a word or an idea to explore in a freewriting. A specific subject may begin to emerge during this writing.

Listing

Freely list ideas as they come to mind. Begin with a concept or a key word related to your assignment and simply start listing additional words or ideas. (Brainstorming, listing ideas with members of a group, is another effective way to search for writing subjects.)

Dialoguing

Create a dialogue between yourself and the intended reader of your piece. The topic of this conversation should be related to your writing assignment. Continue dialoguing until a possible writing idea begins to unfold.

Listening, Participating, Reflecting

Think about possible writing ideas as you read, as you ride or drive to school, as you relax in the evening, and so on. Watch for unusual events, persons, objects, or conversations. Participate in group activities related to your writing assignment. Interview someone who is knowledgeable or experienced about a writing idea. Also talk with friends and family members about possible topics.

Using the "Basics of Life" List

Below you will find a list of the major categories into which most essential things in our lives are divided. The list provides an endless variety of topic possibilities. Consider the fifth category, education. It could lead to the following writing ideas:

- online education
- funding public education
- a new approach in education
- an influential educator

Basics of Life

clothing	**communication**	**exercise**	**health/medicine**
housing	**purpose/goals**	**community**	**entertainment**
food	**measurement**	**arts/music**	**literature/books**
exercise	**machines**	**faith/religion**	**recreation/hobby**
education	**intelligence**	**trade/money**	**personality/identity**
family	**agriculture**	**heat/fuel**	**natural resources**
friends	**environment**	**rules/laws**	**tools/utensils**
love	**science**	**freedom/rights**	**plants/vegetation**
senses	**energy**	**land/property**	**work/occupation**

BOTTOM LINE

Before implementing any prewriting strategy, be sure you thoroughly understand the assignment you've been given. Some assignments allow a lot of freedom in topic choice and approach; others are more directed and specific. A good writer takes these differences into account and uses prewriting strategies accordingly.

Freewriting Guidelines

Freewriting is the writing you do without having a specific outcome in mind. You simply write down whatever comes to mind as you explore potential topics. Freewriting can be combined with any of the other prewriting strategies to help you select, explore, or focus, your writing. If you get stuck at any point during the composing process, you can return to freewriting as a way of generating new ideas.

Reminders

- **Freewriting helps you get your thoughts down on paper.**
- **Freewriting helps you explore these thoughts.**
- **Freewriting helps you make sense out of information you are studying or topics you are researching.**
- **Freewriting may seem awkward at times, but just stick with it.**

The Process

- **Write nonstop and record whatever comes into your mind.** Follow your thoughts instead of trying to direct them.
- **Use a particular topic or assignment as a starting point** or begin with whatever comes to mind.
- **Don't stop to judge, edit, or correct your writing;** that will come later.
- **Keep writing even when you think you have exhausted all of your ideas.** Switch to another mode of thought (sensory, memory, reflective) if necessary, but keep writing.
- **Watch for emerging writing ideas.** Learn to recognize the beginnings of a good idea and then expand on it by recording as many specific details as possible.

INSIDE INFO

Always have a notebook or journal close at hand and write freely in it whenever you have an interesting idea to explore, an important point to remember, or a few random thoughts to reflect upon.

The Result

- **Review your writings and underline the ideas you like.** These ideas may serve as starting points for more-formal writings.
- **Determine exactly what you plan (or are required) to write about;** add specific details as necessary. (This may require a second freewriting.)
- **Listen to and read the freewritings of others;** learn from your peers.

Shaping a Topic

The following strategies will help you develop your topics for writing. If you already have a good "feel" for a particular writing idea, you may attempt only one of these. If you need to explore your idea in some detail, and time permits, you may attempt two or more of the strategies.

Freewriting At this point, you can approach freewriting in two different ways. You can do a *focused freewriting* to see how many ideas come to mind about your topic as you write, or you can approach your freewriting as if it were an instant version of the finished product. An instant version will give you a good feel for your topic and will also tell you how much you know or need to find out about it.

Clustering Try clustering with your specific topic as the nucleus word. This clustering will naturally be more focused or structured than your earlier prewriting cluster. (See page 22 for a model cluster.)

5 W's of Writing Answer the 5 W's—who? what? where? when? why? (and how?)—to identify basic information about your topic.

Directed Writing Do a variation of freewriting by selecting one of the six thinking modes below and writing whatever comes to mind. (Repeat the process as often as you need to, selecting a different mode each time.)

Describe it. What do you see, hear, feel, smell, taste . . . ?

Compare it. What is it like? What is it different from?

Associate it. What connections between this and something else come to mind?

Analyze it. What parts does it have? How do they work (or not work) together?

Apply it. What can you do with it? How can you use it?

Argue for or against it. What do you like about it? Not like about it? What are its good points? Its bad points?

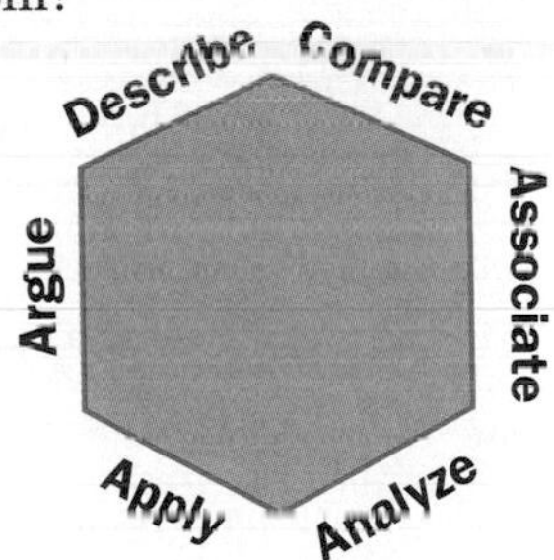

Creating a Dialogue Create a dialogue between two people (one of whom may be you) in which your specific topic is the focus of the conversation. The two speakers should build on each other's comments, reinforce them, or give them a new spin.

Researching and Reflecting For almost all of your academic writing, you will need to research your subject. (See pages 383–397 for different sources of information.) Reserve a special part of a notebook to question, evaluate, and reflect upon your research as it develops. A record of your thoughts and actions during this process will often mean as much or more to you than the actual information you uncover. It helps you make sense of new ideas, refocus your thinking, and evaluate your progress.

Asking Questions

To gain a thorough understanding of a writing idea, it helps to ask questions about it. The basic questions to ask are the 5 W's and H (see page 25). The chart below provides a far more comprehensive set of questions based on the type of analysis practiced by ancient scholars. The chart addresses topics that can be classified as problems, policies, and concepts.

	DESCRIPTION	FUNCTION	HISTORY	VALUE
PROBLEMS	What is the problem? What type of problem is it? What are its parts? What are the signs of the problem?	Who or what is affected by it? What new problems may it cause in the future?	What is the current status of the problem? What or who caused it? What or who contributed to it?	What is its significance? Why? Why is it more (or less) important than other problems? What does it symbolize or illustrate?
POLICIES	What is the policy? How broad is it? What are its parts? What are its most important features?	What is the policy designed to do? What is needed to make it work? What will be its effects?	What brought this policy about? What are the alternatives to this policy?	Is the policy workable? What are its advantages and its disadvantages? Is it practical? Is it a good policy? Why or why not?
CONCEPTS	What is the concept? What are its parts? What is its main feature? Who or what is it related to?	Who has been influenced by this concept? Why is it important? How does it work?	When did it originate? How has it changed over the years? How may it change in the future?	What practical value does it have? Why is it superior (or inferior) to similar concepts? What is its social worth?

Using Graphic Organizers

Graphic organizers can help you gather and organize your details for writing. Clustering is one method (see page 22); these next two pages list other useful organizers. Re-create the organizer on your own paper to do your gathering.

Cause-Effect Organizer

Use to collect and organize details for cause-effect essays.

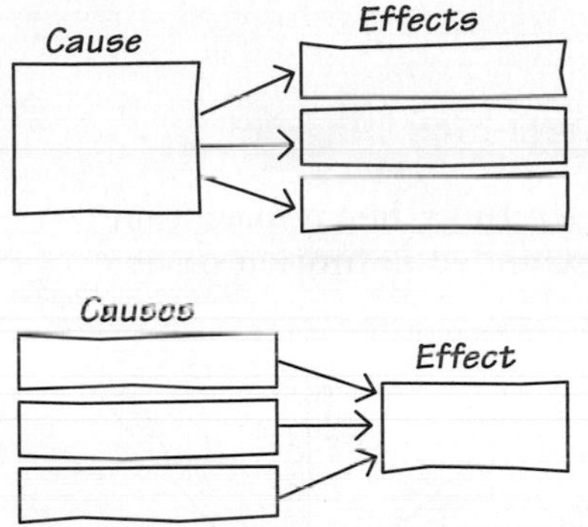

Problem-Solution Web

Use to map out problem-solution essays.

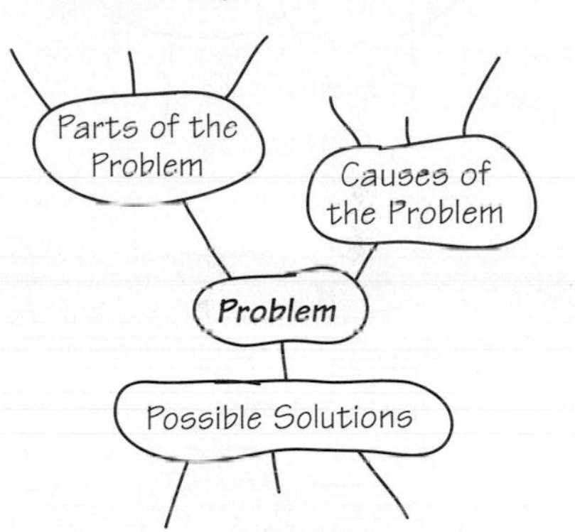

Time Line

Use for personal narratives to list actions or events in the order they occurred.

Subject: ____________________

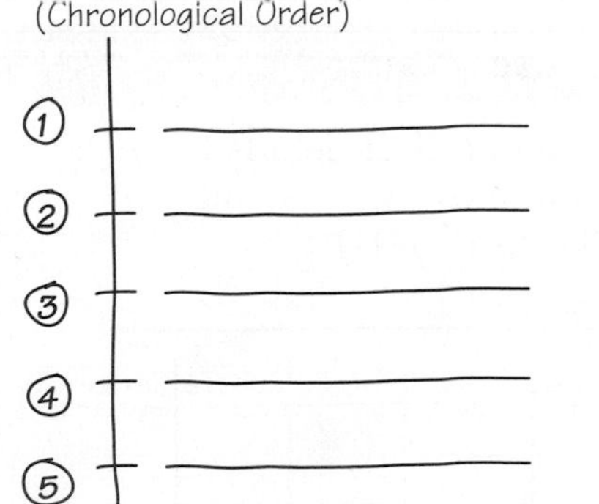

Evaluation Collection Grid

Use to collect supporting details for essays of evaluation.

Subject:

Points to Evaluate	*Supporting Details*
1.	
2.	
3.	
4.	

Venn Diagram

Use to collect details to compare and contrast two topics.

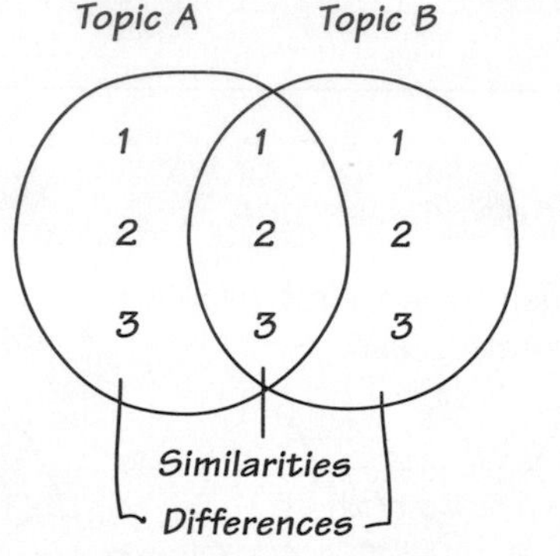

Line Diagram

Use to collect and organize details for academic essays.

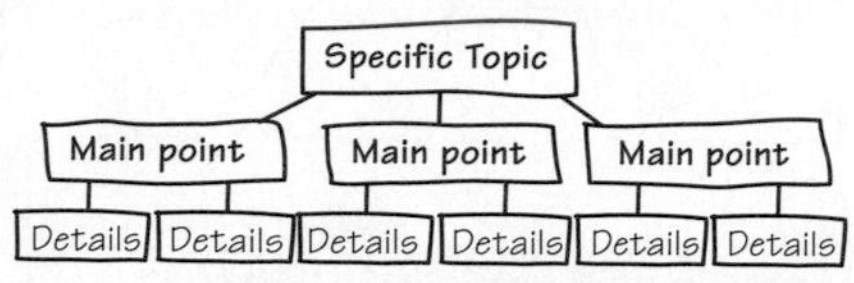

Process (Cycle) Diagram

Use to collect details for science-related writing, such as how a process or cycle works.

Topic:

(Chronological Order)

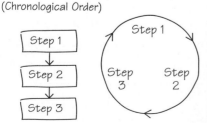

Step 1
Step 2
Step 3

Step 1
Step 2
Step 3

5 W's Chart

Use to collect the *who? what? when? where?* and *why?* details for personal narratives and news stories.

Subject:

Who?	What?	When?	Where?	Why?

Definition Diagram

Use to gather information for extended definition essays.

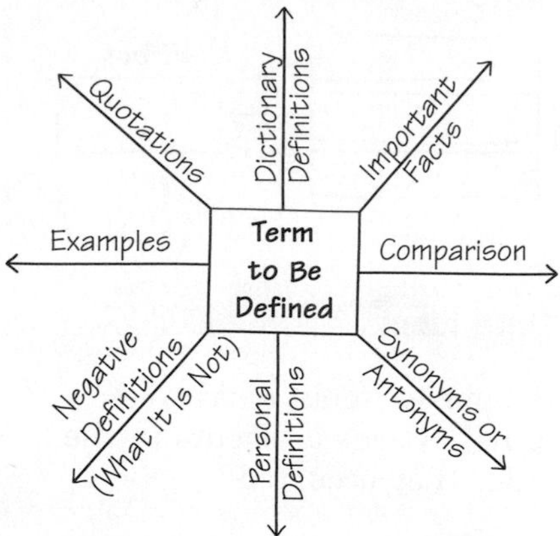

Sensory Chart

Use to collect details for descriptive essays and observation reports.

Subject:

Sights	Sounds	Smells	Tastes	Textures

Taking Inventory

Let's say you still don't feel comfortable with your topic. That is, you've done some searching, and you've discovered some interesting things about your writing idea, but you still don't feel ready to write a first draft. Now may be a good time to see how well *you* match up with your topic. After considering the following questions, you should be able to decide whether to move ahead with your writing or reexamine your topic. (See page 115 for a discussion of these questions related to writing and style.)

Purpose

- What are the specific requirements of this assignment?
- Do I have enough time to do a good job with this topic?
- Am I writing to inform, to analyze, to persuade, or to entertain?

Topic

- How much do I already know about this topic?
- Is additional information available?
- Have I tried any of the shaping activities? (See pages 25–26.)

Audience

- How much does my reader care or already know about this topic?
- How can I create interest in my ideas?

Self

- How committed am I to my writing topic?
- What can I learn or gain by continuing to write on this topic?

Language and Form

- How will I present my ideas: essay, article, editorial?
- Can I think of an interesting lead or opening for my paper?

Continuing the Process

Research If you feel that you need to know more about your topic, continue collecting your own thoughts and/or investigating other sources of information. Remember that it is important (or at least helpful) to investigate a few secondary sources of information. Reading helps stimulate or clarify your thinking about a writing idea.

Review If you feel ready to move ahead, consider reviewing your initial prewriting notes and collecting (graphic organizers, grids, charts, and so on). As you read through this material, circle or underline ideas that seem important enough to include in your writing. Then look for ways in which these ideas connect or relate. This activity will help you focus your thoughts for writing. (See the next page.)

Focusing Your Efforts

All types of writing—research papers, lab reports, responses to prompts, business letters, and so on—have a central thought holding them together. Your early prewriting will probably produce an abundance of information and ideas. As you continue exploring and gathering, you should develop a more focused interest in your subject, which will eventually become the thesis or focus of your writing.

Forming a Thesis Statement

The central thought, or thesis, in a piece of writing usually takes a stand, expresses a feeling, or highlights a feature of a specific topic. Sometimes a thesis statement develops early and easily; sometimes it takes a great deal of reflecting and prewriting; and sometimes it emerges while you are writing your first draft.

Try to state your thesis in a sentence that expresses what you believe and want to explore. Use the following formula:

A manageable or limited subject (multicultural education)
\+ **a specific stand, feeling, or feature**
(is vital to a society made up of many different peoples)

= **an effective thesis statement.**

Thesis Statement: Multicultural education is vital to a society made up of many different peoples.

NOTE: The stronger your thesis statement, the easier it is to bring the rest of your paper into focus. (See page 94 for more information and examples.)

Designing a Writing Plan

With a clear focus in mind, you are ready to make a plan for writing your first draft. Your plan can be anything from a brief list of ideas to a detailed sentence outline. The following guidelines may help:

1. **Study your thesis statement.** It may suggest a logical method of organization for your writing. (See page 96.)
2. **Review the facts and details that support your thesis.** See if an overall pattern of organization begins to emerge.
3. **Consider the patterns of organization listed in the handbook.** (See page 95.)
4. **Organize your ideas into a list or an outline.** (See page 97 for more on outlining.)
5. **If no clear plan presents itself, simply write your first draft to see what unfolds.**

A Guide to Drafting

After the rehearsals, there's a performance. After the drills, there's the first match. After the conditioning, the race begins. And after the prewriting, there's the first draft. If you've done the necessary prewriting, your first draft should go well. You should have more than enough material to shape and expand into an effective piece of writing.

It's important to remember that a first draft is a first look at your developing writing idea. For now, you'll want to concentrate on getting all of your ideas on paper. Use your writing plan (if you have one) as a basic guide for drafting, but also be open to new ideas or directions as they emerge in the heat of composing. Remember that you may have to write more than one draft before your writing really begins to take form.

WHAT'S AHEAD

This chapter offers guidelines and suggestions that will help you develop your initial draft (or drafts). You will find important information related to getting started, continuing, and completing your initial writing.

Writing the Opening

Most writers pay special attention to the opening, its wording and general impact, before they concern themselves with developing a complete draft. Once their opening is set (at least tentatively), they are ready to face the larger task at hand. The opening paragraph or paragraphs should (1) introduce the general subject and spark the reader's interest; (2) establish a tone, direction, and level of language for the writing; and (3) identify or suggest the thesis.

Possible Starting Points

There are many ways to begin an opening paragraph. Several starting points are listed below.

- Open with a fitting quotation.
- Challenge your reader with a thought-provoking question.
- Offer a tantalizing hint of what is to follow.
- Provide important background information.
- Begin with a dramatic anecdote or scenario.
- Start out with an eye-opening statement.

NOTE: If you don't like how the first or second draft of your opening sounds, keep trying. You'll know when you create the right version because it will help you visualize the remainder of your draft.

Sample Opening Paragraph

The writer of the opening paragraph below begins with important background information that effectively leads up to the thesis statement (underlined).

hint of what is to follow

Most children, no matter what their personal or family situation, lead more or less controlled lives. As they grow, they begin to sense the pressure of controlling factors in their lives and start struggling to take control themselves. This can be a difficult process.

background information

In *Native Son* and *Equus,* Richard Wright and Peter Shaffer respectively create two characters who must deal with this struggle. Bigger in *Native Son* and Alan in *Equus* are both entering adulthood and have come to realize that they are controlled by work, religion, and the media.

thesis – In the midst of these characters' efforts to gain control, each of them falls into a tragic situation.

A Closer Look at Openings

If you have trouble coming up with an effective opening paragraph, try the following strategy as a basic guide. Think of this strategy as a starting point—as a way to get something on paper. Afterward, you can work with the opening until it says exactly what you want it to say.

Beginning Strategy

- **First sentence**—Get the reader's attention. Start with a sentence that arouses the reader's curiosity, makes him or her think, and so on.

  Have you ever been in a conversation in which you suddenly feel lost—and out of the loop?

- **Second and third sentences**—Clarify or continue the point made in the first sentence. Offer background information.

  Perhaps you feel that way in your literature class. You may think a poem or a short story means one thing, and then your instructor suddenly pulls out the "hidden meaning."

- **Next sentence or sentences**—Introduce the specific topic of the essay and build up to the thesis statement.

  Joining the conversation about literature may indeed seem daunting, but you can do it if you know what to look for, and what to talk about.

- **Final sentence**—Present the thesis statement. This statement will keep you on track as you develop your essay.

  There are four main perspectives, or strategies, that you can use to converse about literature.

Beginning Approaches to Avoid

- **Obvious or worn-out expressions:**

  "I would like to tell you about . . . "

  "Everybody knows that . . . "

- **Say-nothing sentences:**

  "A and B are alike in some ways and different in others."

  "Crime is an undesirable reality in today's society."

NOTE: The conventional way of approaching the first paragraph is to view it as a "funnel" that narrows to a main point. However, don't feel bound by this conventional pattern, which may sound stale if not handled well.

Developing the Middle

The middle of an essay presents the main points that support your thesis statement. Make sure to use your planning notes (outline, list, cluster) as a general guide for your writing. Here are several different ways to support your thesis.

Summarize: Present only the important ideas.
Explain: Provide important facts, details, and examples.
Quote: Include a direct quotation.
Narrate: Share an anecdote to illustrate or clarify an idea.
Describe: Tell how someone appears or how something works.
Define: Identify or clarify the meaning of a specific term or idea.
Argue: Use logic and evidence to prove something is true.
Compare: Show how two things are alike or different.
Analyze: Examine the parts of something to better understand the whole.
Reflect: Express your thoughts and feelings about something.

INSIDE INFO

For most essays you should use at least two or three methods to support and develop your thesis. For example, in an essay of definition, you might provide a dictionary definition, compare your subject to something similar, and share an anecdote about it.

Build a Coherent Structure

Each middle paragraph should present main points and details that advance your essay logically and coherently.

- Start a new paragraph whenever a shift or change in the essay takes place. A shift occurs when you introduce a new main point or redirect a point of emphasis.
- Arrange middle paragraphs carefully so that each one builds on the preceding paragraph and leads into the next. To do this, link the first sentence of a paragraph to the preceding paragraph, using key words or transitions. (See pages 88–89.)
- Shape each paragraph for unity, coherence, and organization.

BOTTOM LINE

Writing a first draft will tell you two things: (1) whether or not your thesis is valid and (2) whether or not you have enough compelling information (main points and supporting details) to develop it.

Sample Middle Paragraphs

The first middle paragraph of a comparison essay (see the opening paragraph on page 32) focuses on Alan (in *Equus*) and his job as a clerk. This paragraph, at the start, *summarizes* Alan's work experience. It moves on with a *quotation* from the text and concludes with a statement of *analysis*.

> **summary** — Alan is experiencing the pressure of working as a clerk at Bryson's appliance store. The customers are demanding, and the many products and brand names are confusing. He finds that he cannot function in this work environment. Later, under hypnosis, he admits to Dr. Dysart that **quotation** — his "foes" are the myriad of brand names he is challenged to locate and explain to the customers—"The Hosts of Hoover. The Hosts of Philco. **analysis** — Those Hosts of Pifco. The House of Remington and all its tribe!" (73). However, by recognizing the demands of this job, Alan attempts to take some control over his life.

The next paragraph focuses on Bigger (in *Native Son*) and his job as a chauffeur. This paragraph *summarizes* and *analyzes* Bigger's work experience.

> Bigger must also struggle with the pressure and anxiety of his first **summary** — job. Because of his family's desperate financial situation, he is forced to take the one job he is offered by Mr. Dalton. He works as a chauffeur for Dalton's wealthy suburban family. Bigger cannot relate to them. He sees himself as a foreigner, forced to live and work among the privileged. **analysis** — The Daltons tell him where, when, and even how to drive. Bigger struggles; and, like Alan, he cannot deal with the extreme discomfort he is feeling. He quits after only two days on the job. Unlike Alan, however, Bigger does not have the option of getting a job that interests him.

In this paragraph, the writer *compares* the influence of religion on both young men. She also includes a *quotation* from each text as well as personal *analysis*.

> Alan and Bigger also find religion to be a controlling factor in their **comparison** — lives. Alan's mother, Dora, "doses [religion] down the boy's throat" as she **quotation** — whispers "that Bible to him hour after hour, up there in his room" (33). Obviously, Alan's mother believes that he needs the controlling force of religion in his life, so she preaches to him every night. Bigger's mother does not push religion to such an extreme. Instead, she tries to make **quotation** — her son see its value with daily comments such as "You'll regret how you living someday" (13). She tries to show Bigger that religion is a valid way **analysis** — of dealing with a world out of control. In the end, neither boy accepts religion and is left with no spiritual footing or direction.

Bringing Your Writing to a Close

The closing paragraph must tie up loose ends and clarify key points. In a sense, the main part of an essay is a preparation for an effective ending. An effective ending helps the reader reflect on the message of the essay with new understanding and appreciation.

Advice: Because the ending can be so important, draft a variety of possible endings. Choose the one that flows best from the rest of the essay.

Caution:

1. If your thesis is weak or unclear, you will have a difficult time writing a satisfactory ending. To strengthen the ending, strengthen the thesis.
2. You may have heard this formula for writing an essay: "Say what you're going to say, say it, then say what you've just said." Remember, though, if you need to "say what you've just said," say it in new words.

Possible Closings

There are different ways to end an essay. An effective closing usually does some combination of the follow things:

- Restates the thesis.
- Highlights one or more key supporting points.
- Answers any unresolved questions.
- Provides a final bit of analysis or reflection.
- Helps the reader appreciate the importance of the information.
- Relates the essay to the reader's own experience.

Sample Closing Paragraph

restating the thesis	Ultimately, both Alan and Bigger fail to gain real control over the outside forces in their lives.
analysis	In different ways, these two characters are similarly trapped by work, religion, and media pressures. Consequently, both fail in their quest for personal freedom, and the result in each case is devastating. Using television as an escape for his failed ambitions, Alan forfeits his interest in life. Trapped by a media that viciously, and
connection to life	wrongly, condemns him, Bigger tragically loses his life. Both young men, like so many people, become victims of the world in which they live.

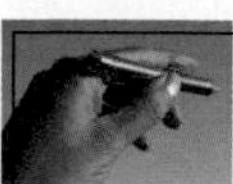

NOTE: The ending is your last chance to gain the reader's acceptance. Be certain to clarify the implications of your thesis and make any connections that will enhance the reader's understanding.

A Closer Look at Closings

If you have difficulty developing an effective closing paragraph, use the strategy below as a basic guide. After you get something on paper, you can work with the closing until it says exactly what you want it to say.

Closing Strategy

- **First sentence**—Remind the reader of the thesis. Start by reflecting on the material you've already presented about it.

  The variety of questions critics might ask about "My Last Duchess" reveals the diversity of critical approaches and the common ground between them.

- **Second and third sentences**—Expand on and clarify the point in your first sentence.

  In fact, interpretive methods actually share important characteristics: (1) a close attention to literary elements such as character, plot, symbolism, and metaphor; (2) a desire not to distort the work; and (3) a sincere concern for increasing interest and understanding of the text.

- **Next sentence or sentences**—Stress the importance of one or more key points that support the thesis.

  In actual practice, critics may develop a hybrid approach to criticism, one that matches their individual questions and concerns about a text.

- **Final sentence**—Add one final thought about the thesis or draw a conclusion from the points you've presented in the writing.

  After learning about some of the questions defining literary criticism, individuals can exercise their own curiosity (and join the ongoing literary dialogue) by discussing a text that genuinely interests them.

If Endings Could Talk

The sample closing above clarifies for the reader the "common ground" between interpretive methods of literary analysis. In effect, it says, "Here's what you need to know." If you would take a quick tour of effective essays, here are some of the things that the final paragraph would say.

- It all comes down to this . . .
- In fact, the opposite is true . . .
- And would you believe . . .
- However, it turns out okay . . .
- It's a strange world, isn't it?
- And there's the difference . . .

Integrating Quotations

Always choose quotations that are appropriate for your writing. Quotations should support your ideas, not replace them.

Strategies for Using Quotations

Use the strategies below to make the most effective use of quoted material in your writing.

- **Use quotations to support your own thoughts and ideas.** Effective quotations can back up your main points or support your arguments.

  Bigger reads about himself in the newspapers and begins to believe certain things that have no basis in truth. He is referred to as someone who looks "as if about to spring upon you at any moment" (260). The papers also remark that Bigger "seems a beast utterly untouched" (260). Unfortunately, he has no control over what is printed or over what other people believe about him.

- **Use quotations to lend authority to your writing.** Quoting an expert shows that you have researched your topic and understand its significance.

  Albert Einstein observed the growth of nuclear power with concern, stating, "I know not with what weapons World War III will be fought, but World War IV will be fought with sticks and stones." His disturbing comment reminds individuals that a nuclear war would result in unthinkable destruction.

- **Use quotations that are succinct and powerful.** Distinctive quotations add value to your writing.

  Pianist Benny Green defines a jazz musician as "a juggler who uses harmonies instead of oranges." The test of jazz is how these harmonies, tossed about seemingly at random, actually hold together in a smooth, if loosely defined, pattern.

Common Quotation Problems to Avoid

Avoid these problems as you choose quotations.

- **Plagiarism**
  Cite sources for all quotations and paraphrases.
- **Long quotations**
  Keep quotations brief and to the point.
- **Overused quotations**
  Use a quotation only when you cannot share its message as powerfully or effectively in another way.

A Guide to Revising

Writer Kurt Vonnegut once told a class of writing students that there are two categories of writers: swoopers and bashers. Swoopers write 17 drafts at high speed and finally say, "I quit. Here, publish this." Bashers, on the other hand, won't move on to the next sentence until they have chiseled and polished the one before it.

Fortunately, there is a third category, halfway between swoopers and bashers. Writers in this group let their thoughts flow freely in the early drafts and then have enough courage and discipline to revise later on.

Courage? Yes, revision takes courage. It's easy to edit and proofread your writing and then turn it in. It's not so easy to improve the core of your writing—the *ideas, organization,* and *voice* that carry your message—before submitting it. Revising is the important process of making changes in your writing until it says exactly what you want it to say.

WHAT'S AHEAD

This chapter introduces valuable revising guidelines and strategies. It also presents examples of revising for the traits as well as guidelines for conducting peer reviews.

Using Basic Revising Guidelines

No writer gets it right the first time. Few writers get it right the second time. In fact, professional writers almost always write a number of revisions before they are satisfied with their work. Don't be surprised if you have to do the same. The guidelines that follow will help you work your first draft into shape.

1. **First look at the big picture.** Read your paper. Decide if the thesis (or focus) is still valid, giving the proper direction for your essay. Or, if your original thinking on your topic has changed, write a new thesis statement.
2. **Then look at specific chunks of information.** Examine the body paragraphs to make sure that they prove or support your thesis. (See page 100.)
3. **Also cut information** that doesn't support your main point; **add information** if you feel additional points need to be made. Make sure that each part of your writing supports the main point you're trying to get across; **rewrite parts** that aren't as clear as you would like them to be or that don't project the appropriate voice.
4. **Review your opening and closing paragraphs** to make sure they introduce and wrap up your thesis effectively.
5. **Finally, refine your writing,** paying careful attention to the quality of your word choice and sentence fluency.

INSIDE INFO

The paragraph is the basic unit in almost all academic writing. Each of your paragraphs should develop an important point related to your subject. In addition, each paragraph should serve as an effective link to the information that comes before it and after it.

Revising on the Run

Writer Peter Elbow recommends "cut-and-paste revising" when you have very little time to make changes in your writing. For example, let's say you are responding to an in-class writing prompt, and you have only a short time to revise your writing. Follow this quick revising technique:

1. Add no new information to your writing.
2. Remove unnecessary facts and details.
3. Find the best possible information and go with it.
4. Arrange the parts in the best possible order.
5. Do what little rewriting is necessary.

A Closer Look at Revising

Know your purpose and your audience. Always know why you are writing—your purpose. Are you sharing information, arguing for or against something, analyzing a process? When you have a clear purpose, it is much easier to know what to change in your writing. Also consider your audience and what they may or may not know about your topic. Lastly, make sure that your writing voice matches the intended audience and purpose.

Escaping the "Badlands"

The final stage of revising is one of the most important in the whole composing process. Why? Because here you can escape the "badlands" of writing: those stretches of uninspired ideas that can make an essay boring. Use these questions to recognize and revise such ideas.

- **Is your topic worn out?** An essay entitled "Lead Poisoning" sounds like a real yawner. With a new twist, you can revive it: "Get the Lead Out!"
- **Is your approach stale?** If you have been writing primarily to please a teacher or to get a good grade, start again. Try writing to learn something or to trigger a particular emotion or action in your reader.
- **Is your voice predictable or fake?** If it is ("Lead poisoning is a serious problem"), start again. This time, be honest. Be real.
- **Does your draft sound boring?** Maybe it's boring because it pays an equal amount of attention to everything. Try skimming through the less significant parts by summarizing information; then focus on the more important parts by sharing specific examples (facts, statistics, anecdotes).
- **Does your essay follow the formula too closely?** For example, the classic five-paragraph essay provides you with a pattern or frame to build on. However, depending on your topic, the pattern may get in the way. Read your draft again, and if your inner voice says "formula," change the structure in some way.
- **Does your writing truly reflect your best efforts?** If not, keep working on it. A real breakthrough may come during your next revision.

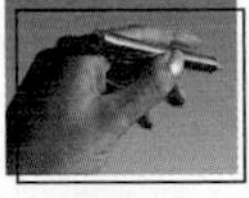

NOTE: Think of revising as an opportunity to energize your writing. If you need to refuel your thinking at any point during the revising process, consider using one of the prewriting activities in this handbook. (See pages 21–30.)

Making Improvements

When you revise a first draft, focus on making improvements to the paper as a whole. You can improve a piece by adding, moving, deleting, or reworking information. (See the next page for examples.)

Adding Information

Add to your writing if you need to . . .

- share more details to make a point,
- clarify or expand an interesting idea, or
- link sentences or paragraphs to improve clarity and flow.

Moving Material

Move text in your writing in order to . . .

- create a clear flow of ideas,
- present points in order, or
- make a dramatic impact.

Deleting Information

Delete material from your draft when the ideas . . .

- do not support your focus or
- are redundant or repetitious.

Reworking Material

Rework sections of writing if they . . .

- are confusing or unclear,
- do not maintain the proper voice, or
- need to be simplified.

Being Your Own Critic

When revising, try to anticipate your reader's concerns. Doing so will help you determine what changes to make. Here are a few basic questions and concerns a reader may have:

- What is the main point of this essay?
- Does the writer's voice sound interested and authoritative?
- Can I follow the writer's ideas easily?
- Does the ending wrap up the essay in a meaningful way?

Revising in Action

The writer of this essay improved the piece by adding, moving, deleting, and reworking parts. See the inside back cover of this book for an explanation of the editing symbols used.

Sample Revision

An important detail is added.

A sentence is moved for clarity.

An unnecessary detail is cut.

A phrase is reworded for appropriate voice.

An idea is added for coherence.

Buckling Up Is Not Enough

During the first lap of a Grand Prix race in Melbourne, Australia, Martin Brundle's car hit another racer at 185 miles per hour. Spinning into the air, Brundle's B&H Jordon broke into pieces, spraying debris across the track. According to The Ultimate Race Car, the unhurt Brundle ran to the pits, climbed into his reserve car, and drove out in time for the restart (Burgess-Wise 139). The race was stopped as the fragments of the car were cleared. This story says a great deal about the Grand Prix's current approach to driver safety, ~~an approach that may surprise people~~. In recent years, Formula One racing has made dramatic improvements in driver safety.

Safety wasn't always a ~~big-time issue~~ primary concern on the Formula One racing circuit. When the Grand Prix began in 1906, the race ran on city streets and country roads, and accidents involving drivers and spectators were common. Modern Grand Prix courses are used only for racing, but they are unlike the ovals used in NASCAR racing. Grand Prix races are held on road courses that include a variety of curves, hills, hairpin turns, and other challenges. The speed of Formula One cars adds another complication. They are the fastest race cars in the world, hurtling through race courses at incredible speeds of more than 180 mph. As a result, the Grand Prix has claimed the lives of dozens of drivers over the years, including 19 racers during the sixties and seventies (Tytler 1). Recently, though, these numbers have been reduced.

Revising for the Traits

As a reviser, your goal is to address the key content issues in your first draft. The next five pages point out some of the areas you should consider in terms of the following traits of writing: *ideas, organization, voice, word choice,* and *sentence fluency.*

Revising for Ideas

The examples below address two important issues related to ideas: the effectiveness of the main point or thesis of the essay and the quality of supporting details.

Evaluating Your Thesis

In the following opening paragraph from an analytical essay, the writer leads up to her thesis statement (underlined).

> Adolescent girls often see teen magazines as handbooks on how to be teenagers. These magazines affect the way they act and look and can exert enormous influence. There are many popular magazines to choose from, and girls who don't really know what they want are the most eager readers.

Discussion: An effective thesis statement clearly states the focus of the essay and suggests a pattern of development for the writing. The above thesis statement does neither. The thesis statement below is stronger and provides direction for the rest of the essay.

Unfortunately, the advice that teen magazines give about self-image, fashion, and boys may do more harm than good.

Checking Your Supporting Details

In the following paragraph from a book review, the writer discusses the overall structure of a particular novel.

> The novel is a collection of tales about men and women who experienced the Vietnam War. Many of the stories tell of the brutal realities of death. O'Brien [the author] holds nothing back—showing us the horror, tragedy, and related black humor of war.

Discussion: This paragraph lacks an essential element of effective writing—*supporting details.* After the second sentence, the review should highlight a few stories from the text. (See below.)

. . . There's Ted Lavender, shot in the head after relieving himself, "zapped while zipping," as one soldier put it. There's also Curt Lemon, blown up into a tree, remembered gruesomely by one soldier singing the song "Lemon Tree." . . .

Revising for Organization

Effective writing has structure. It leads the reader clearly and smoothly from one idea to the next. The examples below address the arrangement of ideas and the use of transitional words and phrases.

Reviewing Your Arrangement of Ideas

In the following paragraph, the writer attempts to classify three main types of government-supported health care:

> There are three types of federal-controlled health-care programs: Medicaid, Medicare, and socialized medicine. Medicaid helps the poor pay for their health care. Medicare is a type of social security that helps people (aged 65 and older) pay their health costs. Socialized medicine, another federal program, pays for everyone's health care through higher taxes. This program pays doctors a flat salary and gives individuals fewer medical choices. In most cases, people are told who they will see and when they will be seen. . . . These government programs may sound effective, but they have many problems.

Discussion: The writing lacks overall focus. It deals with two programs specific to the United States and a third that exists elsewhere. The paragraph should address government-funded health care in general, or the U.S. programs. Also, the idea of "problems" belongs in a different paragraph.

Checking for Transitional Words and Phrases

What follows is the basic frame—the thesis statement and supporting topic sentences—for a cause-effect essay.

Thesis Statement: Wherever graduated driver licensing (GDL) laws are passed, they have had positive effects.

Topic Sentences: The GDL laws, most obviously, provide a long period of restricted, progressive driving. . . .

The new GDL laws also reduce the high cost of insurance for teen drivers. . . .

In addition, the new laws lessen alcohol and drug use among beginning drivers. . . .

Most significantly, the new GDL laws reduce the number of teen fatalities in auto accidents. . . .

Discussion: When reviewing your first draft for organization and coherence, always check for transitional words and phrases. Note how the transitions above (in red) signal that the essay is organized by order of importance. (See pages 88–89 for a list of transitional words and phrases.)

Revising for Voice

The right voice shows that a writer sincerely cares about his or her topic and audience. As you revise the first draft of your essays, make sure that your voice, your special way of stating your ideas, speaks to your audience and matches up with your purpose.

Considering Your Audience

In the opening part of an essay about world hunger and malnutrition, the writer appeals to his audience, his classmates.

> In two days Kamal would have been four years old, but his wasted body now lies under a pile of rocks behind his family's hut. Why did Kamal die? The too-easy answer is malnutrition. A lack of vitamins and protein made him susceptible to an intestinal infection and two fatal weeks of diarrhea. He could have been saved with a simple solution of boiled water, salts, and sugar, which UNICEF distributes in a free kit called "oral rehydration therapy" (ORT). But Kamal's mother, forced to work 15-hour days at home and in the fields, had missed the rural health-care worker's demonstration in the village.

Discussion: The writer of the above essay clearly has his audience in mind as he establishes a dramatic and compelling voice that would appeal to his classmates. If his primary audience had been different, perhaps his instructor, the writer may have used a slightly less passionate voice.

Checking for Purpose

In this passage from an analytical essay, the writer discusses one aspect of his topic—the effects of humors theory on medical diagnoses.

> The humors theory strongly affected how medieval doctors diagnosed illnesses. When someone got sick, doctors tried to figure out why the patient's humors were out of balance, and to what degree. To help them decide, doctors used three diagnostic tools: pulse reading, urinalysis, and astrology. Doctors read the pulse to evaluate the heart and blood, employing a complex classification scheme to measure pulse types and figure out whether such qualities as the strength, duration, regularity, and breadth were normal for the type (Lindberg 335–337).

Discussion: The purpose of analytical writing is to break a topic down to understand it better. The writer must work scientifically—gathering information, testing it, forming conclusions, etc. The clearly academic voice in the passage above is appropriate for this type of writing.

Revising for Word Choice

Carefully chosen words and the proper diction (level of language) help to communicate the message and set an appropriate tone.

Addressing Common Problems with Words

Always correct the following types of word-choice problems.

Replace **vague or uninteresting words and modifiers** with specific words.

A new type of hunter is showing up around our rivers and lakes.

Specific: A new breed of hunter frequents North America's waterways.

Explain **jargon** (technical terminology).

As the *capillaries* bleed, *platelets* work with *fibrinogens* to form a clot.

With explanation: As the capillaries (small blood vessels) bleed . . .

Replace **cliches** (overused phrases) with something fresh and original.

The Hundred Secret Senses leaves no stone unturned about our world.

Original expression: *The Hundred Secret Senses* burrows deeply to uncover our world.

Discussion: Always use specific nouns, action verbs, and precise language.

Checking Your Diction

For most of your writing assignments, you should use either an informal or a formal level of language.

Informal English is characterized by a personal tone, the use of the first-person pronoun *I*, the occasional use of popular expressions, contractions, shorter sentences, and so on.

Inside the bus terminal, I sat with my feet on my suitcase. I didn't want to pay the four quarters for a storage box or turn my back on my belongings. Writing in my notebook became my shield.

Formal English is characterized by an objective tone, attention to appropriate word choice, longer sentences, and so on.

The fourth approach to criticism applies ideas outside of literature to literary works. Because literature mirrors life, argue these critics, disciplines that explore human life help students understand literature.

Discussion: Use informal English for personal narratives, college entrance essays, and personal responses to literature. Use formal English for analytical and persuasive essays, literary analyses, and research papers.

Revising for Sentence Fluency

According to author William Zinsser, writing in which "all the sentences move at the same plodding gait" can be deadly. Such writing lacks variety and style.

Eliminate Sentence Problems

Always check for and correct the following types of sentence problems.

Short, choppy sentences in your writing can be combined for smoother reading.

The tornado destroyed many houses. Some homes just lost their windows. Others lost parts of their roofs.

Combined sentences:

While the tornado destroyed many houses, some homes just lost their windows or parts of their roofs.

Sentence beginnings may sound stilted if too many of them begin in the same way.

The U.S.S. *Constitution*, known as *Old Ironsides*, was launched in 1797. *Old Ironsides* was one of six ships approved by Congress to fight piracy. This ship helped defeat the Barbary pirates during its years of service.

Varied beginnings:

In 1797, the U.S.S. *Constitution*, known as *Old Ironsides*, was launched. Congress had approved this and five other ships to fight piracy. During its years of service, *Old Ironsides* helped defeat the Barbary pirates.

Sentence lengths that are similar may sound robotic. To avoid this problem, write sentences of different lengths.

Amateur photographers once relied on film for taking pictures. In recent years, however, that has all changed. Today's amateurs have replaced film cameras with digital ones. Consumers have gleefully embraced this industry.

Varied lengths:

Amateur photographers once relied on film for taking pictures. That has all changed. Today's amateurs, gleefully embracing changes in the industry, have replaced film cameras with digital ones.

Discussion: Test your writing by reading it out loud. If you stumble or get confused, look for ways to improve the flow of your sentences.

Peer Reviewing

All writers can benefit from an interested audience, especially one that offers constructive and honest advice during a writing project. And who could make a better audience than your peers? The information on the next four pages will help you respond to others' writing, accept constructive criticism, and improve your writing skills while working in a group.

Valuing Feedback

Your fellow writers can tell you what does and doesn't work for them in your writing. This feedback is valuable throughout the writing process, but it is especially helpful during revising. At this point, you need to find out if your writing makes sense, if it holds the reader's interest, and so on.

Some experts go so far as to say that talking about writing is the most important step in the writing process. By sharing ideas and concerns within the group, writing becomes a meaningful process of learning rather than just another assignment. This enthusiasm is bound to have a positive effect on your final products.

> "Comment on what you like in the writing. What you say must be honest, but you don't have to say everything you feel."
>
> —Ken Macrorie

Maintaining Good Relations

To maintain good relations among group members, be specific with your comments or questions about their writing. For example, an observation such as "I'm not sure the closing connects with the thesis of your essay" will mean much more to a writer than a general (negative) comment such as "Your closing is boring" or "Make your closing more relevant." The specific observation helps the writer to deal with a problem in his or her work.

Always base praise on some element or quality in the writing: "The series of questions and answers is an effective way to organize your ideas." (or) "There is an energy in this writing that I really like."

INSIDE INFO

Your ability to make observations will improve with practice. At first, you may comment only on a surprising detail or a point you don't understand. That's fine. Just keep trying and listening.

Guidelines

Peer Reviewing

The guidelines that follow will help you participate in effective group-revising sessions. Work with a group of three to five fellow writers.

THE AUTHOR/WRITER

- **Come prepared with a substantive piece of writing.** Prepare a copy for each group member if this is part of group procedure.
- **Introduce your writing briefly.** Then let your writing stand on its own.
- **Read your copy out loud.** Speak confidently and clearly.
- **As the group reacts to your writing, listen carefully and take brief notes.** Don't be defensive about your writing since this will stop some members from commenting honestly about your work. Answer all questions.
- **Finally, share any specific concerns or problems you have.**

THE GROUP MEMBERS

- **Listen carefully as the writer reads.** Take notes, but make them brief so you don't miss the reading.
- **Imagine yourself to be the audience the writer is addressing in the piece.** If the work is meant for an admissions office, a civic group, or a newspaper, react to the text as if you were that audience.
- **Keep your comments positive, constructive, and concrete.** Instead of "Great job," make a more helpful response: "Countering the opposition early in the argument gives your essay an authoritative tone."
- **Focus on specific observations.** A comment such as "I noticed many 'There are' statements throughout your essay" is more helpful than "Add some style to your writing."
- **Ask questions of the author.** "What do you mean when you say . . . ?" "Where did you get your facts about . . . ?"
- **Listen to other comments and add to them.** Considering everyone's reactions and suggestions can help you and your peers become better writers.

"Keep away from people who try to belittle your ambitions. Small people always do that, but the really great make you feel that you too can become great."

—Mark Twain

Checklist Peer Reviewing

Use the checklist that follows to help you evaluate compositions during peer-reviewing sessions.

_____ **Purpose:** Is the writer's purpose (to analyze, describe, inform, persuade) evident?

_____ **Audience:** Does the writing address a specific audience? Will the reader understand and appreciate this topic?

_____ **Form:** Does the writer present the topic in an effective and appropriate form?

_____ **Content:** Is the thesis, or focus, of the writing clear? Does the writing cover the topic thoroughly?

_____ **Conventions:** Does the writing adhere to the basic conventions of formal or informal English? (Consider sentence fluency, structure, usage, and mechanics.)

_____ **Voice:** Does the writing sound sincere and honest, as if you can "hear" the writer through her or his words?

_____ **Personal Comments:** Does the writing include personal thoughts that enhance the piece overall?

_____ **Final Purpose:** Does the writing succeed in enlightening, persuading, or informing the reader?

Reacting to Writing

Peter Elbow, in *Writing Without Teachers,* offers four types of reactions to consider as you participate in a peer-reviewing session: *pointing, summarizing, telling,* and *showing.*

- **Pointing** refers to "pointing out" words, phrases, or ideas that make a positive or negative impression on you.
- **Summarizing** refers to your general reaction or understanding of the writing.
- **Telling** refers to expressing what happens in the piece: first, then, and later.
- **Showing** refers to expressing your feelings about the piece metaphorically, comparing the writing to a voice quality, a color, a shape, a type of clothing, etc. ("Why do I feel like I've been lectured to in this essay?" [or] "Your writing has a neat, tailored quality to it.")

Using the Traits to Respond

Responders help writers rethink, refocus, and revise their writing. It is especially helpful to base your responses on the traits of writing.

Addressing Ideas, Organization, and Voice

IDEAS: Help the author focus on ideas.

- Can you tell me the main idea of your writing?
- It seems like you're trying to say . . . . Is that right?
- Are these points the main ideas in your writing?
- The most convincing details are . . .
- A few details like . . . may make this part more interesting.
- In my opinion, details like . . . may distract from your main idea.
- Your writing left me thinking . . . . Is that what you intended?

ORGANIZATION: Help the author focus on organization.

- You got my attention in the beginning by . . .
- This sentence seems to state your focus. Is that correct?
- Are the middle paragraphs organized according to . . . ?
- I wonder if a transition is needed between the second and third paragraphs.
- Why did you place the information about . . . in the fourth paragraph?
- Is the purpose of your ending to . . . ?

VOICE: Help the author focus on voice.

- How would you describe your attitude about this topic?
- What audience did you have in mind when you wrote this?
- The sentences that most clearly show your personality are . . .
- The middle part of your essay may be too subjective.
- The third paragraph sounds very formal. Do you think it fits with the rest of your writing?
- The overall feeling I get from your writing is . . .

Reacting to Criticism

You don't have to incorporate all of your classmates' suggestions.

- Trust your own judgment about your writing.
- Determine which issues are most important.
- Pay attention to comments made by more than one responder.
- Get another opinion if you are not sure about something.

A Guide to Editing

Editing is the final step before publishing anything you've written. When you edit, you check your revised writing for "surface errors," or problems with *conventions* (spelling, punctuation, capitalization, and grammar). Your goal is to produce a clean, correct final draft, which is important if you want to be taken seriously. Errors not only cause confusion but also reduce the reader's confidence in your message.

Editing is most easily accomplished with the appropriate tools: a dictionary, a thesaurus, spell- and grammar-checkers, and the "Proofreader's Guide" in this book (pages 509–593). These resources will help you prepare your writing for publication.

WHAT'S AHEAD

The information in this chapter will help you improve your editing and proofreading skills. It contains guidelines for editing and proofreading your writing as well as a list of common errors. The latter can serve as a quick reference for editing and proofreading.

Editing Guidelines
Editing in Action
Common Writing Errors

Editing

The following guidelines will help you edit your revised writing for conventions and then proofread your final copy before submitting it.

SPELLING

1. **Check your writing for spelling errors.**
   - Use the spell-checker on your computer. (It won't, however, catch all of the spelling errors.)
   - Read your writing backward to focus on each word.
   - Circle each spelling you are unsure of.

PUNCTUATION AND CAPITALIZATION

2. **Review each sentence for end punctuation marks.**
3. **Also check each sentence for proper use of commas:** before coordinating conjunctions (*and, but, or,* etc.) in compound sentences, between items in a series, and so on.
4. **Look for apostrophes in possessive expressions and in contractions.**
5. **Examine quoted information or dialogue for proper use of quotation marks.**
6. **Review the text for proper use of capital letters:** first words in sentences; first words in full-sentence quotations; proper names of people, places, and things.

USAGE AND GRAMMAR

7. **Look for the misuse of any commonly confused words:** *there/their/they're; accept/except.* (See pages 551–560.)
8. **Check for subject-verb agreement.** Subjects and verbs should agree in number: singular subjects require singular verbs; plural subjects require plural verbs.
9. **Review for pronoun-antecedent agreement.** A pronoun and its antecedent must agree in number, person, and gender.

FORM

10. **Check the title.** Does it effectively lead into the writing?
11. **Examine any quoted or cited material.** Are all sources of information properly presented and documented? (See pages 333–350 and 361–370.)
12. **Look over the finished copy of your writing.** Does it meet the requirements for a final manuscript?

Editing in Action

Note the editing corrections made in these paragraphs from a student essay. See the inside back cover of this book for an explanation of the editing symbols used.

Let There Be Art

A title is punctuated correctly.

An apostrophe is added to show plural possession.

A comma is placed after a transition.

A spelling error is corrected.

A proper noun is capitalized.

A usage error is corrected.

The Clintondale School Board is proposing to eliminate art classes next year. Last week's Clintondale Gazette quotes the board president, Bill Howland, as saying, "The board needs to decide which programs are necessary and which ones are not" (A5). Superintendent Melvin Ambrose adds that the district should focus on preparing students for exit exams. These concerns are important, but the board should consider just how necessary art really is for students' success.

First of all, art improves visual literacy. The International Visual Literacy Association defines visual literacy as a group of competencies "fundamental to normal human learning" (Avgerinou). Art helps students better understand visual information presented in math, science, English, and social studies. Art also equipps students to understand the images they see on TV and the Internet. In addition, art teaches students how to present their ideas in a visual way. Whether they are creating graphs for science or diagrams for social studies, students need art.

Art also prepares students for business. The business circle for arts education states the following: "Businesses understand that art education strengthens student problem-solving and critical thinking skills . . . " ("Facts"). Art courses ~~coarses~~ require students to solve problems in order to create a finished project. This project-based training is important . . .

Common Writing Errors

Here is a list of the 12 most common errors (other than spelling) to watch for when editing and proofreading your writing. (Corrections are in **red**.)

Sentence Fragment (See page 64.)

, she had a thorough understanding of classical music
Because Zora studied at a conservatory~~.~~

Comma Splice (See page 65.)

Fighting looks like play~~,~~; it teaches cubs important survival skills.

Run-On Sentence (See page 65.)

P
Weather is one cause of famine. ~~p~~olitical strife is another.

Comma Omitted After Long Introductory Phrase (See 512.4.)

Considering all of the incredible hype, the show was a disappointment.

Comma Omitted in a Compound Sentence (See 511.1.)

The first customer came before dawn, and the last one left after midnight.

Commas Omitted Around a Nonessential Element (See 513.2.)

Dr. Lydia Fong, who currently teaches math, has asked for a leave of absence.

Pronoun-Antecedent Agreement Error (See 590.2.)

his or her
Each candidate should report all of ~~their~~ income.

Shift in Person (See page 71.)

they
When people have heart attacks, ~~you~~ experience pain in the left arm.

Subject-Verb Agreement Error (See 588.)

is
The problem with the new facilities ~~are~~ the ventilation.

Shift in Verb Tense (See page 71.)

were
After the school board met, we ~~are~~ allowed to ask questions.

Dangling Modifier (See page 66.)

I found
After studying so long, the exam was a snap.

Faulty Parallelism (See page 71.)

Juma wants to graduate from college, become a volunteer medic, and ~~then he wants to~~ serve humankind in the African sub-Sahara.

A Guide to Publishing

Writer Peter Stillman states, "No piece of writing, regardless of how much you polish and fuss with it, comes out exactly as you want it to." You should know from experience just what Stillman is talking about. Every one of your essays will contain a few passages that just won't say what you want them to say, no matter how many times you rework them. The best you can do is make your writing as clear and correct as possible before publishing it.

The easiest and by far the most helpful form of publishing is sharing a finished project with your classmates. You can also submit a piece of writing to a class portfolio, school newspaper, or literary magazine. If you're really adventurous, submit your writing outside of school, perhaps to a national magazine.

WHAT'S AHEAD

This chapter contains ideas for publishing, for preparing a portfolio, and for submitting your writing to a publisher or an online site.

Publishing Ideas

As you will see in the list below, publishing covers a wide range of ideas. Some are easy to carry out, like sharing your writing with your classmates. Others are more challenging, like entering a writing contest.

PERFORMING
- Sharing with Classmates
- Reading to Other Audiences
- Producing a Video
- Performing Onstage

DISPLAYING
- Bulletin Boards/Display Cases
- Libraries
- Business Windows
- Clinic Waiting Rooms
- Literary/Art Fairs

SELF-PUBLISHING
- Family Newsletter
- Greeting/Special-Occasion Cards
- Personal Web Sites
- Booklets

SUBMITTING (IN SCHOOL)
- School Newspaper
- Literary Magazine
- Classroom Collection
- Class-Project Display
- Writing Portfolio (See next page.)

SUBMITTING (OUTSIDE OF SCHOOL)
- City Newspaper
- Area Historical Society
- Local Arts Council
- Church Publications
- Young Writers' Conferences
- Magazines/Contests
- Online Publications (See page 61.)

TIPS

FOR PUBLISHING

These suggestions will help you prepare your writing for publication.

- Work with your writing from start to finish before you submit it.
- Ask for input and advice throughout the writing process.
- Save all drafts of your writing for reference.
- Carefully edit your work for correctness.
- Present a clean, neat final copy. (See page 60.)
- Know your publishing options.
- Follow the publication's guidelines. (See page 60.)

Preparing a Portfolio

A writing portfolio is a collection of work that shows your skill as a writer. It is different from a writing folder that contains writing in various stages of completion. In most cases, you will be asked to compile a *showcase portfolio*, a collection of your best writing during the quarter or semester. Compiling a showcase portfolio allows you to participate in the assessment process. You decide which pieces to include, reflect upon your writing progress, and make sure the portfolio is arranged correctly. You are in control.

What You Should Include

Most showcase portfolios contain the following basic components. (Check with your instructor for the specific requirements.)

- **A table of contents** listing the pieces included in your portfolio
- **An opening essay or letter** detailing the story behind your portfolio (how you compiled it, what it means to you, etc.)
- **A specified number of finished pieces** representing your best writing in the class (You may be required to include all of your prewriting, drafting, and revising work for some pieces.)
- **A best "other" piece** related to your work in another content area
- **A cover sheet** attached to each piece of writing, discussing the reason for its selection and the work that went into it
- **Evaluation sheets or checklists** supplied by your teacher, to chart the basic skills you have mastered as well as the skills you still need to work on

How You Should Work

Use these tips as a guide as you develop a showcase portfolio.

1. Keep track of all your writing (including planning notes and drafts). This way, when it comes to compiling your portfolio, you will have all the pieces to work with.
2. Make sure that you understand all of the requirements for your portfolio.
3. Use an expandable folder for your portfolio to avoid dog-eared or ripped pages. Keep your papers in a "safe environment."
4. Maintain a regular writing/compiling schedule. It will be impossible to produce an effective portfolio if you approach it as a last-minute project.
5. Develop a feeling of pride in your portfolio. Make sure that it reflects a positive image of yourself. Look your best!

Submitting Writing to a Publisher

The information on this page serves as a basic guide if you are interested in submitting your writing for publication. You may want to talk with your English or composition instructor before you consider this form of publishing.

Q. What types of writing can I submit?

A. There are markets for all types of writing—essays, articles, stories, plays, and poems. Newspapers are most interested in essays and articles. Some magazines publish essays, articles, stories, and poetry; others accept only essays.

Help File

Check the *Writer's Market* or the *Writer's Market: The Electronic Edition* (CD-ROM or online download) to find out who publishes what. If your school library doesn't have either of these resources, your public library will.

Q. Where should I submit my writing?

A. You will probably have better success if you try to publish your work locally. Consider area newspapers and publications of local organizations. If you're interested in submitting something to a national publication, turn again to the *Writer's Market*. It includes a special section devoted to teen and young-adult publications. (See page 58 in this handbook for additional ideas.)

Q. How should I submit my work?

A. Check the publication's masthead for submission guidelines. (The masthead is the small print on one of the opening pages identifying the publisher and editors of the publication, subscription rates, the mailing address, etc.) You can also call the publication or go to its Web site. Most publications expect you to include . . .

- **a brief cover letter** (to a specific editor) identifying the title and form of your writing and the word count;
- **a neatly printed copy of your work** with your name on each page—double-spaced and paper-clipped; and
- **a SASE** (self-addressed stamped envelope) large enough for returning your manuscript after it has been read.

Q. What should I expect?

A. First, you should expect to wait a long time for a reply. (It may take up to two months in some cases.) Second, you should not be surprised or disappointed if your writing is not accepted for publication. Consider it a learning experience and keep submitting.

Publishing Online

The Internet offers many publishing opportunities. There are online magazines, writing contests, and other sites that accept submissions. The questions and answers below will help you publish on the Internet.

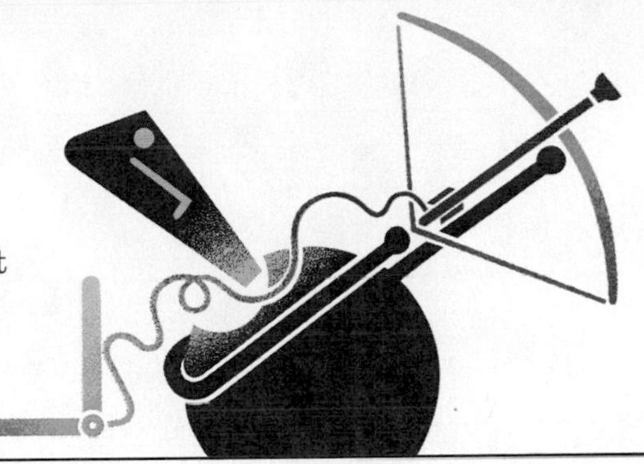

Q. What should I do first?

A. Begin by checking with your instructor to see if your school has its own Internet site where students can post their work. If not, suggest that one be started. Also ask your instructors about Web sites they know of that accept student submissions.

Q. How should I begin my Web search?

A. Use a search engine to find places to publish. Here's one starting point: Refer to the search engine's index of topics and look for an "education" topic; then click on the "K–12" subheading to see what develops. You can also enter "student, publish" as a search phrase and go from there.

Q. Does the Write Source have a Web site?

A. Yes, you can visit our Web site at www.thewritesource.com. Follow the "Publish It" link for a list of other Web sites that accept student submissions.

Q. How should I submit my work?

A. Before you do anything, make sure that you understand the publishing conditions related to a particular site. Then follow these guidelines:

- Include a message explaining why you are contacting the site. Keep your message brief and make your purpose clear.
- Send your work in an appropriate format. Some sites have online forms into which you can paste a text. Others list the electronic file formats they prefer to receive.
- Provide the publisher with correct information for contacting you. E-mail addresses sometimes change, so a site may ask for other information. (However, be careful about handing out personal information.)

Q. What should I expect?

A. Within a week or so of your submission, you should receive a note from the publisher verifying that your work has been received. However, it may take many weeks for the publisher to make a decision about publishing your work. If one site doesn't publish your work, you can always submit it to another.

The Basic **Elements** of Writing

Making Sentences Work

Editor Roscoe Born describes a good sentence as a "rifle shot—one missile, precisely aimed—rather than a buckshot load sprayed in the general direction of the target." This metaphor calls attention to a few key points related to sentence structure: Sentences work when they are clear, direct, and to the point. They work when they have the right sound, balance, and substance; and they work when they move smoothly and fluently from one point to the next. When the sentences in a piece of writing consistently hit the mark, the end result is an effective finished product.

WHAT'S AHEAD

This chapter will help you write "precisely aimed rifle shots." You'll find sets of guidelines to help you write clear, complete, and natural sentences, as well as guidelines to help you write sentences modeled after those of your favorite authors. Turn here whenever you have a question about your sentences.

Writing Complete Sentences

Except in a few special situations, you should use complete sentences when you write. By definition, a complete sentence expresses a complete thought. However, a sentence may actually contain several ideas, not just one. The trick is getting those ideas to work together to form a clear, interesting sentence that expresses your exact meaning.

Among the most common sentence errors that writers make are **fragments, comma splices, rambling sentences,** and **run-ons.**

"A sentence should read as if its author, had he held a plough instead of a pen, could have drawn a furrow deep and straight to the end."

—Henry David Thoreau

Fixing Common Sentence Problems

A **fragment** is a group of words used as a sentence. It is not a sentence, however, because it lacks a subject, a verb, or some other essential part. That missing part results in an incomplete thought.

Fragment: **The mountainous coastline with majestic, fjord-like waterways.** (This phrase lacks a verb.)

Sentence: **The mountainous coastline greets you with majestic, fjord-like waterways.**

Fragment: **If you approach New Zealand's South Island from the southwest.** (This clause is an incomplete thought. The reader needs to know what happens "if you approach New Zealand's South Island from the southwest.")

Sentence: **If you approach New Zealand's South Island from the southwest, the mountainous coastline greets you with majestic, fjord-like waterways.**

Fragment: **We plan to visit the strangely beautiful Lake Taupo area of North Island. Boiling springs, hot geysers, pools of steaming mud, and waterfalls cascading from volcanic peaks.** (This is a sentence followed by a fragment. You can correct this error by combining the fragment with the sentence.)

Sentence: **We plan to visit the strangely beautiful Lake Taupo area of North Island with its boiling springs, hot geysers, pools of steaming mud, and waterfalls cascading from volcanic peaks.**

A **comma splice** is a mistake made when two independent clauses are connected ("spliced") with only a comma. The comma is not enough: a period, semicolon, or conjunction is needed.

Splice: **The commuters had been bottlenecked on the freeway for two hours, the type A's had a crazed look in their eyes, the type B's were napping.**

Corrected: **The commuters had been bottlenecked on the freeway for two hours; the type A's had a crazed look in their eyes, but the type B's were napping.** (A semicolon and the coordinating conjunction *but* have been added to correct the two splices.)

Corrected: **The commuters had been bottlenecked on the freeway for two hours. The type A's had a crazed look in their eyes, but the type B's were napping.** (A period corrects the first splice in this instance.)

A **rambling sentence** is one that seems to go on and on. It is often the result of the overuse of the word "and."

Rambling: **The intruder entered through the window and moved sideways down the hall and under a stairwell and she stood waiting in the shadows.**

Corrected: **The intruder entered through the window. She moved sideways down the hall and under a stairwell where she stood, waiting in the shadows.**

A **run-on sentence** is actually two sentences joined without adequate punctuation or a connecting word.

Run-on: **I thought the test would never end I had a classic case of finger cramps with brain-drain complications.**

Corrected: **I thought the test would never end. I had a classic case of finger cramps with brain-drain complications.** (A period corrects the run-on sentence.)

Sound Advice

When you write dialogue, fragments are not mistakes. In fact, they are often preferable to complete sentences because that's how people talk:

"Hey, Vin! Wing night. McBob's. Seven-thirty."
"Well, if I finish my paper."
"Sure, okay. Later."

Writing Clear Sentences

Writing is thinking. Before you can write clearly, you must think clearly. Nothing is more frustrating for the reader than writing that has to be reread just to understand its basic meaning.

Look carefully at the common errors that follow. Do you recognize any of them as errors you sometimes make in your own writing? If so, use this section as a checklist when you revise. Detecting and correcting these errors will help to make your writing clear and readable.

"If any man wishes to write in a clear style let him first be clear in his thoughts."

—Johann Wolfgang von Goethe

Rewriting for Clarity

Misplaced modifiers are modifiers that have been placed incorrectly; therefore, the meaning of the sentence is not clear.

Misplaced: **The pool staff offers large beach towels to the students marked with chlorine-resistant ID numbers.**
(Students marked with chlorine-resistant ID numbers?)

Corrected: **The pool staff offers students large beach towels marked with chlorine-resistant ID numbers.**

Dangling modifiers are modifiers that appear to modify the wrong word or a word that isn't in the sentence.

Dangling: **Positioning herself to make the winning goal in the water polo match, Juanita's mother yelled from the sideline.**
(The phrase "positioning herself to make the winning goal in the water polo match" appears to modify Juanita's mother.)

Corrected: **Positioning herself to make the winning goal in the water polo match, Juanita heard her mother yelling from the sideline.**

Dangling: **Still failing to understand the concept, the physics teacher gave the students a list of extra reading assignments.**
(In this sentence, it appears as though the professor is "still failing to understand the concept.")

Corrected: **Still failing to understand the concept, the students received a list of extra reading assignments from the physics teacher.**
(Now the phrase clearly modifies those who are "failing to understand"—the students.)

An **incomplete comparison** is the result of leaving out a word or words that are necessary to show exactly what is being compared to what.

Incomplete: **Helium is a lighter gas.**

Clear: **Helium is a lighter gas than oxygen.**

Incomplete: **I get along better with my sister than my brother.** (Do you mean that you get along better with your sister than you get along with your brother, or that you get along better with your sister than your brother does?)

Clear: **I get along better with my sister than I do with my brother.**

Ambiguous wording is wording that is unclear because it has two or more possible meanings. It often occurs when sentences are combined.

Ambiguous: **Carmen decided to have pizza delivered to the lab where she was doing her experiment, which ended in disaster.** (What ended in disaster—Todd's ordering pizza in, or the experiment?)

Clear: **Carmen decided to have pizza delivered to the lab where she was doing her experiment, a decision that ended in disaster.**

An **indefinite reference** is a problem caused by careless use of pronouns. As a result, the reader cannot be sure what the pronoun or pronouns are referring to.

Indefinite: **When the pizza man arrived, she came wheeling around the corner with an enlarged copy of the "No Food in the Lab" rule sheet.** (Who is *she*?)

Clear: **When the pizza man arrived, Ms. Garcia came wheeling around the corner with an enlarged copy of the "No Food in the Lab" rule sheet.**

Indefinite: **As a startled Mr. Pizza Man attempted to slide the pizza next to the test-tube rack, it fell to the floor.** (What fell, the pizza or the rack?)

Clear: **As a startled Mr. Pizza Man attempted to slide the pizza next to the test-tube rack, the rack fell to the floor.**

Writing Natural Sentences

Samuel Johnson, the noted eighteenth-century writer, had this to say about the great temptation to overwrite, using big words, clever words, fancy words: "Read over your compositions and, when you meet a passage which you think is particularly fine, strike it out." For some reason, many people think that writing simply is not writing effectively. Nothing can be further from the truth.

The very best writing is sincere and natural, not fancy and artificial. That's why it is so important to master the art of freewriting. It is your best chance at a personal style. A personal voice will produce natural, honest passages you will not have to strike out. Learn from the following samples, which are wordy and artificial.

> "Confident writers have the courage to speak plainly; to let their thoughts shine rather than their vocabulary."
>
> —Ralph Keyes

Eliminating Overwriting

Deadwood is wording that fills up lots of space but does not add anything important or new to the overall meaning.

Deadwood: **I must tell you that, according to a lot of research out there, excessive partying, plus the chronic sleeping in that goes with it, will almost assuredly result in dismally poor grades.**

Concise: **Excessive partying and chronic sleeping in will probably result in poor grades.**

Flowery language is writing that uses more or bigger words than needed. This writing often contains too many adjectives or adverbs.

Flowery: **The gorgeous beauty of the Great Barrier Reef is fantastically displayed in coral formations of all the colors of the rainbow and in its wonderful, wide variety of tropical fish.**

Concise: **The beauty of the Great Barrier Reef is displayed in rainbow-colored coral formations and in an amazing variety of tropical fish.**

A **trite expression** is one that is overused and stale; as a result, it sounds neither sincere nor natural.

Trite: **In view of the fact that the class is filled, we regret to inform you that we cannot admit you to Anatomy 101.**

Natural: **Unfortunately, because the class is filled, we cannot admit you to Anatomy 101.**

Jargon is language used in a certain profession or by a particular group of people. It is usually very technical and not at all natural.

Jargon: **I'm having conceptual difficulty with these academic queries.**

Natural: **I don't understand these review questions.**

A **euphemism** is a word or phrase that is substituted for another because it is considered a less offensive way of saying something. (Avoid overusing euphemisms.)

Euphemism: **This environmentally challenged room has the distinct odor of a sanitary landfill.**

Natural: **This filthy room smells like a garbage dump.**

A **cliche** is an overused word or phrase that springs quickly to mind but just as quickly bores the user and the audience. A cliche gives the reader nothing new or original to think about and may even be confusing. (See page 124 for more information.)

Cliche: **Advice for applicants: Put your best foot forward!**

Natural: **Advice for applicants: Have confidence that you can succeed!**

Redundancy occurs when words (or synonyms for words) are repeated unnecessarily to add emphasis or to fill up space.

Redundant: **Don't drive through the construction site, and be sure to pick a different route if you want to avoid riding over nails and risking a flat tire.**

Concise: **Don't drive through the construction site if you want to avoid a flat tire.**

Common Redundancies

absolutely essential
advance warning
all inclusive
boiling hot
cash money
climb up
closed fist
close scrutiny
completely filled
crystal clear
empty space
end result
first of all
free gift
grand total
honest truth
ice cold
new and improved
passing fad
spinning around
terrible tragedy
true fact
unsolved mysteries
usual custom

Writing Acceptable Sentences

What Robert Frost says below is very true. Much of the color and charm of literature comes from the everyday habits, the customs, and especially the speech of its characters. It's important to keep that in mind when you write fiction of any kind. However, when you write essays, analyses, and most other assignments, remember that it's just as important to use language that is correct and appropriate.

"You can be a little ungrammatical if you come from the right part of the country."

—Robert Frost

Reworking Careless Writing

Substandard (nonstandard) **language** is language that is often acceptable in everyday conversation and in fictional writing, but seldom in other forms of writing.

Colloquial: Avoid the use of colloquial language, such as *go with* or *wait up*.

Hey, wait up! Cal wants to go with. (Substandard)
Hey, wait! Cal wants to go with us. (Standard)

Double preposition: Avoid the use of certain double prepositions: *off of, off to, from off.*

Pick up the sandwich scraps and dirty clothes from off the floor. (Substandard)
Pick up the sandwich scraps and dirty clothes from the floor. (Standard)

Substitution: Avoid substituting *and* for *to*.

Try and get to class on time. (Substandard)
Try to get to class on time. (Standard)

Avoid substituting *of* for *have* when combining with *could, would, should,* or *might*.

I should of studied for that exam. (Substandard)
I should have studied for that exam. (Standard)

Slang: Avoid the use of slang or any "in" words.

Completely zoned out after watching three solid hours of enterdrainment, Melanie googled yet another celebutante.

A **double negative** is a sentence that contains two negative words used to express a single negative idea. Double negatives are unacceptable in academic writing.

Awkward: **After paying for food and other essentials, I don't have no money left.**

Corrected: **I haven't got any money left. / I have no money left.**

NOTE: Do not use *hardly, barely,* or *scarcely* with a negative; the result is a double negative.

A **shift in construction** is a change in the structure or style midway through a sentence.

Shift in number: **When a person first goes apartment hunting, they ought to look for one that is both comfortable and affordable.**

Corrected: **When a person first goes apartment hunting, he or she ought to look for one that is both comfortable and affordable.** (The pronouns *he* or *she* agree in number with the singular antecedent *person*.)

Shift in tense: **Sheila looked over nine apartments in one weekend before she had chosen one.**

Corrected: **Sheila looked over nine apartments in one weekend before she chose one.** (*Chose* is a past tense verb as is *looked*.)

Shift in person: **You really should check the cupboards, too, or one may be surprised later by mice and other critters.**

Corrected: **You really should check the cupboards, too, or you may be surprised later by mice and other critters.** (Both pronouns are now second person—*you*.)

Shift in voice: **As you continue** (active voice) **to look for just the right place to live, many dirty, dumpy apartments will probably be toured** (passive voice).

Corrected: **As you continue to look for just the right place to live, you will probably tour many dirty, dumpy apartments.** (The verbs *continue* and *will tour* are both active voice.)

Inconsistent (unparallel) construction occurs when the kind of words or phrases being used changes in the middle of a sentence.

Inconsistent: **In my neighborhood, students use free time to shoot hoops, play video games, and eating fast food.** (The sentence switched from the base verbs *shoot* and *play* to the participle *eating*.)

Corrected: **In my neighborhood, students use free time to shoot hoops, play video games, and eat fast food.** (Now all three activities are expressed in a consistent or parallel fashion.)

Combining Sentences

Most mature sentences contain several basic ideas that work together to form a complete thought. For example, if you were to write a sentence about the construction of the Great Wall of China, you would probably be working with several different ideas:

1. The longest and largest construction project in history was the Great Wall of China.
2. The project took 1,700 years to complete.
3. The Great Wall of China is 1,400 miles long.
4. It is between 18 and 30 feet high.
5. It is up to 32 feet thick.

The Combining Process in Action

Of course, you wouldn't express each idea separately like this. Instead, you would combine these ideas (some or all of them) into longer, more mature sentences. Sentence combining is generally carried out in the following ways:

- Use a **series** to combine three or more similar ideas.

  The Great Wall of China is 1,400 miles long, between 18 and 30 feet high, and up to 32 feet thick.

- Use a **relative pronoun** *(who, whose, that, which)* to introduce subordinate (less important) ideas.

  The Great Wall of China, which is 1,400 miles long and between 18 and 30 feet high, took 1,700 years to complete.

- Use an **introductory phrase** or **clause**.

  Having taken 1,700 years to complete, the Great Wall of China was the longest construction project in history.

- Use a **semicolon** (and a conjunctive adverb if appropriate).

  The Great Wall took 1,700 years to complete; it is 1,400 miles long and up to 30 feet high and 32 feet thick.

- Repeat a **key word** or phrase to emphasize an idea.

  The Great Wall of China was the longest construction project in history, a project that took 1,700 years to complete.

- Use **correlative conjunctions** *(either, or; not only, but also)* to compare or contrast two ideas in a sentence.

  The Great Wall of China is not only up to 30 feet high and 32 feet thick but also 1,400 miles long.

- Use an **appositive** (a word or phrase that renames) for emphasis.

  The Great Wall of China—the largest construction project in history—is 1,400 miles long, 32 feet thick, and up to 30 feet high.

Modeling Sentences

What you find when you study the sentences of your favorite authors may surprise you. They use sentences that seem to flow on forever, sentences that hit you right between the eyes, sentences that sneak up on you, and "sentences" that are not, by definition, sentences at all. Writers do occasionally break the rules.

INSIDE INFO

Many authors today write in a relaxed, informal style characterized by sentences with personality, rhythm, and varied structures.

The Modeling Process in Action

You will want to imitate certain sentences because they sound good or make a point so well. This process is sometimes called **modeling**. Here's how you can get started:

- **Reserve** a special section in a notebook or journal to list effective sentences you come across in your reading.
- **List** well-made sentences that flow smoothly, that use effective descriptive words, or that contain original figures of speech (metaphor, simile, personification, and so on).

  He has a thin face with sharp features and a couple of eyes burning with truth oil.

  —Tom Wolfe

- **Study** each sentence so you know how it is put together. Read it out loud. Look for phrases and clauses set off by commas. Also focus on word endings (*-ing, -ed,* etc.) and on the location of articles (*a, an, the*) and prepositions (*to, by, of,* etc.).

  He has a thin face with sharp features and a couple of eyes burning with truth oil.

  —Tom Wolfe

- **Write** your own version of a sentence by imitating it part by part. Try to use the same word endings, articles, and prepositions, but work in your own nouns, verbs, and modifiers. (Your imitation does not have to be exact.) Practice writing several versions.

  He has an athletic body with a sinewy contour and a couple of arms bulging with weight-room dedication.

- **Continue** imitating good sentences. The more you practice, the more you will find professional-sounding sentences in your own essays and stories.

Expanding Sentences

Details seem to spill out of accomplished writers' minds naturally. Readers marvel at how effectively these authors can expand a basic idea with engaging details. Maybe you envy good writers because of this special ability and wish you could write in the same way. The truth is you can, if you practice.

Creating Cumulative Sentences

Above all other types of sentences, the *cumulative sentence* marks an accomplished writer. What you normally find in a cumulative sentence is a main idea that is expanded by modifying words, phrases, or clauses. (See 585.1 for more information.) Here's a sample cumulative sentence with the expanding modifiers coming *after* the main clause (in **red**).

Gina was studying at the kitchen table, memorizing a list of vocabulary words, completely focused, intent on acing tomorrow's Spanish quiz.

Discussion: Notice how each new modifier adds another level of meaning to the sentence. Three modifying phrases have been added. Here's another cumulative sentence with expanding modifiers coming *before* and *after* the main clause (in **red**).

Before every practice, Kesha Sims and Aiko Sato work on free throws, taking 50 shots each.

Discussion: In this case, a prepositional phrase **(Before every practice)** and a participial phrase **(taking 50 shots each)** add important details to the main clause.

Expanding with Details

Here are seven basic ways to expand this main idea: *Tony is laughing.*

1. with **individual words:** *halfheartedly*
2. with **prepositional phrases:** *with his hands on his face*
3. with **absolute phrases:** *his head tilted to one side*
4. with **participial *(-ing* or *-ed)* phrases:** *looking puzzled*
5. with **infinitive phrases:** *to hide his embarrassment*
6. with **subordinate clauses:** *while his friend talks*
7. with **relative clauses:** *who is usually long faced and somber*

Help File

To write stylistic sentences, practice sentence modeling and sentence expanding. Also read often, attentively, noticing the style as well as the content of the text.

Developing Strong Paragraphs

When it comes to writing well, you must remember these two words: support and organization. You need to select details that support your main point, and you need to organize those details effectively. That's where one basic form of writing, the paragraph, comes into play. Paragraphs help you organize your thoughts and make it easier for the reader to follow your line of thinking.

During the sometimes messy revising process, it is the paragraph that enables you to rearrange your details into logical units that deliver a strong, clear message from start to finish. You'll know your writing succeeds when each paragraph works by itself and with the others that come before and after it.

WHAT'S AHEAD

This chapter reviews the parts and types of paragraphs and includes information about understanding and arranging details. You'll find a helpful chart of transitional words and phrases.

The Parts of a Paragraph

Most paragraphs begin with a topic sentence, identifying the topic of the writing. The sentences in the body of the paragraph support or explain the topic, while the closing sentence brings the paragraph to a logical stopping point.

The Topic Sentence ■ The topic sentence tells the reader what your paragraph is about. Here is a formula for topic sentences:

FORMULA

A specific topic
+ a particular feeling or feature about the topic
= an effective topic sentence.

Topic Sentence: **Canada's 29–30 million people** (topic) **can be divided into three main groups: native people, descendents of Europeans, and more recent immigrants** (particular feature).

INSIDE INFO

The topic sentence isn't always the first sentence in a paragraph. It can also appear in the middle or at the end of the paragraph. For example, you can begin a paragraph with details that build up to the summary topic statement. (See the next two pages.)

The Body ■ The body is the main part of the paragraph. It contains all of the information the reader needs to understand the topic. The sentences in the body should contain details that clearly support the topic sentence. Arrange these details in the best possible order.

Body Sentence: **Native people, about 2 percent of the population, are those who came across the Bering Strait from Asia thousands of years ago.**

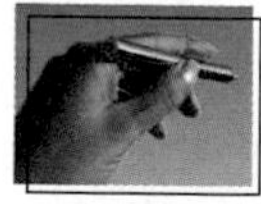

NOTE: Turn to "Arranging Details," pages 84–87, when you have questions about how to organize the details in a paragraph.

The Closing ■ The closing (clincher) sentence comes after all the details have been included in the body of the paragraph. This sentence may (1) remind your reader of the topic, (2) summarize the paragraph, or (3) link the paragraph to the next one.

Closing Sentence: **All three groups contribute to making Canada a rich and interesting culture.**

A Closer Look at Topic Sentences

Where you place the topic sentence in a paragraph depends on the purpose of your writing. The examples below and on the next page show topic sentences placed at the beginning, at the end, and in the middle of paragraphs.

Placing the Topic Sentence First: Put the topic sentence first when you want to be absolutely direct—stating the main idea and then developing it. With this placement, the reader immediately understands the main point and how it relates to the previous paragraph. (The excerpt below, taken from a student writer's essay on Scotland, begins with the last sentence of the paragraph that precedes the model.)

> . . . If what you seek is quiet, peace, and a time to reflect, I can think of no better hideaway than Scotland.
>
> However, the paradox of Scotland is that violence was once the norm in this now-peaceful land. In fact, the country was born, bred, and came of age during war. The Picts were the first inhabitants, fierce men so named by the Romans because tattoos covered their bodies like paint. The mighty Romans could not conquer them, so the Empire had to erect two huge walls to keep them out. Eventually, both walls fell, and the Romans left. By 844, Picts were united with the Scots, invaders from Ireland, under Kenneth MacAlpin, the first king of Scotland. The loosely knit nation of clans then spent nearly the next millennium fighting against the English and each other. But unlike the Irish nationalists, the Scots fell silent after the last uprising was crushed in the eighteenth century.

Placing the Topic Sentence at the End: Put the paragraph's key idea at the end when you want to give details or arguments that build up to it, a strategy particularly useful in persuasive writing. The paragraph below, from a student writer's paper on changes in affirmative action, uses a question to introduce the main idea, but saves the topic sentence for the end.

> How, exactly, has the definition of "affirmative action" changed since the concept became an issue in the 1960s? William Bradford Reynolds, former assistant attorney general in the Civil Rights Division, describes this process in "Affirmative Action and Its Negative Repercussions." When affirmative action started in the '60s, it was meant to help everybody, not just certain ethnic groups. As Reynolds says, it was "originally defined in terms of active recruitment and outreach measures aimed at enhancing employment for all Americans" (38). But in the '70s this broad definition narrowed. Reynolds argues that during that decade, affirmative action turned into a tool for creating racial balance in the workplace. It became a way of enhancing employment opportunities for select groups. After several court battles in the '80s and the Civil Rights Act of 1991, the definition of affirmative action changed again: it came to be seen as a tool of last resort in cases of persistent discrimination. Thus, through four decades of struggle and social change, affirmative action has shifted from its original meaning and purpose.

Placing the Topic Sentence in the Middle: Put the topic sentence in the middle of the paragraph when you want to build up to and then move away from the main idea. Such an approach can let you show two sides of an issue, hinged on a central topic sentence. In the paragraph below, a student writer compares events within a film with those that were part of the filmmaking process.

During the making of *Apocalypse Now,* Eleanor Coppola, wife of the film's director, gathered documentary footage of how the movie was being made. This footage became a separate film called *Hearts of Darkness: A Filmmaker's Apocalypse.* In the first film, the renegade Kurtz has disappeared with his men and native followers into the Cambodian jungle. Having gone insane, he carries on his own war using his own brutal methods. The film's main character, Captain Willard, must "find and terminate" Kurtz. As Willard's search for Kurtz lengthens, the screen fills with flames, smoke, exploding bodies, burning bodies, and blood. However, as *Hearts of Darkness* relates, the horror and insanity portrayed in the fictional *Apocalypse Now* was, in fact, being lived out in the real lives of the production company. In the documentary, director Francis Ford Coppola says about the movie *Apocalypse Now,* "too much money, too much equipment, and little by little we went insane" (*Hearts*). Larry Fishburne, who played one of Willard's men, says in the documentary, "War is fun. You can do anything you want to. That's why Vietnam must have been so much fun for the guys out there" (*Hearts*). Toward the end of the filming of *Apocalypse Now,* Martin Sheen, who played Willard, suffered a life-threatening heart attack. When one of Coppola's assistants sent the news back to the investors in the United States, the director exploded: "Even if Marty dies, he's not dead unless I say he's dead" (*Hearts*).

Creating Coherence

In addition to writing a clear topic sentence, you can do several other things to keep your paragraphs coherent and focused.

- **Monitor the use of tense throughout a paragraph to avoid confusion.** The above paragraph opens and closes in the past tense; references to the screenplays, however, are all in the present tense, as they should be.
- **Use parallel constructions to increase readability and clarity.** Participial phrases such as "portrayed in the fictional *Apocalypse Now*" and "lived out in the real lives of the production company" make the main point of the topic sentence clear.
- **Repeat key words or phrases for added meaning and emphasis.** "Having gone insane" and, later, "little by little we went insane" emphasize the focus of the paragraph.
- **Use transitions to improve the flow of ideas.** Words like "during," "however," and "toward the end" keep the reader on track throughout the paragraph.

Achieving Unity

To achieve unity or coherence, make sure all sentences in the body of a paragraph support the topic sentence. If any sentences shift the focus away from the topic, revise the paragraph in one of the following ways:

- Delete the material from the paragraph.
- Rewrite the material so that it clearly supports the topic sentence.
- Create a separate paragraph for the material.
- Revise the topic sentence so that it relates more closely to the supporting sentences.

Revising for Unity

Examine the following paragraphs about fishing hooks. The original topic sentence focuses on the idea that some anglers prefer smooth hooks instead of barbed hooks. However, the writer doesn't completely develop this idea and changes the focus to the cost of new hooks. In his revised version, the writer restores unity by discussing anglers who prefer smooth hooks in the first paragraph and addressing replacement costs in the second paragraph.

Original (Lacks unity)

According to some anglers who do use smooth hooks, their lures perform better than barbed lures as long as they maintain a constant tension on the line. Smooth hooks can bite deeper than barbed hooks, actually providing a stronger hold on the fish. Some people have argued that replacing all of the barbed hooks in their tackle would be a costly operation.

Revised Version (Shows unity)

According to some anglers who do use smooth hooks, their lures perform better than barbed lures as long as they maintain a constant tension on the line. Smooth hooks can bite deeper than barbed hooks, actually providing a stronger hold on the fish. These anglers testify that switching from barbed hooks hasn't ruined their catch. They land approximately the same number of fish. In fact, they enjoy the sport even more because of the added challenge of playing the fish (maintaining line tension).

Some people have argued that replacing all of the barbed hooks in their tackle would be a costly operation. While this is certainly a concern, people who fish do not necessarily have to replace their hooks. With a simple set of pliers, they can bend down the barbs on most conventional hooks, modifying their existing tackle at no cost.

Types of Paragraphs

There are four types of paragraphs: expository, descriptive, narrative, and persuasive. (Notice how the details support each topic sentence.)

Expository

An **expository paragraph** presents facts, gives directions, defines terms, and so on. It should clearly inform the reader about a specific subject.

"Hope is a dangerous thing," Morgan Freeman tells his fellow inmate in the movie *Shawshank Redemption*. "It can drive a man insane." In this negative view, the prisoner sees hope only as wishful thinking, not determination. Freeman believes that hope cannot coexist with what he calls being institutionalized—accepting fate and living it—and Freeman prefers his world safe, without the disappointments hope brings. When serving a life sentence in jail, this is logical, but not entirely human. In contrast, others have taken a more romantic, optimistic view of hope. Pliny the Elder, a first-century Roman, said, "Hope is the pillar that holds up the world. Hope is the dream of the walking man." This is a grand view, but questionable as well. Finally, Webster defines hope as "a feeling that what is wanted will happen." So which understanding of hope is right? Is it good, bad, or neutral? Hope may indeed run contrary to cultural norms and institutions and at the same time be intrinsic to humanity. In her short fiction, Eudora Welty reveals hope as the reason her heroines break from their cultural expectations. To Welty, hope is a paradox, part of being human and yet a defiance of everyday, normal life.

Descriptive

A **descriptive paragraph** presents a clear picture of a person, a place, a thing, or an idea. It should contain plenty of sensory details.

The new passenger made herself known. She stomped up each stair onto the bus, one hand gripping the steel side bar, the other hand firmly pressed on her cane, a thick walking stick with a worn silver duck's head for a handle. She nodded regally to the driver as her coins clattered into the fare box, then surveyed the bus for the likeliest seat. She started slowly down the center aisle, her wizened hand flitting from the back of one seat to the next. The scent of stale lilacs mingled with a trace of fried onions followed her down the aisle. Finally, she stopped in front of a young girl whose ear was dotted with piercings. The old woman tapped her cane against the girl's booted foot, nudging it aside. The girl wordlessly moved over to the window seat. Leaning on her cane, the old woman sat down gingerly, swinging her legs in after her. She smoothed the front of her coat, made of an expensive fabric that had seen better days. Head erect, cloudy black eyes bright with defiant victory, the old woman stared straight ahead, her left hand, adorned with only a worn gold band, gently caressing the silver duck head. Her highness had claimed her kingdom.

Narrative

A **narrative paragraph** tells a story. It should include details that answer the 5 W's *(Who? What? When? Where?* and *Why?)* about the experience.

In first grade, I learned some of the harsh realities of life. I found out that circuses aren't all they're supposed to be. We were going to the circus for our class trip, and I was really excited about it. Our class worked for weeks on a circus train made of shoe boxes. The day of the trip finally came, and the circus I dreamed of turned out to be nothing but one disappointment after another. First, I couldn't see much of anything. I could just barely make out some tiny figures scurrying around in the three rings. After the first half hour, all I wanted to do was buy a soda and a monkey-on-a-stick and get out of there. Of course, nothing in life is that easy. We weren't allowed to buy anything, so I couldn't have my souvenir; and instead of a cold soda to quench my thirst, I had lukewarm milk that the room mothers had so thoughtfully brought along. I returned to school tired and a little wiser. I remember looking at our little circus train on the window ledge and thinking that I'd rather sit and watch it do nothing than go to another circus.

Persuasive

A **persuasive paragraph** expresses an opinion and tries to convince the reader that the opinion is valid. It should contain supporting points that help solidify your argument.

Spaying or neutering is a humane way to treat the growing problem of unwanted animals in the United States. These simple operations can eliminate aggressive behavior and roaming, reducing the risk that a pet may be hit by a car or injured in a fight with another animal. While "fixing" a pet may make it gentler, it will not eliminate the protective behavior desired of watchdogs. Some say that fixing a cat or dog will make it fat and lazy, but overfeeding and lack of exercise do that. Spaying or neutering a pet may actually protect the animal's health, reducing or eliminating the risk of various cancers. Altered pets, in fact, live long, healthy lives. Perhaps the most compelling reason for altering a pet is to reduce the number of unwanted animals that fill pounds and humane societies. According to the American Humane Society, one dog or cat can be responsible for thousands of puppies or kittens born within a seven-year period. Controlling the pet population can reduce the numbers of homeless dogs and cats that roam city streets and the countryside, just trying to survive. These abandoned animals often revert to the wild, posing a threat or nuisance similar to the one posed by coyotes. It's cruel and even dangerous to allow animals to continue having unwanted litters. By spaying or neutering their pets, people can create a healthier, safer world for domestic animals.

Understanding Details

There are many types of details you can include in paragraphs (and in longer forms of writing). Your reason for writing determines which details are most important to your work. The key types of details are explained below and on the next page.

FACTS are details that can be proven. Facts remain constant, regardless of the type of paragraph you write.

> In 1966, for the first time ever, five African Americans started for the Texas Western Miners in the NCAA basketball championship.
>
> When faced with impeachment as a result of his role in Watergate, President Richard Nixon resigned on August 9, 1974.

STATISTICS present significant numerical information about a chosen topic.

> Making the *Lord of the Rings* films was an epic filmmaking process that included shooting more than 600 million feet of film, using 2,700 special-effects shots, and creating 1,600 pairs of Hobbit feet.
>
> With more than 900 wins and a winning percentage over .800, Tennessee coach Pat Summitt is the winningest coach in college basketball history.

EXAMPLES are individual samples that illustrate a main point.

> During the Victorian period of architecture, the Stick style was often overshadowed by other styles, but it had its own unique characteristics (main point). As its name suggests, the Stick style is known for its stick work, the decorative patterns of boards on a house's exterior. Stick houses were always clad with wood siding. The stick work created horizontal, vertical, or diagonal patterns on the siding, which imitated architecture from medieval Europe.

ANECDOTES are brief stories or "slices of life" that help you make your point. They can illustrate a point more personally than a matter-of-fact listing of details.

> Sometimes people's minds play tricks on them, and they need to take the time to look up information that they think they know. Explaining his embarrassing "potatoe" spelling incident, former vice president Dan Quayle admitted, "I should have caught the mistake on that spelling bee card, but as Mark Twain once said, 'You should never trust a man who has only one way to spell a word.' " When told that it was actually President Andrew Jackson and not Mark Twain he quoted, Quayle said, "I should have remembered that was Andrew Jackson who said that since he got his nickname 'Stonewall' by vetoing bills passed by Congress." Quayle was wrong again. He had confused Andrew Jackson with the Confederate general Thomas Jackson, who received the nickname "Stonewall" during the Civil War.

NOTE: Make sure that an anecdote makes a pertinent point about your specific topic.

Quotations are words from other people that you repeat exactly in your writing. They can provide powerful supporting evidence.

> Sometimes a comic observation can make you think about an important topic. For example, comedian Jay London observed, "I told my therapist I was having nightmares about nuclear explosions. He said, 'Don't worry, it's not the end of the world.' " We laugh at the idea, but when we actually think about it, the statement does remind us that we live in the nuclear age.

Definitions provide the meanings of unfamiliar terms. Definitions may add some clarity to your writing.

> Greener vehicles may run on biodiesel, a renewable fuel derived from vegetable oil or animal fat.

Reasons justify ideas or actions, expand motives, and answer the "Why?" question.

> Filmmakers should not be allowed to make sequels, especially ones with successive numbers in the titles. Producers should know that sequels lose money. Although these movies are made to capitalize on the success of the first film, no sequel has topped an original at the box office. With few exceptions, such as *Godfather II* and *Godfather III*, sequels almost never approach the quality of the original film. With each increasing title number, the film's originality decreases. Did we really need *Jason X* when *Friday the 13th* was enough? Most importantly, for each sequel, you lose one or more "A" stars from the one before it. This clearly makes each movie less watchable.

Summaries give shorter versions of things said, written, or done.

> On March 23, 1775, Patrick Henry gave a speech to the Virginia Convention. He noted his reasons for rebelling against the British Crown—his love for his country, his distrust of British governors, and his hope for others to stand up against oppression. Most remember only his closing remark that summed up his argument—"Give me liberty, or give me death!"

Comparisons show how two topics are similar or different.

> Although they were fought about 40 years apart, the war in Iraq is still similar to the Vietnam War. Most United States citizens did not know where Vietnam was in 1966. In 2006, after three years of war, 63 percent of U.S. citizens ages 18–24 could not find Iraq on a map. The U.S. entered both wars because of a perceived threat: Vietnam because of Communism and Iraq because of terrorism. Both wars were fought against a stubborn enemy that used guerrilla tactics. Early in each war, both Lyndon Johnson and George W. Bush declared that the mission was accomplished. Then, as the wars continued, both saw their approval ratings plummet.

Analyses break down complex wholes into their major parts.

> American government thrives due to the balance of power among its three branches of leadership: the executive (the president), which enforces laws; the legislative (the Congress), which makes laws; and the judicial (the Supreme Court), which interprets laws.

Arranging Details

On the next four pages, you will find sample paragraphs following seven basic methods of organization. Review these samples when you have questions about arranging the details in your own writing.

Classification

Classification is an effective method for explaining a complex term or concept. To classify, you break a topic down into categories and subcategories to help the reader better understand it. The following paragraph classifies the three main types of plastics.

Since the first plastic, cellulose nitrate, was developed more than 100 years ago, this durable material has become an integral part of daily life. Three structurally different plastics are created by chemically changing natural materials or by synthesizing raw materials. The three types are characterized by their molecular structure, which determines how each type reacts to heat. *Thermoplastics* have a branched molecular structure that forms the weakest bond. Pliable at normal temperatures, they melt into a sticky mess with high heat (packaging). Durable *elastomers* have a cross-link structure that allows for flexibility. Once shaped through heating, however, they cannot be reshaped but retain flexibility (tires). *Thermosets,* the most tightly structured plastics, are very hard, with a tightly woven molecular structure that resists reshaping once they are cured. This type of plastic is used to make everything from outlet covers to computer shelves. Different types of plastics, each designed to meet different needs, all play key roles in today's world.

Analogy

An **analogy** is another effective method for explaining a complex or unfamiliar topic. To develop an analogy, you explain the unfamiliar topic in terms of a familiar one. The following paragraph explains the immune system in terms of how the security system in a mall works.

The human body is like a mall, and the immune system is like mall security. Because the mall has hundreds of employees and thousands of customers, security guards must rely on photo ID's, name tags, and uniforms to decide who should be allowed to open cash registers and who should have access to the vaults. In the same way, white blood cells and antibodies need to use DNA cues to recognize which cells belong in a body and which do not. Occasionally security guards make mistakes, wrestling Kookie the Klown to the ground while DVD players "walk" out of the service entrance, but these problems amount to allergic reactions or little infections. If security guards become hypervigilant, detaining every customer and employee, the situation is akin to leukemia, in which white blood cells attack healthy cells. If security guards become corrupt, letting some thieves take a "five-finger discount," the situation is akin to AIDS. Both systems—mall security and human immunity—work by correctly differentiating friend from foe.

"First, work hard to master the tools. Simplify, prune, and strive for order."
—William Zinsser

Chronological Order

Sharing a Story

Chronological (time) **order** is effective for sharing a story or explaining a process. Information is organized according to what happens first, second, third, and so on. The paragraph below uses chronological order to tell about applying for a summer job.

When I applied to work on a mail boat last summer, I went through an unusual application process. Surprisingly, there was no interview for this job. Instead, I had to show that I could leap from boat to pier and back again. On "audition" day, all of the job hopefuls were loaded onto the huge, flat mail boat, which motored away from the dock to start its circle around the large lake. At the first pier, the driver shouted a name. A girl with a long ponytail stepped up and was handed a fake packet of mail and instructed to make the delivery. She mistimed her jump and hit the water with a loud splash. We pulled her in, laughing and sputtering, and the boat continued to the next pier. One by one, we each had to make the jump from boat to pier. Some of us made it, and some of us didn't. I didn't time my return jump quite right and fell into the cold water. Those in the group who made the leap both ways became mail deliverers. I ended up working for a boat rental business instead. That wasn't too bad, but it wasn't as exciting as working on the mail boat. So next year I will again leap at the chance to deliver mail.

Explaining a Process

Chronological order is useful when explaining a process or series of steps. The writer introduces the topic and then describes the process step-by-step.

Perhaps the biggest threat to the nation's freshwater lakes is the process of eutrophication, caused by an excess of nutrients. The process begins at the oligotrophic phase, when water is clear with little aerobic activity. In the second phase, the mesotrophic phase, fertilizers are washed into the water through rain runoff. Rich with nitrates and phosphates, the fertilizers stimulate the growth of algae and other water plants, creating an algal "bloom." By phase three, the eutrophic phase, the bloom has grown to affect the oxygen level in the water in two ways. First, it prevents the water from absorbing light needed for oxygen generation. Second, the algae is broken down by aerobic bacteria that further deplete the oxygen in the water. Left unchecked, the process moves to the hypereutrophic phase, when algae chokes and kills living organisms. The final stage is the dystrophic phase in which water becomes hypoxic, or lacking in enough oxygen to sustain life, and the body of water becomes officially "dead." People in this country must find a way to counteract this process or face losing the nation's clean freshwater supply.

Illustration

Illustration (general to specific) is a method of organization in which a general idea (the topic sentence) is stated and followed with specific details, facts, and examples that clarify or support the idea. The paragraph below opens with a main point about humpback whales and follows with an explanation of the current research on the subject.

> It's hard to say how humpback whales find their way. They may rely on their excellent sense of hearing to pick up low-frequency sound waves that bounce off common ocean features such as rock and coral. Scientists also believe that they may look for familiar landforms. Two researchers recently detected a small amount of magnetic material in humpbacks, which may allow them to migrate by sensing the earth's magnetic field. This may explain why whales get stranded. Some researchers think it's because they are drawn to coasts with low magnetic forces, thinking they are clear waterways. This would also explain how they could follow such precise migration paths.

Climax

Climax (specific to general) is a method of organization in which the specific details lead up to an important summary statement. (If a topic sentence is used, it is placed at the end.) The following paragraph shows the excitement building as the writer waits for a concert to begin.

> As the lights dimmed in the amphitheater, multicolored spotlights began to circle overhead, bouncing off the ceiling and swirling over the heads of the crowd. The sound began to build. At first, it sounded like thunder rumbling in the distance, but soon it grew to a deafening roar. People all around were stamping their feet, clapping their hands, and whistling through their fingers to show that they were ready for the show to begin. The crowd noise was soon drowned out by a blast of bass guitar and drums that seemed to come out of nowhere. Behind a blinding flash of light and a shower of glittering sparks, the band appeared onstage and began to play. At last, the concert had begun.

Help File

When you organize a paragraph from general to specific, you are working **deductively**. Most scientific and informative writing requires deductive reasoning because it helps make complicated material easy to understand. When you organize from specific to general, you are working **inductively**. Inductive reasoning is often used in personal essays and short stories.

Comparison and Contrast

In the paragraphs that follow, the writer **compares** and **contrasts** the literary characters Ulysses and Arthur. More particularly, he is comparing Lord Tennyson's version of these characters in two of Tennyson's poems. The writer covers similarities in the first paragraph and moves on to differences in the next.

In Alfred, Lord Tennyson's "Ulysses" and *Idylls of the King,* the title heroes Ulysses and Arthur are alike in many ways, yet significant differences are apparent. Indeed, both Ulysses and Arthur deal with problems that all men face. Both heroes are disappointed in people. In Ithaca, the Greek hero of the Trojan War rules a "savage race" of people who do not know him and do not appreciate him; while in Britain, Arthur must engage in battle with knights who once loved him. Furthermore, both Ulysses and Arthur must recognize that their sons do not share their ideals. Telemachus is not a hero; he is "centered in the sphere of common duties." Arthur's illegitimate son, Mordred, lacks morals and leads a rebellion against him. Finally, both Ulysses and Arthur face death. The aged Ulysses recognizes that his life is almost over, and in winter, King Arthur is mortally wounded in battle. Clearly, both legendary heroes struggle with universal problems.

Nevertheless, these legendary heroes have distinctly different personalities. Tennyson portrays Ulysses as a self-centered man, while Arthur is a model ruler. Ulysses leaves his subjects in Ithaca before order is fully restored because he finds life too dull there and wants to do some "work of noble note"—possibly to increase his fame. Arthur, on the other hand, loves his people, struggles against evil, and dies trying to restore the glory of the past. In addition, Ulysses draws no emotional response, while Arthur is both hated and loved. Although Ulysses was absent for ten years after the Trojan War, his wife and son are lukewarm toward him and do not beg him to stay at home. Mordred, on the other hand, wickedly plots against the virtuous English king. Sir Bedivere weeps as he carries Arthur out of the church, and the three queens receive the dying king with tears. Finally, the gods seem unimportant to Tennyson's Ulysses, while Arthur is religious. Although Ulysses briefly mentions striving with gods in the past, they do not appear to play a role in his daily life. Arthur, however, is a devout Christian who tries to do the will of God and believes in the power of prayer. It seems fair to conclude that, even though Tennyson's Ulysses and Arthur are similar on the surface, a closer look reveals significant differences.

NOTE: Pay special attention to transitions in the above paragraphs. Transitions are used within each paragraph ("furthermore," "finally," "on the other hand," and so on) and between them ("nevertheless") to move smoothly from one idea or train of thought to the next. (See the next two pages for a list of transitions.)

Using Transitions

Transitions can be used to connect one sentence to another within a paragraph, or to connect one paragraph to another within a longer essay or report. The lists that follow show a number of transitions and how they are used. Each **colored list** is a group of transitions that could work well together in a piece of writing.

Words used to show location

above	around	between	inside	outside
across	behind	by	into	over
against	below	down	near	throughout
along	beneath	in back of	next to	to the right
among	beside	in front of	on top of	under

Above	In front of	On top of
Below	Beside	Next to
To the left	In back of	Beneath
To the right		

Words used to show time

about	during	yesterday	until	finally
after	first	meanwhile	next	then
at	second	today	soon	as soon as
before	to begin	tomorrow	later	in the end

First	To begin	Now	First	Before
Second	To continue	Soon	Then	During
Third	To conclude	Eventually	Next	After
Finally			In the end	

Words used to compare things

likewise	as	in the same way	one way
like	also	similarly	both

In the same way	One way
Also	Another way
Similarly	Both

Words used to contrast (show differences)

but	still	although	on the other hand
however	yet	otherwise	even though

On the other hand	Although
Even though	Yet
Still	Nevertheless

Words used to emphasize a point

again	truly	especially	for this reason
to repeat	in fact	to emphasize	

For this reason	Truly	In fact
Especially	To emphasize	To repeat

Words used to conclude or summarize

finally	as a result	to sum it up	in conclusion
lastly	therefore	all in all	because

Because	As a result	To sum it up	Therefore
In conclusion	All in all	Because	Finally

Words used to add information

again	another	for instance	for example
also	and	moreover	additionally
as well	besides	along with	other
next	finally	in addition	

For example	For instance	Next	Another
Additionally	Besides	Moreover	Along with
Finally	Next	Also	As well

Words used to clarify

in other words	for instance	that is	for example

For instance	For example
In other words	Equally important

Paragraphs

QUICK GUIDE

CHARACTERISTICS: Basically, a paragraph is a unit of thought made up of a group of related sentences. The paragraph . . .

- is organized around one controlling idea that is usually stated in a topic sentence.
- is made up of supporting sentences that develop this main idea.
- rarely stands by itself. It is used with other paragraphs to build a longer piece of writing.
- can be designed for specific functions like opening a piece of writing, closing it, telling a story, describing something, building an argument, etc.

EVALUATING: To decide whether your paragraph is an effective unit of thought, ask these questions:

- What is the topic or controlling idea?
- Is the topic clearly stated?
- Do all phrases and sentences relate to the topic, or do some take a different direction?
- Is the paragraph coherent? Do linking and transitional words show how various elements are related?
- Is the organization clear and the line of thought reasonable and understandable?
- Is the organization effective, utilizing the best method of arranging the details?
- Is the paragraph complete, having enough of the best details to support the topic sentence?

RELATIONSHIP BETWEEN PARAGRAPHS: To decide whether your paragraphs work together, ask these questions:

- Does the opening paragraph introduce the topic and establish the thesis?
- Do the middle paragraphs support and explain the thesis or primary argument of the paper?
- Does each paragraph logically follow the one that precedes it and lead into the one that follows it?
- Does the overall organization of paragraphs build toward the conclusion, or ending paragraph, in a way that's clear and logical?

Mastering the Academic Essay

According to award-winning essayist Lee Gutkind, essay writing is essentially the process of researching, reading, reflecting, and, of course, writing. Essayists immerse themselves in their work, researching a subject from every conceivable angle. Their research usually begins at the library or on the Internet, reading to learn about their subject and to see what has already been written about it. Then they continue to reflect upon the subject and their emerging ideas throughout the process, carefully crafting as many drafts and revisions of the essay as needed.

While you may not have time to immerse yourself so completely in all of your academic writing, you can still approach each new writing task with curiosity and diligence.

WHAT'S AHEAD

This chapter discusses the basic steps in the essay-writing process and provides sample essays, each one using a different approach.

Academic Essays

QUICK GUIDE

As you know, the essay is the primary form of writing in all academic areas. Anytime you are asked to inform, explain, analyze, evaluate, or write persuasively about a topic, you are developing an essay. Refer to the guidelines in this chapter whenever you have a question about the basic essay-writing process. Refer to the index whenever you have a question about a specific type of essay.

1. **Focusing Your Efforts** (next page) Before you begin your essay, gain a clear understanding of your assignment. Then explore and research possible writing ideas. Continue your search until you identify a specific writing idea that you can successfully develop in an essay.
2. **Forming a Thesis Statement** (page 94) Express in a sentence (or two) the specific topic of your writing. A thesis statement establishes the tone and direction for your writing. (Carry out additional research as needed to support your thesis.)
3. **Planning and Organizing Your Essay** (pages 95–97) Either sketch out or carefully plan the basic shape of your essay. Your first job is to establish a pattern of development (comparison, cause-effect, classification, etc.) for your writing.
4. **Writing the Initial Drafts** (pages 98–101) Write as much of your first draft as possible in one sitting, while your thinking and research are still fresh in your mind. This draft is your first complete look at a developing writing idea.
5. **Improving Your Writing** (page 102) Change or revise the content of your essay until you have effectively developed all of your main points. Then turn your full attention to editing your revised writing for style and mechanics.

Insights into Writing

The golden rule of essay writing—one that cannot be overemphasized—is to seek guidance and clarification when you need it. If you ask for help from your instructor and writing peers, you're more likely to produce an essay that you feel good about and that satisfies, or exceeds, the requirements of the assignment.

Focusing Your Efforts

In most cases, you'll be writing an essay in response to a specific assignment. Your instructor will establish some basic parameters, including the purpose of the assignment, a due date, and a minimum page length. On the surface, everything will seem clear enough. But once you actually sit down to write, you may not feel so sure of yourself, and just getting started may become a real struggle. Sound familiar? If so, you need to put your writing tasks in better focus right from the start.

Understanding the Assignment

In order to write with confidence, be certain that you clearly understand the assignment.

- **Analyze** your writing task (prompt) word for word. Locate the key terms (*define, compare, evaluate,* etc.) and make sure you know what they mean.
- **Rephrase** the assignment or question in your own words.
- **Find out** what criteria (rubric) will be used to evaluate your essay.
- **Discuss** the assignment and your plan of action with your instructor and peers.

Selecting a Specific Writing Idea

In most cases, your assignment will address a general subject (or subjects) related to your course work. Your job is to investigate this subject in search of a writing idea for your essay. Continue your research until you discover a manageable or limited topic that interests you and meets the requirements of the assignment. Finally, establish a focus by deciding which specific aspect of the topic you want to explore.

The Selecting Process

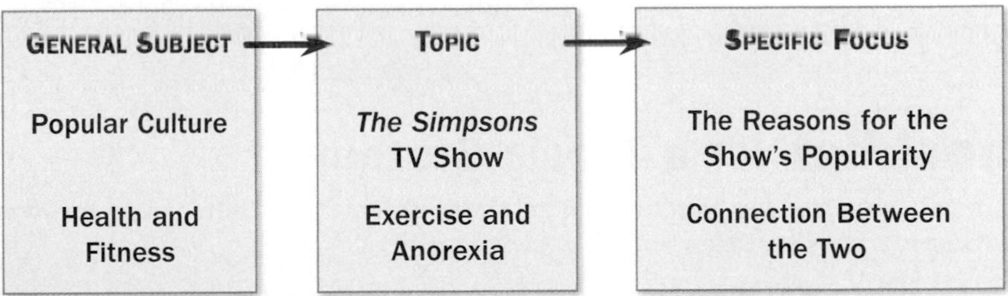

INSIDE INFO

Carry out enough research to expand your knowledge of your writing idea. It is a good plan to collect more facts and details than you will actually need for your writing. (See pages 98–100 for shaping and collecting strategies.)

Forming a Thesis Statement

A **thesis statement** identifies a specific part of your writing topic. The statement declares your unique perspective on the topic. It gives you the necessary focus and direction to develop your essay. As your ideas evolve, you may find it necessary to revise your thesis once or twice. The following information will help you write clear, effective thesis statements.

Stating Your Case

A thesis statement is usually a single sentence and appears in the opening part of an essay. The thesis may be based on a feature of the topic or on a particular stand that you want to defend.

A manageable topic (exercise and anorexia)
+ **a specific feature** (a connection exists between the two)
= **an effective thesis statement.**

Thesis Statement: Evidence suggests that a connection exists between excessive exercise and anorexia, resulting in a condition known as "activity anorexia."

EXAMPLE THESIS STATEMENTS

- **Barbed hooks** (topic) **should be banned from lure fishing to protect undersized fish** (particular stand).
- **Agroterrorism** (topic) **poses a significant threat to the United States** (a specific feature).
- **Isolation, the main theme in Frankenstein** (topic), **plays out in Walton's letters to his sister Margaret** (a specific feature).
- **Though economic sanctions appear to be a powerful peacetime weapon** (topic), **they actually do more harm than good** (particular stand).

Checklist for a Thesis Statement

If you can answer *yes* to each of these questions, then you have written an effective thesis statement:

_____ Does my thesis focus on a specific writing idea?
_____ Does my thesis accurately address the purpose of the assignment?
_____ Is my thesis stated in a clear, direct sentence (or sentences)?
_____ Is my thesis supported by the information I have gathered?
_____ Does my thesis suggest a pattern of development for my essay? (*Comparison, cause-effect,* and *classification* are example patterns.)

Planning and Organizing Your Essay

Think of your working thesis statement as the active ingredient—the yeast—that initiates the whole planning and organizing process. Once you've written this statement, you've established a direction for your essay and can move ahead. The information on the next three pages will help you plan and organize your work.

Organizing Patterns

Almost all academic essays follow a basic pattern of development. As you will see in the charts below, some of these patterns are specific and others are more general. Knowing how these patterns work will help you plan and organize your essays.

Specific Patterns

Types	Organizing Principles
Process (How something works)	Chronological Order (190–192)
Narrative (What happened)	Chronological Order (146–150)
Description (How something/someone appears)	Spatial Order—Location (177–181)
Comparison (How two things are alike/different)	Whole vs. Whole Comparison/Point-by-Point Comparison (194–197)
Cause-Effect (How one thing affects something else)	Identify Cause and Explore Effects/Identify Effect and Explore Causes (208–211)
Problem-Solution (How a problem can be solved)	Study the Problem & Solution(s) (213–218)
Classification (How something can be categorized)	Name Categories, Examine Each One (199–202)
Argumentation (How a position or an opinion can be asserted and supported)	Assert and Support, Counter the Opposition, Reassert Position (240–243)

General Patterns

Types	Organizing Principles
Logical Order	
Working Deductively	Follow an opening thesis with supporting details in the most compelling order (204–206, 237–238).
Working Inductively	Provide examples and details leading up to the main idea (thesis).
Question and Answer	Ask a question (thesis) and answer it in the body of the essay.
Explanation and Analysis	Move back and forth between explanation (or examples) and analysis (270–275, 277–285).

"An effective piece of writing has focus. There is a controlling vision which orders what is being said."
—Donald Murray

Establishing a Pattern of Development

An organizing pattern for your essay is often built into your assignment. For example, you may be asked to develop an argument or to write a process paper. Even when a pattern is not assigned, one may evolve naturally during your initial thinking and planning. If this doesn't happen, look closely at your thesis statement (and supporting information). An effective thesis will almost always suggest an organizing pattern. If it doesn't provide this "controlling vision," consider changing your thesis. The examples below demonstrate how a thesis statement can provide direction and shape for an essay.

Example Thesis

Bigger in *Native Son* and Alan in *Equus* are both entering adulthood and have come to realize that they are tragically controlled by work, religion, and the media.

Discussion: The writer of this thesis is preparing to compare two literary characters. Comparisons are patterned in two different ways: Either you discuss both subjects according to specific criteria (point by point), or you discuss one of the subjects completely and then turn to the other subject (whole vs. whole). Since the example thesis establishes three criteria for comparison—work, religion, and the media—the writer will naturally follow the point-by-point pattern of development. (See pages 194–195 for this essay.)

Example Thesis

Evidence suggests that a connection exists between excessive exercise and anorexia, resulting in a condition known as "activity anorexia."

Discussion: This thesis suggests that the writer is developing a cause-effect essay. Essays following this pattern usually begin with a cause (development, condition, etc.) followed by an explanation of the effects, or they begin with an effect followed by an explanation of the causes. To develop the example thesis, the writer will obviously follow the first route, identifying a cause before carefully examining the effects. (See pages 104–105 for this essay.)

BOTTOM LINE

Remember that you're looking for a basic frame or structure for your essay. Within that general frame, other patterns may come into play. For example, a comparison essay may employ some describing or classifying, and an argumentative essay may organize some of the supporting points in an imagined narrative (scenario).

Outlining Your Ideas

Once you've established a general pattern of development, you're ready to organize the information (main points, supporting details, and so on) that you expect to cover in your essay. You may simply jot down a brief list of ideas or prepare a topic or a sentence outline.

Topic Outline

An outline is an orderly listing of related ideas. In a **topic outline**, each idea is stated as a word or phrase rather than as a complete sentence. To stay focused on the topic of your essay, write your working thesis statement at the top of your paper. Do not attempt to outline your opening and closing paragraphs unless specifically asked to do so.

Thesis statement: Evidence suggests that a connection exists between excessive exercise and anorexia, resulting in a condition known as "activity anorexia."

Introduction

I. Susceptible individuals
   A. Anorexics—people who starve themselves
   B. Compulsive exercisers
   C. "Activity anorexic"—a combination of the two
II. Effects of activity anorexia
   A. Obsess over weight and diet
   B. Risk serious physical problems
   C. Suffer from emotional problems
III. Treatment for the problem
   A. Acknowledge the problem
   B. Undergo intense psychotherapy
   C. Maintain monitored drug therapy

Conclusion

Sentence Outline

A **sentence outline** expresses each idea as a complete sentence, so it naturally contains more detail than a topic outline. It is usually required for longer, more formal writing assignments. (Also see page 352.)

Introduction

I. Susceptible individuals are overly concerned about their weight.
   A. An anorexic knowingly starves her- or himself.
   B. A compulsive exerciser works out excessively to control weight.
   C. A sufferer of "activity anorexia" suffers from both disorders.
II. The symptoms and effects of the condition are unpleasant.
   A. A person with activity anorexia obsesses about weight.
   B. An activity anorexic risks serious physical problems.
   C. A sufferer is also prone to severe emotional problems.
III. Effective treatment is available.
   A. A person must first acknowledge the problem.
   B. Intense psychotherapy addresses complex issues.
   C. A sufferer must also maintain a monitored drug therapy program.

Conclusion

Writing the Initial Drafts

Write your first draft freely, using your outline (or listing) as a general guide. Your goal is not to produce a winning essay the first time through. It can't be done. A first draft is clearly a work-in-progress, or, as writer Donald Murray states, "a vision of what might be." You simply need to get all of your ideas on paper. Then you must revise, developing another draft (or two) before your essay really begins to take shape.

Remember that most academic essays follow a predictable pattern: The opening paragraph introduces the thesis, the body of the essay supports it, and the closing paragraph reaffirms it. (Check below and on the following three pages for information about developing your essay.)

Shaping the Opening Paragraph

Opening paragraphs usually start with general information and end in a specific way. That is, the first part draws the reader into the essay with important ideas related to the topic. The second part states the thesis and leads the reader into the main part of the text. (See the examples on the next page.)

Introduce the topic with . . .

- interesting background information,
- an engaging quotation,
- an illustrative story, or
- a series of questions.

Introductions to Avoid

- Worn-out expressions:

  "In this essay, I will . . . "
  "I would like to tell you about . . . "
  "According to the dictionary, . . . "

- Say-nothing sentences:

  "Subject A and B are alike/different in many ways."
  "World War II was a colossal war . . . "
  "Uncontrollable forest fires devastate the landscape."

INSIDE INFO

Some writers pay special attention to the exact wording of their opening paragraph *before* they draft the rest of their text. Others get everything on paper before they focus a lot of attention on any one part.

Sample Openings

Review these essay openings and those in the "Forms of Writing" section (pages 143–315).

A barrage of news reports continually reminds Americans of the sorry shape they're in: Close to two-thirds of the population is classified by the Center for Disease Control as either overweight or obese. Cases of diabetes have skyrocketed—and not only among adults. Excess weight contributes so much to ill health that it may overtake tobacco as the number one cause of preventable death in this country. Amid such facts and figures, it may be hard to believe that more people than ever are compulsive about following strict exercise regimens to manage their weight. In addition, the number of people with weight-loss eating disorders continues to rise. In fact, growing evidence suggests that a connection exists between excessive exercise and anorexia, resulting in a condition known as "activity anorexia."

Discussion: In the above opening, Kali Alvarez provides interesting facts and figures that lead up to the thesis (*in italics*). She begins with details about obesity that provide a surprising contrast to the essay's topic.

In the dark theater, children sing a haunting tune: "Don't Play with the Alley Children." It's a singsong chant that young Olivia Williams and her friends would sing in their upper-middle-class apartments, while young Cassie Charles and her friends played among the garbage cans below. Though both girls are African Americans, they are divided by their social class, their experience, and their strategies for living in a white world. Then, one New Year's Eve, the grown-up Olivia is stranded in her ad-agency office along with the grown-up Cassie, a cleaning woman. In her play, Sisters, Marsha A. Jackson contrasts the two women's lives, showing how color and gender make two very different women into true sisters.

Discussion: In the above opening, Justin Conley tells how a childhood chant is used to establish the difference between the two main characters in the play. Midway through the paragraph, he transitions effectively to the literary present and the thesis—how two very different women [become] "true sisters."

Since the invention of political systems, people have tried to use money and other gifts to influence the actions of politicians. In New York City in the 1800s, for example, a political group led by William "Boss" Tweed used bribery to corrupt the operations of city agencies and rob the city taxpayers of millions (Martin 434). Tweed died in prison, but the specter of political corruption is alive and well in the United States. Our system allows lobbyists to give gifts and provide favors to members of Congress, a practice that creates a conflict of interest. Do senators and representatives owe more to their constituents or to lobbyists? The best way to remove this conflict from our political system is to ban lobbyists from giving gifts to politicians.

Discussion: In the above opening, Yolanda Curtis shares historical background to effectively introduce her topic. She then uses a rhetorical question to prepare the reader for the essay's thesis.

Developing Your Main Points

How do you develop complete and insightful essays? You gather a good supply of compelling details to support your thesis. Then, in the main part, or body, of your essay, you develop the thesis. You present each main point (as indicated in your outline), expand upon it with supporting facts or examples, and offer additional analysis or commentary as needed.

Adding a Variety of Support

Anyone obsessively concerned with weight control could be susceptible to this condition. An anorexic (approximately 90 percent of whom are female) starves herself to attain some image of perfection. A compulsive exerciser works out excessively for the same reason. Roughly 75 percent of all anorexia sufferers are thought to combine both methods of weight control, often to a detrimental effect ("Overweight"). W. David Pierce, Ph.D., a sociology and neuroscience professor at the University of Alberta, defines the condition in this way: "Activity anorexia is a problematic behavior pattern in which a drastic decrease in eating causes progressively more exercise, which further reduces eating, in a vicious cycle" (qtd. in Dess). The compulsion with appearance and fitness becomes unhealthy, and the cycle of behavior is extremely difficult to break.

Discussion: Kali Alvarez states her main point in the topic sentence above. Then she supports it with *statistics* and a *specific quotation* from an authority.

The action of the play begins on New Year's Eve in Olivia's office at Peat, Montgriff, and Simon, an ad agency in Atlanta, Georgia. Olivia kneels on the floor among boxes and is packing up her office when Cassie arrives singing "I'm Every Woman" at the top of her lungs. The two women could not be more different. Olivia is 30, single, stiff, proper, and sad, listening to MUZAK as she packs up her life. Cassie is 40, a mom, loose and happy, listening to Whitney Houston. As Jackson points out in her notes before the play, "Both characters are intentionally broadly drawn in ACT I, such that the laughter is the medium of entry into the complexity of each character and situation" (104). These two women begin as stereotypes, but when they get stuck together, both characters start to unfold.

Discussion: The paragraph above *paraphrases* the initial action in the play, includes a specific *quotation* from the playwright, and offers the writer's *personal analysis.*

Banning gifts from lobbyists will restore Americans' trust in Congress. Members of Congress must often defend their actions after taking positions favorable to gift-giving lobbyists. In a recent survey, 83 percent of voters said they distrusted lawmakers who accepted gifts from lobbyists (Jones). In the same survey, 64 percent of voters approved a ban on all such gifts. Distrust in public officials has become an epidemic in this country, and gifts from lobbyists to members of Congress increase that distrust. Banning such gifts would create an honest, open environment in which respect for our leaders can grow.

Discussion: Here Yolanda Curtis offers *authoritative facts* as support.

"The only true creative aspect of writing is the first draft. That's when it's coming straight from your head and your heart."

—Evan Hunter

Writing the Closing

Generally speaking, an effective closing adds to the reader's understanding of an essay. The first part of the closing usually reviews (or ties together) important points from the essay, reinforces or stresses one particular point, or reasserts the thesis. The final lines may expand the scope of the text by connecting the essay's message with the reader's experience or with life in general.

Sample Closings

It is a sad commentary on our culture that weight control is so difficult for so many people, especially for those who really do not need to lose weight but are convinced otherwise. When people's attitudes about a healthy body are more in line with reality, perhaps activity anorexia will fade into history. Though science is just beginning to understand the link between mental illness and patterns of behavior, public awareness of activity anorexia may help to stem this affliction.

Discussion: In the above closing, Kali Alvarez first *reflects* on the seriousness of the problem and then *suggests* that public awareness of activity anorexia may help control it.

By the end of their time together, Olivia and Cassie are more than friends: They are sisters. Their theme song no longer is "Don't Play with the Alley Children" but "Blest Be the Tie That Binds." Marsha Jackson has brought two very different women together—two different aspects of the playwright herself. Jackson not only wrote the play but starred as Olivia during its run. As a classically trained playwright and a guiding light in the theater scenes of Atlanta and Houston, Jackson is very much like Olivia. But the loving way in which she writes Cassie's part—and her own experience of being an "alley child" in a white world—show that part of Jackson is and always will be Cassie.

Discussion: In the above closing, the writer first *reflects* on the play's theme and then *expands the scope* of the text by linking the theme to the playwright's life.

When many voters look at Congress, they see an institution in which lobbyists are able to buy power and favorable treatment. Sometimes this is true, and sometimes it isn't. In either case, the ability of lobbyists to give gifts to politicians stirs controversy and contributes to an environment of mistrust that makes it easy for citizens to turn their backs on the political process. Banning these gifts will not only reduce the undue influence of lobbyists, but it will also bring ordinary citizens back into the political process—and that might improve life for everyone.

Discussion: The closing above *restates* the writer's thesis about banning lobbyists' gift giving and then *expands the scope* of the text by predicting the ban's effects.

Improving Your Writing

After you have written one or two early drafts, your most important job is improving the sense and flow of your essay. The best way to do this is to proceed carefully through a series of additional revisions—adding, cutting, and rearranging information as needed.

Checklist for Revising and Editing

Use the following checklist as a general guide when you revise and edit your essays:

_____ **Pace yourself.** If possible, set your draft aside for a day or two before you review it. Everything looks much clearer with a fresh set of eyes. Also make sure that other sets of eyes—including your instructor's—see your work throughout the revising and editing process. (Conferencing is an essential part of the revising process.)

_____ **Think globally at first,** considering the *ideas* and *organization* of your writing. Look for gaps in the overall development of your work. Is your explanation, argument, or analysis complete? Do the basic parts work together and focus on one main point? Does your essay follow one of the basic patterns of development? Do you need to carry out additional research?

_____ **Then carefully examine specific parts** for *ideas* and *organization*. Does the opening paragraph draw the reader into the essay and state your thesis? Have you supported each main point with effective examples and analysis? Does the closing tie up any loose ends and help the reader appreciate the significance of your essay?

_____ **Check for other key traits of writing,** including *voice, word choice,* and *sentence fluency*. Do I sound confident and knowledgeable? Is my voice appropriate for my audience and purpose? Are my nouns and verbs specific? Do my ideas read smoothly?

_____ **Lastly, carry out a close editing** for *conventions*. Check your revised writing for accuracy before preparing a final copy. Also proofread your final copy for errors before submitting it.

INSIDE INFO

On one level, writing an essay is the process of clarifying and fine-tuning your thinking on a subject. On another level, it is the process of informing or persuading your reader. You'll know that you've made enough changes when your essay clearly and accurately reflects your thinking on the topic, and when it answers any questions your reader may have. (For more revising and editing guidelines, see pages 39–56.)

Two Sample Essays

The essays on the following pages are about the same subject, activity anorexia. The first essay is traditional and objective in its approach; the second is more original and personal. Depending upon your writing background and experience, one or the other of these pieces will serve well as a model for your writing. Comprehensive notes precede each model.

Essay I: Notes

Overview: "Exercise and Eating Disorders," starting on the next page, represents a traditional academic essay in terms of approach and structure. The essay follows the thesis-support-summary format:

Paragraph 1: The opening draws attention to the topic and states the thesis.

Paragraphs 2–5: The body of the essay explains the topic and discusses its effects.

Paragraph 6: The closing reflects on the topic and a need for public awareness.

Assessment: This essay is consistently focused on an interesting, timely topic. It follows one pattern of development throughout (the *effects* of activity anorexia) and is clearly based on thorough research and reflection. The text is coherent and unified, the sentence structure is clear and accurate, and in places, the voice is engaging. The result is an effective piece of academic writing.

Suggestions: How might the essay be improved based on the traits of effective writing?

- **Ideas:** Create a more intriguing title. Cite a number of studies about this condition. Discuss the treatment options for the condition more thoroughly.
- **Organization:** Use more transitions within the paragraphs to improve the flow of ideas.
- **Voice:** Use a more caring, concerned tone.
- **Word Choice:** Use fewer "be" verbs (*is, are, was, were,* etc.).

NOTE: Some instructors find the traditional essay format too restrictive. They may encourage you to use a freer, more natural or original approach, demonstrated in the essay at the end of this chapter.

Essay I: Traditional Approach

Kali Alvarez uses the traditional thesis-support-summary format to discuss a serious weight-related condition known as activity anorexia. Notice how this tightly organized essay moves smoothly from one point to the next.

Exercise and Eating Disorders

Opening facts and figures lead up to the thesis (underlined).

A barrage of news reports continually reminds Americans of the sorry shape they're in: Close to two-thirds of the population is classified by the Center for Disease Control as either overweight or obese. Cases of diabetes have skyrocketed—and not only among adults. Excess weight contributes so much to ill health that it may overtake tobacco as the number one cause of preventable death in this country. Amid such facts and figures, it may be hard to believe that more people than ever are compulsive about following strict exercise regimens to manage their weight. In addition, the number of people with weight-loss eating disorders continues to rise. <u>In fact, growing evidence suggests that a connection exists between excessive exercise and anorexia, resulting in a condition known as "activity anorexia."</u>

The key term is defined.

Anyone obsessively concerned with weight control could be susceptible to this condition. An anorexic (approximately 95 percent of whom are female) starves herself to attain some image of perfection. A compulsive exerciser works out excessively for the same reason. Roughly 75 percent of all anorexia sufferers are thought to combine both methods of weight control, often to a detrimental effect ("Overweight"). W. David Pierce, Ph.D., a sociology and neuroscience professor at the University of Alberta, defines the condition in this way: "Activity anorexia is a problematic behavior pattern in which a drastic decrease in eating causes progressively more exercise, which further reduces eating, in a vicious cycle" (qtd. in Dess 1). The compulsion with appearance and fitness becomes unhealthy, and the cycle of behavior is extremely difficult to break.

The symptoms and effects of activity anorexia are unpleasant. A person with the disorder has low self-esteem and constantly worries about weight and diet. She or he often has strange, self-imposed dietary restrictions and is obsessive

Each main point is carefully explained.

about counting calories. This person becomes so compulsive about working off all ingested calories that exercise takes precedence over work, school, friends, and family. Although the workout isn't enjoyable, the person feels guilty for missing even one session. In a short time, the individual considers exercise to be more valuable than food, and extreme weight loss ensues. While this creates a feeling of control, it actually increases the risk of serious medical conditions—bone problems (including osteoporosis and stress fractures), heart trouble, anemia, and, in extreme cases, multiple organ failure that leads to death. Moreover, the emotional toll is high; many people with activity anorexia become socially withdrawn and suffer from depression.

Anorexia drives people to see themselves differently than others see them. For example, Marie (not her real name) said she could look at herself in a mirror, see her ribs jutting out, note her bony arms, trace her sunken cheeks, and still decide she needed to lose another 25 pounds ("The Prison"). Successful weight loss only made her try to lose more. She thought if losing 50 pounds was good, losing 75 pounds would be even better. The cycle is endless.

Information about treatment is paraphrased.

Fortunately, effective treatment for activity anorexia is available. The first step is probably the hardest; as with other addictive behaviors, the key is admitting that you have a problem. Intense psychotherapy that gets the entire family involved is one component of the treatment, preferably administered by a mental health provider who specializes in a bio-behavioral approach to eating disorders (Pierce). Carefully monitored drug therapy is sometimes required for a full recovery, as well.

In closing, the writer reflects on her topic.

It is a sad commentary on our culture that weight control is so difficult for so many people, especially for those who really do not need to lose weight but are convinced otherwise. When people's attitudes about a healthy body are more in line with reality, perhaps activity anorexia will fade into history. Though science is just beginning to understand the links between mental illness and patterns of behavior, public awareness of activity anorexia may help to stem this affliction.

NOTE: The works-cited page is not shown.

> "Work in whatever form interests you. I do suggest that you try your hand at a few forms rather than sticking to just one. A new form can suggest all sorts of new possibilities and can provide a fresh context for your ideas."
>
> —Jack Heffron

Essay II: Notes

Overview: "Too Much of a Good Thing," the essay starting on the next page, is organized according to the writer's unique thought process concerning the topic:

Paragraph 1: The opening clearly personalizes the essay.

Paragraphs 2–3: The writer continues her personal search for information about exercise, which leads to the focus of the essay (at the end of paragraph 3).

Paragraphs 4–8: This section takes on an objective tone as the writer cites experts and studies in the field of anorexia and exercise.

Paragraph 9: The writer identifies and discusses activity anorexia.

Paragraph 10: Next, she shares the story of someone who suffers from this condition.

Paragraph 11: In closing, the writer makes a personal connection with the reader.

Assessment: This essay succeeds in a number of significant ways. (1) "Too Much of a Good Thing" is an intriguing title. (2) The essay flows smoothly, providing compelling information from start to finish. (3) It does not rely on a prefabricated structure (thesis-support-summary). (4) The essay makes excellent use of research, sharing helpful references and many concrete examples (studies). (5) The variety of sentence beginnings and lengths creates a sophisticated level of fluency.

In short, the second essay offers the reader an interesting analysis of a timely topic. It is an engaging piece of writing that originates from thorough planning, drafting, and revising.

Suggestions: How might the essay be improved based on the traits of effective writing?

- **Ideas:** Incorporate an effective unifying motif into the text.
- **Organization:** Reestablish the personal connection in the closing.
- **Voice:** Inject even more personality into the essay.
- **Word Choice:** Vary the use of nouns. (For example, "female" is overused in the seventh paragraph.)

Essay II: Original Approach

Stephanie Lems also explores activity anorexia, but in a less traditional essay structure that reflects her unique perspective on the topic.

Too Much of a Good Thing

The opening anecdote draws the reader in.

I was halfway through my warm-up stretches when I asked myself, "Why do I run? To keep in shape? To lose weight? To have fun? Running is a good thing," I decided, "and I do it for fun." Then I looked down at my shoes that were new only three months earlier, saw their worn edges, and wondered, "So I run just for fun . . . really?"

Background information leads up to the focus of the essay (underlined).

I had done some reading about people who exercise compulsively. One writer had argued that a person in a good exercise program works out regularly to get fit and stay that way. However, exercise becomes compulsive if a person feels driven to work out and lets exercise control his or her life.

Another writer described girls who are both anorexic and addicted to exercise. As I stretched, I thought about the girls I know who run to lose weight, and I wondered whether the writer was correct—whether the two addictions could be connected. After I researched the topic, I realized that when exercise addiction and anorexia are linked, the combination is very dangerous.

Anorexia nervosa, commonly called anorexia, is a syndrome characterized by extreme weight loss. People with anorexia starve themselves to lose weight, because they fear being fat or have distorted images of their own bodies. Anorexic starvation becomes an addiction so strong that an individual can control it only with tremendous personal effort and the help of others.

Experts in the field are quoted.

Marvel Harrison is the national director of Life Balance, a program for people who suffer from eating disorders. She comments on how women with anorexia use exercise: "Women are devoting an incredible amount of energy to controlling their bodies through exercise and diet, obsessing about calories consumed and burned" (qtd. in Despres 3). Women exercise excessively not only to burn calories but also to relieve stress or to get in shape. However, no matter what the motive for excessive exercise, these extreme workouts can become a serious, sometimes deadly disease, especially if anorexia is involved.

Two studies are paraphrased.

A number of scientific studies have found a connection between anorexia and excessive exercise. David Pierce and Frank Epling, researchers from the University of Alberta, used rats to explore the connection. They placed rats in two cages. The rats in the first cage were given a functional running wheel and a reduced diet of one meal per day. The rats in the second cage were given a nonfunctional running wheel and a reduced diet of one meal per day. According to the researchers, the rats with unlimited access to the functional running wheel ran each day, and gradually increased the amount of running; in addition, they started to eat less. At the end of one week, some rats in the first group stopped eating altogether and ran themselves to death. Rats in the second group had a happier ending. Because their running wheel did not function, these rats did not run, soon adapted to their reduced diet, and stayed healthy. Pierce and Epling concluded that given the opportunity to run, rats on a reduced diet would exercise to the point of jeopardizing their health (McGovern 1–2).

All main points are clearly explained.

Clive Long and Jenny Smith, from the Department of Clinical Psychology at St. Andrew's Hospital in Northampton, England, conducted another study. They examined the attitudes and exercise behavior of anorexic females compared with the attitudes and exercise behaviors of nonanorexic females. For two weeks, 21 anorexic females and 45 non-anorexic females participated in the study. During this time, each person recorded details concerning how long she exercised, when she exercised, whether she exercised secretly, and what eating habits she practiced. The participants also evaluated their motives for exercising.

By comparing the anorexic females with the nonanorexic ones, Long and Smith determined that those with anorexia exercised considerably more often, often exercised secretly, and participated in more sports (3). The researchers also found that the individuals with anorexia continued their exercise program even if health issues interfered. Finally, the anorexic women were more hyperactive than those without anorexia, even though the anorexic group ate less food than the other group. The anorexic participants were constantly on the move trying to burn off as many calories as possible.

A key term is defined.

Researchers involved in both studies identified a new disease called "activity anorexia." David Pierce of the Sociology and Neuroscience Department at the University of Alberta defined activity anorexia as "a problematic behavior pattern in which a drastic decrease in eating causes progressively more exercise, which further reduces eating, in a vicious cycle" (qtd. in Dess 1). Among other findings, Pierce and Epling determined that people who are driven to exercise, and who constantly obsess over it, are most likely to develop either anorexia or another type of eating disorder.

Individuals struggling with activity anorexia use exercise not to sustain their health but to control their weight. Renee Despres' article "Burn, Baby, Burn" makes that point when she describes her own struggle with exercise disorder: "I welcomed the chance to burn the calories—400 of them, if I had measured and calculated everything right—in last night's salad. To make sure every last calorie had been burned, I ran for an hour and a half" (5). Activity anorexics assess the exact number of calories in the food they consume, and then they try to exercise enough to burn off all or most of the calories. They exercise not for fun, not for health, but for control.

In closing, the writer pulls the reader into the discussion.

The bad news is that activity anorexia is a significant problem today, but the good news is that we can do something about it. We can learn about the illness and use that information to help others. In addition, we can have the courage to ask ourselves honestly, "Why do I exercise?" The answer to that question will help us better understand ourselves and our health. Our goal must be twofold. First, we must accept ourselves for who we are—every bone, muscle, nerve, and fat molecule. And second, we must use food and exercise responsibly—getting enough, but not too much, of these good things.

NOTE: The works-cited page is not shown.

Writer's Resource

Understanding Style in Writing

Fashion is a cultural phenomenon. If you're in fashion, you dress right, eat right, and play right. Of course, fashion is also a big part of the economy. Our major suppliers of chicness have created a dynamic industry. Wherever fashion goes, most people are sure to follow—no matter what the cost.

Not so with style. Style is more inner-directed. It's based on personal taste and comfort. It always seems to fit. You may love denim; the next person may feel comfortable in something more colorful. That's okay; that's style. Style reflects who you are and changes as you change.

So what does all of this have to do with writing? Well, there is nothing trendy about good writing. It looks and feels like the genuine article and has a long shelf life, all because of its honest, sincere style.

WHAT'S AHEAD

This section provides you with all kinds of information about writing style, including a "short list" of key stylistic reminders, tips for developing a sense of style, plus much more.

Key Stylistic Reminders

If you remember only three things about style, let them be the following three points: *(1) Be purposeful. (2) Be clear. (3) Be sincere.* Almost nothing else matters. Writing with purpose, with clarity, and with sincerity is the key to an effective style. Our best writers have almost always been plain talkers, speaking directly and honestly to the reader. Writers like Mark Twain, Rachel Carson, Kurt Vonnegut, and E. B. White are our role models. Follow their lead, and you are sure to write with style.

■ Be purposeful.

Writing without genuine concern for your topic is like trying to bake bread without yeast. One of the most important ingredients is missing. Good writing begins (and ends) with purpose and commitment. As Vonnegut states, "It is the genuine caring [about a topic], and not your games with language, which will be the most compelling and seductive element in your style." The bottom line is this: If you expect to produce effective writing, select topics that interest you.

NOTE: Let's say that your sociology instructor asks you to write a paper about immigration. But you're not sure which part of this issue interests you most. Use one of the selecting strategies listed in your handbook (pages 22–23) to help you explore possible topics.

■ Be clear.

You may think that style is something you add to your writing with a slick phrase here, a clever aside there. But that is not how style works. In fact, trying to add style usually just clutters things up. It's much more important to be clear and orderly, to keep things simple and direct. Your writing will always be in style if it's easy for your reader to understand and to follow.

> "Have something to say, and say it as clearly as you can. This is the only secret of style."
>
> —Matthew Arnold

■ Be sincere.

Writing works best when it sounds like one person (you) sincerely communicating with another person. It doesn't sound tentative, breezy, or pushy. Nor does it try to impress the reader with a lot of ten-dollar words. It simply rings true. In order to write well—in essays, articles, and narratives—you must be able to use an honest, sincere voice.

Writing That's in Style

Here are two examples of writing that is in style. The first one comes from an essay of definition entitled "The 'New Normal.' " In this excerpt, the writer provides essential background information about the term. This piece exhibits the key elements of stylistic writing: an interesting topic addressed knowledgeably, clearly, sincerely, and with an honest voice.

> After September 11, 2001, Vice President Dick Cheney referred to the security changes that were to be instituted as the "new normal," a phrase that has become common in political discourse. Cheney is often given credit for coining the phrase, but in reality the use of "new normal" can be associated with an earlier disaster, the bombing of the Oklahoma City Alfred P. Murrah Federal Building. During a memorial service in 1997, Paul Heath, president of the Oklahoma City Murrah Building Survivors Association, said the city hoped to find closure, "reaching a new normal" (CNN Interactive).
>
> In terms of security measures, "new normal" means accepting the curtailment of some civil liberties. For instance, security officials have identified nail files, sewing scissors, knitting needles, and pocket knives as potential weapons and banned them from airline flights. A shift in "new normal" occurred in August of 2006 when the British uncovered a terrorist plot to blow up commercial airlines by mixing liquid bomb components. As a consequence, liquids and gels were temporarily not allowed on airplanes; even bottled water was banned . . .

The next piece comes from a position paper discussing peer-to-peer music sharing systems. It, too, addresses a timely, interesting topic that the author knows well. The writer makes a personal connection with the topic and provides sincere, clear analysis.

> My friends and I like music, and we dig through the history of popular tunes from the 1950s to the present looking for connections. Books and magazines are helpful, but the Internet is our main source of information. When we find interesting things, including cuts from old recordings, we share them. What seems like fun to us, unfortunately, is seen as unlawful activity by others. Anyone who uses computer technology like peer-to-peer (P2P) networking to share copyrighted music is risking being sued by the music industry. What the industry is finding out, however, is that prosecuting people who use widely available technology isn't stopping the activity. Recording companies need to understand that they cannot regulate file-sharing technology the way they regulate the sale of physical objects such as tapes and CD's.

Developing a Sense of Style

How can you best develop your writing style, your special way of saying something? You can begin by reading the information below, which explains how accomplished writers learn about and practice stylistic writing. The two pages after that discuss the style matrix as well as specific qualities of effective style.

Becoming a Student of Writing

- **Read widely.** William Faulkner was once asked what advice he would give to young writers. He said, "Read everything—trash, classics, good and bad, and see how they do it. . . . Read! You'll absorb it. Then write." Follow Faulkner's advice and gain an appreciation for the written word in all of its different forms.
- **Be on the lookout** for those unique slices of life that can add so much to your writing. You may enjoy this "slice" recorded in Ken Macrorie's book *Uptaught*:

  > An elderly, sparse man who makes a career out of auditing classes is sitting next to me taking notes on both sides of a paper. Now he turns it upside down and writes over his own notes.

- **Keep track of your reading and observing.** Get into the habit of recording and reflecting upon your experiences. Some of these ideas may later serve as inspiration or models for your own writing.
- **Experiment with a variety of writing forms.** In the process, sharpen your writing abilities: Journaling promotes writing fluency. Corresponding helps you develop your writing voice. Writing articles gives you a sense of form and structure. Crafting poems helps you gain an appreciation for word choice.
- **Write to learn.** Writing helps you examine ideas and feelings more thoughtfully. As Ray Bradbury once said, writing "lets the world burn through you." The more experiences you have as a writer (exploring your personal thoughts), the better able you will be to express yourself intelligently, meaningfully, and stylistically.
- **Understand the basics.** Gain an understanding of the core traits of writing: *ideas, organization, voice, word choice, sentence fluency,* and *conventions.* (Your handbook will help you in all of these areas.) Also begin to build your writing vocabulary. Learn, for example, what it means *to narrate* or *to analyze.* Know the difference between terms like *active* and *passive, abstract* and *concrete.*

Writing with a Plan in Mind

Wise writers think about style *before* they begin to write. You can do the same. Simply ask yourself the key questions below about the writing task at hand. The questions deal with five elements that directly affect writing style.

STYLE MATRIX

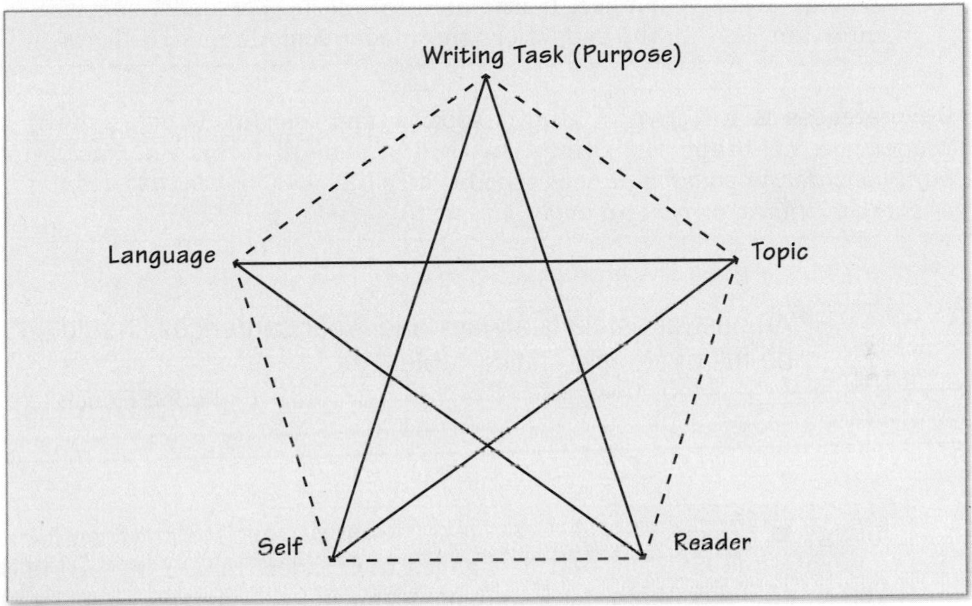

NOTE: The matrix shows how the five elements are interrelated. That is, your understanding of a writing task and your feelings about the topic will affect the way in which you communicate your ideas to the reader.

Asking the Key Questions

Writing Task: What is the purpose of my assignment? Do I understand all of the requirements? Am I writing to inform, to analyze, to persuade, or to entertain?

Topic: What will I write about? Does my topic meet the requirements of my assignment? What will be the specific focus or main point of my writing?

Reader: Who is my reader? Will he or she be interested in my topic? What does this person need to know?

Self: What compels me to write about this topic? What do I hope to gain from this experience?

Language (and Form): How will I present my topic? How will I get and keep the reader's interest? What will I say first, second, and third?

Qualities of Effective Style

Besides being purposeful, clear, and sincere in your writing, use the following qualities to develop a powerful style.

Design ■ Effective writing displays a clear focus and reveals your feelings about your topic. It attempts to inform, persuade, surprise, or entertain, and, in the end, offers the reader something significant.

Concreteness ■ Effective writing is specific and colorful. It helps the reader see, hear, and feel things. Instead of general terms like *race, administrator,* or *emotion*, it uses specific ones like *1500-meter run, dean of student affairs,* or *pent-up anger*.

"An abstract style is always bad. Your sentences should be full of stones, chairs, tables, etc."

—Rudolf Flesch

Energy ■ Effective writing crackles with energy. It shows signs of intensity and emotion, and it engages the reader from start to finish. You build energy into your writing by speaking honestly about your subject and by providing plenty of stimulating, thought-provoking information.

Freshness ■ Effective writing may contain surprises. For example, you may decide to use a sentence fragment (or two) or a long, rambling sentence for dramatic effect. (See page 122 for examples.) Then again, you may develop an idea using a negative definition (what something is not) or a poetic expression.

Coherence ■ Effective writing contains no unnecessary bumps or rough spots. It links important ideas from sentence to sentence and from paragraph to paragraph. It moves smoothly and clearly from the opening paragraph to the closing remarks. Coherence is achieved by working and reworking your ideas many times.

Correctness ■ Effective writing follows the conventions of written English. It attends to every detail, from the accuracy of the facts and details to the proper placement of punctuation marks.

Special Features of Style

A number of features can add style to your writing. One of these features, the metaphor, is discussed below. Other features, including colorful words and repetition, are discussed on the four pages that follow. *But a word of caution:* Your writing will sound forced or artificial if you overuse any of these features.

Writing Metaphorically

A **metaphor** connects an idea in your writing to something new and creates a powerful picture for your reader. (Remember that a metaphor compares two correlated ideas without using *like* or *as*.) In the following examples, notice how the basic ideas come to life when they are stated metaphorically:

BASIC IDEA: Environmentalists are trying to preserve natural resources.
Stated Metaphorically:

Environmentalists are the design engineers for spaceship earth.

BASIC IDEA: There is a lot of activity under the grass.
Stated Metaphorically:
The world is a wild wrestle under the grass. —Annie Dillard

Extending a Metaphor

Sometimes a metaphor serves as the unifying element in a series of sentences. An extended metaphor can expand or clarify an idea in your writing:

His family was a rich **tapestry** of personalities bound together by affection and respect. But the family was at **loose ends** last summer, at least until the reunion in August. Whatever feelings had been **torn** over a divorce . . .

Making Metaphors Work

- **Create original comparisons:** The student who wrote "Halle Berry's last movie sent me to the moon" has spent too much time gazing into space and not enough time creating fresh comparisons.
- **Be clear in your thinking:** The student who wrote the metaphor "Homelessness is a thorn in the city's image" has created a confusing figure of speech. Homelessness may be a thorn in the city's side, but not in its image.
- **Be consistent:** The reporter who wrote "In the final debate, Senator Jones dodged each of his opponent's accusations and eventually scored the winning shot" has created a *mixed metaphor*. He shifts from one comparison (boxing) to another (basketball).

Using Strong, Colorful Words

Suppose, in your mind, you see a soaring power forward, with the ball held high in his right hand, slam home a dunk. Now, suppose you write "The forward scored a basket." How clearly do you think you have communicated this thought? Obviously, not very clearly. Only specific words can create a clear and colorful word picture for your reader.

Choose Specific Nouns: Some nouns are general *(boots, movement, fruit)* and give the reader a vague, uninteresting picture. Other nouns are specific *(desert boots, civil rights, mango)* and give the reader a clear, detailed picture. In the chart that follows, the first word in each category is a general noun, the second is more specific, and the last noun is very specific. Specific nouns can make your writing clear and colorful.

General to Specific Nouns

person	*place*	*thing*	*idea*
woman	school	book	theory
actress	**university**	**novel**	**scientific theory**
Zhang Zi Yi	**Notre Dame**	***Pride and Prejudice***	**relativity**

Use Vivid Verbs: Like nouns, verbs can be too general to create a vivid word picture. For example, the verb *looked* does not say the same thing as *stared, glared, glanced, peeked,* or *inspected.* The statement "Ms. Shaw *glared* at the two goof-offs" is much more vivid and interesting than "Ms. Shaw *looked* at the two goof-offs."

- Whenever possible, use a verb that is strong enough to stand alone without the help of an adverb.

  Verb and adverb: Ricardo fell down in the locker room.
  Vivid verb: Ricardo collapsed in the locker room.

- Avoid overusing the "be" verbs *(is, are, was, were, . . .).* Also avoid overusing *would, could,* or *should.* Often a better action verb can be made from another word in the same sentence.

  A "be" verb: Cole is someone who follows national news.
  A stronger verb: Cole follows national news.

- Use active rather than passive voice. (Use passive voice only if you want to downplay who is performing the action in a sentence. See page 123.)

  Passive voice: Another piercing essay was submitted by Kim.
  Active voice: Kim submitted another piercing essay.

- Use verbs that show rather than tell.

  A verb that tells: Dr. Lewis is very thorough.
  A verb that shows: Dr. Lewis prepares detailed lectures.

SELECT SPECIFIC ADJECTIVES: Use precise, colorful adjectives to describe the nouns in your writing. Strong adjectives make the nouns even more engaging and clear to the reader. For example, the adjectives used in the phrase "*sleek, red* convertible" give the reader a clear picture of the car.

- Avoid using adjectives that carry little meaning: *neat, big, pretty, small, old, cute, fun, bad, nice, good, dumb, great, funny,* etc.

  Overused adjective: His **old** Thunderbird is in storage.
  Specific adjective: His **classic** Thunderbird is in storage.

- Use adjectives selectively. If your writing contains too many adjectives, they will simply get in the way and lose their effectiveness.

  Too many adjectives: A tall, shocking column of thick, yellow smoke marked the exact spot where the unexpected explosion had occurred.
  Revised: **A column of thick, yellow smoke marked the spot where the unexpected explosion had occurred.**

INCLUDE SPECIFIC ADVERBS: Use adverbs when you think they are needed to describe the action in a sentence. For example, the statement "Mayor Meyer *reluctantly* agreed to meet the protesters" tells much more than "Mayor Meyer agreed to meet the protesters." Don't, however, use a verb and an adverb when a single vivid verb would be better. (See pages 118 and 123.)

USE WORDS WITH THE RIGHT FEELING: The words in your writing should also have the right feeling, or *connotation*. The connotation of a word is the sense suggested or implied beyond its literal meaning. (The connotation of the words helps create the mood in a piece of writing.) Notice how the boldfaced words in the following passage connote the distaste that the writer feels for newspaper photographs depicting personal tragedies.

> Too many times I have picked up the evening newspaper to see a photograph of some tortured-looking person **splashed** all over the front page. Usually, this person has just gone through a **trauma**—a car accident, a fire, or a shooting. Newspapers could use a little **discretion** and not choose such pictures to **emblazon** the front page of their papers. It's bad enough that these people have **suffered misfortune**; to have their **grief broadcast** in this vivid way seems very wrong. It **inflates their tragedy** and unnecessarily delays their forgetting and their healing. They will be reminded over and over again by neighbors, friends, coworkers, and well-wishers just how "**terrible**" and "**awful**" and "**frightening**" all of this must have been. They will be **forced to relive** an event weeks and months and perhaps years after it would otherwise have been forgotten. This is the power of the press—**at its worst**.

Using Anecdotes

Writer Donald Murray suggests that people in your writing should communicate important ideas through their actions. Brief slices of life convey the ideas in a lively and interesting manner, sparing the reader a matter-of-fact portrayal.

INSIDE INFO

"Anecdote" is the more technical term for "brief slices of life." *The American Heritage College Dictionary* (4th edition) defines an anecdote as "a short account of an interesting . . . event."

Example I

In the following example, student writer Amy Douma opens her research paper with an anecdote about a homeless man:

> On a chilly February afternoon, an old man sits, sleeping on the sidewalk outside a New York hotel while the lunchtime crowd shuffles by. At the man's feet is a sign that reads: "Won't you help me? I'm cold and homeless and lonely. God bless you." He probably spends his days alone on the street, begging for handouts, and his nights searching for shelter from the cold. He has no job, no friends, and nowhere to turn.

Discussion: This anecdote prepares the reader to explore the questions the writer is attempting to answer in her research paper: Who are the homeless people? What are the reasons for their predicament?

Example II

In this passage, writer Mary Anne Hoff shares the story of a visitor to her childhood home in North Dakota:

> His "bee-yoo-tee-ful" stopped me short. This lanky Mr. Sophisticate from just outside Paris was describing the North Dakota prairie. The wild grasses and big sky, the black-eyed Susan and sagebrush, the hum of dog days were new to him. Now all he could say was "bee-yoo-tee-ful."
>
> Two days later we all huddled around a book about Paris. Our guest pointed to a photo and repeated "bee-yoo-tee-ful." It was the Champs-Elysees at night. The Champs-Elysees and the North Dakota prairie described with the same word? That was when I knew I would like him.

Discussion: This story shares the writer's epiphany far more effectively than a telling statement like "A visitor made me see my North Dakota home in a new way."

Using Repetition

Another important stylistic technique is to repeat similar grammatical structures (words, phrases, or ideas) for the purpose of rhythm, emphasis, and unity. When used effectively, **repetition** can do more to improve your style of writing than just about any other technique.

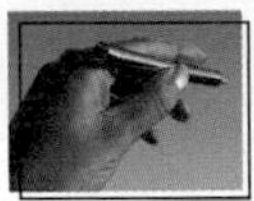

NOTE: The key point to remember when using repetition is to keep the words or ideas *parallel*, or stated in the same way. (As you read the examples below, you will see parallelism in action.)

For Rhythm and Balance: Notice in each of the sentences below how smoothly the repeated words or phrases flow from one to the next. They are in perfect balance.

> **Baseball, football,** and **boxing** are the most popular spectator sports.
>
> The floor was littered with **discarded soda cans, crumpled newspapers,** and **wrinkled clothes.**
>
> Elizabeth wants to **write a Broadway play, make a lot of money,** and **retire to the country.**

For Emphasis and Effect: Notice in the passages below how the repetition of a basic sentence structure adds intensity to the writing.

> The two singers changed styles to match the songs. **They crooned love ballads. They moaned the blues. They scatted to jazz.** Their artistry was in perfect harmony with their material.
>
> **We shall fight on the beaches, we shall fight on the landing grounds, we shall fight in the fields and in the streets, we shall fight in the hills; we shall never surrender.**
>
> —Winston Churchill

For Unity and Organization: Notice in the passage below how the repeated words (in bold) create a poetic effect in this description of a man, his business, and his family.

> **I see Grandfather Aurelio in** the wrinkled black-and-white photo, his eyes young and sharp like mine as he looks beyond the volcanic hills of Sicily, and beyond the Mediterranean toward America.
>
> **I see Grandfather Aurelio in** the folded napkins that bear his name, in the checkered tablecloths and the wooden chairs, in the tin ceiling that he painted gold, and in the whole storefront of his Brooklyn restaurant.
>
> **I see Grandfather Aurelio in** my father's face, the keen eyes and granite jaw, the care lines carved by 50 years of dishes and ovens, the look of love and understanding, as I search beyond these walls for distant shores.
>
> —Joseph Aurelio

Using an Alternative Style

When you write an essay, you are expected to follow some well-established principles: form a thesis, develop main supporting ideas in paragraphs, use complete sentences, and so on. These principles obviously serve you well. But from a stylistic standpoint, it's important to know that there are alternative ways to express yourself effectively. We have listed a few of these alternative techniques below. Experiment with them in your own essays (but only when circumstances are appropriate).

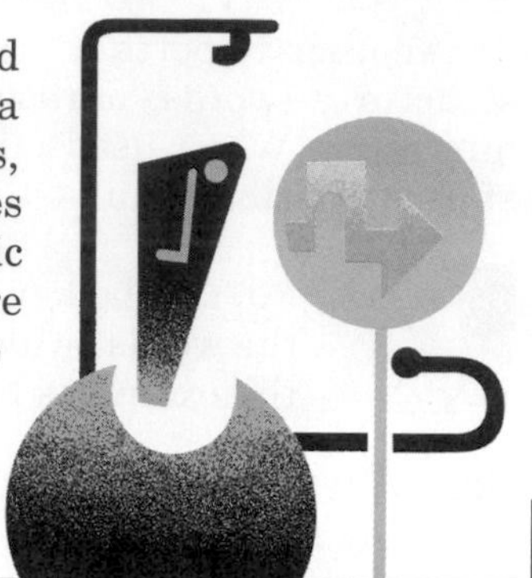

SENTENCE FRAGMENTS: Single words or phrases set off as sentences can have a dramatic effect. Notice below how a feature writer uses a series of imagistic fragments (in bold) to introduce his topic, the city of New Orleans.

> **Riding on the city of New Orleans.** The train has got the disappearing railroad blues. **Green, gold, and purple Mardi Gras beads. Preservation Hall, dirty and small. Old gentlemanly musicians with gnarled hands. When the saints go marching in.** It's hard to be a saint in this city.

MEANDERING SENTENCES: Long, loosely connected sentences provide a powerful sensory experience, immersing the reader in a description, in an action, in an important piece of information, or in a particular train of thought. The following long sentence provides key background information about the Gettysburg Address.

> Considering all that was stacked against Lincoln's address at Gettysburg—the fact that he composed it on the train trip and in his boarding room, that he spoke for five minutes after another person's two-hour speech, and that he believed that "the world will little note nor long remember what we say here"—this speech should have simply slipped into obscurity.

LISTS: Presenting a list of related ideas gives the reader a general, holistic look at a topic. In the opening of her memoir, a retired teacher provides a poetic listing of some of her students. Here is part of that list.

> Maria, my Willa Cather, observing junior high life
>
> Jerry, the Artful Dodger, managing to stay clear
>
> Linda, our Angelfish, eye-catching in every way
>
> Lynn, my Jesse Stuart, strong and silent

Checking for Common Ailments

To write with style, you must know what to look for when a piece doesn't sound smooth or natural. Always check for the ailments listed below and on the following page ("Avoiding Cliches"). Also refer to the information about sentences on pages 64–74.

PRIMER STYLE: If your writing contains many short sentences, one right after another, it may sound like a primary-grade textbook, or "primer."

> A special faculty committee announced a new policy for makeup exams. It seems unreasonable. Students must complete makeup exams within a week. Extensions will be granted only in emergency situations. Emergencies include serious health problems. They also include family crises.

The Cure: The main cure is to combine some of your ideas into longer, smoother-reading sentences. Here's the same passage revised.

> **A special faculty committee announced a new policy for makeup exams that seems unreasonable. Students must complete makeup exams within a week. Extensions will be granted only in emergency situations, including serious health problems and family crises.**

PASSIVE VOICE: If your writing seems slow moving and impersonal, you may have used too many passive verbs. With passive verbs, the subject of the sentence receives the action: *The tree was struck by lightning.* Here's an example passage written in the passive voice.

> The latest poetry jam was enjoyed by everyone. Every reading was greeted with hoots, hollers, and foot stomping. The final performance was the object of the most vocal outpouring by the audience. This poem about "macho men" was shared by Larry Smith.

The Cure: Unless you need a passive verb, change it to the active voice: *Lightning struck the tree.* Here is the passage written in the active voice.

> **Everyone enjoyed the latest poetry jam. Hoots, hollers, and foot stomping greeted each reading. The final performance garnered the audience's most vocal outpouring when Larry Smith shared his poem about "macho men."**

INSECURITY: Does your writing contain many qualifiers (*to be perfectly honest, to tell the truth,* etc.) or intensifiers (*really, truly,* etc.)? Ironically, these words and phrases may suggest that you lack confidence in your ideas.

> I totally and completely agree with Dr. Stark about expanding the course offerings, but that's only my opinion.

The Cure: Never hesitate to say exactly what you mean. Here is one possible revised example.

> **I agree with Dr. Stark about expanding the course offerings.**

Avoiding Cliches

Cliches are comparisons we no longer see as such for their overuse. We use phrases like a chubby man's "spare tire" or the "class clown" without considering their effectiveness.

Sensitive writers try never to use cliches unthinkingly. But sometimes they twist them, stretch them, or turn them upside down to raise the metaphor from the dead. A chubby man's "spare tire" might become the "B. F. Goodrich around his waist."

INSIDE INFO

The word "cliche" is itself a metaphor. Literally, a cliche was a metal plate used in a printing process called "stereotyping." Figuratively, we use the words "cliche" and "stereotype" to refer to words and ideas that are cranked out again and again.

Worn-Out Expressions

Here are a few tired words and phrases you will want to avoid:

- like a house on fire
- kick the bucket
- between a rock and a hard place
- easy as pie
- as good as dead
- up a creek
- throwing your weight around
- wet blanket
- beat around the bush
- piece of cake
- stick your neck out
- green with envy
- burning bridges
- working like a dog
- waging a lonely battle
- planting the seed

Other Types of Cliches

There are other aspects of your writing that may also be tired and overworked. Be alert to these types of cliches as well.

Cliches of Purpose

- Essays to please the instructor
- Sentimental papers mourning over lost loves, gushing about an ideal friend, or droning on about moving experiences
- Short stories with simple lessons at the end

Cliches of Voice

- **The junior analyst:** "I have determined that there are three basic types of newspapers. My preference is for the third."
- **The faceless reporter:** "Overall, homecoming weekend went beautifully. A good time was had by all."
- **The gum-cracking enthusiast:** "I flipped when I saw *Romeo and Juliet.*"

Designing Your Writing

Just as you organize the ideas and details in your essays to make them clear, you arrange the elements and graphic devices on the page to create an appealing design. Design should be both functional (easy to navigate) and attractive (inviting to read). Strong design looks professional, pulls the reader into your document, makes content accessible, and promotes understanding.

Software for word processing and page layout offers countless choices for achieving a particular look. However, it's easy to get carried away; and too much emphasis on design is as bad as none. Remember: When designing a document for presentation, aim for appealing simplicity.

WHAT'S AHEAD

Effective design includes an appropriate format, page layout, typography, and color. This chapter addresses each of these issues as they relate to print materials.

Design Overview

The test of a good page design is its clarity. Always check with your instructor for design requirements. Also consider these guidelines.

Selecting an Appropriate Font

- **Choose an easy-to-read font for the main text.** In most cases, a serif typestyle is best for the text, with sans serif for the headings. Make the headings boldface if they seem to get lost on the paper, and use a 12-point type size for the text of most forms.

  The letters of serif fonts have "tails"—as in this sentence.

  The letters of sans serif fonts are plain, without tails—as in this sentence.

- **Make titles and headings short and to the point.** Headings of equal importance should be stated in the same way. Follow the basic rules for capitalizing titles and headings.

Using Consistent Spacing and Margins

- **Set clear margins.** Use a one-inch margin around each page (top, bottom, left, and right).
- **Hit the tab key, set at five spaces, to indent the first line of each paragraph.**
- **Leave one space after every period.** This will improve the readability of your paper.
- **Avoid placing headings, hyphenated words, and first lines of new paragraphs at the bottom of a page.** Also avoid single-word lines at either the bottom or the top of a page.

Including Graphic Elements

- **Use lists if appropriate.** Use numbered lists for points needing a sequential order. Otherwise, use bulleted lists (like the ones on this page).
- **Include graphics.** Use tables, charts, or illustrations to help make a point. Keep graphics within the text small, and display a larger, complex graphic on its own page.

BOTTOM LINE

Selecting the appropriate design elements will help the reader identify the purpose and message of the document. Effective presentation is key: Keep pages open and balanced, breaking your message into manageable chunks and using consistent visual cues.

Effective Design in Action

The following personal essay by Terence Hatcher demonstrates effective design. The side notes highlight the important design features.

Terence Hatcher
Ms. Brackett
Economics
February 7, 2010

The title is 18-point sans serif type.

Avoiding the Crunch

Let's say that you decide to buy three CD's that are $10 each, and the cashier says, "That will be $30, please. If you don't have $30, just pay a little each month for the next 17 years." Sound ridiculous? Teenagers do it every day, creating credit card debt that will follow them into adulthood.

The main text is 12-point serif type.

Credit card companies are hoping to cash in by targeting students. Plush toys, T-shirts, and snacks are "freebies" intended to lure potential card users. Sociologist Robert Manning states, "The credit card marketers sign high school kids at college fairs. They get paid by the number of applications they turn in" (43). Many students sign up without considering the fine print. For example, while most cards offer an introductory rate of 0 percent, the rate rises to 15 percent after the six-month promotional period. And if you default or fail to pay, the rate skyrockets to 30 percent!

Subheadings are 14-point sans serif.

Doing the Math

What does this mean to you? Let's say you spend $2,000 during the first six months. Then the interest rate zooms up to 15 percent. You decide to start paying off the balance, but you don't have enough money to pay the whole thing. So you pay the monthly minimum of 2 percent or at least $25 a month. How long do you think it would take to pay off the original $2,000 balance? Not only would it take almost 12 years, but you would also end up spending about $4,000! As radio talk-show host Clark Howard says, " . . . what you really need to know is that you are ripping yourself off because you are not paying off that balance" ("In Debt").

Hatcher 2

The chart that follows illustrates the problem with making minimum monthly payments.

A chart adds impact and visual appeal.

$2,000 Credit Card Debt, Paid Off at Minimums

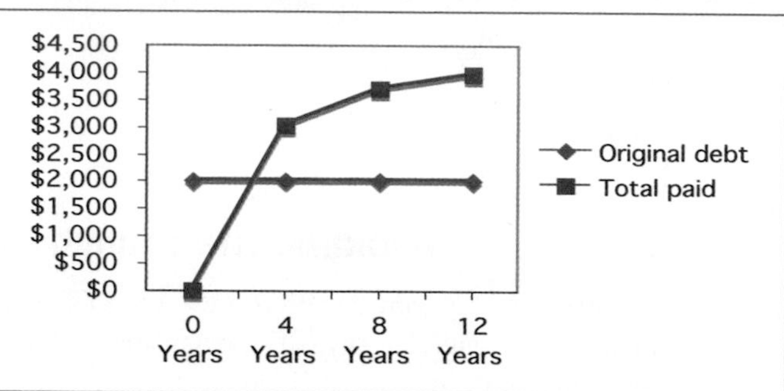

Keeping a Clean Record

"Your credit report is often called your second résumé," according to Dr. Flora Williams in her book *Climbing the Steps to Financial Success* (15). A credit report covers your history of borrowing, bill payment, and debt owed. If you use your credit card irresponsibly, your credit card company will make negative comments on your credit report. Banks, college loan officers, employers, and landlords can request your credit report.

So how do you maintain a positive credit report? Here are four key guidelines:

A bulleted list presents important points clearly.

- Use your credit card wisely. Keep track of what you are buying. Know how long it will take you to pay for each item. Don't be tempted by the latest laptop or video game system that you can't afford.
- Know your credit limit. Going over the limit may result in fines or even cancellation of your account.
- Pay off the balance, or at least more than the minimum.
- Pay on time. This is the simplest way to avoid late fees, increased interest rates, and credit damage.

What is the lesson here? It takes common sense and hard work to avoid the pitfalls of credit card debt. If you read the fine print, spend wisely, and pay promptly, you'll be on your way to building a solid financial foundation.

Adding Graphics

When adding graphics to your writing, make sure you aren't simply "dressing up" the words. Instead, include graphics to add information or enhance the reader's understanding. Follow these guidelines:

Table

Use tables to provide statistics in a compact form. Clearly label rows and columns so that the reader can quickly grasp the information.

COMPARING COUNTRIES			
	Canada	Mexico	United States
Size (Sq. Miles)	3.85 million	759,000	3.8 million
Type of Government	Parliamentary	Republic	Republic
Voting Age	18	18	18
Literacy	99%	87%	98%

Graph

Use graphs to show statistics visually. Line graphs show how quantities change over time. Bar graphs compare and contrast amounts. Pie graphs show the parts of a whole. Be sure to provide a clear title, labels, and a legend (if needed).

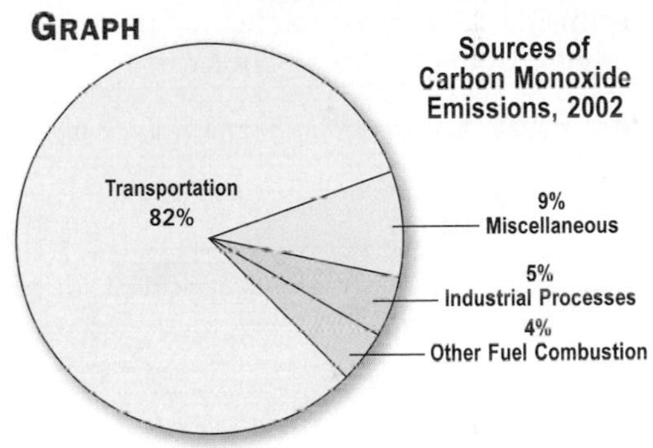

Diagram

Use diagrams to show the parts of something. Include labels or arrows to inform the reader about the parts being shown.

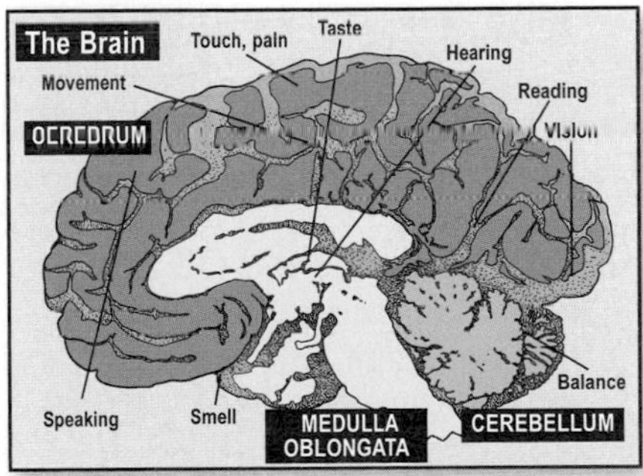

INSIDE INFO

Consider the importance of the graphic when you decide on its size and how and where it should be placed on the page. Place a small graphic on the same page as the reference. Place a large graphic on a separate page.

Page Layout

Page layout—how you arrange material on a page—determines whether your document is attractive, readable, and accessible. Generally, avoid dense blocks of prose, cluttered pages, or largely empty pages.

Layout Decisions

Orientation: Standard orientation for most pages is vertical, called *portrait;* such orientation is used for academic essays, business letters, and more. Other documents, such as pamphlets and Web pages, follow a horizontal orientation, called *landscape*. Select the orientation that best presents the information.

Column types: With *newspaper columns,* text runs continuously from the bottom of one column to the top of the next—useful for pamphlets, booklets, and newsletters. With *parallel columns,* the text in each column remains separate—useful for instructions, résumés, itineraries, and Web pages. Consider these choices:

Basic Page Layouts

- **One column** is standard for most documents.
- **Two columns (even)** balance the page and allow comparisons and contrasts.
- **Two columns (uneven)** provide a larger column for main text and a smaller column for headings, side notes, graphics, and so forth.
- **Three or more columns** break up text into blocks or panels useful for pamphlets, brochures, and newsletters.

Applying Color

Color design is based on the color wheel, which pictures the relationship between colors. Primary colors (red, blue, and yellow) are foundational—not made from blending other colors. Secondary colors are the result of blending two primary colors.

Color Theory

Colors opposite each other on the wheel are complementary. When placed together, these colors "complete" each other, making each appear deeper and richer. In a document's color scheme, complementary colors energize a design.

Those colors located close together on the color wheel have many similarities and subtle variations in content. When used together, related colors keep things calm and balanced, creating harmony.

Color Associations

People often have strong color associations. To develop an effective document design, take such associations into account.

TEMPERATURE: Some colors are warm (yellow, orange, red, brown); others are cool (purple, blue, green). This difference refers, in part, to the emotional tone the colors create.

TONE: Colors have both personal and cultural associations—red with passion, blood, and warnings; blue with sky, water, and stability; green with nature, growth, and cheerfulness.

TIPS

FOR INCORPORATING COLOR

Tie your color scheme to your purpose, audience, and context. Make each color choice an informed choice.

- Select a limited color palette for most documents and avoid confusion caused by clashing colors (such as pink and orange), colors that are misinterpreted by color-blind individuals (red and green), and colors that are hard on the eyes.
- Choose colors to create a mood, draw attention to ideas, and develop subtle effects.
- Employ color to draw the reader's attention to key elements and establish patterns that create a visual logic (headings, bullets, text boxes, tabs, appendices, and so on).
- Create a consistent color pattern throughout a document.
- Use color carefully in academic projects.

Checklist for Document Design

As you plan, develop, test, and refine your design, use this checklist to review your document for effective color, format, page layout, and typography.

Overall Design

_____ The overall design is appropriate for the writing situation, type of document, message, and audience.

_____ If appropriate, the design follows a standard style guide (MLA, APA).

_____ Design elements distinguish the document's topic, main point, and purpose.

_____ The document's format and design make effective use of color; the overall color scheme is both functional and attractive.

Design Features

_____ The layout effectively uses a heading system, lists, margins, columns, and white space to make the message clear and easy to read.

_____ Accent features such as highlighting, underlining, boldface, and italics bring attention to the message and are appropriate to the document's purpose.

_____ Design elements (such as headings, page numbers, and outlines) clearly identify and organize parts of the message.

_____ The document contains all appropriate elements (a title page, table of contents, introduction, outline, appendices, and index).

Fonts and Visuals

_____ The fonts are appropriately sized and attractive, emphasize information as needed, and fit the document's purpose and audience.

_____ The visuals (tables and figures) are well designed and placed to support the message.

Writing Terms and Techniques

As a student of writing, you need to build your writer's vocabulary. For example, you should know what is meant by terms such as *coherence, counterargument,* and *tone* as well as techniques such as *anecdote, irony,* and *parallelism.* You should also be able to recognize the common forms of writing such as *narrative, analytical essay,* and *review.* Whenever you are not sure of a term, technique, or form, turn to this chapter for help.

WHAT'S AHEAD

The following pages contain glossaries of writing terms and writing techniques that you will find useful in your course work. The list of foreign words and phrases will serve as a quick guide to Latin, French, Spanish, Yiddish, and other unfamiliar words you may encounter. Completing the chapter is a survey of writing forms, covering everything from narrative writing to business writing.

Writing Terms

Analysis: Writing that carefully examines and explores a subject with the objective of gaining understanding.

Argumentation: Writing or speaking in which reasons or arguments are presented in a logical way.

Arrangement: The order in which details are placed or arranged in a piece of writing.

Audience: Those people who read or hear what you have written.

Balance: The arranging of words or phrases so that two ideas are given equal emphasis in a sentence or paragraph; a rhythm created by repeating a pattern.

Brainstorming: Collecting ideas by thinking and talking freely and openly about all the possibilities; used most often with groups.

Case study: The story of one individual whose experiences speak for the experiences of a larger group of people.

Central idea: The main point or purpose of a piece of writing, often stated in a thesis statement or topic sentence.

Claim: An assertion or a proposition (thesis) in argumentation, occurring as a claim of fact, value, or policy.

Classification: Writing that breaks a topic down into its most meaningful parts and carefully examines each part.

Coherence: The arrangement of ideas in such a way that the reader can easily follow from one point to the next.

Commentary: Writing that presents a thoughtful reaction to some aspect of life.

Concession: Giving credit to a claim on the opposing side of an argument.

Conventions: The rules and standards of a language.

Counterargument: Defending a position against a significant objection.

Data: Information that is accepted as being true—facts, figures, examples—and from which conclusions can be drawn.

Deductive reasoning: The act of beginning with a general idea and reasoning one's way to a specific point or conclusion.

Definition: Writing that explains, describes, and clarifies a complex concept, an abstract idea, or a complicated idea.

Description: Writing that paints a colorful picture of a person, a place, or a thing.

Details: The words used to describe a person, convince an audience, explain a process, or in some way support the central idea; to be effective, details should appeal to the senses.

Emphasis: Placing greater stress on the most important idea in a piece of writing; emphasis can be achieved by placing the important idea in a special position, by repeating a key word or phrase, or by simply writing more about this idea than the others.

Essay: A piece of prose writing in which ideas on a single topic are presented, explained, argued, or described in an interesting way.

Evaluation: Writing that explores a subject's value, impact, or significance; its strengths and weaknesses; its place in the scheme of things.

Explication: Writing that presents a detailed analysis or thoughtful interpretation of a subject.

Exposition: Writing that explains.

Extended definition: Writing that offers an in-depth definition of a term in order to increase understanding; it can cover several paragraphs and include personal definitions and experiences, similes and metaphors, quotations, and even verse.

Figurative language: Language that goes beyond the immediate meaning of the words used; writing in which a figure of speech is used to heighten the meaning.

Focus: Concentrating on a specific aspect of a topic. (Often called the thesis.)

Form: The arrangement of details into a pattern or style; the way in which the content of writing is organized.

Freewriting: Writing openly and freely on any topic; focused freewriting is writing openly on a specific topic or angle.

Generalization: An idea or a statement that emphasizes the general characteristics rather than the specific details of a topic.

Grammar: The study of the structure and features of a language; it usually consists of rules and standards that are to be followed to produce acceptable writing and speaking.

Idiom: A phrase or an expression that means something different from what the words actually say. An idiom is usually understandable to a particular group of people (using *over his head* for *didn't understand).*

Illustration: Writing that uses an experience to make a point or clarify an idea.

Inductive reasoning: The act of beginning with specific examples or facts and reasoning one's way to a generalization or conclusion.

Inverted sentence: A sentence in which the normal word order is inverted or switched.

Journal: A daily record of thoughts, impressions, and autobiographical information; a journal can be an important source of ideas for writing.

Juxtaposition: Placing two ideas (words or pictures) side by side so that their closeness creates a new, often ironic meaning.

Limiting the subject: Narrowing the subject to a specific topic that is suitable for the writing or speaking task.

Literal: The actual or dictionary meaning of a word; language that means exactly what it appears to mean.

Logic: The science of correct reasoning; correctly using facts, examples, and reasons to support your point.

Narration: Writing that tells a story or recounts an event.

Objective: Relating information in an impersonal manner; without feelings or opinions.

Personal narrative: Personal writing that covers an event in the writer's life; it often contains personal comments, thoughts, and observations.

Persuasion: Writing that is meant to change a reader's thinking or actions.

Point of view: The position or angle from which a story is told.

Position paper: Writing that takes a particular stance on a noteworthy issue (based on extensive analysis), aiming to inform and explain rather than persuade.

Premise: A statement or point that serves as the basis of a discussion or debate.

Process: A method of doing something that involves several steps or stages; the writing process involves prewriting, composing, revising, and proofreading.

Profile: Writing that reveals an individual or re-creates a time period, using interviews and research.

Proposition: The main idea to be discussed in an argument.

Prose: Writing or speaking in the usual or ordinary form; prose becomes poetry when it takes on rhyme and rhythm.

Purpose: The specific reason a person has for writing; the goal of writing.

Reminiscence: Writing that focuses on a memorable past experience.

Report: Writing that results from gathering, investigating, and organizing facts and thoughts on a topic.

Review: Writing that presents a critical evaluation of a literary work or an artistic endeavor.

Revision: Changing a piece of writing to improve it in style or content.

Subjective: Thinking or writing that includes personal feelings, attitudes, and opinions.

Summary: Writing that presents the main points of a larger work in condensed form.

Syntax: The order and relationship of words in a sentence.

Theme: The central idea in a piece of writing (lengthy writings may have several themes).

Thesis statement: A statement of the purpose, intent, or main idea of an essay.

Tone: The writer's attitude toward the subject; a writer's tone can be serious, sarcastic, tongue-in-cheek, solemn, objective, etc.

Topic: The specific subject covered in a piece of writing.

Transitions: Words or phrases that help tie ideas together.

Unity: Writing in which each sentence helps to develop the main idea.

Universal: A topic or an idea that applies to everyone.

Usage: The way in which people use language; language is generally considered to be standard (formal and informal) or nonstandard.

Vivid details: Details that appeal to the senses and help the reader see, feel, smell, taste, and hear the subject being written about.

Writing Techniques

Experiment with these techniques in your own essays and stories.

Allusion A reference to a familiar person, place, thing, or event.

I have feet that put Steven Spielberg's E.T. to shame. They are a tangle of toes held together by bunions.

Analogy A comparison of ideas or objects that are completely different but that are alike in one important way.

The mind of a bigot is like the pupil of the eye: The more light you shine on it, the more it will contract.

—Oliver Wendell Holmes, Jr.

Anecdote A brief story used to illustrate or make a point.

In a passenger train compartment, a lady lit a cigarette, saying to Sir Thomas Beecham, a famous orchestra conductor, "I'm sure you don't object."

"Not at all," replied Beecham, "provided you don't mind if I'm sick."

"I don't think you know who I am," the lady pointed out. "I'm one of the railroad directors' wives."

"Madam," said the conductor, "if you were the director's only wife, I should still be sick." (The story makes a point about the unpleasantness of secondhand smoke.)

Antithesis Using opposite ideas to emphasize a point.

There was no possibility of being hired at the town's cotton gin or lumber mill, but maybe there was a way to make the two factories work for her.

—Maya Angelou, *Wouldn't Take Nothing for My Journey Now*

Colloquialism A common word or phrase suitable for ordinary, everyday conversation but not for formal speech or writing.

y'all listen up **run this by her** **no way**

Exaggeration An overstatement or stretching of the truth to emphasize a point. (See *hyperbole* and *overstatement*.)

The Danes are so full of *joie de vivre* [joy of life] that they practically sweat it.

—Bill Bryson, *Neither Here nor There*

Flashback A technique in which a writer interrupts a story to go back and explain an earlier time or event for the purpose of making something in the present more clear.

I stopped at the gate, panting. Suddenly I was seven years old again, and my brother was there, calling me "chicken" from the edge of the stone well. Then I opened my eyes and I heard only the crickets chirping. The years, the well, and my brother were gone. I turned back to the road, determined to get home before nightfall.

Foreshadowing Hints or clues about what will happen next in a story.

As Mai explained why she had to break their date, she noticed Lamar looking past her. Turning, she saw Meg smiling—at Lamar.

Hyperbole (hi-púr-bə-lē) Exaggeration used to emphasize a point. (See *exaggeration* and *overstatement*.)

We didn't need to [read] because my father has read everything . . . and people in town have said that talking to him about anything is better than reading three books.

—Cynthia Marshall Rich

Irony An expression in which the author says one thing but means just the opposite. (See page 291.)

But then I was lucky enough to come down with the disease of the moment in the Hamptons, which was Lyme disease.

—Kurt Vonnegut

Juxtaposition Putting two words or ideas close together to create a contrasting of ideas or an ironic meaning.

Just remember, we're all in this alone.

—Lily Tomlin

Local color The use of details that are common in a certain place. (The following passage lists foods common to small-town Southern life.)

Folks had already brought over more cakes and pies, and platters of fried chicken and ham, and their good china bowls full of string beans, butter beans, okra, and tomatoes.

—Olive Ann Burns, *Cold Sassy Tree*

Metaphor A figure of speech that compares two things without using the words *like* or *as*.

Perfectionism is the voice of the oppressor, the enemy of the people.

—Anne Lamott, *Bird by Bird*

Overstatement An exaggeration or a stretching of the truth. (See *exaggeration* and *hyperbole*.)

I bet you could set off dynamite in an A & P and the people would by and large keep reaching and checking oatmeal off their lists and muttering "Let me see, there was a third thing, began with an A, asparagus, no, ah, yes, applesauce!"

—John Updike, "A & P"

Oxymoron Connecting two words with opposite meanings.

war for peace **black light** **controlled chaos**

Paradox A true statement that says two opposite things.

The miniature metal toy cars of the 1960s are no longer playthings.

Parallelism Repeating similar grammatical structures (words, phrases, or sentences) to give writing rhythm.

All this waste happens before any lid is popped, any can is opened, or any seal is broken.

—Allison Rozendaal, student writer

Personification A figure of speech in which a nonhuman thing is given human characteristics.

And what I remember next is how the moon, the pale moon with its one yellow eye . . . stared through the pink plastic curtains.

—Sandra Cisneros, "One Holy Night"

Pun A phrase that uses words that sound the same in a way that gives them a funny effect.

I have come to believe that opposing gravity is something not to be taken—uh, lightly.

—Daniel Pinkwater, "Why I Don't Fly"

Sensory details Details that are experienced through the senses to help the reader see, feel, smell, taste, and hear what is being described.

I stood backstage, surrounded by giggles and rustling tulle. The smell of talcum powder, hairspray, and rosin rolled in from the stage. A familiar, acrid taste filled my mouth. The music rose, and the dancers swept onto the stage in a frothy swirl of pink and blue.

Simile A figure of speech that compares two things using *like* or *as*.

They [the old men] had hands like claws, and their knees were twisted like the old thorn trees.

—William Butler Yeats

Slang Informal words or phrases used by a particular group of people.

dis **ain't** **chill out**

Symbol A concrete object used to represent an idea.

hourglass = time passing **dove = peace**

Synecdoche Using part of something to represent the whole.

Idle hands are the devil's playground. (*Hands* represent the person.)

Understatement The opposite of exaggeration. By using very calm language, an author can bring special attention to an object or an idea.

He [our new dog] turned out to be a good traveler, and except for an interruption caused by my wife's falling out of the car, the journey went very well.

—E. B. White, "A Report in Spring"

Foreign Words and Phrases

a cappella (It) without instrumental accompaniment

ad hoc (L) "for this purpose"; for the present matter or situation; temporary

ad infinitum (L) endlessly; forever

ad nauseam (L) to a sickening degree

aficionado (Sp) enthusiast; fan

alfresco (It) in the open air

alma mater (L) "fostering mother"; old school

alpha (Gk) first; the beginning

alter ego (L) another side of oneself

antebellum (L) before the war, especially before the Civil War

a posteriori (L) "from what comes after"; inductive

a priori (L) "from what comes before"; deductive

au contraire (Fr) on the contrary

au courant (Fr) up-to-date; contemporary

avant-garde (Fr) "vanguard"; forward; advanced

beau geste (Fr) noble gesture

bête noire (Fr) "black beast"; pet peeve

blitzkrieg (Gr) a swift, sudden effort, usually in war

bona fide (L) "in good faith"; sincere; genuine

bon appetit (Fr) "good appetite"; enjoy your meal

bon mot (Fr) clever turn of phrase

bon vivant (Fr) a person who has refined tastes

campesino (Sp) peasant farmer

carpe diem (L) "seize the day"; live for today

carte blanche (Fr) "blank document"; unlimited authority or power

cause célèbre (Fr) "celebrated case"; scandal; notorious incident, person, or thing

KEY:				
	Fr	French	L	Latin
	Gk	Greek	R	Russian
	Gr	German	Sp	Spanish
	It	Italian	Y	Yiddish
	J	Japanese		

caveat emptor (L) "let the buyer beware"; buyer takes the risk; no warranty

c'est la vie (Fr) "that's life"

chef d'oeuvre (Fr) masterpiece

chutzpah (Y) gall; daring

circa (L) about; approximately

cogito, ergo sum (L) "I think, therefore I am."

coup de grâce (Fr) a decisive finishing blow, act, or event to end suffering

coup d'etat (Fr) a sudden, decisive exercise of force in politics; overthrow of government

crème de la crème (Fr) "cream of the cream"; the very best

cum laude (L) "with praise"; with honor

déclassé (Fr) fallen in social standing

de facto (L) functioning or existing in fact, or in reality, but not in accordance with the usual or legal process

de jure (L) legally, according to the law

détente (Fr) easing of strained relations

dramatis personae (L) "persons of the drama"; cast of characters

en masse (Fr) in a large group

e pluribus unum (L) "one out of many"

errata (L) a list of errors

ersatz (Gr) fake; imitation

esprit de corps (Fr) common spirit within a group

eureka (Gk) "I have found"; expression of triumph or discovery

ex cathedra (L) "from the chair"; with high authority

exemplum (L) example; model; anecdote

ex officio (L) by virtue of, or because of, one's office or position

ex post facto (L) after the fact or event; retroactive

fait accompli (Fr) accomplished fact

faux pas (Fr) "false step"; a social blunder

fiat (L) "let it be done"; a command; a decree

glasnost (R) "publicity"; openness

habeas corpus (L) "you should have the body"; writ summoning one to court

haute couture (Fr) high fashion

haute cuisine (Fr) elaborate cooking

hoi polloi (Gk) common people, masses

hubris (Gk) exaggerated pride; arrogance

in extremis (L) "in extreme circumstances"

in loco parentis (L) "in place of a parent"; acting as a guardian

in medias res (L) "in the middle of things"

in memoriam (L) "in memory of"; as a memorial to

ipso facto (L) "by the fact (act) itself"; by the nature of the thing; automatically

joie de vivre (Fr) "joy of living"; good spirits; exuberance

kamikaze (J) "divine wind"; suicide pilot

klutz (Y) clumsy person

kudos (Gk) "glory, renown"; fame; honor; accolade

kvetch (Y) complain; carp; gripe

laissez-faire (Fr) "let [people] do [as they wish]"; noninterference

lingua franca (It) "Frankish language"; a common language among people of different tongues

magna cum laude (L) with great honor

magnum opus (L) a masterpiece

mea culpa (L) "my fault"; expressing personal fault or guilt

modus operandi (L) "manner of operating"; a working method or arrangement; a procedure

noblesse oblige (Fr) honorable behavior that is considered to be the obligation of people of noble birth or rank

nom de plume (Fr) pen name

nonpareil (Fr) having no equal

non sequitur (L) "it does not follow"; a response that doesn't follow logically from a previous statement; fallacy

nouveau riche (Fr) the newly rich

par excellence (Fr) above all; superior

per capita (L) "by heads"; for each one

per diem (L) "by the day"

per se (L) "by, of, or in itself, oneself, or themselves"; of its own accord

persona non grata (L) an unacceptable person

pièce de résistance (Fr) the main dish of a meal; the main thing or event

prima facie (L) "on first appearance"; at first glance; self-evident; sufficient to establish a fact

pro forma (L) "for form"; carried out as a formality; for the record

pro rata (L) proportionately

quid pro quo (L) "something for something"; something given for something received

raison d'être (Fr) reason for being

reductio ad absurdum (L) "reduction to absurdity"; disproving an argument by showing its absurd direction

savoir faire (Fr) "knowing how to do"; ability to say and do the right thing

schlemiel (Y) unlucky person; loser

schmaltz (Y) excessive sentimentality

shtick (Y) gimmick; a performer's idiosyncracy

sine qua non (L) "without which not"; like no other; something essential

status quo (L) "the condition in which"; present condition; the state of affairs up to now

summa cum laude (L) with highest honor

tabula rasa (L) "erased tablet"; clean slate

terra firma (L) "solid land"; dry land; solid ground

tête-à-tête (Fr) "head-to-head"; together without intrusion by another

tour de force (Fr) a feat of great strength

veni, vidi, vici (L) "I came, I saw, I conquered."

verbatim (L) "word for word"; exactly as said or written

verboten (Gr) forbidden

vis-à-vis (Fr) "face-to-face"; opposite; in relation to

vox populi (L) "voice of the people"

wanderlust (Gr) desire to travel

Weltschmerz (Gr) "world pain"; world weariness

wunderkind (Gr) prodigy

KEY:			
Fr	French	L	Latin
Gk	Greek	R	Russian
Gr	German	Sp	Spanish
It	Italian	Y	Yiddish
J	Japanese		

Survey of Writing Forms

The following chart classifies many of the different forms of writing. You can learn a great deal about writing by experimenting with a variety of these forms.

Narrative Writing

Remembering & Sharing	Journals • Diaries • Logs • Notebooks
(Exploring Experiences)	Personal Narratives and Essays • Memoirs
Promotes writing fluency.	Descriptive Essays • Freewriting • Listing

Expository & Analytical Writing

Informing & Analyzing	Expository Essays • Process Essays
(Sharing Information)	Essays of Definition • Cause-Effect Essays
Develops organizing skills.	Comparison-Contrast Essays • Summaries Essays of Opposing Ideas • Research Papers

Persuasive Writing

Arguing & Evaluating	Persuasive Essays • Pet Peeves
(Judging the Worth of Something)	Editorials • Personal Commentaries Problem-Solution Essays • Position Papers
Reinforces critical thinking.	Essays of Argumentation

Writing About Literature

Understanding & Interpreting	Journal Entries • Letters to the Author
(Reacting to Texts)	Book Reviews
Fosters critical reading.	Literary Analyses • Dialogues

Creative Writing

Inventing & Imitating	Stories • Patterned Fiction
(Reshaping Ideas)	Free Verse Poetry • Traditional Poetry
Encourages creativity.	Plays • Dialogues • Monologues

Business Writing

Questioning & Answering	Request Letters • Complaint Letters
(Writing to Get a Job Done)	Letters of Application • Memos
Builds real-world writing skills.	E-Mail Messages • Brochures • Résumés

Personal Writing

Personal Writing

Infants perceive themselves as the center of the universe. If they are warm, clean, dry, and full of milk, everything is right with the world. If they are cold or dirty or wet or hungry, everything is wrong. As they grow, their universe expands to take in family, home, neighborhood, community, country, world, and beyond. Even the astronauts who have skipped across the moon began their journeys within themselves.

In the same way, personal writing allows you to explore who you are, where you have been, and where you hope to go. It also helps you connect with the world around you and share the experiences that have made you who you are.

WHAT'S AHEAD

This section in your handbook will help you tell your own stories in reminiscences and personal essays. As you write, expect to gain some interesting insights into your life—past, present, and future.

"The primal story from which all others come, is your own story—your own personal history."

—John Rouse

Personal Writing

QUICK GUIDE

Every time you put fingers to the keyboard (or pen to paper) you disclose something about yourself. It can't be helped. Personal writing, of course, is the most telling type of writing because it is based on your own experiences. As writer John Mayher states, "Our stories point like dreams to certain themes or concerns in our lives, containing either explicitly or implicitly some moral tag, which sums up where we've been."

All personal writing shares the following characteristics:

- **STARTING POINT:** Personal writing begins with a memorable event that you want to explore and share.
- **PURPOSE:** Personal writing helps you make sense out of your experiences. It may also inform or entertain your reader.
- **FORM:** A reminiscence moves in a linear direction, with the details unfolding one after another until the story is told. A personal essay may develop in much the same way, but it will also include explanation and analysis.
- **AUDIENCE:** In most cases, you will be addressing your immediate audience—your writing peers and your instructor.
- **VOICE:** Use your best storytelling voice in a reminiscence. Help the reader relive the experience right along with you. In a personal essay, speak openly and honestly to sincerely share your thoughts and feelings.
- **POINT OF VIEW:** In almost all cases, use the first-person point of view (I) in personal writing. You are, after all, writing about yourself.

INSIDE INFO

Try to picture your subject, a personal experience, as if you were seeing it through the lens of a camera. First pan the camera back and forth. What picture or image appears? Is everything clear? How does this picture make you feel? Then zoom in to get some closer shots. Once you can see a personal experience from different angles, you're ready to write about it.

Guidelines

Writing a Personal Reminiscence

When you write a personal reminiscence, you center on a vivid memory of a defining moment in your life. Consider what moments have made you who you are. Your goal is to select one specific time and re-create it so that it comes alive for the reader. Refer to the steps below and the models on the following pages to help you with your writing.

PREWRITING

Select a topic. Focus on experiences or events that have changed you—the significant moments in your life. Choose one to write about.

Gather details. Review photos and journal entries from that time and speak with others who were there. Then use a sensory chart to record sights, sounds, feelings, smells, tastes, and sensations associated with your experience.

Organize your ideas. Create a time line, telling what happened first, next, and so on. Following chronological order is especially important in the middle of your narrative, while the beginning and ending may shift backward or forward in time.

WRITING

Create a first draft. Let your ideas flow, reviewing your prewriting as needed. Begin by describing the time and place and introducing the people present. Recount details in the order they happened using vivid verbs and natural dialogue. In the ending, reflect on the experience.

REVISING

Review your ideas. *Have I focused on a meaningful experience? Have I included sensory details, action, and dialogue?*

Check your organization. *Does my beginning capture the reader's interest and introduce the moment or event? Do the middle paragraphs follow chronological order? Does the ending reflect on the importance of the experience?*

Revise for voice, word choice, and sentence fluency. *Is my storytelling voice natural? Have I used strong verbs, specific nouns, and vivid modifiers? Do I have a variety of sentence types and lengths?*

EDITING

Edit for conventions. *Have I checked my punctuation, capitalization, spelling, and grammar?*

PUBLISHING

Present your work. Post your reminiscence online or send it to family and friends.

Personal Reminiscence

In the following personal reminiscence, professional writer Jessica Lun She Evans remembers a defining moment in her life. Note how she relates childhood impressions and experiences through an adult perspective.

Coming Home

The writer begins on a universal level and transitions to a specific event.

Our earliest memories are snapshots of who we are. We select these memories, hold on to them, clutch them to our chests, because they define us. We relive these moments a thousand times and dote on them like champions with blue ribbons, or grieve over them like mourners at a grave. I have one such memento moment that I relive: a special afternoon when I first met my little sister.

I was only five, belted into a seat in Grandma and Grandpa's minivan. An air-conditioned breeze poured down over my head like cold water, though the hot August sun streamed through the window and baked my legs. I felt small.

The writer uses physical size as a metaphor for isolation.

For two weeks, I'd been bumping through an adult-sized world. My grandparents' guest bed was two sizes too large; the conversations between them overflowed with polysyllabic words; every chair in their house stranded my feet off the ground. Now, beyond the window in the minivan, a twelve-lane river of semis and cars rushed through a badlands of brick and steel: big brawling Chicago and little bitty me.

"We're almost to O'Hare," Grandpa said proudly, "one of the busiest airports in the world. Look, Jessie!" He pointed out the windshield.

Dialogue allows the reader to experience the event firsthand.

I leaned to see a 747 lumbering through the sky above us. Grandma said, "Maybe that's the one with your mommy and daddy—and your new little sister!" I started to cry. For two weeks, I'd held back, but at last I broke down.

"Oh, don't cry," Grandma said, her large pink hand patting my hot brown knees. "You've been a brave girl so long. Just be brave a little longer."

But it wouldn't be just a little longer. It might be a lot longer. What if I didn't have a mom and dad anymore? What if they'd be so busy with little Kelly that they wouldn't have time for me? What if they loved her more than they loved me?

Fears about the new relationship are shared through the translation of names.

Kelly's Mandarin name was Kun Ro, which meant "gentle girl." My Mandarin name, Lun She, meant "clever debate." What parent would prefer a clever debate to a gentle girl?

Grandma dabbed my eyes with a tissue while Grandpa drove us up a great cement corkscrew and into a giant parking garage. "Remember: White Sox Level, Blue 5," Grandpa said as he pulled into a spot. Grandma undid my seat belt while Grandpa dragged the stroller out of the back of the minivan. As soon as he had it unfolded, I tried to sit down in the stroller but Grandpa pursed his lips. "You're too big now, Jessie. This is for the baby."

The last stroller ride symbolizes the writer's change of position in the family.

"Oh, she won't hurt it," Grandma said. "Let her have one last ride."

During my one last ride, I thought about my new little sister. Mom and Dad had shown me a picture of her: a two-month-old with thick black hair, round cheeks, and a pink jumper. She was sitting up in a crib, propped by the hands of a caretaker, a fuzzy flannel sheet beneath her. I'd stared at that picture for hours, comparing it to my own orphanage photo. I had been about the same size, though I was two months older, with no chubby cheeks and a plain white shirt. In my picture, there were no hands holding me; there wasn't even a sheet stretched across the plywood crib. I was from a poor orphanage in a rural part of the Guanjo province. Kun Ro was from a better orphanage in Beijing.

"Ride's over," Grandpa said as we reached baggage claim. He asked me to get out of the stroller so he could get it ready for the baby. Grandma had brought along a bag of pretzels, but I was too nervous to eat, so she finished them off.

Finally, people started streaming down the hallway ahead of us—lots of Americans, but lots of Chinese as well: businesspeople, tourists, little girls. . . . At last, I saw Mom and Dad, but they didn't see me. They looked glassy-eyed and rumpled. Dad had a belly pouch strapped to him, with the little brown legs of Kun Ro jutting out. I ran to Mom and hugged her and cried. Dad bent down to me and kissed me, and I made sure to hug him in a way that kept the baby from getting between us.

The writer uses physical position to interpret the family relationships.

"Hi, Sweetheart! It's so good to see you. Mom and I've been thinking of you all the time!" Dad whispered in my ear as we hugged. He wiped the tears from my eyes and said, "Have you seen your new sister?"

I hadn't seen more than her legs. I turned now to look down at her. Kun Ro's little face was scrunched up against Dad's chest, as rumpled as his shirt, and her black hair was all matted from being sweaty and cramped. She huddled against Dad's chest as if desperate to stay asleep. One tiny fist was clenched beside her chubby cheek. I poked my finger into her fist, and she opened it and grabbed on and opened her eyes and looked at me.

This shift in perspective changes the writer in a deep way.

Suddenly, we had traded places. I was the baby being brought from China by Mom and Dad. Kun Ro's eyes were my eyes, her crunched up little body was me. I wasn't just receiving a new little sister. I was receiving myself—reliving my own incredible journey from an orphanage on the other side of the world into the arms of my parents. As Kun Ro clung onto my finger, I realized that we were more alike than different.

The writer transitions from a particular event to her life in general.

That was a defining moment, so full of worry that became hope, so full of a sense of loss that became love. It was the moment I became a sister. Through the years, Kelly and I have had the same sorts of fights and feuds as any sisters, but beneath it all there is and always will be the recognition that we are more alike than different. And beneath it all, there is love.

READING FOR BETTER WRITING

1. In the first paragraph, the writer uses the term "memento moment," comparing it to a blue ribbon or a grave marker. What does she mean by a memento moment?
2. In this reminiscence, the writer looks back, relating events from a more mature perspective. Find places in the sample essay in which the writer uses adult ideas to describe childhood experiences. What tensions or possibilities are created by this dual perspective?
3. The writer includes many sensory and memory details that symbolize her feelings of alienation—and of new life. Find at least three examples and indicate how they contribute to the overall mood of the text.

Personal Reminiscence

The writer of this reminiscence, Kristen Crossen, shares an experience that has become something of a family tradition. The piece features the brother-sister relationship.

The Pond in Ralph's Swamp

The opening paragraph sets the scene for the story.

Every one of us has a story about the pond in Ralph's swamp, and it is always the same story—to get across it on some contraption. My dad and Aunt Carol built a log raft that never made it farther than the middle of the pond before it sank. Both of them still laugh and blame the other person when they talk about it. When my two oldest brothers, Bill and Bob, were around ten, they tried to float across in a cow tank. They were successful only a couple of times before the tank tipped and forced them to abandon ship in the center of the pond and slosh through the water to the shore.

"The world seemed so much different when I was away from land and floating in the middle of the pond."

My own pond story happened when I was about seven years old. My brother Darwin, the closest one to my age even though he was seven years my elder, had built a raft that he floated on that pond for the whole summer. It was getting to be fall when I joined Darwin on the raft that day. The oaks had turned a burnt orange color that always reminded me of the pumpkins in our garden, and the maples were McIntosh-apple red. The air smelled like fall, and there was enough of a chill that Mom insisted I start wearing my stocking cap, which was bright yellow with two narrow green stripes and no yarn ball on top.

The writer uses sensory details to allow the reader to experience the event.

I walked back to the pond and found Darwin already out there in the middle, poking at something in the water with a branch.

"Can I come out there?" I called to him.

"Sure, walk on out." Smart aleck.

"No, I mean, will you come and get me?"

Without another word, he turned the raft and began to push with the pole so that he was coming my way. When he got to the shore, he slapped down an old board for me to walk up to keep from getting wet. He reached out a hand covered with a dirty gold barn glove to pull me up beside him. After pulling the board back onto the raft, we pushed off again to the middle.

Memory details show what the sensory details mean.

The world seemed so much different when I was away from land and floating in the middle of the pond. I remember that time out there with Darwin as a quiet moment when I just stared at the woods and the circle of open sky over the pond and started to realize that maybe this brother of mine was my friend, too.

Then, suddenly, Darwin ripped my beloved stocking cap off my head. He held it away from me over his head.

Action helps the writer show instead of tell.

"Give it back!" I shouted, furious.

"Nope." He just grinned.

"I know what I can do with this," he said with the fake brilliance that was supposed to make me think that he hadn't been planning this all along. He stuck the hat on the end of the pole and held it out over the water. I screamed for my dear cap, trying to reach it without falling. I stretched my hand toward the end of the pole, and the farther I reached, the farther he held it away from me.

Dialogue allows the people in the story to speak for themselves.

"Give it back!" I gave another fierce scream.

Just then I reached a little too far and slipped. Darwin grabbed my arm and pulled me back before I had a chance to fall into the water.

He pulled the pole back in. My stocking cap was safe and sound, not a drop of water on it. He flipped it off the end of the pole and into his hands, then put it not so gently on the top of my head, pulling the front flap down over my eyes in his own brotherly show of affection. The war was over. I cooled from furious to just perturbed. The truce was signed as he flipped the edge of my cap back up again so I could see.

The closing reflects upon the significance of the experience.

That day is only an image in my memory now. Five years ago Darwin died in a farm accident on a sunny day in June. I haven't visited the pond in years; my childhood time there with my brother has passed. But I am reminded today by my two nephews that the pond in Ralph's swamp still has a power over us. They tried to cross it on an old raft but didn't get very far before they were knee deep in water and had to slosh back to shore.

Writing a Personal Essay

When you write a personal essay, you go one step beyond reminiscing about a specific event or moment. You select a period in your life, explain and analyze it, and put it into context. As writer Phillip Lopate notes, writing a personal essay is the process of exploring the "stomach growls," the strong feelings you have about some time in your life.

PREWRITING

Select a topic. Think about extended periods of time that have shaped you into the person you are. Complete the sentence "I am who I am because of the period of time when . . . "

Gather events. Use a cluster to think about important events you experienced during the time in question. List sensory and memory details.

Organize the events. Decide on an order for your details. You may write about them in chronological order or share them according to your own order of importance.

WRITING

Create a first draft. In your beginning, focus on the meaning of the time period. In the middle, explain the events according to your organizational plan. In the end, recap how this time period affected you.

REVISING

Check your ideas. *Have I chosen a meaningful time period? Do I provide details to help my reader experience the events?*

Improve your organization. *Does my beginning introduce the time period? Does the middle provide events in the best order? Does the ending sum up the time period? Do I use effective transitions?*

Revise for voice, word choice, and sentence fluency. *Is my storytelling voice inviting and compelling? Have I used active verbs, specific nouns, and strong adjectives? Do my sentences read smoothly, with different beginnings and lengths?*

EDITING

Edit for conventions. *Have I double-checked my punctuation, capitalization, spelling, and grammar?*

PUBLISHING

Create a strong presentation. Format it as a feature article, using photographs and captions. Provide headings and use other graphic elements to lead your reader through the essay. Finally, give copies of your work to family members or friends who were involved in this important time of your life.

Personal Essay

In this essay, Kevin Hoogendoorn explores an experience from his childhood, working cattle on the family farm. Notice how the passage of time has changed the writer's attitude about his subject.

Working Cattle—We'd Hate to Love It

The opening paragraph sets the scene and identifies the subject of the essay.

I grew up on a 400-acre farm five miles southwest of Inwood, Iowa. Our entire crop, and more, was fed to the 1,000 head of finishing cattle we kept on the place. One thousand cattle means a lot of labor, especially when they need to be "worked." Working cattle consists of running them through a process of vaccination, deworming, and implantation. We worked two bunches of cattle twice a year. Four separate days out of the year were set aside for this. Usually it was a Saturday during one of our school vacations. It was a long, hard day.

The essay includes expository and analytical thinking.

We worked the cattle into our barn and then from the small holding pen to another room where there was a self-catching headgate. First, all the boys went outside to chase cattle from the yard into the holding pen. We had a row of feed bunks that formed a wide alley through which we would chase the cattle. As soon as we rounded the corner of the alley, we had a straight shot to the holding pen in the barn. At the corner we would raise a ruckus by hollering, running, and siccing Smokey on the cattle. Smokey was a real cattle dog.

Once we got enough cattle (approximately 30 at a time) in the pen, we would all head to our prospective jobs. The jobs were divided according to age, responsibility, and danger. The oldest boy would chase the cattle, four at a time, toward the holding chute leading to the headgate. The next eldest injected wormers, the next moved along the alley to keep the cattle up and moving, and the youngest pulled the gate rope.

Specific details make the events vivid.

Since I was the youngest, I usually ran the gate. I would hold the gate open and let one steer into the chute. The steer, thinking it was free, would move through the chute and be trapped by the automatic headgate. Kent would slip a holding bar behind the other three cattle while work began on the first. Mom poured Dursban, a delicing agent, on the steer's back. Dave reached through the side and shot Levasole, a wormer, under the skin of the animal's neck. Mom would then hit the steer in the rump with a Red Nose/Virus Diarrhea vaccination. At the same time, Dad would be trying to catch the tossing head to put Ralgro, a steroid implant, in the ear.

As soon as everything was finished, Dad opened the headgate to let the steer out. I then opened the back chute gate to let another one in. Then the process began again.

The digression effectively captures the difficulty of working cattle.

It seems easy writing about it on paper; however, at the time, it seemed like a million things could go wrong, and they usually did. I would let two steers in, Dad would let one out before Mom was done. Needles broke, syringes had to be held in armpits to keep them from freezing, cattle would turn around in the alley, and so on. It was a long, hard day, and when things went wrong, we were further aggravated. Tempers grew short, words were exchanged, and verbal abuse was doled out equally to humans and cattle.

Anecdotes create a personal connection.

At noon we would all troop into the house and eat a huge plate of Mom's hotdish, which would have been cooking in the oven since morning. What a welcome break! After dinner we would try to sneak to the other room to read the paper only to be rousted back out of the house by Dad.

"It amazes me how quirky life is. The things we think we hate, if taken away, we begin to love again."

Working cattle changed as I grew older. I did different jobs, and more jobs, since fewer people were left to work. My last summer before college was really hard on my dad. He asked me to help him, but I decided to get a job with my uncle at Hoogendoorn Construction to establish my own reputation as a worker in the community. That left only my dad to do almost everything by himself. Eventually, he had to sell all of his cattle and retire into "crop only" farming.

In closing, the writer reflects upon this lost time in his life.

It's been three years since I've worked cattle, and I feel an empty spot inside when I think of it. Never again will our entire family get together to do a job the way we did back then. It amazes me how quirky life is. The things we think we hate, if taken away, we begin to love again. I'm sure my father went through this feeling when he left Grandpa's home. I went through it, and my kids will go through it when they leave my home. As time moves on, we must move also.

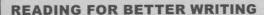

READING FOR BETTER WRITING

1. The writer demonstrates ambivalence about working cattle. Find textual evidence that shows how much he disliked the work; then find evidence that shows how much he enjoyed it.
2. In this essay, the first paragraph transports the reader back in time, and the last brings the reader forward again. How does this temporal frame affect the meaning of the material?
3. The writer's voice has a distinctive quality. How would you describe it? Search the essay for words and sentences that create the voice.

Personal Essay

Novelist Henrik Elsworth created an essay of experience that tells about discovering a serious health issue with one of his sons. The essay provides much vivid detail and thoughtful reflection.

No Longer Alone

The writer creates expectation in the reader and introduces his topic.

When my wife and I started a family, we were determined to make everything perfect. We painted giant murals on the nursery wall, carved wooden blocks that contained the alphabet and animals and musical notes and constellations, bought videos that were supposed to make our children little geniuses. I even quit my editing job so that I could stay home to take care of our children and write novels. For a time, the dream worked, but no dream is perfect. We soon learned that there were problems that murals and blocks couldn't fix.

Anecdotes make the experience vivid.

I first noticed the trouble during day trips in the car. I'd sing "Old MacDonald" to my boys and let them fill in the animals. But my middle son would not respond. I'd say, "Come on, Adam, name an animal. . . . What about a horsey or a pig?" Adam would echo "horseyorpig." He was almost two, and he should have been talking in sentences, but he couldn't even give me an animal for "Old MacDonald."

There were other things he couldn't do either. I tried to teach him the names of things by carrying him on my shoulders around the house and pointing. "What's that?" I would ask, but Adam wouldn't respond. "That's called a door," I would say. "Adore," Adam would echo, but by the time I made another circuit of the room, he would have forgotten.

So, what was the problem? Hearing loss? The ear-nose-throat doctor seemed to think so, and we scheduled Adam for surgery. The doctor gave him an anesthetic that made him lose all muscle tone, and he flopped in our arms like a rag doll. We wept during the surgery, but we told ourselves that soon our son's problems would be over.

Sensory details and metaphors such as "rag doll" help the reader experience the event.

We were wrong. Even after the surgery, Adam didn't progress. By three years old, he was 12 months delayed. My wife arranged for speech therapists and audiologists, and we racked up a thousand dollars a month in medical bills, but nothing helped. By four years old, Adam was 18 months behind his developmental age.

The writer builds the tension as any good storyteller does.

Then I got a phone call from my son's speech therapist. "I think I know what's wrong with Adam."

I was standing in the closet, putting away clothes, and I paused, my hand on the dresser. "What is it?"

"Autism." She said it, and I dropped to the floor.

"That can't be right," I said. "He doesn't rock back and forth; he doesn't hit his head on the floor. . . . "

"There's a broad spectrum to autism," she replied. "There's classic autism—what you're describing—and then there's high-functioning autism, or Asperger's syndrome."

I broke the news to my wife, and we were heartbroken. We went to the library and found books on autism. It was a congenital condition that made a person struggle to understand social situations. People with autism have trouble reading faces, understanding different tones of voice, and even realizing that different people have different thoughts and feelings. As a result, people with autism are trapped in their own world. In fact, the word autism means "alone."

Some resources told us to prepare for institutionalization. We ignored them and sought out new therapies. We filled out hundreds of pages of paperwork to get Adam started in a behavioral therapy program. Our senior therapist arrived, a jolly, red-faced man with a white beard and a round body. He sat down opposite Adam to start therapy, and my wife and I watched nervously. Would he be able to help?

Before the therapist could even begin, Adam reached up, touched the man's beard, and said in awe, "Ho, ho, ho!"

The therapist had made a connection that nobody else could. Over the next couple years of intensive therapy, Adam regained the 18 months he had lost and acquired new skills he needed to enter school with his peers. Adam had come a long way. He had climbed over the wall that kept him from the rest of the world, and he was alone no longer.

The closing focuses on how the experience changed the writer.

I had come a long way, too. When Adam's delays began, I was fearful and ignorant. I didn't know the signs of autism, let alone what it was or what could be done about it. As we worked to help Adam, though, I learned not just about the disease but about my son and myself. I learned that I, too, have traces of this spectrum disorder. It's the reason I can sit by myself for hours and write novels. I learned that many people with autism turn into great scientists, mathematicians, artists, authors, and musicians. Neither of us was alone anymore.

Guidelines

Writing a College-Entrance Essay

The college-entrance essay is perhaps the most important piece of personal writing that a college-bound student encounters. Your college application may ask you to respond to a prompt about who you are and why the particular college or university would be right for you. The key to a successful essay is making a connection with your reader by being honest, positive, and goal oriented. Use the guidelines below to write an effective college-entrance essay.

PREWRITING

Understand the prompt. Each college or university has a different entrance prompt, though all of them aim at finding out whether you would be a good match for the institution. (See the sample prompts on page 158.) Before doing any writing, analyze the prompt:

- **What does the prompt ask about me?** Determine what information the prompt requests: who you are, what you have done, what your goals are, what learning experiences you have had, and so on. This is your focus.
- **What does the prompt ask about the school?** Decide how to demonstrate that you belong at the particular college or in the particular program.
- **What key words does the prompt use?** Look for words such as *recall, describe, explain, share,* or *evaluate* to understand your purpose. You may need to write a response that combines narrative, expository, and persuasive elements.
- **What formal requirements does the prompt include?** Pay attention to any special instructions given in the prompt. Note how long the response should be, what form it should take, or any other submission requirements.

Reflect on your life. Think about your present, your past, and your future. Make a list of words that describe who you are right now. List other words that describe who you wish to become. Then think about experiences that have shaped your life and put you on the path to your future.

Write a focus statement. Create a focus statement that states your personal goal and connects that goal to the college.

A career as a diplomat **(personal goal)**
\+ political science at Indiana University **(college)**

My bilingual background and political activism have pointed me toward a career in diplomacy, and Indiana University's political science programs can guide me to my future.

WRITING

Create a memorable beginning. Remember that admissions personnel read many essays, so you should try to make yours stand out. Here are some strategies for making a strong beginning:

- **Share an anecdote.** Use a story to show who you are.
  I was born into a large family, the last of eight children. Though my parents never went to college, I will be their eighth child to go.
- **Start with a surprising statement.** Provide a single punchy line.
  My whole life comes down to one word: challenge.
- **Begin with appropriate humor.** Show your friendly side.
  Since I've spent seventeen years milking cows, it's only natural that I've had a few conversations with my bovine friends. Over the last year, they've been telling me I should get a degree in agricultural science.

Develop your middle. Support your focus with a variety of details:

- **Personal anecdotes** are stories from your life that prove a point.
- **Facts and statistics** are details that can be proved true or false.
- **Quotations** are the exact words of a person.
- **Similes, metaphors, and analogies** are ways to explain one thing by comparing it to another.

Create a thoughtful ending. Review your focus and why you would be an excellent match for the college you wish to enter.

REVISING

Check your ideas. *Have I answered the prompt? Have I shown clearly who I am and where I am going? Have I highlighted key experiences that have made me who I am? Have I connected my goals with a specific school program?*

Improve your organization. *Does my beginning capture the reader's interest? Does the middle demonstrate my goals? Have I used effective paragraphing and transitions? Does the ending point to a future at the school?*

Revise for voice, word choice, and sentence fluency. *Does my voice sound natural, engaging, and intelligent? Have I chosen precise nouns and active verbs? Do my sentences flow smoothly?*

EDITING

Edit for conventions. *Have I checked my punctuation, capitalization, spelling, and grammar? Have I asked two other people to proofread my work?*

PUBLISHING

Present your work. Prepare your essay according to the instructions given by the college (perhaps including a photo) and send it in.

Sample Prompts

Most college-entrance essay prompts take one of three forms: open-ended prompts, influences in your life, and general-subject prompts. Use the sample prompts below to practice writing a college-entrance essay.

Open-Ended Prompts

Prompts such as these mean you must work extra hard to shape a focused response.

- Please include a personal statement with your application.
- Why is our college a good choice for you?
- Tell us your goals after college. How might one of our programs contribute to those goals?
- Write an essay that introduces you to our admissions department.
- Identify one verb that best describes you and why.

Influences in Your Life

The following prompts ask you to write about people, places, and things that are important to you. Remember to relate their influence to your goal and to how the school can help you meet that goal.

- Describe a creative work in literature, art, music, or science and explain the effect it has had on you.
- Identify a person who has had a significant influence on your life and describe that influence.
- Recall a time of great personal achievement. Indicate what work you did to attain your goal and show how the achievement has shaped your life.

General-Subject Prompts

General-subject prompts ask you to reflect on your thoughts, feelings, and beliefs. They often provide a theme to focus your essay.

- What is the value of community service in our society? Share how it relates to your life and plans.
- Do you believe there is a "generation gap"? Describe the differences between your generation and other generations.
- Think of a time when you have taken a risk: What was the effect (positive or negative) on your life?
- Describe who you are now. Then imagine who you will be in two years (in the middle of your college schooling) and in five years. Explain how you hope your education will affect you.

College-Entrance Essay

David Schaap wrote an essay in response to this prompt: "In 500 words or fewer, explain what you want to study at Burnley College and why."

A New World of Cinema

The writer uses a personal experience to get the reader's attention.

Earlier this year, I met Anastasia Korkoff, a foreign-exchange student from Moscow. As we talked, Anastasia saw a picture of a woman taped on the inside of my locker. "Rachel McAdams!" she said. "I loved *The Notebook!*" We had a sudden connection because of a movie.

The writer explains the point of the experience.

From events like this, I came to realize that film is a major source of shared experience—not just with my friends or with others in this country, but also with people throughout the world. While I had always enjoyed movies as a form of entertainment, I had never realized before how broadly they shape culture, from Miami to Moscow.

Introductory phrases link the paragraphs.

A few weeks later, I explained these ideas to Ms. Crane, my English teacher. She listened, smiled, and suggested that I read the essay "Cinema Is the New Cathedral." As I read the piece, suddenly everything clicked. The writer argued that movies have replaced many other forms of communal experience, and even serve a religious-like function. At that point, I knew that understanding film was critical to understanding culture, both the culture in this country and in others.

The writer offers details that explain his educational goal.

Ever since then, understanding film and filmmaking has been my goal. Entering the film program at Burnley College will help me achieve that goal. I particularly want to study international film and the relationship between a film and its national culture. Also, because films have such a broad international audience, I want to study how Hollywood movies affect cultures outside the United States.

While I'm not sure yet where my film study might lead, I am sure that the trip will be interesting and worth the effort. For example, my mom suggests that I combine film study with communication and think about a career in journalism. My counselor says that the film-study program could be a springboard into the filmmaking industry. But Ms. Crane suggests that I study film and culture, and then teach the subject. Wherever the film-study path leads, I'd like to start the journey at Burnley College.

In closing, the writer links the college with the career path he has chosen.

Report Writing

Report Writing

In report writing, you engage in a search that goes beyond your personal experience. You learn as much as you can about a topic and shape your findings in a way that makes sense and holds the reader's attention. You're interested in sharing information, not in sharing memories.

Reports function in a number of different ways. An interview report, for example, cites the views of a person you have interviewed. A summary report distills the most important elements of a chapter or an article, and a personal research report explains what you have learned about a topic that interests you. What makes any report work is your clear understanding of the information you have gathered.

WHAT'S AHEAD

This section provides guidelines and models for five basic types of report writing: summary report, compiled report, interview report, observation report, and personal research report. Each type of report helps you present information in a different way.

"There's something in life that's a curtain, and I keep trying to raise it."
—Maxine Hong Kingston

Report Writing

QUICK GUIDE

Reports explore timely topics. This type of expository writing appears in many current magazines and on the Internet, addressing the needs and interests of various audiences. The best report writing contains interesting ideas plus personality; it is informative and pleasing to read. At the heart of an effective report are a writer's genuine curiosity about a subject and a sincere commitment to present her or his findings in a professional manner.

All report writing shares the following characteristics:

- **STARTING POINT:** Report writing begins with your interest in a particular person, place, thing, idea, or event.
- **PURPOSE:** The purpose is to learn about a topic of current interest and to educate or enlighten your reader.
- **FORM:** Report writing follows a variety of formats. For example, an interview report may be set up in a basic question-and-answer format. An observation report may simply present sensory details as they were observed. A personal research report may be essentially narrative in structure.
- **AUDIENCE:** In most cases, you will be speaking to your writing peers and your teacher, unless, of course, your report is intended for a school or community publication.
- **VOICE:** A report should speak to the reader sincerely and honestly.
- **POINT OF VIEW:** Most reports use third-person point of view *(he, she, they)*, unless the writer has a strong personal attachment to the subject (as in a personal research report). Then the first-person point of view *(I)* is used.

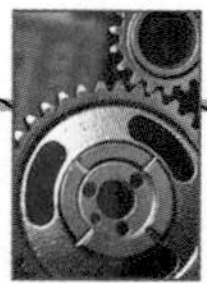

INSIDE INFO

Remember that report writing involves looking outward: observing, listening to, experiencing, and learning about the world around you. As writer Donald Murray states, "Readers hunger for specific information. The more concrete and detailed the information, the more it will interest readers."

Guidelines

Writing a Summary Report

A summary report highlights the main points in a longer text (usually an article or a chapter). To prepare a summary report, you need to ask three questions: *What is the main point of the text? What important information (key facts, statistics, examples, etc.) does the writer use to support this point? What are the most compelling or important features in the selection?*

PREWRITING

Select a topic. If your instructor assigns a text to summarize, move on to the next step. If you must find your own article, search magazines, newspapers, and Web sites related to a particular topic. Also check chapters in your textbooks. Select an article or a chapter that interests you and includes enough details for a summary report.

Find the focus. Read the selection once and write down its focus in one sentence. Rework the sentence until you are satisfied with it.

Gather details. Read the selection again, this time focusing on main points and supporting details. Take notes.

Plan your summary. Read the selection a final time and decide what you want to say first, second, and so on. Create a list or an outline.

WRITING

Write your first draft. Use your planning and organizing as a guide. In the opening, state the focus; in the body, provide main points and a few key details. Sum up the selection in the closing. To avoid plagiarism, use your own words as much as possible. Be sure to cite any words or ideas you use from the original.

REVISING

Check your ideas. *Have I stated the focus of the selection? Have I included main points and a few key details?*

Review your organization. *Does each part (beginning, middle, and ending) work well? Do I use transition words and phrases?*

Revise for voice, word choice, and sentence fluency. *Does my tone match that of the selection? Have I used precise terminology? Do my sentences read smoothly?*

EDITING

Check for conventions. *Have I used correct punctuation, capitalization, spelling, and grammar?*

PUBLISHING

Present your work. Format your writing according to the teacher's specifications, proofread it a final time, and submit it.

Summary Report

In the following summary report, Aleasha Jensen summarizes an article about a historic letter written by Albert Einstein.

His "Greatest Mistake"

The writer identifies the thesis of the original article.

In July of 1939, two men in Long Island sat down to write a document that would usher in the nuclear age. In "Einstein's Letter," Joseph Beeks tells how physicist Leo Szilard prompted Albert Einstein to write a letter Einstein would later consider "the greatest mistake" of his life.

The writer sums up the main points and provides support, with citations.

Two factors had brought Szilard to Einstein's door: The uranium atom was split in December 1938 in Nazi Germany, and the Nazis had ceased selling uranium from the mines they held in Czechoslovakia. These facts convinced Szilard that the Nazis were working to develop an atom bomb (65). However, Szilard's concerns were ignored, and so he asked Einstein to write a letter to President Roosevelt.

After a number of drafts, the two men finally completed a letter dated August 2, 1939. It began by discussing the possibility of a nuclear chain reaction in a large mass of uranium, thus generating tremendous amounts of power and large quantities of new radium-like elements (68). The letter indicated that such a reaction could result in a bomb that would destroy a whole port. Einstein recommended that President Roosevelt fund further experimentation and seek a source of uranium for the United States.

Though the letter was dated August 2, it was not delivered until after Germany invaded Poland on September 1, and World War II began. On October 11, Alexander Sachs, a longtime friend and unofficial advisor to the president, took Einstein's letter to Roosevelt. At first, the president was reluctant, but eventually he created the "Manhattan Project" (69).

The final paragraph puts the issue in perspective.

When the first atom bomb fell on Hiroshima in 1945, Einstein was appalled. He said that men must put an end to war as it no longer makes sense to solve international conflicts through such hostilities (71).

NOTE: The works-cited page is not shown.

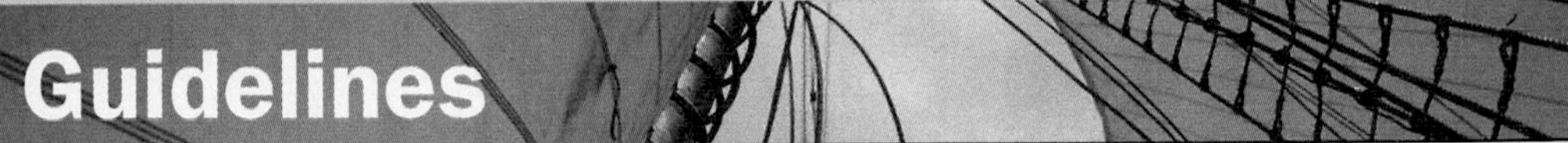

Writing a Compiled Report

A compiled report brings together information from a variety of sources, such as reading material, interviews, questionnaires, Web pages, and so on. Your goal is to inform and/or entertain your reader. Compiled reports often appear in newspapers, magazines, or on the Internet. Refer to the guidelines below and the models that follow.

PREWRITING

Select a topic. If your teacher supplies a topic, move on to the next step. Otherwise, review your textbooks and notes to find a relevant topic that interests you. Find a variety of reliable sources.

Review articles. Search books, periodicals, and the Internet for articles related to your topic. Keep a copy of each article and underline key points.

Write a thesis statement. Decide what main idea about the topic you want to emphasize and put it in a sentence. Be prepared to revise your thesis as you develop your report.

Organize your report. Select key points that support your thesis and details that support each key point. Create a quick list or an outline.

WRITING

Draft your report. Begin with an opening paragraph that introduces the topic and states your thesis. Then provide details according to your plan. (Present information from one source after another, or integrate the details by key points or ideas.) Cite sources to avoid plagiarism.

REVISING

Review your ideas. *Is my thesis statement clear and compelling? Do all my main points support my thesis statement? Have I included enough details? Are all my sources equally authoritative?*

Check your organization. *Does my beginning capture the reader's interest and present the thesis? Does my middle provide strong support? Does my ending revisit the thesis? Do I use my sources in a consistent way?*

Revise for voice, word choice, and sentence fluency. *Have I integrated the voices of the different sources? Have I used precise nouns and active verbs? Do my sentences flow?*

EDITING

Check for conventions. *Have I used correct punctuation, capitalization, spelling, and grammar?*

PUBLISHING

Submit your work. Follow your teacher's formatting requirements, proofread it a final time, and turn it in.

Compiled Report

In the following report, student writer Brittney Paulsen outlines a debate within the hearing-impaired community: whether cochlear implant technology is a boon or an abomination. Brittney uses a variety of sources.

To Hear or Not to Hear

Statistics grab the reader's attention.

A quotation provides context.

The thesis is stated.

About half a million people in the United States are hearing impaired, and a hundred thousand of them are children (*Sound*). According to Eugene Mindel, author of the book *They Grow in Silence,* "With profound hearing loss, the child will be virtually excluded from information and human contact ordinarily available through hearing" (18). To help address this isolation, scientists have developed a new technology: cochlear implantation. A cochlear implant is "an electronic device surgically inserted into the cochlea of a hearing-impaired person, feeding electrical signals from a transmitter outside the scalp into the vestibulocochlear nerve. It does not transmit speech clearly, but provides some awareness of sound in a totally deaf person" ("Cochlear"). While some people hail this new device as a step toward "curing" deafness, many in the hearing-impaired community see it as a new source of isolation and discrimination.

Each paragraph focuses on a different aspect of the issue.

One of the staunch advocates of cochlear implantation is Donna Sorkin, Vice President of Consumer Affairs of the Cochlear Corporation and former Executive Director of the Alexander Graham Bell Association. As a hearing-impaired person with an implant, Sorkin has firsthand knowledge of the device's power. She feels the implant should be seen as a "tool of communication" and not as a source of normal hearing. She supports implantation because it has been shown to significantly improve a recipient's success with speech development (*Sound*). It may have other benefits as well. Many parents of children with implants report that their children seem less hyperactive, less frustrated, and more outgoing. Some even develop interests in music (Christiansen 147).

Cochlear implants have equally staunch critics, however. Nancy Bloch, Executive Director of the National Association of the Deaf, feels that implants are seen as "the panacea for deafness, which serves only to perpetuate and devaluate societal attitudes toward deafness and deaf people." She indicates that though the implant may make a sound *audible*, it often fails to make the sound *intelligible* (*Sound*). In an online forum, one teenager wrote about his frustrations:

> My parents decided to get me a cochlear implant when I was three years old. I have always hated it, but acted like I loved it because it made them happy and proud of me when they see me hear things and my speech was so good. . . . I was always forced to use my speech and hearing therapy. . . . Now I am 16, and I refuse to wear one. . . . I have seen so many kids crying when they can't understand their parents because their parents refuse to learn to sign and don't want their child to sign ("Forum").

An excerpt demonstrates the crux of the issue.

This excerpt shows that the experience of the parent who selects the implant and the experience of the child who gets the implant can be miles apart. The young man's response begs a number of important questions: What rights do children have to accept or refuse implants? Is it wrong for a person to choose to live in silence? And finally, is it appropriate to deny children with implants the use of sign language?

One paragraph focuses on common ground.

Proponents and opponents of implantation both recognize that the implant surgery is expensive and requires lengthy, intensive therapy to work. The mother of one 4-year-old girl who was implanted at 18 months said, "Receiving the implant is like receiving a load of building supplies on a lot. And in a couple of years, you may have a beautiful new house on that lot if you do the work. But if you don't do the work, you'll have just a load of building supplies" (Christiansen 147). Another parent summed it up this way: "The implant is 5 percent, and the other 95 percent is the work you do after the implant" (147).

The closing puts the issue in perspective.

The battle over cochlear implants has just begun. A technology meant to improve the mainstream experience of people who are hearing impaired may actually increase their isolation and augment the discrimination they endure. Some in the hearing impaired community even fear that the device will strand users in a middle ground, neither deaf nor hearing. It is clear that cochlear implants are not a cure-all, but the question remains whether they offer the best alternative to the condition they address.

NOTE: The works-cited page is not shown.

READING FOR BETTER WRITING

Find examples of three types of evidence in this report and indicate how they support the report's thesis.

Compiled Report

The following professional model comes from a journal on the arts in public education. Note how the writer uses different types of evidence, including statistics and anecdotes, to create an informative report.

Painting the Future

A surprising statement leads to the thesis.

In inner-city neighborhoods across the nation, young people are painting on walls and getting applauded for their work. In cities such as New York, Los Angeles, Chicago, Miami, and San Francisco, mural programs teach inner-city youth skills for art and for life. In turn, the young artists teach their cities a thing or two about beauty.

The writer synthesizes information from a variety of sources.

The trend began in 1984 when Philadelphia launched a campaign to "eradicate destructive graffiti and address neighborhood blight," and the Mural Arts Program (MAP) was born. The program's mission was to redirect youth from destroying their neighborhoods to beautifying them (Caldwell). By enlisting young people in creating murals that represented the culture of their neighborhoods, the MAP program helped transform taggers (graffiti makers) into artists. After more than 20 years of operation, MAP has produced more that 2,500 murals. Currently, more than 3,000 youth participate in MAP per year. The program offers classes in schools, detention centers, and homeless shelters ("Art").

Transitions smoothly shift from one part of the report to another.

The power of urban mural programs goes beyond simply preventing delinquency. In one dramatic case, an urban mural project actually helped end rioting in a troubled inner-city neighborhood. In 1991 and 1992, the Adams-Morgan neighborhood of Washington, D.C., home to a number of different ethnic groups and gripped by poverty, erupted in violence. Police tried to address the unrest, but their presence only seemed to deepen tensions (Caldwell).

Enter Byron Peck, a muralist and the director of City Art. He joined forces with local leaders and the Latin American Youth Center to come up with an art project that might bring healing to this wounded neighborhood. The group decided on a mural. The wall-sized painting would need to represent the Latin American, African American, and Asian American residents of the neighborhood. It would also have to be hopeful, showing scenes of beauty and peace. The task force gathered images that represented African Benin, Mayan, and Asian heritage, and they combined them in a pleasing design ("Three Macaws").

Perhaps even more important than the design, though, were the artists. Sixteen local youth volunteered to paint the mural on a wall that is 28 by 35 feet. The young artists learned every step of the craft. They worked with initial sketches and transferred the design to the wall. Afterward, they painted the mural and applied sealant. The participants also learned about project planning, teamwork, budgeting, and commitment. Together, the young artists beautified their neighborhood and learned discipline and self-respect. A wall that once had been defaced became a beautiful expression of the community. The finished work, *The Three Macaws* mural, became a vision of a hoped-for future ("Three Macaws").

The overall organization of this report is chronological.

What began as a movement to reclaim and beautify at-risk neighborhoods has become a source of tourism and new revenue for many of these locations. For example, the Baltimore Mural Program (BMP) has restored and installed lights around the "African Deco" mural masterpieces of Tom Miller due to their cultural significance. The BMP has also commissioned artists to paint murals on concrete pillars beneath the Jones Falls Expressway, thus beautifying the farmer's market there. It has even commissioned two large, student-generated murals for the part of the Gwynns Falls Trail that passes through the Pigtown Industrial Park ("Baltimore"). Sights like these now appear in tourist guides as major attractions (Fodors 638).

A proverb and an idiom are rephrased to express the thesis in a fresh way.

Nearly three thousand years ago, Solomon wrote, "Without vision, the people perish" (Proverbs 29:18). Modern wise men and women are proving that *with* vision—and paint and a few volunteers—the people can flourish. Urban mural projects have taught young people how to paint themselves *out* of a corner and to transform their cities in the process.

NOTE: The works-cited page is not shown.

READING FOR BETTER WRITING

1. Philadelphia's MAP program is presented largely through facts and statistics. Byron Peck's mural program in Washington, D.C., is described through anecdotes. How do these two different types of support affect the reader's impressions of the two different programs?
2. This essay has an expansive and optimistic tone. Find sentences that contribute to this tone. What words, phrases, clauses, and structures help create a sense of optimism?

Guidelines

Writing an Interview Report

Writer William Zinsser states, "Nothing so animates writing as someone telling what he thinks or what he does—in his own words." Zinsser is referring here to an interview report. This form of writing provides information gathered in an interview and allows the reader to "meet" and "listen" to the interviewee. Follow the guidelines below.

PREWRITING

Select a person. If your teacher assigns the topic and asks you to interview a particular person, move on to the next step. Otherwise, brainstorm a list of people knowledgeable in a particular field or involved in a specific event. Choose the one you would like to interview.

Prepare questions. Gather background information about the person and generate a list of thoughtful questions. Avoid questions that can be answered "yes" or "no."

Record information. Take abbreviated notes during the interview and, if your subject agrees, record the exchange. As soon as possible after the interview, write out your notes, filling in any gaps. (As an alternative, conduct an interview via e-mail.)

WRITING

Write your first draft. After reviewing your notes, begin your report by introducing your person and topic. Then include important points from the interview. You may also choose to use a question-and-answer format.

REVISING

Check your ideas. *Have I created an informative, effective interview? Have I accurately quoted the words of the interviewee? Have I anticipated the reader's questions?*

Review your organization. *Does my beginning get the reader's attention and introduce the topic and person? Does the middle provide information in a clear way? Does the ending sum up the interview?*

Revise for voice, word choice, and sentence fluency. *Is the tone of the report appropriate to the topic? Do my sentences read smoothly?*

EDITING

Check for conventions. *Have I used correct punctuation, capitalization, spelling, and grammar?*

PUBLISHING

Present your work. Send a copy of the finished report to the interviewee for comments or a critique. Then share the report aloud with classmates or post it on a blog.

Interview Report

Because of a disturbing childhood experience, college student Benjamin Meyer toured a funeral home and interviewed the director. In the following report, Benjamin shares what he learned.

The Dead Business

The writer starts with background information that creates a personal tone.

"You're going to tour a what?"

"A funeral home."

My friends were shocked. They laughed while describing scenes from *Night of the Living Dead* and *The Shining.*

But their stories didn't frighten me; I feared something else. When I was 10, my grandmother died, and my family drove to the funeral home to view the body. As we entered the place, I noticed the funeral director standing in the corner, looking like an eager-to-please salesman who'd made a deal he didn't deserve. The guy's smile seemed unnatural, almost glib. He didn't seem to care that a stroke had stopped my grandmother's beating heart midway through the doxology that concluded the Sunday evening church service. He didn't seem to care that she and I would share no more cookies, no more coloring books, no more board games, no more laughing. I was 10, very sad, and he didn't seem to care.

Freely using "I," the writer tells the story of his visit and interview.

Now a high school senior, I wanted to tour a different funeral home to work through my earlier experience. While I no longer feared ghouls, I was still nervous while driving to the Vander Ploeg Furniture Store/Funeral Home. I remembered the smile.

I walked inside, not knowing what to expect. Suddenly, a man from behind a desk hopped out of his chair and said, "Hi, I'm Howard Beernink."

He describes the setting.

I looked at the tall, smiling man, paused a moment, and glanced back at the door. His partner had stepped in front of the exit while scribbling on tags that dangled from Lazy Boy rockers. I realized that this interview was something I had to do . . . like getting a tetanus shot.

Howard led me into a room full of furniture where he found a soft, purple couch. We sat down, and he described how the business started.

He relates the early history of the business.

In 1892, pioneers established the town of Sioux Center, Iowa. Winter storms and disease pummeled the tiny community, and soon residents needed someone to bury the dead. A funeral director wasn't available, but a furniture maker was. The furniture maker was the only person with the tools, hardwood, and knowledge to build coffins. As a result, the Vander Ploeg Furniture Store/Funeral Home was born.

The writer summarizes, paraphrases, and quotes from the interview.

Today, starting a funeral home isn't that easy. For example, a funeral home requires the services of an embalmer, and an embalmer must be certified by the state. Most states require a degree from a mortuary college and apprentice work. After that, the individual may be required to earn continuing education credits.

"But why a funeral home director?" I was baffled.

"Because it's a family business." Howard smiled as if he expected my question. "Vander Ploegs and Beerninks have run this place for generations. Today it's difficult to start a funeral home because there are so many of them with long histories and good reputations."

After he answered the rest of my questions, Howard asked if I wanted to see the embalming room.

"Okay," I said, tentatively.

He narrates what happened during the interview.

He led me through doors, down hallways, up a staircase, and into a well-lighted display room containing several coffins. Finally, we entered a small, cold room containing a row of cupboards, a large ceramic table, and a small machine that resembled a watercooler.

"We like to keep the room cold when we're not using it," Howard said.

"What is all this stuff?" I asked.

Howard described why embalming is done and what it involves. The purpose of embalming is to extend the period for viewing the body, and the process includes replacing blood with embalming fluid. He opened a cupboard, pulled out a bottle of fluid and said, "Here . . . smell."

"Smells like cough medicine," I replied.

After he embalms the body, Howard applies makeup so the face appears "more natural." He gets his cosmetics (common powders and tints) from a local store.

"But sometimes we also have to use this," Howard said, pulling out another bottle.

"Tissue builder?" I asked, squinting at the label.

He answered, "We inject it into sunken cheeks of those who have become emaciated.

The writer shares critical information.

When the body is ready for burial, the funeral director must show a price list to the family of the deceased. The Funeral Rule, adopted in 1984 by the Federal Trade Commission, requires that a price list be shown to the family before they see caskets, cement boxes, and vaults. The purpose of the Funeral Rule is to prevent unethical funeral directors from manipulating customers with comments like, "But that's a pauper's casket; you don't want to bury your mother in that. Bury her in this beauty over here." Unfortunately, many of the country's 22,000 funeral homes do not closely follow the Funeral Rule.

"After showing customers where the caskets are, I step away so they can talk among themselves," said Howard. "It's unethical to bother the family at this difficult time."

Before burying a casket, Howard and his partner lower it into either a cement box or a vault. A cement box is a container that's neither sealed nor waterproofed, whereas a vault is both sealed and waterproofed. Howard explained, "Years ago, cemeteries began to sink and cave in on spots, so state authorities demanded containers. Containers make the cemetery look nicer."

After the tour, I asked Howard, "How has this job affected your life?"

He ends the report with a strong quotation and personal reflection.

He glanced at the ceiling, smiled, and said, "It's very fulfilling. My partner and I try to comfort people during a stressful time in their lives, and it strengthens our bond with them."

As I drove away, I thought again about Howard's comment, and about my childhood fear. Howard was right. He doesn't exploit people. Instead, he helps them move on. And while I still fear the pain of saying good bye to someone I love, I don't fear funeral directors anymore. They're just people who provide services that a community needs.

NOTE: **The works-cited page is not shown.**

READING FOR BETTER WRITING

1. This report centers on the writer's own story, reflections, and needs. Discuss how these elements are woven into the report. Are they effective? Why or why not?
2. Examine the opening and the closing. Do they work well together? Do they share a theme for the report? Explain.

Interview Report

Student writer Marsha Lee was assigned an interview on a personal career-related issue. In the report below, she explains how the interview led her to an important decision.

Dramatic Learning

The writer gives background information.

As a first-semester freshman last fall, I arrived on campus with my career track as clear in my head as the highlighted road map that guided me to Reese College. From kindergarten through high school, I liked reading, writing, and doing school plays, so choosing a major was easy: I'd become an English teacher. What I didn't know was which courses I should take.

She introduces her topic and identifies her interviewee.

Then, on the same day I was assigned this interview report, I got an e-mail message from my adviser saying that it was time to choose courses for my sophomore year. So I decided to interview Dr. Angela Wit in the Theater Department. She could tell me which theater courses would help me as an English teacher, and reporting on the interview would help me finish my assignment.

The next morning, I entered Dr. Wit's office and introduced myself. She asked me to sit down, and then she started to talk.

The writer uses quotations that reflect Dr. Wit's ideas and personality.

"Marsha," she said, "you've made a good choice! Middle school students need English teachers who can help them read and write, but they also need English teachers who can help them produce quality plays. Taking theater courses will help you learn that."

"How many courses?" I asked.

"Enough to be a professional educator," she replied.

"And how many is that?" I asked.

Dr. Wit smiled, leaned back in her chair, and asked, "Have you thought about taking a fifth year?" She then delivered a five-minute monologue on how teachers must be professional practitioners in their fields of study. "For you," she said, "that means getting a firm grasp of both the academic and technical aspects of theater. To do that, you should stay a fifth year and finish a theater major, along with your English major." She closed by describing her past student, Mike Krause, an "outstanding young professional" who teaches history and directs first-rate plays at Sylvan Middle School in nearby Jonesburg.

She shares her response and introduces the second interview.

Back in my dorm room, I realized that Dr. Wit had given me raw material for my report but no help selecting courses. Besides, I wanted to graduate in three years! So I decided to do a second interview, this time with the middle school teacher whom Dr. Wit had mentioned, Mike Krause.

The next afternoon, I found Mr. Krause in his last-hour class sitting in front of a puppet stage in the back corner of his classroom. He responded like we knew each other. "Hey, Marsha, over here!" he called. I walked over and he introduced me to five bubbly kids with scissors, colored paper, cloth, and glue. "They're making costumes for a play they wrote about the Lewis and Clark expedition," he said, "and they need your help." Then he walked away.

She summarizes what happened.

The next hour was a whirlwind. I helped make a dress for Sacagawea, rehearsed a dialogue as Martha Washington, and responded to a poem about Sally Hemings and Thomas Jefferson.

After the bell rang and the last student left, Mr. Krause slid into a student's chair and pointed to one nearby. "On the phone you said that you want to talk about theater courses."

"Yes," I said, "and I'd like your ideas."

A long quotation captures Krause's main point.

"I've already given you my best shot," he replied. Mr. Krause then explained why he invited me to visit his class. "I direct school plays at Sylvan," he said, "but the stage isn't where the real theater takes place. The real stuff happens in classrooms like mine where students do theater activities that help them learn history, or science, or whatever. The key to choosing theater courses that will help you teach English is knowing what you need to learn. Today you discovered that you already know a lot about helping kids put on plays. So maybe you should focus on what English teachers must teach, and then select only those theater courses that will help you teach that stuff."

She reflects on both interviews and describes what she learned.

That evening I thought about both interviews. Dr. Wit told me that I have to be a professional in my field, and I agree. But Mr. Krause taught me that my *profession* is education.

When I met with my adviser to choose my fall courses, the choice was easy. In three years I'll graduate and get a job as an English teacher. Meanwhile, I'll finish the prescribed courses and take a few electives like creative dramatics and acting. Oh yes, and for one of the required field experiences in education, I plan to spend a few weeks observing Mr. Krause!

READING FOR BETTER WRITING

1. Does the writer succeed in communicating the ideas and voices of Dr. Wit and Mr. Krause? Explain.
2. Identify the report's theme and explain how the quotations do or do not develop that idea.
3. In the conclusion, does the writer's voice show honest reflection? Explain.

Guidelines

Writing an Observation Report

An observation report is sometimes called a saturation report because it is saturated with sights, sounds, and smells. A well-written observation report inundates the reader with sensations. Some observation reports present a continuous flow of sensory impressions, while others use the more traditional form with a thesis statement and supporting details.

PREWRITING

Select a topic. Choose a location that really appeals to you and meets any requirements established by your teacher.

Take notes. Record as many sensory observations as you can (for at least 15 to 30 minutes) at the location of your choice. Don't forget to record snippets of conversation.

Review your observations. Determine whether you will present your impressions chronologically in a continuous flow or organize them around a specific focus.

WRITING

Write your first draft. Write your first draft freely, working in sensory details as they were recorded or according to your plan and focus.

REVISING

Check your ideas. *Have I accurately recorded my sensory impressions? Does my writing clearly describe a place and the things happening in it?*

Review your organization. *Does my beginning get the reader's attention and introduce my topic? Does the middle present vivid sensations? Does the ending bring the observation to a natural close?*

Revise for voice, word choice, and sentence fluency. *Does my writing capture the feeling of the situation? Have I used precise nouns, active verbs, and modifiers that create a clear picture? Do my sentences read smoothly?*

EDITING

Check for conventions. *Have I used correct punctuation, capitalization, spelling, and grammar?*

PUBLISHING

Present your work. Format your writing according to your teacher's specifications, proofread it a final time, and submit it.

Observation Report

Joel Sorensen is a student who traveled to Santo Domingo to complete a service-learning project. In this report he shares what he observed, what he learned about the local people, and what he learned about himself.

Revelation in Santo Domingo

The writer starts with background information.

It is nearly January, and the evening temperature in Santo Domingo is a sticky 85 degrees. Our youth group waits two hours in the airport for our ride, trying to catch the quick Spanish phrases and brush off men who want to carry our luggage. I expect these things. What I don't expect are the fast food restaurants, the car dealerships, and the cigarette billboards. I have come with fourteen members of a youth group to do a service-learning project for the poor of the Dominican Republic.

He uses present tense to create immediacy.

As I stare out the windows of our van, I soon realize that the wealth does not run deep. Behind large apartment buildings are shoddily constructed shacks, housing people who can only dream of living in the castles in front of them. A block from a sprawling car dealership, people hang out on street corners, unable to buy liquor for their New Year's Eve celebrations. Clusters of people, worn out by want, walk along the highway next to the beautiful expanse of ocean. We pass a city dump overflowing with rubble from Hurricane George. The farther we drive from the airport, the worse the poverty.

A key question offers a focus for the report.

How can such extremes of poverty and wealth, such beauty and ugliness, exist side by side? I can do nothing but stare. Nothing I see seems real.

The writer records his first impressions.

Soon, we enter Los Alcarizos, the suburb of Santo Domingo that will be our home for the next two weeks. Los Alcarizos has a population of about 400,000 people, many of whom are former farmers who squatted here, hoping to make a living in the city, but failed. Our large van crawls along the dirt streets, weaving back and forth to avoid giant potholes. The homes are small and cramped together, only slightly larger than the backyard sheds that house the rakes and lawn mowers of North America's middle class. People sit in front of the shacks, drinking, talking, enjoying each other and the night. Mopeds, driven by young and old, swerve around us. Groups of friends walk along the side of the road. In some shops resembling outdoor newsstands, large speakers blaring merengue music sit on shelves otherwise reserved for alcohol. Other shops have a TV around which men huddle. People are everywhere. We pass two young men along the side of the road, urinating on a tree. Suddenly, I am struck by the fact that these people are real.

The observation deepens with quotations, snapshots of people, and images of buildings.

In the morning, our interpreter Eli brings our group outside the eight-foot cement walls of our camp into the barrio we passed through the night before. Walking the streets of Los Alcarizos feels like a stroll through a film designed to encourage Sunday-school offerings. Rusted tin roofs pop through the trees. Children who see us point and yell, *"Americanos! Americanos!"* A wide-eyed boy stops, looks at me, and exclaims, *"Americano es muy grande!"* Some children raise their hands to their eyes and pretend to snap pictures. Others tug on cameras hanging from our necks, begging to be photographed. A member of our group raises his camera and children scramble to be included. A group of men sit nearby, laughing at their children—and the Americans. A woman breast-feeds her child. We try to talk to those we meet but seldom get past *"Hola, como esta?"* to which we receive an automatic, *"Bien, gracias."* A boy wearing nothing but a long red T-shirt with Michael Jordan's number 23 dangles from the branch of a tree. He looks down at us warily while other children play underneath.

The writer pauses to explain and reflect on his observations.

Many of the homes we pass are partially constructed of cinder block, tin, and wood. Our interpreter explains that the Dominicans buy block when they can afford it and construct the rest of their homes out of whatever they can find. Many homes are pale brown or gray and seem to have bubbled up out of the mud. Other homes are covered by cracked and peeling paint—brilliant pinks, blues, greens, and yellows. In many homes, women mop and sweep with straw brooms. Their effort to clean seems futile given the piles of garbage that surround them in the streets, in a creek that runs parallel to the road, and in the remnants of a broken-down brick building that has somehow been leveled to its windows. Small dogs pick through the trash but find nothing to eat.

Vivid images offer sights, sounds, smells, textures, and tastes.

As the morning temperature begins to rise, we enter the business district of Los Alcarizos. A building like the homes that we have passed is full of chickens. In front of the chicken house, working in a swarm of flies, a butcher chops up chickens for the women who wait to buy them. To the left of the chicken house is a small green pharmacy where a glass case holds pill bottles, squirt guns, and other trinkets. Another store advertises colas for five pesos. On one corner sits a green building with "DISCO" splashed across it in bright blue letters. Across the street, a yellow building, unlike the homes that we pass, has two stories. In front of it dangles a purple and green sign that reads, "Hotel New Jersey."

The writer contrasts a new site with the previous one.

The world that we see on our morning stroll through the streets of Los Alcarizos contrasts sharply with the world that we encounter on our afternoon visit to the beach. Here we still see signs of poverty: vendors selling fried fish (eyeballs and all), children selling brightly colored shells, and adults hawking sunglasses and necklaces. "Cheap, cheap," they all cry out. However, at the beach the poor are only a part of the landscape. The scenery also includes deep-blue water, long white beaches, 20-story hotels, pricey restaurants, and beautiful homes of the upper class. Tourists are everywhere: fat men in tight swimsuits, topless European women with leathery tans, American families playing catch and trying not to look at the Europeans, kids building sand castles, and retirees sipping sodas.

Feeling angry and self-righteous, I want to grab the tourists in their stupid straw hats. I want to yell, "You just don't get it, do you? Can't you see that there are people in this country who are starving?" I want to tell the tourists that they disgust me. I want to lecture them about how their money could help the poor in Los Alcarizos. I want to demand that they see the real Dominican Republic.

And then I realize something. I have seen a family of five that sleeps in a house half the size of my dorm room. I have seen naked children. I have seen men who struggle to provide one meal a day for their families. But the truth is, I don't get it either.

He closes with personal thoughts and self-reflection.

No matter how hard I look, the poverty of Los Alcarizos is not real to me. Real poverty can't be escaped, but this evening, after I finish work, I will escape. I will eat my third meal of the day, while outside the walls of our camp many will struggle for their first. At night, I will lie down under the protection of an armed guard. Then, after two weeks, I will return home to my life as a "poor" high school student, just as the tourists will return to their lives.

Observation Report

Professional writer Randall VanderMey bases this report on the observations he recorded while waiting for a bus in a Greyhound station. As you will see, this report is much more than an as-it-happened record of what the writer saw and heard. It is also a brief documentary of a particular slice of American life.

"Scab!"

The tense tone established in the opening paragraph is maintained throughout the report.

The driver of the airport shuttle bus had to drop me off on the street so as not to cross the line of cross-country bus drivers marching with their picket signs in the dusk. The picketers were angry. Had he turned in at the driveway to the terminal, they would have spat on him and yelled "Scab!" or "Strikebreaker!" Newspapers and TV had carried stories of rocks and bottles being thrown at passenger-filled buses by disgruntled drivers whose demands for decent wages had not been heard. Most of the drivers in other unions were honoring the picket lines. Someday, they knew, they might be in the same fix.

Inside the terminal I sat with my feet on my suitcase. I didn't want to pay four quarters for a storage box and didn't want to turn my back on my belongings. In the strange, tense atmosphere of the bus depot, I wondered if I was better off there or on a bus. Writing notes became my shield.

The detailed sensory account of this experience begins here.

A couple behind me plays Hispanic music for everyone in the terminal to hear. Men go in the men's room and stay there for a strangely long time, punching the button on the electric blow dryer over and over as if to cover up their talk. Near me an old man in a blue baseball cap and blue nylon jacket mumbles to himself as he paces the floor slowly. I hear him say, "My children is all grown up." Another man in a white yachting cap strides around the terminal making a sliding, streaking sound with a metal heel protector that's working its way loose. He seems to like the sound because he keeps walking around on the hard tile floors, over to the video-game room, over to the cafeteria, over to the bathroom, over to the ticket window, around and around in the open spaces in front of the nuns, college kids, young women with children, and Texas farmers waiting for their bus to Dallas. I know where the man in the yachting cap is without even looking up.

A tiny boy, curiosity in a red sweater, is twirling around. Everybody who sees him smiles. A while ago I saw an older man teasing him, saying "Hey, I'm gonna get you" and trying to slip a 10-gallon straw cowboy hat over his ears.

In addition to carefully describing the people and the terminal, the writer includes snippets of actual conversations.

A policeman with a shaved, bumpy head, takes his drawn nightstick into the men's room and brings out, by the elbow, a young man who doesn't seem to know where he is. He cradles a radio in his arm that blasts its music to everyone's discomfort. The cop says, "Didn't I throw you out of here last night? Come on with me."

The guy looks dazed and says, "Where we going?"

The cop says, "We're just going to have a little talk." Turning off the blaring radio, he walks the young man toward the entrance.

Something weird is in the air, as if drugs are being dealt in the bathrooms, though the place remains calm and well lit. The odor of french fries and cleaning solutions fills the air.

The music plays much more softly now, and I hear the dyed-blond lady say to her husband or boyfriend, "Thang you very mush."

A brief personal reflection is provided here.

The iron screen benches are starting to lay a print in my back and rear end, so I shift and squirm. When I bought my ticket at the front counter, I asked the lady who took my money what I'd have to do for two hours and a half. She had laughed and said, "Look at the walls," and she had been right.

The man in the blue baseball cap is mumbling again. But now I see that he's reading the newspaper and seems not to be able to read unless he pronounces the words aloud. I hear him say, "That's a liquidation sale."

The man with the metal heel protector is back again, clicking and shrieking across the tile floor, carrying a blue nylon satchel. Out of the video-game room come noises like echoes in a long hollow pipe. A kid behind the cash register in the cafeteria has neatly combed hair and glasses. He keeps smiling all the time, looking comfortingly sane. Overhead in there, the ceiling-fan blades turn hardly faster than the second hand on a clock.

To conclude, the writer attempts to put this experience into perspective.

It has taken me some time to realize fully how I felt on that hard metal bench for two and a half hours among so many different kinds of people harboring so many different purposes. I said not a word to anyone. Only wrote and wrote. With my eyes and ears I broke into their lives while giving nothing of myself. I got in and got away without any real contact.

I hope the drivers get their money. But I'm not sure my being there helped. I felt like a scab.

Writing a Personal Research Report

A personal research report presents the story of a writer's investigation into a subject of personal interest—perhaps a new technology, a particular place, a current fad, a possible profession, or a certain lifestyle. This type of reporting is based, for the most part, on firsthand methods of research.

PREWRITING

Search for a topic. Think of topics that deeply interest you. Review the "Basics of Life" list (see page 23), page through newspapers and magazines, or search the Internet. Finally, select a topic that makes your pulse quicken.

Explore your topic. Determine what you already know about your topic and what you hope to find out. Find out which people to talk to and which places to visit to get the information you need. Then investigate!

WRITING

Write your first draft. Draft freely, answering the following questions:

1. *Why am I interested in this topic?*
2. *What do I already know about it?*
3. *What do I hope to find out?*
4. *What have I experienced while researching this topic?*
5. *What have I learned?*

REVISING

Check your ideas. *Is my focus clear? Do I answer the five questions above? Have I included the story of my research?*

Review your organization. *Does my beginning introduce the topic and contain a focus statement? Does the middle contain solid supporting details from my explorations? Does the ending reflect on what I've learned?*

Revise for voice, word choice, and sentence fluency. *Does my voice effectively combine narrative and expository elements? Have I used (and defined) precise terminology? Have I used a variety of sentence lengths and types?*

EDITING

Check for conventions. *Have I used correct punctuation, capitalization, spelling, and grammar?*

PUBLISHING

Present your work. Format your work as a feature story and submit it to a school or local newspaper.

Personal Research Report

In this personal research paper, student writer Kim DeRonde investigates the disease that killed three of her grandparents before she had a chance to get to know them.

Three Family Cancers

The writer opens by describing the assignment that brought a serious topic to mind.

One day back in fourth grade, my teacher said, "Use your imagination and make an invention, something new and useful." I grumped all the way home from school. An invention? For what, I thought. What could I invent that we could use? "What about a cure for cancer?" Mom asked.

A few weeks earlier my family had learned that Grandpa DeRonde had cancer, so I went to work imagining my very own miracle cure. I drew a picture of a medicine bottle, similar to a bottle of cough syrup, with a drop of liquid coming out of it. I called my masterpiece, "The Cure for Cancer."

I can remember those school days pretty well, but I can't say the same for three of my grandparents: Grandma and Grandpa DeRonde and Grandpa Vernooy. Before I could grow up and get to know them, their lives were invaded, taken over, and destroyed by different forms of cancer—multiple myeloma, prostate cancer, and lung cancer. Now, years later, I am faced with another assignment that gives me a chance to think about cancer: What is it and what causes it? And what were these cancers like for my grandparents? To get some answers, I reviewed some recent research on cancer and talked with my mother.

Important background information is given.

Cancer, as my family learned firsthand, is a serious killer. In fact, it's the second leading cause of death in the United States. Each year, the disease kills about 555,000 Americans, and doctors discover almost 1.3 million new cases ("American"). Cancer is so powerful because it's not one, but many diseases attacking many parts of the body. All cancers are basically body cells gone crazy—cells that develop abnormally. These cells then clone themselves using an enzyme called *telomerase*. As they multiply like creatures in a sci-fi horror movie, the cells build into tumors, which are tissues that can "invade and destroy other tissues" ("Cancer Facts").

Researchers aren't exactly sure what triggers these cancerous growths, but they think that 80 percent of cancers happen because people come into regular contact with carcinogens, cancer-causing agents. Carcinogens fall into three groups: chemicals, radiation, and viruses. People can be exposed to these carcinogens in many ways and situations. Radiation, for example, devastated the population of Chernobyl, Russia, after the nuclear power plant meltdown. But carcinogens don't cause cancer overnight—even the terrible exposure of such an accident. The cancer may take 30 to 40 years to develop (Nelson).

Note how the writer smoothly incorporates the interview with her mother.

I don't know what carcinogens attacked my Grandma DeRonde, but I do know the result: she developed multiple myeloma. For a multiple myeloma patient, the average period of survival is 20 months to 10 years ("Thalidomide"). When I talked with my mother, she said that my family doesn't really know when Grandma came down with multiple myeloma, but she lived for two years after learning she had it. For two years, she suffered through radiation and chemotherapy treatments, and life seemed measured by the spaces between appointments to check her white-blood-cell count.

What causes multiple myeloma remains a mystery, though its effects are well known. This cancer is a malignant growth of cells in the bone marrow that makes holes in the skeleton. The holes develop mostly in the ribs, vertebrae, and pelvis. Because the holes make the bones brittle, the victim cannot do simple things like drive and cook. In the end, patients fracture bones and die from infection and pneumonia. It was this weakening of the bones, along with the chemotherapy treatments, that made my grandmother suffer.

The writer describes and summarizes each of the three types of cancer.

My Grandpa DeRonde was diagnosed with prostate cancer several years after my grandma died. The doctors began radiation therapy right away, and my family was hopeful because the cancer was caught in its early stages. At first, the cancer seemed to go into remission, but actually cancer cells were invading other sites in his body. Because the cancer spread, the doctors couldn't treat all of it through radiation or surgery. Grandpa lived for only two years after learning he was ill; and during that time, he had many chemotherapy treatments and spent a lot of time in the hospital. On his death certificate, the doctor wrote that Grandpa died of cardiac arrest and carcinoma of the lung, with metastasis.

Like multiple myeloma, prostate cancer is a powerful killer. Even though many technological changes help doctors catch this cancer at an early stage, the number of deaths per year is still going up. Prostate cancer is the second most common cancer in the United States, and experts estimate that it kills more than 30,000 men per year (Michelson 1).

Prostate cancer is a tumor (called a carcinoma) lining the inside of the organ, in this case the prostate gland. Many factors trigger this form of cancer: age, diet, environmental conditions, or maybe just having a cancer-prone family. A survey of more than 51,000 American men showed that eating a lot of fat, found mostly in red meat, can lead to advanced prostate cancer. On the other hand, researchers concluded that fats from vegetables, fish, and many dairy products are probably not linked to the growth of a carcinoma ("Study").

My second grandfather died from a different carcinoma, lung cancer. Doctors found a tumor in the lower lobe of Grandpa Vernooy's right lung, recommended surgery, and removed the lung. The next winter, he weakened, got pneumonia, and died. His doctors believed that his smoking habit caused the cancer. Smoking, in fact, remains the most important factor in lung cancer's development. The truth is that cigarette smoking causes almost half of all cancer cases, even though only one out of ten smokers actually comes down with this disease ("Cigarette").

One grandfather's cancer is linked to smoking—a nonhereditary factor important to the writer.

Some studies have concluded that genetics may play a role in whether a person develops lung cancer or not. A 2006 study suggested that if a person is missing positive genes called tumor suppressor genes, it's bad news. If these genes weren't inherited, or if smoking destroys them, then cancer-related genes are free to do their damage. The study identified another special gene that is inherited from one or both parents and that metabolizes chemicals from cigarette smoke. In this case, if the gene is there, the cancer risk goes up, especially for smokers ("Oncogenes").

I still wish I could cure cancer with a magic miracle liquid in a medicine bottle. But today I understand that cancer is a complicated disease. My grandparents died from three types of the disease—multiple myeloma, prostate cancer, and lung cancer. If it hadn't been for cancerous tumors taking over their bodies, my grandparents might still be alive, and I'd have many more memories of them. Maybe I'd even be sharing with them my plans for college. On the other hand, maybe this paper is a cure of a different type: While it can't change what happened, it can help me understand it.

The writer concludes on a wistful but realistic note.

NOTE: The works-cited page is not shown.

Analytical Writing

Analytical Writing

The word *analysis* means "to break apart" or "to loosen." An effective analysis explores a topic, examines the parts, compares them, and puts them back together again. This cerebral process of breaking down and rebuilding happens everywhere in the world—from the Senate floor to a lecture hall to Al's garage.

Analyses use a variety of mental "muscles." You might break a process into steps, compare and contrast objects, classify strategies or practices, define a complex term, trace the causes and effects of a phenomenon, explain a problem and advocate a solution, or evaluate the merits of a new trend. Whatever strategy you choose for your analysis, in the end, you must demonstrate that you have rigorously worked through the topic and understand it fully.

WHAT'S AHEAD

In this section, you will find guidelines and models for many types of analytical writing: process, comparison, classification, definition, cause and effect, problem and solution, and evaluation.

"Writing is how we think our way into a subject and make it our own."

—William Zinsser

Analytical Writing

QUICK GUIDE

Writers describe analytical writing in a number of ways—digging through a topic, unpacking an idea, crawling through the research. . . . All of these expressions capture the same basic truth: by breaking down a topic and putting it back together, writers come to own the ideas. When you write analytically, consider the following elements.

- **STARTING POINT:** Usually, you are given a specific assignment in which you are asked to examine or investigate a topic related to your course work.
- **PURPOSE:** Your overall purpose is to demonstrate a clear understanding of your topic by breaking it down and reassembling it. Depending on your assignment, you may demonstrate a process, compare two things, define a term, show causes, solve problems, or evaluate a topic.
- **FORM:** The traditional essay form works well for analyses. Identify your thesis in the opening, develop the thesis in the middle, and sum up the main ideas in the closing.
- **AUDIENCE:** Analytical writing is generally intended for your instructor and writing peers.
- **VOICE:** In most types of analytical writing, use formal English. Carefully and correctly phrased, it can be reread many times without sounding tiresome or affected. Avoid slang and colloquialisms.
- **POINT OF VIEW:** Use third-person point of view *(he, she, they)* unless your analysis is clearly based on personal experience.

INSIDE INFO

Directed freewriting, in which you describe your topic, compare it, apply it, and so on, is an effective way to delve into your topic. (See page 25 for more information.) Answering *structured questions* is another useful way to discover what is important or unique about your topic. (See pages 25–26.)

Writing an Analysis of a Process

A process analysis shows the reader how to do something (such as selecting the right telescope) or it explains a particular process (such as the life cycle of a star). Consider the following guidelines and models.

PREWRITING

Select a topic. Think of complex procedures and processes that meet the requirements of your assignment. Choose a topic that interests you.

Gather details. Make certain you understand the process fully. Consult experts, books, magazines, and Web sites. Identify steps or stages in the process.

Focus your analysis. Write a thesis statement that explains the importance of or shares your interest in the process.

Organize your analysis. Make a list or an outline that provides the starting conditions or materials necessary to the process. Follow with the steps or stages in chronological (time) order.

WRITING

Write your first draft. Write your first draft freely, working in details according to your plan. Use time-order transitions (*first, second, third, then, finally,* etc.).

REVISING

Check your ideas. *Have I introduced the process in an interesting way? Does my thesis statement highlight my interest in or note the importance of the process? Do I provide complete steps?*

Review your organization. *Do my beginning and ending work well? Does the middle give steps or stages in chronological order? Do my transitions make the order clear?*

Revise for voice, word choice, and sentence fluency. *Does my writing demonstrate my interest in the topic? Have I used specific nouns and verbs and defined unfamiliar terms? Do I use imperative (command) sentences for giving directions?*

EDITING

Check for conventions. *Have I used correct punctuation, capitalization, spelling, and grammar?*

PUBLISHING

Present your work. Share your analysis with an appreciative audience (such as an astronomy club or online forum for an essay on star formation).

Process Essay

Student writer Kerri Mertz wrote this essay to help nonscientists understand how cancer cells multiply and affect the body.

Wayward Cells

An introductory comparison leads up to the thesis (underlined).

A human body is like a factory, and the body's cells are like workers. If the body is healthy, each cell has an important job and does it correctly. For example, right now red blood cells are running through your arteries carrying oxygen to each body part. Other cells are digesting that steak sandwich you ate for lunch, and others are patching up the cut on your left hand. Each cell knows what to do because its genetic code—or DNA—gives it instructions. However, when a cell begins to function abnormally, it can initiate a process that results in cancer.

The writer describes the first step in the process and cites a potential cause.

The problem starts when one cell "forgets" what it should do. Scientists call this "undifferentiating"—meaning that the cell loses its identity within the body (Pierce 75). Why this happens is somewhat unclear. The problem could be caused by a defect in the cell's DNA code or by something in the environment, such as cigarette smoke or asbestos (German 21). So cancer may happen because of defective genes inside the body, or because of forces outside the body—carcinogens, meaning "any substance that causes cancer" (Neufeldt and Sparks 90). In either case, an undifferentiated cell malfunctions in two ways: (1) by not doing its specified job and (2) by reproducing at the wrong rate.

She describes the next step and its result.

Most healthy cells reproduce rather quickly, but their reproduction rate is controlled. For example, blood cells completely die off and replace themselves within a matter of weeks, but existing cells make only as many new cells as the body needs. The DNA codes tell healthy cells how many new cells to produce. However, cancer cells don't get this message; they lose control and reproduce quickly, with no stopping point, a characteristic called "autonomy" (Braun 3). What's more, their "offspring" exhibit the same qualities, and the resulting overpopulation produces tumors.

She describes the third step—how tumors damage the body.

Tumor cells can hurt the body in a number of ways. First, a tumor can grow so big that it takes up space needed by other organs. Second, some cells may detach from the original tumor and spread throughout the body, creating new tumors elsewhere. This happens with lymphatic cancer—a cancer that's hard to control because it spreads so quickly. A third way that tumor cells can hurt the body is by doing work not called for in their DNA. For example, a gland cell's DNA code may tell the cell to produce a necessary hormone in the endocrine system. However, if cancer damages or distorts that code, sick cells may produce more of the hormone than the body can use—or even tolerate (Braun 4). Cancer cells seem to have minds of their own, and this is why cancer is such a serious disease.

A transition signals a shift in focus—from the illness to its treatment.

Fortunately, there is hope. Scientific research is already helping doctors do amazing things for people suffering with cancer. One treatment that has been used for some time is chemotherapy, or the use of chemicals to kill off all fast-growing cells, including cancer cells. (Unfortunately, chemotherapy can't distinguish between healthy and unhealthy cells, so it may cause negative side effects, such as damaging fast-growing hair follicles, resulting in hair loss.) Another common treatment is radiation, or the use of light rays to kill cancer cells. One of the newest and most promising treatments is gene therapy—an effort to identify and treat chromosomes that carry a "wrong code" in their DNA. Gene therapy is promising because it treats the cause of cancer, not just its effects.

The writer reuses the opening analogy to review main points.

Much of life involves dealing with problems—wayward workers, broken machines, dysfunctional organizations. Wayward cells are just another problem. While this problem is painful and deadly, there is hope. Medical specialists are making progress, and someday, they will help us win our battle against wayward cells.

NOTE: The works-cited page is not shown.

READING FOR BETTER WRITING

Review the transition words and phrases that connect paragraphs and sentences in the essay above. What types of transitions are used? Do they create an effective flow of thought? Explain.

Process Essay

In the following process essay, Bill Baughn describes how one of nature's most devastating forces—a tsunami—develops.

An Unbelievable Force

The introductory paragraph ends with the thesis statement (underlined).

On December 26, 2004, a tsunami struck Indonesia and the coastal areas around the Indian Ocean. A tsunami (the Japanese word for "harbor wave") is one of the most destructive forces in nature, and the Indonesian surge caused devastation as far away as Africa ("Tsunami"). Many people believe that a tsunami is simply a big wave that moves forward until it hits the shore or some other object, but the process is more complex than that. A tsunami is really a huge transfer of energy from the crust of the earth to a body of water.

The middle gives a step-by-step explanation of the process.

Unlike typical ocean waves caused by storms, a tsunami begins when an underwater earthquake causes one tectonic plate to thrust up over another. When the earthquake lifts the continental plate and all the water above it, tremendous energy is released. The force moves upward through the water until it gets near the surface. There, the energy spreads out horizontally like ripples in a pool. This enormous energy is not apparent on the surface, however, and the outwardly spreading waves may be only a few feet high. The power of the tsunami is still under the surface, moving as fast as 500 miles per hour (Castor 25).

As the surge heads toward the shore, the immense energy does not have enough water to carry it. The water nearer the land gets sucked back out to sea to feed the growing wave. Then the wave rushes onshore in the form of a wall of water that can be as high as 90 feet and as wide as several hundred miles. The power of this wall of water can be unbelievable ("Freak").

The closing shares key statistics about the topic.

The tsunami of 2004 was the result of an earthquake that measured 9.3 on the Richter scale, one of the highest readings in 40 years. The surge traveled at about 500 miles per hour but slowed down as it reached shallow water. Its energy shifted from speed to power as it built a wave 65 feet high—a wall of water that carried away trees, buildings, and the lives of an estimated 300,000 people (Lambourne 1–3).

NOTE: The works-cited page is not shown.

Writing an Essay of Comparison

An essay of comparison demonstrates the similarities and differences between two topics. The ultimate challenge is to make the familiar seem new and the new seem familiar. Use these guidelines and the models that follow.

PREWRITING

Select two topics. Consider topics connected to your course work. Make sure they have enough similarities and differences to make an interesting comparison.

Gather details. Create a Venn diagram (see page 28), writing down the similarities between the two topics in the center space and the differences in the outside spaces.

Organize your comparison. Decide if your comparison will be organized topic by topic, point by point, or by addressing similarities first and then differences. Create an outline to organize your essay.

WRITING

Write your first draft. In your first paragraph, introduce your topics and provide a thesis statement that expresses the focus of your comparison. In the middle paragraphs, compare and contrast the two topics. Conclude your essay by revisiting the thesis and by reflecting on the topics.

REVISING

Check your ideas. *Have I created a clear thesis? Have I provided meaningful points of comparison? Is my essay insightful?*

Review your organization. *Have I followed a consistent plan of organization (topic by topic, point by point, or similarities first and then differences)? Do transitions clearly connect the parts of my comparison?*

Revise for voice, word choice, and sentence fluency. *Do I sound knowledgeable and interested? Have I used specific nouns and active verbs? Do I use a variety of smooth-reading sentences?*

EDITING

Check for conventions. *Have I used correct punctuation, capitalization, spelling, and grammar?*

PUBLISHING

Present your work. Format your writing according to the instructor's specifications, proofread it a final time, and submit it for evaluation.

Essay of Comparison

In this essay, student writer Janae Sebranek compares the fate of two tragic characters, Bigger in *Native Son* and Alan in *Equus*.

The opening remarks lead up to the thesis of the essay (underlined).

The writer presents a thoughtful analysis of each character's actions.

Specific references to the texts substantiate key points.

Beyond Control

Most children, no matter what their personal or family situation, lead more or less controlled lives. As they grow, they begin to sense the pressure of controlling factors in their lives, and start struggling to take control themselves. This can be a difficult process. In the works *Native Son* and *Equus*, Richard Wright and Peter Shaffer respectively create two characters who must deal with this struggle. Bigger in *Native Son* and Alan in *Equus* are both entering adulthood and have come to realize that they are controlled by work, religion, and the media. In the midst of these characters' efforts to gain control, each falls into a tragic situation.

Alan works as a clerk at Bryson's appliance store. The customers are demanding, and the many products and brand names are confusing. He finds that he cannot function in this work environment. Later, under hypnosis, he admits to Dr. Dysart that his "foes" are the myriad brand names he is challenged to locate and explain to the customers—"The Hosts of Hoover. The Hosts of Philco. The House of Remington and all its tribe!" (73). Alan decides to look for another job. He likes being around horses, so he pursues and lands a job with a stable owner. He enjoys his job and begins to deal more effectively with work.

Bigger must also struggle with the pressure and anxiety of his first job. Because of his family's desperate financial situation, he is forced to take the one job he is offered, as a chauffeur for Mr. Dalton, a wealthy suburban man. Bigger cannot relate to the Daltons. He sees himself as a foreigner, forced to live and work among the privileged. The Daltons tell him where, when, and even how to drive. Bigger struggles; but, like Alan, he cannot deal with the extreme discomfort he is feeling. He quits after only two days on the job. Unlike Alan, however, he does not have the option of getting a job that interests him.

Alan and Bigger also find religion to be a controlling factor in their lives. Alan's mother, Dora, "doses [religion] down the boy's throat" as she whispers "that Bible to him hour after hour, up there in his room" (33). For a time, Alan is fascinated by the Bible's imagery and ideas, but eventually, his fascination begins to fade.

Each text reference is smoothly integrated into the analysis.

Bigger's mother does not push the issue of religion to the extreme that Alan's mother does. Instead, she tries to make her son see its value with daily comments such as "You'll regret how you living someday" (13). She offers her advice by singing religious songs from behind a curtain in their one-room apartment. She tries to show Bigger that religion is a valid way of dealing with a world out of control. But Bigger rejects her religion, and he is left with no spiritual footing.

Finally, the media takes control of both Alan's and Bigger's lives. Alan's father calls television a "dangerous drug" (27) that can control the mind. Alan still manages to watch television, but only because his mother "used to let him slip off in the afternoons to a friend next door" (31) to watch. Later, while he is under psychiatric care, he watches television every night and eventually finds himself becoming controlled by the medium.

Bigger, in a more tragic way, is also controlled by the media. He reads about himself in the newspapers and begins to believe certain things that have no valid basis. He is referred to as a "Negro killer" who looks "as if about to spring upon you at any moment" (260). The papers remark that Bigger "seems a beast utterly untouched" (260) by and out of place in the white man's world.

The closing remarks focus on the tragic fates of the two characters.

Bigger's ultimate fate is clearly beyond his control. He is falsely accused of raping and killing a woman, and he cannot convince anyone of the truth. Bigger too closely matches the descriptions given in the newspapers, a fact that tragically leads to his death. Alan's fate is different, although tragic in its own right. While in the psychiatric ward, he gains a certain control with the help of therapy and medication. However, he loses his passion for life: "Passion, you see, can be destroyed by a doctor. It cannot be created" (108). This is Alan's personal tragedy.

Ultimately, both Alan and Bigger fail to gain real control over the outside forces in their lives. Alan forfeits his interest in life, and Bigger forfeits life itself. They, like so many people, become victims of the world in which they live.

Essay of Comparison

In the following essay, student writer Rafael Ramirez compares and contrasts Jim Thorpe and Jesse Owens. He uses a point-by-point organizational pattern.

Achieving Greatness

The writer captures the reader's interest and leads up to the thesis statement (underlined).

Who is the greatest American athlete of all time? Most people think of people like Muhammad Ali, Jackie Joyner-Kersey, or Babe Ruth. However, there are two other great American athletes that some people may have forgotten about. These two people caught the world's attention many years ago and still inspire us today. Jim Thorpe and Jesse Owens overcame poverty and prejudice to dominate their sports.

A paraphrase puts information in the writer's own words.

Both of these great athletes started life poor. In 1888, Jim Thorpe was born on a farm near Prague, Oklahoma. His parents named him Wa-tho-huck, a Native American name that means "Bright Path" ("Jim"). Still, he didn't have a bright early life. Thorpe's twin brother, Charlie, died when Jim was nine, and his mother died shortly afterward. Thorpe attended one Indian school after another in Oklahoma, Kansas, and Pennsylvania before his athletic talent was recognized. Jesse Owens also had a tough childhood. He was born in 1913 into a poor Alabama family. They moved north to Cleveland, hoping for a better life, but couldn't find one. During high school, Owens worked so many odd jobs that he couldn't make afternoon practices for the track team. However, track coach Charlie Riley recognized Owens' talent and offered to train him in the morning ("Jesse").

Facts and statistics produce a knowledgeable voice.

As young adults, Thorpe and Owens used their natural talents to achieve greatness. In 1911 and 1912, Thorpe led the Carlisle Indian School varsity football team to victory over powerful teams such as Army, Georgetown, Harvard, and Pittsburgh. Thorpe scored 25 touchdowns and 198 points in his last season, and he was named All-American for two years running ("Jim"). In the same way, Owens became a track star in high school and college. At Cleveland East High School, he tied the world-record time for the 100-yard dash. At Ohio State University, he tied one world record and set three more, all in less than an hour and with an injured back! Owens broke the broad-jump record by placing a handkerchief at the old mark—26 feet 2 1/2 inches—and jumping nearly 6 inches beyond it ("Jesse").

These great American athletes then went on to succeed against the world's best athletes. Jim Thorpe was chosen to represent the United States in the Stockholm Olympics of 1912. There he easily won the pentathlon and set a decathlon score (8,413 points) that wouldn't be topped for 20 years ("Jim"). The king of Sweden even declared Thorpe "the greatest athlete in the world" ("Thorpe"). Twenty-four years later, in 1936, Jesse Owens represented this country in the so-called "Hitler Olympics." Owens won four gold medals, breaking an Olympic record and a world record, but Owens' greatest accomplishment was winning the hearts of the German people. Even Luz Long, the top German long jumper, befriended Jim in front of Hitler. Owens later said, "You can melt down all the medals and cups I have, and they wouldn't be a plating on the 24-karat friendship I felt for Luz Long" ("Track").

Quotations add insight into Owens' personality.

Following their days of Olympic glory, however, Thorpe and Owens both returned to harsh realities. The Olympic committee removed Thorpe's medals because of complaints about his "professionalism." (Professional athletes were not allowed to compete, and Thorpe had earned $15 a week playing minor-league baseball.) Thorpe returned to playing baseball and football, became a Hollywood extra, and finally ended up on the recreation staff of the Chicago Park District ("Jim"). Owens became a "runner-for-hire," racing against ballplayers, motorcycles, or even racehorses ("Biography"). "It was bad enough to have toppled from the Olympic heights to make my living competing with animals," Owens once said, "but the competition wasn't even fair. No man could beat a racehorse, not even for 100 yards" ("Quotes"). Owens eventually launched a new career: motivational speaking.

An explanation clarifies the meaning of a term.

Eventually, these two athletes got the recognition they deserved. In 1976, President Ford gave Owens the Medal of Freedom, the highest honor a civilian can receive ("Biography"). In 1982, 30 years after his death, the Olympic committee returned Thorpe's medals to his family ("Jim"). Jim Thorpe and Jesse Owens overcame poverty and prejudice to become two of the greatest athletes of all time. Their accomplishments live on in the sports they helped to integrate and in the world they helped to change.

The writer revisits the thesis and reflects on the importance of the subjects.

NOTE: The works-cited page is not shown.

Guidelines

Writing an Essay of Classification

To classify a topic is to break it down into its most meaningful parts or to explain how it fits into a larger category or grouping. A classification essay helps the reader understand all the parts and the connections between them.

PREWRITING

Select a topic. Review your course work for topics that have subcategories—types of representative governments, types of bodily defenses against disease, kinds of carbohydrates, types of reed instruments, and so on. Select a topic that fits the assignment and has several categories (three to six) to explore in a meaningful essay.

Gather details. Collect enough information to develop an interesting essay.

Plan your analysis. Decide what is most important about your topic, establish your focus, and outline your essay.

WRITING

Write your first draft. Create an opening that introduces the topic and presents your thesis, previewing how you will classify the topic. Continue by discussing the categories and supporting your thesis with details you've gathered. Sum up your essay in a way that leaves the reader with a new understanding of the topic.

REVISING

Check your ideas. *Do I have an interesting overall topic? Have I clearly analyzed the different parts of it? Have I provided many interesting details?*

Review your organization. *Does each part (beginning, middle, and ending) work well? Do I use transition words and phrases to connect the parts?*

Revise for voice, word choice, and sentence fluency. *Do I sound interested in and knowledgeable about the topic? Have I used precise language and defined any unfamiliar terms? Have I used a variety of sentences?*

EDITING

Check for conventions. *Have I used correct punctuation, capitalization, spelling, and grammar?*

PUBLISHING

Present your work. Consider illustrating your essay with photos or drawings and share your work with classmates who have a similar interest. You may choose to give an oral presentation or publish your essay on a Web site.

Essay of Classification

In the following essay, Davis Ryan writes about his passion: orchids. He identifies and describes four distinct methods by which orchids are pollinated.

The Secret Lives of Orchids

An engaging and thoughtful introduction leads up to the thesis (underlined).

Flowers have one main job: to attract pollinators. For most flowers, bright colors catch the pollinator's eye, sweet odors draw the creature's nose (or antennae), and delicious nectar rewards the pollinator for visiting. One peculiar family of flowers, however, has taken the art of seduction to a new level. Orchids have four unique ways to attract pollinators: olfactory assaults, animal mimicry, insect trapping, and self-pollination.

Each paragraph in the middle focuses on a specific category.

For one group of orchids, the traditional smell factor takes a completely different twist. For example, many orchids of the *Bulbophyllum* species smell and look like rotting meat. That's because their chief pollinators are flies and carrion beetles. These carnivorous insects find the *Bulbophyllum beccarii* irresistible, though some human observers have compared the smell to "a herd of dead elephants" (Horak 121). Other orchids mimic the smell of more popular flowers and plants in their environment, hence stealing traffic from the competition. One such orchid, nicknamed the "Sharry Baby," smells like chocolate, thus attracting the pollinators of their rivals (Orlean).

Words such as "elaborate," "shivers," and "duped" create a strong voice.

Other types of orchids exhibit elaborate animal mimicry that leads to pollination. Orchids of the genus *Oncidium* attract their pollinators by taking the shape and color of the pollinators' rival insects. The flower even shivers antagonistically in the wind. When the bee attacks this floral lure, the duped creature gets covered in pollen and flies away only to make the same mistake again. This type of mimicry is called *pseudoantagonism* ("Oncidiums"). Other orchids seem to make love instead of war. In Australia alone, more than 100 species of orchids not only look like their pollinators but also exude the insects' sex pheromones. The female insect pollinators gather the pheromone to wear like perfume, and the males court the flowers (Peakall 5).

While some orchids lure pollinators through mimicry, others demonstrate downright entrapment. *Cypripedium* orchids—commonly called *lady slippers*—have pouchlike structures that capture insect visitors. Some simply have a slippery "landing strip" above the pouch, causing visiting insects to tumble in and get covered with pollen. Others do the trick with clever trapdoors ("Pollination"). Perhaps the cleverist lady slipper, though, produces an intoxicant that insects seek out. They get "drunk," tumble into the pouch, stagger around awhile, and finally drag themselves out, only to do the same thing again (Orlean).

Transitions signal the shift from category to category and example to example.

Another group of orchids—those living in places without insects—rely on self-pollination. The *Holcoglossum amesianum* lives on tree trunks a mile above sea level in China. Few insects, fewer animals, and a windless season from February to April mean that this plant has had to adapt to these conditions. The orchid has the ability to twist its anther 360 degrees in order to pollinate its stigma ("Hermaphroditic"). Botanists point out that this method does not allow for cross-pollination, thereby making the species vulnerable to disease, but for the orchids this risk is preferable to immediate extinction.

The ending sums up the analysis and provides a final insight.

With strange smells, animal disguises, elaborate traps, and even floral acrobatics, orchids display four bizarre forms of pollination. These strategies aren't particularly effective, though. During one 15-year study, only 23 orchids out of 1,000 were pollinated. However, each of those 23 orchids produced millions of seeds. In her book *The Orchid Thief*, Susan Orlean writes, "One pod has enough seeds to supply the world's prom corsages for the rest of eternity."

NOTE: **The works-cited page is not shown.**

READING FOR BETTER WRITING

1. Which of the forms of pollination is most surprising to you? Why?
2. The writer uses outright and implied personification to make orchids seem to act intentionally. Find three examples. How does this personification affect the overall tone of the essay?

Essay of Classification

In this essay, John Van Rys classifies four types of literary criticism.

Four Ways to Talk About Literature

The opening paragraph effectively draws the reader into the essay.

The word "literature" sounds daunting to some people—a word that should be spoken with the nose raised and an affected English accent spilling out of one's mouth. But literature does not have to be daunting. Readers can join the conversation about literature by employing one (or more) of the four basic approaches to literary criticism.

Each new category, or approach, is clearly identified.

Text-centered approaches focus on the literary piece itself. Often called formalist criticism, this approach claims that the structure of a work and the rules of its genre are crucial to its meaning. The formalist critic determines how various elements (plot, character, language, etc.) reinforce the meaning and unify the work. For example, the formalist may ask the following questions concerning Robert Browning's poem "My Last Duchess": How do the main elements in the poem—irony, symbolism, and verse form—help develop the main theme (deception)? How does Browning use the dramatic monologue genre in this poem?

Audience-centered approaches focus on the "transaction" between text and reader—the dynamic way the reader interacts with the text. Often called rhetorical or reader-response criticism, these approaches see the text not as an object to be analyzed, but as an activity that is different for each reader. A reader-response critic might ask these questions of "My Last Duchess": How does the reader become aware of the duke's true nature, if it's never actually stated? Do men and women read the poem differently? Who were Browning's original readers?

How each approach functions (to interpret a poem) is a primary feature in the essay.

Author-centered approaches focus on the origins of a text (the writer and the historical background). For example, an author-centered study examines the writer's life—showing connections, contrasts, and conflicts between his or her life and the writing. Broader historical studies explore social and intellectual currents, showing links between an author's work and the ideas, events, and institutions of that period. Finally, the literary historian may make connections between the text in question and earlier and later literary works. The author-centered critic might ask these questions of "My Last Duchess": What were Browning's views of marriage, men and women, art, class and wealth? As an institution, what was marriage like in Victorian England (Browning's era) or Renaissance Italy (the duke's era)?

Subcategories are identified and analyzed to give the complete picture.

The fourth approach to criticism applies ideas outside of literature to literary works. Because literature mirrors life, argue these critics, disciplines that explore human life can help us understand literature. Some critics, for example, apply psychological theories to literary works by exploring dreams, symbolic meanings, and motivation. Myth or archetype criticism uses insights from psychology, cultural anthropology, and classical studies to explore a text's universal appeal. Moral criticism, rooted in religious studies and ethics, explores the moral dilemmas literary works raise. Marxist, feminist, and minority criticism are, broadly speaking, sociological approaches to interpretation. While the Marxist examines the themes of class struggle, economic power, and social justice in texts, the feminist critic explores the just and unjust treatment of women as well as the effect of gender on language, reading, and the literary canon. The critic interested in race and ethnic identity explores similar issues, with the focus shifted to a specific cultural group.

Such ideological criticism might ask a wide variety of questions about "My Last Duchess": What does the poem reveal about the duke's psychological state and his personality? How does the reference to Neptune deepen the poem? What does the poem suggest about the nature of evil and injustice? In what ways are the Duke's motives class based and economic? How does the poem present the duke's power and the duchess's weakness? What is the status of women in this society?

The closing paragraph explores the "common ground" between the critical approaches.

No single approach to literature is the correct one. Any approach, or a combination of a few or all of them, can open wide the meaning of a text. An interpretive method is valid as long as it has the following characteristics: (1) a close attention to literary elements such as character, plot, symbolism, and metaphor; (2) a desire to understand the work without distortion; and (3) a sincere interest in connecting the work to life and meaning. Each of the four approaches to literature is simply a tool in the hands of readers, a tool to be applied as needed to work through a text.

Guidelines

Writing an Essay of Definition

An essay of definition clarifies a complex concept *(inflation)*, an abstract idea *(hope)*, or a complicated ideal *(democracy)*. An extended essay of definition goes beyond the basic definition of a concept or an idea. It also includes synonyms, antonyms, etymology, comparisons, examples, anecdotes, and analysis. Follow the guidelines below.

PREWRITING

Select a topic. Choose a term or concept that meets the requirements of your assignment. Make certain your topic is thought provoking.

Gather details. Create a definition diagram (see page 28), supplying various types of definitions for your term. Consult the dictionary and thesaurus as well as Web sites and magazine articles to broaden your understanding of the word.

Plan your analysis. Decide on a main focus or thesis for your essay and develop a plan, determining where you want your essay to begin and how you want it to progress.

WRITING

Write your first draft. Identify your term and indicate its significance. Then flesh out the basic definition with a variety of details and ideas. Finally, connect your ideas, synthesizing a new view of the term for your reader.

REVISING

Check your ideas. *Have I clearly introduced and defined my term? Have I included a variety of details? Does my essay show the term in a new light?*

Review your organization. *Does each part (beginning, middle, and ending) work well? Do I use transition words and phrases to connect the parts?*

Revise for voice, word choice, and sentence fluency. *Do I sound interested in the topic and knowledgeable about it? Have I used precise words and defined any unfamiliar terms? Have I used a variety of sentences?*

EDITING

Check for conventions. *Have I used correct punctuation, capitalization, spelling, and grammar?*

PUBLISHING

Present your work. Present your work to your class, as well as to anyone else who would be interested in the term or concept. Consider including photographs or illustrations with the final version of your essay.

Essay of Definition

Words mean different things to different people. In this essay, student writer Kirsten Zinser takes a whimsical approach to defining the word *eclectic*. The personal approach she uses tells us as much about her as it does about the word she defines.

A Few of My Favorite Things

The introduction piques the reader's interest.

Purple cows, purple bruises, jet fuel, boxes on skateboards, dresses with bells, a dog named Tootsie, a neighbor named Scott, a song about meatballs, a certain good-night kiss, a broken swing. What have all these to do with each other? Nothing.

Go-carting, Handel's *Messiah*, a blue bike, pump organs, box cities, twelfth grade . . . "What do these have to do with each other?" you wonder. Like I said, nothing. My memories, like the things I enjoy, can only be described as one thing: *eclectic*. This paper, however, is not about my life; it's about my fascination with a word.

Before defining the word, the writer asks the reader to say it and feel it.

E-clec-tic. Say it out loud, savoring each syllable—*e . . . clec . . . tic.* Notice the different positions of your tongue. Odd how a word made of nothing more than clicking noises conveys meaning. I love to say the word. The lips do absolutely no work.

Now try to say it with your lips separated as little as possible. It still works. All the work is done on the inside, a dance of the muscular tongue on the teeth. If I were a ventriloquist, I would use the word as often as possible. Notice how the sound emerges as you form the letters. *E*—here it comes right down the center, *cl*—out from either side, *e*—an open corridor, *c*—the sound cut off, *ti*—the sound explodes past the tongue and over the teeth until pinched off with the last—*c*.

A dictionary definition is given.

Webster defines *eclectic* as selecting or choosing elements from different sources or systems. *Eclectic* implies variety. What a grand way of saying variety. Variety sounds so generic; so discount. But *eclectic* is rich with imaginative sound.

The writer describes a highly imaginative experience.

If I could get inside the word, I would find air so pure it would sting my lungs. I imagine the space inside the walls of the word to be like a long hallway that differs in shape every few feet. At one point, the distance between the walls would offer so much space, you could run and jump with little caution. In the next few feet, the walls would be so close together, that you would need to crawl on your belly to pass through. A few feet later, open space again, and so on. You would need to be limber to move through the many different-shaped spaces within the word.

Zinser describes her earliest history with the word.

For me, *eclectic* is one of those words that isn't simply used to describe something. It is a word that fits my soul. When I was young and first heard the word, I said it all the time, though I did not really understand its meaning. Then, as I began to internalize its definition, something inside me vowed allegiance. I knew this word would become not only a part of my vocabulary, but a part of my life.

The writer's "loyalty" to the word is described.

And so I pledge my loyalty to the variety of life. To enjoy theater, music, science, the outdoors, sports, philosophy, everything—this is my strategy. I want to be mature enough to carry on a conversation at elite restaurants, and young enough to squish my toes in thick mud. I want to be wild enough to walk on top of tall fences, and wise enough to be afraid of falling.

When I have a house of my own, I want an eclectic house with an old lamp here, a new dresser there, a vintage couch with a knitted afghan. The walls crowded with paintings, pictures, and stencils. Wild plants filling a yard of fragrant, clipped grass and popping up in unexpected places in the gravel driveway. Or perhaps I'll ditch the possession thing and root myself in the poetry of life, soaking in everything by osmosis, but being owned by nothing. I'll adopt a policy of "no policy." I won't be eclectic based on the things I possess, but on the experiences that I have.

The conclusion echoes the beginning and rounds out the discussion.

Purple cows, purple bruises, jet fuel, boxes on skateboards, dresses with bells, a dog named Tootsie, a neighbor named Scott, a song about meatballs, a certain good-night kiss, a broken swing. "But these have nothing to do with each other," you say. Precisely.

READING FOR BETTER WRITING

1. This essay doesn't simply define the term *eclectic*. It embodies the term. List the eclectic types of support the writer uses.
2. The voice of this essay contributes powerfully to its effect. The author herself is an example of the term *eclectic*. Pinpoint words, phrases, and clauses that contribute to the eclectic voice.

Essay of Definition

In the following essay, student writer Christia Wood explains multiple definitions for the word *romance*.

"Isn't It Romantic?"

The first paragraph identifies the topic and states the focus of the essay.

When someone uses the word *romance*, the images that come to mind are long-stemmed roses, soft music, and chocolates in a heart-shaped box. *Romance* has more meanings than *love*, however. It may also refer to a family of languages, a heroic tale, or a particular period in the arts.

In the first case, *Romance* (with a capital R) refers to languages that have descended from Latin. These include French, Italian, Portuguese, Spanish, and even Romanian, among others. Because Latin was the language of the Roman Empire, the term "Romance" reflects those origins.

Each middle paragraph helps define the topic.

After the fall of the Roman Empire, and during the Middle Ages, fantastic tales of heroism, adventure, and the supernatural became popular in Europe. Troubadours and traveling actors spread stories of noble knights battling evil ogres, dragons, and other monsters. Because many of these tales originated in southern Europe, where the Romance languages were spoken, the stories were called romances.

Often, these romances featured a damsel in distress, who was rescued by a knight according to a code of chivalry. In France, especially, chivalric tales became extremely popular. In these stories, knights would dedicate themselves to the honor of a lady, as in the story of Sir Lancelot and Queen Guinevere. It isn't difficult to see, then, where the link between courtship, love, and *romance* began.

Later, during the early nineteenth century, poets such as Wordsworth, Coleridge, Byron, Keats, and Shelley used the term *Romantic* to refer to a new type of poetry. They were reacting against the previous period, the Age of Reason. Poetry of the Romantic period sought to regain a sense of wonder and intense feeling. It focused on nature rather than on science, on human emotions and human rights rather than on the progress of nations.

The closing reviews the word's key meanings and tells how they relate to modern usage.

Romance means much more than just hearts and flowers. It can refer to languages descended from Latin, to heroic tales, and to a particular period of poetry. Running through all of these is the thread of love, so that meaning of *romance* has its place, too.

Guidelines

Writing a Cause-Effect Essay

A cause-effect essay provides a careful examination of the relationship between events. Some essays focus on a single cause and a single effect. Others focus on multiple causes or multiple effects. Let the following information guide your writing.

PREWRITING

Select a topic. Search for a cause-effect relationship in the material you are studying currently, perhaps the cause of a social movement or the effect of a specific diet regimen. Review textbooks, magazines, and Web sites for possible topics.

Gather details. Create a cause-effect chart (see page 27) to collect information about your topic. Write down more details than you'll use.

Find a focus. Review your chart and determine which cause(s) and effect(s) you will cover. Then develop a thesis statement that names your topic and gives your essay its focus.

Plan your analysis. Create an outline. Provide details in the order that best fits your topic—beginning with cause(s) and leading to effect(s), or beginning with effect(s) and returning to cause(s).

WRITING

Write your first draft. Begin by introducing the topic and providing your thesis statement. Present the cause(s) and effect(s) in the middle paragraphs and analyze the connection between them. End by summarizing the analysis.

REVISING

Check your ideas. *Have I clearly analyzed the causal connection? Do my details support the main connection? Is my essay informative?*

Review your organization. *Does my beginning forecast the cause-effect relationship? Have I chosen the best organizational structure for my middle paragraphs? Have I use causal transitions* (for example, because, as a result, due to)?

Revise for voice, word choice, and sentence fluency. *Does my analysis sound thorough and knowledgeable? Have I used (and defined) precise terminology? Do my sentences flow smoothly?*

EDITING

Check for conventions. *Have I used correct punctuation, capitalization, spelling, and grammar?*

PUBLISHING

Present your work. Consider finding an online forum that deals with your topic. Upload your work and invite comments.

Cause-Effect Essay

In the following essay, student writer Jessica Radsma explains the cause behind some intriguing medical practices of the past. She argues that the cause of these practices was the doctors' belief in "humors."

A reference to a film introduces the topic and leads up to the thesis (underlined).

The Humors Theory

In the film *Sense and Sensibility*, an early nineteenth-century English doctor treats his feverish patient, Marianne, by making an incision in her arm and draining some of her blood. The procedure was called *bloodletting*, a widespread medical practice meant to address the imbalance of fluids that caused the illness. The cause of such a bizarre treatment was the humors theory, a theory that strongly affected medical practice from ancient times to the nineteenth century. The humors theory was a simple concept that had far-reaching implications in diagnosing and treating illness.

Radsma summarizes the cause-effect thinking that once governed medical practice.

First, what was the humors theory? Doctors thought that the body held four liquids, or "humors," namely blood, phlegm, black bile, and yellow bile. The unique balance or mix of these four fluids created a person's temperament and affected his or her appearance (Lindberg 332). For example, doctors thought that the domination of blood made someone sanguine, fat and jolly. The domination of phlegm made a person phlegmatic, lazy and sleepy. A lot of black bile created a cold fish, a melancholy person—pensive and solitary. Finally, a lot of yellow bile made a person choleric, quick to get angry (Bettman 72). People became ill when their normal combination of humors was upset in some way.

Belief in the humors theory leads to the use of three diagnostic tools.

The humors theory strongly affected how the medical profession diagnosed illness. When someone got sick, doctors tried to figure out why the patient's humors were out of sync, and to what degree. To help them decide, practitioners used three diagnostic tools: pulse reading, urinalysis, and astrology. Doctors read the pulse to check out the heart and blood. In fact, they came up with a complex classification scheme to measure pulse types and figure out whether such things as the strength, duration, regularity, and breadth were normal for the type (Lindberg 335–337). Examining urine, too, was a way of checking how the humors were working. Urine was checked for color, consistency, odor, and clarity (Lindberg 335). In fact, doctors were trained to detect

Humors theory (the cause) leads to both helpful and foolish practices (the effects).

A quotation from an old medical text adds an authoritative note.

as many as 18 colors in this precious liquid. The instrument used, the urine glass, was divided into four even parts, each standing for a part of the body. For example, if the urine at the top was cloudy, the patient was thought to have head trouble (Bettman 73). Finally, because doctors believed that the heavens influenced the human body, they also connected the unbalanced humors to planetary influences (Lindberg 339).

Humors theory affected how doctors treated illness as well. Having figured out why and how far the humors were out of balance, the practitioner would try to restore order using a variety of treatments, some surprisingly helpful and others outright quackery. Some helpful prescriptions included changes in diet or daily activities, as well as medicines (age-old remedies tested by experience). But the doctors' faith in the humors also caused foolish practices, like bloodletting, or phlebotomy, to restore the balance of the humors. Since doctors believed that the four humors were linked by tubes, bloodletting would release excess bodily fluids. As a medieval medical guidebook put it, "Bleeding soothes rage, brings joy unto the sad, / And saves all lovesick swains from going mad" (Rapport and Wright 84). Bloodletting was a tune-up when the humors were out of sync, a procedure often done in spring and fall (with the help of astrology) to "attune the humors to new climactic conditions" (Bettman 74–75).

Though the humors theory may sound bizarre to people today, it actually represented a step beyond superstition. Instead of blaming supernatural forces for all illness, proponents of the humors theory believed that chemical imbalances caused illness. This unusual theory really was a precursor to modern medicine.

NOTE: **The works-cited page is not shown.**

READING FOR BETTER WRITING

1. How does the writer establish a knowledgeable-sounding, interested voice in this essay?
2. Does the writer primarily appeal to logos, ethos, or pathos in this essay? Explain. (See page 231 for help.)

Cause-Effect Essay

In the following expository essay, the writer identifies the effects of Charlemagne's unification of Europe. The notes in the left margin explain the key parts of the essay.

Charlemagne

The opening paragraph introduces the topic and states the thesis (underlined).

"By the sword or the cross," proclaimed Charles the Great, one of the most fearless and colorful leaders of the Middle Ages. Better known as Charlemagne, this leader utilized both the sword and the cross to become the first crowned emperor of the Holy Roman Empire, a political area including most of Western and Central Europe. During his 32-year rise to power, he was able to unify the nations of that area into a strong, single entity. Charlemagne's unification of Europe brought peace to all the people, stabilized the European economy, and promoted education.

The middle paragraphs provide background information and discuss three effects.

Charles was the son of Pippin, king of the Franks, whose title he inherited in 768. With this responsibility, Charles developed the leadership and management skills he eventually used to rule much of Europe. He gained control of European lands by political maneuvering, waging war, and spreading Christianity to unite the people under a common religion. Charles earned the reputation of being a fair-minded, diplomatic leader (Judd). In the year 800, Pope Leo III crowned Charles as Emperor *Carolus Magnus*. That Latin name translates to *Charlemagne* in Old French. Charlemagne brought about solidarity among kingdoms and unified continental Europe.

One of Charlemagne's greatest gifts was his skillful peacemaking ability. Prior to his reign, civil uprisings erupted continually as peasants grew weary of funding military campaigns by paying heavy taxes or forfeiting their land. Charlemagne organized the resources of each region to avoid heavy taxing. He started by collecting tolls, custom duties, and tributes from conquered peoples and distributing the funds to the regions where they were most needed (Judd). Charlemagne endeared himself to his subjects when he showed mercy to captured invading troops. When peasant and nobleman alike realized that they were being treated fairly, a feeling of trust and peace spread throughout Europe.

The writer uses facts and paraphrases to develop his thesis.

In order to maintain peace, Charlemagne soon realized that he needed to stabilize the economy in the entire region. He divided larger parcels of land into more manageable estates that were self-contained and administered by a steward or caretaker. Each estate had a bustling center of commerce surrounded by a market, church, guilds, and public buildings. The remaining land was rented to the farmers who produced the crops that fed the people living on the estate. In return, the stewards provided protection and administered justice. The changes instituted by Charlemagne created an intricately balanced system of commerce and trade and stabilized the European economy (Axelrod).

With peace and a more stable economy in place, Charlemagne was then able to concentrate his efforts on education. He assembled the greatest minds of the entire region into an "academy" whose members traveled with and advised Charlemagne. Artists, scientists, and teachers, who were educated at the monasteries, were sent to other regions to share their knowledge. Due to Charlemagne's efforts, education was promoted and learning flourished throughout his empire.

The final paragraph ties all the key points together and connects with the thesis statement.

Charlemagne died in 814 at the age of 72. During his reign as king of the Franks and as emperor, he succeeded in unifying Europe, leaving behind a legacy of peace, economic stability, and an appreciation for the value of education. He cherished the written word and preserved the rich culture of his era. Although historians may judge Charlemagne as a foreign invader rather than a hero, it is difficult to imagine how Europe would have developed without the influence of this dynamic leader who lived "by the sword or the cross."

NOTE: The works-cited page is not shown.

READING FOR BETTER WRITING

1. What is the writer's intention or purpose in this essay?
2. Analyze the writer's use of verbs. Are there a lot of "be" verbs, strong action verbs, slow-moving passive verbs? How do the verbs affect the overall voice?

Writing a Problem-Solution Essay

A problem-solution essay closely examines all aspects of a problem and then suggests a reasonable solution. The effectiveness of a problem-solution essay depends on the writer's ability to understand a topic in all of its complexity.

PREWRITING

Select a topic. Consider major problems that leaders or scientists face or have encountered in the past. Search resources for complex and important problems that would allow for an in-depth analysis.

Gather details. Create a problem-solution chart (see page 227) to help you consider all aspects of the problem and solution.

Write a thesis statement. Create a sentence or two that provides a compelling insight into the problem and its solution.

Outline your essay. Arrange the main points and accompanying details that support your thesis. Make sure to explore all facets of the problem before presenting the solution.

WRITING

Write your first draft. Introduce the problem and your thesis. Provide important background about the problem and fully explain the issues involved. Then shift to discussing the solution. In the ending, reflect on the probable success and the limitations of the solution.

REVISING

Check your ideas. *Have I discussed all aspects of the problem? Have I realistically presented the solution? Have I addressed significant objections?*

Review your organization. *Does my beginning introduce the problem and explain its importance? Does the middle provide sufficient background and clearly present the solution? Does the ending sum up the analysis?*

Revise for voice, word choice, and sentence fluency. *Have I created an interested and knowledgeable voice? Have I defined technical terms and concepts? Do I use precise nouns and active verbs? Have I included a variety of sentences?*

EDITING

Check for conventions. *Have I used correct punctuation, capitalization, spelling, and grammar?*

PUBLISHING

Present your work. If you have addressed a historical problem, post your work on a Web site dedicated to that time period. If you have tackled a current problem, consider formatting your work as a letter to the editor. Then send it to a local paper.

Problem-Solution Essay

Jennifer Tomlinson's problem-solution essay focuses on the problem of antibiotic resistance. She clearly explains the problem before advocating a set of clear, reasonable steps to solve it.

A surprising statistic grabs the reader's interest.

The thesis statement (underlined) focuses on the problem.

The writer defines the term *broad-spectrum antibiotic*.

A paragraph focuses on how resistance forms.

Another paragraph explains how resistance is spread.

Bacteria Fight Back

In the United States, doctors inappropriately prescribe antibiotics 50 million times a year (Lieberman and Wootan). Why? Simply put, there is no cure for the common cold or the flu, but suffering patients beg for a prescription, and they get antibiotics, even though these drugs are powerless against viral infections. The overuse of antibiotics has resulted in the development of bacterial strains that are resistant to these drugs, a serious threat to world health.

Antibiotics interfere with "a specific bacterial enzyme or process" and thereby kill the bacteria or inhibit its reproduction (Salyers and Whitt 152). The most effective antibiotics attack multiple bacteria strains without harming human cells or causing serious side effects. These "broad-spectrum antibiotics" allow doctors to treat an infection without identifying an exact strain of bacteria (Salyes and Whitt 154). Some of the most effective antibiotics, however, are losing their potency due to the development of resistant strains.

Bacteria develop antibiotic resistance when a spontaneous mutation provides accidental protection for a given cell (Bren). The mutation may prevent the antibiotic from crossing the outer membrane of the bacteria, may pump the antibiotic out as soon as it enters, or may even "sequester" the antibiotic in a safe compartment within the cell. Some mutations also produce enzymes that neutralize the antibiotic or keep it from activating ("Bugs"). Though these mutations are accidental, they quickly provide the cell with a survival advantage.

When a bacterium has spontaneously developed a defense against a given antibiotic, use of the antibiotic actually selects the cell for survival. Nonresistant bacteria die, but the "superbug" lives on to reproduce rampantly. Because bacteria can reproduce in 20 minutes, one cell can give way to hundreds of generations of superbugs within a single day

("Resistant"). Bacteria can also pass their resistance on to other strains. Simply by brushing up against each other, bacteria can exchange plasmids, the compartment that holds their chromosomes. In this way, antibiotic resistance can pass from one strain of bacteria to a completely different strain ("Bugs").

A historical case study demonstrates the growing problem.

Although scientists and physicians knew about antibiotic resistance before the 1970s, the problem was not recognized as serious until the 1990s. In a study of *Bacteroides* strains, a type of bacteria that can lead to infections in the blood, scientists "found that before 1970, about 25 percent of the strains were resistant to tetracycline, and none were resistant to erythromycin. By the late 1990s, over 80 percent of the *Bacteroides* strains were resistant to tetracycline, and nearly one-third were resistant to erythromycin" (Salyers and Whitt 180).

The negative effects of the problem show its seriousness.

Antibiotic resistance leads to prolonged illnesses, higher health-care costs, and sometimes even death (Spelhaug). Because the very use of antibiotics stimulates the development of resistant strains, the most virulent bacteria often stalk hospital halls. In the 1990s, the bacteria *S. aureus*—also known as MRSA—was most commonly contracted by patients with extensive hospital stays. Twenty-one percent of the MRSA cases resulted in the death of the patient because there were no antibiotics available to fight the bacteria (Salyers and Whitt 169).

The writer shifts to solutions.

One way to solve the problem of antibiotic resistance is to develop new antibiotics. "The need for research directed toward development of new antibiotics has never been greater" (Cassell and Mekalanos 77). However, antibiotic development is a costly and lengthy process. One new antibiotic costs an average of $800 million to create, and the development process takes about 10 years (Finkelstein 6). Also, new antibiotics may not be as convenient as the former variety. Stronger antibiotics would not be available in pill form, but would instead need to be injected directly into the patient's bloodstream (Spelhaug).

The writer outlines clear, easily implemented steps to solve the problem.

Instead of waiting for pharmaceutical companies to develop new antibiotics, the public should take three simple steps to slow down the development of resistant bacteria. The first step is hand washing. Washing hands, especially after using the restroom and before eating anything, reduces the amount of bacteria entering a person's body and lowers the chance of passing bacteria to other people ("Antibiotic Resistance").

The second step to controlling the spread of resistant strains is to stop asking for antibiotic prescriptions for colds and the flu. One study estimates that during the last decade, 90 percent of the people who received an antibiotic prescription for a sore throat actually were suffering from a viral infection (Spelhaug). Instead of guzzling antibiotics, these patients should have been guzzling water, which is cheaper and more effective in fighting viruses.

The third step to controlling antibiotic resistance is to take antibiotics exactly as prescribed by the doctor. In a study performed by the Mayo Clinic, 31 percent of patients claimed that they do not regularly finish their full course of antibiotics. One in every four people interviewed have even saved extra antibiotics for future use (Spelhaug). By stopping short of the full course or by taking antibiotics in small amounts later, the patient is simply killing off the least resistant bacteria and leaving the most resistant bacteria to multiply (Bren).

The writer puts the current crisis in historical perspective.

Nearly 70 years ago, Howard Florey and Ernst Chain developed the first antibiotic, penicillin, and ushered in a new age of disease control (Bellis). Now, the misuse of antibiotics is threatening to end that age. "Although defining the precise public health risk of emergent antibiotic resistance is not simple, there is little doubt the problem is global in scope and very serious" (Cassell and Mekalanos 78). While drug companies work on new antibiotics, the public needs to fight bacteria through hand washing, accepting the doctor's advice about whether an antibiotic is needed, and taking the medications exactly as prescribed. Following these simple procedures can safeguard the health of the individual—and of our whole species.

NOTE: The works-cited page is not shown.

READING FOR BETTER WRITING

This essay uses a great deal of technical language. How does the writer deal with the technical terms? What effect does the use of this language have on the writer's voice?

Problem-Solution Essay

In the following problem-solution essay, Jacqueline Wojcik focuses on the desperate plight of Cuban refugees. She spends half of her essay clearly explaining the problem before she argues for a specific solution.

The writer begins with a commanding vision.

Ninety Miles to Freedom

On a clear day, natives of Havana, Cuba, can look across a 90-mile stretch of the Gulf of Mexico and see the skyscrapers in Miami, Florida. The sight of freedom compels some people to climb aboard boats or rafts to try to reach Miami—a decision that more often than not proves unsuccessful or even fatal. In addition to battling winds and waves in their homemade crafts, Cuban refugees also must battle a United States policy that makes their perilous decision even more desperate.

The thesis statement (underlined) outlines the problem.

The first paragraph provides background and gives an example.

To understand the plight of Cuban refugees, one merely needs to consider a typical escape attempt. On March 18 of 2004, eight Cubans started paddling in the Gulf of Mexico, bound for Florida. They had constructed a crude vessel by tying inner tubes together. Large waves, a deficient water supply, and the blazing sun killed five of the eight. One of the survivors, Milena Gonzalez Martinez, had to watch her husband succumb to delusions and drown. "He kept jumping up and down and saying we should jump into the water and swim for shore. I told him to calm down, hang on to the raft. But he kept jumping off. The waves were high, and he swallowed a lot of water" (qtd. in Olmeda). Even though she survived this harrowing journey, Mrs. Martinez did not reach the United States or gain refugee status. She was picked up by the U.S. Coast Guard and returned to Cuba—there to face prosecution and possible imprisonment.

The next paragraph gets at the crux of the problem.

Mrs. Martinez was returned to Cuba due to a policy instituted by President Bill Clinton on May 2, 1995. The so-called "Wet Foot/Dry Foot" policy stated that if people fleeing Cuba set foot on U.S. soil, they would be treated as refugees, but if they were intercepted by the Coast Guard at sea, they would be returned to Cuba ("U.S.-Cuba"). This policy was a response to the 1994 "mass exodus" of 40 thousand Cubans due to Fidel Castro's proclamation that all Cubans could leave if they so wished. It was a shrewd move by Castro. By releasing this tide of refugees, he forced the United States to take responsibility for patrolling his borders and keeping his citizens in place.

The writer uses definitions to provide a pivot point for her essay.

The "Wet Foot/Dry Foot" policy may seem like a reasonable reaction to these events, especially during the current attempts to seal the U.S. southern border. However, the policy ignores the distinction between immigrants (illegal and otherwise) and refugees. According to *Webster's*, an immigrant is merely "a person who comes to a country to take up permanent residence," while a refugee is "one who flees . . . a foreign country or power to escape danger or persecution." Under these definitions, Cubans are refugees deserving help—not hindrance. To put the matter another way, this is not an immigration problem; it is a humanitarian crisis.

The writer provides more support for her claim of injustice.

The injustice of the "Wet Foot/Dry Foot" policy has also encouraged a dangerous business: human trafficking. Immigration and Naturalization Service spokesman Mike Gilhooly estimates that 80 percent of Cubans who try to escape have to pay from $1,000 to $9,000 a head for their journeys. In November 1999, the ill-fated crossing of Elian Gonzales cost $14,000 and 11 lives, including that of Elian's mother (Robinson 29).

The essay anticipates and answers the reader's main objections.

Supporters of the "Wet Foot/Dry Foot" policy argue that if Cuban refugees were welcomed into the United States, they would either become a permanent burden on the U.S. welfare system or would move into the job market, depriving citizens of employment. These fears are at best overstated and at worst downright false.

Yes, the influx of refugees does burden the welfare system—temporarily. Refugees, unlike immigrants, are eligible for welfare as soon as they come into the United States (Simon 9). That is because their situation is so desperate. When Cuban refugees reach U.S. shores, they are without any possessions and sometimes without any native family or friends. They need to buy food and clothing while they search for a job. However, according to the Cato Institute, the "total per capita government expenditures on immigrants are much lower than those for natives, no matter how immigrants are classified [refugee or immigrant]" (Simon 4). In addition, refugees are 1.5 times more likely to become citizens than any other type of new arrival (Fix 7). The welfare burden created by refugees is small and temporary—an investment that pays dividends as refugees assimilate, get jobs, and pay taxes.

An excerpt answers the objection with authority.

The eventual success of the refugee population concerns other proponents of the "Wet Foot/Dry Foot" policy. They fear that refugees will take jobs away from U.S. citizens. However, a study by the Cato Institute and the National Immigration Forum demonstrated that this fear is unfounded:

> Immigrants do not cause native unemployment, even among low-paid or minority groups. [. . .] The explanation is that new entrants not only take jobs, they make jobs. The jobs they create with their purchasing power, and with the new businesses which they start, are at least as numerous as the jobs which the immigrants fill. (Simon 9)

The writer carefully documents sources.

Since most Cuban refugees do not speak English, the first jobs they take are often the difficult minimum-wage positions that citizens shun. "Many refugees . . . arrive and find that, at least temporarily, they no longer are qualified to be doctors, lawyers, nurses, teachers, or engineers. Language is the biggest barrier. Just as often they need additional college credits or certification" (Steele). Armando Flores worked with an engineering degree in Cuba. Now, in Florida, he drives an airport shuttle. Is he upset? No. He says, "I'm so happy to be here, I'll never go back to Cuba" (qtd. in Steele). Of course, he spends the money he makes on food, clothing, and shelter, creating more jobs for others.

The ending sums up the essay and provides a larger context for the ideas.

To summarize, the "Wet Foot/Dry Foot" policy should be rescinded because it is unjust and is based on unfounded fears. Whenever people flee tyranny, danger, and persecution, the United States should help them, not hinder them. Of course, the nation's response to humanitarian crises is spotty at best. Though the United States sent troops to end the ethnic cleansing in Kosovo, the country turned a blind eye to the ethnic cleansing in Darfur. While the United States has opened doors to Hmong refugees, it has closed them to Cubans. It's time for the "Wet Foot/Dry Foot" policy to end, and time for the United States to return to a more empathetic credo:

> Give me your tired, your poor,
> Your huddled masses yearning to breathe free,
> [. . . . .]
> Send these, the homeless, tempest-tost to me,
> I lift my lamp beside the golden door! (Lazarus 14)

NOTE: The works-cited page is not shown.

Writing an Essay of Evaluation

In an essay of evaluation, a writer acts like a roving critic, exploring the worth of an event, a trend, a product, a decision, or so on. The essay explores the topic's value, impact, and significance; its strengths and weaknesses; its place in the scheme of things.

PREWRITING

Select a topic. Write *people, places, events,* and *trends* on a piece of paper turned lengthwise. Then list topic ideas under each heading. Choose a topic that fits the scope of your assignment.

Research the topic. Conduct primary research by experiencing the topic firsthand—interviewing people, visiting places, attending events, trying out trends. Also carry out secondary research by consulting periodicals, books, and Web sites.

Organize your essay. Write a thesis statement and list points that support it. Then turn the list into an outline for your essay.

WRITING

Write your first draft. Grab the reader's interest and introduce your topic. Then explore the topic fully, demonstrating its value and importance, its strengths and weaknesses. In the ending, place the topic in a greater context for the reader and provide a final evaluation.

REVISING

Check your ideas. *Have I selected an interesting topic that fits the assignment? Have I based my evaluation on primary and secondary research? Have I included a variety of details to support my position? Have I shared significant judgments or insights?*

Review your organization. *Does my beginning introduce the topic in an engaging way? Does the middle thoroughly explore the topic? Does the ending create a clear evaluation? Do I use transitions between paragraphs and sentences?*

Revise for voice, word choice, and sentence fluency. *Have I used precise nouns and active verbs? Have I included a variety of sentences?*

EDITING

Check for conventions. *Have I used correct punctuation, capitalization, spelling, and grammar?*

PUBLISHING

Present your work. Find a forum that accepts reviews and essays—perhaps online, in a magazine or fanzine, or in a school or local newspaper. Then format and submit your work.

Essay of Evaluation

In this essay of evaluation, Joyce Lee slogs through the quagmire of modern reality TV shows. With diverse examples and a lively voice, this essay explains and critiques this pop-culture phenomenon.

Keeping It Real?

Vignettes grab the reader's interest.

A family confronts its deepest secrets as tears fall and fists fly. Diverse groups of people in a closed environment compete and scheme against each other, using whatever means they can to come out on top. Verbal fireworks explode as two litigants debase each other in front of a judge. Private issues? Absolutely. But these intensely personal conflicts are presented before an audience of millions. Welcome to a bizarre, pugilistic world in which ordinary people humiliate themselves for valuable prizes and a little fame. Welcome to reality TV.

The writer presents a stylized thesis (underlined).

Background is provided.

Reality TV is not a new concept. As early as 1948, Allen Funt's *Candid Camera* presented real people in silly situations. In 1950, game shows like *Beat the Clock* and *Truth or Consequences* showed contestants doing silly stunts to win cash and prizes. Even *American Idol* can trace its roots to 1948's *Ted Mack's Original Amateur Hour* and *Arthur Godfrey's Talent Scouts* (David 12).

Early reality shows were silly, light entertainment, but then a serious stab at reality TV was taken by PBS in 1973, when it presented *An American Family*. This was the first show to place a camera inside a family's home and closely observe the family members' lives. The show became unexpectedly dramatic as America watched the Loud family disintegrate right on the TV screen ("American"). That was the beginning of the modern idea of reality TV, and as the century turned, the genre really caught on, reaching new heights of comedy and drama—both unexpected and intentional.

The writer analyzes the success of reality TV shows.

Reality TV usually places ordinary people in extraordinary circumstances. As Andy Warhol said in 1968, "In the future everyone will be world-famous for 15 minutes" (qtd. in Paulson). Reality TV specializes in getting viewers to identify with participants and vicariously live through them. According to the sensitivity theory put forth by Steven Reiss and James Wiltz of Ohio State University, there are 16 basic desires that create joy: power, curiosity, independence, status, social contact, vengeance, honor, idealism, physical exercise, romance, family, order, eating, acceptance, tranquility, and saving. These two psychologists theorize that "we embrace television viewing as a convenient, minimal effort means of vicariously experiencing the 16 joys repeatedly" (Reiss).

Transitions help the reader track the argument.

Though some reality TV shows play on the viewers' empathy, others play on their antipathy. Shows such as *Fear Factor* routinely require participants to degrade themselves by eating live bugs or smearing their bodies with noxious substances. Brad Waite of Central Connecticut State University calls this phenomenon "humilitainment" ("Reality Check"). The appeal of such programs may simply be the "gaper's block" phenomenon: People can't look away from a car wreck. Or the appeal may be darker—the *schadenfreude* of taking pleasure in another's misery (David 14).

Each paragraph evaluates a different aspect of the topic.

Another reason for the popularity of reality TV is its apparent unpredictability. Most reality shows follow a contest format, combining the characters and plots of a soap opera with the uncertainty of a football game. Often, participants, judges, or even the audience "vote people off" the show, providing an even greater sense of uncertainty and participation. However, the uncertainty is often an illusion. Story editors plan episodes to create conflict. They also work with more than a hundred hours of film to cut a single one-hour episode. In this way, the story editors often manipulate character development, create stronger emotional responses, and present an altered reality (Eidlestein).

Cost may be the other driver in the proliferation of reality TV shows. In his *Washington Post* article "Reality Is Only an Illusion, Writers Say," William Booth suggests that reality programs have proliferated because they are cheap to produce, but they still bring in huge audiences. In a time when the average TV sitcom star can demand hundreds of thousands of dollars *per episode*, why wouldn't studio executives leap at the chance to have a large, interesting cast for free?

The writer sums up the evaluation.

Real or not, "reality TV" shows no signs of slowing down. As long as people want to root for the underdog or watch people air their dirty laundry or seek romance, reality TV will be a reality of modern life.

NOTE: The works-cited page is not shown.

Essay of Evaluation

In this essay of evaluation, Julie Ooms explores the strange new world of computer athletics. Throughout her essay, she assesses the worth of this new trend, but her final page provides one long, complex evaluation.

Cyberathletics: The Spectator Sport of the Future

The essay begins with an interesting definition, which leads to the thesis statement (underlined).

In 2005, *The Independent*, a newsmagazine in London, informed the public of a new word added to the English language: "cyberathlete." According to the magazine, a cyberathlete is a professional player of computer games ("Cyberathlete"). As crazy as that concept might sound to some people, to others, it's only a matter of time before cyberathletes and their digital arenas become as much a part of everyday life as quarterbacks and football fields.

The writer provides a broad overview of the trend.

Cyberathletics has been gaining popularity and media coverage steadily since the official conception of professional video gaming in 1996. From that time to the present, cyberathletic tournaments have popped up on every continent except Antarctica. Events have received increasing coverage not only in magazines that target gaming enthusiasts but also in periodicals like the *Boston Globe, Time, ESPN The Magazine, Business Week,* and the *Washington Post*. The world of professional video gaming is apparently worth popular—and often prestigious—attention.

Statistics demonstrate the growing support of the trend.

The attention is hardly surprising, considering the statistics. In June of 2005, *ESPN The Magazine* reported that the upcoming Cyberathletics Professional League (CPL) Extreme Summer Championships would include "7,300 registered gamers, 60 countries, more than $200,000 in prize money and 40,000 online fans." That same year, *60 Minutes* reported "worldwide sales of video game consoles and software are expected to reach $35 billion this year—that's more than twice the revenue of the NFL, the NBA, and Major League Baseball combined." With hundreds of millions of people buying and playing video games worldwide, CBS calls the rise of cyberathletics, and the mutation of video gaming into a spectator sport, "inevitable" ("Cyber").

Early video gaming started with simple games like Pong and Atari, played on TV screens via one- or two-player consoles with joysticks and a few buttons. Cyberathletics employ PC's and mice, and gamers from all over the world compete through Internet connections and Web-wide gaming forums. In fact, that's how most organized gaming in the United States happened at first, online. However, in 1996, a man named Angel Munoz quit his job as an investment banker and organized the first offline CPL tournament, known as "The FRAG" (The Foremost Roundup of Advanced Gamers). On October 31, 1997, gamers came from all over the United States and the world to the InfoMart in Dallas, Texas, and set up their desktops (the event was strictly BYOC—Bring Your Own Computer) in a 12,000-square-foot room at the back of the InfoMart. Tables for two gamers each were set up on the concrete floor, and booths for vendors lined the walls. Three hundred gamers attended the event, which is considered by members to have laid the foundation for the development of what is now recognized worldwide as the Cyberathletic Professional League, the world's leading professional computer gaming league ("History").

The writer explains how the trend began.

The second tournament, called simply "The CPL Event," took place at the same InfoMart in July of 1998. The third, dubbed "The FRAG 2," occurred in October of the same year—this time, at a bigger venue in Dallas because the event had outgrown its humble quarters at the InfoMart. It has done nothing but grow since ("History").

Such growth has enabled some people to actually earn their living playing video games, thus becoming cyberathletes. The best cyberathlete in the world is an American named Jonathan Wendel (or "Fatal1ty," his screen name, by which online gamers know him). Wendel has been pro since he was 18 and has won world championships in four different video games and over $300,000 in tournament prize money in that time. He's traveled to six of the seven continents at no personal expense, has played in Moscow's Red Square and on the Great Wall of China, and is inundated with fans wherever he goes ("Cyber"). He is treated just like a baseball, football, or soccer star.

The writer gives an example of a cyberathlete superstar.

Can video gaming really be considered a sport? Wendel told *60 Minutes* that video gaming is "all about hand-eye coordination, reflexes, timing, strategy, being quick on your feet, being able to think fast. . . . You have to be doing everything" ("Cyber"). In this way, it shares in the physical and mental demands of more traditional sports. David Laprod, a writer for the cyberathlete's magazine *Adrenaline Vault*, says that "like football or pool, *Deathmatch* requires strategic

The writer poses the reader's questions and then answers them.

thinking, the embellishment of defensive boundaries, and precision point coordination. Like a marathon, it requires endurance in the pursuit of the highest frag count [or score]. And like a win-or-lose 10th frame strike, the participants must keep their cool." Apparently, then, experts agree that competitive video gaming is, indeed, a sport, an increasingly popular and profitable one at that.

Comparisons between cyberathletics and traditional sports strengthen the evaluation.

Is it really okay for cyberathletes to spend hours trying to kill people in a virtual gaming world? Most gamers compare video gaming to professional sports, this time focusing on the violence inherent in many athletic events. "You're trying to get to a point," Wendel says. "Like, I mean, football. Why are you hitting the guy? That's not right. But people will accept it, because that's part of the game" ("Cyber"). If we can endorse football violence, virtual violence must be okay as well. Another reason to endorse cyberathletics, notes Laprod, is the fact that the sport is gender neutral. Competitive gaming allows both male and female cyberathletes to compete on the same plane, in the same tournaments, for the same prizes, something football has never and likely will never achieve without the invention of some sort of miracle steroid ("The FRAG").

The trend is placed in the context of global communication networks.

Why are cyberathletics taking over the world? Perhaps the most obvious reason is the massive growth of communication over the past few decades. Edward Castronova, an Indiana University professor who studies the economics and sociology of video games, feels that cyberathletics represent a very broad communication phenomenon. If we can instantly chat online or via cell phone from our living room in northwest Iowa with our loved one in the Netherlands, it's not surprising that we can blast to death the virtual manifestation of a South Korean video gamer known online as "Apoc." Professional video gaming encourages a weird sort of camaraderie among participants (Castronova).

The writer addresses concerns about reality versus fantasy.

Are we simply, then, giving up on reality? All the battles are virtual, all the names are made up, all the weapons are comprised of a certain number of colored pixels on a computer screen. In actual football games, people get hurt because they're actually out there *doing* something, interacting with their fellow human beings on a physical level. The football player and the cyberathlete both have their minds focused on the game while they're playing, but the football player feels the contact. He moves, performs real actions that have real consequences in the real world. The video gamer, though he (or she) might jerk occasionally in his (or her) chair, is a sedentary figure with twitching fingers; the only sound is the rapid clicking of a mouse.

The writer outlines a complex personal evaluation of the trend.

We need to be careful of what we're endorsing. As a frequent critic of professional sports and the absurd salaries paid to the players, I am inclined to applaud cyberathletics as a phenomenon destined to put all those too-rich, iron-pumping athletes in their places—a sort of ultimate "revenge of the nerds." But do we really need another set of professional athletes? Even more worrisome is the effect video gaming has on people; I've seen it happen to my cousins. Video gaming entices the player with an escape that is horrifically similar to that of a drug. It seems that the more dire we think our situation is and the less we want to deal with what's going on in our lives, the more we turn to something that could take us away, even for a little while.

The final paragraph puts the full evaluation into perspective.

Cyberathletes are undoubtedly talented people who work extremely hard to get where they want to be. Cyberathletics certainly has its upsides, forging bonds between people across oceans and national borders. However, we need to be careful about what we let control us, our economy, and our leisure time. Perhaps the very essence of a cultural phenomenon is its ability to overtake people before they're even aware of what's happened. However, the first step on the road to discerning the good and the bad about anything, including cyberathletics, is learning about it. It's immeasurably better, however "inevitable" the growing prominence of cyberathletics may be, to know what's happening, to remain informed as the phenomenon changes and grows, and to make sure you're always aware that your name is, in fact, John Smith, and not "Cybersmith of Havoc."

NOTE: **The works-cited page is not shown.**

READING FOR BETTER WRITING

This essay presents a multifaceted evaluation, at times defending and even praising the movement of cyberathletics, and at times presenting strong cautions. Would the essay be stronger or weaker if it had a single point of view? Explain.

Using Graphic Organizers

Graphic organizers can help you think through your analytical writing. At a glance, you will know what to do when you are asked to compare, classify, define, evaluate, and so on.

Process Analysis

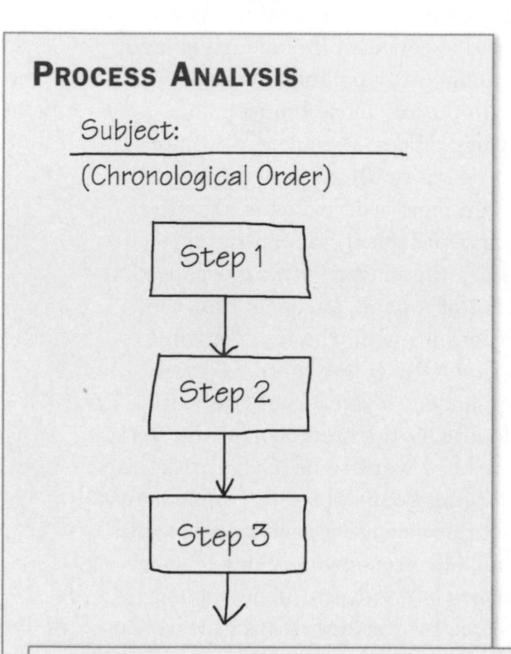

Comparison

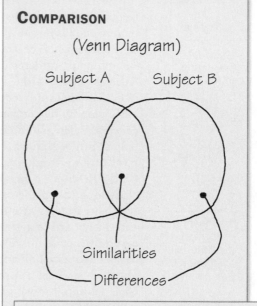

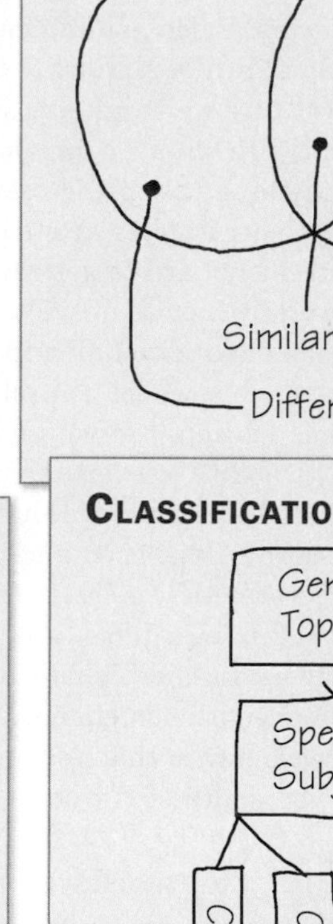

Comparison

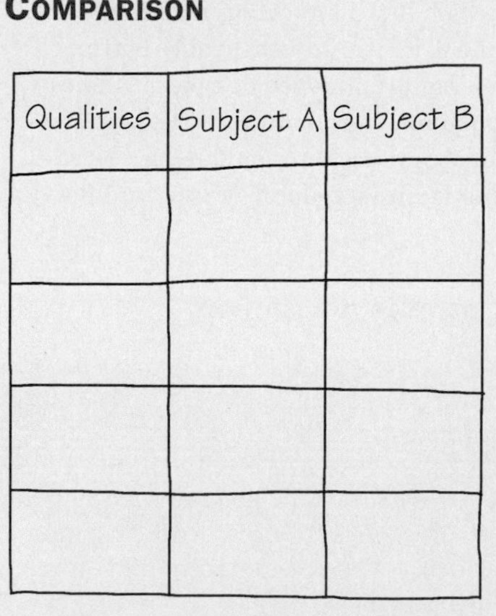

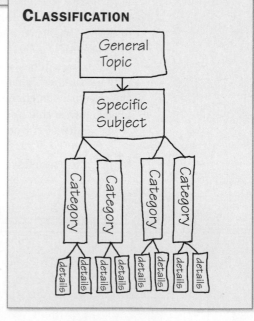

Classification

Cause and Effect

Subject:

Causes	Effects
(Because of . . .)	(. . . these conditions resulted)
•	•
•	•
•	•

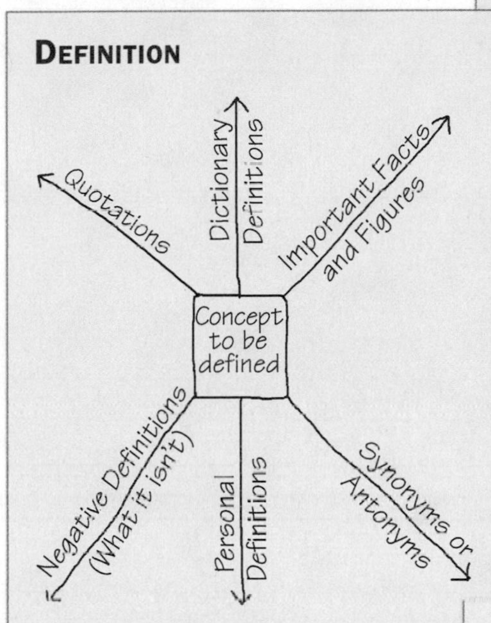

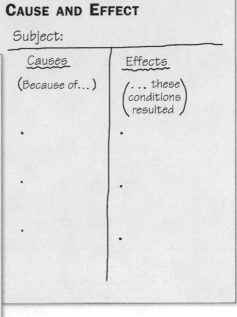

Evaluation Collection Grid

Subject:

Points to Evaluate	Supporting Details
1.	
2.	
3.	
4.	
5.	

Problem and Solution

Causes of the Problem

Parts of the Problem

Problem

Future Implications

Possible Solutions

Persuasive Writing

Persuasive Writing

Sir Isaac Newton devised three laws of motion: an object at rest remains at rest unless acted on by an external force; the force applied to an object equals its mass times its acceleration; and for every action, there is an equal and opposite reaction. Newton might as well have been postulating the three laws of persuasion:

1. An opinion at rest remains at rest unless acted on by an argument.
2. The force of an argument equals its mass times its acceleration.
3. For every argument, there is a counterargument.

Like physics, persuasive writing is dynamic. Thomas Paine wrote a little persuasive pamphlet called *Common Sense* and sparked democratic revolutions in the West. Karl Marx wrote a persuasive pamphlet called *The Communist Manifesto* and sparked equal and opposite revolutions in the East. Persuasive writing, when done well, can change the world.

WHAT'S AHEAD

Persuasive writing takes many forms, from a brief, tightly crafted editorial to a longer, looser commentary about life. In addition to these two forms, this chapter also includes essays of argumentation and position papers.

"I would rather try to persuade a man to go along, because once I have persuaded him, he will stick. If I scare him, he will stay just as long as he is scared, and then he is gone."

—Dwight D. Eisenhower

Persuasive Writing

QUICK GUIDE

Preparing a persuasive essay is much like preparing for a debate. You study an issue from different perspectives, establish a main argument, and gather support. You also plan a strategy to counter the opposition, and so on. When writing persuasively, always keep your silent debating opponent in mind.

All persuasive writing shares the following characteristics:

- **STARTING POINT:** In persuasive writing, you begin with a strong feeling about an important issue, one about which there are significant differences of opinion.
- **PURPOSE:** Your goal is to convince readers to agree with your argument (or to accept its validity).
- **FORM:** Most persuasive writing follows a predictable pattern: An opinion is expressed and fully supported. Opposing arguments are addressed. Then, in closing, the opinion is reasserted with added extensions or insights.
- **AUDIENCE:** Always have a clear sense of your readers, whether writing peers or a more general audience. What do they already know about the topic? What objections may they have to your opinion?
- **VOICE:** Speak with confidence and assurance, but also be reasonable and fair in your comments. This will help you gain the confidence of your readers.
- **POINT OF VIEW:** Use the third person *(he, she, they)* in most persuasive writing. However, in personal commentaries and in persuasive essays stemming from direct experience, the first person *(I)* may be appropriate.

INSIDE INFO

Try a prewriting activity. Create a *dialogue* between two people who disagree about your topic. Play the dialogue out to a logical stopping point, or simply *list* arguments for your opinion in one column and arguments against it in another column. Both activities will help you gain control of your topic.

Rhetoric and Persuasion

In Ancient Greece, thinkers such as the Sophists and Aristotle devised a system of persuasion called *rhetoric*. The word *rhetoric* comes from the Greek word *rhetor*, which means "orator." At that time, written documents were rare, so most persuasion was done orally. Over the course of the next 2,500 years, rhetoric came to encompass all aspects of persuasion, including written argumentative essays.

Aristotle and Rhetoric

In *The Art of Rhetoric,* Aristotle presented a triad (triangle) that showed the three fundamental components of rhetoric. Each component has its own persuasive appeal.

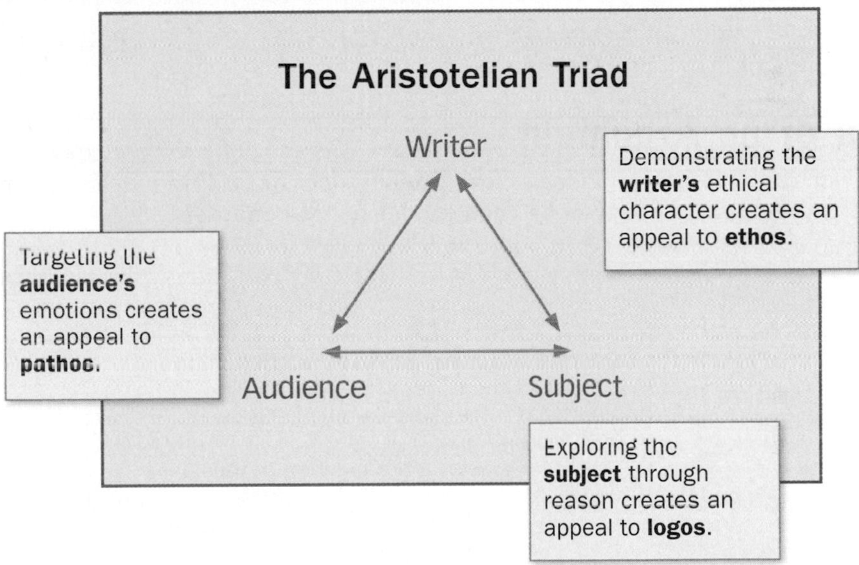
The Aristotelian Triad
Writer
Audience
Subject
Demonstrating the writer's ethical character creates an appeal to ethos.
Targeting the audience's emotions creates an appeal to pathos.
Exploring the subject through reason creates an appeal to logos.

Aristotle also delineated three different genres of rhetoric, which address the past, the present, and the future.

Genres of Rhetoric		
Past ⟷	Present ⟷	Future
Forensic rhetoric is used by judges and lawyers to show the truth or falsity of events in the past.	*Epideictic rhetoric* is used by public figures at ceremonies to praise or blame some event in the present.	*Deliberative rhetoric* is used by leaders and lawmakers to forecast what should be done in the future.

Canons of Rhetoric

About 400 years after Aristotle, the Roman rhetorician Quintilian outlined five canons of oratory (speech making). The five canons connect generally with the steps in the writing process:

Canons		Process
Invention	Gathering and assembling details	Prewriting
Arrangement	Developing the parts of the argument	Writing
Style	Carefully constructing parts and sentences	Revising
Memory	Mastering every word of the argument	Editing
Delivery	Presenting the argument to an audience	Publishing

Parts of an Argument

Classic rhetoric also provides a clear progression for building an argument, a structure generally followed by each model in this chapter.

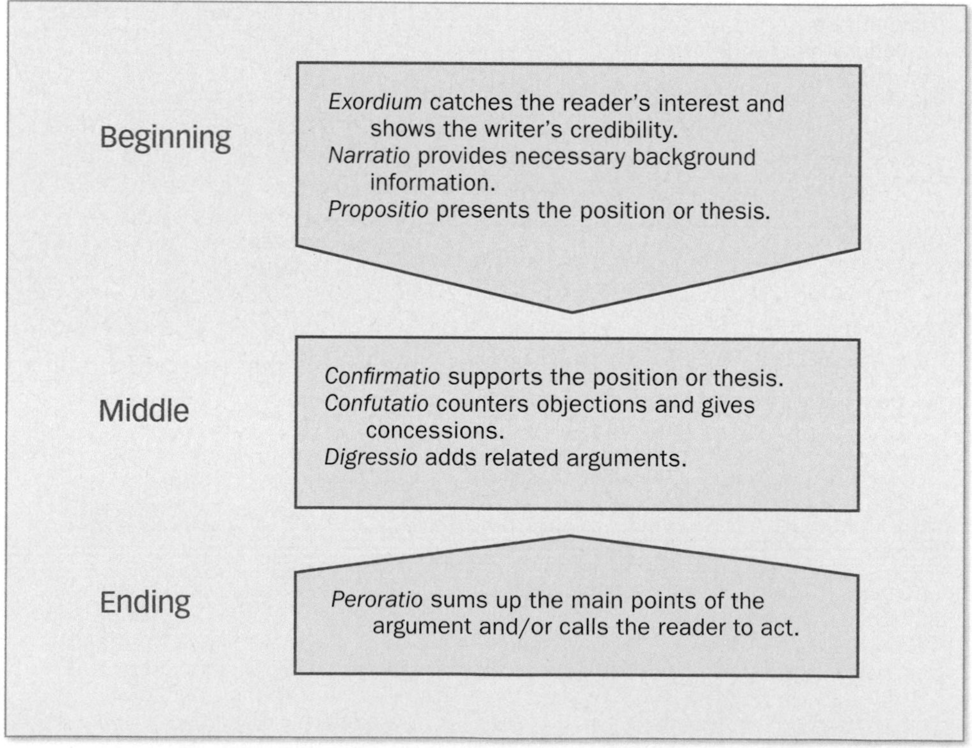

Beginning
Exordium catches the reader's interest and shows the writer's credibility.
Narratio provides necessary background information.
Propositio presents the position or thesis.
Middle
Confirmatio supports the position or thesis.
Confutatio counters objections and gives concessions.
Digressio adds related arguments.
Ending
Peroratio sums up the main points of the argument and/or calls the reader to act.

Guidelines

Writing an Editorial

An editorial is a persuasive essay expressing an opinion about a timely issue. Editorials usually appear in newspapers, magazines, or blogs, and they are written in a style that is direct, clear, and confident. Use vigorous prose and short paragraphs. Refer to the guidelines below.

PREWRITING

Select a topic. Review magazines, newspapers, and Web sites, watching for controversial issues in the news. Select a topic that you have strong feelings about.

Research the topic. Read factual articles related to the topic and form your opinion. Then review opinion pieces on both sides of the issue and revise your opinion as needed.

Create a position statement. Write a single sentence that succinctly and powerfully presents your position.

WRITING

Write your first draft. Grab the reader's interest and provide your position statement. Then develop your argument by incorporating strong supporting details and countering any significant objections. End with a clear restatement of your position and, if appropriate, a call to action.

REVISING

Check your ideas. *Do I have strong feelings about my topic? Is my position clear? Have I included sufficient support?*

Review your organization. *Does my beginning capture my reader's interest and provide my position? Does the middle present a rigorous argument? Does the ending restate my position statement in bold terms?*

Revise for voice, word choice, and sentence fluency. *Does my voice sound concerned but also reasonable? Have I avoided inflammatory language? Do my sentences create a logical progression of thought?*

EDITING

Check for conventions. *Have I used correct punctuation, capitalization, spelling, and grammar?*

PUBLISHING

Present your work. Format your work according to the submission guidelines of your school or local newspaper. Then submit your editorial.

Editorial (Point)

The editorial page of a newspaper and the op-ed page (opposite the editorial page) often include pieces that present opposing positions on a topic. The editorial below, by David Mills, expresses a strong opinion about the best strategy for winning the war on terror. The editorial on the facing page expresses a different opinion.

Winning the War on Terror (Point)

The editorial begins with an effective metaphor—a paper tiger.

Before the war on terror began, a terrorist leader such as Osama bin Laden considered the United States a "paper tiger," ferocious to look at and listen to but unable to stand up to attack or adversity. The coordinated attacks of 9/11 (2001) struck at the heart of U.S. government and financial power, with the hope of burning down that paper tiger. Nearly 3,000 U.S. citizens died that day. The U.S. military response in Afghanistan and Iraq proved that the terrorists were wrong. By taking an aggressive stance against terrorism, the United States shows that it is a very real tiger.

A historical analogy sheds light on the current crisis.

This is a familiar pattern. On December 7, 1941, Prime Minister Hideki Tojo of Japan believed that one stunning surprise attack could cripple the U.S. Navy. About 2,500 U.S. citizens died that day. Though Tojo believed this move to be a masterstroke, his great admiral Yamamoto realized it was a terrible blunder: "I fear that we have awakened a sleeping giant and filled him with a terrible resolve." He was right. Franklin Delano Roosevelt, who had faced the Great Depression with the line "The only thing we have to fear is fear itself," proved true to his word, leading the United States into a war on two fronts.

The writer calls the reader—and the nation—to action.

Now, this nation must bring down terrorism by denying the enemies the one weapon they possess: terror. If the government ignores or tries to reason with the terrorists, it only encourages them. By proving to be a true tiger, taking the fight to the networks of terror in the enemies' own backyards, the United States demonstrates the futility of attacks like those on September 11.

The paper-tiger metaphor and another historical reference create a strong ending.

It's a matter of fight or flight. Both of these adrenaline responses make the heart pump furiously. However, the flight response only strengthens our enemies. The fight response calls this nation to face the true paper tiger—the shadowy network of killers—and see how quickly it caves in. The best way to win this war is to take away the one weapon the enemies have—terror—and make preemptive attacks against them.

Editorial (Counterpoint)

The following editorial by Anna Johnson was published as a counterpoint to the editorial on the facing page.

Winning the War on Terror (Counterpoint)

The beginning makes a reference to the previous editorial.

When people talk about the war on terror, they often draw parallels with other wars the United States has faced—Vietnam, World War II, or the Civil War. These were conflicts between nations or states. The war on terror is a conflict between a state and extremist groups.

The writer draws a different historical analogy.

The best historical analogy occurred in 1993, with the standoff between the FBI and the Branch Davidians near Waco, Texas. The charismatic leader of the Davidians, David Koresh, preached an extremist faith that portrayed the United States government as the "spawn of Satan" and armed adherents for a final fiery apocalypse. On April 19, the FBI fulfilled Koresh's terrible prophecies by storming the compound with tanks and tear gas. The attack resulted in a fire that killed 76 Branch Davidians. Two years later, in retaliation for the attack, Timothy McVeigh blew up the Oklahoma City Federal Building and killed 168 people.

The writer attacks the opposing position.

This kind of war is a war against extremist ideologies. As the government's experience with David Koresh demonstrated, increasing pressure on extremists only increases their determination. When a terrorist leader calls the U.S. government the "Great Satan," a response of "shock and awe" only lends credence to the terrorist's views. The Davidian standoff also demonstrated that crushing one group of extremists may make them martyrs that inspire another individual or group.

This paragraph calls the reader to follow a different path.

The United States cannot combat extremists by becoming extremists. It cannot combat terrorists by using terror. Instead, it must use the greatest weapons it possesses: law, diplomacy, democracy, and capital. This nation must fight the war on terror by showing a better way, by building coalitions, not destroying them.

A return to 9/11 puts the argument in context.

On September 12, 2001, the headline of *Le Monde*, the French national newspaper, read, "Nous Sommes Tous Américains" or "We Are All Americans." In the months that followed, though, we gradually lost the support of the world. Instead of targeting the lives of terrorist foes, the answer lies in targeting the hearts and minds of the world.

Guidelines

Writing a Personal Commentary

A personal commentary reflects on a current trend or a fundamental issue. Think of this form as one step removed from an editorial. An editorial usually attacks or applauds a specific event or situation. A commentary speaks more evenhandedly about some aspect of contemporary life. This type of writing succeeds best when it is thoughtful and thought provoking and when the commentator reveals a personal connection to the topic. Follow these guidelines to create a personal commentary.

PREWRITING

Select a topic. Think about new developments or, in the words of William Faulkner, "eternal verities." What inspires you? What aggravates you? Choose a topic that engages you—head, heart, body, or spirit.

Wrestle with the topic. Explore the issue through freewriting or another prewriting strategy. Ask difficult questions about the topic and search for answers. State a possible focus for your commentary—a sentence (or two) expressing the main point you want to convey.

WRITING

Write your first draft. Explore your topic. Use a "peripatetic" approach. (Peripatetic philosophers such as Socrates wandered in search of the truth). Include a beginning, a middle, and an ending, but make sure they work together to lead the reader on a journey of discovery.

REVISING

Check your ideas. *Have I selected an engaging topic? Have I provided a unique insight into the topic? Is my writing reflective and thoughtful?*

Review your organization. *Does my beginning invite the reader on the journey? Does the middle provide a thoughtful path? Does the ending reflect on my main ideas or add an insight?*

Revise for voice, word choice, and sentence fluency. *Does my voice sound reflective? Have I used precise words? Does the commentary have an effective flow?*

EDITING

Check for conventions. *Have I used correct punctuation, capitalization, spelling, and grammar?*

PUBLISHING

Present your work. Share your commentary on a personal blog or post it with an online writing community.

Personal Commentary

In this commentary, Rob King reflects on a discussion he had with a colleague about seeing past the barriers between them.

The personal voice draws the reader in.

The writer uses a conversation to frame his thoughts.

Eye to Eye

I recently had a heart-to-heart conversation with a friend—I, a white male liberal, and she, a black female conservative. As a writer and editor of textbooks, I had steered the discussion toward one of my pet topics: English dialects. I floated out the notion that Shakespeare's greatness came in part from the fact that Elizabethan English was still so rough, so formless. When Shakespeare needed a word, he invented one. He changed nouns to verbs and verbs to adjectives, crammed together words that had never before been used, and thereby introduced the great English hits "gloomy," "luggage," "hobnob," "madcap," "eyeball," and 1,700 others.

I complained to my friend that Standard English had none of that fluidity, that spice. The place where English is still dynamic is in the dialects, such as Creole and African American Vernacular English and Spanglish. "That's where you'll find your modern Shakespeares," I told my friend, and then went one step too far: "It's a shame that these kids with this rich heritage language are stuck having to learn Standard English."

I could tell by my friend's frown that she was unimpressed with my argument. "Sure, Shakespeare could write dialect," she said, "but he could also write speeches for kings. He might've been a rube from Stratford, but he couldn't have made it in London if he hadn't also learned the Queen's English."

A fair point, but I wasn't going to concede my argument just yet. When people discuss the barriers to success in our society, they often focus on prejudice and poverty but ignore language. However, linguists agree that dialects such as African American Vernacular English have distinct vocabulary, grammar, and conventions. The differences are as pronounced as those between American English and British English. To paraphrase George Bernard Shaw, America is a nation divided by a common language.

In 1945, a Yiddish linguist named Max Weinreich joked that "a language is a dialect with an army." There's a lot of

The commentary presents interesting concepts, examples, anecdotes, and quotations.

truth in that point. Danish and Norwegian are two different languages, even though they are completely understandable to speakers of each. The reason for the "separate" languages is that each nation has its own army. Mandarin and Cantonese are dialects of Chinese even though speakers of each cannot understand one another. That's because there isn't a Mandarin army and a Cantonese army, but only a Chinese one. I wanted to make this point to my friend. "A person who speaks African American Vernacular English at home has to speak and write a completely different dialect at school. It's not fair," I said. Once again, I carried my point a step too far: "They wouldn't have to if they had their own army."

My friend smiled and shook her head. "But we don't have an army, so we have to learn Standard English." She went on to tell me that, in the black community, Standard English was sometimes called the "cash language"—the dialect a person needed to learn to get a job or go to college. "That's the reality. To tell black kids that they don't have to learn the cash language is shutting them out of society."

This quotation reveals a turning point in the conversation.

She reminded me that this language barrier has been faced by every ethnic group that ever fought for acceptance in the United States: Irish, German, Chinese, Hispanic. Each ethnic group may have its own language or dialect, but all the groups must have one language as well. "Standard English doesn't belong just to white people. It belongs to everybody."

I made one last-ditch effort: "Martin Luther King, Jr., said he dreamed of a society in which children weren't judged by the color of their skin, but by the content of their character."

I should have known better than to use King against my friend. She said, "If black kids don't have to learn what white kids have to learn, if they don't have to achieve what white kids have to achieve, then that's the end of King's dream." Her next comment finally got me to shut up. "White guilt does not help anybody, Rob. It just makes you feel terrible, and it keeps us down. It's prejudice. Look me in the eye. Not as a white man looking at a black woman, but as a person looking at a person."

In closing, the writer expresses his new understanding.

It's amazing how insidious prejudice can be, how it can hide in the guise of liberal generosity. But the truth isn't in our hearts; it's in our eyes. I started this commentary by referring to it as a heart-to-heart conversation, but I guess I should have called it an eye-to-eye conversation.

Writing an Essay of Argumentation

An essay of argumentation presents a sensible discussion of a topic based on thorough research and logical thinking. This type of essay centers on a debatable proposition and a carefully crafted argument featuring convincing supporting evidence and reasonable counters to opposing points of view. The essay should enlighten as well as persuade. Follow these guidelines.

PREWRITING

Select a topic. Review your texts or class notes for topics. Also consider issues you hear debated locally or nationally. Find a topic that is serious, specific, timely, and debatable.

Research the topic. Begin by writing down your first thoughts. Then collect as much information as necessary through reading, interviewing, observing, and so on.

Develop a proposition. Write down the proposition that you want to defend. Then list at least three solid arguments supporting it. Also write down arguments against it and ways to counter them.

WRITING

Write your first draft. Introduce your topic and lead to your proposition. In the middle paragraphs, argue by providing a variety of support and answering major objections. In the ending, summarize your argument and make a final case for your proposition.

REVISING

Check your ideas. *Is my proposition clearly stated and debatable? Have I included a variety of compelling support? Have I countered significant objections?*

Review your organization. *Do I have a strong beginning, middle, and ending? Have I built my argument in the most logical, convincing way? Do I use transitions to connect the ideas in my sentences and paragraphs?*

Revise for voice, word choice, and sentence fluency. *Does my voice sound both knowledgeable and persuasive? Does my word choice demonstrate my thorough understanding of the topic? Have I created sentences that flow smoothly?*

EDITING

Check for conventions. *Have I used correct punctuation, capitalization, spelling, and grammar?*

PUBLISHING

Present your work. Read your essay to your class, or stage a debate between yourself and someone who holds an opposing view.

Essay of Argumentation

This essay by student writer David DeHaan provides a convincing argument for banning the barbed hook from sportfishing.

Evening the Odds

A new breed of hunter dwells among North America's hidden waterways. Armed with an $80.00 rod and reel, $90.00 hip waders, and a wide array of lures ranging from glowing gadgets to old-fashioned worms, today's fishing enthusiast has an arsenal well beyond the bent nail and old twine that Huck Finn used for jigging. Today, however, people who fish carry one piece of equipment that is outdated: the barbed hook, which is still added to almost every lure produced commercially. This mechanism continues to plague the sport of fishing by damaging young fish stocks. Barbed hooks should be banned from lure fishing to protect fish that are not yet ready for anglers to keep.

The opening comments draw the reader into the main point of the argument (underlined).

A smooth (barbless) fishing hook is much easier to remove from a fish's mouth than a barbed hook. A smooth hook comes out cleanly, leaving only a small puncture, and giving anglers the opportunity to release undamaged fish. A properly set barbed hook, on the other hand, often inflicts serious injury to the jaw of the fish. While this is not a problem for the larger keepers, it does have serious consequences for smaller fish that should be released back into the waterway. Many of these small fish are kept because the anglers know that releasing them would be inhumane, while others are released with portions of their jaws missing, unable to feed properly. By improving the angler's chances of safely releasing unwanted fish, barbless hooks help to preserve our limited fish stocks.

An objection is effectively addressed.

Supporters of barbed fishing hooks say that banning the hooks would decrease the number of fish they are able to land. They claim that enjoyment of the sport would be limited by the increased difficulty of keeping fish on the line. They are at least partially correct; playing a fish is difficult without a barb. However, this does not have to limit the enjoyment of the sport.

When sportsmen stop to reflect on why they find fishing so enjoyable, most realize that what they love is the feel of a fish on the end of the line, not necessarily the weight of the fillets in their coolers. Fishing has undergone a slow evolution during the last century. While fishing used to be a way of putting food on the table, today's motivation may be for the relaxation that it provides. The barbed hook was invented to increase the quantity of fish a person could land in order to help feed a family. This need no longer exists, and so barbed hooks are no longer necessary.

Each new claim is thoroughly explored.

According to some anglers who do use smooth hooks, their lures perform better than barbed lures as long as they maintain a constant tension on the line. Smooth hooks can bite deeper than barbed hooks, actually providing a stronger hold on the fish. These anglers testify that switching from barbed hooks has not noticeably reduced the number of fish that they are able to land. In their experience, enjoyment of the sport is actually heightened by adding another challenge to playing the fish (maintaining line tension).

Some people have argued that replacing all of the barbed hooks in their tackle would be a costly operation. While this is certainly a concern, barbed hooks do not necessarily require replacement. With a simple set of pliers, the barbs on most conventional hooks can be bent down, providing a cost-free method of modifying one's existing tackle. These modified hooks are also much safer to use. Young children who are just learning to fish may be in danger with barbed fishhooks. While the possibility of snagging someone still remains with a smooth hook, the hook is much easier to remove from skin, clothing, and branches.

In closing, the writer emphasizes a key point.

Because most people do not need to fish for food, barbed hooks are no longer needed. Just as in any other sport, enjoyment comes from being able to achieve a goal despite considerable difficulty. If anglers chose their equipment solely on the quantity of fish they were able to land, we would all be fishing with dragnets. While everyone agrees that nets take the sport out of fishing, they must realize that barbed hooks do the same thing. Fishing with smooth hooks is a way of caring for and conserving fish stocks while still maintaining the enjoyment of sportfishing for the angler.

READING FOR BETTER WRITING

The voice of this piece is calm and sensible, yet concerned. Would the essay be more persuasive if the writer used more emotion? Less emotion? Why?

Essay of Argumentation

In this essay, Thea Karas defends her position against the use of economic sanctions as a political tool.

Sanctions Won't Solve Political Problems

The beginning introduces the topic and states the position (underlined).

In July of 1941, the United States imposed economic sanctions against Japan, banning exports to the country and freezing any of its assets that were under U.S. control. These sanctions were meant to stop Japanese military aggression in Asia. On December 7, 1941, however, Japan attacked the U.S. naval base at Pearl Harbor. Instead of reducing aggression, the sanctions had helped push both nations into a war. Though economic sanctions appear to be a powerful peacetime weapon, they actually do more harm than good.

The first middle paragraph provides one reason sanctions do not work.

Economic and political sanctions often prolong bad situations rather than end them. Political sanctions usually come about when an international dispute cannot be resolved by discussion and compromise. In order for one nation to get what it wants, it reduces or stops trade with another nation. It may also freeze any assets the "offending" nation has invested in its country. In 1962, for example, Communist leader Fidel Castro took power in Cuba. His government took control of U.S. businesses there. The United States imposed sanctions, cutting trade with Cuba, hoping the action would speed the fall of Castro's government ("United States Sanctions"). More than 40 years later, the sanctions remained in place, and Castro remained in power.

More middle paragraphs provide clear reasons for the position.

One reason that sanctions are often ineffective is that they reduce dialogue between disputing nations. Instead of searching for common ground, one side imposes sanctions, which rely on unilateral force and provoke anger, and that only makes matters worse. For the duration of the sanctions, talks are focused almost exclusively on the removal of the sanctions rather than on seeking common ground.

Another reason for the ineffectiveness of sanctions is that they often harm innocent victims, yet they have little or no effect on the lives of those in power. In August of 1990, the United Nations imposed sanctions on Iraq following its invasion of Kuwait. The sanctions shut off the sale of broad categories of goods to Iraq and prohibited Iraq from selling its oil on the international market. In place for more than 10 years, the sanctions led to a near collapse of the Iraqi economy ("Iraq"). It has been reported that hundreds of thousands of Iraqis died because of malnutrition or lack of medical care. Meanwhile, Iraqi president Saddam Hussein and other Iraqi leaders lived in luxury, unaffected by the embargo. There was no reason for Hussein to bend to international will because he and those closest to him were not suffering.

This paragraph presents the writer's most important reason.

The most important reason a country should think twice before applying sanctions is that they may backfire. For example, when the United States enforced sanctions against Cuba, Cuba simply increased its trade with Mexico, Canada, and the Soviet Union (Cordenas 238). Thus, the United States lost out. This pattern is especially common when the international community disagrees with the sanctions and the nation that instituted the sanctions finds itself isolated from the rest of the world.

Another paragraph defends the position against an important objection.

Those who support sanctions insist that they represent a useful tool in international diplomacy that is preferable to war. In 1953, when the United States realized it would not win the Korean conflict, it ceased military action against communist North Korea but left strong economic and political sanctions in place. Fifty years later, partly as a result of these sanctions, the people of North Korea are starving, the dictator Kim Jong-Il holds absolute power, and North Korea is considered part of the "Axis of Evil" due to its support of terrorism and its breaking of the nuclear nonproliferation treaty. Kim Jong-Il has indicated that if North Korean nuclear tests resulted in U.N. sanctions, he would consider the sanctions an "act of war" ("Report for Congress" 6). The fifty years that could have been spent reducing the differences between the two nations have actually broadened them. Sanctions have driven North Korea and the United States closer to war, not away from it. Now, only multilateral talks can diffuse the crisis.

The ending restates the position and personalizes the argument.

When two friends disagree, they can negotiate, or they can use manipulative games to try to "win" the argument. The latter passive-aggressive behavior doesn't work for friends, and it doesn't work for nations, either. In international disputes, economic sanctions all too often put nations on a path to something far worse, a military conflict.

NOTE: The works-cited page is not shown.

Guidelines

Writing a Position Paper

A position paper presents a thorough, extensive analysis of a noteworthy issue. This analysis stems from the writer's position, or stance, on the issue. The goal of a position paper is to trace a particular line of thinking on a topic. Follow these guidelines.

PREWRITING

Select a topic. Think of current developments in the news (decisions, laws, advancements, or controversies) that you feel strongly about. Also review course materials for ideas. Choose a topic that fits the assignment.

Conduct research. Note what you already know about your topic and state an initial position. Then investigate, checking a variety of primary and secondary resources. Take thorough notes and document sources.

Organize your thinking. As necessary, revise your position statement to reflect your continuing research. Then create an outline with the main support points for your position.

WRITING

Write your first draft. Create a beginning that introduces the issue and states your position, a middle that gives support and answers objections, and an ending that inspires the reader to accept the validity of your point of view.

REVISING

Check your ideas. *Have I clearly stated my position? Does my support demonstrate thorough research? Do I defend my position against objections?*

Review your organization. *Does each part of my essay work well (beginning, middle, and ending)? Does the middle logically organize my support? Does my ending convince the reader to accept my point of view?*

Revise for voice, word choice, and sentence fluency. *Have I created a persuasive voice? Do I use precise nouns and active verbs? Do I effectively use different types and kinds of sentences?*

EDITING

Check for conventions. *Have I used correct punctuation, capitalization, spelling, and grammar?*

PUBLISHING

Present your work. Share your work with others interested in the issue. Moderate a discussion based upon the position you have presented.

Position Paper

In the following position paper, Molly Rich argues about the unhealthy effects of our new Internet society. She states her position in the beginning, reviews both sides of the issue, and then returns to her position by the end of the essay.

The writer begins with a barrage of Internet terms and catch phrases.

The position statement is given (underlined).

A historic study provides important background.

Other research validates the initial study.

The Internet and Social Interactions

The world is always on. The revolution will not simply be televised but uploaded, downloaded, podcasted, and blogged. Cell phones, e-mail messages, pagers, instant messages, MySpace—"broadcast yourself" should be the credo not just for YouTube but for the whole planet. Human beings are connected in more ways now than ever before, and yet some researchers fear that all of this connection has left people strangely disconnected. As the baud rate of bits exchanged has skyrocketed, the quality of interpersonal relationships has reached new lows.

The concern began in 1998 with the publication of a seminal work on Internet use and social interaction. Robert Kraut, a professor of human-computer interaction at Carnegie Mellon University, published a study of the effects of Internet usage on social behaviors. The sample included 93 diverse Pittsburgh families who did not have Internet access in their homes. Participants completed surveys that measured the communication among family members, the extent of one's local and distant social ties, and one's social support. The respondents also took tests that analyzed their loneliness, stress, and depression. Afterward, participants received two years of free Internet access in their homes. During those two years, the participants agreed to have their Internet usage monitored. At the end of the two years, the participants of the study retook the tests and resubmitted the surveys. The results showed that "greater use of the Internet was associated with small but statistically significant declines in social involvement" (Kraut et al. 1025).

These results have been corroborated by other researchers. Norman Nie of Stanford University published a study in 2005 that showed an even more pronounced effect. Nie's online study included 4,839 respondents who all submitted detailed logs of their activities for the same day in two succeeding years. The study showed that 31 percent of the U.S. population were frequent Internet users. When compared with infrequent users, these people spent 70 minutes less per day in family interactions (Dixon). Nie sees this latest development as the continuation of a long trend of isolation. "It's a history that began with the Industrial Revolution, when the male started to leave the house to earn a living and was not teaching his son how to carry on his craft. Now we have very few remaining institutions that are face to face" (qtd. in Dixon). Nie's report, however, did indicate that over half of the time that Internet users spent online was spent in communicating with others (Dixon).

A quotation from an expert lends authority.

Perhaps the weakening of family and face-to-face interactions is balanced by a strengthening of connections with others. In 2004, Nojin Kwak of the University of Michigan reported, "Overall, dial-up modem users are more interactive with others and more knowledgeable about current affairs than nonusers of the Internet" (qtd. in Wadley). The effect is even more pronounced among broadband users, who can more easily communicate with each other through multimedia formats.

The writer considers the other side of the argument.

Could it be that the Internet can actually increase an individual's interpersonal interaction, self-esteem, and social enjoyment? Many shy individuals who would never speak up in face-to-face interactions lead a lively social life on the Internet. One such person comments, "When we feel we are unheard in relationships, we experience depression. Our voices go underground. [However, online] we feel freer—we bring our voices onto the screen" (qtd. in Silverman 781). These individuals are thus freed psychologically and are more apt to speak exactly what they feel.

Through e-mail and chat rooms, the Internet also helps people expand social networks and keep in touch with their distant family members and friends (Olson and Olson 500). Individuals can meet others online who share similar interests and hobbies, or who have had similar experiences such as sexual abuse and grief. These people thus can exchange and provide much needed social support for one another (Bargh and McKenna 62). Instant messaging programs let people feel very connected because "symbols next to the list of participants show who is online, who is 'away,' and who has signed off. This combines awareness

Sources are cited throughout the paper.

of others' activity state as well as access in real time for informal immediate responses" (Olson and Olson 503).

The writer counters the opposing view.

Other researchers, however, stress the superficial nature of relationships created online. Robert Kraut and one of his colleagues, Sara Kiesler, pointed out in a follow-up explanation to their original findings that "most online relationships formed by the participants in our field trial resulted primarily in informational support rather than emotional support, tangible aid, or companionship" (783). Chat rooms and services such as MySpace excel at connecting people with similar interests, but the reality of the people on the other end of the fiber-optic cable is sometimes uncertain. Users create screen names and personas, reinventing themselves into idealized people that may not reflect who they really are. Ananga Sivyer, a health writer for *Lifescape Magazine,* points out the danger of this practice: "In some cases, the difference between invented Internet personas and the factual truth of an individual can lead to unwelcome self-concept issues and further social withdrawal as the Internet image pulls from social reality into an isolated realm of keyboard, screen, and preferred self" (Sivyer). In the virtual world, perhaps the best that can be achieved is virtual friendship.

The final paragraph powerfully restates the writer's position.

The Internet has created many new ways to connect people, but using these new connections has caused people to abandon richer forms of communication. Face-to-face interaction includes sight, sound, smell, and touch. The unique, bubbly laugh of a friend cannot be replaced by a simple LOL. The uproar of friends crammed onto a couch and dragging steaming slices of pizza out of boxes while reliving a fabulous concert cannot be replaced by individuals sitting alone in their basements listening to downloaded music. And the perils aren't limited to leisure time. According to Nie, "The workplace is one of the richest social environments we now have, and I worry it will be the next to go. . . . We need a national dialogue about how we invent new institutions" (qtd. in Dixon). Yes, people may be more connected now than at any other time in history, but if we have forsaken quality interactions for quantity of interactions, we are more alone than ever before.

NOTE: The works-cited page is not shown.

Position Paper

In the following position paper, high school senior Yolanda Torrez argues for the use of random drug testing to assure that high school athletes do not use performance-enhancing drugs.

Stop Steroids Cold

A national news story introduces the topic and leads up to the position statement (underlined).

In 2005, scandal rocked the world of professional baseball as allegations of the use of steroids and other performance-enhancing drugs hit the headlines. Responding to pressure by Congress, major league baseball instituted standards for testing players for the use of these drugs ("Baseball Battles"). However, the controversy extends far beyond the baseball diamond. Steroids and other drugs that quickly build muscle mass and make athletes stronger and faster have permeated virtually all levels of athletics. For example, in the last five years, steroid use among high school athletes in New Jersey has doubled to 6 percent ("School Tackles"). That means a typical high school football team includes a few users. <u>The best way to prevent the use of performance-enhancing drugs in our schools is to institute random drug tests for all high school athletes.</u>

A topic sentence introduces the main idea of each middle paragraph.

To begin, random testing is needed because steroid use can be hard to detect. When young people participate in sports, they build muscle mass naturally, so large muscles are not always recognized as a symptom. Also, because steroids and other performance-enhancing drugs are illegal, most student athletes realize that getting caught with them would mean immediate expulsion from sports. As a result, students will do everything they can to cover up their use. Peer pressure only reinforces the silence (Smith 26). However, drug tests can quickly and easily detect steroids in a minimally intrusive fashion. Once a student is identified as a user of performance-enhancing drugs, he or she can receive treatment and put an end to steroid use.

The body of each paragraph supports the paragraph's topic sentence.

Random testing also makes it easier for young athletes to resist the temptation of performance-enhancing drugs. Most student athletes participate in sports because they love them. If athletes know that testing positive could put them on the sidelines, they are more likely to resist the pressure to bulk up with performance-enhancing drugs. By acting as a deterrent, testing makes it easy for student athletes to resist peer pressure to use steroids and other enhancers (Smith 27).

Athletes who do not want to risk their school sports careers are more likely to say "no" because of the random testing.

The middle paragraphs build to the most important reason.

Most importantly, instituting testing can protect young athletes from physical and mental harm. Performance-enhancing drugs can cause a broad range of serious health issues, from liver damage and heart attack to certain types of cancer. In addition, these drugs can affect mental health, causing unprovoked rage and violence among users. Sometimes the mood swings lead to depression and even suicide. That fact makes these drugs doubly deadly. Fortunately, if treatment is provided soon enough, most of these health issues can be avoided or reversed ("Anabolic").

Significant objections are addressed.

Some critics of random drug testing fear a "slippery slope," saying that the schools are assuming too much control over students. They cite, for example, the town of El Dorado, Kansas, which in 2006 instituted random drug testing not only for high school athletes, but for any high schoolers or middle schoolers involved in any activity—or even attending any activity ("Kansas"). Clearly, this level of intrusion is excessive, but most schools that institute a random drug-testing policy do not go to such extremes. A carefully designed policy that limits random drug testing to high school athletes and limits the tests to performance-enhancing drugs will not create a "slippery slope" leading to testing every student for every drug.

Other critics feel that random testing for performance-enhancing drugs violates student privacy rights. According to the American Civil Liberties Union (ACLU), "Policies like random drug testing force students to prove their innocence, [and] strip our youth of their Fourth Amendment rights to be free from unreasonable search and seizure" ("Test"). However, the courts disagree. In 1995, in the Supreme Court case known as Vernonia School District v. Wayne Acton, the courts ruled that schools could test entire athletic teams even if no specific individual was suspected of using drugs. Another ruling in 2002 extended the rights of schools to test for drugs, and in 2005 alone, the federal government offered $7.5 million in grant money to assist schools in setting up random drug-testing programs ("Kansas").

Again, the key to success is to carefully set up the random drug-testing program to limit its intrusion in the lives of students. If no individuals are targeted, but rather whole teams are tested, no one should feel singled out. In fact, random testing ensures a level playing field, eliminating potential bias against students. In a recent survey of track athletes at Fillmore High, 78 percent said they were not bothered by the privacy issues of drug testing. "It makes the sport fair for everyone," said junior Megan Krupinski. Random drug testing is a way of publicly telling athletes that adults care about what students do in their private lives and want to see them make good decisions.

One way to lessen the punitive feeling of random drug testing is to pair the program with an educational effort. For example, the National Institute of Health has launched a program titled ATLAS (Adolescents Training and Learning to Avoid Steroids). The program features seven highly interactive sessions led by football coaches and student athletes, focusing on the dangers of steroid use and on alternatives for building muscle and stamina. Dr. Linn Goldberg of Oregon Health Sciences University in Portland helped develop the program, and he comments on the success of the approach: "It's kids talking to kids; that's an important ingredient in our program" ("Steroid Prevention"). A combination of awareness efforts such as ATLAS and random drug-testing programs provide both a "carrot and a stick" to get student athletes off steroids, and keep them off.

The position is restated.

Random testing for high school athletes is the best way to prevent kids from using steroids. Right now, all across the United States, thousands of kids are risking their lives for the sake of bigger muscles. Carl Colton, coach of the Fillmore High School wrestling team, said, "Pro sports have, for a long while, forgotten the reason for competition—the love of the game, the pursuit of excellence. Instead of our high school athletes learning from drug-using pros, the pros ought to learn from our kids." The best way to reverse the current trend is to make random drug testing of high school athletes mandatory, but do it in a way that protects everyone's civil rights. It's time to level the playing fields again, without steroids.

The paragraph sums up the support and ends with a final thought.

NOTE: The works-cited page is not shown.

Thinking Through an Argument

A convincing argument requires a clear, substantial claim; thoughtful qualifiers; varied kinds of solid evidence; and perceptive concessions.

Making and Supporting a Point

MAKING CLAIMS: A claim, or proposition, is the main point in argumentative writing. Three categories of claims are fact, value, and policy.

Claims of fact state or claim that something is true or not true.
Cigarette smoking is a leading cause of cancer.

Claims of value state that something has or does not have worth.
The new on-campus housing plan lacks vision.

Claims of policy assert that something ought to be done or not done.
A semester of community service ought to be a graduation requirement.

USING QUALIFIERS: Qualifiers are terms that make a claim more flexible. Note the difference between the two claims below.

The policies regulating illegal immigration need reform.
Some policies regulating illegal immigration need reform.

"Some" makes a qualified claim, rather than an all-or-nothing claim. Here are some useful qualifiers:

almost	if . . . then . . .	maybe	probably
often	in most cases	might	usually

ADDING SUPPORT: Your claim or proposition needs evidence for support; the more kinds of evidence you offer, and the stronger the evidence, the more solid your argument will be. Here are some types of evidence:

Prediction: Opportunities in science will continue to decline.

Observation: I see more and more unemployed chemists.

Statistics: Washington is going to cut $30 million in research in the next budget.

Comparison: The stature of science has declined since the '60s.

Expert Testimony: Placement Director Juarez reported, "Physics majors find . . . "

Demonstration: At a recent seminar, the regional job market in the sciences was a leading topic of discussion.

Analysis: This situation is the result of . . .

MAKING CONCESSIONS: Concessions are "points" that you let the other side score. Making a concession often adds believability to your overall claim. Here are some expressions for making concessions:

admittedly	granted	I cannot argue with
even though	I agree that	while it is true that

Using Evidence and Logic

To develop an effective, convincing argument, you must think and write logically. You must draw reasonable and sensible conclusions from solid evidence. Furthermore, you must be able to recognize and avoid fallacies of thinking, or false arguments, in your work. By fallacies, we mean the habits of fuzzy or illogical thinking that may crop up in your writing if you are not careful. (They also crop up in advertisements, political appeals, and such.) Learn about the common fallacies by reading the descriptions below. Then make sure to avoid them in your own thinking and writing.

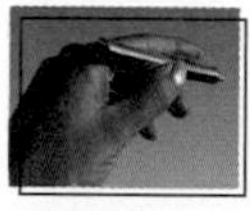

NOTE: When you develop an argument, appeal to your readers' good sense and reason, and not to their emotions.

Fallacies of Thinking

Appeal to Ignorance

This logical fallacy suggests that since no one has ever proved a particular claim, it must be false. Appeals to ignorance unfairly shift the burden of proof onto someone else.

Show me one study that proves cigarettes lead to heart disease.

Appeal to Pity

This fallacy may be heard in courts of law when an attorney begs for leniency because his client's mother is ill, his brother is out of work, his cat has a hair ball, and blah, blah, blah. The strong tug on the heartstrings can also be heard in the classroom.

Student: "May I have an extension on this paper? I worked on it all weekend, but it's still not done."

Bandwagon

Another way to avoid using logic in an argument is to appeal to everyone's sense of wanting to belong or be accepted. By suggesting that everyone else is doing this or wearing that or going there, you can avoid the real question: "Is this idea or claim a good one or not?"

Everyone walked out of the meeting. It was the smartest thing to do.

Broad Generalization

A broad generalization takes in everything and everyone at once, allowing no exceptions. For example, a broad generalization about voters might be, "All voters spend too little time reading and too much time being swayed by 30-second sound bites." It may be true that quite a few voters spend too little time reading about the candidates, but it is unfair to suggest that this is true of all voters. Here's another example:

Young adults can't manage money.

Circular Thinking

This fallacy consists of assuming, in an argument, the very point you are trying to prove. Note how circular this sort of reasoning is:

I hate my first-hour class because I'm never happy when I'm there. (But what's wrong with the class?)

Either-Or Thinking

Either-or thinking consists of reducing a solution to two possible extremes: "America: Love It or Leave It." "Put up or shut up." This fallacy of thinking eliminates every possibility in the middle.

Either this community provides light-rail transportation, or it will be impossible to expand in the future.

Half-Truths

Avoid building your argument with evidence that contains part of the truth, but not the whole truth. These kinds of statements are called half-truths. They are especially misleading because they leave out "the rest of the story." They are true and dishonest at the same time.

The new work-for-welfare bill is good because it will get people off the public dole. (Maybe so, but it may also cause undue suffering to some truly needy individuals.)

Oversimplification

Beware of phrases like "It all boils down to . . . " or "It's a simple question of . . . " Almost no dispute is "a simple question of" anything. Anyone who feels, for example, that capital punishment "all boils down to" a matter of protecting society ought to question a doctor, an inmate on death row, the inmate's family, a sociologist, a religious leader, etc.

Capital punishment is a simple question of protecting society.

Slanted Language

By choosing words that carry strong positive or negative feelings, a person can distract the audience, leading them away from the valid arguments being made. A philosopher once illustrated the bias involved in slanted language when he compared three synonyms for the word *stubborn:* "I am *firm*. You are *obstinate*. He is *pigheaded*."

No one in his right mind would ever agree to anything so ridiculous.

Testimonial

If the testimonial or statement comes from a recognized authority in the field, great. If it comes from a person famous in another field, beware.

Sports hero: "I've tried every cold medicine on the market, and—believe me—nothing works like Temptrol."

Writing About Literature

Writing About Literature

What exactly is **literature**? Is it a long, complicated novel by Dostoyevsky, a series of perceptive poems by Dickinson? Yes, of course. How about a play by Shaw or some short stories by Cisneros? These, too, are literature.

Literature is fiction, drama, poetry, and much more: It is the body of high-quality, imaginative writing, well formed and rich in content. But that is only part of the story. Until you interact with it and form some new understandings, literature is mere words on paper.

You can't approach a piece of literature casually and expect to uncover its meaning. You create meaning by sifting the text through your own thoughts and feelings, by reading it (more than once), by discussing it, and by writing about it.

WHAT'S AHEAD

This section provides guidelines and models for three basic types of writing about literature: personal responses, reviews, and literary analyses. Each type involves thinking about and reacting to a piece of literature in a different way. Also included is an extensive glossary of literary terms.

"I am a part of all that I have read."
—John Kieran

Writing About Literature

QUICK GUIDE

Each piece of literature presents you with a slice of human experience as imagined (or perceived) by the author. When you read, study, and write about a particular selection, you gain insight into a new world and discover how it matches up with your own experience.

- **STARTING POINT:** Writing about literature begins when you are asked to react to or analyze a literary work (or some other artistic endeavor, such as a live performance).
- **PURPOSE:** The goal is to share your understanding of the literary work, and this "understanding" will be influenced by the particular writing task.
- **FORM:** Personal responses can be journal entries, poems, personal reflections, and so on. Reviews are brief essays, loosely structured blends of information and commentary. Analyses are carefully planned academic papers, following the traditional essay form.
- **AUDIENCE:** For the most part, you're addressing your writing peers and your instructor. Some of your reviews, however, may be intended for publication.
- **VOICE:** Speak from both the heart and the mind in personal responses. Reviews may or may not be heartfelt; analyses seldom are.
- **POINT OF VIEW:** Generally speaking, use first-person point of view *(I)* for personal responses and third-person *(he, she, they)* for most reviews and for analyses.

INSIDE INFO

To write effectively about literature, you must be a critical reader, carefully noting your thoughts, feelings, and questions as you go along. It's good practice to read a selection once to get an overall impression of the text. Then go back a second time (and a third, if necessary), looking for answers to your questions. Also note the connections between different characters or parts, and discern any patterns of development.

Writing a Personal Response

A response to literature is your reply to whatever a selection says to you. A response may be a journal entry (or a series of entries) about a compelling idea in the text. It may be a poem expressing your feelings about the selection. It may also be an essay examining your personal connection to the piece, and so on. Your goal is to interact with a text in a meaningful way. Refer to the guidelines below and the models that follow.

PREWRITING

Select a text. In most cases, you will respond to a piece of literature that is part of your course work.

Read the selection. Carefully read the text (more than once), noting your thoughts, feelings, and questions as you go along. Make your initial notations right in the text if you own the book. Otherwise, take notes in your notebook.

Assess your notes. Review your notes and select one idea to develop, keeping in mind any requirements established by your instructor. Plan and organize your details to fit the form of your response.

WRITING

Develop your response. Follow your plan or write freely and naturally as thoughts come to mind. Make specific references to the text as needed.

REVISING

Check your ideas. *Have I created an effective, complete response? Does my response reflect my thoughts and feelings about the text? Have I accurately recorded any references from the text?*

Review the organization. *Does my response include a clearly developed beginning, middle, and ending?*

Revise for voice, word choice, and sentence fluency. *Does my voice match the purpose of my response? Have I used specific words? Do my sentences read smoothly?*

EDITING

Check for conventions. *Have I used correct punctuation, capitalization, spelling, and grammar?*

PUBLISHING

Present your work. Proofread the final copy of your response if, in fact, you are turning it in. Also consider sharing it with your classmates.

Starting Points for Journal Responses

The following reader-response questions will help you react thoughtfully to the literature you read. This list should be used only when you need a starting point for writing. Your own thoughts are always the best source of ideas for your journal.

Making Connections

1. What are your feelings after reading the opening chapter(s) of this book? After reading half the book? After finishing the book?
2. What connections are there between the book and your life?
3. In what ways are you like any of the characters? Do any of the characters remind you of other people? Explain.
4. What effect does the book have on your personal beliefs?
5. What is the most important word in the book (or in a particular chapter or section)? The most important passage? The most important event? Explain.

Points of Interest

6. What parts of this book are worth reading again and again? Why?
7. What parts (aspects, elements) detract from the book's overall effectiveness? Why?
8. What patterns have you discovered in the text (characterization, plot development)?
9. What surprised you in the book? Why?
10. What confuses you or makes you wonder about the book?

Careful Reflection

11. What is the significance of the title?
12. What dominant themes run through the text?
13. What thoughts do you have about the author?
14. What do you know now that you didn't know before?
15. What questions do you have after reading this book?

TIPS

FOR JOURNAL WRITING

- **Try writing nonstop.** Set a goal of writing 10 to 15 minutes at a time.
- **Push an idea as far as you can.** Uncover more of your thoughts by exploring an idea from many different angles. (Keep asking yourself "Why?" as you write.)
- **Review your entries.** Mark sections that seem significant, surprising, or insightful. Continue writing about these ideas in later entries or use them as starting points for future writing.

Personal Response

In this response, Elizabeth Delaney explores the effect that her own feelings and experience have on her interpretation of literature. Notice how effectively the writer moves between her personal experience and the two texts she compares.

Summer Undergoes a "Metamorphosis": The Function of Experience in Forgiveness

The opening remarks set the tone for an honest and thoughtful response.

At first I thought my reaction to Edith Wharton's *Summer* was too close, too personal, to ever allow me to form a coherent, reasonable response. It was not until reading "The Metamorphosis" by Franz Kafka that I was able to assign some rationality to my feelings. I finally realized the extent to which experience shapes our understanding and appreciation of literature. In both *Summer* and "The Metamorphosis," the reader is forced to grapple with issues of fallibility and forgiveness; however, the two works present the issues in such different environments that I was initially unable to see the connection.

During my reading of *Summer,* a flood tide of half-suppressed, half-forgotten emotions washed over me, and I instinctively reached out in empathy to Charity Royall and Lucius Harney. I found that Lucius's actions were regrettable and wounding, but understandable and excusable. Others in my class saw him as cruel and wholly condemnable. I could forgive Lucius because I have forgiven someone whose relationship with me was very similar to Lucius's relationship with Charity; and while I ache with Charity over her loss, I can also understand her pride in relinquishing him.

The writer makes a link between her own life and the literature.

Because of my closeness to the situation described in *Summer,* I was angry when it was suggested that Lucius was so entirely reprehensible, particularly when Charity's "heart felt strangely light" (p. 151) during the days after sending her letter of release to him. I wanted to know, if "she did not even reproach him in her thoughts" (p. 157), why should we? But as my classmates condemned Lucius Harney for his insensitivity, weakness, and duplicity, I began to wonder if I was the one who was blind—if I had glossed over Lucius's behavior in an attempt to justify my own feelings toward my past.

Furthermore, Charity's frequent denial of her insecurities and faults forced me to reexamine my own rationale for the value of my past relationship. I was in emotional turmoil over the worth of my memories and experience. One part of me debated whether I was being honest or not—forgiving Lucius only out of the need to excuse myself for cherishing someone who had truly hurt me.

A connection between the two texts is made.

Reading "The Metamorphosis" gave me new insights into my response to *Summer* because a natural relationship between experience and forgiveness suddenly became clear. During class, the same unsympathetic attitude that had angered me a week earlier, crept unconsciously into my feelings toward Gregor Samsa. But just as I was able to understand Charity and Lucius, others in the class were able to understand and forgive Gregor because of their experiences with a loved one like him. The reactions of my classmates illuminated the value of Gregor's choices. It was pivotal that "he thought of his family with tenderness and love" (p. 127), losing perspective on his own life in an effort to sustain and respect them.

As I began to relate to Gregor, I discovered the correlation between his behavior and Charity's. Just as Charity was blind to her own motivation, Gregor judged his father's greed to be "unexpected thrift and foresight" (p. 96).

The writer reflects on her new understanding.

My view of Kafka has obviously undergone a "metamorphosis," just as my personal response to *Summer* has changed. Instead of fearing my reactions and debating their worth, I now welcome my feelings and accept that my own experience naturally plays an important role in my understanding of literature. I have also learned, rather sheepishly, that I am often too quick to judge characters with whom I sense no common ground. Acknowledging this fallibility, I no longer trust my instant conclusions, especially when my own experience does not resemble a character's situation, but I seek to exercise compassion and to forgive.

READING FOR BETTER WRITING

1. What is the focus of Elizabeth Delaney's personal response to *Summer*? How does her response differ from her classmates' response?
2. In the closing paragraph, what new understanding does Delaney express?

Personal Response

Heather Bachman's response to *Alice's Adventures in Wonderland* focuses on the theme of childhood imagination. She completed this writing for a class in which she was studying children's literature.

Down the Rabbit Hole

The opening paragraph establishes the essay's focus.

Lewis Carroll's *Alice's Adventures in Wonderland* is a charming reminder of the imaginary world of children. Following a white rabbit, Alice and the reader are led to a dreamlike land of unusual characters and odd animals. I have always had an active imagination, and this book made me smile many times as I remembered my own fantastical excursions.

After her experiences in Wonderland, Alice begins to think "very few things were really impossible." Drinking a special liquid makes her shrink, and a nibble of sweet cake causes her to grow. Alice begins to expect the unusual; there's no limit to her dreams. I, too, have proposed some unusual ideas, and even believed (sort of) that they could come true. For an English project many years ago, I was required to make three wishes. My third wish surprised the teacher because I wanted my own planet. All the animals of the world could live on my planet, safe from oil spills and hunters. The teacher commented, "Never has a student wished for something quite so large!"

After her experiences in Wonderland, Alice begins to think "very few things were really impossible."

The writer relates aspects of her own life to Alice's imaginary world.

Alice meets many animals that chatter with her. I especially like her discussions with the lory, dodo, crabs, and other creatures. What child hasn't imagined that animals can talk? My cat, who is 17, has spent many hours by my side and shared in all of my secrets (without ever telling a soul). Bobcat's rich purr tells me, "Everything will be okay." Whenever he enters a room, his raspy meow seems to ask, "Are you going to pet me now, or should I just hop into your lap?" Perhaps my feeling that animals can talk did not fade with the end of childhood.

Alice experiences Wonderland on many levels. When she is tiny, she converses with the curious caterpillar. Tall and willowy, she has a bird's perspective. It is amazing how different the world can be from different points of view. I remember crawling around, long after I had learned to walk. I saw my house in a whole new way. Table legs became mighty tree trunks. The shag carpet felt like grass. When I flew in an airplane, the cars far below were tiny, colorful bugs. Fields of corn, wheat, and soybeans were patches on a giant green quilt. At other times, I did more than change position—I became a different creature. My sister and I spent hours being dolphins and mermaids in our grandfather's pool. We kept our legs tight together, swimming in graceful arches. To a child, the world is never boring—with just a little help from her imagination.

Wonderland is teeming with bizarre creatures. The Queen of Hearts introduces Alice to Gryphon, a mythical beast that is part lion and part eagle. As a child, I dreamt about having my own Pegasus, the gorgeous winged horse of mythology. I sketched my perfect Pegasus and imagined a world of impossible animals, like quirky birds with musical beaks.

One of my favorite scenes in this book is the croquet match with the Queen of Hearts. I can see Alice struggling with her flamingo/mallet only to discover the hedgehog/ball has wandered off. Children know how to give inanimate objects life. A little girl, dreaming of having a pony, rides a stick in her backyard. The garden hose coils like a python about to strike! A pencil suddenly becomes a friendly lizard, especially when the homework seems boring. In Wonderland, Alice may give up the wild game of croquet, but I won't ever forget that wonderful scene.

The closing remarks include an important quotation from the text.

Alice's sister knew that the young girl "would keep, through all her riper years, the simple and loving heart of her childhood . . . the dream of Wonderland long ago . . . and find pleasure in . . . simple joys, remembering her own child-life, and the happy summer days." My childhood imagination, too, has not faded. I will not forget my journeys into backyard jungles or my faithful steeds of polished wood. Creativity and imagination are precious, in literature and in life.

READING FOR BETTER WRITING

1. What is the focus of this response? What examples from the text and the writer's own life support this focus?
2. What can you conclude about the sentence fluency in this response? Are the sentence beginnings and lengths varied enough? Do the sentences read smoothly? Explain.

Guidelines

Writing a Book Review

Charles Dickens once said, "There are books of which the backs and covers are by far the best parts." Undoubtedly, you have equally strong opinions about many of the books you have read, or have tried to read. When you write a review, you pass judgment on a book (or some other literary or artistic endeavor) and point to specific parts to support your opinion. Your goal is to help readers decide whether the work is something they want to read for themselves. Use the guidelines below and the models that follow to help you write a review.

PREWRITING

Select a topic. The topic of your review should be a book that you have recently read and have strong feelings about.

Collect details. Gather your initial thoughts and feelings about the book through freewriting or clustering. List the book's strengths and its weaknesses. Take special note of lines from the text that you may want to include in your review.

Focus your efforts. Read your notes and plan your review. Here's a possible format: In your opening, provide background information that leads up to the thesis or focus statement. Follow with a brief plot summary plus a discussion of two or more of the text's significant features. Conclude with your overall judgment.

WRITING

Draft your review. Develop your first draft according to your plan. Gain the reader's interest with a strong opening.

REVISING

Consider your ideas. *Is the thesis or focus of my review clear and compelling? Does my review highlight main features of the book? Have I made enough specific references to the text?*

Check the organization. *Does my beginning capture the reader's interest and present the thesis or focus? Does the middle provide strong support? Does the closing present my overall judgment of the book?*

Revise for voice, word choice, and fluency. *Do I sound interested in and knowledgeable about the book? Does my review read smoothly?*

EDITING

Check for conventions. *Have I used correct punctuation, capitalization, spelling, and grammar?*

PUBLISHING

Submit your review. Share your review with your class or a larger audience.

Book Review: Nonfiction

In this review, Malaya Alexander discusses *Seabiscuit* by Laura Hillenbrand. Notice that the reviewer focuses much of her attention on the surprising notoriety of a special horse during the Depression.

A Game-Legged Pony

The first part introduces the novel and gives the thesis statement (underlined).

It is the Great Depression. Unemployment rises to 25 percent, the average family income drops 40 percent, and dictators control Germany, Italy, and Russia. Franklin Delano Roosevelt tries to speak hope into American living rooms, and Hollywood produces thousands of escapist movies. But in 1938, newspaper coverage of Hitler and F.D.R. and Clark Gable slumps. The hottest story is a horse named Seabiscuit (xvii). In her book *Seabiscuit,* Laura Hillenbrand tells how a surprising cow pony teaches the world about finding victory in defeat.

The first middle paragraphs summarize the main events in the novel.

The book traces the life of Seabiscuit, a broken-down three-year-old racehorse. Though he is the son of the fast and temperamental racehorse named Hard Tack, Seabiscuit has none of his sire's sleek beauty. Hillenbrand describes Seabiscuit as "blunt, coarse, rectangular, stationary. [. . .] His stubby legs were a study in unsound construction, with squarish, asymmetrical 'baseball glove' knees that didn't quite straighten all the way, leaving him in a permanent semi-crouch" (33). The horse has had a hard life, running more races in two years than most horses run in a lifetime. By his third year, he seems used up and useless, and many people think him lame.

The writer includes some of the author's creative descriptions.

Along comes the wealthy Charles Howard, who "had a weakness for lost causes" (6). He sees potential in Seabiscuit and purchases him. Howard gives the horse over to the care of Tom Smith, who is himself a lost cause—an old washed-up horse trainer who rarely speaks and who "had a colorless translucence about him that made him seem as if he were in the earliest stages of progressive invisibility" (20). For a jockey, Howard lines up a luckless firebrand named Red Pollard, who literally wanders penniless up to the stable after having crawled out of a car wreck. As Hillenbrand puts it, "The scattered lives of Red Pollard, Tom Smith, and Charles Howard had come to an intersection" (95). They glimpse greatness in this broken-down horse, and as they nurture Seabiscuit, they begin to discover greatness in themselves.

The middle paragraphs include paraphrased material.

A string of race wins follows, in Detroit, in Cincinnati, and all through the racecourses of California. During that time, Seabiscuit's star is rising, and the handicap weights he carries become heavier and heavier—often 20 to 30 pounds more than any other horse in the field. In his six years of racing, he goes on to beat the Triple Crown winner, War Admiral, in a head-to-head race considered the greatest race in the sport's history.

The later middle paragraphs use events and quotations to demonstrate the main theme.

Seabiscuit is, on the surface, a book about winning, but Hillenbrand also provides much compassionate commentary about losing. The reason this horse captures the imagination of Depression-era America is that he looks like a commoner, a "cow pony" that has more heart than the most beautiful thoroughbred. While people in the '30s are reading stories about Horatio Alger and his rise from poverty, they are seeing a real-life Horatio Alger in this "mean, restive, and ragged" horse (31). Hillenbrand carries the theme further, showing how Smith and Pollard and even Howard himself find new life through this amazing animal.

The ending of *Seabiscuit* perfectly demonstrates the theme of victory from defeat. After pulling up lame in a race in 1939, the six-year-old Seabiscuit is considered finished. So, too, is his longtime rider, Red Pollard, who has suffered such terrible injuries in track accidents that doctors tell him he will never ride a horse again. "We were a couple of old cripples together," said Red (296). But during that year, he and the old horse both recover. They return in 1940 to race at Santa Anita, with Seabiscuit carrying 130 pounds—more than 15 pounds over what the second and third place horses had to carry, though they were only half the age of Seabiscuit.

The ending applies the theme to life in general.

During the same year that Seabiscuit makes his comeback, the novelist F. Scott Fitzgerald lies on his deathbed and says, "There are no second acts in American lives." He is wrong. Reading the story of Seabiscuit proves that there are third acts and fourth acts and fifth acts, too. That's a horse that all of us can cheer for.

Book Review: Fiction

In this review, Jacqueline Williams examines a novel about the Vietnam War called *The Things They Carried* by Tim O'Brien. Williams approaches this novel (and her review) with some skepticism since there has already been so much written about this tragic time. But, as you will see, she concludes that O'Brien's book is a valuable addition to the literature about the Vietnam experience.

The Truth in Tim O'Brien's *The Things They Carried*

The opening remarks establish the reviewer's connection with her subject.

Unlike the traditional college student, I come to Vietnam-era movies and novels with skepticism . . . and annoyance. Having been a college sophomore when the Vietnam conflict finally ended (or at least U.S. involvement in it), I know what Vietnam was like. My husband was in the army from 1970 to 1974, and I had several friends whose brothers served in Nam. I know it was awful. I know how kids' minds were messed up by the whole ordeal, if not their bodies. More than 30 years have passed since the war, and I just do not want to relive or deal with it anymore. Even the title of O'Brien's novel bothered me, *The Things They Carried,* since it obviously refers to the emotional and psychological effects of Vietnam.

The focus of the review is identified.

Those were my feelings as I began to read this book. To my surprise, by the time I had finished O'Brien's work, I had a broader and deeper understanding of how Vietnam affected those who fought in it. Although I grimaced when reading his graphic descriptions of the horrible acts committed, I knew that the author was not embellishing the story with gore or using obscenities gratuitously. O'Brien, I think, tells these stories for therapeutic purposes—his and ours: he confronts his own personal ghosts, and he forces his reader to face them as well.

A brief plot summary is provided.

The novel is actually a collection of interrelated tales about men and women who experienced Vietnam directly or indirectly. Many of the stories tell of the brutal realities of death and how soldiers meet it and deal with it. There's Ted Lavender, shot in the head after relieving himself, "zapped while zipping," as the other soldiers put it. There's Curt Lemon, blown up into a tree, remembered gruesomely by one soldier in singing the song "Lemon Tree." There's Kiowa, sucked down into a "_____ field." And there's the Vietcong soldier that the narrator himself kills. With each of these deaths, O'Brien holds back no punches—showing us the horror, tragedy, and related black humor of war.

A major theme in this book—change—is analyzed.

He shows us how Vietnam changes the living. One strange story, for example, tells about Mary Anne Bell, an all-American girl smuggled into Nam by her boyfriend. In a horrifying way, she gets swallowed up by the war; in fact, this "Barbie Doll" seems to thrive on it. Another powerful change happens to Norman Bowker, who goes home eaten by guilt for Kiowa's death. All he can do, trapped in his hometown, is drive the loop around the lake over and over . . . until he kills himself. But maybe the biggest change happens to the narrator himself. Early in the novel, we see him struggle with his draft notice. He is all idealism and innocence. By the end of the novel, we see that the war has cost him both, and that they have been replaced only by personal loss and the knowledge of his own capacity for evil.

In closing, the reviewer addresses the relevance and the importance of her subject.

The truth O'Brien seeks is not in the events that he details, but in the emotions, attitudes, and feelings that his stories project. The stories look at courage and fear and how the imagination helps us understand and shape the truth. The novel is an illustration of how "story truth is truer than happening truth." As a fiction writer who experienced Vietnam, O'Brien wants to confront us with the imaginative truth of it all, not just the hard facts.

Tim O'Brien captured my attention, even when I didn't want him to. After so many years, Vietnam is still an important daily reality for millions of Americans, and really for the whole nation. The tales in *The Things They Carried* drive home that truth. In fact, they give the reader a "truth goose," a disturbing, but important dose of war and its wide-ranging effects.

READING FOR BETTER WRITING

1. What personal ghost does the writer come to terms with in this review?
2. Do you agree that "story truth is truer than happening truth"? Explain.

Film Review

In the film review below, David Schaap analyzes Stephen Spielberg's film *War of the Worlds* by asking key questions about the filmmaker's strategies and their effects.

Terror on the Silver Screen: Who Are the Aliens?

The writer introduces the filmmaker and film; he then describes a pivotal scene.

In Steven Spielberg's 2005 movie, *War of the Worlds,* Ray Ferrier and his two children flee their New Jersey home in a stolen minivan. To escape outer-space aliens who are destroying houses and killing people from their enormous three-legged machines, this father, son, and daughter lurch through scene after scene of 9/11-type destruction. At one point the daughter surveys the violence, panics, and shrieks, "Is it the terrorists?"

He cites an important quotation and explores its significance.

The girl's question nudges the audience to ask the same question, "Are the aliens terrorists?" That would make sense. Often filmmakers will play off the audience's real-life emotions to give them a sensational imaginary experience as well as a glimpse at their real world. In this case, by suggesting that the alien's imaginary attack resembles the Al Qaeda's 9/11 attack, Spielberg could be doing two things: (1) heightening fear of the alien characters and (2) suggesting a political theme.

Two questions focus the writer's analysis.

But is Spielberg's *War of the Worlds* this type of film? First, does the film inspire fear by suggesting that the alien's attack is similar to Al Qaeda's attack? And second, does the film's alien attack represent a future terrorist invasion of the United States?

He answers the first question and offers supporting details.

The answer to the first question is *yes.* Spielberg inspires fear of his outer-space aliens by their resemblance to 9/11 terrorists. In a series of scenes, he shows a crashed airliner like the ones used on 9/11, a wall covered with posters of missing loved ones, and mobs of ash- and dust-covered characters like those escaping the collapsing World Trade Center. Because the film takes place in the United States, viewers subconsciously further fear the aliens' violence.

He answers the second question by explaining the film's focus.

However, do the aliens invading the United States represent Al Qaeda fighters? Not really. The aliens are Spielberg's universal stand-in for whatever strikes fear into viewers' hearts. This film does not examine the political, psychological, or cultural roots of any problem. The film's focus is on the *effect* of violence, not the *identity* of the perpetrators. *War of the Worlds* is about *terror,* not *terrorists.*

Writing a Limited Literary Analysis

A limited literary analysis presents your thoughtful interpretation of a literary work. A short poem may be analyzed line by line for more than one element (perhaps the interplay between style and theme); whereas the analysis of a longer work should focus on one aspect of the plot, setting, theme, characterization, or style. Use only ideas from your own critical reading of the text. Refer to the guidelines below and the models that follow.

PREWRITING

Select a text. In most cases, you will be provided with a list of titles or authors to choose from. If you have any questions, consult your classmates or your instructor.

Read (or reread) the selection. Read the text carefully to ensure that you have a good working knowledge of its contents. Take detailed notes as you read.

Consider your options. Examine the features of the literary work. Are you drawn to a certain character? Are you interested in one of the themes? Do you appreciate the style? (See page 286 for ideas.)

Establish a thesis. Write a sentence or two expressing the main point you want to emphasize in your analysis. Plan and organize your writing accordingly. (Be sure that you can support your thesis with direct references to the text.)

WRITING

Draft your analysis. Develop your first draft, based on your plan. Identify your thesis in your opening.

REVISING

Review your ideas. *Is my thesis statement clearly stated? Do all of my main points support it? Have I used direct references from the text?*

Check the organization. *Does my analysis form a meaningful whole with fully developed beginning, middle, and closing parts? Do I use transitions to connect main ideas and to help build a coherent essay?*

Revise for voice, word choice, and sentence fluency. *Have I used an engaging and appropriate voice (formal or semiformal)? Have I expressed my ideas using specific nouns and verbs? Do my sentences flow smoothly?*

EDITING

Check for conventions. *Have I used correct punctuation, capitalization, spelling, and grammar?*

PUBLISHING

Submit your work. Proofread your final copy before sharing it.

Limited Literary Analysis

In the following essay, Joelle Lee analyzes *Sisters*, a play by Marsha A. Jackson. As you will see, the student writer focuses her analysis on the development of the two main characters.

Stuck with Each Other

The beginning catches the reader's interest, introduces the play, and states the thesis (underlined).

In the dark theater, children sing a haunting tune: "Don't Play with the Alley Children." It's a singsong chant that young Olivia Williams and her friends would sing in their upper-middle-class apartments, while young Cassie Charles and her friends played among the garbage cans below. Though both girls are African Americans, they are divided by their social class, their experience, and their strategies for living in a white world. Then, one New Year's Eve, the grown-up Olivia is stranded in her ad-agency office along with the grown-up Cassie, a cleaning woman. In her play *Sisters,* Marsha A. Jackson contrasts the two women's lives, showing how color and gender make two very different women into true sisters.

The first middle paragraph sets the scene.

The action of the play begins on New Year's Eve in Olivia's office at Peat, Montgriff, and Simon, an ad agency in Atlanta, Georgia. Olivia kneels on the floor among boxes and is packing up her office when Cassie arrives singing "I'm Every Woman" at the top of her lungs. The two women could not be more different. Olivia is 30, single, stiff, proper, and sad, listening to MUZAK as she packs up her life. Cassie is 40, a mom, loose and happy, listening to Whitney Houston. As Jackson points out in her notes before the play, "Both characters are intentionally broadly drawn in Act I, such that the laughter is the medium of entry into the complexity of each character and situation" (104). These two women begin as stereotypes, but when they get stuck together, both characters start to unfold.

A storm begins outside, lightning strikes, and the power in the building goes out. Olivia and Cassie, alone in the building, must rely on each other. They walk down twenty flights of stairs so that Olivia can drive Cassie home, but Olivia has forgotten her car keys, and the storm has turned into a blizzard. All traffic is stopped, and the trains that Cassie would ride aren't running because of the blackout.

The women climb back up the stairs, and Cassie reluctantly helps Olivia pack up her office while the two women unpack their lives. Olivia reveals that she is leaving because she has hit the "glass ceiling" and, despite her hard work, is getting passed over for promotions. Cassie says that Olivia's ambition is a curse: "Being ungrateful for what you got, and wishing for things you can't have. If that ain't a curse, I ain't seen one" (134). Cassie has her own hang-ups. She has taken care of others her whole life: first her grandmother and now her son. Olivia points out, "Who's taking care of you, Cassie? You've been so busy working, trying to convince yourself you don't deserve a life, you didn't even feel it when you gave up" (144). As they talk, Olivia and Cassie grow to understand each other.

Direct references to the play are made.

Jackson seems to be showing that the things that keep people apart—walls and alleys, work and money—aren't as powerful as the forces that draw them together. Simply by setting these two women in the same space, Jackson undoes the years and dollars that had kept them apart. Stuck with each other on New Year's Eve, Olivia and Cassie create their own celebration. They trade stories, listen to music, dance, and even make resolutions. Olivia resolves to find her way in a "white man's world" and have fun doing it. Cassie resolves to start her own cleaning business and move up in the world.

By the end of their time together, Olivia and Cassie are more than friends: They are sisters. Their theme song no longer is "Don't Play with the Alley Children" but "Blest Be the Tie That Binds." Marsha Jackson has brought two very different women together—two different aspects of the playwright herself. Jackson not only wrote the play but starred as Olivia during its run. As a classically trained playwright and a guiding light in the theater scenes of Atlanta and Houston, Jackson is very much like Olivia. Yet the loving way in which she develops Cassie's part, and her own experience of being an "alley child" in a white world, show that part of Jackson is and always will be Cassie.

The writer provides thoughtful analysis in the final two paragraphs.

Limited Literary Analysis

The analysis below is based on Sara Volle's close reading of the following passage from *The Scarlet Letter* by Nathaniel Hawthorne. In this analysis, Volle explores how Pearl takes steps toward growing up.

"Hester and Pearl"

Pearl, whose activity of spirit never flagged, had been at no loss for amusement while her mother talked with the old gatherer of herbs. At first, as already told, she had flirted fancifully with her own image in a pool of water, beckoning the phantom forth, and—as it declined to venture—seeking a passage for herself into its sphere of impalpable earth and unattainable sky. Soon finding, however, that either she or the image was unreal, she turned elsewhere for better pastime. She made little boats out of birch-bark, and freighted them with snail-shells, and sent out more ventures on the mighty deep than any merchant in New England; but the larger part of them foundered near the shore. She seized a live horseshoe by the tail, and made prize of several five-fingers, and laid out a jelly-fish to melt in the warm sun. Then she took up the white foam, that streaked the line of the advancing tide, and threw it upon the breeze, scampering after it with winged footsteps, to catch the great snow-flakes ere they fell. Perceiving a flock of beach-birds, that fed and fluttered along the shore, the naughty child picked up her apron full of pebbles, and, creeping from rock to rock after these small sea-fowl, displayed remarkable dexterity in pelting them. One little gray bird, with a white breast, Pearl was almost sure, had been hit by a pebble, and fluttered away with a broken wing. But then the elf-child sighed, and gave up her sport; because it grieved her to have done harm to a little being that was as wild as the sea-breeze, or as wild as Pearl herself.

Her final employment was to gather sea-weed, of various kinds, and make herself a scarf, mantle, and a head-dress, and thus assume the aspect of a little mermaid. She inherited her mother's gift for devising drapery and costume. As the last touch to her mermaid's garb, Pearl took some eel-grass, and imitated, as best she could, on her own bosom, the decoration with which she was so familiar on her mother's. A letter,—the letter A,—but freshly green, instead of scarlet! The child bent her chin upon her breast, and contemplated this device with strange interest; even as if the one only thing for which she had been sent into the world was to make out its hidden import.

Child's Play

A brief summary of the passage leads up to the thesis (underlined).

In this passage from chapter 15 in *The Scarlet Letter* entitled "Hester and Pearl," Pearl amuses herself down at the margin of the sea. The narrator recalls Pearl's fixation with the image she sees upon peeping into the tide pool. Pearl then turns "elsewhere for better pastime"—floating birch-bark boats in the tide and assailing various marine creatures. Finally, she costumes herself in seaweed, complete with a "freshly green" letter A affixed to her bosom. <u>These actions reveal some of the steps that Pearl takes in the process of growing up.</u>

Each middle paragraph develops a main point.

One thing that comes across quite effectively in this passage is Pearl's incredible energy; she is indeed a child whose "activity of spirit never flagged." The way in which the narrator speaks of the child's "activity of spirit" is exceptionally precise. This energy also sets Pearl apart from the "deformed old figure" of Roger Chillingworth, described earlier in the chapter. Through this implicit juxtaposition of the fanciful child with the jaded physician, the reader is, among other things, positioned to recognize the ways in which an understanding of "innocence," as opposed to "sinfulness" or "maturity," becomes complicated.

Specific references to the passage are made.

Like Eve in *Paradise Lost,* Pearl "flirted fancifully with her own image in a pool of water." In the previous chapter, Pearl sees in the pool "the image of a little maid." Like many children who create imaginary friends, "having no other playmate," Pearl invites her reflection to "take her hand and run a race with her." At this point it seems as if Pearl has not yet made the distinction between herself and the "little maid" in the water before her. But this childlike belief is soon shattered as Pearl finds "that either she or the image was unreal."

A definition adds authority to the analysis.

As Pearl turns elsewhere "for better pastime," she first makes birch-bark boats and freights them with snail shells. The narrator playfully compares this sort of amusement to "ventures on the mighty deep" undertaken by "merchant[s] in New England." However, the "larger part" of Pearl's boats "foundered near the shore." One of the primary definitions of the word "foundered" describes a vessel that has been sunk or wrecked. Like the "little maid" who would not take her hand and play, Pearl's imaginative maritime ambitions go somewhat amiss, and she moves on to other activities. Seizing "a live horseshoe [crab] by the tail," Pearl makes "prize of several five-fingers [starfish]," and lays out "a jellyfish to melt in the warm sun." All of these things—the crab, the starfish, and the jellyfish—are living organisms that, in all likelihood, are either killed or severely injured by Pearl's flippant exploitation of them as she plays. In this way, Pearl continues, even augments, the pattern of destruction first wrought on pieces of birch bark and snail shells.

Pearl's next diversion appears, at least initially, as her most mean-spirited act thus far. Upon "perceiving a flock of

The writer links this passage to the complete novel.

Each of Pearl's actions is examined.

beach-birds . . . the naughty child picked up her apron full of pebbles, and, creeping from rock to rock after these small sea-fowl, displayed remarkable dexterity in pelting them." It is important to observe in this scene the way "amoral" attributes are ascribed to Pearl. Elsewhere in *The Scarlet Letter* she is described as an "imp," a "fairy," or "wild" and "bird-like." In this case, Pearl is spoken of as "the naughty child." However, this moral categorization seems to be used in an ironic way: For the seven-year-old Pearl, "good" and "evil," "moral" and "amoral" need not be so distinct. Yet what is remarkable about this incident is how Pearl, upon breaking a bird's wing, demonstrates a profound sense of remorse for her action, "because it grieved her to have done harm to a little being that was as wild as the sea-breeze, or as wild as Pearl herself." In the words of Prince Hamlet, "aye, there's the rub." For it is only when Pearl can somehow identify with the creature to which she has done harm, that she sighs and gives up her sport.

Perhaps a subtle lesson is offered in the way Pearl responds to the wound she has inflicted upon this "little gray bird, with a white breast." In many ways, Pearl's ambush of the flock of beach birds resembles how the close-knit New England town has also "displayed remarkable dexterity" in ostracizing Hester. The woman is ill-treated by the townspeople and cruelly regarded as "the Other" largely because the community cannot explicitly identify with her particular sin of adultery. Pearl has no qualms about other destructive behavior such as laying out a jellyfish "to melt in the warm sun." But when her play comes to harming a bird, a creature so inextricable from Pearl's very existence, the "sport" is promptly abandoned. Members of the community seem to have forgotten the words of Paul to the Romans: "All have sinned and fall short of the glory of God." If a child can identify with a bird, then surely the townspeople should have the capacity to recognize that they are sinners, too, and, as a result, should respond more sympathetically to Hester.

Of course, Hester's sin is public. Both Pearl and the scarlet letter are constant reminders of this. Yet Pearl does something remarkably curious at the end of the passage: Out of seaweed, she adorns herself in "mermaid's garb," fashioning a "mantle, and a head-dress." Then, "as the last touch," she takes some eel-grass and imitates "on her own

One telling action is carefully analyzed.

bosom, the decoration with which she was so familiar on her mother's. A letter,—the letter A,—but freshly green, instead of scarlet!" This is one of the most poignant scenes in all of *The Scarlet Letter*. There is an amazing redemptive quality to Pearl's act of replicating "on her own bosom" the letter A. In one sense, it shows how Pearl is still a child, just beginning her process of growing up. As children do, Pearl conspicuously imitates her mother, both in "devising drapery and costume" and, most significantly, by including in it the letter A.

Pearl's letter may very well be of "hidden import," but it does connote a sense of rebirth, hope, and growth. In some ways, the green letter signifies redemption, a reversal of the dishonorable meaning of Hester's scarlet letter. Later in this chapter, Hester realizes that, perhaps, along with Pearl's deep interest in the scarlet letter rests "a purpose of mercy and beneficence." The way Pearl contemplates the letter, "as if the one only thing for which she had been sent into the world was to make out its hidden import," shows her to be a child who knows more than she says, more than she even realizes.

In closing, the writer puts the passage's importance into perspective.

Chapter 15 is very much about Hester and Pearl, particularly the tensions that arise as Pearl plays and interacts with her surroundings. In this particular passage, the reader watches Pearl grow and develop through her play. Later in the chapter, the reader watches Hester struggle to relate to Pearl. She muses that Pearl "might already have approached the age when she could have been made a friend, and intrusted with as much of her mother's sorrows as could be imparted." Yet this chapter ends with Hester threatening to shut the "naughty" Pearl in a "dark closet," which serves as a reminder that, no matter how uncannily wise Pearl might seem, she is still a seven-year-old "whose activity of spirit never flagged."

READING FOR BETTER WRITING

Compare the merits of an in-depth analysis of part of a text with those of a general analysis of an entire novel.

Guidelines

Writing an Extended Literary Analysis

An extended literary analysis presents a critical understanding of a literary work (or works) based primarily on your own interpretation of the text. It also contains the viewpoints of important critics, either to support your own ideas or to offer alternative interpretations. An effective extended analysis synthesizes information from multiple sources into a thoughtful, unified essay. Refer to the guidelines below and the models that follow.

PREWRITING

Select a text. You may be given a list of titles (or authors) to consider. If so, choose a work that matches up well with your own beliefs and thoughts, or a literary work that challenges your principles or experience.

Read (or reread) the selection. Read carefully to ensure a good working knowledge of the literary work. Note any "telling" thoughts or passages in the text.

Gather details. During your information gathering, generate personal responses, review class notes, refer to secondary sources, and so on.

Establish a thesis. Choose a suitable thesis for your essay, a sentence (or two) that states your main point and exhibits your critical understanding of the text. Plan and organize the rest of your analysis accordingly.

WRITING

Draft your analysis. Shape your first draft according to your plan. Develop each key idea, working in direct references to the text and to secondary sources when appropriate.

REVISING

Review the ideas. *Does my thesis statement show insight? Do my main points support the thesis? Have I used references from the text and secondary sources?*

Check the organization. *Does my analysis form a meaningful whole with fully developed beginning, middle, and closing parts? Do I use transitions to connect main ideas and to help build a coherent essay?*

Revise for voice, word choice, and sentence fluency. *Do I sound knowledgeable about and interested in my analysis? Have I explained any unusual terms? Do my sentences flow smoothly?*

EDITING

Check for conventions. *Have I used correct punctuation, capitalization, spelling, and grammar?*

PUBLISHING

Submit your work. Carefully proofread the final copy of your analysis and follow any formatting guidelines established by your instructor.

Extended Literary Analysis

In this analysis, Sonya Jongsma explores a major theme in the nineteenth-century novel *Frankenstein* by Mary Shelley. Notice that the writer cites a number of important literary critics and displays a thorough understanding of the text, from the plot structure to the characters' motives.

Mary Shelley's *Frankenstein:* Friendship, Alienation, and Relationship Dynamics

The opening paragraph establishes the thesis of the analysis (underlined).

Mary Shelley's *Frankenstein* is one of the most well-known novels of the Romantic era. The story is one that has seeped into the popular imagination, albeit as a completely confused version. The novel's prophetic voice continues to be echoed today in modern science fiction, showing the impact of scientific knowledge on human life and institutions. Although scientific progress and the pride that often accompanies it are important and often understood to be the main purpose of the novel, *Frankenstein* also focuses on alienation and the human need for friendship. <u>The theme of friendship and alienation is clearly played out in Walton's letters to his sister, in Frankenstein's cautionary tale, and in the story of the monster.</u>

Frankenstein begins with four letters from Walton to his sister Margaret. Walton is on a voyage to the North Pole. Although he looks forward to discovering "the wondrous power which attracts the needle" (Shelley 14), and he is aglow with anticipation of the completion of the journey and the resulting glory and fame that await him, he admits that he has one want that he has "never yet been able to satisfy" (Shelley 17): he has no friend. He bemoans this fact and shares with his sister his feelings about friendship. Walton sees a friend as someone who can participate in his joy when he is glowing with the enthusiasm of success, and someone who can sustain him when he is feeling dejected because he has failed to accomplish his goals. He says, "I need a great enough friend who would have sense enough not to despise me as romantic, and affection enough for me to endeavor to regulate my mind" (Shelley 18).

A secondary source provides authoritative support.

Robert Kiely, in a collection of essays titled *The Romantic Novel in England,* says Mary Shelley shows the Coleridgean side of herself in this novel. He says, "She sees a friend as a balancing and completing agent, one who is sufficiently alike to be able to sympathize and understand, yet sufficiently different to be able to correct and refine" (167).

The writer examines the novel's structure in terms of its relationship to the thesis.

Specific text references are cited throughout the analysis.

This view is carried out even in the structure of the novel itself. It is written as three stories, with the monster's story at the center, surrounded by Frankenstein's personal story as told to Walton, and framed by Walton's narrative, which takes the form of a letter addressed to his sister. According to Mary Poovey, in *The Proper Lady and the Woman Writer,* focusing on a network of personal relationships enabled Shelley to write a credible story as a woman. She says, "Shelley is able to create her artistic persona through a series of relationships rather than a single act of self-assertion; and she is freed from having to take a single, definitive position on her unladylike subject" (31).

The stories take the form of three confessions, each one to a person with whom the confessor has an unusually close tie. In the case of the monster's story, the tie is the creature-creator relationship. In Frankenstein's story, it is the common bond, held by himself and Walton, of wholehearted commitment to a "glorious enterprise." Each hopes to bring himself fame and glory for some unprecedented scientific discovery. Finally, Walton and his sister share a close family bond.

Mary Wollstonecraft, in *A Vindication of the Rights of Woman,* says, "The most holy band of society is friendship . . . this is an obvious truth" (113). Wollstonecraft continues to explain, asserting that friendship is a special, rare kind of love because it is more than just appetite or emotion. This kind of friendship is evidenced in the early relationship between Frankenstein and Elizabeth (his sister by adoption), and it is such a friendship that Walton desires to have with Frankenstein.

In Walton's fourth letter to his sister, he relates how he has met a stranger drawn on a sled over the ice. He writes, "I said in one of my letters, dear Margaret, that I should find no friend on the wide ocean; yet I have found a man who, before his spirit had been broken by misery, I should have been happy to have possessed as the brother of my heart" (Shelley 26).

Walton tells Frankenstein about his burning desire to reach the North Pole with this stranger. Frankenstein, in turn, sees himself mirrored in Walton's single-minded pursuit of this quest. Walton then tells him that simply achieving his goals will not make him happy, sharing his conviction that a man without a friend "could boast of little happiness" (Shelley 27).

Frankenstein agrees, and says a person isn't whole if he doesn't have someone who is "wiser, better, dearer" than himself to "lend his aid to perfectionate our weak and faulty natures" (Shelley 28). Frankenstein once had such friends, but now he has lost them and can't begin life anew. He then tells Walton his story, explaining the origins of his desire for scientific knowledge and how his passion to create a living being has had disastrous consequences.

In her book *Women in Romanticism*, Meena Alexander describes Frankenstein's act of creation as an attempt to usurp the natural relationship between parents and child. She says, "Victor has abandoned the monster in his helpless infancy" (28); he alienates his creation because he is repulsed by its hideousness. Frankenstein tries to create something without the benefit of the natural family structure, and then he fails to support his creature with a personal relationship after it is "born."

The connection between the writer's ideas and those of a critic strengthens the analysis.

Kiely also sees Frankenstein's scientific experiment as unnatural because he usurps the power of women by trying to create a new species that would "bless him as its creator and source" (164). In doing such a thing, Kiely says, Frankenstein eliminates the need for woman in the creative act. He also neglects his relationship with Elizabeth during his two-year period of time-consuming, obsessive work in the laboratory.

One wonders why Frankenstein doesn't marry Elizabeth earlier and, with her cooperation, finish his work more quickly and pleasurably. After all, if the two are soul mates and have shared all things since childhood, this would be the logical step. But Frankenstein neither marries his best friend and true love nor confides in her about his real purpose and plan.

Kiely says Frankenstein's actions are "the supreme symbol of egotism, the ultimate turning away from human society and into the self which must result in desolation" (167). Having moved away from family, friends, and fiancee to perform his "creative" act in isolation, Frankenstein later witnesses in horror the monster, in an exaggerated reenactment of his own behavior, eliminate his younger brother, his dearest friend, and his beloved Elizabeth.

After Frankenstein's story is told, he explains to Walton that he can never have a close friend again. He asks Walton bitterly, "Think you that any can replace those who are gone? Can any man be to me as Clerival was; or any woman another Elizabeth?" He says friends like these "know our infantine dispositions, which, however they may be afterwards modified, are never eradicated; and they can judge of our actions with more certain conclusions as to the integrity of our motives" (Shelley 204).

Hatcher 2

A careful examination of two characters reveals an important insight.

Frankenstein's story serves well as a cautionary tale and helps prevent Walton from making the same mistakes. Unlike Frankenstein, Walton sees the possible consequences of continuing his quest and abandons it for the greater good of those who are close to him, his sister and his crew. But Frankenstein himself has not learned from his story—he still considers his purpose one "assigned by Heaven" and asks Walton to undertake his unfinished work, to prevent the monster from living as an "instrument of mischief" (Shelley 210).

The monster returns after Frankenstein's death and in an impassioned outburst explains the agony he has gone through because of his murderous acts. He compares himself to Satan in his fall from glory and accepts the fact that he will never find sympathy. The monster is content to suffer alone, although, he says, "even that enemy of God and man had friends and associates in his desolation; I am alone" (Shelley 213).

In closing, the writer reaffirms her thesis.

Shelley successfully proposes the importance of friendship to living creatures. The monster's loneliness and alienation lead to his destructive rampage, which he himself says would not have happened if he had had a companion. Frankenstein, although a proponent of the power of friends to balance and refine a person, neglects his friendships and suffers the consequences. Finally, Walton's newfound friendship with Frankenstein does provide needed guidance. Walton learns from Frankenstein and stems his ambition, placing the higher priority on his relationships, both with his sister and with his crew.

Works Cited

Alexander, Meena. *Women in Romanticism: Mary Wollstonecraft, Dorothy Wordsworth and Mary Shelley.* Savage, MD: Barnes and Noble Books, 1989. Print.

Kiely, Robert. *The Romantic Novel in England.* Cambridge: Harvard UP, 1972. Print.

Poovey, Mary. *The Proper Lady and the Woman Writer.* Chicago: U of Chicago P, 1984. Print.

Shelley, Mary. *Frankenstein.* London: Penguin Books, 1992. Print.

Wollstonecraft, Mary. *A Vindication of the Rights of Woman. The Norton Anthology of English Literature.* Ed. M. H. Abrams. New York: W. W. Norton and Company, 1993. 101–126. Print.

Extended Literary Analysis

In this essay, Sara Volle analyzes the character Rosalind in the play *As You Like It* by William Shakespeare, bringing to light the differences between men and women as explored by the playwright. Volle cites a number of important literary critics in her analysis.

"Doublet and Hose": The Implications of Rosalind's Disguise in *As You Like It*

In the opening, key background information leads up to the thesis (underlined).

Rosalind's disguise is part of Shakespeare's effort to explore the differences between men and women. Through her disguise as Ganymede, Rosalind is able to "gain extraordinary access" to Orlando (Berggren 22). Their ensuing friendship and the deconstruction of gendered stereotypes serves to validate Orlando and Rosalind's marriage. As is true of most Shakespearean comedies, *As You Like It* is largely a play about the union of opposites. <u>In disguise, Rosalind takes on both masculine and feminine characteristics and, in the process, gains valuable insights into her own personality.</u>

Specific references to the text are integrated into the analysis.

Why does Rosalind choose to disguise herself in the first place? The choice to sport "doublet and hose" is initially made as a means of protection. After being banished by Duke Frederick, Rosalind and Celia determine to join Duke Senior in the Forest of Arden. Yet Rosalind fears for their security, saying: "Alas, what danger it will be to us,/Maids as we are, to travel forth so far!/Beauty provoketh thieves sooner than gold" (1.3.108–110). Celia suggests they dress in "poor and mean attire," to which Rosalind interjects the idea of disguising herself as a man because she is "more than common tall" (1.3.115). Rosalind dons her masculine disguise with "high spirits, making fun of men's appearances of courage at the same time" (Novy 190). This disguise soon becomes Rosalind's most valuable tool for manipulating characters and situations in order to assert her own needs and desires.

In the closing lines of Act I, Celia says, "Now go [we in] content/To liberty, and not to banishment" (1.3.137–138). Indeed, both Rosalind and Celia enjoy a greater degree of liberty in the forest. Rosalind in particular obtains this liberty through her masculine disguise and the power with which

Secondary sources add authority to the analysis.

it endows her. Through her disguise, Rosalind is allowed to criticize some of the gender limits society has placed on her. This is accomplished "both by [her] words and by [her] competence in the masculine disguise that removes some of these limits" (Novy 7). Yet the masculine disguise is problematic and complicated by the ways it can work to undermine female assertiveness: "It permits us to take anything a woman says or does while in disguise as only part of a role to be discarded" (Novy 7).

There are repeated reminders in *As You Like It* that Rosalind is a woman playing the part of a man. She says to Celia, "I could find in my heart to disgrace my man's apparel and to cry like a woman; but I must comfort the weaker vessel, as doublet and hose ought to show itself courageous to petticoat; therefore courage, good Aliena" (2.4.4–8). Rosalind's realization that she must comfort the "weaker vessel" is most likely a Biblical allusion to 1 Peter 3:7: "Husbands, in the same way, show consideration for your wives in your life together, paying honor to the woman as the weaker vessel." In her new disguise, Rosalind is thus fulfilling her new place in a position that men have historically occupied. A few lines later, Rosalind implores the shepherd Corin to "Bring us where we may rest and feed./Here's a young maid with travel much oppressed,/And faints for succor" (2.4.73–74). While these words could very well be true of Rosalind, she utters them strictly on behalf of Celia, the young maid, and "here begins the comic irony introduced by Rosalind's assumption of male attire" (Knowles 96).

A Biblical allusion is noted.

Rosalind also "borrows" from the myth of Ganymede in order to successfully execute her disguise. When Rosalind expresses her desire to dress in "doublet and hose," the first question Celia asks is, "What shall I call thee when thou art a man?" (1.3.123). Rosalind responds, "I'll have no worse a name than Jove's own page,/And therefore look you call me Ganymede" (1.3.124–125). Ganymede was, according to legend, "A beautiful boy, beloved by Zeus, who (in the form of an eagle) carried him off and made him his cupbearer" (Knowles 64). The name seems particularly appropriate when one considers that Ganymede has traditionally been "thought to represent intelligence, or rational thought; more elaborately his name was thought to derive from two Greek

An allusion to Greek mythology is explored.

words meaning to joy or rejoice, and advice or counsel, and this was extended to suggest that he led people to love of divine truth" (Knowles 64). Indeed, throughout the play, Rosalind embodies these characteristics of intelligence, joy, wisdom, and truth.

The writer demonstrates a clear and thoughtful understanding of the text.

As much as Rosalind strives to stay in her masculine character, she cannot deny her feminine temperaments. Rosalind's first questions for Celia about Orlando are "Doth he know that I am in this forest and in man's apparel? Looks he as freshly as he did the day he wrestled?" (3.2.229–231). The first of Rosalind's questions could possibly be her way of "testing" the situation to determine if Orlando knows about her disguise; in this way, Rosalind is perhaps discerning whether or not she can use the disguise to her advantage. Her second question—"Looks he as freshly as he did the day he wrestled?"—speaks of Rosalind's concern with outward appearances. This accusation has usually fallen on Orlando, as he predominantly displays the quality of a Petrarchan lover whose "blazon-like poems about Rosalind" tend to overidealize the object of his infatuation (Novy 28). Yet the audience sees in Rosalind's question that she too is guilty of such overidealization and needs to establish a friendship with Orlando before true mutuality can be realized in their relationship.

The way in which Celia describes Orlando's dress and Rosalind's reaction to this description is revealing in regards to Rosalind's acceptance of traditional gender roles in a male-female relationship. Celia tells Rosalind that Orlando "was furnish'd like a hunter," to which Rosalind replies, "O ominous! he comes to kill my heart" (3.2.245–246). In this way, Rosalind is reinforcing a patriarchal view of love: She sees man as the hunter, the pursuer, and the woman as the pursued. Rosalind's pun on the word "hart" (a male deer) furthers the notion that it is the man's duty to pursue the woman. The analogy of hunting implies that the hunter is ultimately in control of the situation. As a female, Rosalind allows Orlando such control, although through her disguise, she initially asserts control, telling Celia, "I will speak to him like a saucy lackey, and under that habit play the knave with him" (3.2.295–297).

An analogy is analyzed.

Some of Rosalind's lines suggest her understanding of a more malleable sense of gender identity. Rosalind refers twice to the "hare" and once to the "hyena"; such use of animal lore is effective as Rosalind "alludes to her role as sexual chameleon" (Harley 335). When Orlando asks Rosalind (disguised as Ganymede), "Are you native of this place?" Rosalind responds, "As the cony that you see dwell where she is kindled" (3.2.338–340). Later on, Rosalind says of Phebe, "Her love is not the hare that I do hunt" (4.3.18). In another instance, Rosalind says to Orlando, "I will laugh like a hyena, and that when thou are inclin'd to sleep" (4.1.155–156). With these references, Rosalind is capitalizing on traditionally held lore in order to establish her fluctuating sexual identity. Both the hare and the hyena were thought to be hermaphroditic animals. Rosalind's allusion to them is another way of emphasizing her "symbolic role as a reconciler of opposites, an agent of harmony" (Harley 337). Through Rosalind and her disguise, dualities such as male and female are both "represented and resolved" (Harley 337).

An allusion to traditional lore is explored.

Despite the instances in which Rosalind is conspicuously feminine, she also embodies characteristically masculine traits. For example, when Rosalind eagerly listens to Le Beau's description of the upcoming wrestling match between Orlando and Charles, Touchstone marvels, "It is the first time that ever I heard breaking of ribs was sport for ladies" (1.2.138–139). In response, Rosalind implores, "But is there any else longs to see this broken music in his sides? Is there yet another dotes on rib-breaking?" (1.2.141–143). This taste for violence is a particularly masculine quality attributed to Rosalind—thus demonstrating the futility in thinking of Rosalind or any other woman in purely feminine terms. Much of *As You Like It* shows that such conceptions are valid but ultimately disabling, as females such as Rosalind clearly display both feminine and masculine qualities.

The topic sentences effectively link main ideas in the analysis.

Rosalind uses the freedom she has while in disguise to deconstruct Orlando's idealistic images of her. She reminds Orlando of the less-than-idyllic characteristics of women, ironically declaring, "I thank God I am not a woman, to be touch'd with so many giddy offenses as [my uncle] hath generally tax'd their whole sex withal" (3.2.347–350). Orlando begs Rosalind to elaborate on the "principal evils" that her uncle "laid to the charge of women" (3.2.351–352).

Rosalind articulates the faults of her sex when she tells Orlando of how she allegedly "cured" a similar lover:

Following MLA guidelines, a longer quotation is set off from the rest of the text.

> He was to imagine me his love, his mistress; and I set him every day to woo me. At which time would I, being but a moonish youth, grieve, be effeminate, changeable, longing and liking, proud, fantastical, apish, shallow, inconstant, full of tears, full of smiles; for every passion something, and for no passion truly any thing, as boys and women are for the most part cattle of this color. (3.2.407–415)

In order for Orlando and Rosalind to enjoy a truly mutual relationship, Orlando must accept Rosalind for the human that she is. Rosalind helps Orlando to come to this understanding through her disguise: "Ganymede's 'Rosalind' is a blend of such misogynistic stereotypes as the scold, the fickle, or the cruel Petrarchan mistress, and the shrewish cuckold maker" (Shapiro 124).

In closing, the writer reflects on the significance of Rosalind's role-playing.

Rosalind's disguise allows both her and Orlando the opportunity to cultivate a friendship without being confined by the long-established barriers that exist between men and women. In this way, "theatrical disguise robs courtship of the artificial exaggeration of masculine and feminine difference sustained in the skirmishes between Phebe and Silvius" (Dusinberre 251). It is necessary, however, that Rosalind relinquish her disguise at the end of the play. While "disguise is first used to crystallize rivalry between the woman's self-image and the man's desires," it must be surrendered to "bring consummation both to man and woman, so that rivalry can be transcended as cooperation brings fulfillment" (Hayles 66). Because of this realized mutuality, Hymen's words at the end of the play—"Then is there mirth in heaven/When earthly things made even/ Atone together" (5.4.108–110)—can ring true. Indeed, a harmony is reached at the end of the play as opposites are reconciled in marriage (Beckman 46). This harmony would not have been possible without Rosalind's earlier disguise.

NOTE: The works-cited page is not shown.

READING FOR BETTER WRITING

Select a quotation from the text in Volle's analysis. Would it have been wiser to paraphrase the ideas? Discuss your reasons.

Ideas for Literary Analyses

The ideas listed below will help you choose a focus for your analysis.

THEME: Write about one of the themes presented in your selection.

- Is the author saying something about ambition, courage, etc.?
- Does the selection show you what it is like to experience racism, loneliness, and so on?
- Does the author say something about a time and place in history?

CHARACTERIZATION AND PLOT: Explore aspects of character and plot development.

- What motives determine a character's course of action?
- What are the most revealing aspects of one of the characters? (Consider her or his thoughts, words, and actions.)
- What external conflicts affect the main character? (Consider conflicts with other characters, the setting, objects, and so on.)
- What internal conflicts challenge the main character? (Consider the thoughts, feelings, and ideas that affect him or her.)
- How is suspense built into the story?
- Do any twists or reversals in the plot add to the story?
- Does the text exhibit traits of a quest, a comedy, a tragedy, or an ironic twist on one of these patterns of development?

SETTING: Analyze the role of the setting in the story.

- What effect does the setting have on the characters? The plot? The theme?
- Has the setting increased your knowledge of a specific time and place?
- Is the setting new and thought provoking?

STYLE: Give special attention to the author's style of writing.

- What feeling or tone is created in the selection? How is it created?
- Does an important symbol add meaning to the selection?
- Do figures of speech like metaphors, similes, and personification add to the writing?

AUTHOR: Focus on the life and times of the author.

- How does the text reflect the author's experience or beliefs?
- How does this text compare to other works by the author?
- How does the literary work represent the author's particular time, place, and culture?

NOTE: You can also address a particular form of *criticism*. (See page 297.)

LITERARY TERMS

Allegory is a story in which people, things, and actions represent an idea or a generalization about life; allegories often have a strong moral, or lesson.

Allusion is a reference in literature to a familiar person, place, or thing.

Anadiplosis is the repetition of the last word of one clause at the beginning of the following clause.

Analogy is a comparison of two or more similar objects, suggesting that if they are alike in certain respects, they will probably be alike in other ways, too.

Anaphora is the repetition of a group of words at the beginning of successive clauses.

Anecdote is a short summary of an interesting or humorous, often biographical incident or event.

Antagonist is the person or thing working against the protagonist, or hero, of the work.

Asyndeton is the omission of conjunctions between related clauses, as in "I came, I saw, I conquered."

Caricature is a picture or an imitation of a person's features or mannerisms exaggerated to appear comic or absurd.

Character sketch is a short piece of writing that reveals or shows something important about a person or fictional character.

Characterization is the method an author uses to reveal or describe characters and their various personalities.

Climax is the turning point, and usually the most intense point, in a story.

Comedy is literature with a love story at its core. The basic plot often develops in this way: an old, established society tries to prevent the formation of a new one (the union of a young couple). The young couple succeed in the end. In comedy, human errors or problems may appear humorous.

Conflict is the problem or struggle in a story that triggers the action. There are five basic types of conflict:

Person vs. Person: One character in a story has a problem with one or more of the other characters.

Person vs. Society: A character has a problem with some element of society: the school, the law, the accepted way of doing things.

Person vs. Self: A character has a problem deciding what to do in a certain situation.

Person vs. Nature: A character has a problem with some natural happening: a snowstorm, an avalanche, the bitter cold, etc.

Person vs. Fate (God): A character must battle what seems to be an uncontrollable problem.

Context is the set of facts or circumstances surrounding an event or a situation in a piece of literature.

Convention is an established technique or device in literature or in drama. *Deus ex machina* (see below) is a common convention in Greek and Roman drama.

Denouement (dā´no͞o-mäN´)is the final solution or outcome of a play or story.

Deus ex machina (dā´ əs ĕks mä´ kə-nə) is a person or thing that suddenly appears, providing a solution to a difficult problem. The person or thing is lowered to the stage by means of a crane in classic drama.

Dialogue is the conversation carried on by the characters in a literary work.

Diction is an author's choice of words based on their correctness, clarity, or effectiveness.

Archaic words are words that are old-fashioned and no longer sound natural when used, as "I believe thee not" for "I don't believe you."

Colloquialism is an expression that is usually accepted in informal situations and certain locations, as in "He really grinds my beans."

Jargon (technical diction) is the specialized language used by a specific group, such as those who use computers: *override, interface, download.*

Profanity is language that shows disrespect for someone or something regarded as holy or sacred.

Slang is the language used by a particular group of people among themselves; it is also language that is used in fiction and special writing situations to lend color and feeling: *awesome, chill out.*

Trite expressions are those that lack depth or originality, are overworked, or are not worth using in the first place.

Vulgarity is language that is generally considered common, crude, gross, and, at times, offensive. It is sometimes used in fiction to add realism.

Didactic literature instructs or presents a moral or religious statement. It can also be, as in the case of Dante's *Divine Comedy* or Milton's *Paradise Lost,* a work that stands on its own as valuable literature.

Drama is the form of literature known as plays; but drama also refers to the type of serious play that is often concerned with the leading character's relationship to society.

Dramatic monologue is a literary work (or part of a literary work) in which a character is speaking about him- or herself as if another person were present. The speaker's words reveal something important about his or her character.

Elizabethan literature generally refers to the prose and poetry created during the reign of Elizabeth I (1558–1603).

Empathy is putting yourself in someone else's place and imagining how that person must feel. The phrase "What would you do if you were in my shoes?" is a request for one person to empathize with another.

Epic is a long narrative poem that tells of the deeds and adventures of a hero.

Epigram is a brief, witty poem or expression often dealing with its subject in a satirical manner.

> **"There never was a good war or a bad peace."**
>
> —Ben Franklin

Epitaph is a short poem or verse written in memory of someone.

Epithet is a word or phrase used in place of a person's name; it is characteristic of that person: Alexander the Great, Material Girl, Ms. Know-It-All.

Essay is a piece of prose that expresses an individual's point of view; usually, it is a series of closely related paragraphs that combine to make a complete piece of writing.

Exaggeration (hyperbole) is overstating or stretching the truth for special effect.

> **"That story is as old as time."**

Exposition is writing that is intended to clarify or explain something that might otherwise be difficult to understand; in a play or novel, it would be that portion that helps the reader to understand the background or situation in which the work is set.

Expressionism is a highly emotional form of dramatic expression exploring the ultimate nature of human experience. The expressionist playwrights focused on subconscious feelings and desires.

Fable is a short fictional narrative that teaches a lesson. It usually includes animals that talk and act like people.

Falling action is the action of a play or story that works out the decision arrived at during the climax. It ends with the resolution.

Farce is literature based on a highly humorous and highly improbable plot.

Figurative language is language used to create a special effect or feeling. It is characterized by figures of speech or language that compares, exaggerates, or means something other than what it first appears to mean. (See "Figure of speech.")

Figure of speech is a literary device used to create a special effect or feeling by making some type of interesting or creative comparison. The most common types are *antithesis, hyperbole, metaphor, metonymy, personification, simile,* and *understatement.*

Antithesis is an opposition, or a contrast, of ideas.

> **"It was the best of times, it was the worst of times, it was the age of wisdom, it was the age of foolishness . . . "**
>
> —Charles Dickens, *A Tale of Two Cities*

Hyperbole (hī-pûr´ bə-lē) is an exaggeration, or overstatement.

> **"I have seen this river so wide it had only one bank."**
>
> —Mark Twain, *Life on the Mississippi*

Metaphor is a comparison of two unlike things in which no word of comparison (*as* or *like*) is used.

Metonymy (mə-tŏn′ ə-mē) is the substituting of one word for another that is closely related to it.

"The White House has decided to provide a million more public service jobs." (*White House* is substituting for *president*.)

Personification is a literary device in which the author speaks of or describes an animal, object, or idea as if it were a person.

"The rock stubbornly refused to move."

Simile is a comparison of two unlike things in which a word of comparison (*like* or *as*) is used.

"She stood in front of the altar, shaking like a freshly caught trout."
—Maya Angelou, *I Know Why the Caged Bird Sings*

Understatement, or **litotes,** is stating an idea with restraint (holding back) to emphasize what is being talked about. Mark Twain once described Tom Sawyer's Aunt Polly as being "prejudiced against snakes." Since she could not stand snakes, this way of saying so is called understatement.

Flashback is going back to an earlier time (in a story) for the purpose of making something in the present clearer.

Foreshadowing is giving hints of what is to come later in a story.

Genre refers to a category or type of literature based on its style, form, and content. The mystery novel is a literary genre.

Gothic novel is a type of fiction that is often characterized by gloomy castles, ghosts, and supernatural or sensational happenings—creating a mysterious and sometimes frightening story. Mary Shelley's *Frankenstein* is probably the best-known gothic novel still popular today.

Hubris, derived from the Greek word *hybris,* means "excessive pride." In Greek tragedy, hubris is often viewed as the flaw that leads to the downfall of the tragic hero.

Imagery is the words or phrases a writer selects to create a certain picture in the reader's mind. Imagery is usually based on sensory details.

"The sky was dark and gloomy, the air was damp and raw, the streets were wet and sloppy."
—Charles Dickens, *The Pickwick Papers*

Impressionism is the recording of events or situations as they have been impressed upon the mind as feelings, emotions, and vague thoughts; in contrast, realism deals with objective facts. A writer shares his boyhood impressions of winter:

" . . . we waited to snowball the cats. Sleek and long as jaguars and horrible-whiskered, spitting and snarling, they would slink and sidle over the white back-garden walls, and the lynx-eyed hunters, Jim and I, fur-capped and moccasined trappers from Hudson Bay, off Mumbles Road, would hurl our deadly snowballs at the green of their eyes. The wise cats never appeared."
—Dylan Thomas, *A Child's Christmas in Wales*

Irony is using a word or phrase to mean the exact opposite of its literal or normal meaning. There are three kinds of irony:

dramatic irony, in which the reader or the audience sees a character's mistakes or misunderstandings, but the character him- or herself does not;

verbal irony, in which the writer says one thing and means another ("The best substitute for experience is being sixteen"); or

irony of **situation,** in which there is a great difference between the purpose of a particular action and the result.

Local color is the use of details that are common in a region of the country.

> **"Mama came out and lit into me for sitting there doing nothing. Said I was no-count and shiftless and why hadn't I gathered eggs and . . . "**
>
> —Olive Ann Burns, *Cold Sassy Tree*

Malapropism is the type of pun, or play on words, that results when two words become jumbled in the speaker's mind. The term comes from a character in Sheridan's comedy *The Rivals.* The character, Mrs. Malaprop, is constantly mixing up her words, as when she says "as headstrong as an allegory [she means alligator] on the banks of the Nile."

Melodrama is an exaggerated form of drama (as in television soap operas) characterized by heavy use of romance, suspense, and emotion.

Miracle play is a medieval drama based on Biblical events (creation, the Flood, the life of Christ, and so on) or on the life of a saint or martyr. The term is also used for any type of religious drama in the medieval period.

Mood is the feeling a piece of literature arouses in the reader: happiness, sadness, peacefulness, and so on.

Moral is the particular value or lesson the author is trying to get across to the reader. The "moral of the story" is a common phrase in Aesop's fables.

Morality play is a type of allegorical drama (fifteenth century) making a moral or religious point. A morality play—*Castle of Perseverance, Everyman,* and so on—gives appreciable shape to abstract concepts.

Motif is an often-repeated idea or theme in literature. In *The Adventures of Huckleberry Finn,* Huck is constantly in conflict with the "civilized" world. This conflict becomes a motif throughout the novel.

Myth is a traditional story that attempts to explain a natural phenomenon or justify a certain practice or belief of a society.

Narration is writing that relates an event or a series of events: a story.

Narrator is the person who is telling the story.

Naturalism is an extreme form of realism in which the author tries to show the relation of a person to the environment or surroundings. Often, the author finds it necessary to show the ugly or raw side of that relationship.

Neoclassicism is the period of English literature (through the eighteenth century) influenced by classical arts and literature.

Novel is a lengthy fictional story with a plot that is revealed by the speech, action, and thoughts of the characters.

Novella is a prose work longer than the standard short story, but shorter and less complex than a full-length novel.

Oxymoron is a combination of contradictory terms, as in *jumbo shrimp.*

Parable is a short, descriptive story that illustrates a particular belief or moral.

Paradox is a statement that seems contrary to common sense yet may, in fact, be true: "The coach considered this a good loss."

Parody is a form of literature intended to mock a particular literary work or its style; a comic effect is intended.

Pathos is a Greek root meaning *suffering* or *passion.* It usually describes the part in a play or story that is intended to elicit pity or sorrow from the audience or reader.

Periphrasis is circumlocution. It is the use of longer phrasing when a shorter form could be used (for example, passive voice).

Persona is the voice or personality an author assumes for a particular purpose or character, which may or may not be anything like the author's personality.

Picaresque novel (pik´ ə-rěsk´) is a novel consisting of a lengthy string of loosely connected events. It usually features the adventures of a rogue, or scamp, living by his wits among the middle class. Mark Twain's *Huckleberry Finn* is a picaresque novel.

Plot is the action or sequence of events in a story. It is usually a series of related incidents that build upon one another as the story develops.

Plot line is the graphic display of the action or events in a story: *exposition, rising action, climax, falling action,* and *resolution.*

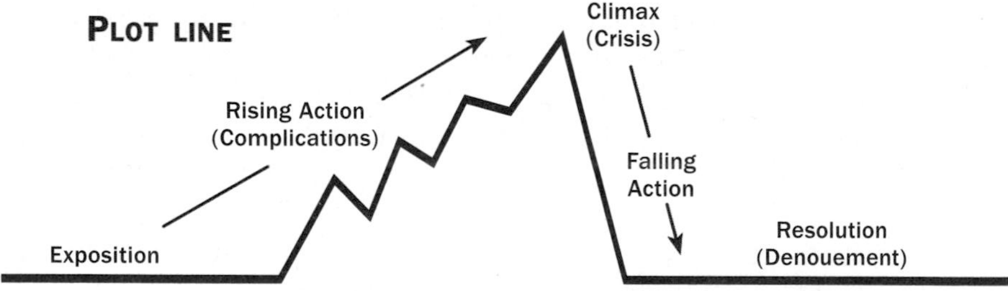

Poetic justice is a term that describes a character "getting what he deserves" in the end, especially if what he deserves is punishment. The purest form of poetic justice results when one character plots against another but ends up being caught in his or her own trap.

Poetry is an imaginative response to experience reflecting a keen awareness of language. (See pages 295–296 for poetry terms.)

Point of view is the vantage point from which the story is told. In the first-person point of view, the story is told by one of the characters: "I don't know what I'm doing tonight. What about you?" In the third-person point of view, the story is told by someone outside the story: "The simple fact is he lacked confidence. He would rather do something he wasn't all that crazy about doing than risk looking foolish."

Protagonist is the main character or hero of the story.

Pseudonym (also known as "pen name") means "false name" and applies to the name a writer uses in place of his or her given name. George Eliot is the pseudonym of the novelist Ann Evans.

Pun is a word or phrase that is used in such a way as to suggest more than one possible meaning. Words used in a pun are words that sound the same (or nearly the same) but have different meanings.

Quest features a main character who is seeking to find something or achieve a goal. In the process, this person encounters and overcomes a series of obstacles. In the end, she or he returns, having gained knowledge and experience as a result of the adventures.

Realism is literature that attempts to represent life as it really is.

Reminiscence is writing based on the writer's memory of a particular time, place, or incident. "Memoir" is another term for reminiscence.

Renaissance, which means "rebirth," is the period of history following the Middle Ages. This period began late in the fourteenth century and continued through the fifteenth and sixteenth centuries. Milton (1608–1674) is often regarded as the last of the great Renaissance poets. The term now applies to any period of time in which intellectual and artistic interest is revived or reborn.

Resolution, or denouement, is the portion of the play or story in which the problem is solved. It comes after the climax and falling action and is intended to bring the story to a satisfactory end.

Rising action is the series of conflicts or struggles that build a story or play toward a climax.

Romance is a form of literature that presents life as we would like it to be rather than as it actually is. Usually, it has a great deal of adventure, love, and excitement.

Romanticism is a literary movement with an emphasis on the imagination and emotions.

Sarcasm is the use of praise to mock someone or something, as in "He's a real he-man," "She's a real winner."

Satire is a literary tone used to ridicule or make fun of human vice or weakness, often with the intent of correcting or changing the subject of the satiric attack.

Setting is the time and place in which the action of a literary work occurs.

Short story is a brief fictional work. It usually contains one major conflict and at least one main character.

Slapstick is a form of low comedy that makes its appeal through the use of exaggerated, sometimes violent action. The "pie in the face" routine is a classic piece of slapstick.

Slice of life is a term that describes the type of realistic or naturalistic writing that accurately reflects what life is like. This is done by giving the reader a sample, or slice, of experience.

Soliloquy is a speech delivered by a character when he or she is alone on stage.

Stereotype is a pattern or form that does not change. A character is "stereotyped" if she or he has no individuality and fits the mold of that particular kind of person.

Stream of consciousness is a style of writing in which the thoughts and feelings of the writer are recorded as they occur.

Structure is the form or organization a writer uses for her or his literary work. There are a great number of possible forms used regularly in literature: parable, fable, romance, satire, farce, slapstick, and so on.

Style is the author's use of words, phrases, and sentences to form his or her ideas. Style is also the qualities and characteristics that distinguish one writer's work from the work of others.

Symbol is a person, a place, a thing, or an event used to represent something else: the dove is a symbol of peace. Characters in literature are often symbols of good or evil.

Theme is the statement about life a particular work is trying to get across to the reader. In stories written for children, the theme is often spelled out clearly at the end. In more complex literature, the theme is embedded in the story.

Tone is the overall feeling, or effect, created by a writer's use of words. This feeling may be serious, mock-serious, humorous, satiric, and so on.

Total effect is the general impression a literary work gives the reader.

Tragedy is a literary work in which the hero is destroyed by some character flaw and by forces beyond his or her control.

Tragic hero is a character who experiences an inner struggle because of a character flaw. That struggle ends in the defeat of the hero.

Transcendentalism is a philosophy that requires human beings to go beyond (transcend) reason in their search for truth. An individual can arrive at the basic truths of life through spiritual insight if he or she takes the time to think seriously about them.

POETRY TERMS

Alliteration is the repetition of initial consonant sounds in words such as "rough and ready." An example of alliteration (from "Runaway Warning" by Anne-Marie Oomen) is underlined below:

"Our gang paces the pier like an old myth . . . "

Assonance is repetition of vowel sounds without repetition of consonants.

"My words like silent rain drops fell . . . "

—Paul Simon, "Sounds of Silence"

Ballad is a poem in verse form that tells a story.

Blank verse is an unrhymed form of poetry. Each line normally consists of 10 syllables in which every other syllable, beginning with the second, is stressed. Since blank verse is often used in very long poems, it may depart from the strict pattern from time to time.

Caesura (sĭ-zho͞orʹ ə) is a pause or sudden break in a line of poetry.

Canto is a main division of a long poem.

Consonance is the repetition of consonant sounds. Although it is similar to alliteration, consonance is not limited to the first letters of words:

" . . . and high school girls with clear skin smiles . . . "

—Janis Ian, "At Seventeen"

Couplet is two lines of verse the same length that usually rhyme.

End rhyme is the rhyming of words that appear at the ends of two or more lines of poetry.

Enjambment (ĕn-jămʹ mənt) is the running over of a sentence or thought from one line to another.

Foot is the smallest repeated pattern of stressed and unstressed syllables in a poetic line. (See "Verse.")

Iambic: an unstressed followed by a stressed syllable **(rĕ péat)**

Anapestic: two unstressed followed by a stressed syllable **(ĭn té rrúpt)**

Trochaic: a stressed followed by an unstressed syllable **(óld ĕr)**

Dactylic: a stressed followed by two unstressed syllables **(ó pĕn lў̆)**

Spondaic: two stressed syllables **(heárt breák)**

Pyrrhic: two unstressed syllables (Pyrrhic seldom appears by itself.)

Free verse is poetry that does not have a regular meter or rhyme scheme.

Heroic couplet (closed couplet) consists of two successive rhyming lines that contain a complete thought.

Internal rhyme occurs when the rhyming words appear in the same line of poetry: **"You break my eyes with a look that buys sweet cake."**

Lyric is a short verse that is intended to express the emotions of the author; quite often, these lyrics are set to music.

Meter is the patterned repetition of stressed and unstressed syllables in a line of poetry.

Onomatopoeia (ŏn′ ə-măt′ a-pē′ ə) is the use of a word whose sound suggests its meaning, as in *clang, buzz,* and *twang.*

Refrain is the repetition of a line or phrase of a poem at regular intervals, especially at the end of each stanza. A song's refrain may be called the chorus.

Repetition is the repeating of a word, a phrase, or an idea for emphasis or for rhythmic effect within a poem or prose.

"His laugh, his dare, his shrug / sag ghostlike . . . "

Rhyme is the similarity or likeness of sound existing between two words. *Sat* and *cat* are perfect rhymes because the vowel and final consonant sounds are exactly the same.

Rhymed verse is verse with end rhyme; it usually has regular meter.

Rhythm is the ordered or free occurrence of sound in poetry. Ordered sound creates metered rhythm; freely occurring sound creates free verse.

Sonnet is a poem consisting of 14 lines of iambic pentameter. There are two popular forms of the sonnet, the Italian (or Petrarchan) and the Shakespearean (or English).

Italian (Petrarchan) sonnet has two parts: an octave (eight lines) and a sestet (six lines), usually rhyming *abbaabba, cdecde.* Often, a question is raised in the octave and answered in the sestet.

Shakespearean (English or Elizabethan) sonnet consists of three quatrains and a final rhyming couplet. The rhyme scheme is *abab, cdcd, efef, gg.* Usually, the question or theme is set forth in the quatrains while the answer or resolution appears in the final couplet.

Stanza is a division of poetry named for the number of lines it contains.

Couplet: two-line stanza
Triplet: three-line stanza
Quatrain: four-line stanza
Quintet: five-line stanza
Sestet: six-line stanza
Septet: seven-line stanza
Octave: eight-line stanza

Synecdoche (sĭ-nek′ də-kē) is using part of something to represent the whole: "All hands on deck." ("Hands" is being used to represent the whole person.)

Verse is a metric line of poetry. It is named according to the kind and number of feet composing it: iambic pentameter, anapestic tetrameter, and so on. (See "Foot.")

Monometer: one foot
Dimeter: two feet
Trimeter: three feet
Tetrameter: four feet
Pentameter: five feet
Hexameter: six feet
Heptameter: seven feet
Octometer: eight feet

Critical Approaches to Literary Analysis

Each of the following approaches represents a theory of literary interpretation. You will notice similarities between some of the theories.

Deconstruction suggests that meanings derived during a reading are neither obvious nor neutral. It presupposes that unessential features of a text betray the "main" message and sees all writing as a complex historical, cultural process rooted in the relations of texts to each other and the institutions and conventions of writing.

Feminist Criticism focuses on the place of women in society and examines how a text sustains or challenges the accepted structure of society.

Formalism emphasizes a close reading of a text (the words themselves) and the analysis of its form in order to understand its meaning.

Historical Biographical Criticism sees a literary work as a reflection of the author's life in the life of the characters.

Marxist Criticism focuses on the exploitation of the masses and on forcing particular values and beliefs onto other social groups. It explores how different classes of people are represented in literature.

Moral Philosophical Criticism sees the function of literature as teaching morality.

Mythological Archetypal Criticism explores archetypal patterns in literature.

New Criticism argues that meaning is produced by the words on the page and rejects the importance of the author's intention or factors "outside" the text. (See "Formalism.")

New Historicism examines a text alongside other texts of the period.

Poststructuralism follows the principles of structuralism and questions them. It investigates existing social structures and seeks to analyze how their knowledge and truths are constructed to favor some groups and not others. (See "Deconstruction.")

Psychoanalytic Criticism explores the relationship between culture and the personal identity of a character(s) in a text. It attends to the role of the subconscious in the author, reader, and characters in a text.

Reader Response shares a personal reaction to a literary work.

Semiotics grows out of formalism and approaches a text as a collection of elements drawn from a social system—forms of dress, speech, and so on. It explores how characters, settings, actions, and so on, are structured and examines a text as representing certain cultural ideas. (See "Structuralism.")

Structuralism analyzes systems or structures that make a text possible and demonstrates how texts are constructed to make meaning. It is similar to but more philosophical than formalism.

Business Writing

Business Writing

You write essays, develop research papers, and respond to writing prompts. These are important practical types of writing that you develop in school. Be prepared. You'll continue to do a lot of writing after you've completed your technical or university schooling. As writer Patricia T. O'Conner states, "Because of computers, we're suddenly a nation of writers." Engineers, mechanics, lawyers, physicians, fitness trainers—everyone is "wired in" and writing letters, reports, proposals, news briefs, and so on.

Even if you remain a student for several more years, you'll find yourself using forms of workplace communication. You'll write business letters and e-mail messages, develop multimedia presentations, and create proposals and résumés.

WHAT'S AHEAD

This chapter serves as a basic guide to business writing. Sample letters will help you communicate effectively with everyone from city officials to scholarship committees. The sample résumé will help you make a favorable impression when you apply for part-time work, a summer job, or an internship. There's even a special set of guidelines to help you master memos and e-mail messages.

"Be yourself. Above all, let who you are, what you are, what you believe shine through every sentence you write."

—John Jakes

Business Writing

QUICK GUIDE

All business writing, whether it is a letter, a résumé, or a memo, shares the following characteristics:

- **IDEAS:** Business writing begins with your need to communicate an important idea to another person ("I would like to apply for, request, inform you, . . . "). The purpose is to discuss, announce, clarify, or confirm a specific business-related matter. Always provide your audience with the necessary information to act upon your request, concern, or announcement.

- **ORGANIZATION:** Business writing is a highly structured and practical form of communication. The beginning, middle, and ending parts must include specific types of information.

- **VOICE:** Express yourself concisely, and courteously. Think of your writing as one part of a purposeful and sincere conversation with your reader. Use the personal pronouns *I* and *my* in person-to-person communication and *we* and *our* in messages in which you are representing your company or department.

- **WORD CHOICE:** Use specific words that clearly communicate your message. Explain any specialized words or phrases.

- **SENTENCE FLUENCY:** Express your ideas in easy-to-follow sentences. Business people appreciate a "quick read."

- **CONVENTIONS:** Make sure that your business writing follows the accepted standards of the language. Carelessly written letters or résumés send the wrong message.

- **PRESENTATION:** When it comes to business writing, it's important to follow the basic standards of form and style (as outlined in this chapter). People expect letters, memos, and résumés to be presented in recognizable formats.

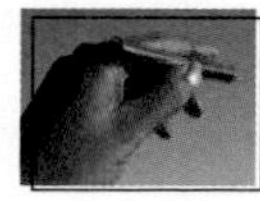

NOTE: Writers of business messages must know why they are writing (the purpose), what they are writing (the details), how to present the message (the accepted form), and how to send it (mail, e-mail, fax). One final thought—always make a copy of your writing and file it for future reference.

Writing the Business Letter

Business letters are written for specific reasons: to make a request, to order materials, to file a complaint, to apply for a job, and so on. A business letter is usually concise and to the point. Preferably, it should fit on one page and follow a specific pattern of form, style, and spacing, as you'll see in the guidelines below.

Full Block

BC Box 143
Balliole College
Eugene, OR 97440-5125
August 29, 2007

Ms. Alida Mandez
Ogg Hall, Room 222
Balliole College
Eugene, OR 97440-0222

Dear Ms. Mandez:

As the president of Balliole's Earth Care Club, I'd like to welcome you to college. I hope that your freshman year is a great learning experience both inside and outside the classroom.

That learning experience is the reason I'm writing to encourage you to join the Earth Care Club. As a member, you could participate in the educational and action-oriented mission of the club. The club has most recently been involved in the following:

- assisting with recycling on campus
- promoting cloth rather than plastic bag use among students
- advising the college administration on landscaping, renovating, and building for energy efficiency
- planning the annual Earth Day celebration

What environmental concerns and activities would you like to focus on? Bring them to the Earth Care Club. Simply complete the enclosed form and return it by September 4. Then watch the campus news for details on our first meeting.

Yours sincerely,

Katherine Mioto
Katherine Mioto
President

KM:kr
Encl. membership form
cc: Esther du Toit, membership committee

Semi-Block

BC Box 143
Balliole College
Eugene, OR 97440-5125
August 29, 2007

Ms. Alida Mandez
Ogg Hall, Room 222
Balliole College
Eugene, OR 97440-0222

Dear Ms. Mandez:

As the president of Balliole's Earth Care Club, I'd like to welcome you to college. I hope that your freshman year is a great learning experience both inside and outside the classroom.

That learning experience is the reason I'm writing—to encourage you to join the Earth Care Club. As a member, you could participate in the educational and action-oriented mission of the club. The club has most recently been involved in the following:

- assisting with recycling on campus
- promoting cloth rather than plastic bag use among students
- advising the college administration on landscaping, renovating, and building for energy efficiency
- planning the annual Earth Day celebration

What environmental concerns and activities would you like to focus on? Bring them to the Earth Care Club. Simply complete the enclosed form and return it by September 4. Then watch the campus news for details on our first meeting.

Yours sincerely,

Katherine Mioto
Katherine Mioto
President

KM:kr
Encl. membership form
cc: Esther du Toit, membership committee

Format Guidelines

- Use a consistent style: semi-block or full block.
- Use a type size and style that make reading easy.
- Use left and right margins of 1 to 1.5 inches.
- Center the letter vertically (top to bottom) on the page, leaving margins of 1 to 1.5 inches.
- If you develop a personal letterhead, keep the design simple.

Parts of a Business Letter

Writers use business letters to request information, to apply for a job, and to file a complaint. The basic format of an effective letter is similar whether it is sent through the regular mail or delivered via e-mail.

- The **heading** includes the writer's complete address, either on company stationery, in a word-processing template, or typed out manually. The heading also includes the day, month, and year. If the address is part of the letterhead, place only the date in the upper left corner.
- The **inside address** includes the recipient's name and complete address. If you're not sure who should receive the letter or how to correctly spell someone's name, you can call the company to ask. If a person's title is a single word or very short, include it on the same line as the name, preceded by a comma. If the title is longer, put it on a separate line under the name.
- The **salutation** is the greeting. Follow the recipient's name with a colon, not a comma. Use *Mr.* or *Ms.* with the person's last name, unless you happen to be well acquainted with the person. (Do not guess at whether a woman prefers *Miss* or *Mrs.)* If the person's gender is not obvious from the name, you may use the full name in the salutation—for example, *Dear Pat Johnson.* If you don't know the recipient's name, use one of these salutations:
  - Dear Manager:
  - Dear Sir or Madam:
  - Attention: Customer Service
  - Attention: Personnel Director
- The **body** is the main part of the letter. It is organized into three parts. The beginning states why you are writing, the middle provides the needed details, and the ending focuses on what should happen next. Double-space between the paragraphs and do not indent. If the letter is longer than one page, put the reader's name at the top left margin, the page number in the center, and the date at the top right margin of all subsequent pages.
- The **complimentary closing** ends the message. Use *Sincerely* or *Yours truly* followed by a comma. Capitalize only the first word.
- The **signature** makes the letter official. Leave four blank lines between the complimentary closing and your typed name. Write your signature in that space.
- The **notes** tell who authored the letter (uppercase initials and a colon), who typed the letter (lowercase initials), who received a copy (after *cc:*), and what enclosures are included (after *Enclosure* or *Encl:*).

Letter of Inquiry or Request

Mandisa Kwafume, student liaison for the band boosters club, wrote this letter to solicit advertising revenue from the business community.

Heading

Plains Union High School Band Boosters Club
676 Highway R
Dry Plains, TX 78112
October 3, 2007

Four to Seven Spaces

Inside address

Rex Neinheus
Area Aquatics
1322 Main Street
Dry Plains, TX 78113

Double Space

Salutation

Dear Mr. Neinheus:

Double Space

Body
The writer explains why she is writing, provides details, and suggests a next step.

I am writing on behalf of the Plains Union High School Band Boosters Club. Perhaps you are aware that the high school presents several concerts and plays throughout the year. Did you also know that many local businesses advertise in the programs for these events?

Purchasing an ad in one or more of the programs is an effective form of advertising. The performers' family and friends read the programs and notice the businesses advertising in them. They'll make an effort to patronize a business that supports the school.

Enclosed you will find an insertion order for any size advertisement you care to place. You may provide camera-ready copy, or we will design something for you. Please be sure to indicate which program(s) you prefer for your ad.

Thank you for supporting the arts at Plains Union High School.

Double Space

Complimentary closing

Sincerely,

Signature

Mandisa Kwafume

Four Spaces

Mandisa Kwafume, Student Liaison

Double Space

Initials
Copies
Enclosure

MK: jb
cc: Ms. Felicia Goodman, President
Encl: insertion order

The Letter of Complaint

One type of letter you'll write now and in the future is the complaint letter. When a mistake happens that affects you—a defective product, poor service, a negative housing condition—you often need to write a letter to correct the situation. Elaine Hammons wrote the following letter to complain about a defective product.

2112 Jefferson Park Avenue #10
Charlottesville, VA 22903-5790
April 11, 2007

The Shoe Company
123 West Adams
Beaverton, OR 97005-9870

Dear Customer Service Department:

The **opening** describes the problem.

On February 22, I bought size 8 Jump Max running shoes for $64.95 at the Runner's Roost in Walker, Virginia. The store was going out of business, but the salesperson told me that your guarantee would still apply.

The **middle** discusses the action taken.

I wore the shoes for four weeks with no problem. However, on April 7, I noticed a loss of cushioning in my left shoe.

I spoke to Suzanne in your customer service department yesterday, and she told me to send the shoes and related details to her attention.

The **closing** identifies the preferred solution.

I am enclosing my Jump Max running shoes along with a copy of the canceled check to show proof of purchase. Please send me a new pair of shoes in the same model and size. I've enjoyed using your products in the past, and I expect to use them in the future.

Sincerely,

Elaine Hammons

Elaine Hammons

Encl: shoes, check copy

Letter of Application

Louis Roberts wrote the following letter to apply for a research internship position.

24 Hampshire Street
Skones, MT 59781
February 2, 2007

Brian Allman, Director
Office of Biomedical Studies
Medical College of Butte
540 Kings Row
Butte, MT 59702

Dear Mr. Allman:

The **opening** introduces the writer as well as the purpose of the letter.

Please find enclosed my official application for your High School Summer Research Internship Program, as well as the names and contact information for two references. I believe I am qualified for this internship and would love the opportunity to work with the mentors at the Medical College of Butte.

The **middle** paragraphs discuss background, qualifications, and long-range goals.

I developed my interest in biochemistry and cell biology in my high school science classes this past year. In these classes, we planned and executed several research experiments related to allergic reactions, and I would like to continue to investigate the physiology behind these "overreactions" of the immune system.

This internship would be the first step in my ultimate goal of becoming an immunologist. I realize how intensive the training for such a career is, and I can't think of a better introduction to it than this internship.

The **closing** adds information and thanks the reader.

If you have any specific questions for me, please e-mail me at lrbts@email.net or call me at (406) 555-0515. Thank you for your consideration, and I hope to hear from you soon.

Sincerely,

Louis Roberts

Louis Roberts

Encl: application, references

The Recommendation Request Letter

Letters of recommendation are required for almost all applications to universities as well as for many scholarship, internship, and employment applications. You may make your request in person, but a courteous and clear letter or e-mail message makes the request official and provides the person with the necessary information to complete the task. Christina Lee wrote the following letter of request to her high school history teacher and coach.

2456 Charles Street
Koren, WI 53801
October 10, 2007

Mrs. Veronica Ochoa
History Department
Central High School
2125 Pine Street
Koren, WI 53801

The **opening** asks the person to write a letter.

Dear Mrs. Ochoa:

As we discussed last week, I would like you to write a letter of recommendation for me. You, as well as anyone else in our high school, know my potential as a college student.

The **middle** provides background information.

As my instructor for AP History and Introductory Psychology, you are familiar with my academic abilities and classroom performance. And as my cross-country coach, you know my work habits and drive. I am interested in attending LaSalle University in Philadelphia, a school with strong history and communications departments, two areas of special interest to me. As part of the application process, the university requires a letter of recommendation from one of my instructors.

The **closing** provides the necessary information for the letter.

Please address your letter to the Admissions Office, LaSalle University, 1901 West Olney Avenue, Philadelphia, Pennsylvania 19141. The letter must be sent by November 10. Thank you for your help.

Sincerely,

Christina Lee

Christina Lee

Preparing a Letter for Mailing

Letters sent through the mail will get to their destinations faster if they are properly addressed and stamped. Always include a ZIP code.

Addressing the Envelope

Place the return address in the upper left corner, the destination address in the center, and the correct postage in the upper right corner. Some word-processing programs will automatically format the return and destination addresses.

CHRISTINA LEE
2456 CHARLES ST
KOREN WI 53801

MRS VERONICA OCHOA
HISTORY DEPARTMENT
CENTRAL HIGH SCHOOL
2125 PINE ST
KOREN WI 53801

There are two acceptable forms for addressing the envelope: the traditional form and the form preferred by the postal service.

TRADITIONAL FORM	POSTAL SERVICE FORM
Liam O'Donnell	LIAM O'DONNELL
Macalester College	MACALESTER COLLEGE
Admissions Office	ADMISSIONS OFFICE
1600 N. Grand Ave.	1600 N GRAND AVE
St. Paul, MN 55105-1801	ST PAUL MN 55105-1801

Following U.S. Postal Service Guidelines

The official United States Postal Service guidelines are available at any post office or online at www.usps.org.

- Capitalize everything in the address and leave out commas and periods.
- Use the list of common state and street abbreviations found in the *National ZIP Code Directory* or on page 535 of this book.
- Use numbers rather than words for numbered streets (for example, 42ND AVE or 9TH AVE NW).
- If you know the ZIP + 4 code, use it.

Interviewing Tips

A letter of application and résumé introduce you and provide background information to a prospective employer or school official. If the person wants a closer look at the real you, he or she may request an interview. Here are some tips to help you get ready:

Before an Interview

THINK ABOUT YOURSELF.

What are your goals? Strengths? Weaknesses?

THINK ABOUT THE OFFICIAL OR EMPLOYER.

Why is the organization interested in you?
What are the business's goals? Products? Services? Plans?

THINK ABOUT THE INTERVIEW.

What questions can you expect: Reason for seeking the job? Interest in the school? Qualifications for the scholarship?
Does the employer or official want to see work samples or a portfolio?

THINK ABOUT QUESTIONS YOU HAVE.

What does the job involve? What are the hours?
How many scholarships are available?
How competitive is admission into the school?

During an Interview

BE ATTENTIVE.

Introduce yourself to the office staff and say why you're there.
Complete forms neatly and quietly.
Shake hands and look the interviewer in the eye.
Listen carefully.

BE CLEAR.

Answer questions clearly and briefly.
Restate questions in your own words if you are unsure about what the interviewer means.
State your strengths and how you use them.

BE FLEXIBLE.

Rephrase a response if it seems unclear.
Expect the unexpected and be open to new lines of thinking.

After an Interview

BE POLITE.

Shake hands and thank each person involved in the interview.
Write a follow-up letter. (See the next page.)

Writing the Follow-Up Letter

What should you do after an interview? Pace the floor and chew your nails? No. As soon as possible after the interview, get to work writing a follow-up letter that will help an employer or official make a final decision in your favor. After her interview for a summer job, Teri Michaels sent the following letter.

606 Church Street
Spring Lake, NY 10970
April 22, 2007

Mr. Peter Snyder
Turtle Bay Marina
231 Lakeshore Drive
Lake Ripley, NY 12265

The **opening** thanks the person for the interview.

Dear Mr. Snyder:

Thank you for the interview yesterday. I enjoyed meeting you and learning about your boat rental business. I also appreciated talking with the returning crew members at your marina and hearing about their duties.

The **middle** confirms your interest in the position or program.

I think that I could make a significant contribution at Turtle Bay Marina. As you know, I have experience operating speed boats, pontoon boats, and jet skis. I also have good communications skills, which will help me explain to renters how to start and drive the different boats. As I mentioned in our interview, I can work every Saturday and Sunday, the busiest days at your marina. Since I am saving for college, the more hours I can work, the better. I would be available to start on June 10.

The **closing** provides contact information.

I appreciate your considering me for this summer position. If you have any further questions, please contact me at 231-6700 or e-mail me at tmichaels@global.com.

Sincerely,

Teri Michaels

Teri Michaels

Guidelines

Résumé

The purpose of a résumé is to interest an employer or an official enough to call you for an interview. Instead of simply telling about yourself in a letter, use a special résumé format to highlight your skills, knowledge, work experience, and education, especially as they relate to the position for which you're applying. Prepare a basic version of your résumé. Then, depending upon the requirements of each position, customize your objective, highlight various experiences, and focus on particular abilities that match the employer's expectations.

PREWRITING

Think about your abilities, experiences, and accomplishments.

Gather details that will create a complete picture of you. Include classes or training taken outside of school, achievements, and other experience such as volunteer work, club duties, and so on.

WRITING

Use a traditional résumé format and organize the information into these parts:

- Personal contact information
- Objective
- Qualifications
- Specific work experience
- Education
- References (Be sure to get permission from each person you wish to use as a reference. Then, each time you apply for a job, remind the people so they will be prepared for a phone call.)

REVISING

Improve your résumé by asking yourself these questions: *Have I included specific, accurate, and complete information? Have I presented information in a parallel, consistent manner? Have I given the most important information first? Have I used a business-like writing style? Have I used words appropriate to the reader? Have I defined any unfamiliar technical terms?*

EDITING

Check for errors in punctuation, mechanics, and grammar.

Ask someone else to look over your résumé as well.

PUBLISHING

Use text features such as boldface, columns, bullets, and white space to make your résumé attractive and readable.

Sample Résumé

A strong résumé is specific, not generic. Here is how one student presented himself in his search for summer employment on a landscaping crew.

The **beginning** provides contact information and the objective.

The **middle** lists key details.

The **ending** notes that references are available.

Delmer Sobodian

250 Lowe Avenue • Sherwood Heights, MI 49065
Phone 517-555-1662 E-mail delsob@themailstop.com

Objective: Seeking full-time summer employment on a landscaping crew.

Qualifications:
- Experienced with landscaping materials and plants
- Teamworker
- Fast learner
- Good physical condition

Experience:

May–October and winter holiday season 2006
Garcia's Gardens & Gifts
Part-time yard worker and cashier. Became familiar with different kinds of plants, trees, and shrubs and their care.

October 2005–March 2006
Shop A Lot supermarket
Part-time stocker and cashier. Often did heavy lifting.

Education: Will graduate from Cayman High School in June; plan to attend Tuyo Community College this fall to work on a degree in horticulture.

Member of our school's chapter of the National FFA Organization; assisted in yearly sale of native-species plants to raise funds for our chapter.

References: Available upon request.

Memo

Memos are short messages in which you ask and answer questions, describe procedures, give short reports, and remind others about deadlines and meetings. Memos are important to the flow of information within any organization. Many routine memos in schools and workplaces are distributed electronically, with hard copies posted on bulletin boards or sent by interoffice mail.

PREWRITING

Consider your audience by thinking about who will receive your memo and why.

Determine your purpose and jot down your reason for writing the memo.

Gather necessary details based on what your reader needs to know.

WRITING

Prepare the heading by typing "Memo" and centering it. Use a preprinted memo form or include a heading that contains the following information:

Date: The month, day, and year
To: The reader's name
From: Your first and last name (You may initial it before sending.)
Subject: The memo's topic in a clear, simple statement

Organize the body into three parts:

Beginning: State why you are writing the memo.
Middle: Provide all the necessary details. Consider listing the most important points rather than writing them out.
Ending: Focus on what happens next—the action or response you would like from the reader or readers.

REVISING

Improve your writing by asking yourself these questions related to ideas, organization, voice, word choice, and sentence fluency: *Is my topic clear? Is my purpose obvious? Do I have an effective beginning, middle, and ending? Is my memo as brief as possible? Have I used a positive, friendly tone? Have I explained any unfamiliar terms? Does my memo read smoothly?*

EDITING

Check for conventions. Correct any errors in punctuation, grammar, and mechanics.

Prepare a final copy of your memo and proofread it before distributing it.

Sample Workplace Memo

Ben Braun, an assistant to the personnel director, typed up this memo about the company's monthly staff improvement meetings.

Memo

The **heading** identifies the date, recipients, sender, and subject.

Date: October 22, 2007

To: Inter-Tech Staff

From: Ben Braun, Assistant to the Personnel Director

Subject: New Technology

The **beginning** states why you are writing.

Our next staff-development meeting will be held on Thursday, November 8, at 9:00 a.m. in the new training center.

The **middle** shares the necessary details.

The guest at that meeting will be Dr. G. F. Hollis, a professor at City Technical College. She will speak on the latest technology and how we can expect it to affect us and our work.

Dr. Hollis is planning a winter-term training program that will cover all facets of office technology and communication. Those attending the meeting will receive additional information about that upcoming program.

This meeting is intended for those in Level 5 and employees interested in writing data-sharing software.

The **ending** makes a call for action.

Please sign up with me before the end of the day on Friday, November 2, if you plan to attend the meeting.

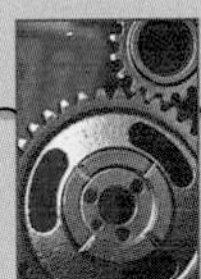

INSIDE INFO

A memo is less formal than a letter and can vary in length from a few sentences to a multipage report. Your goal is to share information clearly and effectively.

E-Mail Message

Electronic mail is a fast, convenient way to communicate in the workplace. It saves paper and allows many people to share information simultaneously. Increasingly, e-mail is used not only within the office, but also to communicate with customers and business partners.

PREWRITING

Consider your audience and your purpose for sending the message.

Gather details based on what the reader needs to know.

WRITING

Organize the body into three parts:

Beginning: Complete your e-mail header, making sure your subject line is clear. Expand on the subject in the first sentences of your message. Get right to the point.

Middle: Supply all the details of your message while keeping your paragraphs short. Double-space between paragraphs. Try to limit your message to one or two screens and use numbers, lists, and headings to organize your thoughts.

Ending: Let your reader know what follow-up action is needed and when; then end politely.

REVISING

Improve your writing by asking yourself these questions: *Is my message accurate, complete, and clear? Is my message as brief and concise as possible? Do I have an effective beginning, middle, and ending? Is my tone appropriate for the topic and the reader?*

Improve your style. Ask yourself these questions related to word choice and sentence fluency: *Have I used clear, everyday language? Does my message read smoothly?*

EDITING

Check for conventions. Correct any errors in grammar, punctuation, and mechanics before sending your e-mail message.

TIPS

FOR EFFECTIVE E-MAIL

- **Never use all capital letters** in an e-mail message; people feel you are shouting at them.
- **Follow grammar conventions.**
- **Proofread.** Because e-mail is so fast, it's easy to dash off a message and overlook a typo, a wrong word, or a missing word.

Sample E-Mail Message

Following an unpleasant experience at a local automobile dealership, Emiko Tikaram decided to contact the manufacturer directly to voice her concerns. She copied the general manager of the dealership, as well.

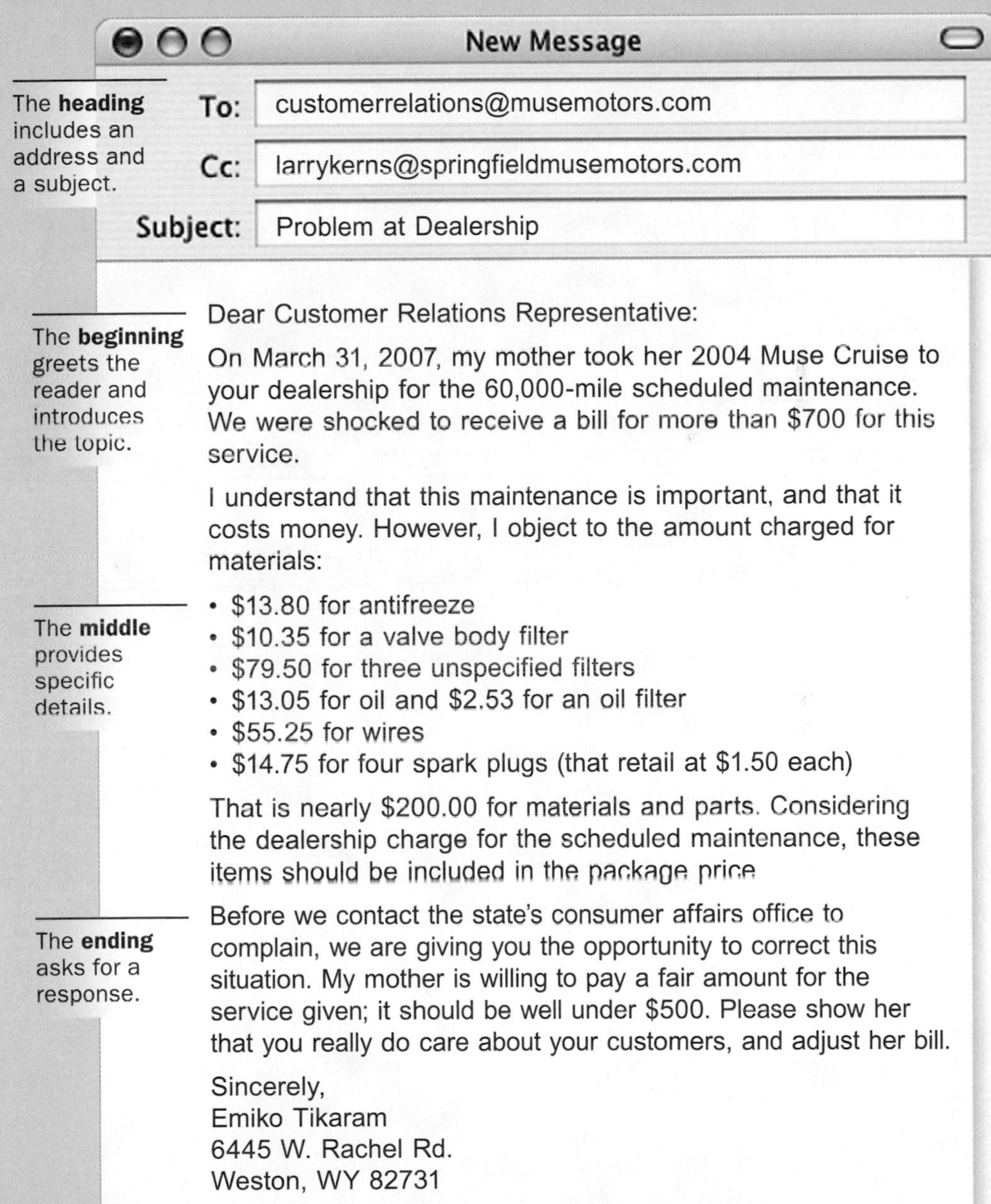

New Message

The **heading** includes an address and a subject.

To: customerrelations@musemotors.com

Cc: larrykerns@springfieldmusemotors.com

Subject: Problem at Dealership

The **beginning** greets the reader and introduces the topic.

Dear Customer Relations Representative:

On March 31, 2007, my mother took her 2004 Muse Cruise to your dealership for the 60,000-mile scheduled maintenance. We were shocked to receive a bill for more than $700 for this service.

The **middle** provides specific details.

I understand that this maintenance is important, and that it costs money. However, I object to the amount charged for materials:

- $13.80 for antifreeze
- $10.35 for a valve body filter
- $79.50 for three unspecified filters
- $13.05 for oil and $2.53 for an oil filter
- $55.25 for wires
- $14.75 for four spark plugs (that retail at $1.50 each)

That is nearly $200.00 for materials and parts. Considering the dealership charge for the scheduled maintenance, these items should be included in the package price.

The **ending** asks for a response.

Before we contact the state's consumer affairs office to complain, we are giving you the opportunity to correct this situation. My mother is willing to pay a fair amount for the service given; it should be well under $500. Please show her that you really do care about your customers, and adjust her bill.

Sincerely,
Emiko Tikaram
6445 W. Rachel Rd.
Weston, WY 82731

The Research Center

Writing the Research Paper

One of your finest achievements as a student will be to write a compelling research paper, since doing so demands that you apply so many skills: thinking, speaking, reading, and writing. More than that, the research paper challenges you to take charge of your own learning. You're the leader. It's your topic, your curiosity, and your energy that make things happen. Writing a research paper requires effective time management, too, because there are so many stages and steps involved in the process. If you can write a quality research paper, you'll know you can manage other complex and time-consuming academic tasks in high school and beyond.

WHAT'S AHEAD

This section of your handbook explains the steps in the research-writing process, from prewriting through the final proofreading.

NOTE: This chapter can be used with either the MLA or APA documentation style.

Research Overview

When you write a research paper, you ask important questions, search systematically for answers, and share your conclusions with the reader. In other words, this task is all about curiosity, discovery, and dialogue.

Starting Point

The assignment usually relates to a course concept, so consider what your teacher wants you to learn and how your project will be evaluated. Then take ownership of the project by looking for an angle that truly makes the research your own.

Purpose

The project requires you to carry out research and share the results. Your specific goal is to establish and support a position worth sharing with others.

Form

The traditional research paper is an extended essay (at least five pages), complete with thesis, supporting paragraphs, a thoughtful conclusion, integrated sources, and careful documentation. However, you may be asked to shape your research into something more visual, perhaps a multimedia presentation.

Audience

Normally, your research paper is intended for your instructor and writing peers. Sometimes, however, your audience may be more specific (all Floridians, women with eating disorders, high school athletes, and so on).

Voice

The tone should be semiformal or formal, but ask your teacher for specific requirements. In any research paper, maintain a thoughtful, confident tone. After all, your research has made you somewhat of an authority on the topic.

Point of View

In most cases, your teacher will expect you to remain objective in a research paper, relating information in an impersonal manner, and keeping the focus where it belongs—on the topic. Another form of research, the I-Search paper, is much more personal, more of a story of the researcher's searching adventure. An I-Search paper is written from the first-person point of view.

NOTE The best research writing centers on your ideas, ideas you develop through thoughtful engagement with sources. In poor research writing, the sources dominate, and the writer's perspective disappears.

Steps in the Process

The process of writing a research paper starts with selecting an interesting topic and doesn't end until you print out and proofread the final copy. The next eight pages take you through the research-writing process.

Prewriting

Finding a Research Topic

1 SELECT AN INTERESTING SUBJECT.

In most cases, you will be expected to focus on a subject connected to your course work. However, if the assignment is more open-ended, begin your subject search by thinking about books you have read and movies you have seen. Also consider controversial or intriguing topics in the news and things that are important in your daily life. Ask yourself what you need or want to know: *What are the best career opportunities for young people? What are the real costs and benefits of a college education? Are we doing enough (or too much) to protect our endangered natural resources?*

Whatever the case, you need to find a subject that interests you and seems practical for the time and resources available. (See pages 22–23 for ideas on selecting a subject.) *Remember:* Meaningful research starts with a personal need or desire to know.

2 THINK ABOUT YOUR SUBJECT.

Once you've selected a general subject, you need to explore it further. You can start by taking out your writer's notebook and writing down everything you know (and don't know) about your subject. You might use the basic *who, what, when, where, why,* and *how* questions:

I already know . . .
I want to find out *who* . . .
I want to discover *what* . . .
I want to learn *when* . . .
I want to know *where* . . .
I want to understand *why* . . .
I want to find out *how* . . .

Also talk with other people about your subject—instructors, parents, grandparents, community leaders, local experts, whoever is available. And don't forget to do some exploratory reading. A brief Web search or an encyclopedia review can give you a reliable overview of your subject and lead to related topics. You may also choose to review magazines, newspapers, videos, CD's, and other such sources of information. (See page 25 as you attempt to "shape" your subject.)

3 LIMIT YOUR SUBJECT.

Once you've done all your preliminary thinking, you need to take steps to find a limited topic. Let's say you've always been interested in social issues; recently, you saw a special on television about global problems resulting from population explosion. You were surprised to learn that there are more people alive on the planet now than have died since the time of the Egyptian pyramids. And since you need a topic for your research paper, you've decided that writing a paper on some aspect of this subject would be a good idea. Clearly, it's a timely, worthwhile subject, and because you also have a personal interest in it, it makes perfect sense as a research topic.

So, with a general subject area in mind, you're ready to begin the process of zeroing in on a specific, limited topic, one you can adequately cover in a 5- to 10-page research paper (or whatever length you are assigned). This is how your process of limiting might go:

Global problems
- **Population explosion and poverty**
  - **Social needs because of poverty**
    - **Governments' inability to meet these needs**
      - **Individuals who are tackling the problem**

4 WRITE A THESIS STATEMENT.

With a limited topic in hand, you'll next want to compose a sentence to serve as the controlling idea for your research. This sentence is often called the **thesis statement**, a sentence that states what you believe your research will prove. Even though your original thesis statement may change as you do more research, it will guide you and make your research more productive. Here, and on the following page, you'll find a number of tips to help you develop a useful thesis statement.

1. Consider carefully the general information you've already gathered about your subject and decide what specifically you would like to cover in your research.

   Individuals who are solving the problem of poverty due to overpopulation

2. Put your idea in the form of a question.

   How are individuals tackling the social needs of the poverty stricken?

3. Now turn your question into a sentence that states exactly what you would like to say about your subject.

   Individuals are applying business strategies to tackle the social needs of the poor.

Guidelines

For Writing a Thesis Statement

A good thesis statement tells the reader what your topic is and, more importantly, it reveals how you plan to treat your topic. It also serves as a personal guide to help you focus on your topic throughout the research process. In addition, your thesis helps you to prioritize your research time, as you decide whether to read a particular book or skim it, photocopy an article or take a few notes on it, view a video in its entirety or fast-forward to the conclusion.

THE PROCESS AT WORK

A thesis statement is usually a single sentence that contains two main elements: a limited topic plus a specific feeling or attitude toward that topic. To arrive at a final thesis, you might follow this process:

- **Select a general subject.** — Global problems
- **Narrow your subject.** — Social needs due to poverty
- **Select a working thesis.** — Individuals who are tackling social needs
- **Put your thesis in the form of a question.** — How are individuals tackling this problem?
- **Compose a final thesis statement.** — Individuals are applying business strategies to tackle the social needs of the poor.

Checklist for a Thesis Statement

_____ My thesis statement focuses on a single, limited topic.

_____ My thesis is stated in a clear, direct sentence (or sentences).

_____ The thesis conveys my point of view or attitude about the topic.

_____ I have access to enough good information to support my thesis statement.

_____ The thesis predicts a research paper that meets all the requirements of the assignment.

Searching for Information

5 PREPARE A PRELIMINARY BIBLIOGRAPHY.

Continue to look for information related to your thesis statement. As you find good sources of information, keep track of them on your computer or on 3- by 5-inch cards. Arrange the cards in alphabetical order by the authors' last names. If a source does not identify its author, alphabetize it by the first word in the title (not including *A, An,* or *The*). Number each card in the upper right-hand corner.

Bornstein, David (2)
How to Change the World: Social Entrepreneurs and the Power of New Ideas
Oxford UP
New York. 2004
Print

Sample Bibliography Card

Problems related to overpopulation (2)
* Widespread hunger
* Not enough health care
* Poor education
* Unchanging poverty
* High crime rates
* Damaged environment

How to Change the World page 2

Sample Note Card

6 READ AND TAKE NOTES.

As you begin reading the material listed in your bibliography, take notes, including quotations related to your specific thesis.

- Keep notes on cards of the same size and style. (Arranging and referencing a stack of differently sized cards can be troublesome.)
- Write down important details and quotations, along with the page numbers where this information can be found. Also place the number of the related bibliography card in the upper right-hand corner.
- Place quotation marks around word-for-word quotations.
- Use an ellipsis (. . .) if you omit words in a quotation. Use brackets [like this] around words you add to a quotation. (See pages 527–528.)
- Look up the definitions of any unfamiliar words. If a particular word is important to your topic, copy its definition onto a note card.
- Give each card a descriptive heading (a word or phrase to highlight the main idea of that note card: *Problems related to overpopulation*).

Note Taking: A Closer Look

This is a good time to develop your skimming talents. Look over the table of contents, the index, and a sample paragraph or two before deciding to read a source in its entirety.

Summarize ■ To summarize, reduce what you have read to a few important points using your own words.

Paraphrase ■ To paraphrase, restate what you have read using your own words. Put quotation marks around key words or phrases you borrow directly from a source.

Quote Directly ■ To quote someone directly, record the statement or idea word for word and put quotation marks before and after.

7 Collect information from primary sources.

If possible, collect firsthand information about your topic by conducting interviews, passing out questionnaires, or making your own observations. Remember to plan interview questions in advance and to put the person at ease during the interview. If you use a questionnaire, design it carefully so the results will be valid.

Designing a Writing Plan

8 Write your working outline.

Organize your note cards into their most logical order and use them to construct a working outline. List each descriptive heading as a main point or subpoint on that outline. Number them all as shown on page 97.

9 Continue developing your research.

Search for any additional information you need to develop your thesis. Reconsider the thesis statement you wrote in step 4. If your thoughts about it have changed, this is the time to revise it.

10 Revise your outline.

Revise your working outline to reflect any new information you find. Your outline serves as a blueprint for your final paper, a blueprint that can be improved upon.

"The guiding question in research is 'So What?' Answer that question in every sentence and you will become a great scholar; answer it once a page in a ten-page paper and you'll write a good one."

—Donald N. McCloskey

Writing the First Draft

11 WRITE THE INTRODUCTION.

The introduction does two things. The first part gains the reader's attention with an interesting, surprising, or personal bit of information about your topic. The second part identifies the specific thesis of your research. Here are several ways to begin:

- Offer a revealing story or quotation.
- Give important background information.
- Share a series of interesting or surprising facts.
- Provide important definitions.
- State your reason for choosing this subject.

12 WRITE THE BODY.

The next step is to write the main part of your research paper, the part that supports or proves your thesis. There are two ways to proceed. You may write freely and openly, or you may work systematically, carefully following your notes and working outline.

WRITING FREELY AND OPENLY

This method allows you to put your outline and note cards aside and write as much of the paper as you can, drawing on the information you have absorbed during your research. Refer to your note cards only when you need specific facts, figures, or quotations.

After you have completed this first writing, review your outline and note cards to see if you have missed or misplaced any important points. Then resume writing, filling in or reorganizing ideas as you go along.

WRITING SYSTEMATICALLY

This method involves carefully following your working outline and note cards right from the start. Begin by laying out the first section of note cards (those covering the first main point in your working outline). Write your first main point and then support it with facts and details from the appropriate note cards. Repeat this process until you have covered all the main points in your outline.

TIPS

FOR RESEARCH WRITING

- **Use your own words as much as possible.** Use direct quotations only when they fit your intent perfectly and would lose their impact if paraphrased.
- **Present your own ideas honestly and clearly.** Although you must consider the research of others as you consult journal articles, books, newspapers, etc., be sure to analyze this information and offer your personal perspective on the topic.
- **Avoid fragments, abbreviations, or slang** ("you know," "no way," "forget it") in your writing. Work to maintain a formal to semiformal style.
- **Drop statements that you cannot support with facts.**

13 WRITE THE CONCLUSION.

The final section, or conclusion, of your paper should leave the reader with a clear understanding of the significance of your research. Review the important points you have made and draw a final conclusion. In a more personal approach, you may discuss how your research has strengthened or changed your thinking about your subject.

> "[Good] writing is concise. A sentence should contain no unnecessary words, a paragraph no unnecessary sentences, for the same reason that a drawing should have no unnecessary lines and a machine no unnecessary parts."
>
> William Strunk

Revising

14 REVISE YOUR FIRST DRAFT AT LEAST TWICE.

Revise your paper once to make sure you have covered all of the main points and effectively supported them in an organized way. Revise a second time to make sure that your words are clear and specific and that your sentences are smooth reading. (See pages 39–52 for help.)

15 DOCUMENT YOUR SOURCES.

Assemble your "Works Cited" page (MLA style) or "References" list (APA style), including all of the sources you have cited in your paper. You must give credit in the body of your paper for ideas and direct quotations taken from these sources. Also be certain to accurately represent/reproduce borrowed ideas/quotations. (See the MLA or APA section for specific guidelines.)

"Only the hand that erases can write the true thing."
—Meister Eckhert

Preparing the Final Paper

16 Edit your final revision.

Check and correct punctuation, capitalization, usage, and grammar. (See pages 53–56 for help.)

17 Prepare your final copy.

If you use a computer, print your final copy on a good-quality printer. Do not justify your right margin. Leave a margin of one inch on all sides (except for page numbers). Double-space your entire paper, including long quotations and the works-cited page or reference list.

Number your pages from the first page of your paper through the works-cited or reference pages. Place the page numbers in the upper right-hand corner, one-half inch from the top and even with the right-hand margin. If using MLA style, type your last name before each page number. If using APA style, type a short title (first two or three words) in the upper left-hand corner.

18 Add identifying information.

MLA style requires your name, the instructor's name, the course title, and the date in the upper left corner of the first page of your paper. (Begin one inch from the top and double-space this information.) Center the title (double-space before and after); then type the first line of the paper. (See page 352 if your teacher requires a separate title page.)

APA style requires a title page and an abstract. (See pages 372–373 for guidelines and examples.)

19 Type your final outline.

If you need to submit a final outline, make sure it follows the final version of your paper. (See page 352.) Double-space your outline and number its pages with lowercase Roman numerals.

20 Check your paper from start to finish.

When you hand in your paper, it should be neat, clean, error free—and on time!

Writing Responsibly

A research paper, like any other type of meaningful writing, should be a personal process of discovering new information. Once you've collected the information, you need to make it part of your own thinking. Examine the points on which your sources agree and disagree and decide which ones offer the best arguments. You can then determine how these findings stand up to your own thinking. Research becomes your own when you . . .

- have a genuine interest in your topic,
- give yourself enough time to learn about it,
- involve yourself in active, thorough research, and
- make your own voice the primary voice in your writing.

WHAT'S AHEAD

This chapter will help you understand how to accurately and smoothly incorporate other people's ideas and words into your research paper. The concepts and strategies here form a basis for the chapters about MLA and APA style that follow.

Avoiding Plagiarism

You owe it to your sources, your reader, and yourself to give credit for other people's words and ideas used in your writing. Not only is this the legal thing to do, it's also the smart thing to do. Citing sources adds authority to your writing. Using sources without giving credit is called *plagiarism*, the act of presenting someone else's ideas as your own. Don't plagiarize.

Forms of Plagiarism

- **Submitting another writer's paper:** The most blatant form of plagiarism is to put your name on someone else's work (another student's paper, an essay bought from a "paper mill," the text of an article from the Internet, and so on).
- **Using copy-and-paste:** It is unethical to copy phrases, sentences, or larger sections from a source and paste them into your paper without giving credit for the material. Even if you change a few words, this is still plagiarism.
- **Neglecting necessary quotation marks:** Whether you quote just a phrase or a larger section of text, you must put the exact words of the source in quotation marks and cite them.
- **Paraphrasing without citing a source:** Paraphrasing (rephrasing ideas in your own words) is an important research skill. However, paraphrased ideas must be credited to the source, even if you entirely reword the material.
- **Confusing borrowed material with your own ideas:** While taking research notes, it's important to identify the source of each idea you record. Then you will know whom to credit as you write your paper.

Other Source Abuses

- **Using sources inaccurately:** Make certain your quotation or paraphrase accurately reflects the meaning of the original. Don't twist someone else's words to support your own ideas.
- **Overusing source material:** Your paper should be primarily your thoughts and words, supported by outside sources. If you simply string together quotations and paraphrases, your own voice will be lost.
- **"Plunking" source material:** When you write, smoothly incorporate any outside material. Dropping in quotations or paraphrases with no introduction or comment creates choppy, disconnected writing.
- **Relying too heavily on one source:** If your writing is dominated by one source, your reader may doubt the depth and integrity of your research.

Examples of Plagiarism

The brief passage below is taken from the essay "The State" by Randolph Bourne published in 1919. Examples of how the passage might be plagiarized follow below.

Essay Passage

Psychologists recognize the gregarious impulse as one of the strongest primitive pulls which keeps together the herds of different species of higher animals. Mankind is no exception. Our pugnacious evolutionary history has prevented the impulse from ever dying out. This gregarious impulse is the tendency to imitate, to conform, to coalesce together, and is most powerful when the herd believes itself threatened with attack. Animals crowd together for protection, and men become most conscious of their collectivity at the threat of war.

Using Copy-and-Paste without Quotation Marks and Citation

Obviously, **psychologists recognize the gregarious impulse as one of the strongest primitive pulls which keeps together the herds of different species of higher animals. Mankind is no exception. Our pugnacious evolutionary history has prevented the Impulse from ever dying out.** It would seem we are destined to war and war again.

Using Key Words without Quotation Marks and Citation

Obviously, a sense of common identity nurtures **the gregarious impulse** among **different species of higher animals.** Human beings are also prone to this herd instinct, and our history of conflict **has prevented the impulse from ever dying out.** It would seem we are destined to war and war again.

Paraphrasing without Citation

Experts say that one of the strongest, most basic instincts is the herd instinct that keeps groups of higher animals together. Human beings are also prone to this herd instinct. Our history of warfare has helped to continue that need to gather and live together. And this impulse is always the most powerful when a group feels threatened by attack. Just as animals huddle together for safety, human beings gain a new sense of unity in time of war.

Using an Author's Idea without Citation

The herd instinct is powerful, both in animals and in human beings. It is what holds a society together, especially in times of danger. When threatened, it is only natural for creatures to crowd together, finding safety in numbers. This explains why people within a society feel such a sense of unity and purpose during times of war.

Writing Paraphrases

QUICK GUIDE

In a report or research paper, you share your ideas about an important topic, supporting your thoughts with details and information from other sources.

There are two ways to share a source's information: (1) quoting directly and (2) paraphrasing the material. When you quote directly, you include the exact words of the author and put quotation marks around them; when you **paraphrase**, you use your own words to restate the author's ideas.

1. **To paraphrase, skim the selection first to get the overall meaning.** (Concentrate on the main ideas, not on the details.)
2. **Then read the selection carefully,** paying particular attention to key words and phrases. (Check the meaning of any unfamiliar words.)
3. **Next, try listing the main ideas on a piece of paper**—without looking at the selection.
4. **Review the selection again** so that you have the overall meaning clearly in mind as you begin to write.
5. **Write your paraphrase,** using your own words to restate the author's ideas. Keep the following points in mind:
   - Stick to the essential information.
   - State each important idea as clearly and concisely as possible.
   - Put quotation marks around key words or phrases taken directly from the source. (See 523.3.)
   - Arrange the ideas into a smooth, logical order. (Your version of the author's views should be easier to read or as easy to read as the original.)
6. **Check your final work** by asking these questions:
   - Does my paraphrase clearly state the author's ideas and point of view?
   - Have I quoted a key word or phrase only as necessary?
   - Have I included the essential main ideas, leaving out the unnecessary details?
   - Could another person understand the author's message by simply reading my paraphrase?

Examples of Paraphrases

The passage below is taken from page 26 of a book entitled *The Brain at Work* by R. Jennings. Following the excerpt are two examples of how this passage could be paraphrased and credited.

Book Excerpt

The human brain, once surrounded by myth and misconception, is no longer such a mystery. It is now understood to be the supervisory center of the nervous system that controls all voluntary (eating and thinking) and most involuntary behavior (blinking and breathing).

The brain functions by receiving information from nerve cells located throughout the body. Recent research has revealed exactly what happens when information first reaches the brain. It has been discovered that the cells that receive the information in the cortex of the brain are arranged in a regular pattern in columns. The columns are, in turn, arranged into a series of "hypercolumns." Each cell within each column has a specific responsibility to analyze certain kinds of incoming information. Within the columns, the analysis follows a formal sequence.

Eventually, the information is relayed to the higher centers of the brain where a complete picture is assembled. The brain then either sends a return message or stores the information for later use. A return message travels through the body in the form of electrical and chemical signals via billions of nerve cells (neurons). When the message reaches its destination, muscles or glands respond with the appropriate reaction.

Basic Paraphrase

The human brain controls all voluntary and most involuntary behavior. The process begins when the brain receives information from nerve cells located throughout the body. This information is analyzed by brain cells arranged in a series of columns with each cell having a specific responsibility for certain kinds of incoming information. After analysis, the information is sent to the higher centers of the brain where a complete picture is put together. The brain then either stores that information for later use or sends a return message to the muscles and glands, which react appropriately (Jennings 26).

Paraphrase with Quotation

The human brain controls all voluntary and most involuntary behavior. The process begins when the brain receives information from nerve cells located throughout the body. "[T]he cells that receive the information in the cortex of the brain are arranged in a regular pattern in columns. [. . .] Each cell within each column has a specific responsibility to analyze certain kinds of incoming information." After analysis, the information is sent to the higher centers of the brain where a complete picture is put together. The brain then either stores that information for later use or sends a return message to the muscles and glands, which react appropriately (Jennings 26).

Using Quoted Material

QUICK GUIDE

A quotation can be a single word or an entire paragraph. You should choose quotations carefully and keep them as brief as possible. Be sure that the wording, capitalization, and punctuation of direct quotations are the same as in the original work. Clearly mark changes for your reader: (1) changes within the quotation are enclosed **[like this]** in brackets; explanations are enclosed in parentheses at the end of the quotation before the closing punctuation **(like this)**.

- **SHORT QUOTATIONS:** If a quotation is four typed lines or fewer, work it into the body of your paper and put quotation marks around it.

- **LONG QUOTATIONS:** Quotations of more than four typed lines are generally introduced by a colon and set off from the rest of the text, indenting each line one inch (10 spaces) and double-spacing the material. When quoting two or more paragraphs, indent the first line of each paragraph an extra quarter inch (3 spaces). Do not use quotation marks.

  After the final punctuation mark of the quotation, leave two spaces and insert the appropriate parenthetical reference.

- **PARTIAL QUOTATIONS:** If you want to leave out part of a quotation, use an ellipsis to show the omission. An ellipsis is three periods with a space before and after each one.

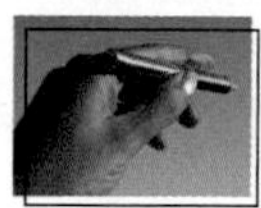

NOTE: Anything you take out of a quotation should not change the author's original meaning.

- **ADDING TO QUOTATIONS:** Use brackets [like this] to signify any material you add to a quotation to help clarify its meaning.

- **QUOTING POETRY:** When quoting up to three lines of poetry, use quotation marks and work the lines into your writing. Use a slash (/) to show where each line of verse ends. For verse quotations of four lines or more, indent each line one inch (10 spaces) and double-space; do not use quotation marks.

  To show that you have left out a line or more of verse, make a line of spaced periods the approximate length of a complete line of the poem.

MLA Documentation Style

Most academic disciplines have their own manuals of style for research paper documentation. The Modern Language Association (MLA) style manual, for example, is widely used in the humanities (literature, history, philosophy, etc.), making it the most popular manual in high-school and college writing courses. Clearly, it's a documentation style you will want to become familiar with.

As with any research-paper style, the MLA style uses a clearly defined system for documenting sources. As a writer, it's your responsibility to understand and apply the system consistently from start to finish. (For complete information on the MLA style, refer to the latest version of the *MLA Handbook.*)

WHAT'S AHEAD

This chapter provides you with guidelines for citing sources according to the MLA style manual, including a special section on citing sources from the Internet, and a Web site address for obtaining updated information.

Citing Sources

Guidelines for In-Text Citations

The simplest way to credit a source is to insert the information (usually the author and page number) in parentheses after the words or ideas taken from that source. These in-text citations (often called "parenthetical references") refer to the "Works Cited" page at the end of your paper. (See page 338.)

Points to Remember

- Make sure each in-text citation clearly points to an entry in your list of works cited. Use the word or words by which the entry is alphabetized.
- Keep citations brief and integrate them into your writing. (See pages 334–337.)
- When paraphrasing, make it clear where your borrowing begins and ends. Use stylistic cues to distinguish the source's thoughts ("Kalmbach points out . . . ") from your own ("I believe . . . ").
- For inclusive page numbers larger than 99, give only the two digits of the second number (113–14, not 113–114).
- At the end of a sentence, place your parenthetical reference before the end punctuation.

Model In-Text Citations

One Author: A Complete Work

You must give the author's last name in a parenthetical citation unless it is already mentioned in the text. An in-text citation could name an editor, a translator, a speaker, or an artist, instead of an author, if that is how the entry is listed in the works-cited section.

With Author in Text (This is the preferred method.)

In *No Need for Hunger*, Robert Spitzer recommends that the U.S. government develop a new foreign policy to help Third World countries overcome poverty.

Without Author in Text

***No Need for Hunger* recommends that the U.S. government develop a new foreign policy to help Third World countries overcome poverty (Spitzer).**

NOTE: Do not offer page numbers when citing complete works, articles in alphabetized encyclopedias, one-page articles, and unpaginated sources.

One Author: Part of a Work

List the necessary page numbers in parentheses if you borrow words or ideas from a particular source. Leave a space between the author's last name and the page reference. No abbreviation or punctuation is needed.

With Author in Text

Bullough writes that genetic engineering was dubbed "eugenics" by a cousin of Darwin's, Sir Francis Galton, in 1885 (5).

Without Author in Text

Genetic engineering was dubbed "eugenics" by a cousin of Darwin's, Sir Francis Galton, in 1885 (Bullough 5).

Two or More Works by the Same Author(s)

In addition to the author's last name(s) and page number(s), include a shortened version of the title of the work when you are citing two or more works by the same author(s).

With Author in Text

Wallerstein and Blakeslee claim that divorce creates an enduring identity for children of the marriage (*Unexpected Legacy* 62).

Without Author in Text

These children are intensely lonely despite active social lives (Wallerstein and Blakeslee, *Second Chances* 51).

NOTE: When including both author(s) and title in a parenthetical reference, separate them with a comma, as shown above.

A Work by Two or Three Authors

Give the last names of every author in the same order that they appear in the works-cited section. (The correct order of the authors' names can be found on the title page of the book.)

Students learned more than a full year's Spanish in 10 days using the complete supermemory method (Ostrander and Schroeder 51).

A Work by Four or More Authors

Give the first author's last name as it appears in the works-cited section followed by *et al.* (meaning *and others*).

Communication on the job is more than talking; it is "inseparable from your total behavior" (Culligan et al. 111).

A Work Authored by an Agency, a Committee, or Another Organization

If a book or other work was written by an organization, it is said to have a *corporate author.* If the corporate name is long, include it in the text (rather than in parentheses) to avoid disrupting the flow of your writing. After the full name has been used at least once, use a shortened form in subsequent references. For example, *Task Force* may be used for *Task Force for Economic Growth.*

The thesis of the Task Force's report is that economic success depends on our ability to improve large-scale education and training (113–14).

An Anonymous Work

When there is no author listed, give the title or a shortened version of the title as it appears in the works-cited section.

Statistics indicate that drinking water can make up 20 percent of a person's total exposure to lead (*Information* 572).

Two or More Works Included in One Citation

To cite multiple works within a single parenthetical reference, separate the references with a semicolon.

In Medieval Europe, Latin translations of the works of Rhazes, a Persian scholar, were a source of medical knowledge (Albala 22; Lewis 266).

A Work Referred to in Another Work

If you must cite an indirect source (information from one source that is quoted from another source), use the abbreviation *qtd. in* (quoted in) before the indirect source in your reference.

Paton improved the conditions in Diepkloof (a prison) by "removing all the more obvious aids to detention. The dormitories are open at night: the great barred gate is gone" (qtd. in Callan xviii).

Quoting Verse

Do not use page numbers when referencing classic verse plays and poems. Instead, cite them by division (act, scene, canto, book, part) and line, using Arabic numerals for the various divisions, unless your instructor prefers Roman numerals. Use periods to separate the various numbers.

In the first act of the play named after him, Hamlet comments, "How weary, stale, flat and unprofitable, / Seem to me all the uses of this world" (1.2.133–134).

NOTE: A slash, with a space on each side, shows where a new line of verse begins.

Quoting Verse *(continued)*

If you are citing lines only, use the word *line* or *lines* in your first reference and numbers only in additional references.

In book five of Homer's *Iliad*, the Trojans' fear is evident: "The Trojans were scared when they saw the two sons of Dares, one of them in fright and the other lying dead by his chariot" (lines 22–24).

Verse quotations of more than three lines should be indented one inch (10 spaces) and double-spaced. Do not add quotation marks. Each line of the poem or play begins a new line of the quotation.

In "Song of Myself" poet Walt Whitman claims to belong to everyone:

> **I am of old and young, of the foolish as much as the wise,**
> **Regardless of others, ever regardful of others,**
> **Maternal as well as paternal, a child as well as a man,**
> **Stuffed with the stuff that is coarse, and stuffed with the stuff that is fine, (16:326–329)**

Quoting Prose

To cite prose from fiction, list more than the page number if the work is available in several editions. Give the page reference first, and then add a chapter, section, or book number, if appropriate.

In *The House of the Spirits*, Isabel Allende describes Marcos, "dressed in mechanic's overalls, with huge racer's goggles and an explorer's helmet" (13; ch. 1).

When you are quoting any sort of prose that takes more than four typed lines, indent each line of the quotation one inch (10 spaces) and double-space it; do not add quotation marks. In this case, you put the parenthetical citation (the page and chapter number) outside the end punctuation mark of the quotation itself.

Allende describes the flying machine that Marcos has assembled:

> **The contraption lay with its stomach on terra firma, heavy and sluggish and looking more like a wounded duck than like one of those newfangled airplanes they were starting to produce in the United States. There was nothing in its appearance to suggest that it could move, much less take flight across the snowy peaks. (12; ch. 1)**

TIPS

FOR CITING PARAPHRASED MATERIAL

To make it clear where you have borrowed information from outside sources, always use quotation marks for exact words. For paraphrases, use wording that indicates where your borrowing starts and a parenthetical reference to show where it ends.

Guidelines

MLA Works-Cited List

The works-cited section lists all of the sources you have cited (referred to) in your text. It does not include sources you may have read but did not refer to in your paper. Begin your list on a new page and number each page. The guidelines that follow describe the form of the works-cited section.

1. Type the page number in the upper-right corner, one-half inch from the top of the page, with your last name before it.
2. Center the title *Works Cited* (not in italics) one inch from the top; then double-space before the first entry.
3. Begin each entry flush with the left margin. If the entry runs more than one line, indent additional lines one-half inch (five spaces) or use the hanging indent function on your computer.
4. Double-space lines within each entry and between entries.
5. List each entry alphabetically by author's last name. If there is no author, use the first word of the title (disregard *A, An, The*).
6. Identify the medium of publication for each work (Print, Web, Television, DVD, etc.).

■ This is a basic entry for a book:

Author's last name, First name. *Book Title*. City: Publisher, date. Medium.

Opie, John. *Ogallala: Water for a Dry Land*. Lincoln: U of Nebraska P, 1993. Print.

NOTE: Use a single space after all punctuation in a works-cited entry.

■ This is a basic entry for a periodical:

Author's last name, First name. "Article Title." *Periodical Title* date: page nos. Medium.

Stearns, Denise Heffernan. "Testing by Design." *Middle Ground* Oct. 2000: 21–25. Print.

■ This is a basic entry for an online entry:

Author's last name, First name. "Title." *Site Title*. Site Sponsor. Date of posting or last update. Medium. Date accessed.

Tenenbaum, David. "Dust Never Sleeps." *The Why Files*. U of Wisconsin, Board of Regents. 28 July 1999. Web. 26 April 2010.

NOTE: In online entries, include the URL (after the date accessed) only if your reader cannot find the source without it.

Works-Cited Entries: Books

The entries on pages 340–342 illustrate the information needed to cite books, sections of a book, pamphlets, and government publications. The possible components of these entries are listed in order below:

1. **Author's name**
2. **Title of a part of the book** (an article in the book or a foreword)
3. **Title of the book**
4. **Name of editor or translator**
5. **Edition**
6. **Number of volume**
7. **Name of series**
8. **Place of publication, publisher, year of publication**
9. **Page numbers** (if only a part of the work is cited)
10. **Medium** ("Print")

NOTE: In general, if any of these components do not apply, they are not included in the works-cited entry. However, in the rare instance that a book does not state publication information, use the following abbreviations in place of information you cannot supply:

n.p.	No place of publication given
n.p.	No publisher given
n.d.	No date of publication given
n. pag.	No pagination given

Additional Guidelines

- List only the city for the place of publication. If several cities are listed, give only the first.
- Additionally, note that publishers' names should be shortened by omitting articles (*a*, *an*, *the*), business abbreviations (*Co.*, *Inc.*), and descriptive words (*Books, Press*). Cite the surname alone if the publisher's name includes the name of one person. If it includes the names of more than one person, cite only the first of the surnames. Abbreviate University Press as UP. Also use standard abbreviations whenever possible. (See pages 535 and 536.)

"My idea of research is to look at the thing from all sides; the person who has seen the animal, how the animal behaves, and so on."

—Marianna Moore

A Work by One Author

Baghwati, Jagdish. *In Defense of Globalization*. New York: Oxford UP, 2004. Print.

Two or More Books by the Same Author

List the books alphabetically according to title. After the first entry, substitute three hyphens for the author's name.

Dershowitz, Alan M. *Rights from Wrongs*. New York: Basic Books, 2005. Print.

---. *Supreme Injustice: How the High Court Hijacked Election 2000*. Oxford: Oxford UP, 2001. Print.

A Work by Two or Three Authors

Haynes, John Earl, and Harvey Klehr. *In Denial: Historians, Communism, & Espionage*. San Francisco: Encounter Books, 2003. Print.

NOTE: List the authors in the same order as they appear on the title page. Reverse only the name of the first author.

A Work by Four or More Authors

Schulte-Peevers, Andrea, et al. *Germany*. Victoria: Lonely Planet, 2000. Print.

A Work Authored by an Agency, a Committee, or Another Organization

Exxon Mobil Corporation. *Great Plains 2000*. Lincolnwood: Publications Intl., 2001. Print.

An Anonymous Book

***Chase's Calendar of Events 2002*. Chicago: Contemporary, 2002. Print.**

A Single Work from an Anthology

Mitchell, Joseph. "The Bottom of the Harbor." *American Sea Writing*. Ed. Peter Neill. New York: Library of America, 2000. 584–608. Print.

Two or More Works from the Same Anthology or Collection

Cite the collection once with complete publication information (see *Forbes* below). Then cite individual entries (see *Joseph* below) by listing the author, title of the piece, editor of the collection, and page numbers.

Forbes, Peter, ed. *Scanning the Century*. London: Penguin, 2000. Print.

Joseph, Jenny. "Warning." Forbes 335–36.

One Volume of a Multivolume Work

Cooke, Jacob Ernest, and Milton M. Klein, eds. *North America in Colonial Times*. Vol. 2. New York: Scribner's, 1998. Print.

NOTE: If you cite two or more volumes in a multivolume work, give the total number of volumes after each title. Offer specific references to volume and page numbers in the parenthetical reference in your text, like this: (5:112–14).

Salzman, Jack, David Lionel Smith, and Cornel West. *Encyclopedia of African-American Culture and History*. 5 vols. New York: Simon, 1996. Print.

An Introduction, a Preface, a Foreword, or an Afterword

To cite the introduction, preface, foreword, or afterword of a book, list the author of the part first. Then identify the part by type, with no quotation marks or underlining, followed by the title of the book. Next, identify the author of the work, using the word *By*. (If the book author and the part's author are the same person, give just the last name after *By*.) For a book that gives cover credit to an editor instead of an author, identify the editor as usual. Finally, list any page numbers for the part being cited.

Barry, Anne. Afterword. *Making Room for Students*. By Celia Oyler. New York: Teachers College, 1996. Print.

Lefebvre, Mark. Foreword. *The Journey Home*. Vol. 1. Ed. Jim Stephens. Madison: North Country, 1989. ix. Print.

Second and Subsequent Edition

An edition refers to the particular publication you are citing, as in the third (3rd) edition.

Joss, Molly W. *Looking Good in Presentations*. 3rd ed. Scottsdale: Coriolis, 1999. Print.

An Edition with Author and Editor

The term *edition* also refers to the work of one person that is prepared by another person, an editor.

Shakespeare, William. *A Midsummer Night's Dream*. Ed. Jane Bachman. Lincolnwood: NTC, 1994. Print.

A Translation

Lebert, Stephan, and Norbert Lebert. *My Father's Keeper*. Trans. Julian Evans. Boston: Little, 2001. Print.

An Article in a Familiar Reference Book

It is not necessary to give full publication information for familiar reference works (encyclopedias, dictionaries). List the edition and publication year. If an article is initialed, check the index of authors for the author's full name.

Lum, P. Andrea. "Computed Tomography." ***World Book.*** **2000 ed. Print.**

A Government Publication

State the name of the government (country, state, and so on) followed by the name of the agency. Most federal publications are published by the Government Printing Office (GPO).

United States. Dept. of Labor. Bureau of Labor Statistics. ***Occupational Outlook Handbook 2000–2001.*** **Washington: GPO, 2000. Print.**

A Book in a Series

Give series name and number (if any) before the publication information.

Paradis, Adrian A. ***Opportunities in Military Careers.*** **VGM Opportunities Series. Lincolnwood: VGM Career Horizons, 1999. Print.**

A Book with a Title Within Its Title

If the title contains a title normally in quotation marks, keep the quotation marks and italicize the entire title.

Stuckey-French, Elizabeth. ***"The First Paper Girl in Red Oak, Iowa" and Other Stories.*** **New York: Doubleday, 2000. Print.**

If the title contains a title that is normally italicized, do not italicize that title in your entry:

Harmetz, Aljean. ***The Making of*** **The Wizard of Oz:** ***Movie, Magic, and Studio Power in the Prime of MGM.*** **New York: Hyperion, 1998. Print.**

A Pamphlet, Brochure, Manual, or Other Workplace Document

Treat any such publication as you would a book.

Grayson, George W. ***The North American Free Trade Agreement.*** **New York: Foreign Policy Assn., 1993. Print.**

If publication information is missing, list the country of publication [in brackets] if known. Use *n.p.* (no place) if the country or the publisher is unknown and *n.d.* if the date is unknown, just as you would for a book.

Pedestrian Safety. **[United States]: n.p., n.d. Print.**

Works-Cited Entries: Periodicals

The possible components of periodical entries are listed in order below:

1. **Author's name** (last name, first name)
2. **Title of article** (in quotation marks)
3. **Name of periodical** (italicized)
4. **Series number or name** (if relevant)
5. **Volume number** (for a scholarly journal)
6. **Issue number**
7. **Date of publication** (abbreviate all months but May, June, July)
8. **Page numbers**
9. **Medium** ("Print")

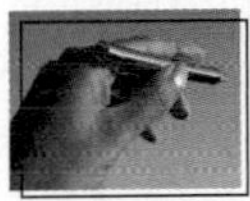

NOTE: If any of these components do not apply, they are not listed.

An Article in a Weekly or Biweekly Magazine

List the author (if identified), article title (in quotation marks), publication title (italicized), full date of publication, and page numbers for the article. Do not include volume and issue numbers. End with the medium.

Goodell, Jeff. "The Uneasy Assimilation." *Rolling Stone* 6–13 Dec. 2001: 63–66. Print.

An Article in a Monthly or Bimonthly Magazine

As for a weekly or biweekly magazine, list the author (if identified), article title (in quotation marks), and publication title (italicized). Then identify the month(s) and year of the issue, followed by page numbers for the article. Do not give volume and issue numbers. End with the medium.

"Patent Pamphleteer." *Scientific American* Dec. 2001: 33. Print.

An Article in a Scholarly Journal

Rather than month or full date of publication, scholarly journals are identified by volume number. List the volume number immediately after the journal title, followed by a period and the issue number, and then the year of publication (in parentheses). End with the page numbers of the article, as usual, followed by the medium.

Chu, Wujin. "Costs and Benefits of Hard-Sell." *Journal of Marketing Research* 32.2 (1995): 97–102. Print.

A Printed Interview

Begin with the name of the person interviewed.

Cantwell, Maria. "The New Technocrat." By Erika Rasmusson. *Working Woman* Apr. 2001: 20–21. Print.

NOTE: If the interview is untitled, *Interview* (no italics) follows the interviewee's name.

A Newspaper Article

Bleakley, Fred R. "Companies' Profits Grew 48% Despite Economy." *Wall Street Journal* 1 May 1995, Midwest ed.: 1. Print.

NOTE: Cite the edition of a major daily newspaper (if given) after the date (1 May 1995, Midwest ed.: 1). If a local paper's name does not include the city of publication, add it in brackets (not underlined) after the name.

To cite an article in a lettered section of the newspaper, list the section and the page number (A4). If the sections are numbered, however, use a comma after the year (or the edition); then indicate sec. 1, 2, 3, and so on, followed by a colon and the page number (sec. 1: 20). An unsigned newspaper article follows the same format:

"Bombs—Real and Threatened—Keep Northern Ireland Edgy." *Chicago Tribune* 6 Dec. 2001, sec. 1: 20. Print.

A Newspaper Editorial

If an article is an editorial, put *Editorial* (no italics) after the title.

"Hospital Power." Editorial. *Bangor Daily News* 14 Sept. 2004: A6. Print.

A Letter to the Editor

To identify a letter to the editor, put *Letter* (no italics) after the author's name.

Sory, Forrest. Letter. *Discover* July 2001: 10. Print.

A Review

Begin with the author (if identified) and title of the review. Use the notation *Rev. of* (no italics) between the title of the review and that of the original work. Identify the author of the original work with the word *by* (no italics). Then follow with publication data for the review.

Olsen, Jack. "Brains and Industry." Rev. of *Land of Opportunity,* by Sarah Marr. *New York Times* 23 Apr. 1995, sec. 3: 28. Print.

NOTE: If you cite the review of a work by an editor or a translator, use *ed.* or *trans.* instead of *by.*

An Unsigned Article in a Periodical

If no author is identified for an article, list the entry alphabetically by title in your list of works cited (ignoring any initial *A, An,* or *The*).

"Feeding the Hungry." *Economist* 371.8374 (2004): 74. Print.

An Article with a Title or Quotation Within Its Title

Morgenstern, Joe. "Sleeper of the Year: *In the Bedroom* Is Rich Tale of Tragic Love." *Wall Street Journal* 23 Nov. 2001: W1. Print.

NOTE: Use single quotation marks around the shorter title if it is a title normally punctuated with quotation marks.

An Article Reprinted in a Loose-Leaf Collection

The entry begins with original publication information and ends with the name of the loose-leaf volume (*Youth*), editor, volume number, publication information including name of the information service (SIRS), and the article number.

O'Connell, Loraine. "Busy Teens Feel the Beep." *Orlando Sentinel* 7 Jan. 1993: E1+. Print. *Youth.* Ed. Eleanor Goldstein. Vol. 4. Boca Raton: SIRS, 1993. Art. 41.

An Article with Pagination That Is Not Continuous

For articles that are continued on a nonconsecutive page, whatever the publication type, add a plus sign (+) after the first page number.

Garrett, Robyne. "Negotiating a Physical Identity: Girls, Bodies and Physical Education." *Sport, Education & Society* 9 (2004): 223+. Print.

Works-Cited Entries: Online Sources

Online sources fall into three general categories: Nonperiodical sources (such as common Web sites), scholarly articles published or republished online, and periodicals collected in a database. The following guidelines explain the contents of each type of reference.

Nonperiodical Sources

1. **Author's name**
2. **Title of work, in quotation marks** (article or section) **or italics** (larger work)
3. **Title of site** (if separate from the work), **italicized**
4. **Version or edition**
5. **Site sponsor or publisher** (or "N.p.")
6. **Date of publication** (or "n.d.")
7. **Medium of publication** ("Web")
8. **Date of access**

NOTE: Do not include the URL (Web address) unless your reader cannot find the source without it, or your instructor requires it. In that case, remove the medium and list the URL within angle brackets (< >) after the date of access. If you must break a long URL across lines of text, do so only after a double or single slash, and do not add a hyphen.

Scholarly Articles Published or Republished Online

1. **Information for print version** (without the medium "Print")
2. **Medium of publication** ("Web")
3. **Date of access**

Periodicals in a Database

1. **Information for print version** (without the medium "Print")
2. **Title of database** (italicized)
3. **Medium of publication** ("Web")
4. **Date of access**

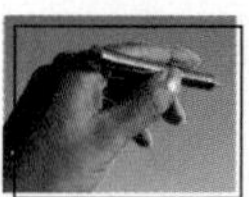

NOTE: If no page numbers are available for an article in a database, use the abbreviation "n. pag."

A Personal Site

After the author's name, list the site title (italicized) or a description such as *Home page* or *Online posting* (no italics), whichever is appropriate. Follow with the date of publication or most recent update, if available, the medium, and your date of visit.

Mehuron, Kate. Home page. N.p., 30 Sept. 2004. Web. 31 Jan. 2010.

A Professional Site

Generally, no author is identified for a professional site, so the entry begins with the article or site title. Use the copyright date if no date of update is given. Conclude with the medium and your date of access.

"Challenges." *BP Global.* BP p.l.c., 2005. Web. 17 June 2009.

An Article in an Online Periodical

Begin with the author's name, the article title in quotation marks, the italicized name of the site, and the date of publication. Include page numbers (or other sections) if numbered. Close with the medium and date of access.

Dickerson, John. "Nailing Jello." *Time.com.* Time, 5 Nov. 2001. Web. 9 Dec. 2009.

An Article in an Online Reference Work

Unless the author of the entry is identified, begin with the entry name in quotation marks. Follow with the usual online publication information.

"Eakins, Thomas." *Britannica Online Encyclopedia.* Encyclopedia Britannica, 2008. Web. 26 Sept. 2009.

An Article from an Online Service

Begin with the information for the print source, followed by the database name (in italics), the medium, and the date of access.

Davis, Jerome. "Massacre in Kiev." *Washington Post* 29 Nov. 1999, final ed.: C12. *ProQuest.* Web. 28 Dec. 2008.

An Online Governmental Publication

As with a governmental publication in print, begin with the name of the government (country, state, and so on) followed by the name of the agency. After the publication title, add the electronic publication information.

United States. Dept. of Labor. Office of Disability Employment Policy. *Emergency Preparedness for People with Disabilities.* Apr. 2004. Web. 12 Sept. 2009.

When citing the Congressional Record, the date, page numbers, and medium are all that is required.

***Cong. Rec.* 5 Feb. 2002: S311–15. Web.**

An Online Multimedia Resource: Painting, Photograph, Musical Composition, Film or Film Clip, Etc.

After the usual information for the type of work being cited, add electronic publication information.

Goya, Francisco de. *Saturn Devouring His Children.* 1819-1823. Museo del Prado, Madrid. Web. 13 Dec. 2009.

An E-Mail Communication

Identify the author of the e-mail, and then list the subject line of the e-mail as a title, in quotation marks. Next, include a description of the entry, including the recipient—usually *Message to the author* (no italics), meaning you, the author of the paper. Finally, give the date of the message and the medium of delivery.

Barzinji, Atman. "Re: Frog Populations in Wisconsin Wetlands." Message to the author. 1 Jan. 2010. E-Mail.

TIPS

FOR FINDING UPDATED CITING INFORMATION

Because the Internet continues evolving, details of documentation style for online sources sometimes change as well. For the latest information, visit **thewritesource.com**.

Other Sources: Primary, Personal, and Multimedia

The following examples of works-cited entries illustrate how to cite sources such as television or radio programs, films, live performances, works of art, and other miscellaneous nonprint sources.

A Periodically Published Database on CD-ROM, Diskette, or Magnetic Tape

Citations for materials published on CD-ROM, diskette, or magnetic tape are similar to those for print sources, with these added considerations:

1. The publisher and vendor of the publication may be different, in which case both must be identified.
2. Because of periodic updates, multiple versions of the same database may exist, which calls for citation if possible of both the date of the document cited and the date of the database itself.

"Bunker Hill Monument to Get $3.7M Makeover." *Boston Business Journal* 13 June 2005. CD-ROM. *Business Dateline*. ProQuest. July 2005.

Malleron, Jean-Luc, and Alain Juin. *Database of Palladium Chemistry*. Version 1.1. Burlington, MA: Academic Press, 2002. CD-ROM.

Computer Software

If you use an encyclopedia or other reference book recorded on disk, use the form below. If available, include publication information for the printed source.

***Microsoft Encarta Deluxe 2005*. Redmond: Microsoft, 2005. DVD.**

A Television or Radio Program

"Another Atlantis?" *Deep Sea Detectives*. The History Channel. 13 June 2005. Television.

A Film

The director, distributor, and year of release follow the title. Other information may be included if pertinent.

***The Aviator*. Dir. Martin Scorsese. Perf. Leonardo DiCaprio. Miramax Films, 2004. DVD.**

A Video Recording

Cite a filmstrip, slide program, videocassette, or DVD just as you would a film.

***Beyond the Da Vinci Code.* A&E Home Video, 2005. DVD.**

An Audio Recording

If you are not citing a CD, indicate LP, Audiocassette, or Audiotape. If you are citing a specific song on a musical recording, place its title in quotation marks before the title of the recording.

Welch, Jack. *Winning.* Harper Audio, 2005. Audiotape.

An Interview by the Author (Yourself)

Brooks, Sarah. Personal interview. 15 Oct. 2009.

Artwork on Display

Titian. *The Entombment.* 1520? The Louvre, Paris.

A Cartoon or Comic Strip (in Print)

Luckovich, Mike. "The Drawing Board." Cartoon. *Time* 17 Sept. 2001: 18. Print.

Letter Received by the Author (Yourself)

Thomas, Bob. Message to the author. 10 Jan. 2010. Letter.

A Lecture, a Speech, an Address, or a Reading

If there is a title, include it in quotation marks after the speaker's name.

Annan, Kofi. Oslo City Hall, Oslo, Norway. 10 Dec. 2001. Lecture.

A Map or Chart

Follow the format for an anonymous book, adding *Map* or *Chart* (no italics).

***Wisconsin Territory.* Map. Madison: Wisconsin Trails, 1988. Print.**

NOTE: The availability of information on computer networks can change from day to day, so we strongly recommend that you print out a copy of the material you are accessing. For additional information on citing sources in MLA style, visit our Web site at www.thewritesource.com/mla.htm.

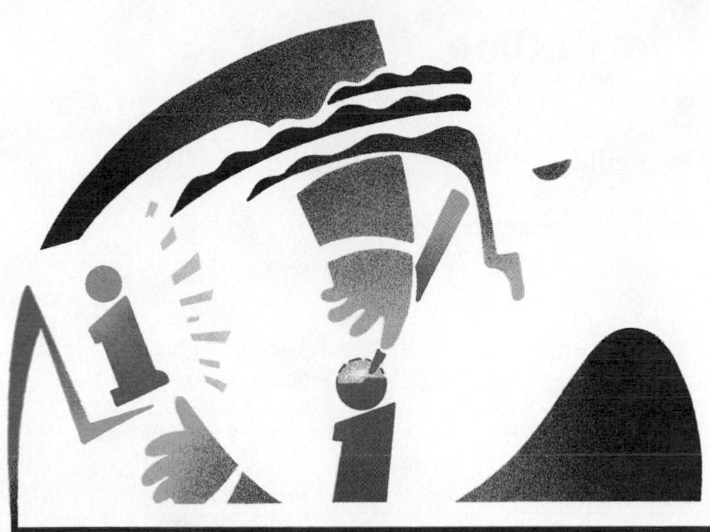

MLA Research Paper

Writer and teacher Ken Macrorie says, "Good writing is formed partly through plan and partly through accident." His words certainly apply to the process of writing a research paper. Producing an effective finished product requires a great deal of planning, from selecting and researching an intriguing topic to organizing your ideas for writing. But a truly memorable paper is also born of wrong turns, unexpected discoveries, and of your own thoughts and feelings developed during the research process.

As you read the sample MLA paper that follows, keep Macrorie's quotation in mind. Is Fidel Novielli's research paper the result of careful planning? Is it also an expression of the writer's thoughts and feelings about his topic?

WHAT'S AHEAD

Novielli's paper deals with an important social issue: the rise of private entrepreneurs who tackle public problems. As you will see, he refers to a variety of sources, including books, magazines, and Web sites, in his research. The sample paper also demonstrates MLA documentation style.

Title Page and Outline

Research Paper

Works-Cited Page

Title Page and Outline

MLA style does not require a title page or an outline. However, if you are instructed to include a title page or an outline with your paper, use the examples below as a guide.

Title Page

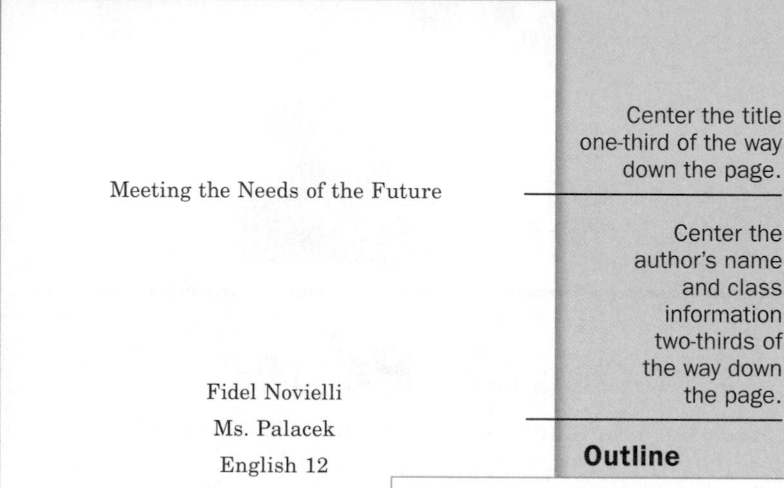

Meeting the Needs of the Future

Fidel Novielli

Ms. Palacek

English 12

23 February 2010

Center the title one-third of the way down the page.

Center the author's name and class information two-thirds of the way down the page.

Outline

Novielli i

Meeting the Needs of the Future

THESIS STATEMENT: "Social entrepreneurs" have begun to apply business strategies to human problems, with impressive results.

I. The root problem is that social systems are about 300 years behind the times.
   A. The Industrial Revolution made businesses competitive and innovative.
   B. Government and other social systems remained uncompetitive.
   C. For 300 years, business evolved in expertise and inventiveness, while social systems became increasingly less cost-effective by comparison.

II. About 25 years ago, this began to change dramatically.
   A. Faced with such need and opportunity, social entrepreneurs began to appear.
   B. Bill Drayton founded Ashoka to help foster social capitalism.
   C. His goal is to change the world.

Center the title one inch from the top of the page. Double-space the outline. If the outline is longer than one page, number its pages with lowercase Roman numerals (i, ii, iii, and so on).

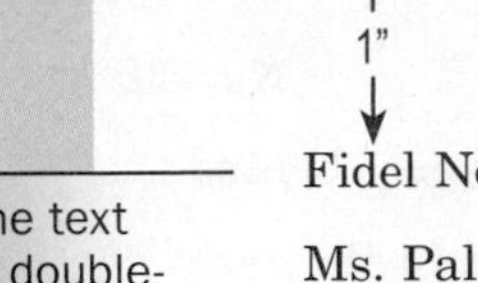

Novielli 1

The text is double-spaced throughout.

Fidel Novielli

Ms. Palacek

English 12

23 February 2010

Meeting the Needs of the Future

The introduction grabs the reader's attention with a dramatic comparison.

In a small community, when tragedy strikes, everyone knows it, and everyone can see how best to chip in and help. In our global community, tragedy strikes somewhere every day, but knowing how to respond is much more difficult. Even in the wealthiest countries, far too many social needs remain unmet. In the United States alone, 13.8 million American children live with hunger, and nearly 20 million have little or no health care ("Childhood"). Globally, 30,000 children die each day from malnutrition and disease ("Global").

The introduction ends with the paper's thesis (underlined).

Faced with numbers like these, an individual might be tempted to despair and cry out, "I'm only one person. What can I do?" Fortunately, a new breed of concerned citizenry has begun to demonstrate that one person can do a lot, given a little imagination and determination. In the business world, these qualities have long been recognized as the features of an entrepreneur. Now "social entrepreneurs," sometimes called "social capitalists," have begun to apply business strategies to human problems, with impressive results.

The writer explains the problem being addressed.

According to Bill Drayton, founder of Ashoka, an organization that promotes social entrepreneurship, the root

Novielli 2

problem is that social systems are about 300 years behind the times. When the Industrial Revolution started in the early 1700s, the business sector became competitive and innovative. However, government and other social systems remained uncompetitive, supported by taxes or donations and bolstered by tradition. As business continued to evolve in expertise and influence over the centuries, social systems fell further and further behind in their cost-effectiveness (Hammonds).

Worse, industrialization brought new challenges that the old social systems were simply not equipped to handle. As futurists Alvin and Heidi Toffler explain, society became increasingly urban, drawing people away from farms and villages to work in factories. The social support of rural communities, with their multigenerational families, did not carry over to the cities, where many people had relocated, living alone or in a "nuclear family" of father, mother, and a few children (19–24). As any Dickens novel reveals, and every modern metropolitan newspaper repeats, far too often this relocation has resulted in poverty, crime, and disease.

A source is introduced, paraphrased, and identified by page numbers.

The author refers to common knowledge to support his point.

Drayton believes that roughly 25 years ago, this situation began to change dramatically. The social sectors started applying the lessons of business. In his words, "It was like hearing the ice breaking up at the end of winter in a lake. Creak, creak, groan, crash! The need was so big, the gap so huge, the opportunity to learn right before people's eyes" (Hammonds). Faced with such need and opportunity, a new breed of entrepreneur began to emerge, this time in the citizen sector. Drayton created Ashoka as a means of fostering this

An exact quotation adds voice and authority to the paper.

social entrepreneurship on a global scale. His goal is literally to change the world.

Background information supports a statement made in the previous paragraph.

If that seems audacious, it is important to understand Drayton's vision and his experience. As one former employer explains, "Everything that Drayton did he worked to solve fundamentally." In other words, Drayton believes in attacking the root of a problem. For example, while serving as assistant administrator for the Environmental Protection Agency, he successfully championed a "bubble" method of cheaply and effectively combating pollution. Under this plan, pollution is tackled as a whole, rather than as individual processes. Instead of dictating specific details for reducing emissions, the plan gives each business an emissions target, and that business can determine the most cost-effective way to meet that goal. Businesses can even trade gains at one location against shortfalls at another, to bring the overall level of pollution down. This "bubble and trading" plan quickly became the official policy of the United States. Since then, it has also been included as a central part of the Kyoto Protocol for international emissions, and the European Parliament has adopted it for their global emissions-trading market (Bornstein 53–58).

It is this sort of "fundamental solution" thinking that characterizes social entrepreneurship and that distinguishes it from traditional charity. Traditional charity tends to be a one-sided, top-down approach to solving a problem. This approach involves the haves handing something down to the have-nots. And more often than not, it focuses on a crisis. Social capitalism, on the other hand, seeks to change the situation that causes the need. It looks for opportunities by which the needy can better themselves. In the process, society benefits as well.

Specific examples illustrate the thesis.

Consider the example of Erzsébet Szekeres of Hungary, whose son Tibor was born with microcephalus (an abnormally small skull) and severe mental retardation. Under the strain of caring for Tibor during his early years, Szekeres' marriage and career began to suffer. Friends and family urged the woman to put her son in a state institution and go on with her life. Szekeres saw, however, that these institutions were little more than prisons where the severely handicapped were shut away from public view. She dreamed of a group home where people like Tibor could care for themselves, with assistance, and even have meaningful work.

The author includes details for support.

It took years of determined effort on Szekeres' part to make that dream a reality. Often, the government itself opposed her efforts, because she was not a member of the health-care profession. Eventually, however, with two loans from disability organizations, she purchased an abandoned farming cooperative and turned it into a community for the disabled. Today, this facility includes dorm-style rooms, a cafeteria, a community room where dances are held and movies are shown, and work facilities where people like her son earn money by assembling curtain clips and other such assembly-line jobs. To date, Szekeres has created 21 such institutions across Hungary, where more than 600 multiply disabled people live and work. Her efforts are even changing the way the state itself deals with the handicapped (Bornstein 98–116).

Novielli 5

Perhaps an even clearer example of social capitalism is shown in the food-bank program created by Wojciech Onyszkiewicz in Poland. During the years that Soviet communism ruled Poland, the very existence of poverty was denied. After the fall of the Soviet Union, it was estimated that 20 percent of the population lived below the poverty line, and 31 percent of those living in poverty were in multi-child families. While rural communities often had a surplus of food, there were no systems in place for getting it to urban populations ("Ashoka"). In addition, rural citizens were not happy about giving charity to people they perceived as "parasites" (Bornstein 201). On the other hand, these same rural people envied the opportunities for education and culture that were available to urban citizens.

Ideas from two different sources are worked smoothly into the text.

Onyszkiewicz came up with a plan in which rural communities donate excess food for urban use, and in exchange, rural children travel to the cities to help distribute that food, visit museums, attend sessions of parliament, and take part in other such activities ("Ashoka"). Under a similar plan, Onyszkiewicz organized computer training for rural children by recruiting physically disabled computer users from the city. In exchange for their expertise, these city dwellers are able to visit the countryside. Villagers prepare wheelchair ramps and arrange outdoor activities that the urbanites could not otherwise experience (Bornstein 201). In both of these cases, "commodities" are exchanged in a very capitalistic manner, and important human needs are met.

Each paragraph contains a topic sentence and supporting details.

Ashoka itself is actually another example of social capitalism at work. The organization's goal is to identify promising social entrepreneurs in the earliest stages of their work and to provide support to help that work flourish. While some of this support is monetary, a small stipend to allow the blossoming entrepreneur to work full-time on the project, most of it is less tangible. Ashoka fellows "get support, ideas, and, quite literally, protection," as in the case of a Brazilian whose work in drug rehabilitation resulted in attacks by local police. The organization took the case to the local governor, and the attacks stopped (Hammond). What makes this support capitalistic is that by applying it early in the work of a social entrepreneur, Ashoka gets the greatest "return" on its investment—the most good for the least assistance.

In the closing paragraphs, the writer reflects on the topic.

These are only a few examples from thousands of programs around the world. (Ashoka alone has more than 1,500 fellows.) Social entrepreneurs are tackling problems at all levels, from helping inner-city students fill out college applications to training health-care workers who will minister to millions of AIDS victims in South Africa, from establishing a market for "fair-trade" coffee to electrifying rural Brazil. It is no exaggeration to say that such efforts often lift entire communities out of poverty. Each year, the number of social-entrepreneurship programs continues to grow. Since 2004, Fast Company and the Monitor Group have given awards recognizing the 25 best social entrepreneurs each year ("25"). The competition is stiff, and the stories of the finalists are every bit as inspiring as those of the award winners.

Novielli 7

Bill Drayton believes that the next step in this social evolution is a partnering of business and social entrepreneurs. One such example involves the Mexican cement company Cemex, which promotes a savings program for families to build home additions. As a result, family crowding is reduced and neighborhoods are improved, while Cemex reaches a market it would not have otherwise (Hammond). Drayton sees this sort of partnership as only natural. It was the splitting of business and social concerns 300 years ago that was unnatural. Eventually, he believes, everyone will be a change-maker, and as a result, everyone will feel that his or her life has meaning.

A final connection with the reader is made.

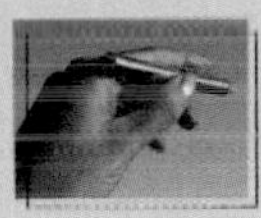

NOTE: The list of works cited for this paper appears on page 360.

Analyzing the Research Paper

A paper such as "Meeting the Needs of the Future" both informs and challenges the reader. Consider the following questions as you review the author's handling of this social issue.

- Why do you think the writer chose a problem-and-solution organization for this paper?
- What is your reaction to Bill Drayton's view of history?
- Why might some people prefer the term "social entrepreneur" and others the term "social capitalist"?
- What important social issues are you aware of in your own city, state, or region? How might you learn more about those issues?

Novielli 8

A separate page alphabetically lists sources cited in the paper.

Double spacing is used throughout, and second and third lines are indented five spaces.

Works Cited

"Ashoka Fellow Profile—Wojciech Onyszkiewicz." *Ashoka.* Ashoka Fellows, 1995. Web. 23 Feb. 2010.

Bornstein, David. *How to Change the World: Social Entrepreneurs and the Power of New Ideas.* New York: Oxford, 2004. Print.

"Childhood Hunger in the United States." *Learn About Hunger.* America's Second Harvest, 2006. Web. 19 Feb. 2010.

"Global Hunger Facts." *Fast.* Concern Worldwide, 2006. Web. 20 Feb. 2010.

Hammonds, Keith H. "A Lever Long Enough to Move the World." *Fast Company* Jan. 2005: 61. Print.

Toffler, Alvin, and Heidi Toffler. *Creating a New Civilization.* Atlanta: Turner, 1995. Print.

"25 Entrepreneurs Who Are Changing the World." *Fast Company* Jan. 2006. Web. 19 Feb. 2010.

APA Documentation Style

Those who write in the social sciences—psychology, sociology, political science, education, journalism, or public health—usually refer to the style guidelines found in the fifth edition of the *Publication Manual of the American Psychological Association* (APA). While those guidelines are intended primarily for preparing manuscripts for journal publication, they are also commonly used for student research papers and dissertations.

WHAT'S AHEAD

This chapter provides guidelines and models for citing sources according to APA style, both in the text of the paper and in your list of references. For instructions on formatting the paper itself, see the overview and example paper on pages 372–382. Also visit the "APA Style" page at thewritesource.com for further citation examples and updates regarding APA format.

Citing Sources: In-Text Citations

Reference List: Guidelines

Reference Entries: Books

Reference Entries: Periodicals

Reference Entries: Online Sources

Reference Entries: Other Sources

Citing Sources

In-Text Citations

In-text citations must include the author and date of the sources, either within the sentence or in parentheses. Each citation must be matched to an entry in the alphabetized list of references at the end of your paper.

According to a 2002 essay by Patrick Marshall . . .

According to a recent essay by Patrick Marshall (2002) . . .

According to a recent essay (Marshall, 2002) . . .

One Author

Place the author's last name and the date of the work in parentheses. If you cite a specific part, give the page number, chapter, or section, using the appropriate abbreviations (p. or pp., chap., or sec.).

. . . Bush's 2002 budget was based on revenue estimates that "now appear to have been far too optimistic" (Lemann, 2003, p. 48).

NOTE: When citing two works by the same author published in the same year, arrange them alphabetically by title in the reference list. Add a small *a* after the date of the first work, a small *b* after the second, and so on. Then use these letters in your in-text citations.

Gene therapy holds great promise for the future (Gormann, 2000a).

Two Authors

If a work has two authors, identify both in every citation of that work. Separate their names with an ampersand in any parenthetical reference.

A rise in global temperature and a decrease in atmospheric oxygen led to the mass extinction during the Late Permian Period (Huey & Ward, 2010).

Three to Five Authors

Mention all authors—up to five—in the first citation of a work.

Love changes not just who we are, but who we can become, as well (Lewis, Amini, & Lannon, 2010).

After the first citation, list only the first author followed by *et al.* (meaning *and others*).

These discoveries lead to the hypothesis that love actually alters the brain's structure (Lewis et al., 2010).

Six or More Authors

If your source has six or more authors, refer to the work by the first author's name followed by "et al." in all parenthetical references. However, be sure to list all the authors (up to seven) in your reference list.

Among children 13 to 14 years old, a direct correlation can be shown between cigarette advertising and smoking (Lopez et al., 2004).

A Work Authored by an Agency, a Committee, or Another Organization

The organization name acts as the author name. For the first citation, place abbreviations in square brackets; then use only the abbreviation.

First text citation: (National Institute of Mental Health [NIMH], 2010)

Subsequent citations: (NIMH, 2010)

A Work with No Author

If your source lists no author, use the first two or three words of the title (capitalized normally) instead.

. . . including a guide to low-impact exercise ("Staying Healthy," 2004).

A Work Referred to in Another Work

When using a source that is referred to in another source, try to find and cite the original. If that isn't possible, credit the source by adding "as cited in" within the parentheses.

. . . theorem given by Ullman (as cited in Hoffman, 2010).

NOTE: Your reference list will have an entry for Hoffman (not Ullman).

Two or More Works in One Reference

When citing two or more works within one parenthetical reference, list the sources in alphabetical order, separating them with semicolons.

These near-death experiences are reported with conviction (Rommer, 2000; Sabom, 1998).

NOTE: Arrange two or more works by the same author(s) by year of publication, separated by commas. (McIntyre & Ames, 1992, 1995)

Personal Communications

Cite letters, e-mail messages, phone conversations, and so on, as "personal communications," with their full date. Do not list them in your references.

The management team expects to finish hiring this spring (R. Fouser, personal communication, December 14, 2009).

Reference List

The reference list includes all of the retrievable sources cited in a paper. It begins on a separate page and follows the format below.

Page Numbers Continue the numbering scheme from the paper: place the running head (short title) in the upper left corner.

Title Place the title "References" approximately one inch from the top of the page and center it.

Entries List the entries alphabetically by author's last name. If no author is given, then list by title (disregarding *A, An,* or *The*).

- Double-space between all lines (including between the title "References" and the first entry).
- Capitalize only the first word (and any proper nouns) of book and article titles; capitalize the names of periodicals in the standard upper- and lowercase manner.
- Begin each entry at the left margin and indent additional lines of the entry five to seven spaces. (See the examples below.)

FORMAT FOR A BOOK ENTRY

Author's last name, Initials for first name and middle name. (year).
Book title. Location: Publisher.

NOTE: For the location, give the city and the postal abbreviation for the state. Outside of the United States, include the state or province and the country.

FORMAT FOR A PERIODICAL ENTRY

Author's last name, Initials. (date). Article title. _Periodical Title, volume number_ (issue number if paginated by issue), page numbers.

FORMAT FOR AN ONLINE PERIODICAL ENTRY

Author's last name, Initials. (date). Article title. _Periodical Title, volume number_ (issue number), pages. doi:code.

NOTE: If no DOI (digital object identifier) is available, use a "Retrieved from URL" statement instead. If the content is likely to change, use a "Retrieved date from URL" format.

Reference Entries: Books

The entries on pages 365–366 illustrate the information needed to cite books, sections of books, articles in reference books, and government publications on the "References" page in documented writing.

A Book by One Author

Guttman, J. (1999). *The gift wrapped in sorrow: A mother's quest for healing.* Palm Springs, CA: JMJ Publishing.

A Book by Two or More Authors

Lynn, J., & Harrold, J. (1999). *Handbook for mortals: Guidance for people facing serious illness.* New York, NY: Oxford University Press.

NOTE: Follow the first author's name with a comma; then join the two authors' names with an ampersand (&) rather than "and." List up to seven authors; abbreviate subsequent authors as "et al."

An Anonymous Book

If an author is listed as "Anonymous," treat it as the author's name. Otherwise, follow this format:

***American Medical Association essential guide to asthma.* (2003). New York, NY: American Medical Association.**

A Chapter from a Book

Tattersall, I. (2002). How did we achieve humanity? In *The monkey in the mirror* (pp. 138–168). New York, NY: Harcourt.

A Single Work from an Anthology

Nichols, J. (2005). Diversity and stability in language. In B. D. Joseph & R. D. Janda (Eds.), *The handbook of historical linguistics* (pp. 283–310). Malden, MA: Blackwell.

NOTE: When editors' names appear in the middle of an entry, follow the usual order: initial first, surname last.

One Volume of a Multivolume Edited Work

Salzman, J., Smith, D. L., & West, C. (Eds.). (1996). *Encyclopedia of African-American culture and history* (Vol. 4). New York, NY: Simon & Schuster Macmillan.

A Group Author as Publisher

Amnesty International. (2000). *Hidden scandal, secret shame: Torture and ill-treatment of children.* New York, NY: Author.

NOTE: If the publication is a brochure, identify it as such in brackets after the title.

An Edited Work, One in a Series

When a work is part of a larger series or collection, make a two-part title of the series and the particular volume you are citing.

Hunter, S., & Sundel, M. (Eds.). (1998). *Sage sourcebooks for the human services: Vol. 7. Midlife myths: Issues, findings and practice implications.* Newbury Park, CA: Sage Publications.

An Edition Other Than the First

Trimmer, J. (2001). *Writing with a purpose* (13th ed.). Boston, MA: Houghton Mifflin.

An Article in a Reference Book

Lewer, N. (1999). Non-lethal weapons. In *World encyclopedia of peace* (pp. 279–280). Oxford, UK: Pergamon Press.

NOTE: If no author is listed, begin the entry with the title of the article.

A Technical or Research Report

Ball, J., & Evans Jr., C. (2001). *Safe passage: Astronaut care for exploration missions.* Washington, DC: Institute of the National Academics.

A Government Publication

National Renewable Energy Laboratory. (2003). *Statistical wind power forecasting for U.S. wind farms* (NREL Publication No. CP-500-35087). Springfield, VA: U.S. Department of Commerce.

NOTE: If the document is not available from the Government Printing Office (GPO), the publisher would be either "Author" or the separate government department that published it.

Reference Entries: Periodicals

The entries on pages 367–368 illustrate the information needed to cite articles in magazines, scholarly journals, abstracts, newspaper articles, and reviews. The general form for a periodical entry is this:

Author's last name, Initials. (year, Month day). Article title. *Periodical Title, Vol. no.*, pages.

A Magazine Article, Author Given

Silberman, S. (2001, December). The geek syndrome. *Wired, 9*(12), 174–183.

A Magazine Article, No Author Given

Arctic ozone wiped out by solar storms. (2005, March). *New Scientist, 185*(2490), 17.

An Article in a Scholarly Journal, Consecutively Paginated

Epstein, R., & Hundert, E. (2002). Defining and assessing professional competence. *JAMA, 287*, 226–235.

NOTE: Here are the features of a basic reference to a scholarly journal:

- last name and initial(s) as for a book reference,
- year of publication,
- title of article in lowercase (except for the first word and proper nouns), not italicized or in quotation marks,
- title and volume number of journal italicized, and
- inclusive page numbers.

A Journal Article, Paginated by Issue

Lewer, N. (1999, summer). Nonlethal weapons. *Forum, 14*(2), 39–45.

NOTE: When the page numbering of the issue starts with page 1, the issue number (not italicized) is placed in parentheses after the volume number.

A Journal Article, Two Authors

Newman, P. A., & Nash, E. R. (2005). The unusual Southern Hemisphere stratosphere winter of 2002. *Journal of the Atmospheric Sciences, 62*(3), 614–628.

A Journal Article, More Than Seven Authors

Watanabe, T., Bihoreau, M-T., McCarthy, L., Kiguwa, S., Hishigaki, H., Tsuji, A., . . . James, M. (1999, May 1). A radiation hybrid map of the rat genome containing 5,255 markers. *Nature Genetics*, 22, 27–36.

An Abstract of a Scholarly Article (from a Secondary Source)

Yamamoto, S., & Nakamura, A. (2000). A new model of continuous dust production from the lunar surface. *Astronomy & Astrophysics, 356,* 1112–1118. Abstract taken from CDS Bibliographic Service, 2005.

NOTE: When the dates of the article and the secondary-source abstract differ, the reference in your text would cite both dates, the original first, separated by a slash (2000/2005). When the abstract is obtained from the original source, the description "Abstract" is placed in brackets following the title (but before the period).

A Newspaper Article, Author Given

Stolberg, S. C. (2002, January 4). Breakthrough in pig cloning could aid organ transplants. *The New York Times,* pp. 1A, 17A.

NOTE: For newspapers, use "p." or "pp." before the page numbers; if the article is not on continuous pages, give all the page numbers, separated by commas.

A Newspaper Article, No Author Given

AOL to take up to $60 billion charge. (2002, January 8). *Chicago Tribune,* sec. 3, p. 3.

A Letter to the Editor

Cohen, E. (2005, May 9). Don't overlook benefits of medical spending [Letter to the editor]. *The Milwaukee Journal Sentinel,* p. 9A.

NOTE: The "A" means that the letter is in the newspaper's A section.

A Review

Updike, J. (2001, December 24). Survivor/believer [Review of the book *New and Collected Poems* 1931–2001]. *The New Yorker,* 118–122.

A Newsletter Article

Newsletter article entries are very similar to newspaper article entries; only a volume number is added.

Teaching mainstreamed special education students. (2002, February). *The Council Chronicle, 11,* 6–8.

Reference Entries: Online Sources

APA style prefers a reference to the print or fixed-media form of a source, even if the source is available online. Even if an online article has been changed from the print version or has additional information, follow the same general format for the author, date, and title elements of print sources, but follow it with a DOI (if possible) or a "Retrieved from" statement.

See the "APA Style" page at thewritesource.com for additional examples.

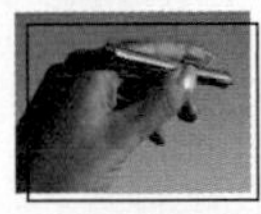

NOTE: If you must break a URL across lines of text in an APA formatted paper, do so only after a double or single slash or before a period.

Online Document:

Author, A.A. (year). *Title of work.* doi or "Retrieved from" statement.

Bittlestone, R. (2005). *Odysseus unbound.* doi:10.2277/0521853575

American Psychological Association. (2000, January). Successful aging: The second 50. *APA Monitor.* Retrieved May 6, 2010, from http://www.apa .org/monitor/jan00/cs.html

Periodical, Different from Print Version or Online Only

Author, A., & Author, B. (year, month day). Title of article, chapter, or Web page. *Title of Periodical, volume number,* inclusive page numbers if available. doi or "Retrieved from" statement.

Nicholas, D., Huntington, P., & Williams, P. (2001, May 23). Comparing web and touch screen transaction log files. *Journal of Medical Internet Research,* 3. Retrieved Nov. 15, 2009, from http://www.jmir .org/2001/2/e18/index.htm

NOTE: When citing additional information (podcast, map, etc.) that has been included in the online version, use the description "Supplemental material" in brackets after the article title.

A Document from an Online Database

If the database identifies the print source, list that information only. Add a "Retrieved from" statement only if the source cannot be found otherwise or is likely to change (such as a wiki page).

Author, A., & Author, B. (year). Title of article. *Title of Periodical, volume number,* inclusive page numbers.

Belsie, Laurent. (1999). Progress or peril? *Christian Science Monitor, 91*(85), 15.

NOTE: If the document cited is an abstract, include [Abstract] after the title.

Reference Entries: Other Sources

The following citation entries are examples of audiovisual media sources and sources available electronically.

A Television or Radio Broadcast

Crystal, L. (Executive Producer). (2005, February 11). *The newshour with Jim Lehrer* [Television broadcast]. New York, NY, and Washington, DC: Public Broadcasting Service.

An Audio Recording

Give the name and function (author, speaker, performer, compiler, and so on) of the originators or primary contributors. Indicate the recording medium (CD, record, cassette, and so on) in brackets, following the title.

Kim, E. (Author, Speaker). (2000). *Ten thousand sorrows* [CD]. New York, NY: Random House.

A Motion Picture

Give the name and function of the director, producer, or both. If the motion picture's circulation was limited, provide the distributor's name and complete address in parentheses.

Jackson, P. (Director). (2003). *The lord of the rings: Return of the king* [Motion picture]. United States: New Line Productions, Inc.

A Lecture, Speech, Reading, or Dissertation

For an unpublished paper presented at a meeting, indicate when the paper was presented, at what meeting, in what location.

Lycan, W. (2002, June). *The plurality of consciousness.* Paper presented at the meeting of the Society for Philosophy and Psychology, New York, NY.

For an unpublished doctoral dissertation, place the dissertation's title in italics, even though the work is unpublished. Indicate the school at which the writer completed the dissertation.

Roberts, W. (2001). *Crime amidst suburban wealth* (Unpublished doctoral dissertation). Bowling Green State University, Bowling Green, OH.

APA Research Paper

As with any important writing project, it may help to examine a model research paper. Reviewing the student paper in this chapter will give you a firsthand look at how the APA guidelines work in actual practice.

Begin by looking over the entire paper, from the abstract to the graphics to the reference page. Notice how the report is constructed and how the pieces fit together. Then do a closer reading of the abstract and the first few pages, examining the side notes and parenthetical references. Finally, continue to refer to the model as you put your own paper together.

WHAT'S AHEAD

The chapter begins with an overview of the APA paper format, followed by a sample student paper. For details on in-text citations and preparing the list of references, see pages 362–370.

APA Paper Format

This overview gives formatting guidelines for a student research paper, not for an article to be submitted to a journal. Ask your teacher for special requirements he or she may have.

- **Title Page** On the first page, include your paper's title, your name, and your school's name on three separate lines. Double-space and center the lines beginning approximately one-third of the way down from the top of the page. Place the running head (an abbreviated title) after the phrase "Running head:" in the upper left corner and place the page number 1 in the upper right.

- **Abstract** On the second page, include an abstract—a 150- to 250-word paragraph summarizing your paper. Place the title *Abstract* approximately one inch from the top of the page and center it. Include the running head (without that identifier) upper left and page number 2 upper right.

- **Body** Format the body of your paper as follows:

  Margins: Leave a one-inch margin on all four sides of each page (1-1/2 inches on the left for papers to be bound).

  Running Head and Page Numbers: Continue the running head (without that identifier) throughout in the upper left corner and the page number in the upper right.

  Line Spacing: Double-space your entire paper, unless your teacher allows single spacing for tables, titles, and so on.

  Headings: The first is centered, boldface, upper- and lowercase. The second is flush left, boldface, upper- and lowercase. The third is indented, boldface, lowercase paragraph style ending with a period. The fourth is like the third, but italicized as well.

- **In-Text Citations** Within your paper, give credit by including the author and year in a citation. For quotations and other specific references, add the page number to the citation. (See page 311.) If a quotation runs 40 words or more, type it in block style, five spaces in from the left margin, with all lines flush left along that new margin. If it is more than one paragraph, indent the first line of the second and later paragraphs another five spaces.

- **References** Place full citations for all sources in an alphabetized list at the end of your paper. Start this list on a separate page. Center the title *References* approximately one-inch from the top of the page. (See pages 313–319.)

Sample APA Research Paper

Student writers Thomas Delancy and Adam Solberg wrote the following research paper based on an experiment that they conducted in a psychology course. This model paper can be used . . .

- to study how a well-written research paper, based on experimentation, structures and builds a discussion from start to finish;
- to examine how sources are used in social-science research writing (see pages 374–380); and
- to review the format and documentation practices of APA style.

Title Page

Place the running head (an abbreviated title) in the upper left corner, and the page number 1 in the upper right.

Running head: RUNNING ON EMPTY 1

Running on Empty:

The Effects of Food Deprivation on

Concentration and Perseverance

Thomas Delancy and Adam Solberg

Dordt College

Center the full title, authors, and school name on the page. Do not list the instructor's name or course title.

Abstract

RUNNING ON EMPTY 2

Abstract

This study examined the effects of short-term food deprivation on two cognitive abilities—concentration and perseverance. Undergraduate students (N = 51) were tested on both a concentration task and a perseverance task after one of three levels of food deprivation: none, 12 hours, or 24 hours. We predicted that food deprivation would impair both concentration scores and perseverance time. Food deprivation had no significant effect on concentration scores, which is consistent with recent research on the effects of food deprivation (Green, Elliman, & Rogers, 1995). However, participants in the 12-hour deprivation group spent significantly less time on the perseverance task than those in both the control and 24-hour deprivation groups, suggesting that short-term deprivation may affect some aspects of cognition and not others.

In the abstract, summarize the problem, participants, hypotheses, methods used, results, and conclusions.

The title is centered one inch from the top. The text is double-spaced throughout.

Running on Empty: The Effects of Food Deprivation on Concentration and Perseverance

The introduction states the topic and the main questions to be explored.

Many things interrupt people's ability to focus on a task. To some extent, people can control the environmental factors that make it difficult to focus. However, what about internal factors, such as an empty stomach? Can people increase their ability to focus simply by eating regularly?

The researchers supply background information by discussing past research on the topic.

One theory that prompted research on how food intake affects the average person was the glucostatic theory, which suggested that the brain regulates food intake (and hunger) in an effort to maintain a blood-glucose set point. This theory seemed logical because glucose is the brain's primary fuel (Martinez, 2004; Pinel, 2000). The earliest investigation of this theory found that long-term food deprivation (36 hours or more) was associated with sluggishness, depression, irritability, reduced heart rate, and inability to concentrate (Keys, Brozek, Henschel, Mickelsen, & Taylor, 1950). Since then, research has focused mainly on how nutrition affects cognition. However, as Green, Elliman, and Rogers (1995) point out, the effects of food deprivation on cognition have received comparatively less attention in recent years, leaving room for further research.

Clear transitions guide the reader through the researchers' reasoning.

According to some researchers, most of the results so far indicate that cognitive function is not affected significantly by short-term fasting (Green et al., 1995, p. 246). Others have noted slight impairment of spatial sense and response speed, though not of accuracy, in subjects facing moderately difficult tasks after short-term fasting (Doniger, Simon, & Zivotofsky, 2006, p. 815). However, no study has tested perseverance,

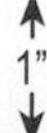

despite its importance in cognitive functioning. Perseverance may be a better indicator than achievement tests in assessing growth in learning and thinking abilities, as it helps in solving complex problems (Costa, 1984). Testing as many aspects of cognition as possible is key because the nature of the task is important when interpreting the link between deprivation and cognitive performance (Smith & Kendrick, 1992).

The researchers support their decision to focus on concentration and perseverance.

Therefore, the current study helps us understand how short-term food deprivation affects concentration on and perseverance with a difficult task. Specifically, participants deprived of food for 24 hours were expected to perform worse on a concentration test and a perseverance task than those deprived for 12 hours, who in turn were predicted to perform worse than those who were not deprived of food.

The researchers state their initial hypotheses.

Method

Headings and subheadings show the paper's organization.

Participants

Participants included 51 undergraduate student volunteers. The mean college grade point average (GPA) was 3.19. Potential participants were excluded if they were dieting, menstruating, or taking special medication. Those who had ever struggled with an eating disorder were excluded, as were potential participants who were addicted to nicotine or caffeine.

The experiment's method is described, using the terms and acronyms of the discipline.

Materials

Concentration, speed, and accuracy were measured using a numbers-matching test that consisted of 26 lines of 25 numbers each. Scores were calculated as the percentage of correctly identified pairs out of a possible 120. Perseverance was measured with a puzzle that contained five octagons, which were to be placed on top of each other in a specific way to make the silhouette of a rabbit. However, three of the shapes were slightly altered so that the task was impossible. Perseverance scores were calculated as the number of minutes that a participant spent on the puzzle task before giving up.

Procedure

Passive voice is used to emphasize the experiment, not the researchers; otherwise, active voice is used.

At an initial meeting, participants gave informed consent and supplied their GPA's. Students were informed that they would be notified about their assignment to one of the three groups and were given instructions.

Participants were then randomly assigned to one of the experimental conditions using a design based on the GPA's (to control individual differences in cognitive ability). Next, participants were informed of their group assignment and reminded of their instructions. Participants from the control group were tested at 7:30 p.m. on the day the deprivation started. Those in the 12-hour group were tested at 10:00 p.m. on that same day. Those in the 24-hour group were tested at 10:40 a.m. on the following day.

The experiment is laid out step-by-step, with time transitions like "then" and "next."

At their assigned time, participants arrived at a computer lab for testing. After all participants had completed the concentration test and their scores were recorded, participants were each given the silhouette puzzle. They were told that (1) they would have an unlimited amount of time to complete the task and (2) they were not to tell any other participant whether they had completed the puzzle or simply given up.

Attention is shown to the control features.

This procedure prevented group influence. Any participant still working on the puzzle after 40 minutes was stopped.

Results

The writers summarize their findings.

Perseverance data from one control-group participant were eliminated, and concentration data from another control-group participant were dropped. The average concentration score was 77.78 (SD = 14.21), which was very good considering that anything over 50 percent is labeled "good" or "above average." The average time spent on the puzzle was 24.00 minutes (SD = 10.16).

"See Figure 1" sends the reader to a figure (graph, photograph, chart, or drawing) contained in the paper.

We predicted that participants in the 24-hour deprivation group would perform worse on the concentration test and the perseverance task than those in the 12-hour group, who in turn would perform worse than those in the control group. A one-way analysis of variance (ANOVA) showed no significant effect of deprivation condition on concentration, $F(2,46) = 1.06$, $p = .36$ (see Figure 1). Another one-way ANOVA indicated a significant effect of deprivation condition on perseverance time, $F(2,47) = 7.41$, $p < .05$. Post hoc Tukey tests indicated that the 12-hour

Figure 1.

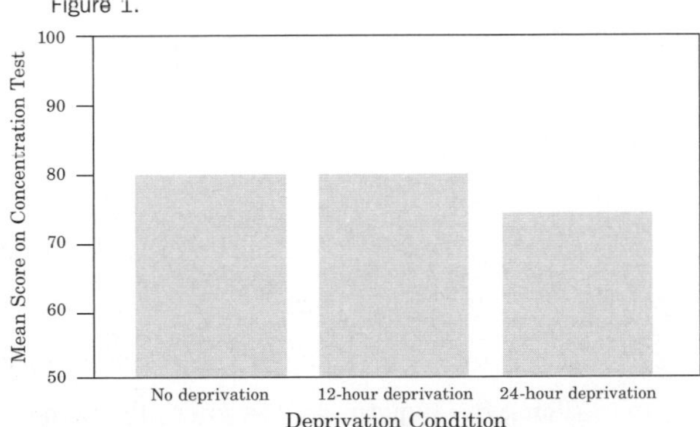

All figures are numbered in the order that they are first mentioned in the paper.

Figure 2.

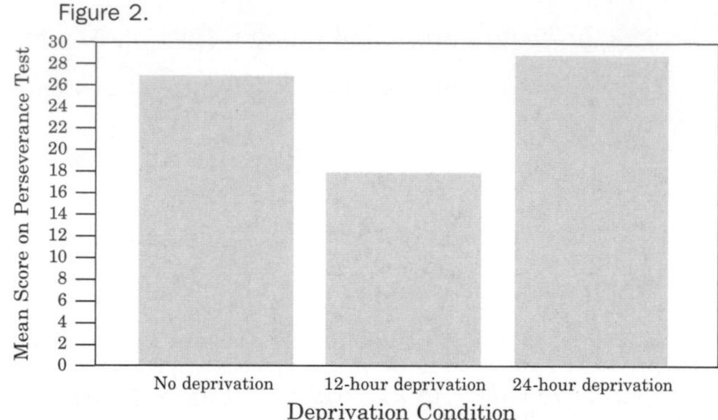

deprivation group (M = 17.79, SD = 7.84) spent significantly less time on the perseverance task than either the control group (M = 26.80, SD = 6.20) or the 24-hour group (M = 28.75, SD = 12.11), with no significant difference between the latter two groups (see Figure 2). Unexpectedly, food deprivation had no significant effect on concentration scores. Overall, we found support for our hypothesis that 12 hours of food deprivation would significantly impair perseverance when compared to no deprivation. Unexpectedly, 24 hours of food deprivation did not significantly affect perseverance relative to the control group.

Discussion

The researchers restate their hypotheses, the results, and go on to interpret those results.

The purpose of this study was to test how different levels of food deprivation affect concentration on and perseverance with difficult tasks. We predicted that the longer people had been deprived of food, the lower they would score on the concentration task, and the less time they would spend on the perseverance task. In this study, those deprived of food did give up more quickly on the puzzle, but only in the 12-hour group. Thus, the hypothesis was partially supported for the perseverance task. However, concentration was found to be unaffected by food deprivation, and thus the hypothesis was not supported for that task.

The writers speculate on possible explanations for the unexpected results.

In terms of concentration, the findings of this study are consistent with those of Green et al. (1995), where short-term food deprivation did not affect some aspects of cognition, including attentional focus. The findings on perseverance, however, are not as easily explained. We surmise that the participants in the 12-hour group gave up more quickly on the perseverance task because of their hunger. But those in the 24-hour group failed to yield the same effect. We postulate that this result can be explained by the concept of "learned industriousness," wherein participants who perform one difficult task do better on a subsequent task than participants who never did the initial task (Eisenberger & Leonard, 1980; Hickman, Stromme, & Lippman, 1998). Another possible explanation is that the motivational state of a participant may be a significant determinant of behavior under testing (Saugstad, 1967; Yang & Hamilton, 2002).

Research on food deprivation and cognition could continue in several directions. First, other aspects of cognition may be affected by short-term food deprivation, such as reading comprehension or motivation. Perhaps, then, the motivation level of food-deprived participants could be effectively tested. Second, longer-term food deprivation periods, such as those experienced by people fasting for religious reasons, could be explored. It is possible that cognitive function fluctuates over the duration of deprivation. Third, and perhaps most fascinating, studies could explore how food deprivation affects learned industriousness.

The conclusion summarizes the outcomes, stresses the experiment's value, and anticipates further advances on the topic.

In conclusion, the results of this study provide some fascinating insights into the cognitive and physiological effects of skipping meals. Contrary to what we predicted, a person may indeed be very capable of concentrating after not eating for many hours. On the other hand, when performing a tedious task that requires perseverance, one may be hindered by not eating for a short time, as shown by the 12-hour group's performance on the perseverance task. Many people have to deal with short-term food deprivation, either intentional or unintentional. This research and other research to follow will contribute to knowledge of the disadvantages—and possible advantages—of skipping meals. The mixed results of this study suggest that we have much more to learn about short-term food deprivation.

RUNNING ON EMPTY 10

References

Costa, A. L. (1984). Thinking: How do we know students are getting better at it? *Roeper Review, 6,* 197–199.

Doniger, G. M., Simon, E. S., & Zivotofsky, A. Z. (2006). Comprehensive computerized assessment of cognitive sequelae of a complete 12-16 hour fast. *Behavioral Neuroscience, 120,* 804–816.

Eisenberger, R., & Leonard, J. M. (1980). Effects of conceptual task difficulty on generalized persistence. *American Journal of Psychology, 93,* 285–298.

Green, M. W., Elliman, N. A., & Rogers, P. J. (1995). Lack of effect of short-term fasting on cognitive function. *Journal of Psychiatric Research, 29,* 245–253.

Hickman, K. L., Stromme, C., & Lippman, L. G. (1998). Learned industriousness: Replication in principle. *Journal of General Psychology, 125,* 213–217.

Keys, A., Brozek, J., Henschel, A., Mickelsen, O., & Taylor, H. L. (1950). *The biology of human starvation* (Vol. 2). Minneapolis: University of Minnesota Press.

Martinez, R. J. (2004). Repeated fasting/refeeding elevate glucose levels. *Behavior Research, 62,* 459–464. Retrieved September 29, 2005, from http://www.behaviorresearch.com/041204.html

Pinel, J. P. (2000). *Biopsychology* (4th ed.). Boston: Allyn & Bacon.

Saugstad, P. (1967). Effect of food deprivation on perception-cognition: A comment [Comment on the article by David L. Wolitzky]. *Psychological Bulletin, 68,* 345–346.

Smith, A. P., & Kendrick, A. M. (1992). Meals and performance. In A. P. Smith & D. M. Jones (Eds.), *Handbook of human performance: Vol. 2. Health and performance* (pp. 1–23). San Diego: Academic Press.

Yang, W., & Hamilton, J. B. (2002). Effect of food deprivation on motivation. *Psychology Research Today, 38,* 15–32. Retrieved October 11, 2005, from http://www.psychrt .com/journals/yang38425.html

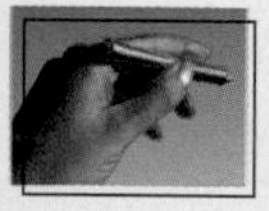

NOTE: Always check for specific guidelines set by your instructor, which take precedence over the guidelines in the APA manual. Also visit the "APA Style" page at **thewritesource.com** for further citation examples and updates regarding APA format.

Using the Library

In this information age, the best place to acquire knowledge is still the library. Users can find books and periodicals to borrow, log on to the Internet and subscription services, and get the help of a librarian or an information specialist when doing research.

Libraries house vast collections of information, in almost limitless formats, that cannot be found elsewhere. Knowing what is available at a library—and how to find it—is vital to any writer. This chapter will lead you in the right direction.

WHAT'S AHEAD

Discover the essentials of using the library as you read each of the following sections.

Library Holdings

Using the Electronic Catalog

Using Call Numbers

Finding Articles in Periodicals

Selecting Reference Works

Library Holdings

A library offers material that is both in-depth and reliable. While libraries are changing every day, their basic components remain the same.

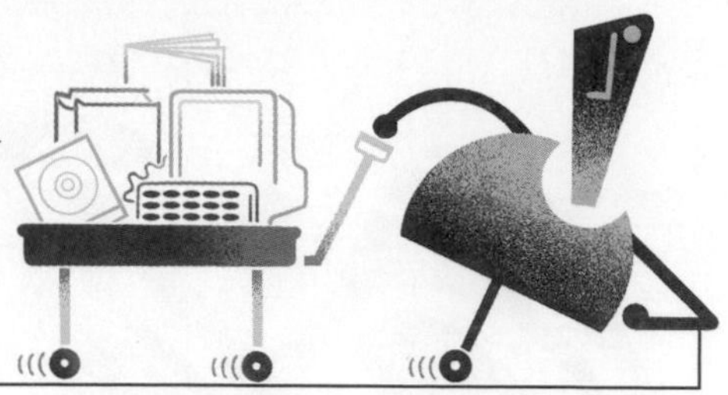

The Basic Components

Librarians: Librarians are information experts who manage the library's materials, guide you to resources, and help you perform online, CD-ROM, and database searches.

Catalogs: Catalogs are databases that guide you to the materials you need. Most library catalogs are computerized databases, although manual card catalogs still exist, alone or alongside computerized catalogs in some places. In addition, most large college and university libraries catalog materials according to the Library of Congress classification system, whereas most public high schools and local libraries use the Dewey decimal system.

Collections: A library's collection is all the materials it contains. It varies greatly from one library to the next, but the collection usually includes the following:

- **books**—fiction and nonfiction
- **periodicals**—magazines, journals, newspapers, microfilm, CD-ROM's
- **reference materials**—directories, indexes, handbooks, encyclopedias, abstracts, and almanacs
- **audiovisual and multimedia materials**—videotapes, CD's, audiotapes, microfilm, laser discs
- **special collections**—government and historical documents, pamphlets, local history, artwork, rare books, artifacts, archive materials
- **computer resources**—the catalog itself, connections to the campuswide network and to interlibrary loan, online databases, Internet access, and links with document delivery services

Using the Electronic Catalog

An electronic catalog, also called an online public access catalog (OPAC) or a computer catalog, contains all the information you need to use your library efficiently. Most computer catalogs are easy to use; just follow the instructions on the screen. Each system does vary a bit, so ask for help if you're not sure how to use it. Below is a typical start-up screen.

Start-up Screen

```
Welcome to the Rapid City
Online Public Access Catalog
Databases:
    1. author, title, subject searching
    2. general periodical index
    3. information about system libraries

To make a selection, type a number
and then press [RETURN]>>>
```

Using Keyword Searches

With the first database shown on the screen above, you could find an item by doing a keyword search. This means that if you know only part of the title or author's name, you can still find the work.

Keyword Searches for Titles

If you know only one word in an item's title, use it as your keyword. The computer will show you all titles that contain the word, and you can scan the list to find the title you're looking for.

NOTE: If you know several words in a title, use all of them; the computer will give you a shorter list to scan. (Use the most unusual word if you are limited to one keyword.)

Keyword Searches for Authors

If you know only an author's last name, the computer will show you all authors with that last name. You can scan the list to find the author you're looking for. (Some computer catalogs can find your author even if you know only the first few letters of the name, or if you spell the name incorrectly.)

Keyword Searches for Subjects

If you want to search by subject, use a keyword just as you would in a regular subject search. However, a keyword search often turns up a longer list of books than a regular subject search would yield.

Refining a Keyword Search

Computer catalogs vary. Some allow you to refine (broaden or narrow) your keyword search using ordinary words and phrases. Other search systems allow you to use "Boolean operators"—the words *and*, *or*, and *not*. Examples of how Boolean operators work are shown below.

Keywords you enter:	The computer will show you . . .
civil war	listings that contain the words **civil war**.
civil war and **United States**	listings that contain both **civil war** and **United States**; this might be the U.S. Civil War or other civil wars in which the United States played a role.
civil war or **rebellion**	listings that contain either **civil war** or **rebellion**; this would be civil wars anywhere, as well as events that were called rebellions instead of wars.
civil war not **United States**	listings that contain **civil war** but not **United States** (in other words, civil wars outside the United States).

Reading the Catalog Record

In the illustration below, the labels identify the types of information provided for a particular resource, in this case, a book. Once you identify the book you need, jot down the call number. You will use this to locate the book on the shelf.

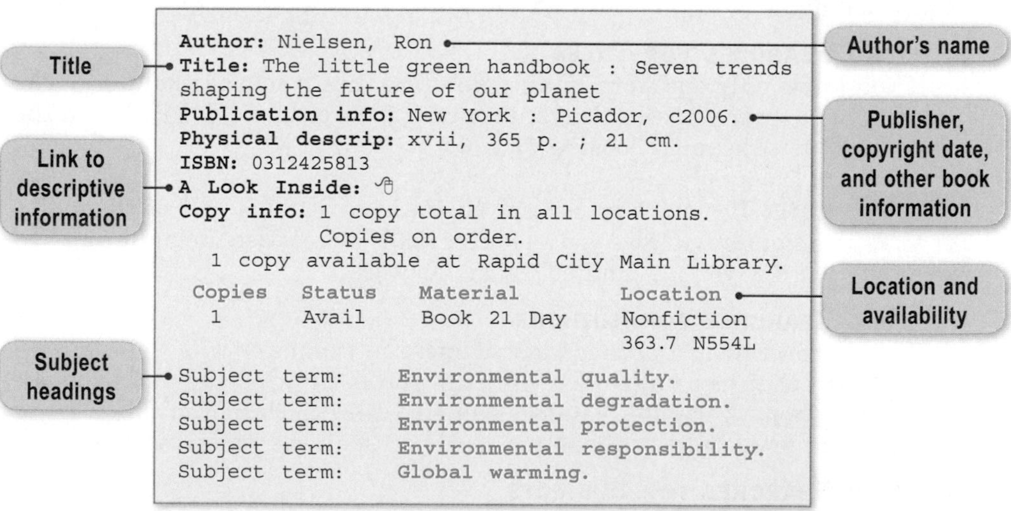

Using Call Numbers

All nonfiction books in the library are arranged on the shelves according to call numbers. In public libraries, call numbers are usually based on the Dewey decimal classification system, which divides nonfiction books into 10 subject categories.

NOTE: Fiction books and biographies are not classified according to the Dewey decimal system. Most fiction is shelved in a separate section of the library, alphabetized by the author's last name. (However, classic fiction is classified as literature and shelved according to the appropriate Dewey decimal class number.) Biographies, too, are in a separate section and are shelved alphabetically by the last name of the person written about.

The Dewey Decimal System

000–099 **Computers, Information, and General Reference** ■ Computer science, journalism, encyclopedias, handbooks, periodicals, newspapers, and other books on many subjects

100–199 **Philosophy and Psychology**

200–299 **Religion** ■ Books on religions or religious topics

300–399 **Social Sciences** ■ Books on education, government, law, economics, and other social sciences

400–499 **Language** ■ Dictionaries and books about grammar

500–599 **Science** ■ Books about biology, chemistry, all other natural sciences, and math

600–699 **Technology** ■ Books about engineering, inventions, and medicine; cookbooks

700–799 **Arts and Recreation** ■ Books on painting, music, and other arts; sports and games

800–899 **Literature** ■ Poetry, plays, essays, and famous speeches

900–999 **History and Geography**

The 10 major subject classes are broken down into divisions, sections, and subsections—each with its own topic and number. Here is an example.

Divisions of the Dewey Decimal Class Number

900	History	Class
970	History of North America	Division
973	History of the United States	Section
973.7	History of the U.S. Civil War	Subsection
973.74	History of Civil War Songs	Sub-subsection

To find a book in the library, read the call number carefully. Note that 973.2 is a higher number than 973.198 and will come after it on the shelf.

Finding Articles in Periodicals

Many libraries subscribe to online databases that allow you to search for articles in magazines, newspapers, and journals. You can read the entire text of some articles; for other articles, only an abstract (summary) is provided. Access the databases on the library computers.

Periodical indexes are another option for locating information in periodicals. You will find these indexes in the reference or periodical section of the library. Some are available as printed volumes; others are on CD-ROM or online.

The *Readers' Guide to Periodical Literature*

The *Readers' Guide to Periodical Literature* is available in nearly all libraries and indexes articles that appear in widely read magazines. Begin by finding the volume that covers the time period you are researching. Use the following guidelines to help you look up your topic:

- Search for articles alphabetically by topic and by author.
- Check articles listed under subtopics.
- Follow cross-references to related topic entries.

Most libraries have other indexes, too, including the *General Periodicals Index*, and the index for the *New York Times*.

Sample *Readers' Guide* Format

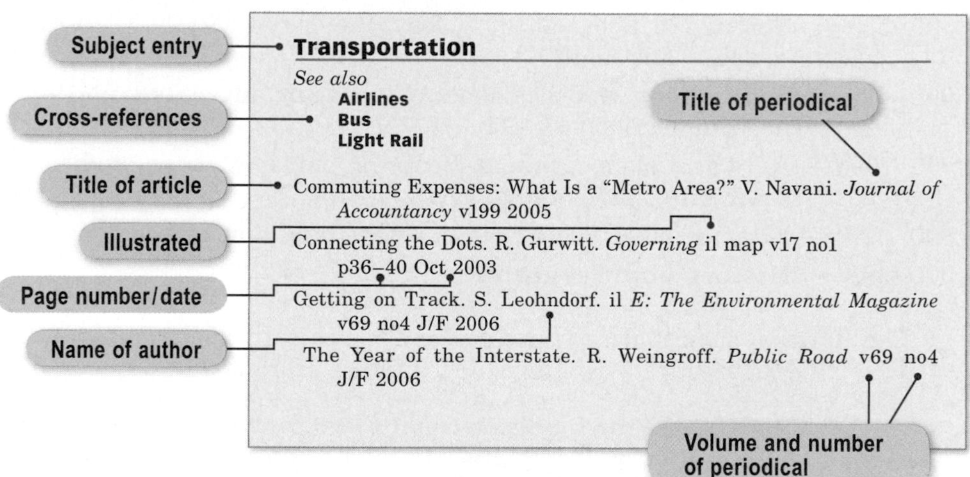

Locating Articles

After you find a listing on your topic, write down the essential information: the name and issue date of the magazine, and the title and page numbers of the article. You may need to ask a librarian to get the periodical for you. Your library may have periodicals in printed form, on CD-ROM or microfilm.

Selecting Reference Works

Whatever your specific needs, reference works can provide a myriad of details about many topics. The key is learning how to get the most of these materials without spending too much time in the process. Three very common reference works are encyclopedias, thesauruses, and dictionaries.

Using Encyclopedias

Libraries usually have several sets of encyclopedias. (Review each set and decide which one best serves your needs.) Topics are arranged alphabetically. At the end of an article, there is often a list of related articles. You can read these other articles to learn more about your topic.

The index, which is usually in a separate volume or at the end of the last volume, can help you find out more about your topic. The index lists every article that contains information about a topic. For example, if you look up "newspapers" in the index, you would find a list of articles—"United States Media," "Freedom of the Press," etc.—that include information on that topic.

Using a Thesaurus

A thesaurus is, in a sense, the opposite of a dictionary. You go to a dictionary when you know the word but need the definition. You go to a thesaurus when you know the general definition but need a specific word. For example, you might want a noun that means *fear*—the kind of fear that causes worry. You need the word to complete the following sentence:

Dana experienced a certain amount of ________ over the upcoming exam.

If you have a thesaurus in dictionary form, simply look up the word *fear* as you would in a dictionary. If, however, you have a traditional thesaurus, first look up your word in the index. You might find this entry:

FEAR 860
Fearful painful 830
timid 862

The numbers in the index entry (for example, 860) are guide numbers, not page numbers. When you look up number 860 in the thesaurus, you will find a long list of synonyms for *fear.* You may need to look up the synonyms in a dictionary in order to decide which is right for your sentence. *Anxiety* means "a state of uneasiness, worry, and fear"; it's a good choice.

Dana experienced a certain amount of anxiety over the upcoming exam.

Using a Dictionary

A dictionary gives many types of information, including the 10 types listed below.

Spelling Not knowing how to spell a word can make it difficult for you to look it up in the dictionary, but not impossible. You will be surprised at how quickly you can find most words by simply sounding them out.

Capitalization If you're not sure whether a word should be capitalized, check a dictionary.

Syllabication A dictionary tells you where you may divide a word. The centered dots in the entry word show precisely where you can make an end-of-line division.

Pronunciation A dictionary tells you how to pronounce a word and also provides a key to pronunciation symbols, usually at the bottom of the page.

Parts of Speech A dictionary tells you what part(s) of speech a word is, using these abbreviations:

n	noun	**tr.v**	transitive verb	**adj**	adjective
pron	pronoun	**interj**	interjection	**adv**	adverb
intr.v	intransitive verb	**conj**	conjunction	**prep**	preposition

Etymology Many dictionaries give etymologies (word histories) for at least some words. They tell what language an English word came from, how the word entered our language, and when it was first used.

Special Uses Different kinds of labels tell about special uses of words.

- **Usage labels** tell how a word is used: slang, nonstandard (nonstand.), dialect (dial.), etc.
- **Geographic labels** tell the region or country in which a word is used: New England (NewEng.), Canada (Can.), etc.

Synonyms and Antonyms Some dictionaries list both synonyms and antonyms of words. (Of course, the best place to look for these is in a thesaurus.)

Illustrations If a definition is difficult to make clear with words alone, a picture or drawing is provided.

Meanings Many dictionaries list all the meanings of a word. Some list meanings chronologically, with the oldest meaning first, followed by newer meanings. Other dictionaries list a word's most common meaning first, followed by less common meanings. Always read all the meanings listed to make sure you are using the word appropriately.

SAMPLE DICTIONARY PAGE

GUIDE WORDS

SYNONYMS

MEANING

USAGE

SPELLING OF RELATED FORMS

ETYMOLOGY (HISTORY)

PRONUNCIATION

SPELLING AND CAPITAL LETTERS

SYLLABICATION AND PART OF SPEECH

ILLUSTRATION

Botany Bay-•-Botswana 168

Botany Bay An inlet of the Tasman Sea in SE Australia.

botch (bŏch) *tr.v.* **botched, botch•ing, botch•es 1.** To ruin through clumsiness. **2.** To make or perform clumsily; bungle. **3.** To repair or mend clumsily. ❖ *n.* **1.** A ruined or defective piece of work: *"I have made a miserable botch of this description"* (Nathaniel Hawthorne). **2.** A hodgepodge. [ME *bocchen,* to mend.] **—botch′er** *n.* **—botch′y** *adj.*

SYNONYMS *botch, blow, bungle, fumble, muff* These verbs mean to harm or spoil through inept or clumsy handling: *botch a repair; blow an opportunity; bungle an interview; fumbled my chance; muffed the painting job.*

bot•fly also **bot fly** (bŏt′flī′) *n.* Any of various stout two-winged flies, chiefly of the genera *Gasterophilus* and *Oestrus,* having larvae that are parasitic on various animals.

both (bōth) *adj.* One and the other; relating to or being two in conjunction: *Both guests came.* ❖ *pron.* The one and the other: *Both are mad.* ❖ *conj.* Used with *and* to link two things in a coordinated phrase or clause: *both he and I.* [ME *bothe* < ON *bādhar.* See **to-** in App.]

USAGE NOTE *Both* is used to indicate that the action or state denoted by the verb applies individually to each of two entities.

Bo•tha (bō′tə, -tä′), **Louis** 1862–1919. South African general and first prime minister of South Africa (1910–19).

Botha, Pieter Willem b. 1916. South African prime minister (1978–89) who upheld apartheid.

both•er (bŏth′ər) *v.* **-ered, -er•ing, -ers** *—tr.* **1.** To disturb or anger, esp. by minor irritations; annoy. **2a.** To make agitated or nervous; fluster. **b.** To make confused or perplexed; puzzle. **3.** To intrude on without warrant; disturb. **4.** To give trouble to. *—intr.* **1.** To take the trouble; concern oneself. **2.** To cause trouble. ❖ *n.* A cause or state of disturbance. ❖ *interj.* Used to express annoyance or mild irritation. [Prob. < dialectal *bodder,* poss. of Celt. orig.]

both•er•a•tion (bŏth′ə-rā′shən) *n.* The act of bothering or the state of being bothered. ❖ *interj.* Used to express annoyance or irritation.

both•er•some (bŏth′ər-səm) *adj.* Causing bother.

Both•ni•a (bŏth′nē-ə), **Gulf of** An arm of the Baltic Sea between Sweden and Finland.

Both•well (bŏth′wĕl′, -wəl, bŏth′-), 4th Earl of. Title of James Hepburn. 1536?–78. Scottish noble and third husband of Mary Queen of Scots, whose second husband, Lord Darnley, he murdered (1567).

bo tree (bō) *n.* See **pipal.** [Partial transl. of Sinhalese *bo-gahu,* tree of wisdom (because it was the tree under which the Buddha was enlightened) : *bo,* wisdom (< Pali *bodhi* < Skt. *bodhiḥ,* enlightenment; see **bheudh-** in App.) + *gaha,* tree.]

bot•ry•oi•dal (bŏt′rē-oid′l) also **bot•ry•oid** (bŏt′rē-oid′) *adj.* Shaped like a bunch of grapes. Used esp. of mineral formations: *botryoidal hematite.* [< Gk. *botruoeidēs* : *botrus,* bunch of grapes + *-oidēs,* -oid.] **bot′ry•oi′dal•ly** *adv.*

bo•try•tis (bō-trī′tĭs) *n.* **1.** Any of various fungi of the genus *Botrytis* responsible for numerous fruit and vegetable diseases. **2.** Noble rot. [NLat., genus name < Gk. *botrus,* bunch of grapes.]

Bot•swa•na (bŏt-swä′nə) Formerly **Bech•u•a•na•land** (bĕch-wä′nə-lănd′, bĕch′o͞o-ä′-) A country of S-central Africa; gained independence from Great Britain in 1966. Cap. Gaborone. Pop. 1,443,000. **—Bot•swa′nan** *adj. & n.*

Botswana

Using Other Reference Works

You will find the following items in the reference section, too.

Almanacs are regular (usually annual) publications listing facts and statistics. Originally, almanacs were used as community calendars and basic information books. Today they're broader in scope and cover everything from politics to sports.

The World Almanac **and** ***Information Please® Almanac*** both present information on many topics such as business, politics, history, religion, social programs, sports, education, and the year's major events.

Atlases are books of detailed maps and related information. They include information on countries, transportation, languages, climate, and more.

The Rand McNally Commercial Atlas and Marketing Guide includes maps of the United States and its major cities as well as information on transportation and communication, economics, and population. ***Street Atlas USA*** on CD-ROM allows you to call up street maps for any place in the United States.

Biographical Dictionaries contain minibiographies of many famous people, usually listed in alphabetical order.

Current Biography is published monthly and annually. Each article includes a photo of the individual, a biographical sketch, and information concerning the person's birth date, address, occupation, and so on.

Directories are lists of people and groups. (Directories are now widely used on the Internet.)

The ***National Directory of Addresses and Telephone Numbers*** provides nationwide coverage of companies, associations, schools, and so on.

Guides and Handbooks offer guidelines and models for exploring a topic, a program, an area of knowledge, or a profession.

Occupational Outlook Handbook, published by the Department of Labor, explores the job market—where jobs are or will be and how to prepare for the workplace.

Yearbooks cover major developments in specific areas of interest during the previous year.

Statistical Abstract of the United States: The National Data Book provides statistical information about the United States, from population figures to data on geography, social trends, politics, employment, and business.

Using the Internet

The increasing speed of Internet connections makes this resource more and more inviting as a means of research and communication. By navigating the Internet, you can find government publications, articles from periodicals, encyclopedia entries, business reports, and much more. Unfortunately, the Internet is an unregulated, open exchange of information—meaning that anyone can create and post Web content. So you will also find a lot of unreliable, questionable information. It is your responsibility to determine the validity of the sites you explore.

This chapter will help you use the Internet intelligently and efficiently. Among other things, you will learn about evaluating sources of information as well as conducting thoughtful research.

WHAT'S AHEAD

Discover the essentials of using the Internet as you review each of the following sections.

Evaluating Sources of Information

You may find a lot of information about a particular topic, either on the Internet or in printed materials. Before you use any source, you must decide whether or not the information is dependable. Use the following questions to help you determine the reliability of your sources.

Is the source a primary source or a secondary source?

You can usually trust information you've collected firsthand (interviews, surveys, original documents, lab results), but be careful with secondary sources (information others have gathered and interpreted). Although many secondary sources are reliable, others may contain outdated or incorrect information.

Is the source an expert?

An expert knows more about a subject than other people. Government and education sites are usually reliable, as are most nonprofit organization sites and professional business sites. If you aren't sure about a source's authority, ask a teacher or librarian what he or she thinks.

Are the author's sources documented?

Reputable authors clearly document the sources they used to create content. Look for a bibliography, footnotes, or Web links that substantiate the information.

Is the information accurate?

Sources that people respect are usually very accurate. For news, try to find the original source, if possible. Big-city newspapers (*New York Times* or *Chicago Tribune*) and well-known Web sites (CNN or ESPN) are reliable sources of information. Little-known sources that do not support their facts or that contain errors may not be reliable. Be especially cautious about the accuracy of information on the Internet. If you can find the same information at more than one reliable site, it is probably accurate.

"Research is formalized curiosity. It is poking and prying with a purpose."
—Zora Neale Hurston

Is the information fair and complete?

A reliable source should provide information fairly, covering all sides of a subject or an issue. If a source presents only one side of a subject, its information may not be accurate. Politicians and advertisers often present just their side of a subject to make themselves sound better. Avoid sources that are one sided and look for those that are balanced.

Is the information current?

Usually, you want to have the most up-to-date information about a subject. Sometimes information changes, and sources can become outdated quickly. Check the copyright page in a book, the issue date of a magazine, and the posting date of online information.

Is contact information for the site provided?

A respectable Web site provides a phone number, physical address, and an e-mail address to enable users to contact the people behind the URL. Be wary of a site that doesn't provide at least one contact option.

Is the content well written?

Beware if there are more than a few typographical errors or grammar mistakes in the text of a Web site. If the author doesn't care enough to present correct copy, she or he may not have been careful about the validity of the ideas presented.

BOTTOM LINE

Keep the following five points in mind whenever you evaluate the usefulness of a source: Is the information (1) reasonable, (2) reliable, (3) accurate, (4) current, and (5) complete?

Researching on the Internet

Finding appropriate information is the most important part of online research. Once you find the information you need, you can save the results for later use.

Locating Information

There are several ways to find relevant and trustworthy information.

Using a Search Engine

If you don't have any Internet addresses for your topic, a search engine can help you look for sites.

- **Browser Searching** Some browsers have an Internet-search function built into them. Just type words about your topic into the address bar or search bar, then press "Return" or "Enter," and your browser will supply a list of suggested sites. Select one of those links to load that site.
- **Web Search Engines** The Web offers many different search engines. (See the Write Source site, www.thewritesource.com, for a recommended list.) Some use robot programs to search the Internet; others accept recommendations submitted by individuals; most combine these two approaches. When you type a term into a search engine's input box, the search engine scans its database for matching sites. Then the engine returns recommendations for you to explore. (Most search engine sites also provide topic headings you can explore yourself rather than trusting the engine to do your searching.)

TIPS

FOR DOING A WORD SEARCH

Mastery of search engines lies in how you phrase your searches. Check the engines' instructions to learn how to best use them.

- **Enter a single word** to seek sites that contain that word or a derivative of it. The term *apple* yields sites containing the word *apple, apples, applet,* and so on.
- **Enter more than one word** to seek sites containing any of those words. The words *apple* and *pie* yield sites containing *apple* only and *pie* only, as well as those containing both words (together or not).
- **Use quotation marks** to find an exact phrase. The term *"apple pie"* (in quotation marks) yields only sites with that phrase.
- **Use Boolean symbols (+ or -)** to shape your search. The phrase *+apple +pie* (without quotation marks) yields sites containing both words, though not necessarily as a phrase. The phrase *+apple -pie* yields sites with *apple* but not *pie.*

Using an Internet Address

Sometimes you already have the address of an Internet location, perhaps from a book, a periodical, or a teacher. Type the address into the bar at the top of your browser window; then press the "Enter" or "Return" key to load it.

Conducting a Page Search

To find information quickly within a file, use the available document search functions. Just as your word processor can seek a particular word within a document, most Web browsers can "scan" the text of an Internet document. See your browser's help files to learn how.

Following Links

If you find good data on a particular Web page, you might benefit from following the links it offers for further information. These links may lead to the sources of the site's information or to more in-depth material.

Saving Information

There are several ways to preserve information once you find it. Here are four of them.

- **Bookmark** Your Web browser can save a site's address for later use. Look for a "bookmark" or "favorites" option on your menu bar. (Keep in mind that sites change, so a bookmark may become outdated.)
- **Printout** You can print a hard copy of an Internet document to keep. Be sure to note the details you'll need for citing the source in your work.
- **Electronic Copy** You can save an Internet document to your computer or to a disc as text. Web browsers allow you to save a page as "source," which preserves the formatting. Unless your browser can create a "Web archive," however, you must save the page's graphics separately.
- **E-mail** One quick way of saving is to send the current page address as e-mail to your personal account. That's especially helpful when you're not at your own computer.

Communicating on the Internet

Writers usually thrive in a community of other writers, and the Net allows such a community to converse in many ways. Many of the most common ways are listed below. Discuss these different options with your instructors and classmates.

E-MAIL

You can send and receive electronic mail at Web sites that provide free e-mail accounts.

CHAT ROOMS

Chat rooms are sites where people can hold real-time conversations. You can find them through any search engine; most are identified by topic. Pay attention to your Netiquette (see the next page) if you wish to be taken seriously and benefit from a chat room.

INSTANT MESSAGING

Instant messaging is a form of real-time communication, achieved with specific computer programs that let the user know when certain other individuals are online and available for a dialogue.

BLOGS

Short for "Web log," a blog is analogous to an online journal. Writers provide commentary on their personal lives or public events on a Web site accessible to the world. Blog writers often invite feedback.

MAILING LISTS

Mailing lists are group discussions of a topic by e-mail, often managed by an automated program. The messages come directly to your e-mail account. Check a search engine to find an automated mailing list about your topic.

MESSAGE BOARDS

Many organizations on the Internet provide online message boards devoted to one topic or another. Some message boards are open to the public; others are "members only." On message boards, people post items for others to read and respond to. Some college courses are conducted online in a message-board format.

ONLINE WRITING LABS

Some schools maintain an online writing lab (OWL) on their Web site or Internet server. An OWL can be a great place to post your work-in-progress and have it critiqued by other writers and teachers. Ask your teacher if your school has such a site.

Using Netiquette

Chatting and posting messages on the Internet pose special challenges. It's almost as immediate as speaking face-to-face, except for missing the visual or audio clues, such as facial expressions and tone of voice. These missing clues mean that the intent of a message can be misunderstood. To help solve this problem, Net users have developed "Netiquette." Proper Netiquette will help you communicate effectively online.

- **Message Clarity** The most important part of Netiquette is being careful as you write. Make your message as clear as possible before you send it. And don't assume that the recipient will remember a previous e-mail or posting; add a reminder about the topic in your message. When responding to a message, it may also help to quote part of it in your response.
- **Subject Line** Include an accurate subject line that identifies your topic. Update the line if your e-mail exchange results in a number of replies.
- **Emoticons** Often, to add a certain tone to part of an online message, people use smiley faces or other emoticons. These sideways faces :-) are made up of keyboard characters. Limit emoticons to your personal correspondence.
- **Net Abbreviations** To speed the flow of communication, people on the Net use many abbreviations: LOL for "laughing out loud," TTFN for "ta-ta for now," etc. If you see an abbreviation you don't recognize, you may politely ask the user what it means. These expressions are most suited to informal communications.
- **Don't SHOUT** On the Internet, words in capital letters mean SHOUTING. Don't send your messages in all capital letters. Such messages are hard to read, and people consider them rude.

NOTE: You can, however, use all capitals to represent the titles of publications that are normally italicized. For lighter emphasis, bracket the words in asterisks.

- **Long Messages** If your message is long (100 lines or more), it's polite to add "Long Message" to the subject line. That way people are prepared before they open the text itself.
- **Accuracy** Though writing e-mail and other electronic feedback is easy and fast, don't let that be an excuse for sloppiness. Proofread your messages; check spacing between words and between sentences. Follow correct punctuation rules and use paragraphs just as you would in a nonelectronic message.

The Tools of Learning

Critical Reading

You've just been given a reading assignment in your literature class: the first 360 lines of John Milton's *Paradise Lost, Book 1.* After heaving a big sigh, do you (A) raid the fridge; (B) find a comfortable chair, preferably a recliner; (C) put on your favorite tunes; or (D) all of the above? Any of these choices will almost surely lead to a nice nap with dreams of spring break, and your reading of *Paradise Lost* will never happen.

Save the recliner for magazines, or a just-published mystery. *Paradise Lost*, one of the greatest pieces of literature ever written, cannot be approached casually. It is a long, complex epic poem, and reading it is a formidable academic task. You need to prepare.

WHAT'S AHEAD

This chapter offers helpful strategies and advice for completing challenging reading assignments, no matter if you are reading great works of literature or difficult nonfiction texts.

Reading to Learn

Whenever you are asked to read a complex assignment, you should do three things before you begin:

- create an appropriate environment,
- gather the necessary tools, and
- allow sufficient time to accomplish the work.

Preparing to Read

Consider the environment. Your goal is to be comfortable—but not too comfortable. So cancel the easy chair. Slide up to a well-lighted desk or table where you can read and write efficiently. (Have paper, pen, dictionary, and other reference books handy as well.)

It's okay to have water, juice, or coffee at hand but forget the music (an exception might be instrumental music to help block out any annoying background noise). Make sure the room temperature is relatively cool, since warm rooms are notoriously sleep inducing. The point is, you need all your powers of concentration focused on the task at hand. Never begin a major reading session when you are overly hungry or tired, either.

This may seem too obvious, but be sure that you know exactly what the assignment is and when it is due. Finally, have all your class materials close at hand (notebook, assignment sheet, handouts, etc.).

TIPS

FOR STUDY-READING

- **Read in 30- to 45-minute spurts,** followed by short breaks.
- **Sit up straight** in your chair (don't get too comfortable).
- **React to the text** by making observations, questioning certain parts, noting main points, and so on.
- **Connect new concepts to ideas or experiences** that you are familiar with.
- **Underline, highlight, star, circle**—whatever—but only if the book belongs to you.
- **Draw** helpful pictures or diagrams in your notes.
- **Stop and freewrite** at different points during the reading.
- **Predict** what will come next.
- **Read especially difficult parts out loud.**
- **Use your senses**—try to visualize your subject.
- **Take turns reading out loud with a partner.**
- **Make up possible test questions.** Write them in your notes.

Using PQ4R

There are a number of study-reading techniques with unusual titles—SQ3R and PQRST, to mention two of them. Well, here's one more: PQ4R. It stands for *preview, question, read, recite, review,* and *review again*. All of these techniques are designed to make you an "active" rather than a "passive" reader and learner.

P

Preview

When you preview a reading assignment, you are attempting to get a general picture of what the assignment is about. Look briefly at each page, paying special attention to the headings, chapter titles, illustrations, charts, graphs, and so on. It's also a good idea to skim the first and last paragraphs on each page.

Previewing gives you a chance to familiarize yourself with the reading's main ideas. Consider writing a brief outline of the assignment, jotting down section titles and paragraph headings as the major and minor points. As you do the actual reading, you can fill in your outline with additional supporting ideas and details.

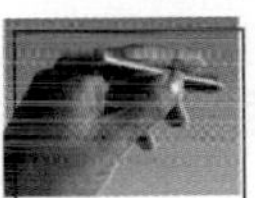

NOTE: Previewing serves two important purposes: (1) It gives you the big picture, and (2) it gets you into the assignment. Sometimes getting started is the hardest part.

Q

Question

Asking questions may be the most important step in the study-reading process. Start with questions about what you hope to find out (or need to know) from the reading material. One quick way to do this is to turn the headings and subheadings into questions. For example, if you're reading a biology text and run across the heading "The Metabolism of the Red Cedar," you may be prompted to ask, "A tree has a metabolism?" Or, if you think more as a scientist does, you may ask, "Is a tree's metabolism similar to a human's?"

Another way to generate questions is to imagine a specific test question for each of the major points. In fact, once you get to know your instructor, this can be a useful way to approach a reading assignment.

R

Read

Read the assignment carefully from start to finish. However, before you begin, you need to clear your mind and eliminate distractions. Turn your cell phone off and notify your friends and family members that you are not to be disturbed.

Once you get into the actual reading, ask questions as you go along: *What does this mean? What is the author saying here? How does this connect to the previous material?* These types of questions force you to think about what you're reading, which will enhance your understanding. After you have completed the first reading, try to answer your questions.

Also react to the text in other ways: Take notes on important points, write brief summaries, underline or circle key passages and significant words (but only if you own the text or are reading a copy). Be sure that you use a well-organized and consistent method of note taking. (See pages 415–418 for a guide to note taking.)

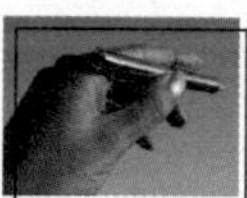

NOTE: If you feel that you're beyond your limit of understanding, don't panic. Challenging reading assignments are designed to make you a better thinker. Simply raise any unanswered questions in the next class discussion.

R

Recite

Reciting is often overlooked in the study-reading process. It is just what it sounds like—repeating, out loud, what you have just learned from your reading.

One way to approach this step is to stop at the end of each page, section, or chapter, and answer the *who? what? when? where? why?* and *how?* questions about the reading. As you recite the answers, you are in effect testing yourself on what you have just read. It will be clear what you do and do not understand, and what you may want to reread. Repeating ideas out loud not only tests what you are able to recall immediately, but also provides audio reinforcement, which helps you remember the material.

Reciting works well in a group study session as well. Let each group member recite what he or she remembers about a certain section of the assignment.

Review

Before you finish, you need to review or summarize what you have just read. If you have questions to answer or a short paper to write, do it now. If not, consider preparing an outline, flash cards, illustrations, graphic organizers, etc., to use as study tools in the future.

If you can't review your reading immediately, try to do so within a day. Research shows that reviewing within 24 hours helps move information from your short-term to your long-term memory. Whenever you review reading material, consider the special memory techniques that follow:

R

Memory Techniques

- Relate the material to your life.
- Recite ideas and facts.
- Try to relax; you'll remember more.
- Put the material in your own words.
- Write about what you have read.
- Draw diagrams, illustrations, clusters.
- Study with a classmate or teach someone the material.
- Visualize what you read.
- Use acronyms, rhymes, raps, and flash cards.
- Ask others about the memory techniques they use.
- Study when you are the most alert.

Review Again

If the material you've read is something you will be tested on weeks later, you need to continue to review on a regular basis—maybe once a week. These follow-up reviews can be very short (4 to 5 minutes) and can take place nearly anywhere—while you're waiting for the bus, riding in a car, or finishing your lunch. You can review anywhere you're able to pull out a notebook or a few note cards without causing a distraction.

You can also review with classmates whenever time permits. Agree to show up for class a few minutes early and ask each other practice test questions. Send your classmates e-mail messages with questions or observations when you've got a few extra minutes; they can return messages at their convenience. If it works, do it.

Reacting to Different Texts

It's critical that you react to challenging reading material as you go along. This may include everything from questions you have to key passages or important points you want to remember. If you own the text or are reading a copy, you can make some of your comments right on the page. Otherwise, record your reactions in your notebook. Sample reactions are provided below and on the next two pages.

Reacting to Poetry

"Sonnet 18" is a poem by William Shakespeare. The notes on the copy of the poem below show one student's reaction to it. The student makes observations, asks questions, reacts to word choice, and so forth. Whenever you read a challenging poem, try to react to it in several different ways.

Sonnet 18

an English sonnet—14 lines with 3 quatrains and 1 final rhyming couplet

Theme: the stability of love

Shall I compare thee to a summer's day?
Thou art more lovely and more temperate:
Rough winds do shake the darling buds of May,
And summer's lease hath all too short a date:

Everything changes. Summer always comes to an end.

Sometime too hot the eye of heaven shines,
And often is his gold complexion dimm'd;
And every fair from fair sometime declines,
By chance, or nature's changing course untrimm'd:

But thy eternal summer shall not fade,
Nor lose possession of that fair thou ow'st;
Nor shall Death brag thou wander'st in his shade,
When in eternal lines to time thou grow'st:

What would this poem sound like written in modern language?

So long as men can breathe, or eyes can see,
So long lives this, and this gives life to thee.

The last quatrain and couplet mean that, unlike summer, this person's beauty won't fade. It lives on because of this sonnet.

Reacting to Fiction

The excerpt below comes from Nathaniel Hawthorne's novel *The Scarlet Letter*. The side notes show how one student reacted to this reading. He makes observations, defines unfamiliar words, and asks questions. Whenever you are reading a challenging piece of fiction, take time to react to it in a similar way.

From *The Scarlet Letter*, Chapter 2, "The Market-Place"

When the young woman—the mother of this child—stood fully revealed before the crowd, it seemed to be her first impulse to clasp the infant closely to her bosom; not so much by an impulse of motherly affection, as that she might thereby conceal a certain token, which was wrought or fastened into her dress. In a moment, however, wisely judging that one token of her shame would but poorly serve to hide another, she took the baby on her arm, and, with a burning blush, and yet a haughty smile, and a glance that would not be abashed, looked around at her townspeople and neighbors. On the breast of her gown, in fine red cloth, surrounded with an elaborate embroidery and fantastic flourishes of gold thread, appeared the letter A. It was so artistically done, and with so much fertility and gorgeous luxuriance of fancy, that it had all the effect of a last and fitting decoration to the apparel which she wore; and which was of a splendor in accordance with the taste of the age, but greatly beyond what was allowed by the sumptuary regulations of the colony.

Hester seems ashamed but still proud.

She makes her mark of shame look gorgeous.

The young woman was tall, with a figure of perfect elegance, on a large scale. She had dark and abundant hair, so glossy that it threw off the sunshine with a gleam, and a face which, besides being beautiful from regularity of feature and richness of complexion, had the impressiveness belonging to a marked brow and deep black eyes. She was lady-like, too, after the manner of the feminine gentility of those days; characterized by a certain state and dignity, rather than by the delicate, evanescent, and indescribable grace, which is now recognized as its indication. And never had Hester Prynne appeared more lady-like, in the antique interpretation of the term, than as she issued from the prison. Those who had before known her, and had expected to behold her dimmed and obscured by a disastrous cloud, were astonished, and even startled, to perceive how her beauty shone out, and made a halo of the misfortune and ignominy in which . . .

Hawthorne's language sounds "lady-like."

"Evanescent" means "quickly disappearing."

What is a "halo of the misfortune and ignominy"?

Reacting to Nonfiction

The excerpt below comes from Henry David Thoreau's essay "Civil Disobedience." The side notes show how one student reacted to this reading. She makes observations, asks questions, summarizes certain parts, and connects ideas to other subjects. Whenever you are reading a challenging nonfiction text, take time to react to it in a similar way.

Excerpt from "Civil Disobedience"

Under a government which imprisons any unjustly, the true place for a just man is also in prison. The proper place today, the only place which Massachusetts has provided for her freer and less desponding spirits, is in her prisons, to be put out and locked out of the State by her own act, as they have already put themselves out by their principles. It is there that the fugitive slave, and the Mexican prisoner on parole, and the Indian come to plead the wrongs of his race, should find them; on that separate, but more free and honorable ground, where the State places those who are not with her, but against her—the only house in a slave State in which a free man can abide with honor. If any think that their influence would be lost there, and their voices no longer afflict the ear of the State, that they would not be as an enemy within its walls, they do not know by how much truth is stronger than error, nor how much more eloquently and effectively he can combat injustice who has experienced a little in his own person. Cast your whole vote, not a strip of paper merely, but your whole influence. A minority is powerless while it conforms to the majority; it is not even a minority then; but it is irresistible when it clogs by its whole weight. If the alternative is to keep all just men in prison, or give up war and slavery, the State will not hesitate which to choose. If a thousand men were not to pay their tax bills this year, that would not be a violent and bloody measure, as it would be to pay them, and enable the State to commit violence and shed innocent blood. This is, in fact, the definition of a peaceable revolution, if any such is possible. If the tax-gatherer, or any other public officer, asks me, as one has done, "But what shall I do?" my answer is, "If you really wish to do anything, resign your office." When the subject has refused allegiance, and the officer has resigned his office, then the revolution is accomplished. But even suppose blood should flow. Is there not a sort of blood shed when the conscience is wounded? Through this wound . . .

Side notes:

I think of Martin Luther King and Ghandi when I read this part about a "just man in prison."

Thoreau writes long, rambling sentences.

What does Thoreau mean by "truth is stronger than error"?

Thoreau believes that being in the minority is not a reason to give up.

Is Thoreau concerned more with rebelling against the government or with speaking against slavery?

Critical Listening and Note Taking

Experts have long told us that people remember only about half of what they hear, even if they're tested immediately after hearing it. A couple of months later, that percentage drops to 25 percent. That may be no big deal if you're listening to a prime-time sitcom, but if you only remember 25 percent of what you heard in a history class, you may be in big trouble.

Listening is a skill, and like all other skills, it can be improved with time and practice. The same is true for note taking. In fact, the two skills work hand in hand: You will be a better listener if you take good notes, and you will take better notes if you listen carefully. In addition, if you read carefully, you will enhance both of these skills.

WHAT'S AHEAD

This section of your handbook introduces guidelines and strategies designed to improve both your listening and note-taking skills.

Improving Critical Listening Skills

Listening is much more than sitting up straight, looking in the direction of the person speaking, and following the gist of what is being said. Critical listening involves thinking. It is an active process.

Lots of things can interfere with listening. Some distractions, like outside noise or the temperature of a classroom, may be out of your control. But other things, like staying up too late, overeating before a class, or daydreaming, are within your power to control. What you need is a positive attitude and some guidelines to follow.

Listening Guidelines

■ Prepare to listen and keep a goal in mind.

Think ahead about what you may hear and keep an open mind about the speaker and the topic. Take time to identify the purpose of your listening (to gather information for tests, to learn how to . . . , etc.).

■ Listen carefully.

Listen not only to what the speaker is actually saying but also to what the speaker is implying (saying between the lines). The speaker's voice, facial expression, and gestures help communicate his or her message.

■ Listen for the facts.

Listen to find out the *who? what? when? where? why?* and *how?* of what the speaker says. This will give you the important facts and help you to arrange them in a memorable way.

■ Separate fact from opinion.

Listen for bias or opinion disguised as fact.

■ Listen for signals.

Your instructor will often tell you exactly what is important. She or he may not use a megaphone to say, "Now hear this!"—but it may be almost as obvious.

Examples: And don't forget to __________________.
Remember, the best way to __________ is ________.
The two reasons are ____________________.
Three characteristics are __________________.
This all means that ______________.
The bottom line is ________________________.

■ Listen for patterns of organization.

Textbooks and lectures often follow "patterns of organization." If you can discover how a speaker has organized information and where she or he is going with the material, you have important clues to follow. Discovering a speaker's pattern of organization can greatly enhance your ability to learn by listening.

Five Basic Patterns of Organization

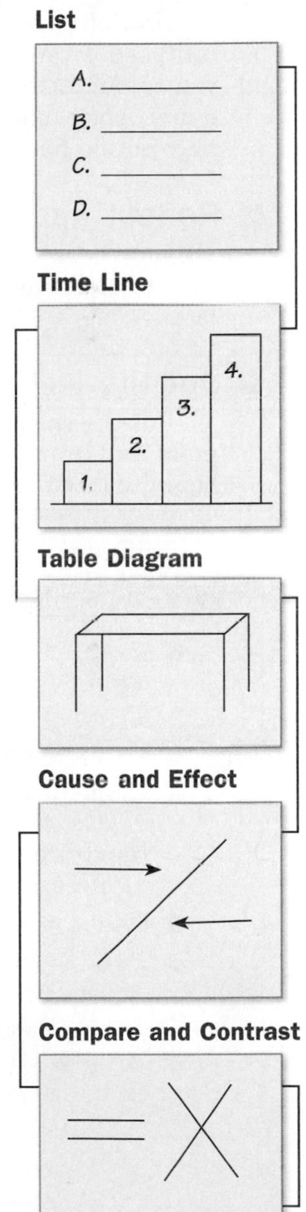

Listing In this pattern, the speaker introduces a list of items to be discussed. For example, a biology teacher might say, "There are four types of simple cells." The listing pattern can be visualized by a column of lines and letters (or numerals).

Time-Sequence In this pattern, events are presented in time order. How-to presentations are always in time sequence. Time sequence is also important in discussions of history and current events, in explanations of processes in science and math, and in the study of literature. Visualize this pattern as steps that build upon one another.

General-Statement-Plus-Examples In this pattern, the speaker begins with a general statement such as "Children, even the very young, can easily show their understanding of spatial relationships." Examples are then given to support this general statement. You can visualize this pattern as a tabletop (generalization) being supported by table legs (examples).

Cause-and-Effect This pattern can be worked in two directions. A speaker can present a cause that led to a specific result, or effect; or a speaker can present a result (an effect) that followed an event (a cause). In either case, the speaker is stressing a relationship; one thing happens because something else happened. You can visualize this pattern as a slanted line being pushed from either side.

Comparison-and-Contrast In this pattern, the speaker explains something by telling how it is similar to (comparison) or different from (contrast) another thing. Visualize this pattern as two lines going in the same direction for comparison and two lines going in different directions for contrast.

■ Listen for details.

Don't be satisfied with understanding the general meaning of a story or a lecture. Pay full attention to what a speaker is saying. If you allow the details to slip through the cracks, you are less likely to remember what is being said. Details, examples, and anecdotes help a lecture come alive, and they also provide "hooks" for your memory.

■ Listen to directions.

How often have you sat down, ready to begin an assignment, only to be confused because you could not remember exactly what the teacher asked you to do? Listening carefully to directions is basic. You may be able to e-mail your teacher later to ask for the directions again, but he or she may not be too impressed.

■ Reflect upon what is being said.

How does this material relate to you? How might you use it in the future? Relating information to your personal life will help you recall it later.

■ Put the lecture into your own words.

Put the speaker's statements into your own words. Identify each main point and draw conclusions about the importance of each. In this way you begin to "own" the material.

When the Lecturer Talks Fast

- **Prepare well before class.** In a class where the instructor covers material quickly, you may get lost . . . unless you've read or previewed the appropriate pages or assignment.
- **Use a system of shorthand.** (See page 418.)
- **Lock into the speed.** Did you know that it's actually easier to concentrate and grasp information when the speaker uses rapid-fire delivery? You are less likely to be distracted or to daydream. So let the speed help you stay focused.
- **Use a recorder.** (See page 420.)
- **Talk to the teacher.** Ask questions before, during, and after class about points that you don't understand, and don't be afraid to ask her or him (politely) to slow down.
- **Meet with other students from the class;** compare and exchange notes.

Taking Notes

Note taking is an active approach to learning, one that gets you personally involved in the learning process and helps you focus on the most important information. It is not simply hearing and writing; note taking is listening, thinking, reacting, questioning, summarizing, organizing, listing, labeling, and illustrating. The following tips will help you to improve your note-taking skills.

Preparing for the Presentation

- **Use a notebook or a three-ring binder.** If you use a binder, you can punch holes in handouts and add them to your notes in the appropriate places.
- **Keep the course outline in the front of your notebook.** At a glance you'll be able to see where you are, where you've been, and where you're going.
- **Label and date your notes for each class period.** If you are using loose-leaf paper, number and date each page.
- **Write your name and phone number in your note holder.** Then, if you leave it behind, there's a good chance that it will be returned to you.
- **Learn the common words and jargon of the course.** Write accurate definitions of these words and learn them.
- **Request a seat change if needed.** Position yourself so that you have no trouble paying attention to the lecturer, viewing the board or overhead screen, participating in discussions, and so on.
- **Have a positive attitude.** Sit up straight and focus your attention on the teacher. You'll learn more.
- **Do the assigned reading before class.** Then you can follow the lecture and be prepared when the teacher asks a question.

Sound Advice

If your teacher writes anything on the board—a word, a formula, a definition—copy it accurately word for word. It will probably show up on an exam.

Taking Notes During the Presentation

- **Use one side of your paper only.** This will make it possible later on to line up sheets of notes and see the flow of ideas.
- **Write all assignments and test dates in one place in your notebook.** That way you'll always know where to find this information.
- **Use a note-taking guide.** Choose the guide that best fits your needs, or create a variation of your own. (See pages 415–418.)
- **Leave wide margins or skip lines between main ideas.** Don't cram a lot of words on a page. Leave room to add study notes when you're reviewing later.
- **Condense information.** Use phrases and lists rather than recording complete sentences.
- **Write legibly and in ink.** If you have a laptop or notebook computer, try using it to take notes. (See page 419.)
- **Star, underline, or check important points.** Teachers often signal exactly what it is they want you to remember. Don't rely on your memory. Mark it right away.
- **Use abbreviations and symbols for common words.** See the chart on page 418 for tips on how to build your own system.
- **Draw simple illustrations, charts, or diagrams.** You will remember main points better if you add visuals to words.

Following Up After the Presentation

- **Read over your notes soon after the lecture.** Then, if something is unclear or doesn't make sense, you can make a point of asking about it.
- **Jot down key words in the left-hand column.** This system will help you to pinpoint what is important.
- **Cover your notes and restate concepts for each key word.** An early review of your notes will help to "fix" them in your mind.
- **Relate new information to what you know or have experienced.** Associating what you've learned with what you already know will help you retain the new information.
- **Review your notes periodically.** Remembering what you learned at the beginning of the semester will help you understand concepts introduced later on.
- **Make note cards for important points in your notes.** Reviewing with flash cards is particularly useful when you must memorize a lot of material.

Using a Note-Taking Guide

Note taking helps you listen in class, organize your teacher's ideas, and remember what was said. However, there are pitfalls. You can take so many notes that you are overwhelmed when it comes to reviewing them, or you can take notes in such a haphazard fashion that it's impossible to follow them. That's when a note-taking guide comes into play. The right guide can help you coordinate your textbook, lecture, and review notes into an efficient system.

Keeping Text and Presentation Notes Together

If the lecturer closely follows the textbook, try using your reading-assignment notes as a classroom note-taking guide. As you follow your reading notes, you will be prepared to answer your teacher's questions and take additional notes as well. Simply jot down anything that clarifies the material for you. Combining your reading and classroom notes in this way will give you one set of well-organized study notes.

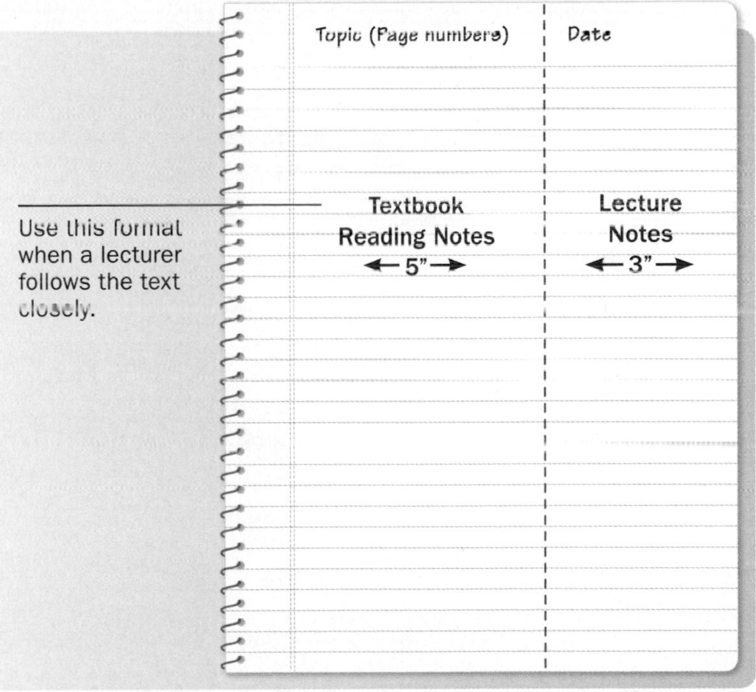

NOTE: Use the left two-thirds of your paper for reading notes; use the right one-third for class notes.

Adding a Review Column

If you want to keep all your notes together, you can add a third column at the right of your page. Leave this review column blank during class; but afterward, read through your notes and summarize the ideas in key words and phrases. This will help you review and remember the material.

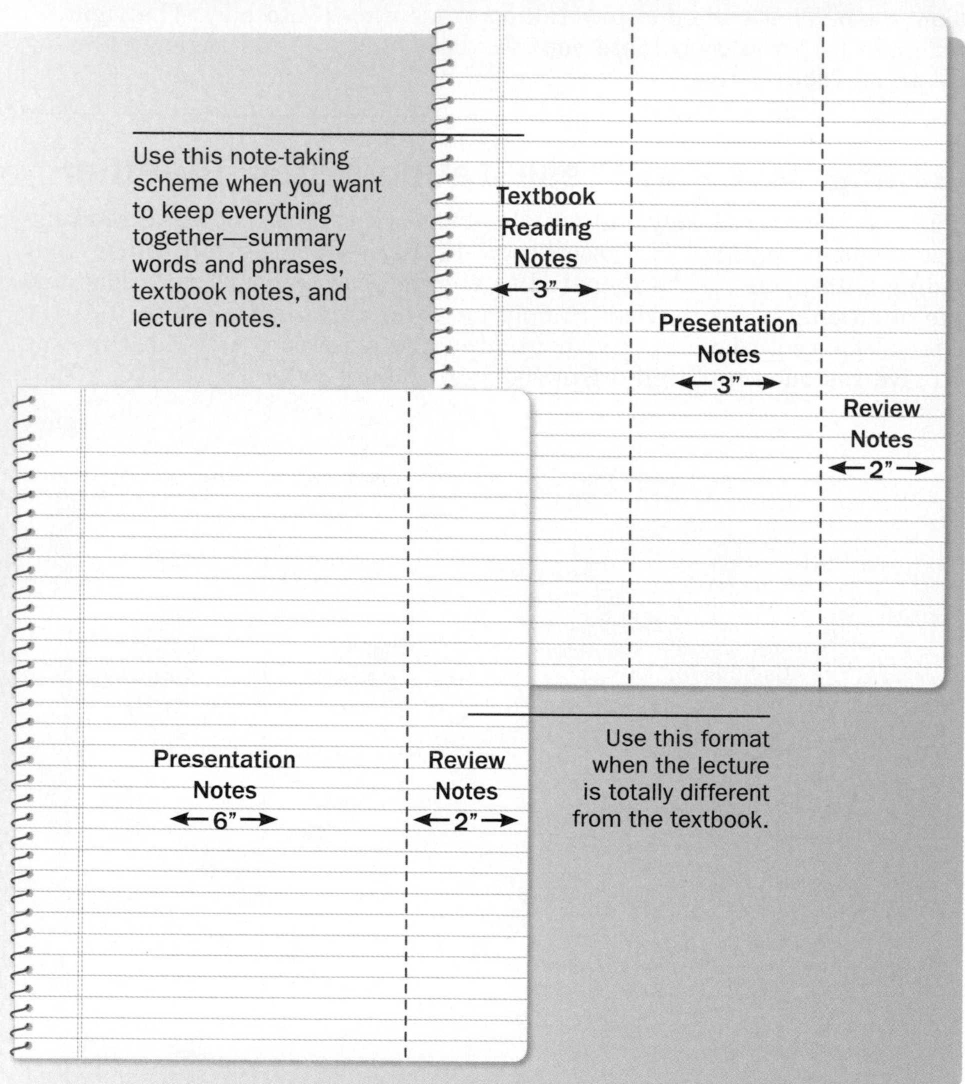
Use this note-taking scheme when you want to keep everything together—summary words and phrases, textbook notes, and lecture notes.
Textbook Reading Notes
← 3" →
Presentation Notes
← 3" →
Review Notes
← 2" →
Presentation Notes
← 6" →
Review Notes
← 2" →
Use this format when the lecture is totally different from the textbook.

Keeping Presentation and Text Notes Separate

If your teacher does not base his or her presentation on the class text, you may want to keep your class and textbook notes separate. In that case, your class notes will have only two columns—a wide left column for lecture notes and a narrow right column for review notes.

Creating a Mind Map

A mind map is a creative, nonlinear organization of material. You can create one during a lecture and use it later as a review tool. Starting at the center with a key idea such as "Stamp Act" or "Aerodynamics," you create a map by adding related details on branches.

Mind maps work well because they use both sides of your brain, the logical left side and the creative right side. They force you to be more than a passive recorder of information; and, when you're finished, they reinforce information for you in a fresh way.

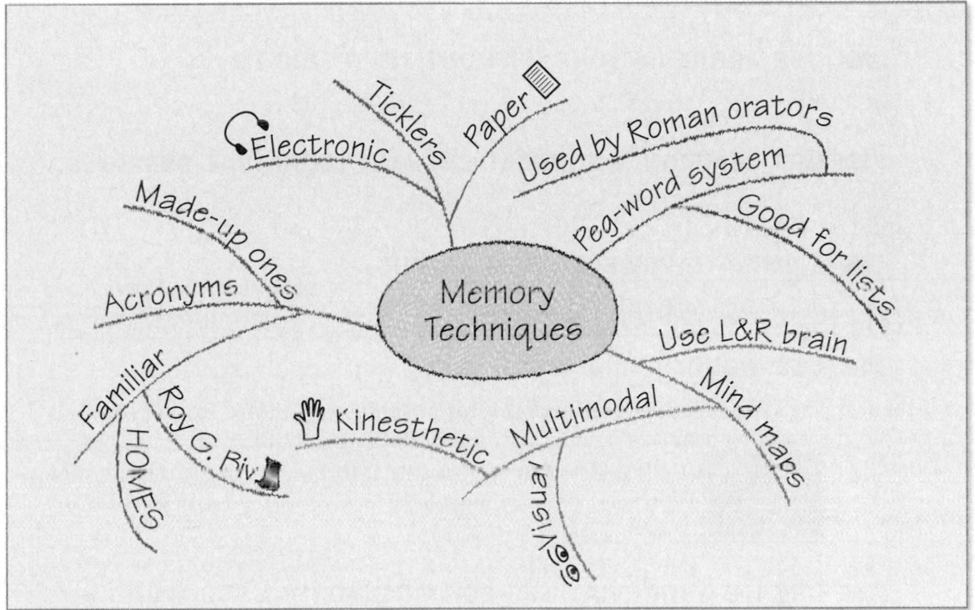

TIPS

FOR DRAWING MIND MAPS

- Write your topic in the center of the paper. Draw a circle or box around it.
- Draw subtopic lines emanating from the main topic. Write a condensed thought of three or four words above each line. Further subdivisions and examples should branch off from the subtopics.
- Add graphics, arrows, question marks, stick figures, drawings—anything that will fix an idea in your mind.
- Afterward, color-code or emphasize important concepts.

Creating a Shorthand System

QUICK GUIDE

You will be taking a lot of notes during your high school and college career. To make the process more efficient, start now to develop your own shorthand system. Here are some guidelines.

OMIT ALL ARTICLES *(a, an, the)*.

USE ABBREVIATIONS WITHOUT THE PERIODS.

lbs st pres Jan wk gov US

USE COMMON MATHEMATICAL AND TECHNICAL SYMBOLS.

+ - = % # < > ÷ × ∴ $ ||

ELIMINATE VOWELS FROM WORDS.

mdl for *middle* *psbl* for *possible*

USE WORD BEGINNINGS.

intro for *introduction* *psych* for *psychology* *info* for *information*

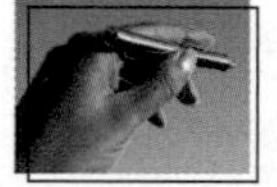

NOTE: Use your abbreviations consistently. Otherwise, you will end up wondering if *psych* means *psychology, psychiatry,* or *psychic.*

CREATE ABBREVIATIONS FOR COMMONLY USED WORDS in a particular course. Write these words and their abbreviations at the front of your notebook or binder.

PNS for *parasympathetic nervous system*
QE for *quadratic equation*

KEEP ADDING TO YOUR PERSONAL SHORTHAND SYSTEM. Here are some examples to get you started:

w/	with	w/o	without
ex.	example	b/c	because
b4	before	SB	should be
SNB	should not be	2	two, to, too
etc.	and so on	♀	female
&	and	♂	male

Electronic Note Taking

Even though you may never want to rely totally on electronic methods of note taking (laptop or recorder), they can prove extremely useful in certain situations. Read the suggestions that follow.

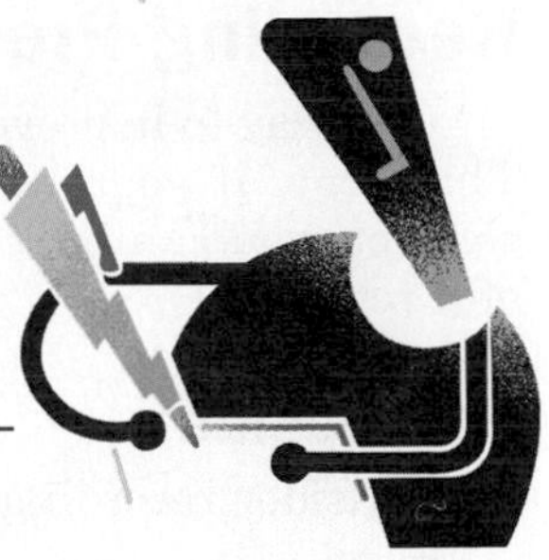

Using a Laptop

With the popularity of laptop computers, more and more students are taking notes electronically instead of in longhand.

The Upside

- You can record more information than you can in longhand.
- You can search your notes electronically for key words.
- After class, you can reorganize your notes quickly in any way you choose.
- Many word-processing programs allow you to compose notes in outline form, making them easier to review.

The Downside

- Despite the advances, nothing is as light, portable, or dependable as plain old paper and pen or pencil.
- It's easy to get behind if you don't have an efficient technique.
- Your battery may run out at some crucial moment.
- Finally, your computer can crash, leaving you with no notes at all.

TIPS

FOR TAKING NOTES ON A LAPTOP

- Read your laptop computer manual for tips on battery conservation. Turning down your backlighting will save battery power, as will using certain word-processing programs rather than others.
- Use lots of paragraphs so that your notes will not become one long, formidable block of words. Use the "return" button.
- Save your file periodically throughout the lecture.
- Print out a copy of your notes at the end of each lecture.
- Make a full backup of the folder containing all your notes.
- Rely on the ultimate backup—paper and pen. Don't leave home without them.

Recording Presentations

One way to improve and supplement your note taking is to record lectures. That way, if you miss a point or two or don't understand an important concept, you can hear it again. (Make sure your instructor permits the use of a recorder.)

The Upside

Consider recording a lecture in any of the following situations:

- **The class material is technical or unfamiliar to you.** Hearing it a second time may help you understand the material.
- **You have to be absent from class.** Just make sure the friend who is recording for you is familiar with all the features on your recording device and knows exactly what to do.
- **You want a backup to your notes.** Then, if you come across something puzzling in your notes, you can listen to that part of the lecture a second time.
- **You need to maximize time.** Instead of listening to your favorite music, listen to a lecture from one of your classes as you run, walk, or work out.

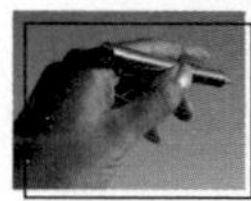

NOTE: As a courtesy, ask your teacher's permission before you record the first time. Usually, recording is not a problem; but in rare instances, the teacher may either object to having the class recorded or may ask you to turn off the recorder during the class discussion.

The Downside

Recording a lecture may seem like a surefire way to get every last word; but before you throw your notebooks away, consider the following:

- **Recording encourages daydreaming or half-listening.** Knowing that you have the lecture recorded can encourage you to zone out. Continue to take notes so this does not happen.
- **Listening to a recorded lecture takes time**—a lot of time. Reviewing a good set of notes can be a much more efficient use of your time.
- **Recording devices are machines,** and the cardinal rule with machines is that if they can malfunction, they will. Always double-check the obvious:
  - Are the batteries fresh or fully charged?
  - Is the record button on?
  - Is the volume adequate?
  - Can the recorder microphone pick up the speaker clearly?

Writing to Learn

Writing to learn is writing that helps you understand the subjects you are studying. When you write to learn, you are *not* trying to show how well you can express yourself or how much you already know about a topic; instead, you are writing to clarify your thinking and gain new understandings. As writer and teacher Anne Ruggles Gere says, "Writing to learn focuses on better thinking and learning. To be sure, students who use writing as a way of learning often produce better written products, but this is a side benefit, not the chief purpose."

Many educators believe that writing to learn is the best way to learn in any class, from math to music. Most writing-to-learn activities, such as entries in a learning log, are short, spontaneous, and exploratory. Other forms, such as summaries and paraphrases, are more carefully planned. Writing to learn is seldom, if ever, graded for mechanical errors.

WHAT'S AHEAD

This chapter includes guidelines and examples for four different types of writing to learn. Once you learn about these forms of writing, be sure to use them as soon as possible.

Writing in Learning Logs

Writing a Summary

Writing a Paraphrase

Writing an Abstract

"The discipline of real learning consists of the self and the others flowing into each other."

—Ken Macrorie

Writing in Learning Logs

Writing about a new concept so you can understand and remember it better—that's what writing to learn is all about. It's really that simple. When you write to learn, you are writing to learn more. Keeping a learning log may be the best way to learn anything. The guidelines below offer different approaches to help you get started with your own learning log. Also review the sample entries on the next page.

Guidelines for Keeping a Learning Log

A learning log gets you actively involved in your course work and gives you the opportunity to explore important ideas freely and naturally. It is a place where you can dig deeper into what you have learned from lectures, class discussions, group projects, experiments, and reading assignments.

- **Write about class activities—**anything from a class discussion to an important exam. Consider what was valuable, confusing, interesting, humorous, worth remembering, etc.
- **Personalize new ideas and concepts.** Consider how this new information relates to what you already know.
- **Evaluate your progress in a particular class.** Consider your strengths, your weaknesses, your relationship with members of the class.
- **Discuss your course work with a particular audience:** a young child, a foreign exchange student, an object, an alien from another planet.
- **Question what you are learning.** Dig deeply into the importance of the concepts presented. (One way to do this is to write a dialogue.)
- **Confront ideas that confuse you.** Back them into a corner until you finally grasp their meaning.
- **Develop a mock essay test.** Answer one or more of the questions yourself.
- **Keep a record of your thoughts and feelings.** This can be especially helpful during an extended lab or research assignment.
- **Start a glossary** of new or unfamiliar vocabulary words. Use these words in your log entries.
- **Argue for or against a topic**—any idea or position that comes up in a discussion, in your reading, or in a lecture.

Learning-Log Entries

The sample learning-log entries below were written in response to a newspaper article (company merger), a literary work *(Canterbury Tales)*, and a class lecture (chemistry). Notice how each entry is personalized.

Response to a Newspaper Article

I just read an article by Ellen Goodman. It's interesting how cautiously she responds to the news of a gigantic merger between a phone company and a cable TV company, which will form an electronic superhighway. She recalls how the concrete highway system of the 1950s brought unintended consequences such as smog, traffic jams, and drive-by shootings. Similarly, the electronic superhighway system may deliver more data than meaning, more commerce than education, and more isolation than community. It's an interesting thought.

Response to Chaucer's *Canterbury Tales*

I think the order in which characters appear in the *Prologue* helps the reader compare and contrast the different characters. If the Miller did not follow the Knight, then the parody would have been much more difficult to see, and if the Reeve did not follow the Miller, then his tale would have lost most of its revenge themes. Even the Franklin's tale is connected to the previous tale told by the Squire. Order is very important in connecting the themes in *The Canterbury Tales*. I guess that's true in all things, from commercials to baseball lineups to lunch menus. By organizing ideas in a certain order, different components can be compared more easily and special connections become more apparent.

Response to a Chemistry Lecture

Our teacher used the *Hindenburg* as an example of how noble gases are different from other elements. The *Hindenburg* was a zeppelin—a huge, cylinder-shaped flying balloon that could carry passengers. It was filled with hydrogen—not a noble gas—which reacted with oxygen in the air, causing the zeppelin to burn. Thirty-six people died. If helium had been used instead, it also would have kept the zeppelin airborne, but it wouldn't have burned. This is because it is a noble gas, meaning it doesn't interact with other elements. That's why balloons and dirigibles use helium now, not hydrogen. This got me thinking about how what you don't know can hurt you. Chemistry can actually be useful in real life!

Writing a Summary

A summary is a condensed version of another text. An effective summary gleans the key factual information from an original document and does not contain personal opinions or evaluations. Your instructors may ask you to write summaries of books, book chapters, lectures, or portions of your class notes. Summarizing calls on your ability to comprehend, analyze, synthesize, and evaluate information—all important thinking skills. Developing your summarizing skills will prime you for success in college and beyond.

Guidelines for Writing a Summary

- **Skim the selection** first to get the overall meaning.
- **Read the selection carefully,** paying particular attention to key words and phrases. (Check the meaning of any words you're unsure of.)
- **List the main ideas** on your own paper without looking at the selection.
- **Review the selection** a final time so that you have the overall meaning clearly in mind as you begin to write.
- **Write a summary** of the major ideas, using your own words except for those few words in the original that cannot be changed. Keep the following points in mind as you write:
  1. Write an opening (topic) sentence that clearly states the main idea of the original selection.
  2. Include each important idea in a supporting sentence.
  3. Stick to the essential information. Names, dates, times, places, and similar facts are usually essential; examples, descriptive details, and adjectives are usually not needed.
  4. Write a concluding sentence that ties all of your thoughts together and brings the summary to an effective end.
- **Check your summary** for accuracy and conciseness. Ask yourself the following questions:
  1. Have I included all of the main ideas?
  2. Have I cut or combined most of the descriptive details? (Your summary should be about one-half the length of the original.)
  3. Will a reader understand the main points of the original simply by reading my summary?

Summary Writing in Action

A student wrote this summary of the chapter entitled "How Can X Be Summarized?" from *Twenty Questions for the Writer* by Jacqueline Berke.

Original Summary

> According to Jacqueline Berke, one of the greatest challenges to the intellect is to digest complex written communications and to boil them down to manageable size. The author says she will treat summary as a significant and recurring question. The chapter goes on to offer examples of summaries, showing the different styles in which they can be written and the different purposes they can serve. In all summaries, however, the key to success is repeated rereading and accurate critical thinking. Under the first main heading, "Summarizing Ideas," Berke offers a long, hard paragraph by John Stuart Mill . . .

The preceding summary includes more information than is necessary and resembles a paraphrase more than it does a summary. (For information on paraphrasing, see page 427.)

In the student's second attempt, she simply highlights the main points and purpose of the chapter, freely rearranging ideas for the sake of clarity. Before writing her summary, she made a quick list of key words and phrases that would capture the essence of Berke's chapter.

Improved Summary

> Summary, according to Jacqueline Berke in chapter 7 of *Twenty Questions for the Writer*, is the process of distilling "the heart of the matter" from any detailed piece of written prose. In all three types of summaries for which she offers examples—summaries of ideas, of plots (also called a synopsis), and of events—Berke stresses that summary is a demanding process of analysis and careful and sustained critical thinking. The quality of a summary, she says, is not determined by its length; a summary by nature must be a condensation of the original. But depending on one's purpose, whether subjective and evaluative or objective and descriptive, a summary may be fairly involved, or it may be extremely brief. The chapter concludes with a section of in-class and out-of-class assignments.

This revised summary gets to the "heart of the matter" quickly, just as Berke recommends. It doesn't waste time on illustrations, examples, and other minor points, but carefully focuses on the essence of the chapter's content.

Additional Summaries

Many of the summaries that you write will have an objective, academic tone. A personal summary, on the other hand, is an excellent way to learn about a subject by relating it to your own life.

Objective Textbook Summary

When humans or other vertebrates are in a dangerous or stressful situation, a chain reaction is set in motion. First, the central nervous system stimulates the adrenal medulla to release the hormones epinephrine and norepinephrine into the bloodstream. The whole sympathetic nervous system is activated, in fact, and even more norepinephrine is released. These two hormones—epinephrine and norepinephrine—make the heart pump faster and faster. At the same time, the pressure inside the blood vessels increases. This causes the blood to circulate more rapidly throughout the whole body. Another organ, the liver, releases extra glucose or blood sugar into the bloodstream. The blood vessels in the muscles dilate in response to the increased blood supply. The muscles are supplied with extra oxygen and glucose and are prepared to either fight or run away. Because the body does not have time to eat, digest, or eliminate food, the supply of blood to the kidneys, stomach, and intestines is greatly reduced.

Personal Summary

I remember our biology instructor talking about the "fight or flight" syndrome. I always wondered what causes this whole chain of events to kick in. Why does it happen? What happens? All I have to do is remember the last time I walked into a class unprepared and the instructor said the dreaded words—chapter exam. I could feel those hormones kicking in. My heart started thumping, my muscles tightened, and if somebody had offered me my favorite snack, I would not have responded. My body was psyched to either fight or flee; instead, I was trapped in an overheated classroom with nothing but a pen and regrets for not having studied. Sometimes I think our ancestors had it easier. They could take physical advantage of all that activity within the sympathetic nervous system. I wonder if the increased heart rate and blood pressure improve thinking and remembering in any way.

INSIDE INFO

Another way to get the most out of a learning opportunity is to do a summary "on the run." It's called a *stop 'n' write* and can be done during a reading assignment or class discussion. By stopping to write, you're forced to reflect on what you've just read or heard.

Writing a Paraphrase

A paraphrase is a type of summary that is written in your own words. It is particularly good for clarifying the meaning of a difficult or symbolic piece of writing (poems, proverbs, documents). Because a paraphrase often includes your interpretation, it is sometimes longer than the original.

Guidelines for Writing a Paraphrase

- Skim the passage or selection quickly.
- Then read the passage carefully, noting key words and ideas.
- Look up any unfamiliar words.
- Summarize each main idea in the passage in a clear statement.
- Expand or amplify the text to make it clearer, but be sure to maintain the meaning and tone of the original text.

Original Passage

Each man has his own vocation. The talent is the call. There is one direction in which all space is open to him. He has faculties silently inviting him thither to endless exertion. He is like a ship in a river; he runs against obstructions on every side but one; on that side all obstruction is taken away, and he sweeps serenely over a deepening channel into an infinite sea.

—Ralph Waldo Emerson, "Spiritual Laws"

Notice that the paraphrase that follows "translates" some of the archaic language *(faculties, thither)* by putting the passage into words that make sense to the modern reader. Notice, too, how the paraphrase changes the problematic masculine pronouns in the original to gender-inclusive plurals, while still retaining Emerson's meaning.

Paraphrase

Everyone has a calling in life. Our abilities and talents and energies silently call us to work at developing them further. People who respond to their calling are like ships in a river flowing toward the sea. There are banks on both sides, and only one direction in which to move with ease. These people will only run into obstacles if they try to change directions. And, like ships moving surely through a channel to the sea, people following their true calling will move with great peace of mind toward the open water of unlimited possibilities.

Writing an Abstract

The abstract is a summary that presents an overview of an article or a report. Many journals publish abstracts of all the articles in an issue. If you are looking for information on a particular subject, an abstract can help you determine whether the article is worth reading in its entirety. In addition, many collections of abstracts are available in databases that you can search using keywords. When you are asked to write an abstract of a paper or project, follow the guidelines below.

Guidelines for Writing an Abstract

- Using a copy of the paper, review and highlight the key information.
- Begin by writing a thesis statement (article's purpose).
- Summarize key points in the order they appear in the paper.
- Include only essential information, methods, and results.
- Limit your abstract to one paragraph of 100–150 words.
- Avoid technical terms, specific quotations, and interpretations.

ABSTRACT

Running on Empty 2

Abstract

This study examined the effects of short-term food deprivation on two cognitive abilities—concentration and perseverance. Undergraduate students (*N*-51) were tested on both a concentration task and a perseverance task after one of three levels of food deprivation: none, 12 hours, or 24 hours. We predicted that food deprivation would impair both concentration scores and perseverance time. Food deprivation had no significant effect on concentration scores, which is consistent with recent research on the effects of food deprivation (Green, Elliman, & Rogers, 1995). However, participants in the 12-hour deprivation group spent significantly less time on the perseverance task than those in both the control and 24-hour deprivation groups, suggesting that short-term deprivation may affect some aspects of cognition and not others.

The abstract at the left is taken from the APA research paper, "Running on Empty: The Effects of Food Deprivation on Concentration and Perseverance" (see pages 373–382). In 115 words, it explains the scope and purpose of the paper. The abstract summarizes the problem being studied, including participants in the study, research methods, results, and conclusions.

Building a College-Sized Vocabulary

Increasing your vocabulary, the words you understand and use comfortably, will improve your reading, writing, and speaking skills. As your vocabulary grows, your reading rate and comprehension level will grow, too.

One of the most natural and effective ways to improve your vocabulary is to read. That means reading whatever you *need* to read and whatever you *want* to read. However, building your vocabulary through reading is a gradual process. You can start building a better vocabulary today by using the strategies discussed on the following pages. Making a daily commitment to this process will vastly improve the scope and depth of your vocabulary.

WHAT'S AHEAD

This chapter serves as a basic vocabulary guide, helping you broaden your understanding of the language and your ability to communicate. Included is information on using context clues, using a thesaurus, and figuring out difficult words by learning prefixes, suffixes, and roots.

Building Your Vocabulary

QUICK GUIDE

Many experts say that the single most important thing that you can do to improve your grades is to enlarge your vocabulary. Here are some ways to do that:

- **USE CONTEXT:** Begin by studying a new word in its context. (See pages 431–432.) Look for clues within the phrases surrounding the word in question. You'll be amazed at how many definitions you can figure out on your own.
- **LEARN COMMON WORD ROOTS, PREFIXES, AND SUFFIXES.** With a knowledge of these, you can often infer the meaning of a word. (See pages 434–444.)
- **KEEP A VOCABULARY NOTEBOOK.** Include the definition, the pronunciation, and the part of speech for each word. If you encountered the new word in your reading, copy the sentence it came from into your notebook. Words learned in context are more likely to be remembered than words learned in isolation.
- **USE FLASH CARDS.** Print the new word on the front of an index card with the definition on the back. Carry the cards with you and flip through them from time to time.
- **USE YOUR DICTIONARY (PRINT OR ONLINE).** If you look up a word more than once, include it in your flash cards.
- **LEARN THE ORIGINS OF WORDS.** Pay attention to the etymologies (origins of words) in the dictionary. Many of these are interesting enough to help you remember a word.
- **USE A THESAURUS (PRINT OR ONLINE).** Use a thesaurus to find all the synonyms for a common word, such as *think*. For starters, there's *consider, believe, imagine,* and *suppose;* but remember, these words are not interchangeable. Learn the subtle differences between these words to appreciate their connotation and appropriate use.
- **CONSIDER FOREIGN LANGUAGES.** Use your knowledge of foreign languages to decode and remember new words. For example, if you remember that the Spanish word "amigo" means "friend," you can guess the meaning of the word "amity" (peaceful relations or friendship).

Using Context

When you come across a word you don't know, do you stop to look it up? That's a good idea, but it's not always necessary. Sometimes you can figure out the meaning of a word through its context, the words surrounding it. You already do this naturally, but becoming conscious of various context clues will improve this skill enormously. Become familiar with the different types of clues and look for them when you come across unfamiliar words in your reading.

Types of Context Clues

DEFINITIONS OR DESCRIPTIONS: This is the most obvious type of clue. The sentence itself tells you what the word means. The tip-off for this type of clue is often one of the "be" verbs *(am, is, are, was, were)*.

> A **zealot** is someone who is enthusiastic about a cause or an activity in a way that goes far beyond ordinary interest.

SYNONYMS: A familiar word follows and defines the first.

> Sometimes individuals display **altruistic**, selfless behavior toward complete strangers who are in great need.

COMPARISONS: A comparison is made that helps you define the word. Comparisons are often signaled by the word *like* or *as*.

> As the people who supported the Vichy government in France during World War II discovered, a postwar wrath often falls on those who have **collaborated** with the enemy.

CONTRASTS: A contrast helps you define the word. Contrasts are often signaled by words such as *although, but, on the other hand,* or *on the contrary*.

> Although modern medicine has proven very effective in dealing with acute conditions and traumas, it has not been as successful in treating **chronic** conditions for which surgery or medication are problematic.

RESTATEMENTS: A term is restated in other words. Demonstrative pronouns such as *this, that,* and *those* may signal restatements, as do appositives, which are set off by commas, parentheses, and dashes.

> Thousands of otherwise healthy adults suffer from **agoraphobia**. This fear of open spaces has been successfully treated by a variety of methods from medication to behavioral therapy.
> (A demonstrative pronoun signals the restatement.)

> In an age of computers, typewriters have almost become an **anachronism**, a thing of the past.
> (An appositive signals the restatement.)

Items in a Series: Even if you don't recognize all the items in a series, you can assume that they are all part of the same family.

> **Cantatas, concertos, oratorios, sonatas,** and **suites**—all of these were part of the enormous output of Baroque composer Johann Sebastian Bach.

Tone and Setting: Picturing the scene set by the writer will often provide helpful clues to a word's meaning.

> During the long and tedious trial, the jury was **sequestered** day and night from the public, in quarters where there were no televisions, radios, or daily newspapers.

Cause and Effect: From a cause-and-effect sequence in a sentence, you can often deduce the meaning of a word.

> Because genetic mutations can be caused by the effects of chemicals, radiation, or even ordinary heat on DNA, reliable genetic research requires constant **vigilance**.

INSIDE INFO

Context clues do not always appear immediately before or after the word you are studying. In a lengthy piece of writing, the clues may appear a few paragraphs later (or earlier).

Now You Try It

Read the passage below taken from Jack London's *Call of the Wild.* Notice the boldfaced words. Then look for direct and indirect clues to their meanings. With your new understanding of context clues, you will be able to define a greater number of unfamiliar words.

They made Sixty Miles, which is a fifty-mile run, on the first day; and the second day saw them booming up the Yukon well on their way to Pelly. But such splendid running was achieved not without great trouble and **vexation** on the part of Francois. The **insidious** revolt led by Buck had destroyed the **solidarity** of the team. It no longer was as one dog leaping in the traces. The encouragement Buck gave the rebels led them into all kinds of petty **misdemeanors**. No more was Spitz a leader greatly to be feared. The old awe departed, and they grew equal to challenging his authority. Pike robbed him of half a fish one night and gulped it down under the protection of Buck. Another night Dub and Joe fought Spitz and made him forego the punishment they deserved. And even Billee, the good-natured, was less good-natured, and whined not half so **placatingly** as in former days. Buck never came near Spitz without snarling and bristling **menacingly**. In fact, his conduct approached that of a bully, and he was given to swaggering up and down before Spitz's very nose.

Using a Thesaurus

A thesaurus is, in a sense, the opposite of a dictionary. You refer to a dictionary when you know the word but need the definition. You go to a thesaurus when you know the definition but need the word. As a reference tool, a thesaurus is a treasure chest of *synonyms*, words with similar meanings.

Locating Word Lists

Go to a thesaurus when you have a word in mind, but it doesn't exactly fit. For example, let's say you're writing an essay on *Hamlet* and need a word for *fear* (a certain kind of fear) to complete the following sentence:

Hamlet delays his revenge out of ____________ that the ghost may be an evil spirit sent to deceive him.

For a thesaurus in dictionary form, simply look up *fear* alphabetically. If, however, you have a traditional thesaurus, you must first look up your word in the alphabetical index at the back of the book. Using guide numbers, the index will point you to entries in the body of the thesaurus. There you will find a list of synonyms for *fear: timidity, fearfulness, diffidence, apprehensiveness, solicitude, anxiety, misgiving, mistrust, suspicion, qualm.* From these, you can choose a word to complete the sentence:

Hamlet delays his revenge out of <u>suspicion</u> that the ghost may be an evil spirit sent to deceive him.

Choosing Synonyms

The key to getting the most out of a thesaurus is learning to choose a synonym that fits the situation.

- Review the entire list of synonyms in an entry before making a decision.
- Choose the best word by considering these factors:
  1. Which word feels like it fits best in the context of your sentence?
  2. What are the connotations of these various words?
  3. What are the fine distinctions in meaning and emphasis between these words?
  4. What level of diction do these words belong to, and what level is appropriate for your piece of writing?

NOTE: Most word-processing programs have a built-in thesaurus. Use this tool to answer any vocabulary questions that you have when drafting and revising online.

Using Word Parts

Another useful tool for building your reading vocabulary is the ability to divide unfamiliar words into their basic parts so that you can examine each—namely, the *prefix, suffix,* and *base*. For this technique to work, you need to know the meanings of commonly used word parts and how they work together. Notice the examples below.

Prefixes ■ A **prefix** is a word part added to the beginning of a base word:

Prefix	Base Word	New Word
a (not)	**typical**	**atypical**
di (two)	**oxide**	**dioxide**
meta (beyond)	**physical**	**metaphysical**

The prefix *a* means "not." Knowing this meaning tells you that *atypical* means "not typical."

Suffixes ■ A **suffix** is a word part added to the ending of a base word:

Base Word	Suffix	New Word
assist	**ant** (one who)	**assistant**
duck	**ling** (small)	**duckling**

The suffix *ant* means "the performer or agent of a task." Knowing this meaning tells you that *assistant* means "someone who assists."

Roots ■ A **root** is a base upon which a word is built:

Root	Meaning	Word
biblio	(book)	**bibliophile**
phile	(love)	

Knowing that the root *biblio* means "book" and *phile* means "love" tells you that *bibliophile* means "someone who loves books."

INSIDE INFO

You already know and use many common prefixes, suffixes, and roots every day. To increase your speaking and writing vocabulary, study the meanings of those prefixes, suffixes, and roots that are not familiar to you. The following pages contain nearly 500 of them! Scan a page until you come to a word part that is "new." Learn its meanings and at least one of the example words listed. Then apply your knowledge as you encounter new words in your textbooks, in your favorite magazines, and on the Internet.

Prefixes

Prefixes are those "word parts" that come before the root words (*pre* = "before"). Depending upon its meaning, a prefix changes the intent, or sense, of the base word. As a skilled reader, you will want to know the meanings of the prefixes you will come across most often.

a, an [not, without] amoral (without a sense of moral responsibility), atypical, atom (not cutable), apathy (without feeling), anesthesia (without sensation)

ab, abs, a [from, away] abnormal, abduct, absent, avert (turn away)

acro [high] acropolis (high city), acrobat, acronym, acrophobia (fear of height)

ambi, amb [both, around] ambidextrous (skilled with both hands), ambiguous, amble, ambient (on all sides)

amphi [both] amphibious (living on both land and water), amphitheater

ante [before] antedate, antebellum, anteroom, antecedent (happening before)

anti, ant [against] anticommunist, antidote, anticlimax, antacid

be [on, away] bedeck, belabor, bequest, bestow, beloved

bene, bon [well] benefit, benefactor, benevolent, benediction, bonanza, bonus

bi, bis, bin [both, double, twice] bicycle, biweekly, bilateral, biscuit, binoculars

by [side, close, near] bypass, bystander, by-product, bylaw, byline

cata [down, against] catalog, catastrophe, catapult, cataclysm

cerebro [brain] cerebrospinal, cerebellum, cerebrum, cerebral

circ, circum [around] circular, circumspect, circumference, circumnavigate

co, con, col, com [together, with] copilot, conspire, collect, compose

contra, counter [against] controversy, contradict, counterpart, contraindicate

de [from, down] demote, depress, degrade, deject, deprive, devoid, deviate

deca [ten] decade, decathlon, decapod (ten feet), decagon, decagram

di [two, twice] divide, dilemma, dilute, ditto, dioxide, dipole, digraph, diplopia (vision disorder, seeing two images)

dia [through, between] diameter, diagonal, diagram, dialogue (speech between people)

dis, dif [apart, away, reverse] distinguish, dismiss, distort, diffuse

dys [badly, ill] dyspepsia (digesting badly), dystrophy, dysentery, dysfunction

em, en [in, into] embrace, enslave

epi [upon] epidermis (upon the skin, outer layer of skin), epitaph, epithet

eu [well] eulogize (speak well of, praise), euphony, eugenics, euphoria

ex, e, ec, ef [out] ex-mayor, expel (drive out), exorcism, eject, eccentric (out of the center position), efflux

extra, extro [beyond, outside] extraordinary (beyond the ordinary), extrovert, extracurricular, extraneous

for [away, off] forswear (to renounce an oath), forgo, forlorn

fore [before in time] forecast, foretell (to tell beforehand), foreshadow

hemi, demi, semi [half] hemisphere, demitasse, semicircle (half of a circle)

hex [six] hexameter, hexagon

homo [man] Homo sapiens, homicide (killing man)

hyper [over, above] hypersensitive (overly sensitive), hyperactive

hypo [under] hypodermic (under the skin), hypothesis

il, ir, in, im [not] illegal, illegible, irregular, incorrect, immoral

in, il, im [into] inject, inside, illuminate, illustrate, impose, implant, imprison

infra [beneath] infrared, infrastructure

inter [between] intercollegiate, interfere, intervene, interrupt (break between)

intra [within] intramural, intravenous (within the veins), intracellular

intro [into, inward] introduce, introvert (turn inward), introspection

macro [large, excessive] macrodent (having large teeth), macrocosm

mal [badly, poorly] malady, maladjusted, malnutrition, malfunction

meta [beyond, after, with] metaphor, metamorphosis, metaphysical

mis [incorrect, bad] misuse, misprint

miso [hate] misanthrope, misogynist

mono [one] monoplane, monochrome, monotone, monocle

multi [many] multiply, multiform

neo [new] neopaganism, neoclassic, neologism, neophyte

non [not] nontaxable (not taxed), nontoxic, nonexistent, nonsense

ob, of, op, oc [toward, against] obstruct, offend, oppose, occur

oct [eight] octagon, octave, octopus, octane, octameter

paleo [ancient] paleoanthropology (pertaining to ancient man), paleontology (study of ancient life-forms)

para [beside, almost] parasite (one who eats beside or at the table of another), paraphrase, paramedic, parallel, parody

penta [five] pentagon (figure or building having five angles or sides), pentameter, pentathlon

per [throughout, completely] pervert (completely turn wrong, corrupt), perfect, perceive, permanent, persuade

peri [around] perimeter (measurement around an area), periphery, periscope, pericardium, period

poly [many] polygon (figure having many angles or sides), polygamy, polyglot, polychrome

post [after] postpone, postwar, postscript, posterity

pre [before] prewar, preview, precede, prevent, premonition

pro [forward, in favor of] project (throw forward), progress, promote, prohibition

pseudo [false] pseudonym (false or assumed name), pseudoscientific, pseudopodia

quad [four] quadruple (four times as much), quadriplegic, quadratic, quadrant

quint [five] quintuplet, quintuple, quintet, quintile

re [back, again] reclaim, revive, revoke, rejuvenate, retard, reject, return

retro [backward] retrospective (looking backward), retroactive, retrorocket

se [aside] seduce (lead aside), secede, secrete, segregate

self [by oneself] self-determination, self-employed, self-service, selfish

sesqui [one and a half] sesquicentennial (one and one-half centuries)

sex, sest [six] sexagenarian (sixty years old), sexennial, sextant, sextuplet, sestet

sub [under] submerge (put under), submarine, subhuman, substitute, subsoil

suf, sug, sup, sus [from under] suffer, sufficient, suggest, support, suspect, suspend

super, supr [above, over, more] supervise, superman, supernatural, supreme

syn, sym, sys, syl [with, together] synthesis, synchronize (time together), synonym, sympathy, symphony, system, syllable

trans, tra [across, beyond] transoceanic, transmit (send across), transfusion, tradition, transform

tri [three] tricycle, triangle, tripod, tristate

ultra [beyond, exceedingly] ultramodern, ultraviolet, ultraconservative

un [not, release] unfair, unnatural, unbutton

under [beneath] underground, underlying

uni [one] unicycle, uniform, unify, universe, unique (one of a kind)

vice [in place of] vice president, vice admiral, viceroy

Numerical Prefixes

Prefix	Symbol	Multiples and Submultiples	Equivalent	Prefix	Symbol	Multiples and Submultiples	Equivalent
tera	T	10^{12}	trillionfold	centi	c	10^{-2}	hundredth part
giga	G	10^{9}	billionfold	milli	m	10^{-3}	thousandth part
mega	M	10^{6}	millionfold	micro	u	10^{-6}	millionth part
kilo	k	10^{3}	thousandfold	nano	n	10^{-9}	billionth part
hecto	h	10^{2}	hundredfold	pico	p	10^{-12}	trillionth part
deka	da	10	tenfold	femto	f	10^{-15}	quadrillionth part
deci	d	10^{-1}	tenth part	atto	a	10^{-18}	quintillionth part

Suffixes

Suffixes come at the end of words. Very often a suffix will tell you what kind of word it is part of (noun, adverb, adjective, and so on). For example, words ending in *-dom* are usually nouns, words ending in *-ly* are usually adverbs, and words ending in *-able* are usually adjectives.

able, ible [able, can do] capable, agreeable, edible, visible (can be seen)

ade [result of action] blockade (the result of a blocking action), lemonade

age [act of, state of, collection of] salvage (act of saving), storage, forage

al [relating to] sensual, gradual, manual, natural (relating to nature)

algia [pain] neuralgia (nerve pain)

an, ian [native of, relating to] African, Canadian

ance, ancy [action, process, state] assistance, allowance, defiance, truancy

ant [agent, one who] assistant, servant

ary, ery, ory [relating to, quality, place where] dictionary, bravery, dormitory

ate [cause, make] liquidate, segregate

cian [having a certain skill or art] musician, beautician, magician, physician

cule, ling [very small] molecule, ridicule, duckling, sapling

cy [action, function] hesitancy, prophecy, normalcy (function in a normal way)

dom [quality, realm, office] freedom, kingdom, wisdom (quality of being wise)

ee [one who receives the action] employee, nominee (one who is nominated), refugee

en [made of, make] silken, frozen, oaken (made of oak), wooden, lighten

ence, ency [action, state of, quality] difference, conference, urgency

er, or [one who, that which] baker, miller, teacher, racer, amplifier, doctor

escent [in the process of] adolescent (in the process of becoming an adult), obsolescent

ese [a native of, the language of] Japanese, Vietnamese

esis, osis [action, process, condition] genesis, hypnosis, neurosis, osmosis

ess [female] actress, goddess, lioness

et, ette [a small one, group] midget, octet, baronet, majorette

fic [making, causing] scientific, specific

ful [full of] frightful, careful, helpful

fy [make] fortify, simplify, amplify

hood [order, condition, quality] womanhood, manhood, brotherhood

ic [nature of, like] metallic, heroic, poetic

ice [condition, state, quality] justice, malice

id, ide [a thing connected with or belonging to] fluid, fluoride

ile [relating to, suited for, capable of] juvenile, senile (related to being old), missile

ine [nature of] feminine, genuine, medicine

ion, sion, tion [act of, state of, result of] contagion, aversion, infection

ish [origin, nature, resembling] foolish, Irish, clownish (resembling a clown)

ism [system, manner, condition, characteristic] alcoholism, heroism, Communism

ist [one who, that which] violinist, artist, dentist

ite [nature of, quality of, mineral product] Israelite, dynamite, graphite, sulfite

ity, ty [state of, quality] captivity, clarity

ive [causing, making] abusive, exhaustive

ize [make] emphasize, publicize, idolize

less [without] baseless, careless (without care), artless, fearless, helpless

ly [like, manner of] carelessly, fearlessly, hopelessly, shamelessly

ment [act of, state of, result] contentment, amendment (state of amending)

ness [state of] carelessness, restlessness

oid [resembling] asteroid, spheroid, tabloid

ology [study, science, theory] biology, anthropology, geology, neurology

ous [full of, having] gracious, nervous, spacious, vivacious (full of life)

ship [office, state, quality, skill] friendship, authorship, dictatorship

some [like, apt, tending to] lonesome, threesome, gruesome

tude [state of, condition of] gratitude, aptitude, multitude (condition of being many)

ure [state of, act, process, rank] culture, literature, rupture (state of being broken)

ward [in the direction of] eastward, forward, backward

y [inclined to, tend to] cheery, crafty, faulty

Roots

Knowing the root of a difficult word can go a long way toward helping you figure out its meaning, even without a dictionary. Because improving your vocabulary is so important to success in all your classes (and beyond school), learning the following roots will be very valuable.

acer, acid, acri [bitter, sour, sharp] acerbic, acidity (sourness), acrid, acrimony

acu [sharp] acute, acupuncture

ag, agi, ig, act [do, move, go] agent (doer), agenda (things to do), agitate, navigate (move by sea), ambiguous (going both ways), action

ali, allo, alter [other] alias (a person's other name), alibi, alien (from another place), alloy, alter (change to another form)

altus [high, deep] altimeter (a device for measuring heights), altitude

am, amor [love, liking] amiable, amorous, enamored

anni, annu, enni [year] anniversary, annually (yearly), centennial (occurring once in 100 years)

anthrop [man] misanthrope (hater of mankind), anthropology (study of mankind), philanthropy (love of mankind)

antico [old] antique, antiquated, antiquity

arch [chief, first, rule] archangel (chief angel), architect (chief worker), archaic (first; very early), monarchy (rule by one person), matriarchy (rule by the mother)

aster, astr [star] aster (star flower), asterisk, asteroid, astronomy (star law), astronaut (star traveler, space traveler)

aud, aus [hear, listen] audible (can be heard), auditorium, audio, audition, auditory, audience, ausculate

aug, auc [increase] augur, augment (add to; increase), auction

auto, aut [self] automobile (self-moving vehicle), autograph (self-writing), automatic (self-acting), autobiography, author

belli [war] rebellion, belligerent (warlike or hostile), bellicose

biblio [book] Bible, bibliography (writing, list of books), bibliomania (craze for books), bibliophile (book lover)

bio [life] biology (study of life), biopsy (cutting living tissue for examination), biography

brev [short] abbreviate, brevity, brief

cad, cas [to fall] cadaver, cadence, caducous (falling off), cascade

calor [heat] calorie (a unit of heat), calorify (to make hot), caloric

cap, cip, cept [take] capable, capacity, capture, reciprocate, accept, except, forceps

capit, capt [head] decapitate (to remove the head from), capital, captain, caption

carn [flesh] carnivorous (flesh-eating), incarnate, reincarnation

caus, caut [burn, heat] caustic, cauldron, cauterize (to make hot, burn)

cause, cuse, cus [cause, motive] because, excuse (to attempt to remove the blame or cause), accusation

ced, ceed, cede, cess [move, yield, go, surrender] procedure, proceed (move forward), cede (yield), concede, intercede, precede, recede, secede (move aside from), success

centri [center] concentric, centrifugal, centripetal, eccentric (out of center)

chrom [color] chrome, chromosome (color body in genetics), monochrome (one color), polychrome

chron [time] chronological (in order of time), chronometer (time-measured), chronicle (record of events in time), synchronize (make time with, set time together)

cide, cise [cut down, kill] suicide (self-killer), homicide (man, human killer), pesticide (pest killer), germicide (germ killer), insecticide, decide (cut off uncertainty), precise (cut exactly right), incision, scissors

cit [to call, start] incite, citation, cite

civ [citizen] civic (relating to a citizen), civil, civilian, civilization

clam, claim [cry out] exclamation, clamor, proclamation, reclamation, acclaim

clud, clus, claus [shut] include (to take in), conclude, recluse (one who shuts himself away from others), claustrophobia (abnormal fear of being shut up, confined)

cognosc, gnosi [know] recognize (to know again), incognito (not known), prognosis (forward knowing), diagnosis

cord, cor, cardi [heart] cordial (hearty, heartfelt), concord, discord, courage, encourage (put heart into), discourage (take heart out of), core, coronary, cardiac

corp [body] corporation (a legal body), corpse, corpulent

cosm [universe, world] cosmos (the universe), cosmic, cosmonaut, microcosm, cosmopolitan (world citizen), macrocosm

crat, cracy [rule, strength] democratic, autocracy

crea [create] creature (anything created), recreation, creation, creator

cred [believe] creed (statement of beliefs), credo (a creed), credence (belief), credit (belief, trust), credulous (believing too readily, easily deceived), incredible

cresc, cret, crease, cru [rise, grow] crescendo (growing in loudness or intensity), concrete (grown together, solidified), increase, decrease, accrue (to grow)

crit [separate, choose] critical, criterion (that which is used in choosing), hypocrite

cur, curs [run] current (running or flowing), concurrent, concur (run together, agree), incur (run into), recur, occur, courier, precursor (forerunner), cursive

cura [care] curator, curative, manicure (caring for the hands)

cycl, cyclo [wheel, circular] Cyclops (a mythical giant with one eye in the middle of his forehead), unicycle, bicycle, cyclone (a wind blowing circularly, a tornado)

deca [ten] decade, decalogue, decathlon

dem [people] democracy (people-rule), demography (vital statistics of the people: deaths, births, etc.), epidemic (on or among the people)

dent, dont [tooth] dental (relating to teeth), denture, dentifrice, orthodontist

derm [skin] hypodermic (injected under the skin), dermatology (skin study), epidermis (outer layer of skin), taxidermy (arranging skin, mounting animals)

dict [say, speak] diction (how one speaks, what one says), dictionary, dictate, dictator, dictaphone, dictatorial, edict, predict, verdict, contradict, benediction

doc [teach] indoctrinate, document, doctrine

domin [master] dominate, dominion, predominant, domain

don [give] donate, condone

dorm [sleep] dormant, dormitory

dox [opinion, praise] doxy (belief, creed, or opinion), paradox (contradictory), orthodox (having the correct, commonly accepted opinion), heterodox (differing opinion)

drome [run, step] syndrome (run together, group of symptoms), hippodrome (a place where horses run)

duc, duct [lead] induce (lead into, persuade), seduce (lead aside), produce, reduce, subdue, aquaduct (water leader or channel), viaduct, conduct, conduit, duke

dura [hard, lasting] durable, duration, endurance

dynam [power] dynamo (power producer), dynamic, dynamite, hydrodynamics

endo [within] endoral (within the mouth), endocardial (within the heart), endoskeletal

equi [equal] equinox, equilibrium

erg [work] energy, erg (unit of work), allergy, ergophobia (morbid fear of work), ergometer, ergograph

fac, fact, fic, fect [do, make] factory (place where workmen make goods of various kinds), fact (a thing done), manufacture, amplification, confection

fall, fals [deceive] fallacy, falsify

fer [bear, carry] ferry (carry by water), coniferous (bearing cones, as a pine tree), fertile (bearing richly), defer, infer, refer

fid, fide, feder [faith, trust] confidante, Fido, fidelity, confident, infidelity, infidel, federal, confederacy

fila, fili [thread] filament (a threadlike conductor heated by electrical current), filter, filet, filibuster, filigree

fin [end, ended, finished] final, finite, finish, confine, fine, refine, define, finale

fix [fix] fix, fixation (the state of being attached), fixture, affix, prefix, suffix

flex, flect [bend] flex (bend), reflex (bending back), flexible, flexor (muscle for bending), inflexibility, reflect, deflect

flu, fluc, fluv [flowing] influence (to flow in), fluid, flue, flush, fluently, fluctuate (to wave in an unsteady motion)

form [form, shape] form, uniform, conform, deform, reform, perform, formative, formation, formal, formula

fort, forc [strong] fort, fortress (a strong point), fortify (make strong), forte (one's strong point), fortitude

fract, frag [break] fracture (a break), infraction, fragile (easy to break), fraction (result of breaking a whole into equal parts), refract (to break or bend)

gam [marriage] bigamy (two marriages), monogamy, polygamy (many spouses or marriages)

gastr(o) [stomach] gastric, gastronomic, gastritis (inflammation of the stomach)

gen [birth, race, produce] genesis (birth, beginning), genetics (study of heredity), eugenics (well-born), genealogy (lineage by race, stock), generate, genetic

geo [earth] geometry (earth measurement), geography (earth writing), geocentric (earth-centered), geology

germ [vital part] germination (to grow), germ (seed, living substance, as the germ of an idea), germane

gest [carry, bear] gestation, congestive (causing clogging), congest (bear together, clog)

gloss, glot [tongue] glossary, polyglot (many tongues), epiglottis

glu, glo [lump, bond, glue] glue, agglutinate (make to hold in a bond), conglomerate (bond together)

grad, gress [step, go] grade (step, degree), gradual (step-by-step), graduate (make all the steps, finish a course), graduated (in steps or degrees), progress

graph, gram [write, written] graph, graphic (written, vivid), autograph (self-writing, signature), photography (light-writing), graphite (carbon used for writing), phonograph (sound-writing), bibliography, telegram, diagram

grat [pleasing] congratulate (express pleasure over success), gratuity (mark of favor, a tip), grateful, ingrate (not thankful)

grav [heavy, weighty] grave, gravity, aggravate, gravitate

greg [herd, group, crowd] gregarian (belonging to a herd), congregation (a group functioning together), segregate (tending to group aside or apart)

helio [sun] heliograph (an instrument for using the sun's rays to send signals), heliotrope (a plant that turns to the sun)

hema, hemo [blood] hemorrhage (an outpouring or flowing of blood), hemoglobin, hemophilia

here, hes [stick] adhere, cohere, cohesion

hetero [different] heterogeneous (different in birth), heterosexual (with interest in the opposite sex)

homo [same] homogeneous (of same birth or kind), homonym (word with same name or pronunciation as another), homogenize

hum, human [earth, ground, man] humus, exhume (to take out of the ground), humane (compassion for other humans)

hydr, hydra, hydro [water] dehydrate (take water out of, dry), hydrant (water faucet), hydraulic, hydraulics, hydrogen, hydrophobia (fear of water)

hypn [sleep] hypnosis, Hypnos (god of sleep), hypnotherapy

ignis [fire] ignite, igneous, ignition

ject [throw] deject, inject, project (throw forward), eject, object

join, junct [join] adjoining, enjoin (to lay an order upon, to command), juncture, conjunction, injunction, conjunction

juven [young] juvenile, rejuvenate (to make young again)

lau, lav, lot, lut [wash] launder, lavatory, lotion, ablution (a washing away), dilute (to make a liquid thinner and weaker)

leg [law] legal (lawful, according to law), legislate (to enact a law), legislature, legitimize (make legal)

levi [light] alleviate (lighten a load), levitate, levity (light conversation, humor)

liber, liver [free] liberty (freedom), liberal, liberalize (to make more free), deliverance

liter [letters] literary (concerned with books and writing), literature, literal, alliteration, obliterate

loc, loco [place] locality, locale, location, allocate (to assign, to place), relocate (to put back into place), locomotion (act of moving from place to place)

log, logo, ology [word, study, speech] catalog, prologue, dialogue, logogram (a symbol representing a word), zoology (animal study), psychology (mind study)

loqu, locut [talk, speak] eloquent (speaking well and forcefully), loquacious (talkative), colloquial (talking together; conversational or informal), soliloquy, locution

luc, lum, lus, lun [light] translucent (letting light come through), lumen (a unit of light), luminary (a heavenly body; someone who shines in his profession), luster (sparkle, shine), Luna (the moon goddess)

magn [great] magnify (make great, enlarge), magnificent, magnanimous (great of mind or spirit), magnate, magnitude, magnum

man [hand] manual, manage, manufacture, manacle, manicure, manifest, maneuver, emancipate

mand [command] mandatory (commanded), remand (order back), mandate

mania [madness] mania (insanity, craze), monomania (mania on one idea), kleptomania, pyromania (insane tendency to set fires), maniac

mar, mari, mer [sea, pool] marine (a sailor serving on shipboard), marsh (wetland, swamp), maritime (relating to the sea and navigation), mermaid (fabled marine creature, half fish)

matri [mother] matrimony (state of wedlock), matriarchate (rulership of women), maternal (relating to the mother), matron

medi [half, middle, between, halfway] mediate (come between, intervene), medieval (pertaining to the Middle Ages), mediterranean (lying between lands), mediocre, medium

mega [great] megaphone (great sound), megalopolis (great city, an extensive urban area including a number of cities), megacycle (a million cycles), megaton

mem [remember] memo (a reminder, a note), commemoration (the act of remembering by a memorial or ceremony), memento, memoir, memorable

meter [measure] meter (a metric measure), voltameter (instrument to measure volts), barometer, thermometer

micro [small] microscope, microfilm, microcard, microwave, micrometer (device for measuring small distances), omicron, micron (a millionth of a meter), microbe (small living thing)

migra [wander] migrate (to wander), emigrant (one who leaves a country), immigrate (to come into the land to settle)

mit, miss [send] emit (send out, give off), remit (send back, as money due), submit, admit, commit, permit, transmit (send across), omit, intermittent (sending between, at intervals), mission, missile

mob, mot, mov [move] mobile (capable of moving), motionless (without motion), motor, emotional (moved strongly by feelings), motivate, promotion, movement, demote

mon [warn, remind] monitor, monument (a reminder or memorial of a person or event), premonition (forewarning), admonish (warn)

mor, mort [mortal, death] mortal (causing death or destined for death), immortal (not subject to death), mortality (rate of death), mortician (one who prepares the dead for burial), mortuary (place for the dead, a morgue)

morph [form] amorphous (with no form, shapeless), metamorphosis (a change of form, as a caterpillar into a butterfly), morphology

multi [many, much] multifold (folded many times), multilinguist (one who speaks many languages), multiped (an organism with many feet), multiply

nat, nasc [to be born, to spring forth] innate (inborn), natal, native, nativity, renascence (a rebirth, a revival)

neur [nerve] neuritis (inflammation of a nerve), neuropathic (having a nerve disease), neurologist (one who practices neurology), neural, neurosis, neurotic

nom [law, order] autonomy (self-law, self-government), astronomy, gastronomy (stomach law, art of good eating), economy

nomen, nomin [name] nomenclature, nominate (name someone for an office)

nov [new] novel (new, strange, not formerly known), renovate (to make like new again), novice, nova, innovate

nox, noc [night] nocturnal, equinox (equal nights), noctilucent (shining by night)

numer [number] numeral (a figure expressing a number), numeration (act of counting), enumerate (count out, one by one), innumerable

omni [all, every] omnipotent (all-powerful), omniscient (all-knowing), omnipresent (present everywhere), omnivorous

onym [name] anonymous (without name), pseudonym (false name), antonym (against name, word of opposite meaning), synonym

oper [work] operate (to labor, function), cooperate (work together), opus (a musical composition or work)

ortho [straight, correct] orthodox (of the correct or accepted opinion), orthodontist (tooth straightener), orthopedic (originally pertaining to straightening a child), unorthodox

pac [peace] pacifist (one for peace only, opposed to war), pacify (make peace, quiet), Pacific Ocean (peaceful ocean)

pan [all] Pan-American, panacea (cure-all), pandemonium (place of all the demons, wild disorder), pantheon (place of all the gods in mythology)

pater, patr [father] paternity (fatherhood, responsibility, etc.), patriarch (head of the tribe or family), patriot, patron (a wealthy person who supports, as would a father)

path, pathy [feeling, suffering] pathos (feeling of pity, sorrow), sympathy, antipathy (against feeling), apathy (without feeling), empathy (feeling or identifying with another), telepathy (far feeling, thought transference)

ped, pod [foot] pedal (lever for a foot), impede (get the feet in a trap, hinder), pedestal (foot or base of a statue), pedestrian (foot traveler), centipede, tripod (three-footed support), podiatry (care of the feet), antipodes (opposite feet)

pedo [child] orthopedic, pedagogue (child leader, teacher), pediatrics (medical care of children)

pel, puls [drive, urge] compel, dispel, expel, repel, propel, pulse, impulse, pulsate, compulsory, expulsion, repulsive

pend, pens, pond [hang, weigh] pendant (a hanging object), pendulum, suspend, appendage, pensive (weighing thought)

phil [love] philosophy (love of wisdom), philanthropy, philharmonic, bibliophile, Philadelphia (city of brotherly love)

phobia [fear] claustrophobia (fear of closed spaces), acrophobia (fear of high places), aquaphobia (fear of water)

phon [sound] phonograph, phonetic (pertaining to sound), symphony (sounds with or together)

photo [light] photograph (light-writing), photoelectric, photogenic (artistically suitable for being photographed), photosynthesis (action of light on chlorophyll to make carbohydrates)

plac, plais [please] placid (calm, peaceful), placebo, placate, complacent (pleased)

plu, plur, plus [more] plural (more than one), pluralist (a person who holds more than one office), plus (indicating that something more is to be added)

pneuma, pneumon [breath] pneumatic (pertaining to air, wind, or other gases), pneumonia (disease of the lungs)

pod (see *ped*)

poli [city] metropolis (mother city, main city), police, politics, Indianapolis, megalopolis, Acropolis (high city, upper part of Athens)

pon, pos, pound [place, put] postpone (put afterward), component, opponent (one put against), proponent, expose, impose, deposit, posture (how one places oneself), position, expound, impound

pop [people] population (the number of people in an area), populous (full of people), popular

port [carry] porter (one who carries), portable, transport (carry across), report, export, import, support, transportation

portion [part, share] portion (a part, a share, as a portion of pie), proportion (the relation of one share to others)

prehend [seize] apprehend (seize a criminal), comprehend (seize with the mind), comprehensive (seizing much, extensive)

prim, prime [first] primacy (state of being first in rank), prima donna (the first lady of opera), primitive (from the earliest or first time), primary, primal, primeval

proto [first] prototype (the first model made), protocol, protagonist, protozoan

psych [mind, soul] psyche (soul, mind), psychiatry (healing of the mind), psychology, psychosis (serious mental disorder), psychotherapy (mind treatment), psychic

punct [point, dot] punctual (being exactly on time), punctuation, puncture, acupuncture

reg, recti [straighten] regiment, regular, rectify (make straight), correct, direct, rectangle

ri, ridi, risi [laughter] deride (mock, jeer at), ridicule (laughter at the expense of another, mockery), ridiculous, derision

rog, roga [ask] prerogative (asking before, privilege), interrogation (the act of questioning), derogatory

rupt [break] rupture (break), interrupt (break into), abrupt (broken off), disrupt (break apart), erupt (break out), incorruptible (unable to be broken down)

sacr, sanc, secr [sacred] sacred, sacrosanct, sanction, consecrate, desecrate

salv, salu [safe, healthy] salvation (act of being saved), salvage, salutation

sat, satis [enough] satiety (gratified to or beyond capacity), saturate, satisfy (to give pleasure to, to give as much as is needed)

sci [know] science (knowledge), conscious (knowing, aware), omniscient (knowing everything)

scope [see, watch] telescope, microscope, kaleidoscope (instrument for seeing forms), periscope, stethoscope

scrib, script [write] scribe (a writer), scribble, inscribe, describe, subscribe, prescribe, manuscript (written by hand)

sed, sess, sid [sit] sediment (that which sits or settles out of a liquid), session (a sitting), obsession (an idea that sits stubbornly in the mind), possess, preside (sit before), president, reside, subside

sen [old] senior, senator, senile (old, showing the weakness of old age)

sent, sens [feel] sentiment (feeling), consent, resent, dissent, sentimental (having strong feeling or emotion), sense, sensation, sensitive, sensory, dissension

sequ, secu, sue [follow] sequence (following of one thing after another), sequel, consequence, subsequent, prosecute, consecutive (following in order), second (following first), ensue, pursue

serv [save, serve] servant, subservient, servitude, preserve, conserve, reservation, service, conservation, observe, deserve

sign, signi [sign, mark, seal] signal (a gesture or sign to call attention), signature (the mark of a person written in his own handwriting), design, insignia (distinguishing marks), significant

simil, simul [like, resembling] similar (resembling in many respects), assimilate (to make similar to), simile, simulate (pretend, put on an act to make a certain impression)

sist, sta, stit [stand] assist (to stand by with help), persist (stand firmly, unyielding, continue), circumstance, stamina (power to withstand, to endure), status (standing), state, static, stable, stationary, substitute (to stand in for another)

solus [alone] solo, soliloquy, solitaire, solitude

solv, solu [loosen] solvent (a loosener, a dissolver), solve, absolve (loosen from, free from), resolve, soluble, solution, resolution, resolute, dissolute (loosened morally)

somnus [sleep] insomnia (not being able to sleep), somnambulist (a sleepwalker)

soph [wise] sophomore (wise fool), philosophy (love of wisdom), sophisticated (world-wise)

spec, spect, spic [look] specimen (an example to look at, study), specific, spectator (one who looks), spectacle, aspect, speculate, inspect, respect, prospect, retrospective (looking backward), introspective, expect, conspicuous

sphere [ball, sphere] sphere (a planet, a ball), stratosphere (the upper portion of the atmosphere), hemisphere (half of the earth), spheroid

spir [breath] spirit (breath), conspire (breathe together, plot), inspire (breathe into), aspire (breathe toward), expire (breathe out, die), perspire, respiration

string, strict [draw tight] stringent (drawn tight, rigid), strict, restrict, constrict (draw tightly together), boa constrictor (snake that constricts its prey)

stru, struct [build] construe (build in the mind, interpret), structure, construct, instruct, obstruct, destruction, destroy

sume, sump [take, use, waste] consume (to use up), assume (to take, to use), sump pump (a pump that takes up water), presumption (to take or use before knowing all the facts)

tact, tang, tag, tig, ting [touch] tactile, contact (touch), intact (untouched, uninjured), intangible (not able to be touched), tangible, contagious (able to transmit disease by touching), contiguous, contingency

tele [far] telephone (far sound), telegraph (far writing), telegram, telescope (far look), television (far seeing), telephoto (far photography), telecast, telepathy (far feeling)

tempo [time] tempo (rate of speed), temporary, extemporaneously, contemporary (those who live at the same time), pro tem (for the time being)

ten, tin, tain [hold] tenacious (holding fast), tenant, tenure, untenable, detention, retentive, content, pertinent, continent, obstinate, contain, abstain, pertain, detain

tend, tent, tens [stretch, strain] tendency (a stretching, leaning), extend, intend, contend, pretend, superintend, tender, extent, tension (a stretching, strain), pretense

terra [earth] terrain, terrarium, territory, terrestrial

test [to bear witness] testament (a will, bearing witness to someone's wishes), detest, attest (bear witness to), testimony

the, theo [God, a god] monotheism (belief in one god), polytheism (belief in many gods), atheism, theology

therm [heat] thermometer, therm (heat unit), thermal, thermos bottle, thermostat, hypothermia (subnormal temperature)

thesis, thet [place, put] antithesis (place against), hypothesis (place under), synthesis (put together), epithet

tom [cut] atom (not cutable, smallest particle of matter), appendectomy (cutting out an appendix), tonsillectomy, dichotomy (cutting in two, a division), anatomy (cutting, dissecting to study structure)

tort, tors [twist] torture (twisting to inflict pain), retort (twist back, reply sharply), extort (twist out), distort (twist out of shape), contort, torsion (act of twisting, as a torsion bar)

tox [poison] toxic (poisonous), intoxicate, antitoxin

tract, tra [draw, pull] tractor, attract, subtract, tractable (can be handled), abstract (to draw away), subtrahend (the number to be drawn away from another)

trib [pay, bestow] tribute (to pay honor to), contribute (to give money to a cause), attribute, retribution, tributary

turbo [disturb] turbulent, disturb, turbid, turmoil

typ [print] type, prototype (first print, model), typical, typography, typewriter, typology (study of types, symbols), typify

ultima [last] ultimate, ultimatum (the final or last offer that can be made)

uni [one] unicorn (a legendary creature with one horn), unify (make into one), university, unanimous, universal

vac [empty] vacate (to make empty), vacuum (a space entirely devoid of matter), evacuate (to remove troops or people), vacation, vacant

vale, vali, valu [strength, worth] equivalent (of equal worth), valiant, validity (truth, legal strength), evaluate (find out the value), value, valor (value, worth)

ven, vent [come] convene (come together, assemble), intervene (come between), venue, convenient, avenue, circumvent (come or go around), invent, convent, venture, event, advent, prevent

ver, veri [true] very, aver (say to be true, affirm), verdict, verity (truth), verify (show to be true), verisimilitude

vert, vers [turn] avert (turn away), divert (turn aside, amuse), invert (turn over), introvert (turn inward), convertible, reverse (turn back), controversy (a turning against, a dispute), versatile (turning easily from one skill to another)

vic, vicis [change, substitute] vicarious, vicar, vicissitude

vict, vinc [conquer] victor (conqueror, winner), evict (conquer out, expel), convict (prove guilty), convince (conquer mentally, persuade), invincible (not able to be conquered)

vid, vis [see] video (television), evident, provide, providence, visible, revise, supervise (oversee), vista, visit, vision

viv, vita, vivi [alive, life] revive (make live again), survive (live beyond, outlive), vivid, vivacious (full of life), vitality, vivisection (surgery on a living animal)

voc [call] vocation (a calling), avocation (occupation not one's calling), convocation (a calling together), invocation (calling in), evoke, provoke, revoke, advocate, provocative, vocal

vol [will] malevolent, benevolent (one of goodwill), volunteer, volition

volcan, vulcan [fire] volcano (a mountain erupting fiery lava), vulcanize (to undergo volcanic heat), Vulcan (Roman god of fire)

volu [turn about, roll] voluble (easily turned about or around), voluminous (winding), convolution (a twisting or coiling)

vor [eat greedily] voracious, carnivorous (flesh-eating), herbivorous (plant-eating), omnivorous (eating everything), devour (eat greedily)

zo [animal] zoo (short for zoological garden), zoology (study of animal life), zoomorphism (attributing animal form to God), zodiac (circle of animal constellations), protozoa (one-celled animals)

INSIDE INFO

By learning two or three new word parts a day (and a word that each is used in), you will soon become a word expert. For example, by learning that *hydro* means "water," you have a good start at adding dozens of words to your vocabulary: *hydrogen, hydrofoil, hydroid, hydrolysis, hydrometer, hydrazide, hydrophobia, hydrochloride, hydrosphere, hydrokinetic, hydroponics,* etc.

Speaking Effectively

You use your speaking skills every day—occasionally to give a traditional formal speech, and more often to accomplish one of the following activities:

- Talking one-on-one with students or teachers, inside and outside the classroom
- Interviewing people to get information and ideas about a topic you're researching; or being interviewed for an internship, an assistantship, or a job
- Giving oral reports on research projects or class work
- Participating in class discussions

WHAT'S AHEAD

This chapter provides guidelines for handling any of the above-mentioned speaking activities, including a special section on adding "style" to your formal speeches.

Preparing a Speech

A speech is an opportunity for both learning and teaching. The success of this opportunity depends on how well you pay attention to the occasion, audience, and purpose. *How does your speech relate to the other activities in the class (the occasion)? How does it relate to your listeners? How does it relate to the assignment (the purpose)?* The guidelines that follow should help.

Choosing the Topic

When you may choose any topic, select one that meets the guidelines of the assignment and helps the class learn something new and interesting.

- Address the topic from a compelling angle, one that engages you and your audience.
- Develop the topic by consulting current, reliable sources of information.

Selecting the Form and Style

Students and instructors are in the classroom to explore and learn together. Make the experience worthwhile by following these guidelines:

- Keep your speech concise and to the point.
- Organize the speech so clearly that listeners get the point immediately.
- Use humor (when appropriate), insightful quotations, clarifying examples, interesting anecdotes.
- Speak honestly and sincerely.
- Show that you care about your audience by discussing real issues, finding strong support, and presenting an effective speech.

Choosing the Method of Delivery

Use the method of delivery that is appropriate for the occasion, audience, purpose, topic, and the time you have to prepare the speech.

- **Impromptu presentation:** Use this method when you have little time to prepare (effective for introductions and other brief presentations when you're thoroughly familiar with the topic).
- **Outlined speech:** Use this method when you have more time and want to shape the speech carefully (effective for reports or speeches when you want to ask for and respond to audience feedback).
- **Written speech:** Use this method when you want precision and formality (effective for reports containing complex arguments or technical information). See pages 452–454 for a model manuscript speech.

Writing the Speech

The way you gather information and organize your ideas depends primarily on the kind of speech you're giving and your method of delivery. For example, if you're giving a 5-minute impromptu speech during a meeting of students in the Amnesty International Club, you probably have no time to gather information, and only a few minutes to organize your thoughts. On the other hand, if you're giving an oral report on a research project in history class, you should have plenty of time to search for information, to write out your speech in manuscript form, and to rehearse your delivery.

The important step in writing any speech is searching for information. See pages 25–28 in the handbook. After collecting enough facts and details, organize your ideas into a speech with an introduction, a body, and a conclusion.

Planning the Introduction

The introduction establishes a tone and sets the direction of your speech by

- getting your audience's attention and introducing the topic,
- stating your central idea or purpose,
- briefly identifying the main points, and
- making your audience interested in what you have to say.

NOTE: An introduction that clearly sets out a speech's framework is particularly important in reports or presentations where your audience needs help to follow complex arguments and understand detailed, technical information.

To capture your audience's attention, use one or more of the following strategies:

- an interesting quotation,
- an amazing fact or a startling statement,
- a funny story or personal anecdote,
- an illustration or a colorful visual aid,
- a series of questions,
- a short history of the topic, or
- a strong statement demonstrating the topic's relevance to important political, social, or scientific issues.

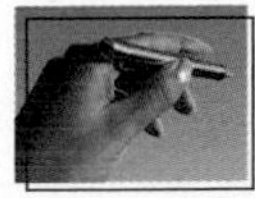

NOTE: In a project or research report, consider "hooking" your audience in the introduction by showing how the information that you will present connects to the subject your class is studying, or to projects other students are doing.

Developing the Body

The body of your speech contains the main message, including the primary arguments and supporting evidence. As a result, the way you organize your information is important. There are seven common ways of organizing information in the body of your speech.

1. **ORDER OF IMPORTANCE:** Arrange information according to its importance: least to greatest, or greatest to least.

   A speech in Life Skills outlining the choices college students must make in order to graduate in four years

2. **CHRONOLOGICAL ORDER:** Arrange information according to the order in which events take place.

   An evaluation of a two-week environmental-studies project during which you spent an hour a day at a nature preserve observing migrating geese

3. **COMPARISON/CONTRAST:** Give information about subjects by comparing them (showing similarities) and contrasting them (showing differences).

   A report to a government class comparing and contrasting Proposition 209 (the California civil rights initiative) with the current California civil rights laws

4. **CAUSE AND EFFECT:** Give information about an event, a phenomenon, or a problem by showing (1) the situation's causes and (2) its effects.

   A lab report explaining your chemistry project and its results

5. **SPATIAL:** Arrange information about subjects according to where things are in relation to each other.

   A guide's presentation to prospective freshmen on a walking tour of the campus

6. **TOPICAL:** Arrange your ideas in related groups according to themes or topics in your speech.

   A speech in art in which you role-play a famous artist, showing slides of "your" paintings and discussing recurring themes

7. **PROBLEM/SOLUTION:** Describe a problem and then present a solution to solve it.

   A report in psychology class discussing the problem of youth violence and the value of learning conflict resolution as a solution

Creating the Conclusion

A good conclusion completes the argument or thesis while it also helps your audience understand

- what they have heard,
- why it's important, and
- what they should do about it.

Rehearsing and Delivering the Speech

Good speakers understand that preparing the script for delivery, revising it as necessary, and rehearsing repeatedly are necessary steps in the speaking process. Just how you prepare the script for delivery depends on your speech. The following information should help get you started.

For an **impromptu speech**, think about your purpose and write an abbreviated outline that includes the following:

- Your opening sentence
- Two or three phrases, each of which summarizes one main point
- Your closing sentence

I. Opening Sentence
II. Phrase #1
Phrase #2
Phrase #3
III. Closing Sentence

For an **outline speech**, one that you have time to research and rehearse, think about your purpose, topic, and audience. Then outline your speech as follows:

- As opening statement in sentence form
- All your main points in sentence form
- Quotations written in full
- All supporting numbers, technical details, and sources listed
- Closing statement in sentence form
- Notes indicating visual aids you plan to use

I. Introduction
A. Point with support
B. Point (purpose or thesis)
II. Body (with 3 to 5 main points)
A. Main point with details
B. Main point with details
C. Main point with details
III. Conclusion
A. Point (restatement of thesis)
B. Point (possible call to action)

For a **written speech**, use the guidelines below and write out the speech exactly as you plan to give it (for a model, see pages 452–454):

- Pages or cards double-spaced
- Pages or cards numbered
- Abbreviations used only when you plan to say them (*FBI, YMCA,* but not *w/o*)
- Each sentence complete on a page—not running from one page to another
- All difficult words marked for pronunciation
- Script marked for interpretation (see symbols on page 450)

Rehearsing the Speech

Rehearse your speech until you're comfortable with it. Ask a classmate or friend to listen and offer feedback, or use a tape recorder or video recorder so you can hear and see yourself. Practice these techniques:

- Stand, walk to the lectern or front of the room, and face the audience with your head up and back straight.
- Speak loudly and clearly.
- Don't rush. Take your time and look at your notes (or your script) when you need to.
- Think about what you're saying so your audience hears the feeling in your voice.
- Use the symbols for interpretation (illustrated below).
- Talk with your hands, using specific gestures that help you communicate.
- Communicate with your eyes and facial expressions by looking at the audience as you speak.
- Rehearse with any audiovisual equipment, displays, or props that you plan to use during your speech.
- Conclude the speech by picking up your materials and walking to your seat. Or, if your speech is a report on a research project, be prepared to stay in front of the room to answer questions regarding your research project.

Marking for Interpretation

As you decide what changes you need to make in your speech, note them on your copy. Do the same for changes in delivery. Putting notes about delivery techniques on your paper is called "marking your copy" and involves using a set of symbols to represent voice patterns. These symbols will remind you to pause in key places during your speech or to emphasize a certain word or phrase. Here is a list of copy-marking symbols.

INFLECTION *(arrows)* .... for a rise in pitch, for a drop in pitch.

EMPHASIS *(underlining or boldface)* .... for additional drive or **force**.

COLOR *(wavy line or italic)*.................. for additional feeling or *emotion*.

PAUSE *(dash, diagonal, ellipsis)* .... for a pause—or / break . . . in the flow.

DIRECTIONS *(brackets)* .... for movement [*walk to chart*] or use of visual aids [*hold up chart*].

Using Visual Aids

While writing (or outlining) your speech, think about visual aids that would get the audience's attention and help them understand the message. For example, in a speech on outsourcing call centers, Hillary Gammons used two overheads that helped her audience listen to the speech and follow her logic: (1) arguments for outsourcing call centers and (2) arguments against outsourcing call centers. To see how Gammons used the overheads, read the notes beside the text of her speech. (See pages 452–454.)

Model Overheads

COMPANY ARGUMENTS FOR OFFSHORING CALL CENTERS

- Saves 20 to 40 percent on labor costs
- Frees resources for other business priorities
- Benefits from time-zone differences
- Employs skilled, motivated workers
- Provides added security in most cases

ARGUMENTS AGAINST OFFSHORING CALL CENTERS

- Takes away domestic jobs
- Undermines customer satisfaction and loyalty
- Reduces levels of service
- Decreases quality of staffing as market demands increase

Model Speech

"Call-Center Controversy" is a speech by student writer Hillary Gammons who presents a balanced look at the pros and cons of international outsourcing focusing on call centers. Watch how she hooks her audience by beginning with several anecdotes. The model below would be appropriate in a communications class or in a history, economics, or sociology class.

NOTE: In the speech text, the speaker included no page numbers for sources; however, in case an audience member requested the information, she kept the information in her outline (not shown here).

Call-Center Controversy

The speaker introduces the topic (with two anecdotes) and states the focus of the speech (underlined).

Eric Hendon desperately needs to change his flight itinerary due to an emergency at home, so he calls the airline customer-service number to arrange for an earlier flight. Cailin Anderson is struggling with her home-office computer software, so she calls the toll-free help desk, hoping for a quick fix. As soon as Eric and Cailin hear the voice on the other end of the phone, they know they are now facing challenges possibly as daunting as their original problems. That's because they have each been connected to a representative at a call center on the other side of the world. Eric's and Cailin's frustrating experiences are duplicated again and again as more and more companies in the United States ship certain jobs overseas. The practice of offshoring, using an international source to perform a particular task, may be beneficial for companies, but the benefits are not always passed along to the customers.

She quotes a reliable source to show the significance of the topic.

Offshoring is not always well received by domestic workers because they feel that they are losing much-needed jobs. According to *Forbes* magazine, "By 2015, experts predict that 3 million U.S. white collar jobs will be farmed out to other countries," up from several hundred thousand today. On the other hand, companies feel offshoring is beneficial because it allows them to pay better salaries to highly skilled domestic workers and use other resources to focus on more important aspects of business. Less-complicated tasks such as customer service and order taking are delegated to call centers overseas. Interestingly, Keith Dawson of *Call Center Magazine* notes that the call-center industry in the United States is one of high turnover and that more of these jobs are lost to automation than they are to offshoring. So is the controversy really centered around lost jobs, or is there more to the story? Dawson states, "For most Americans, a negative view of offshore call handling is less a measure of anger at job loss than it is anger at the company for sticking them with substandard service because they've chosen the lowest-cost provider."

The speaker uses statistics.

Although companies can enjoy a significant savings of 20 to 40 percent through overseas call centers, there can be a hidden price. Even though most workers in the call centers are well trained and educated, English is often not their native language. This creates communication difficulties for both the customer and the worker. In addition to language barriers, cultural differences also add to the confusion. Kenneth Beare of Dialogue Consulting, LLC, explains that cultural differences affect many areas of conversation including vocabulary and set phrases, degrees of formality, and literal translations. For example, in some cultures when a person says "Yes," they're really saying "I hear you," not necessarily "I agree with you." Ultimately, the challenges created by these combinations of differences can result in irritated customers and a loss of customer loyalty. Cheaper labor becomes costly when it results in lost sales. An article in *CIO* magazine entitled "Lost in Translation" tells the story of a manager at Lehman Brothers who decided to outsource the company's internal help desk to a vendor in India. He thought it would be "a pretty straightforward affair," but he didn't appreciate the complexity of the calls. Unfortunately, he discovered "service levels were abysmal" and Lehman Brothers wasn't saving money. In less than a year, the manager brought the help-desk call center back to New York.

She shares anecdotal evidence from an authority.

Despite the risks, some companies find advantages to implementing offshoring. For example, major time-zone differences sometimes allow companies to provide 24-hour service because the customer's off hours are the peak hours for international call centers. Also, workers in developing nations pay for their training in the call-center industry and are highly motivated by the opportunity of having a career. According to Outsourcing International, LLC, this allows companies to hire workers overseas who may be more skilled than their current on-site workers, at about one-fifth the cost.

India is currently the hub for offshore call centers, although the Philippines and several countries in Africa are emerging markets. Because of India's history with British rule, English is a familiar language to people living there. In addition, India's currency is presently valued at a much lower rate than that of more developed nations. Because of India's success, the country's workforce is becoming more educated. This competition may lead to higher quality services, but it will also lead to higher incomes and ultimately higher prices. Gartner Media, a provider of research and analysis of global information technology, cautions that India's supply of skilled workers is not unlimited. In the future, Indian companies may be forced to recruit increasingly less qualified people to meet the demands. Less qualified people may lead to poorer service.

Other experts are cited.

According to Gartner Media, an increase in less qualified staff jeopardizes security issues and "increases the risk of fraud and theft of confidential data." In a survey conducted by *Call Center Magazine,* Dawson states, "Three quarters of the business-to-business callers we surveyed said that they thought it was somewhat or very risky to exchange data with an offshore center." Offshore call centers were then asked what precautions and procedures were in place to insure security. Surprisingly, it was discovered that many offshore centers take greater security measures than call centers in the United States. "In other words," Dawson concludes, "despite what an American business caller thinks is the case, they [sic] appear to be more likely to suffer a data breach calling a center in Texas than they are in Manila." It seems that at least some of the offshore call-center controversy is based on perceptions, rather than on reality.

The speaker focuses on how both sides can come together.

In the new global economy, offshore appears to be here to stay, despite its challenges. Companies in developed nations need to monitor and manage the quality of the services provided by their offshore call centers. Developing nations need to provide advancement opportunities for their skilled workers, while still maintaining competitive pricing and security. Both need to consider the customer first because the customer is ultimately the driving force of the industry. Technology has created the global market, but without a satisfied customer, success is still a world away.

A Closer Look at Style

More than any other president since the 1950s, John F. Kennedy is remembered for the appealing style and tone of his speeches. By looking at sample portions of his speeches, you should get a better feel for how style and tone can help strengthen the spoken word. By using special stylistic devices (allusion, analogy, anecdote, etc.), you can improve the style and impact of your speech.

By using special appeals (democratic principle, common sense, pride, and so on), you can control the tone or feeling of what you have to say. (The type of appeal used is listed above each Kennedy speech excerpt.)

Allusion is a reference to a familiar person, place, or thing.

Appeal to the Democratic Principle

One hundred years of delay have passed since President Lincoln freed the slaves, yet their heirs, their grandsons, are not fully free (Radio and Television Address, 1963).

Analogy is a comparison of an unfamiliar idea to a simple, familiar one. The comparison is usually quite lengthy, suggesting several points of similarity. An analogy is especially useful when attempting to explain a difficult or complex idea.

Appeal to Common Sense

In our opinion the German people wish to have one united country. If the Soviet Union had lost the war, the Soviet people themselves would object to a line being drawn through Moscow and the entire country defeated in war. We wouldn't like to have a line drawn down the Mississippi River . . . (Interview, November 25, 1961).

Anecdote is a short story told to illustrate a point.

Appeal to Pride, Commitment

Frank O'Connor, the Irish writer, tells in one of his books how as a boy, he and his friends would make their way across the countryside and when they came to an orchard wall that seemed too high and too doubtful to try and too difficult to permit their voyage to continue, they took off their hats and tossed them over the wall—and then they had no choice but to follow them. This nation has tossed its cap over the wall of space, and we have no choice but to follow it. Whatever the difficulties, they will be overcome (San Antonio Address, November 21, 1963).

Antithesis is balancing or contrasting one word or idea against another, usually in the same sentence.

Appeal to Common Sense, Commitment

Mankind must put an end to war, or war will put an end to mankind (Address to the U.N., 1961).

Irony is using a word or phrase to mean the exact opposite of its literal meaning, or to show a result that is the opposite of what would be expected or appropriate, an odd coincidence.

Appeal to Common Sense

They see no harm in paying those to whom they entrust the minds of their children a smaller wage than is paid to those to whom they entrust the care of their plumbing (Vanderbilt University, 1961).

Negative definition is describing something by telling what it is *not* rather than, or in addition to, what it *is.*

Appeal for Commitment

. . . members of this organization are committed by the Charter to promote and respect human rights. Those rights are not respected when a Buddhist priest is driven from his pagoda, when a synagogue is shut down, when a Protestant church cannot open a mission, when a cardinal is forced into hiding, or when a crowded church service is bombed (United Nations, September 20, 1963).

Parallel structuring is the repeating of phrases or sentences that are similar (parallel) in meaning and structure; **repetition** is the repeating of the same word or phrase to create a sense of rhythm and emphasis.

Appeal for Commitment

Let every nation know, whether it wishes us well or ill, that we shall pay any price, bear any burden, meet any hardship, support any friend, oppose any foe, in order to assure the survival and the success of liberty (Inaugural Address, 1961).

Quotations, especially of well-known individuals, can be effective in nearly any speech.

Appeal for Emulation or Affiliation

At the inauguration, Robert Frost read a poem which began “the land was ours before we were the land's”—meaning, in part, that this new land of ours sustained us before we were a nation. And although we are now the land's—a nation of people matched to a continent—we still draw our strength and sustenance . . . from the earth (Dedication Speech, 1961).

Rhetorical question is a question posed for emphasis of a point, not for the purpose of getting an answer.

Appeal to Common Sense, Democratic Principle

“When a man's ways please the Lord,” the Scriptures tell us, “he maketh even his enemies to be at peace with him.” And is not peace, in the last analysis, basically a matter of human rights—the right to live out our lives without fear of devastation—the right to breathe air as nature provided it—the right of future generations to a healthy existence (Commencement Address, 1963)?

Conducting Interviews

The idea of the interview is simple: You talk with someone who has expert knowledge or has had important experiences with your topic. For example, for a botany paper, you might discuss the benefits of forest fires with a forest ranger or botanist. An interview can be as informal as a phone call or an e-mail message to ask a few questions, or as complex as a videotaped interview on location.

Preparing for an Interview

1. **Know the person and the subject that you will discuss.** Come to the interview informed so that you can build on what you know.
2. **Schedule the interview thoughtfully.** Set it up at the interviewee's convenience. Explain who you are, what your purpose is, the topics you'd like to cover, and how long it may take.
3. **Write out some questions ahead of time.** This will give the interview some structure and help you cover the necessary topics.
   - Review the types of questions that you can ask, including the 5 W's and H (*who? what? when? where? why?* and *how?*).
   - Think about the specific topics you want to cover in the interview and draft related questions for each topic.
   - Organize your questions in a logical order so that the interview moves smoothly from one subject to the next.
   - Supply a list of your basic questions, ahead of time, to allow the person time to plan thoughtful responses.
   - Understand open and closed questions. Closed questions ask for simple answers; open questions ask for an explanation.

     Closed: ***How did you vote on the recent budget proposal?***

     Open: **Can you describe the process the Congress went through to arrive at the current budget?**
   - Avoid slanted or loaded questions that suggest you want a specific answer.

     Slanted: ***Don't you agree that liberal politicians are spending our country into bankruptcy? Won't conservative politicians' approach to slashing social programs hurt the family?***

     Better: **What are some key differences between liberal and conservative political positions on spending?**
4. **Write the questions on the left side of the page.** Leave room for quotations, information, and impressions on the right side.
5. **Be prepared.** Take pens and paper. If you plan on taping the interview, get permission ahead of time. Take along a tape recorder or camcorder with blank tapes and extra batteries.

Doing the Interview

1. **Begin by reminding the person why you've come.** Provide whatever background information is necessary to help him or her feel comfortable and ready to focus on the specific topic.
2. **If the person gives permission, tape the interview.** However, make sure the recording equipment doesn't interfere. If you are videotaping the interview, set your camcorder on a tripod at a comfortable distance from the interviewee. If you are using a recording device, place it off to the side so that its presence isn't a distraction. Try to use a tape recorder with a counter. Then, when the interviewee makes an interesting or important point, jot down the number. Later, you'll be able to find these points quickly.
3. **Write down key information.** Even if you are using a recorder, note descriptive words for the voice, actions, and expressions of the interviewee.
4. **Listen actively.** Use body language (from nods to smiles) to show you're listening. Pay attention not only to what the person says but how she or he says it. If you don't understand something, ask politely for clarification.
5. **Be flexible.** If the person looks puzzled by a question, rephrase it or ask another. If the discussion gets off track, redirect it. Based on the interviewee's responses, ask follow-up questions that occur to you at that moment in order to dig deeper. (Don't be handcuffed by the questions you wrote out before the interview.)
6. **Be tactful.** If the person avoids a difficult question, politely rephrase it, ask for clarification, or return to it later.

INSIDE INFO

Anticipate that important points may come up late in the interview as the person develops a trust in you.

Following Up on the Interview

1. **Review all your notes and fill in responses you remember but couldn't record at the time.** If you recorded the interview, replay it and listen carefully for key points.
2. **Thank the person with a note or phone call.** Also get clarification on points or statements you still have questions about.
3. **Share the outcome of the interview.** That might be a digital recording of the interview, the report you hand in, or a copy of the speech you present or article you publish.

Multimedia Reports

The word *media* means "a channel or system of communication." A multimedia presentation—using *more* than one way to communicate—can help people absorb information better than a simple speech or essay can. By engaging multiple senses, you are more likely to hold the attention of your audience.

Multimedia presentations differ slightly from interactive reports. When you use some sort of visual (including a computer screen) to present the major points of a speech, that is a multimedia presentation. An interactive report is an electronic file that computer users access on their own. The file contains links that the viewers can explore at their own pace.

You can create a multimedia report using various kinds of software. Once you learn how the software works, use your imagination and a good plan to turn a basic report or speech into something that connects with your audience.

WHAT'S AHEAD

Follow some general guidelines to add the power of a computer to your reports.

Guidelines

Multimedia Presentation

Giving an oral report with the help of visuals and sound results in a multimedia presentation. You might use an audio recording to illustrate a point, or support your ideas with posters, photographs, charts, and other graphics. With a computer, you can move from page to page, reinforcing and clarifying information on a screen for your audience.

Writing Guidelines

PREWRITING

1. **Select a topic** that is right for your audience and appropriate for a multimedia presentation.
2. **Gather details** about your topic in the same way you would if you were writing a report or preparing a speech.

WRITING AND REVISING

3. **Design your pages.** Use an appropriate tone for your topic and your audience—businesslike for a serious topic, lighthearted for a humorous presentation, and so on. Remember, visuals should never detract from your message. They should add to or highlight important points.
4. **Create a new page** for each main idea in your outline. (See the storyboard on the facing page.) Insert separate pages for statements or quotations that need emphasis. If an idea has several parts, present them one at a time on the same page if your software allows it. Each click of the mouse should reveal a new detail.
5. **Check pages for readability and accuracy.** The words on-screen must be clear, concise, and correct. Listeners need to quickly grasp your message.
6. **Fine-tune your presentation.** Practice delivering your presentation while clicking through the multimedia pages. Present it to a trial audience (a group of friends or family). Also add sound and animation if they enhance your message.

EDITING AND PROOFREADING

7. **Prepare a final version** by checking spelling, punctuation, usage, and other mechanics. Remember: On-screen errors are glaringly obvious.

Creating a Presentation Storyboard

The storyboard below represents a plan to convert the argumentative essay "Sanctions Won't Solve Political Problems" (pages 242–243) into a computerized multimedia presentation. The boxes refer to the visual and auditory components of each screen page.

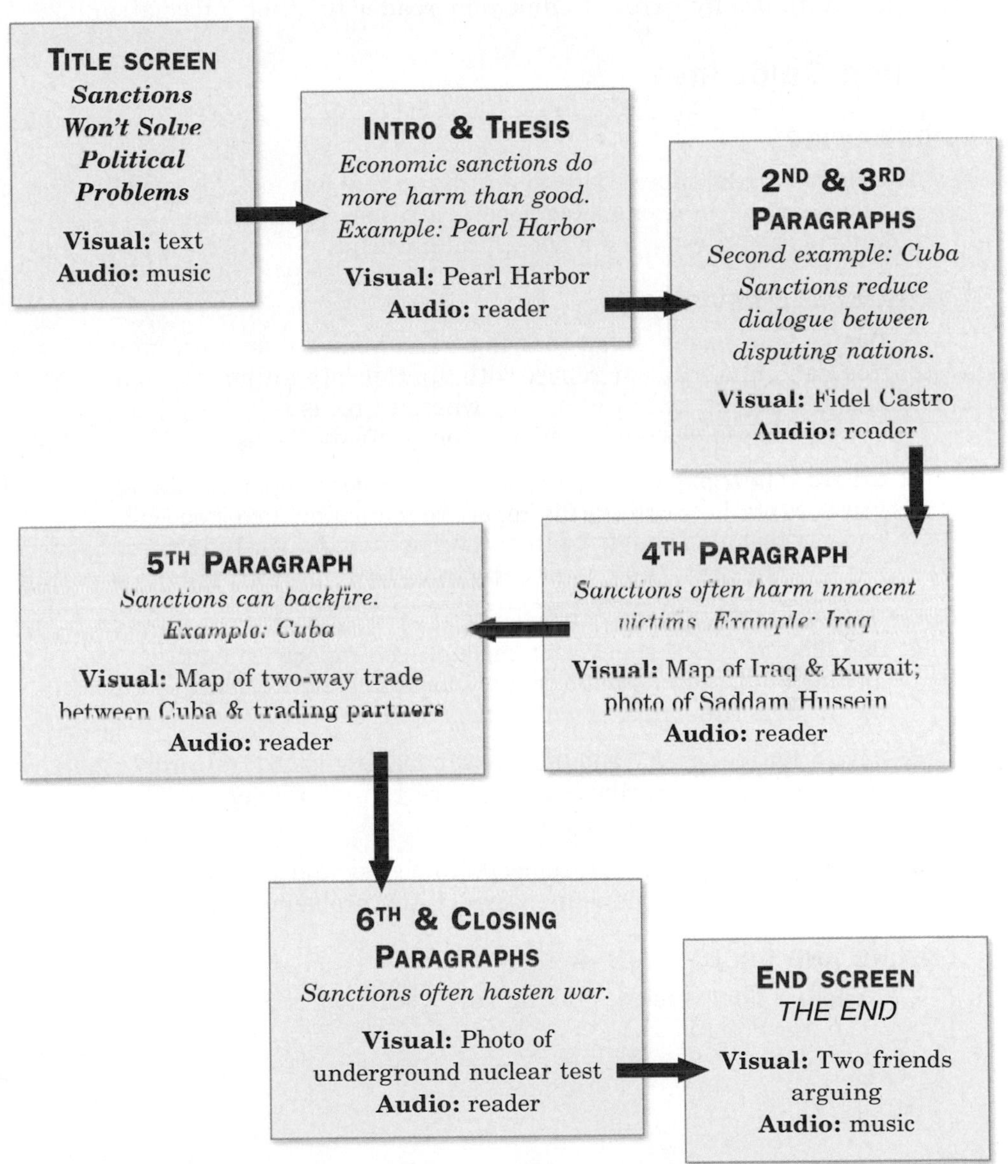

TITLE SCREEN
Sanctions Won't Solve Political Problems
Visual: text
Audio: music
INTRO & THESIS
Economic sanctions do more harm than good.
Example: Pearl Harbor
Visual: Pearl Harbor
Audio: reader
2ND & 3RD PARAGRAPHS
Second example: Cuba
Sanctions reduce dialogue between disputing nations.
Visual: Fidel Castro
Audio: reader
4TH PARAGRAPH
Sanctions often harm innocent victims. Example: Iraq
Visual: Map of Iraq & Kuwait; photo of Saddam Hussein
Audio: reader
5TH PARAGRAPH
Sanctions can backfire.
Example: Cuba
Visual: Map of two-way trade between Cuba & trading partners
Audio: reader
6TH & CLOSING PARAGRAPHS
Sanctions often hasten war.
Visual: Photo of underground nuclear test
Audio: reader
END SCREEN
THE END
Visual: Two friends arguing
Audio: music

Guidelines

Interactive Report

An interactive report allows a computer user to access your work on his or her own time, reviewing points or moving around between the most interesting features. Special software presents information in an interactive format and enables you to use hypertext to link your reader to other information.

Writing Guidelines

PREWRITING

1. **Select a topic** appropriate to an interactive format. You may also start with a completed report: a research paper, an informational essay, or a speech manuscript.

WRITING AND REVISING

2. **Design your pages.** Keep your topic and your audience in mind. You can enhance your report with appropriate animation and sound (such as a click or a beep when a link is selected), but don't let these elements distract from your message.
3. **Create a new page** for each main idea in your report. Because you will not be reading this report to your audience, you will have to include enough text for thorough coverage. If an idea has several parts, and your software allows, present the parts on-screen one at a time.
4. **Use links** to guide the reader through the report. In addition, include outside links as necessary for notes, definitions, sound recordings, film clips, or Web sites.
5. **Revise for readability and accuracy,** checking that the words on-screen are clear, concise, and correct. Your reader must grasp your message easily.
6. **Fine-tune the report.** Ask someone to access and read your work; then invite comments. Correct any problems you discover.

EDITING AND PROOFREADING

7. **Prepare a final version,** making sure your text is free of mechanical errors.

Creating an Interactive Storyboard

The storyboard below represents a plan to convert the argumentative essay on pages 242–243 into a computerized interactive report. The text for each page must be expanded, and links will allow navigation through the report and also connect the reader to additional information (boxes with dashed lines).

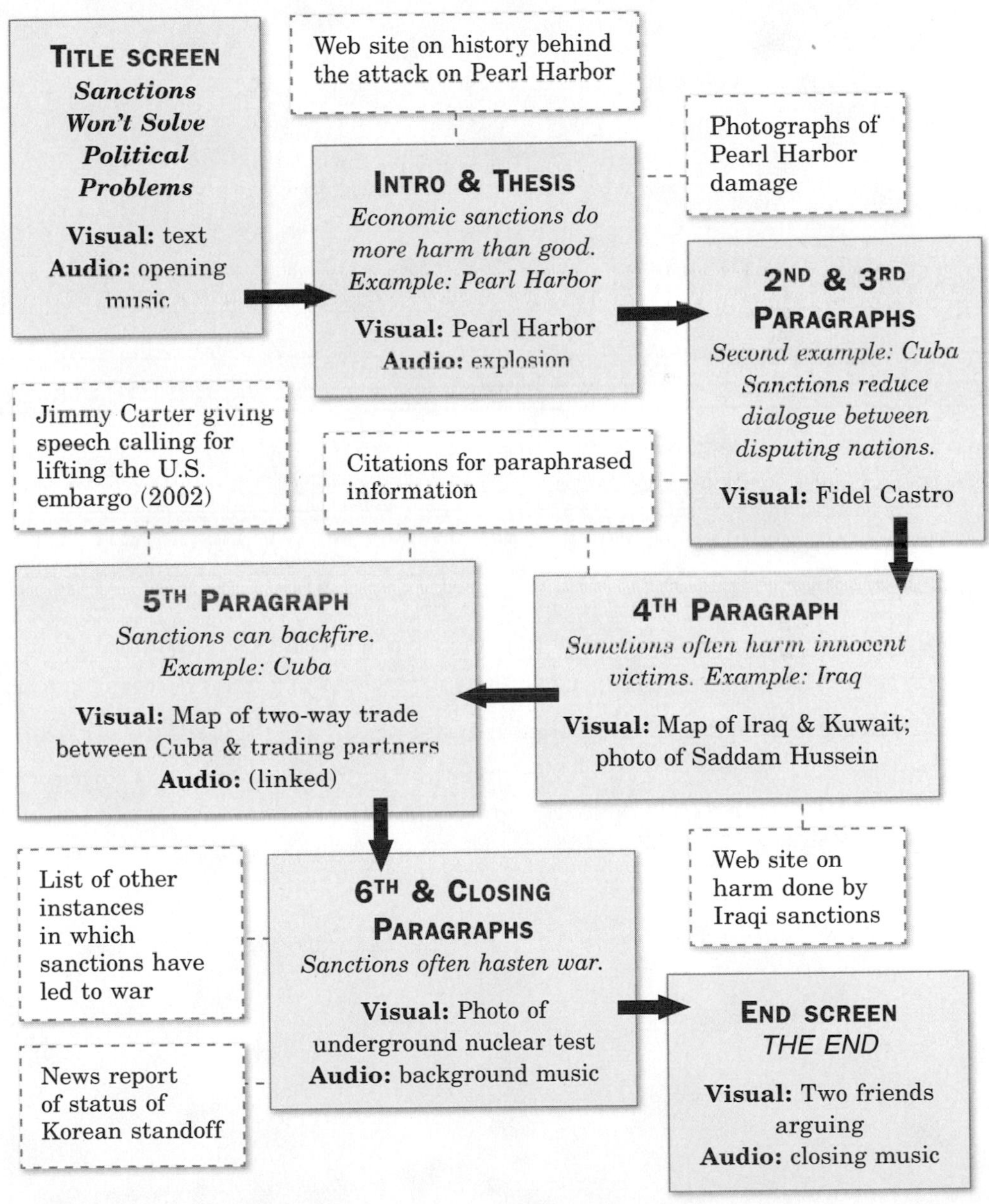
TITLE SCREEN
Sanctions Won't Solve Political Problems
Visual: text
Audio: opening music
Web site on history behind the attack on Pearl Harbor
Photographs of Pearl Harbor damage
INTRO & THESIS
Economic sanctions do more harm than good.
Example: Pearl Harbor
Visual: Pearl Harbor
Audio: explosion
2ND & 3RD PARAGRAPHS
Second example: Cuba
Sanctions reduce dialogue between disputing nations.
Visual: Fidel Castro
Jimmy Carter giving speech calling for lifting the U.S. embargo (2002)
Citations for paraphrased information
5TH PARAGRAPH
Sanctions can backfire.
Example: Cuba
Visual: Map of two-way trade between Cuba & trading partners
Audio: (linked)
4TH PARAGRAPH
Sanctions often harm innocent victims. Example: Iraq
Visual: Map of Iraq & Kuwait; photo of Saddam Hussein
Web site on harm done by Iraqi sanctions
List of other instances in which sanctions have led to war
News report of status of Korean standoff
6TH & CLOSING PARAGRAPHS
Sanctions often hasten war.
Visual: Photo of underground nuclear test
Audio: background music
END SCREEN
THE END
Visual: Two friends arguing
Audio: closing music

The Testing Center

Writing on Demand

An early rock 'n' roll song opens with this famous line: "Time is on my side, yes it is." That may have been true decades ago in the context of the song, but it certainly isn't true for you today. You have, among other things, schoolwork, after-school activities, jobs, and home commitments to deal with. To succeed, or even to survive, in today's busy world, you must manage your time effectively.

How important is time? Just think about the writing you do in school. To develop a strong analysis or research paper, you must think "long term" to break the project into smaller tasks and establish a writing timetable. Conversely, when you are involved in writing on demand (timed writings), you must think "short term," to allot appropriate, though brief chunks of time for planning, writing, and reviewing your work.

WHAT'S AHEAD

This chapter will help you with your writing on demand in class and on exams. Included is an effective strategy for analyzing a prompt, plus guidelines for planning, writing, and reviewing a response.

Analyzing a Prompt

Writing on demand starts with a prompt. You may be asked to write from your own experience or to support your point of view on a relevant topic or text; you may also be asked to read one or more documents (often short passages) and respond to them. The first step in responding to a writing prompt is to carefully analyze the prompt. *(Spend approximately 5 minutes on this step.)*

Answering the STRAP Questions

To analyze a prompt effectively, use the **STRAP** questions below. (Some prompts may not include answers for every **STRAP** question. Use your judgment to answer those questions.)

Subject: **What topic should I write about?**

Type: **What form of writing should I create (essay, letter, editorial)?**

Role: **What position should I assume as the writer (student, friend, employee, citizen)?**

Audience: **To whom am I writing (instructor, parents, classmates, employer, official)?**

Purpose: **What is the goal of my writing (discuss, persuade, respond, explain, analyze)? (See the next page.)**

Sample Prompts

Subject
Type
Role
Audience
Purpose

Swordfish populations are declining due to overfishing. Local restaurants are campaigning for people to choose other fish on the menu. As a **concerned citizen,** write a letter to the local newspaper editor asking readers to support or oppose this campaign.

Go Tell It on the Mountain is James Baldwin's account of a Southern family's move to Harlem and young John's struggle with his identity. Write an essay that compares John's feelings about white people to those of Gabriel (his stepfather) and to those of Richard (his natural father). Try to quote the characters in your response.

INSIDE INFO

Responses to prompts are evaluated on clarity, consistency, level of detail, and appropriateness. While correctness is important, evaluators do not expect perfect papers.

Understanding the Purpose of a Prompt

Key words help you determine the purpose of a prompt. Pay special attention to them when you analyze a prompt. Key words tell you how to present all the information needed to write an essay answer. Studying these terms carefully is the first step in writing worthwhile responses to prompts.

Analyze ■ To analyze is to break down a problem or situation into separate parts or relationships.

Classify ■ To classify is to place persons or things (especially animals and plants) together in a group because they share similar characteristics. Science uses a special classification or group order: phylum, class, order, family, genus, species, and variety.

Compare ■ To compare is to use examples to show how things are similar and different, placing the greater emphasis on similarities.

Define ■ To define is to give the meaning for a term. Generally, it involves identifying the class to which a term belongs and telling how it differs from other things in that class.

Describe ■ To describe is to give a detailed sketch or impression of a topic.

Discuss ■ To discuss is to review an issue from all sides. A discussion answer must be carefully organized to stay on track.

Evaluate ■ To evaluate is to make a value judgment by giving the pluses and minuses along with supporting evidence.

Explain ■ To explain is to bring out into the open, to make clear, and to analyze. This term is similar to *discuss* but places more emphasis on cause-effect relationships or step-by-step sequences.

Justify ■ To justify is to tell why a position or point of view is good or right. A justification should be mostly positive—that is, the advantages are stressed over the disadvantages.

Prove ■ To prove is to bring out the truth by giving evidence to back up a point.

Review ■ To review is to reexamine or to summarize the key characteristics or major points of the topic. Generally speaking, a review presents material in the order in which it happened or in decreasing order of importance.

State ■ To state is to present a concise statement of a position, fact, or point of view.

Summarize ■ To summarize is to present the main points of an issue in a shortened form. Details, illustrations, and examples are usually not given.

Trace ■ To trace is to present—in a step-by-step sequence—a series of facts that are somehow related. Usually the facts are presented in chronological order.

Planning a Response

After answering the **STRAP** questions, you need to plan your response. You should do two important things: Write a thesis (focus) statement and gather details to support it. *(Spend approximately 5 minutes on this step.)*

Writing a Thesis (Focus) Statement

Your thesis statement should highlight a particular feature or feeling about the topic or take a specific stand. The thesis must also address the purpose and goal of the prompt. (You may even restate part of the prompt in your thesis.)

Sample Thesis Statement

You can make a life-changing difference in your community (a particular feeling) **by volunteering to give blood** (specific topic).

Gathering Details

Use a graphic organizer such as a Venn diagram, a cluster, or a list to gather details that support your thesis statement.

Venn Diagram

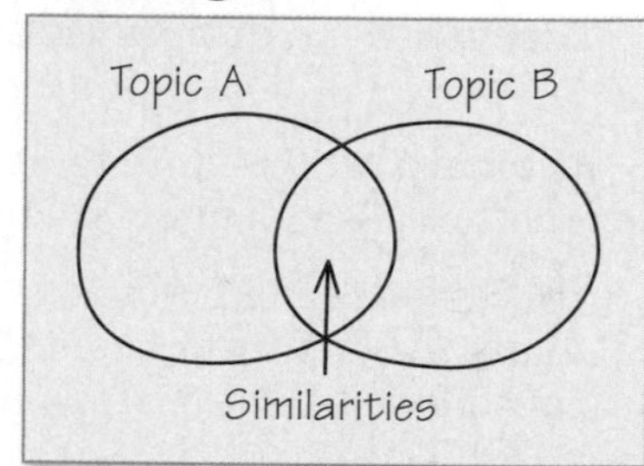

Cluster

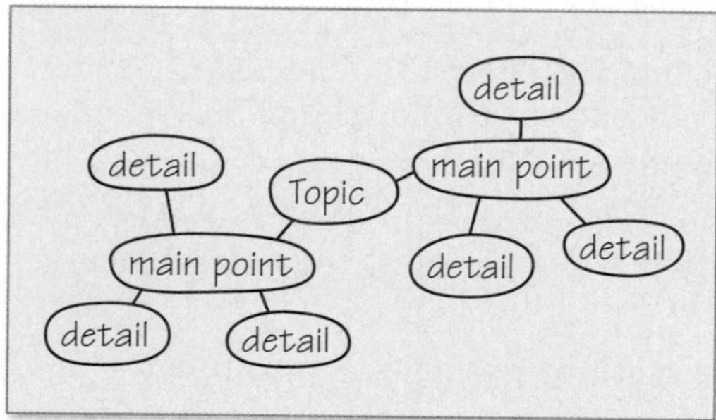

Quick List

1. First Point
   - Detail
   - Example
2. Second Point
   - Detail
   - Example

T-Bar

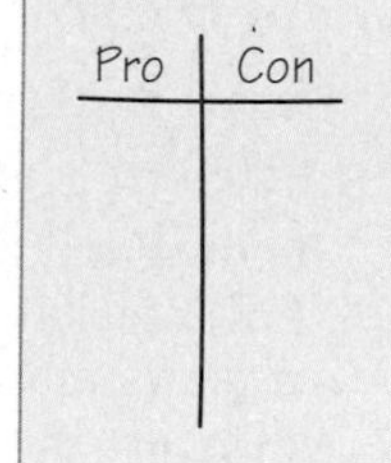

INSIDE INFO

Some prompts ask you to look at two sides of a controversial issue and write persuasively in support of one side. After considering both sides, you'll need to choose the one that is most reasonable. Your initial thinking will also prepare you to respond to the weaker side. Addressing an important objection can strengthen your argument. A *T-Bar* chart (see above) can help you quickly list details for and against your point of view.

Writing a Response

Once you have answered the **STRAP** questions and planned your response using a graphic organizer, you can begin writing. *(Spend the main portion of your time on this step.)* As you write, keep the following points in mind:

- **Stay focused.** Keep your main idea or argument in mind as you write. Your key points should clearly support your argument.
- **Answer a significant objection.** Make your argument stronger by responding to a likely objection. (Check your T-Bar chart.)
- **Summarize your argument.** In your final paragraph, summarize your main point and supporting reasons to make a final plea to the reader.

Sample Persuasive Prompt

A recent documentary about young people highlighted ways that high school students are making a difference in their communities. As a high school student, write a letter to your school newspaper that invites students to get involved in a positive way in your community.

Sample Response

Dear Editor:

The beginning paragraph draws the reader in and states the thesis.

How would you like to help save lives without spending years training to be a doctor, a nurse, or a firefighter? You can make a life-changing difference in your community by volunteering to give blood.

The first middle paragraphs express reasons for supporting the position.

While surgery, accidents, and illness can all bring someone to the point of death, a transfusion can change that outcome. In addition, modern medicine is able to separate blood into its components: platelets, plasma, stem cells, and so on. So someone who is a hemophiliac (a person whose blood lacks enough clotting potential) and a person being treated for cancer can both be helped. Stem-cell therapies are being used to treat a variety of illnesses. One donation of blood may actually save a number of lives because of the many ways blood can be used.

The process of giving blood only takes about 20 minutes. Snacks and juice are provided at the donation site. You need a valid ID and a parental permission slip if you are under 18.

Students must be at least 16 years old, weigh at least 110 pounds, and be in good health.

There are both tests and restrictions in place to keep the nation's blood supply safe. Those who have had a tattoo or a body piercing (not including ears) are not allowed to give blood for one year owing to the risk of blood infections with those activities. Those on medication or those who have traveled abroad should talk to the technicians to find out if they can safely donate blood.

The final middle paragraph cites objections and responds to them.

You may be someone who would like to give blood, but you fear the process. You may worry about getting AIDS or just hate needles. You may think you'll feel faint or be at risk until your blood supply is back to normal. The donor program has anticipated all these concerns. The needles used are new and sterile, so you won't contract AIDS or any other blood-borne disease. The needles are also extremely sharp and generally cause little discomfort. Finally, about one pint of blood is taken, so your blood supply is not drastically reduced. Just remember, your discomfort will be outweighed by the lifesaving gift you are offering.

The ending restates the writer's position and makes a call to action.

Our student council supports the annual blood drive. The donation center is in the school gym on the last Friday in October. I gave last year. It felt great to help someone I didn't even know. Get in line early to give the gift of life.

Sincerely,

Veronica Heath

Veronica Heath

Link to the Traits

Focus on three key traits when crafting a timed response: *ideas, organization,* and *voice*. Certainly *word choice, sentence fluency,* and *conventions* are also important in making your response as clear and as error free as possible. But when it comes to writing on demand, focus most of your attention on the first three traits.

Reviewing a Response

Before you begin a writing test, find out if you are allowed to make changes to your draft copy. If changes are allowed, make them neat and clear. *(Use the final 5 minutes to check your writing for clarity and conventions.)*

Revising Guide

Carefully review and revise your response using the **STRAP** questions below as a guide. Limit the types of revisions you make, since there won't be time for significant rewriting.

STRAP Questions

Subject: **Have I responded to the topic of the prompt? Do all my main points support my position?**

Type: **Have I responded in the form requested (essay, letter, editorial, article, report)?**

Role: **Have I assumed the role called for in the prompt?**

Audience: **Have I addressed the audience identified in the prompt?**

Purpose: **Does my response accomplish the goal indicated in the prompt?**

Editing Guide

After revising, be sure to read through your response one final time. Neatly correct any errors in conventions: punctuation, capitalization, spelling, and grammar. Use the following checklist as a guide.

Checklist for Editing

_____ Have I used end punctuation for every sentence?

_____ Have I capitalized all proper nouns and the first word of every sentence?

_____ Have I spelled all words correctly?

_____ Have I made sure my subjects and verbs agree?

_____ Have I used the right words *(to / too / two, there / their / they're)*?

Sample Prompts

For practice during the school year, respond to some of the prompts listed below. Make sure to complete your response within the time limit set by your instructor. (Remember to get started by using the **STRAP** questions to analyze the prompt.)

Analytical Prompts

- The First Amendment of the Constitution guarantees freedom of expression. The framers of the Constitution believed this freedom essential to a strong democracy. Write an essay that explains how freedom of expression contributes to democracy.
- Cell phones provide an incredible amount of convenience, but they cause problems, too. People who use their phones in inappropriate settings can cause problems. Write a set of guidelines for the safe and respectful use of cell phones.
- According to Mark Twain, "We find not much in ourselves to admire; we are always privately wanting to be like somebody else. If everybody was satisfied with himself there would be no heroes." Write a letter to Twain explaining your own definition of a hero, including examples of people you consider heroic.

Persuasive Prompts

- You have learned that your town is planning to use 10 acres of a 100-acre city park to build affordable housing for low-income families. Write an editorial supporting or opposing the plan.
- As a class project, your English instructor wants to view and analyze a current movie. In preparation for this unit, she would like students to recommend a movie to study. In a memo or an e-mail message, convince your instructor to use the movie of your choice.

Literary Prompts

- A focal point of literary analysis is an author's use of symbols in the development of a piece of literature. Write a brief essay, considering the significance of one or two symbols in a short story or novel that you have recently read.
- Historical biographical criticism views a literary work as a reflection of the author's life in the life of one or more of the characters. Explore the relationship of an author with one or more of the characters in a novel of your own choosing.

Answering Document-Based Questions

In one of your classes, perhaps a history class, you may be asked to respond to a document-based question (DBQ), often as part of an exam. A DBQ requires that you analyze a series of related documents that may include excerpts from books, magazines, Web pages, diaries, or other text sources. Visual documents, such as photographs, maps, editorial cartoons, tables, graphs, or time lines, may also be included.

In most cases, a DBQ asks you to write an essay, drawing information from the documents as well as from material you have previously learned. Sometimes you may be asked to glean information from one or more documents and present it in a different form, perhaps as a graph or a table. In either situation, you must work quickly and accurately because time is not on your side: You may have no more than 60 minutes to form your response.

WHAT'S AHEAD

This chapter will help you respond to document-based questions. It offers responding tips plus a sample DBQ with corresponding documents and response essay.

Responding Tips

A document-based question asks you to read, think, and write as a historian, social scientist, or physical scientist. You work with primary and secondary sources, compare documents, form a position, support that position, cite sources, and so on. Use the following tips as a guide to help you effectively respond to DBQ's.

Before you write . . .

- **Read all the information thoroughly.** Review the introduction to the topic, the DBQ, and all the documents.
- **Be sure you understand the question or prompt.** Focus on the cue words, such as *compare, explain,* and *define,* that indicate the type of thinking and writing that is expected. Consider using a strategy to help you understand the prompt (see page 466 for information on **STRAP** questions).
- **Analyze each document.** Consider how the documents relate to and differ from each other. Be especially alert to documents that present opposing points of view.
- **Form a position or take a stand.** After analyzing the documents and rereading the DBQ, form a thesis or focus statement to guide your writing. (See page 30.)
- **Gather and organize your support.** Plan your response, gleaning facts, examples, and quotations from the documents to support your thesis. Use a quick list or some other graphic organizer to help you organize your support.

As you write . . .

- **Form your beginning paragraph.** Provide a few introductory sentences that gain the reader's attention and introduce the topic. Then state your thesis.
- **Develop the body of your response.** Support your thesis with key points, examples (including quotations from the documents), and explanations.
- **Write a concluding paragraph.** Briefly restate or expand upon the thesis.

After you write . . .

- **Check for clarity and coherence.** Make sure that your response reads clearly and logically, but limit yourself to essential changes. You won't have time to do a lot of rewriting.
- **Edit for conventions.** Correct any errors in punctuation, capitalization, spelling, and grammar.

Sample Documents

The documents below and on the next three pages deal with the issue of health care and the increasing costs associated with it. In the past decade, the costs have risen dramatically, putting both insurance and treatment out of reach for many people. Carefully review these documents and related tasks; then examine the sample DBQ and response on pages 479–480.

Document One

The High Cost of Health Care

Ask many people in this country today what worries them most, and sooner or later you'll get to the subject of health care. While today's advanced health-care technologies and procedures offer an unprecedented ability to keep people healthy, the cost of these technologies and procedures is skyrocketing. And with employers increasingly unwilling to shoulder the burden of health insurance coverage, many people who might benefit from modern health care are unable to afford it.

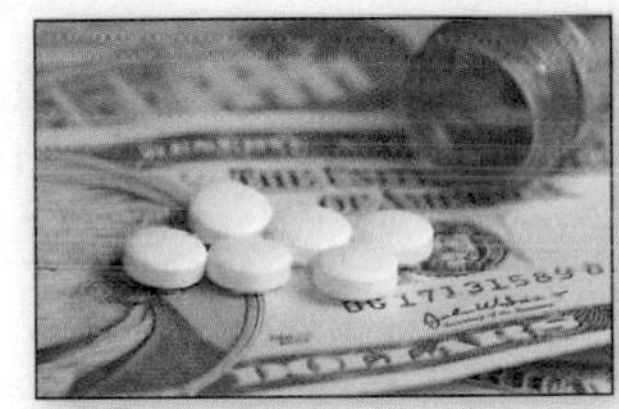

In the not too distant past, most employers offered their workers health insurance packages that allowed people and their families to maintain their health. But in an effort to cut costs and increase profits, many businesses have asked their employees to pick up a greater portion of the health insurance tab—or have cut health-care benefits altogether. Workers have few options—pay high premiums on their own, apply for limited benefits issued by the government, or simply live insurance free and hope to stay healthy.

Source: Hill, Ennis. *A System in Crisis.* Health Solutions Press, 2003.

Task: Summarize the relationship between businesses and the health-care crisis.

Many businesses used to pay for health insurance for their employees. But insurance is expensive, and many businesses are cutting or eliminating health benefits. That makes it harder for workers to get the health care they need.

Only the most important information is included in the summary.

Document Two

Varied Views on the Health-Care Crisis

"We are proud to offer a broad range of medical treatment to our customers, and we are constantly working to expand coverage while keeping premium costs as low as possible."

Alan Singer, Health Insurance Council

"While I understand the needs of my patients, my costs are going up as well. Last year I paid $60,000 in malpractice insurance premiums."

Dr. Joanna Voss, orthopedic surgeon

"I pay $1,200 per month for health insurance for me, my wife, and my son. And I only bring home about $400 per week from my full-time job. Do the math."

Will Cartwright, security guard

"We'd like to offer our employees better health insurance, but the cost of premiums is going up. If I offer everyone health insurance, I may well have to go out of business."

Susan Chin, bookstore owner

"We feel that technology offers us promise. Using computers to manage and distribute medical records effectively, we can dramatically cut health-care costs."

Anna Lopez, health insurance claims adjuster

"The bottom line is that treatment comes first. I cannot and will not turn a patient away because he or she does not have insurance."

Dr. Bill Craig, general practitioner

Source: Comments from the Norfolk Regional Health Care Symposium, July 2005

Task: Make a chart showing the perspectives of consumers, doctors, and insurance companies on the health-care crisis.

Phrases are all that is needed to list answers in a chart.

Consumers	Doctors	Insurance Companies
– forced to choose between health care and other expenses	– pinched by costs of their own insurance – dedicated to patient care	– working to cut the cost of insurance – proud of helping people stay healthy

Document Three

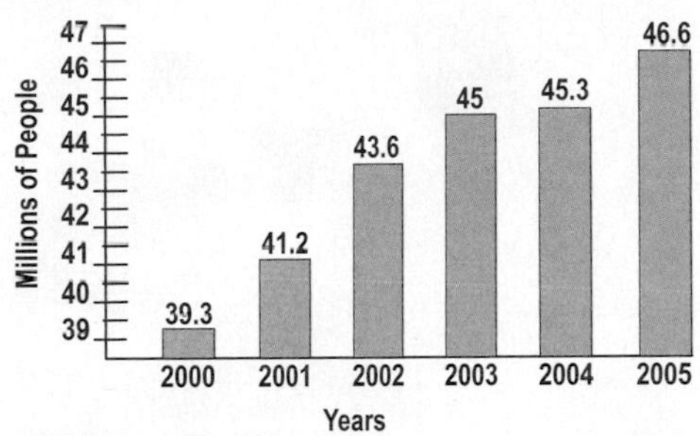

Task: Express the total increase in uninsured people from 2000 to 2005 as a simple number and as a percentage increase.

Graph information is changed to text form.

The total number of people in the United States who did not have health insurance increased by 7.3 million from 2000–2005. Reflected as a percentage, the growth of uninsured Americans was 18.5 percent.

Document Four

Task: Explain how the cartoonist feels about the health-care industry.

An inference is used to interpret the cartoon.

The cartoonist is saying that the health-care industry cares more about money than making people healthy.

DOCUMENT FIVE

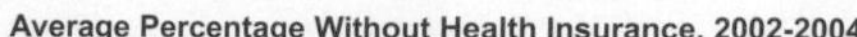

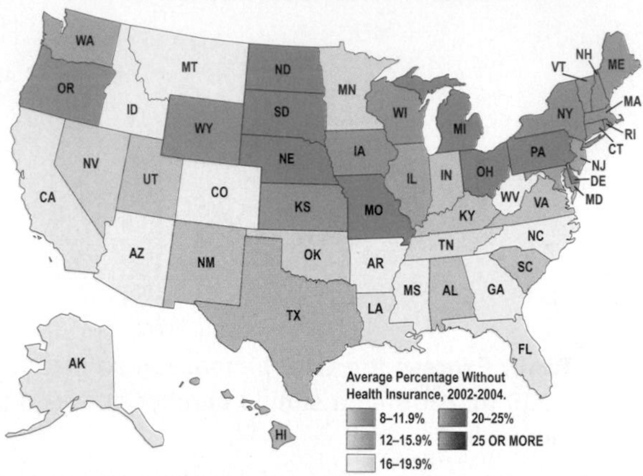

Task: Based on this map, identify state or regional trends in health insurance coverage.

Statistics are used to make some generalizations.

Overall, states in the Northeast and Midwest seem to be doing the best job of providing their residents with health insurance. In the South and the West, rates of uninsured tend to be higher. The state with the lowest percentage of uninsured is Minnesota. The state with the highest percentage of uninsured is Texas.

DOCUMENT SIX

The quest to reform the health insurance industry could take years—maybe even decades. But meanwhile, there is plenty that United States citizens can do to lower the cost of health care. As a nation, U.S. citizens are remarkably unhealthy. By quitting smoking, losing weight, exercising more, and eating balanced diets, they can become dramatically healthier. This improved fitness would lead to a reduction of health-care costs, not just for individuals but for the nation as a whole.

Task: How does the writer propose to reduce health-care costs?

The writer encourages people to improve their fitness levels.

Sample DBQ and Response

The document-based question below asks the writer to respond to the health-care crisis. The sample response that follows draws key facts and details from the documents.

Document-Based Question

The United States is a wealthy nation, but unfortunately many of its citizens cannot afford health care. How extensive is this crisis and what can be done to solve it?

Develop an essay in response to the above question, drawing on information from the six documents and from your own knowledge of the issue.

The High Cost of Health Care

Documents 1, 2, 3, 5, and 6 The opening defines the health-care problem and outlines the thesis.

Can you afford to get sick? That's a question more and more United States citizens are asking themselves. Faced with rising health-care costs and deprived of the solid insurance packages once offered by employers, many cannot afford health care. Even those who can are struggling under expensive premiums and prescription drugs. Will Cartwright, who told his story at the recent Norfolk Health Care Symposium, is a typical example of those burdened by a health-care system in crisis. He earns $400 a week as a security guard, and his health insurance costs $1,200 per month. Cartwright's plight is common, and a solution to the health-care crisis remains elusive.

Today, more and more U.S. citizens are unable to afford health care. From 2000 to 2005, federal, state, and local governments all worked to address the health-care crisis. Meanwhile, the number of uninsured people rose from 39.3 million to 46.6 million—an 18.5 percent increase. The hardest hit areas include the South and West; people in the Northeast and Midwest are more likely to be insured. But even in Minnesota, where the percentage of insured is highest, over 8 percent of people are not insured.

Health-care consumers aren't the only ones feeling pressured by health-care costs. Physicians have seen dramatic rises in malpractice insurance. And many have been forced to pass these increases on to their patients. Employers are feeling the pinch as well. While some employers cut their contribution to employee health

Document 2
The problem is viewed from all angles.

insurance to increase their profits, many employers still want to provide their workers with good coverage. It's just becoming harder to do. As premium costs rise, business owners are often forced to cut their health-care expenses or risk losing their businesses. Even insurance companies, often portrayed negatively, are struggling. They are proud to offer quality care but have trouble getting that care to the people who need it.

Documents 2, 4, 6, and prior knowledge
Solutions are examined.

As the health-care crisis worsens, consumers, legislators, health-care practitioners, and health-care insurance representatives are desperately looking for a solution. The range of solutions is varied, from dramatic reforms to small, incremental ones. Among the former, the idea of a single national health insurance program, like that in Canada and many European countries, has been one of the most often proposed. Its proponents argue that cutting down the number of insurance providers will dramatically reduce paperwork and streamline operations, saving billions in costs.

A powerful ending paragraph summarizes the situation and leaves the reader with something to think about.

At the other end of the spectrum is a simple solution that many say could have dramatic results: making people in this country healthier. Proponents of this solution argue that by forcefully addressing public health issues such as smoking, obesity, nutrition, and physical fitness, the United States could dramatically reduce its dependence on the health-care system.

As people search for a solution to the health-care crisis, the goal is clear—a system that offers quality care to all of our citizens. But for those struggling with or locked out of the health-care system, the solution may come too late.

Checklist Reviewing Your Response

_____ Do I fulfill the requirements outlined in each document task?
_____ Does my opening contain a clear thesis statement?
_____ Do all the ideas in my essay support my thesis statement?
_____ Do I refer to information from all the documents?
_____ Do I include some of my own knowledge about this topic?
_____ Do I restate or expand upon my thesis in my conclusion?
_____ Have I checked my punctuation, grammar, and spelling?

Taking Exit and Entrance Exams

Teachers and administrators use exit and entrance exams to assess your ability to use skills and strategies in a subject area such as English or mathematics. Many school districts use exit exams to determine if students are qualified to graduate from high school. Scores on entrance exams such as the SAT and ACT help college admissions departments determine whether a student meets a school's admission standards.

Most exit and entrance exams include components designed to test your writing skills. You may also be asked to respond to writing prompts and answer objective questions that test your revising and editing skills.

WHAT'S AHEAD

In this chapter, you'll learn strategies and skills that will help you succeed on the writing portion of exit and entrance exams. Everything from answering multiple-choice questions to responding to literary prompts is covered.

Multiple-Choice Questions

For writing-related multiple-choice questions, you must decide if a sentence or a passage contains some type of error. You may be asked to identify the error (if one exists) or correct it.

Testing Conventions

Some questions on exit and entrance exams ask you to edit sentences for conventions: punctuation, capitalization, spelling, usage, and grammar. Read each question and each possible answer carefully. The following examples are typical conventions questions.

Respond to the directions accompanying each of the following sentences.

1. *Dover High School starts the last week in August and Seth Jones High School begins the first week in September.*

   The best punctuation for the underlined section is

   A. August, and
   B. August and,
   C. August. and
   D. NO CHANGE

   ■ The focus is punctuation (compound sentences), and the answer is **A**.

2. *Charise says that her three brothers-in-law hope to start a Web-based company that will market their ideas.*

   The correct spelling for the underlined noun is

   A. brother-in-laws
   B. brothers'-in-law
   C. brothers-in-laws
   D. NO CHANGE

   ■ The focus is plurals, and the answer is **D**.

3. *The customs agent looked at the passport and asked the man, How long will you be staying in New York?*

   The correct punctuation for the underlined section is

   A. "How . . . New York"?
   B. "how . . . New York"?
   C. "How . . . New York?"
   D. NO CHANGE

   ■ The focus is punctuation (dialogue), and the answer is **C**.

4. *The decision to change the import tariff on wool products was not spontaneus, for it came after five months of extensive research and debate.*

Which underlined word is spelled incorrectly?

A. tariff
B. spontaneus
C. extensive
D. All three are correct.

- The focus is spelling, and the answer is **B**.

5. *None of the 85 people on the boat were willing to get into the water once the shark was sighted.*

The correct choice for the underlined word is

A. was
B. are
C. is
D. NO CHANGE

- The focus is grammar (verb tense and subject-verb agreement), and the answer is **D**.

6. *After hiking more than four miles out of the way due to a washed-out trail, the tired group of campers couldn't hardly take another step.*

The correct way to write the underlined section is

A. could hardly take
B. couldn't take
C. Both A and B
D. NO CHANGE

- The focus is grammar (double negatives), and the answer is **C**.

TIPS

FOR ANSWERING MULTIPLE-CHOICE QUESTIONS

- **Read the question completely.** Do not try to answer a question until you understand all of its parts.
- **Study all the answers.** Sometimes there is more than one correct answer, or there is no correct answer. The correct response may be "All of the above," "None of the above," or "A and B."
- **Eliminate obviously wrong answers.** Cross out answers you know are incorrect before making your final choice.
- **Avoid guessing.** Most entrance exams penalize incorrect answers as a way to discourage guessing.

Testing Sentence-Revision Skills

Other multiple-choice questions may test your ability to revise sentences. These questions cover such skills as combining sentences, fixing ambiguous wording, creating parallel structure, correcting dangling modifiers, and eliminating sentence errors.

Read the following sentences and choose the best revision. If the original is the best choice, the answer is D.

1. *Demonstrating a new out-of-bounds play, we sat on the bleachers to watch the basketball coach.*

A. To watch the basketball coach, we sat on the bleachers demonstrating a new out-of-bounds play.
B. We sat on the bleachers to watch the basketball coach demonstrating a new out-of-bounds play.
C. Watching the basketball coach demonstrating a new out-of-bounds play, we sat on the bleachers.
D. NO CHANGE

■ The focus is misplaced modifiers, and the answer is **B**.

2. *On Saturday morning, Thomas ate breakfast and then he put the finishing touches on his science project and then he walked to Dunn's Hardware to start his new job.*

A. Thomas ate breakfast and then he put the finishing touches on his science project. Then he walked to Dunn's Hardware to start his new job.
B. Thomas ate breakfast. Then he put the finishing touches on his science project. He walked to Dunn's Hardware to start his new job.
C. Thomas ate breakfast, put the finishing touches on his science project, and then walked to Dunn's Hardware to start his new job.
D. NO CHANGE

■ The focus is rambling sentences and creating parallel structure, and the answer is **C**.

3. *Before we started our workout. We jogged around the track.*

A. Before we started our workout, we jogged around the track.
B. We jogged around the track before we started our workout.
C. Both A and B
D. NO CHANGE

■ The focus is fragments and combining, and the answer is **C**.

4. *Caroline won more trophies than any other team member.*

A. Caroline won the most trophies.
B. Caroline won more trophies than any other team member won.
C. Caroline won even more trophies than any other team member.
D. NO CHANGE

■ The focus is incomplete comparisons, and the answer is **B**.

5. *The thunderstorm roared through town, soaking the clothes on the line and leaving them dripping wet.*

A. soaking the clothes on the line and leaving them dripping.
B. soaking the dripping wet clothes on the line.
C. leaving the clothes on the line dripping.
D. NO CHANGE

■ The focus is avoiding redundancy, and the answer is **C**.

6. *The girls' soccer team happy to have new uniforms will play in the postseason tournament.*

A. The girls' soccer team, happy to have new uniforms will play in the postseason tournament.
B. The girls' soccer team happy to have new uniforms, will play in the postseason tournament.
C. The girls' soccer team, happy to have new uniforms, will play in the postseason tournament.
D. NO CHANGE

■ The focus is restrictive and nonrestrictive clauses and phrases, and the answer is **C**.

7. *The jet airplane is huge. The plane has two levels for passengers. It can hold as many as 850 people.*

A. The huge jet airplane has two levels for passengers and can hold as many as 850 people.
B. The jet airplane is huge and has two levels for passengers. It can hold as many as 850 people.
C. The jet airplane is huge. It has two levels for passengers and can hold as many as 850 people.
D. NO CHANGE

■ The focus is combining sentences, and the answer is **A**.

Testing Paragraph-Revision Skills

Some questions are based on an extended reading sample. These questions test your paragraph-revising skills. It is important to read the sample carefully and refer to it as you try to answer the questions.

Sample Test Essay

(1) After World War II, the United States and the Soviet Union engaged in the cold war, the cold war was a protracted political struggle over who would become the dominant world power. *(2)* The two countries competed in a variety of venues. *(3)* Their most dramatic competition was the so-called "space race," the battle to see who could attain supremacy in the exploration of outer space.

(4) In 1957, Russia's launch of *Sputnik 1,* the world's first artificial satellite, shocked the world. *(5)* Suddenly the launch of *Sputnik* created fears that the Soviet Union would develop space weaponry that would give it a military edge. *(6)* These weapons have rarely been used. *(7)* The launch also shook the United States to its core. As the first nation to develop nuclear weapons, the United States had enjoyed military superiority because of nuclear weapons.

(8) The United States developed its own space program. *(9)* Soon, the program began to focus on an almost unbelievable goal—taking human passengers to the moon and bringing them back. *(10)* The program developed to reach the moon was known as *Apollo.* *(11)* The first Apollo mission ended in tragedy during a launch simulation when the command module caught fire on the launchpad, killing all three members of the crew. *(12)* Subsequent tests proved successful, and in 1969, *Apollo 11* landed two U.S. astronauts on the moon. *(13)* Around the world, millions watched the event live on television.

(14) Several lunar landings gave the United States a key victory in the space race, but another program helped maintain U.S. dominance. *(15)* In 1981, the United States launched the first reusable space shuttle, signaling the next phase in space exploration. *(16)* More importantly, the United States and the Soviet Union finally began to cooperate on space exploration.

1. *Which part of sentence 1 should be deleted?*

A. After World War II
B. engaged in the cold war
C. the cold war was
D. NO CHANGE

■ The focus is correcting comma splices, and the answer is **C**.

2. *Which of the following would make the best addition to the beginning of sentence 8?*

A. In response to *Sputnik,*
B. The Soviets fought back,
C. First of all,
D. In conclusion,

■ The focus is effective use of transitions, and the answer is **A**.

3. *Which of the following sentences should be deleted?*

A. Sentence 2.
B. Sentence 6.
C. Sentence 11.
D. Sentence 15.

■ The focus is details appropriate to the topic sentence, and the answer is **B**.

4. *Which revision would improve this essay?*

A. Switch sentence 5 with sentence group 7.
B. Switch sentence 1 with sentence 3.
C. Switch sentence 11 with sentence 15.
D. Switch sentence 15 with sentence 16.

■ The focus is clear organization, and the answer is **A**.

5. *Which sentence would make the best conclusion to this passage?*

A. The moon would never again be explored.
B. Space exploration was no longer important.
C. The *Apollo* program was no longer significant.
D. The space race was over, but the exploration of space would continue.

■ The focus is effective closings, and the answer is **D**.

Testing Editing Skills

Some writing tests assess your editing skills. These questions require you to find a usage or grammatical error in a sentence.

In the following sentences, choose the underlined section that contains an error. If there is no error, choose D.

1. *Jerome, Baker, or Steve are not ready to board the train for New York.*
   A: are; B: to board; C: for

   D LEAVE AS IS

   ■ The focus is subject-verb agreement, and the answer is **A**.

2. *Jumping off the fence, Kaylee she landed badly and twisted her ankle.*
   A: off the fence; B: she; C: and

   D LEAVE AS IS

   ■ The focus is double subjects, and the answer is **B**.

3. *The massive size of the huge volcanic cloud blotted out the sun for three days.*
   A: huge; B: blotted; C: three

   D LEAVE AS IS

   ■ The focus is wordiness or redundancy, and the answer is **A**.

4. *After practice, Bill timidly asked the director if he found his playbook.*
   A: After; B: timidly; C: his

   D LEAVE AS IS

   ■ The focus is indefinite pronoun reference, and the answer is **C**.

5. *This summer, Lanata plans to play tennis, movies, and go swimming.*
   A: This summer,; B: movies,; C: swimming.

   D LEAVE AS IS

   ■ The focus is parallel structure, and the answer is **B**.

6. *After his friends described the roof at the new ballpark, Mr. Abar decided he should probably go watch the opening of the roof himself.*
   A: Mr.; B: decided; C: he should probably go watch the opening of the roof himself.

   D LEAVE AS IS

   ■ The focus is ineffective writing, and the answer is **C**.

Writing Tests Based on Prompts

Some state and district exit exams require you to respond to a writing prompt in the form of an essay, a narrative, or a letter. You may be prompted to write from your own experience, or you may be asked to read one or two short passages and respond to them. These exams are usually timed, but some states and districts give students as much time as they need.

College entrance tests such as the ACT and SAT also include a timed writing section. The prompts on these tests ask you to support your point of view on a topic. The essays are evaluated on clarity, consistency, level of detail, and appropriateness. While correctness is important, evaluators understand that you are working within a limited time frame.

Early in the initial planning stage, use the **STRAP questions** to analyze the writing prompt.

Subject: **What topic (career, community) should I write about?**
Type: **What form (essay, editorial, report) of writing should I create?**
Role: **What position (friend, employee) should I assume as the writer?**
Audience: **Who (classmates, community members) is my intended reader?**
Purpose: **What is the goal (persuade, evaluate, explain, tell) of my writing?**

TIPS

FOR PREPARING FOR EXIT OR ENTRANCE EXAMS

Understand the basic forms of writing. Be sure that you know how to write the following:

- **Expository essay** to share information or explain a process
- **Persuasive essay** to share an opinion or defend a position
- **Personal (biographical) narrative** to share your own or another's experience
- **Business letter** to ask for or share information or take a stand
- **Literary analysis** to explore themes of literature

Follow the writing process.

- **Prewrite.** Take some time to plan your response. (See the **STRAP** questions above.) Write a thesis or focus statement and jot down supporting ideas in a simple outline.
- **Write.** Begin in an interesting way and state your thesis or focus; include details and examples to support your thesis in the middle part; and restate your main ideas in the closing.
- **Revise and edit.** Make as many revisions and corrections as time allows.

Reviewing a Prompt and Response

The following prompt is similar to what you would find on an entrance or exit exam. Review it and the student response.

Sample Prompt

Former Green Bay Packers coach Vince Lombardi knew about teamwork. According to Lombardi, "People who work together will win, whether it be against complex football defenses, or the problems of modern society." Drawing on your experience, write an essay for your classmates explaining how a project you worked on benefited from teamwork.

Sample STRAP Answers and Quick List

The student writer analyzed the prompt using the **STRAP** questions, wrote his position, and created a quick list. (Other graphic organizers can also be used to plan a response.)

Subject: Value of teamwork
Type: Essay of exposition
Role: Student
Audience: Classmates
Purpose: Explain a personal experience.
Position: Teamwork makes a big project go smoothly.

Quick List
- The benefit concert demanded more than I could handle alone.
- I needed volunteers for the many tasks.
- A dedicated group got the job done.

Sample Response

Next, the student developed his response. He paid as much attention to each part—the beginning, the middle, and the ending—as time permitted.

Teamwork at Work

After volunteering at the Mendon Brook Food Bank last summer, I decided to organize a classical concert to benefit the facility. I thought it would be something I could accomplish on my own, but doing the project taught me a valuable lesson: sometimes it takes more than one person to get the job done. The food bank benefit concert succeeded because a talented group of people combined their skills and worked as a team.

The **opening** leads to a position statement (underlined).

At first, I thought that I could easily organize the benefit concert by myself. As a member of the school orchestra, I had played violin in concerts for six years. I felt confident playing in public and had even performed in several benefit concerts. In addition, I knew other musicians who could help me realize my goal.

Middle paragraphs share examples of teamwork to support the main idea.

As I began to work, I realized the project was too big for just one person. It takes more than music to make a concert happen. I was able to put together a group of musicians and choose selections to perform, but I needed to find a venue, generate publicity, and even provide catering for people who attended. I quickly became overwhelmed and asked some friends and relatives for help.

My friend Carla, who is a fantastic writer and artist, handled the publicity like a professional. James, who had a summer job at a local college, found a hall we could use for free. Anna and her mother, who both love to cook, took charge of the catering. My dad found volunteers from work to serve as ushers. As the project progressed, we all ended up pitching in to do a little of everything.

The **closing** restates the lesson learned through this experience.

In the end, the benefit concert was a great success, raising $700 for the Mendon Brook Food Bank. I also benefited because I learned the value of teamwork. The next time I need to tackle a project, I'll try the team approach. When it comes to doing a big job, the skills and energy of a group of people accomplish more than one person could ever accomplish alone.

Now You Try It

Use the STRAP questions to analyze the following prompt. Then create a position statement and quick list and begin your response. Finish writing, revising, and editing in the time your teacher provides.

Imagine that the Senate wants to require that all people serve their country prior to pursuing college or a career. Would you support compulsory two-year service to the country for graduating seniors? The service could be community- or military-based. Write a letter to your senator supporting your position.

Responding to Literature

Prompts may be based on literature that you have read prior to the exam or on selections that you read during the test. Here are some tips on writing responses to literature.

- **Write a thesis (focus) statement.** Reword the prompt so that it applies to the literature you're writing about.
- **Briefly outline your main points.** Support your thesis statement with convincing details.
- **Avoid summarizing the literature.** Follow your outline; don't simply retell a story or paraphrase a poem.
- **Include comments on the author's techniques.** Point out literary devices (symbols, repetition, metaphors, word choice) that discuss the author's purpose.
- **Make direct references to the text.** Quote or paraphrase important excerpts to support your analysis.

Sample Prompt and Reading Selections

Time and mortality are common themes in literature. Both of the poems that follow deal with these themes, and each also says something about art itself. In "When I Have Fears That I May Cease to Be," John Keats writes about a poet's eagerness to capture his thoughts on paper. In "Languages," Carl Sandburg describes how all languages change with time. Discuss what these two poems, taken together, have to say about time and human expression.

When I Have Fears That I May Cease to Be

When I have fears that I may cease to be
Before my pen has glean'd my teeming brain,
Before high piled books, in charact'ry,
Hold like rich garners the full-ripen'd grain;
When I behold, upon the night's starr'd face,
Huge cloudy symbols of a high romance,
And think that I may never live to trace
Their shadows, with the magic hand of chance;
And when I feel, fair creature of an hour!
That I shall never look upon thee more,
Never have relish in the faery power
Of unreflecting love!—then on the shore
Of the wide world I stand alone, and think
Till Love and Fame to nothingness do sink.

—John Keats (1795–1821)

Languages

There are no handles upon a language
Whereby men take hold of it
And mark it with signs for its remembrance.
It is a river, this language,
Once in a thousand years
Breaking a new course
Changing its way to the ocean.
It is mountain effluvia
Moving to valleys
And from nation to nation
Crossing borders and mixing.
Languages die like rivers.
Words wrapped round your tongue today
And broken to shape of thought
Between your teeth and lips speaking
Now and today
Shall be faded hieroglyphics
Ten thousand years from now.
Sing—and singing—remember
Your song dies and changes
And is not here tomorrow
Any more than the wind
Blowing ten thousand years ago.

—Carl Sandburg (1878–1967)

Sample STRAP Answers and Quick List

Subject: Time and human expression in "When I Have Fears . . ." and "Languages"
Type: Essay
Role: Reader
Audience: Testers
Purpose: Analyze

Position: Both poems are positive statements about eternity.

Quick List

1. Keats feels the tension of limited time.
   - Too many ideas, eternal "symbols," mortal love
   - He takes comfort in eternity.
2. Sandburg describes continual change.
   - Languages change and die like rivers.
   - Sing because today will soon be gone.

Sample Response

Next, the student developed his response. He paid as much attention to each part—the beginning, the middle, and the ending—as time permitted.

Inevitable Change

The **opening** introduces both poems and ends with a thesis statement (underlined).

John Keats' famous sonnet "When I Have Fears That I May *Cease to Be*" may seem extremely dark and pessimistic. It may seem to end on an especially negative note about the pointlessness of effort in the face of eternity. Likewise, Carl Sandburg's "Languages" might be interpreted as a depressing recognition of mortality in the face of endless change. Upon careful reading, however, these two works reveal something different. <u>Both poems are actually positive statements about life and eternity.</u>

The first **middle paragraph** discusses one poem.

Keats' opening line "When I have fears . . . " begins in tension. The first three quatrains reveal fear that there won't be time to write all the thoughts of his"teeming brain," to explore "huge . . . symbols of a high romance," and to enjoy simple, "unreflecting love." In the final couplet, Keats' answer to these fears is to "stand alone" on the "shore of the wide world" until all tension fades. The suggestion is that it fades in the face of eternity.

Similarly, Sandburg's poem ends with a statement that may seem bleak. He says, "Your song . . . / . . . is not here tomorrow" and compares it to "the wind/Blowing ten thousand years ago." Within the context of the whole poem, however, we can see that Sandburg celebrates life. He describes language as a living river, unable to be controlled. He says, "Sing—and singing—remember." What we are to remember is that life itself is change.

The **ending** revisits the thesis statement.

Together, these two poems reveal that eternity need not frighten us. It is only when we fear our mortality that we either grow tense at the shortness of time—as in Keats' poem—or try to resist change—as in Sandburg's. By accepting our mortality, the authors suggest, we become free to sing and love and explore and grow—to enjoy to the fullest our time on earth.

Taking Advanced Placement* Exams

Most college-bound students have had the nightmare that they showed up for an exam without having studied. The only way to prevent that nightmare from becoming a reality is to prepare. Those who prepare for the Advanced Placement English exams feel confidence instead of dread, and their preparation pays off in their scores.

Successful preparation is the opposite of "cramming." Those who spend a caffeine-fueled night of sleepless study prior to the exam do a disservice to themselves. Yes, you should review this chapter and other chapters in "The Testing Center" before taking the exams. But you'll be even better prepared if you keep up with your course work throughout the year, make a habit of critical reading and responding, and learn the techniques of rhetoric and persuasion. The Advanced Placement English exams test your ability to read, think, and write, so the best way to prepare for the exams is to routinely do these three things.

WHAT'S AHEAD

This chapter provides general preparation advice and specific guidelines for the AP English exams.

General Exam Preparation

AP English Language and Composition

AP English Literature and Composition

General Exam Preparation

The AP English exams use objective questions and on-demand writing. To prepare for the exams, do the following:

1. **Practice critical reading.** Use these questions.

___ **Ideas**

What is the *topic?*
What is the *purpose* (informational, persuasive, literary)?

- For *informational writing,* what sorts of details are used, and how do they support the thesis?
- For *persuasive writing,* what combination of ethos, logos, and pathos develops the position? (See page 231.)
- For *literature,* how do the plot, settings, characters, and conflicts affect the theme?

What is the *context?*

___ **Organization**

What is the *overall structure* of the work?
How does each *paragraph* function?
Where does the work *shift in meaning?*

___ **Voice**

What is the *tone* (the author's attitude toward the topic)?
What is the *formality* (the author's relationship to the reader)?

___ **Word Choice**

What are the *key words* in the text?

___ **Sentence Fluency**

What is remarkable about the *sentence style?*
What *literary* or *rhetorical devices* does the writer use?

2. **Understand literary analysis.** Study literary and poetry terms and "Critical Approaches to Literary Analysis" (pages 287–297).
3. **Understand rhetoric and persuasion.** Study "Rhetoric and Persuasion," "Thinking Through an Argument" and "Fallacies of Thinking" (pages 231–232 and 251–253).
4. **Practice responding to prompts.** Write essays in response to the prompts in this handbook. (See pages 472, 492, 500, and 505.)
5. **Study exemplary models.** Review the essays in this handbook and seek out your own exemplary models of writing.

AP English Language and Composition

The AP English Language and Composition exam focuses on your ability to read and respond to essays, letters, speeches, and other nonfiction prose. It has two sections: multiple-choice questions and on-demand writing.

Section I

This section counts as 45 percent of the exam grade. It includes five or six passages, each of which is followed by multiple-choice questions (55 in all). You have 60 minutes to complete this section (10 minutes per passage).

Guidelines for Section I

- **Read questions first.** Then you know what to watch for.
- **Note question order.** Often the first question asks about the first line. Usually questions follow the order of the passage.
- **Treat each passage separately.** The passages are not connected.
- **Be patient with short passages.** They may take as long or longer to analyze than long passages.
- **Pay attention to footnotes.** If there is a footnote, often there will be a question about it.
- **Analyze ideas and organization.** Questions often focus on specific ideas and how they contribute to the whole passage. Think of what each idea accomplishes—summing, supporting, contrasting, questioning, and so on.
- **Analyze voice.** Questions may ask about the writer's tone (feeling about the topic) or formality (relationship with the audience).
- **Analyze word choice and sentence fluency.** Questions may focus on the writer's sentence style or on figures of speech used by the writer.
- **Answer easy questions first.** Eliminate obviously incorrect answers.

Sample Prompt, Passage, and Questions

Read the following passage from Ralph Waldo Emerson's essay "The American Scholar." Then answer the questions that follow.

The theory of books is noble. The scholar of the first age received into him the world around; brooded thereon; gave it the new arrangement of his own mind, and uttered it again. It came into him, life; it went out from him, truth. It came to him, short-lived actions; it went out from him, immortal thoughts. It came to him, business; it went from him, poetry. It was dead fact; now, it is quick thought. It can stand, and it can go. It now endures, it now flies, it now inspires. Precisely in proportion to the depth of mind from which it issued, so high does it soar, so long does it sing.

Or, I might say, it depends on how far the process had gone, of transmuting life into truth. In proportion to the completeness of the distillation, so will the purity and imperishableness of the product be. But none is quite perfect. As no air-pump can by any means make a perfect vacuum, so neither can any artist entirely exclude the conventional, the local, the perishable from his book, or write a book of pure thought, that shall be as efficient, in all respects, to a remote posterity, as to contemporaries, or rather to the second age. Each age, it is found, must write its own books; or rather, each generation for the next succeeding. The books of an older period will not fit this.

Yet hence arises a grave mischief. The sacredness which attaches to the act of creation,—the act of thought,—is transferred to the record. The poet chanting, was felt to be a divine man: henceforth the chant is divine also. The writer was a just and wise spirit: henceforward it is settled, the book is perfect; as love of the hero corrupts into worship of his statue. Instantly, the book becomes noxious: the guide is a tyrant. The sluggish and perverted mind of the multitude, slow to open to the incursions of Reason, having once so opened, having once received this book, stands upon it, and makes an outcry, if it is disparaged. Colleges are built on it. Books are written on it by thinkers, not by Man Thinking; by men of talent, that is, who start wrong, who set out from accepted dogmas, not from their own sight of principles. Meek young men grow up in libraries, believing it their duty to accept the views, which Cicero, which Locke, which Bacon, have given, forgetful that Cicero, Locke, and Bacon were only young men in libraries, when they wrote these books.

1. **Which of the following literary techniques is featured most heavily in the first paragraph?**
- **a.** caesura
- **(b.)** anaphora
- **c.** rhyme
- **d.** satire

2. **The phrase, *"brooded thereon"* (line 2), means**
- **a.** "grew depressed."
- **(b.)** "pondered."
- **c.** "ignored."
- **d.** "hatched out."

3. **The transitional thought between paragraphs one and two can best be phrased as**
- **a.** "the best minds always speak the best truth."
- **b.** "truth is life reflected upon."
- **c.** "poetry is more true than life."
- **(d.)** "the depth of reflection determines the quality of utterance."

4. **The author views the human masses as**
- **(a.)** resistant to change.
- **b.** the final arbiter of knowledge.
- **c.** "Man Thinking."
- **d.** devoted to truth.

5. **The word "dogmas" in line 28 is contrasted with which of the following:**
- **a.** individual talent.
- **b.** sensory observations.
- **(c.)** personal principles.
- **d.** book learning.

6. **The overall theme of the passage is**
- **a.** books preserve knowledge for later generations.
- **(b.)** every generation needs to write new books.
- **c.** books are imperfect vehicles for knowledge.
- **d.** books should be banned.

Section II

This section counts as 55 percent of the exam grade. It contains three writing prompts, each of which is usually based on a short passage that you must respond to critically. You have 120 minutes to complete this section. Watch for these types of prompts:

1. A **rhetorical analysis prompt** asks you to analyze the rhetorical devices used in a given passage (essay, letter, speech, etc.). Watch for these key words: *rhetorical, analyze, methods, purpose, strategies, devices,* and *evaluate.*
2. A **position prompt** asks you to agree or disagree with the writer's stance in a given passage (essay, letter, speech, etc.). (See pages 231–232 and 244–253.) Watch for these key words: *support or dispute, agree or disagree,* and *qualify.*
3. A **synthesis prompt** asks you to read multiple sources and then state and develop a position based on a number of them. (See "Answering DBQ's" on pages 473–480 for more help.) Watch for these key words: *synthesize, combine, cite sources, formulate,* and *propose.*

Guidelines for Section II

- **Plan your time.** Spend 5 to 10 minutes in prewriting, 20 to 25 minutes in writing, and 5 minutes in revising and editing each response (about 40 minutes per prompt).
- **Analyze the prompt.** Use a strategy such as answering the **STRAP** questions. (See page 466.)
- **Read the passage and annotate it.** Underline or star important concepts or sentences.
- **Form a thesis and list support.** Try to list three to five supporting points.
- **Write a brief opening.** Restate the prompt and present your thesis. (Do not spend extra time on an elaborate opening.)
- **Leave a blank line between paragraphs** to aid revision.
- **Develop the middle.** Start each middle paragraph with a main point and then provide supporting details. Refer to the text and give citations. Paraphrase and elaborate as needed.
- **Write a brief closing.** Summarize your thesis.
- **Revise and edit your work.** Quickly check your thesis and support. Read through to refine transitions and correct errors.

INSIDE INFO

Every AP prompt requires you to write persuasively—to take a position and support it. Even if the prompt says "discuss," your response should present a strong position.

Sample Position Prompt and Excerpt

Ralph Waldo Emerson, a nineteenth-century essayist and lecturer, began an essay entitled "History" with the following observation:

> "There is one mind common to all individual men. Every man is an inlet to the same and to all of the same. He that is once admitted to the right of reason is made a freeman* of the whole estate. What Plato has thought, he may think; what a saint has felt, he may feel; what at any time has befallen any man, he can understand."

Support, dispute, or qualify Emerson's assertion based on your own reading, observations, and experiences.

Quick List

More info doesn't mean better info.
- Online info overwhelms.
- People choose badly.
- They find what they seek.
- They need wisdom.

Sample Response

A brief introduction identifies the thesis (underlined).

Easy Access

Emerson believed in his day that any man could access the accumulated wisdom of the ages. In today's world, access to information is ridiculously easy, but improved access does not necessarily mean better information nor enhanced judgment.

Each paragraph develops a main supporting point.

Online encyclopedias, high-powered search engines, blogs, and public-domain e-books are just some of the ways in which Emerson's vision of easy information access remains true. A person can search a university library's holdings using his or her laptop while sipping a latte at a coffee shop. If someone wants to know what Jane Austen, Socrates, or Madonna has to say about love, their thoughts are instantly accessible. If the Dark Ages were so named because of their isolation from the light of previously discovered knowledge, then indeed we are in the brightest of all ages since much of what has ever been known is just a click away.

Yet will anyone recognize the difference between Madonna and the Mahatma? Will anyone read the ancient philosophers in preference to watching the movie Old School? When there

Key points from the passage are cited.

is a Shakespeare channel, how many viewers will regularly tune in? Emerson believed each person could be "admitted to the right of reason," yet in today's world, it's hard to imagine that many people are queuing up at the entrance to Reason Land. The glamour and glitter of movie stars and professional athletes have everyone's attention.

Once people step through one of the many modern information portals, how will they sift through all of the information? One problem with so many different channels, blogs, and "experts" is the ease with which people can find someone who confirms their own prejudices. If someone thinks invading Iraq was a mistake, he or she can easily find 50 "authorities" to agree with this point of view. People find strength in those 50 by ignoring the 50 who say the opposite. The broadband of available opinion has the paradoxical effect of narrowing our thought: Individuals tend to listen to whoever thinks or sounds the most like them.

Instead of becoming "freemen" of the estate of ideas, people keep repurchasing the same sliver of opinion they already owned. They are not enriched by the wealth of fact and opinion available in modern society if they never consider positions contrary to their own.

The writer uses a main theme from a contemporary novel to make his point explicit.

Perhaps more important than how little people listen to others is how little they care about them. Atticus Finch told Scout in To Kill a Mockingbird that she would never understand her first-year teacher until she "looked at things from her point of view." A little more than a year ago Hurricane Katrina destroyed the city of New Orleans and much of the surrounding area. A thinking person would look at those pictures and at the very least donate some money for relief. Unfortunately, some looked at those broken lives and thought, "How stupid to build a city below sea level, and how stupid those people are for living there." They could find commentators to agree with them. That's not what a "saint" would say about Katrina's victims.

The closing comments revisit the thesis.

Even though the wisdom of the ages is available at our fingertips, even though the information portals are all open, people will not be admitted to Emerson's reasonable utopia until they open their hearts and minds to many points of view. Jimi Hendrix said, "Knowledge speaks, but wisdom listens." Hendrix listened to Otis Redding, Bob Dylan, and Francis Scott Key. Admittance to the "right of reason" requires this type of openness and thought.

AP English Literature and Composition

The AP English Literature and Composition exam focuses on your ability to read and analyze imaginative literature from various periods throughout history. The exam has two sections: The first features multiple-choice questions, and the second features on-demand writing.

Section I

This section counts as 45 percent of the exam grade. It includes five or six excerpts from literature, each of which is followed by multiple-choice questions about it (55 questions in all). You have 60 minutes to complete this section (about 10 minutes per excerpt).

Guidelines for Section I

- **Read questions first.** Then you know what to watch for.
- **Note question order.** Often the first question asks about the first line. Usually questions follow the order of the excerpt.
- **Consider each excerpt in isolation.** They are not connected.
- **Take time with short excerpts.** They may take as long or longer to analyze than long passages.
- **Read footnotes.** Often there will be questions about them.
- **Analyze ideas and organization.** Some questions address how one part affects the whole work. Is a sentence or paragraph *pivotal,* does it *contradict* something else, does it *epitomize* an idea, does it *signal a shift* in thinking?
- **Analyze voice.** Some questions ask about tone (the writer's feeling about the topic) or mood (the feeling the reader takes away from the passage).
- **Analyze word choice and sentence fluency.** Some questions ask about sentence style or literary devices such as images, symbols, or metaphors.
- **Answer easy questions first.** Eliminate incorrect answers.

SAMPLE PROMPT, PASSAGE, AND QUESTIONS

In this selection from Shakespeare's *Julius Caesar,* Mark Antony speaks to the Roman crowd just after Caesar's death. Read the selection carefully. Then answer the questions that follow.

Good friends, sweet friends, let me not stir you up
To such a sudden flood of mutiny.
They that have done this deed are honourable:
What private griefs they have, alas, I know not,
That made them do it; they're wise and honourable,
And will, no doubt, with reasons answer you.
I come not, friends, to steal away your hearts:
I am no orator, as Brutus is;

But, as you know me all, a plain blunt man,
That love my friend; and that they know full well
That gave me public leave to speak of him:
For I have neither wit, nor words, nor worth,
Action, nor utterance, nor the power of speech,
To stir men's blood: I only speak right on;
I tell you that which you yourselves do know;
Show you sweet Caesar's wounds, poor dumb mouths,
And bid them speak for me: but were I Brutus,
And Brutus Antony, there were an Antony
Would ruffle up your spirits, and put a tongue
In every wound of Caesar, that should move
The stones of Rome to rise and mutiny.

1. Antony's primary purpose in this speech is
- **a.** to express sorrow.
- **b.** to praise Caesar.
- **(c.)** to foment rebellion.
- **d.** to apologize.
- **e.** to seek clarification.

2. His tone is mainly
- **a.** angry.
- **b.** pensive.
- **(c.)** ironic.
- **d.** sorrowful.
- **e.** didactic.

3. In his address to the Roman people, Antony makes the most significant use of
- **a.** understated commands.
- **b.** direct threats.
- **(c.)** indirect accusations.
- **d.** references to past heroics.
- **e.** expressions of self-loathing.

4. "Private griefs" (line 4) means:
- **a.** "heartfelt resentments."
- **b.** "personal anguish."
- **(c.)** "individual grievances."
- **d.** "physical ailments."
- **e.** "nagging confusion."

5. "Show you sweet Caesar's wounds, poor dumb mouths" (line 16) best demonstrates which poetic device:
- **a.** allusion
- **(b.)** metaphor
- **c.** hyperbole
- **d.** antithesis
- **e.** metonymy

6. Which of the following would be an inaccurate comment about the passage?
- **a.** It is written in blank verse.
- **b.** It is a soliloquy.
- **c.** It makes reference to a skilled orator.
- **(d.)** It abounds in metaphoric language.
- **e.** It concludes in much the same way as it begins.

Section II

This section counts as 55 percent of the exam grade. You have 120 minutes to respond to each of three prompts by creating a literary analysis. Usually, the test includes two types of prompts:

1. **Text-specific prompts** ask you to analyze pieces of fiction or poetry provided on the test.
2. **Open-ended prompts** ask you to analyze a particular device used in one or two major literary works from your own reading or from a list of works provided. Don't analyze movies or TV shows.

Guidelines for Section II

- **Come prepared.** Before the exam, list important works you have read. Commit to memory three important quotations and three important moments in each of these works.
- **Plan your time.** Spend 5 to 10 minutes in prewriting, 20 to 25 minutes in writing, and 5 minutes in revising and editing each response (about 40 minutes per prompt).
- **Analyze the prompt.** Use a strategy such as answering the **STRAP** questions. (See page 466.)
- **Read the passage and annotate it** (for text-specific prompts). Underline or star important concepts or sentences.
- **Form a thesis and list support.** Try to list three to five supporting points.
- **Write a brief opening.** Present your thesis. (Do not spend extra time on an elaborate opening.)
- **Leave a blank line between paragraphs** to aid revision.
- **Develop the middle.** Do not spend time summarizing the plot. Assume the reader is familiar with the work. Start each middle paragraph with a main point and provide support from the literature. Refer to the text (and for text-specific prompts, make sure to give citations).
- **Write a brief closing.** Summarize your analysis.
- **Revise and edit your work.** Quickly check your thesis and support. Read through to refine transitions and correct errors.

INSIDE INFO

Prompts often focus on these types of literary devices or issues:

allusion	conflict	metaphor	motivation	setting
characters	climax	mood	resolution	symbolism

Lists of possible selections include works such as the following:

Adventures of Huckleberry Finn	*Death of a Salesman*
Beloved	*Macbeth*

Sample Prompt and Poem

Read the following poem by W. B. Yeats and discuss how the poet explores the connection between beauty and work.

Adam's Curse[1]

We sat together at one summer's end, *
The beautiful mild woman, your close friend,
And you and I, and talked of poetry.
I said: "A line will take us hours maybe;
Yet if it does not seem a moment's thought,   Key
Our stitching and unstitching has been naught.
Better go down upon your marrow-bones
And scrub a kitchen pavement, or break stones
Like an old pauper, in all kinds of weather;
For to articulate sweet sounds together
Is to work harder than all these, and yet   Poetry
Be thought an idler by the noisy set
Of bankers, schoolmasters, and clergymen
The martyrs call the world."
                                        And thereupon
That beautiful mild woman for whose sake
There's many a one shall find out all heartache
On finding that her voice is sweet and low
Replied, "To be born woman is to know—
Although they do not talk of it at school—   Beauty
That we must labour to be beautiful."
I said, "It's certain there is no fine thing
Since Adam's fall but needs much labouring.
There have been lovers who thought love should be
So much compounded of high courtesy
That they would sigh and quote with learned looks
Precedents out of beautiful old books;
Yet now it seems an idle trade enough."   Love
We sat grown quiet at the name of love;
We saw the last embers of daylight die, *
And in the trembling blue-green of the sky
Symbol → A moon, worn as if it had been a shell
Washed by time's waters as they rose and fell
About the stars and broke in days and years.
I had a thought for no one's but your ears:
That you were beautiful, and that I strove
To love you in the old high way of love;
That it had all seemed happy, and yet we'd grown
As weary-hearted as that hollow moon.

—W. B. Yeats

[1] After the fall from paradise, God's curse upon Adam is that he must work for a living.

Quick List

The curse is to work hard, but labors turn to dust.
–Poets strive to make poetry.
–Women strive to look beautiful.
–Some people strive for love.
–Time destroys beauty.
–Adam's curse shows human condition.

Sample Response

The opening identifies the poet and poem and states the thesis (underlined).

A longer quotation is given as an excerpt. All quotations are cited.

The writer connects different parts of the poem.

Labor, Beauty, and Time

In "Adam's Curse," William Butler Yeats uses the biblical story of the fall of Adam to demonstrate the human condition. Adam's curse means that human beings must work hard in all endeavors, including art, and that in time, even our finest creations will fade.

During a conversation with two women, a poet suggests that writing poetry takes hard work and time:

> I said, "A line will take us hours maybe;
> Yet if it does not seem a moment's thought,
> Our stitching and unstitching has been naught" (lines 4-6).

Hours of labor are compressed into a moment, though the world at large dismisses the resulting beauty as the work of idlers. The poet adds, with a touch of sarcasm, that one might as well scrub floors or break rocks since hard labor like this is recognized by the world.

One of the poet's companions, described as a "beautiful mild woman" (2, 16), extends the observation. She says that just as poets labor to create beautiful words, women "must labour to be beautiful" (21). The world at large also disregards the hours of work that go into creating physical beauty: "they do not talk of it at school" (20). In reference to his other companion, the poet says near the end of the poem, "I had a thought for no one's but your ears: / That you were beautiful" (35, 36). The operative word is "were." Despite all the time and work that she may have spent striving for beauty, in the end, her beauty had faded.

Each middle paragraph builds the writer's case using examples from the poem.

Yeats extends this observation by focusing on those who have made an art of love. He speaks of those who strive to create love "compounded of high courtesy" (25) by quoting "with learned looks / Precedents out of beautiful old books" (26). The poet himself is one such man. He tells his lover or wife, "I strove / To love you in the old high way of love" (36-37). But time has eroded the beauty of the love he had tried to build, leaving both of them "weary-hearted."

The writer uses rhetorical analysis, focusing on symbols and their meaning.

The power of time then is central to this poem. Yeats compares time to the waves of the sea, which "rose and fell / About the stars and broke in days and years" (33-34). Just as waves wear down seashells, time wears down all things that are beautiful. Yeats symbolizes beautiful things with the moon—worn hollow by time. So, too, Yeats sets the poem "at one summer's end" (1) and at the close of a day, as "the last embers of daylight die" (30). The death of the day and of the season symbolize the perishable nature of all beauty.

The writer gives an original interpretation.

But why is it that any "fine thing/ . . . needs much labouring" (23–24)? The title and the poet both point to Adam's curse, which banished him from the Garden of Eden. The suggestion is that whenever humans strive to create beauty, they are trying to recapture a vision of paradise. Yet many hours of labor can produce perhaps a moment's glimpse of that lost world.

In closing, the writer relates the poem to its creator.

Yeats is not interested in the world as it is, in "bankers, schoolmasters, and clergymen" (14). He is interested in visions that go beyond what is taught in school. For Yeats, the labor involved in creating something beautiful, and the recognition that beautiful things cannot last, only makes the beauty more intense and precious. Though this poem might seem a complaint about living under Adam's curse, Yeats would not be able to stand living any other way.

NOTE: To learn more about rhetorical analysis, see "Literary Terms" (pages 287–294), "Poetry Terms" (pages 295–296), and "Critical Approaches to Literary Analysis" (page 297).

Proofreader's Guide

"Cut out all those exclamation marks. An exclamation mark is like laughing at your own joke."
—F. Scott Fitzgerald

Marking Punctuation

Period

509.1 At the End of a Sentence

Use a **period** at the end of a sentence that makes a statement, requests something, or gives a mild command.

(Statement) **The man who does not read good books has no advantage over the man who can't read them.** —Mark Twain

(Request) **Please bring your folders and notebooks to class.**

(Mild command) **If your topic sentence isn't clear, rewrite it.**

NOTE: It is not necessary to place a period after a statement that has parentheses around it and is part of another sentence.

My dog Bobot (I don't quite remember how he acquired this name) is a Chesapeake Bay retriever—a hunting dog—who is afraid of loud noises.

509.2 After an Initial or an Abbreviation

Place a period after an initial or an abbreviation.

Ms. Sen. D.D.S. M.F.A. M.D. Jr. U.S. p.m. a.m.

Edna St. Vincent Millay Booker T. Washington D. H. Lawrence

NOTE: When an abbreviation is the last word in a sentence, use only one period at the end of the sentence.

Jaleesa eyed each door until she found the name Fletcher B. Gale, M.D.

509.3 As a Decimal Point

A period is used as a decimal point.

New York City has a budget of $46.9 billion to serve its 8.1 million people.

Question Mark

510.1 Direct Question

Place a **question mark** at the end of a direct question.

Now what? I wondered. Do I go out and buy a jar of honey and stand around waving it? How in the world am I supposed to catch a bear?

—Ken Taylor, "The Case of the Grizzly on the Greens"

Where did my body end and the crystal and white world begin?

—Ralph Ellison, *Invisible Man*

When a question ends with a quotation that is also a question, use only one question mark, and place it within the quotation marks.

On road trips, do you remember driving your parents crazy by asking, "Are we there yet?"

NOTE: Do *not* use a question mark after an indirect question.

Marta asked me if I had finished my calculus homework yet.

Also, when a single-word question like *how, when, or why* is incorporated into a sentence, question marks (and capitalization) are not necessary.

The questions we need to address at the next board meeting are not *why* or *whether,* but *how* and *when.*

510.2 To Show Uncertainty

Use a question mark within parentheses to show uncertainty.

This summer marks the 20th season (?) of the American Players Theatre.

NOTE: Do not use a question mark in this manner for formal writing.

510.3 Short Question Within a Sentence

Use a question mark for a short question within parentheses.

We crept so quietly (had they heard us?) past the kitchen door and back to our room.

Use a question mark for a short question within dashes.

I'm pleased to introduce Nancy—did I mention that she's a doctor?—and her husband, Antwon.

Exclamation Point

510.4 To Express Strong Feeling

Use the **exclamation point** (sparingly) to express strong feeling. You may place it after a word, a phrase, or a sentence.

Su-su-something's crawling up the back of my neck!

—Mark Twain, *Roughing It*

Comma

511.1 Between Two Independent Clauses

Use a **comma** between two independent clauses that are joined by a coordinating conjunction (*and, but, or, nor, for, yet, so*).

> **I wanted to knock on the glass to attract attention, but I couldn't move.**
>
> —Ralph Ellison, *Invisible Man*

NOTE: Do not confuse a sentence containing a compound verb for a compound sentence.

> **The Indians took the canoes close to the shore and stepped out into the icy river.**
>
> —Margaret Craven, *I Heard the Owl Call My Name*

511.2 To Separate Adjectives

Use commas to separate adjectives that *equally* modify the same noun.

NOTE: Do not use a comma between the last adjective and the noun.

> **Bao's eyes met the hard, bright lights hanging directly above her.**
>
> —Julie Ament, student writer

To Determine Equal Modifiers

To determine whether the adjectives in a sentence modify a noun equally, use these two tests.

1. Reverse the order of the adjectives; if the sentence is clear, the adjectives modify equally. (In the example below, *hot* and *crowded* can be reversed, and the sentence is still clear; *short* and *coffee* cannot.)

    Matt was tired of working in the hot, crowded lab and decided to take a short coffee break.

2. Insert *and* between the adjectives; if the sentence reads well, use a comma when *and* is omitted. (The word *and* can be inserted between *hot* and *crowded,* but *and* does not make sense between *short* and *coffee.*)

511.3 To Separate Contrasted Elements

Use commas to separate contrasted elements within a sentence.

> **Since the stereotypes were about Asians, and not African Americans, no such reaction occurred.**
>
> —Emmeline Chen, "Eliminating the Lighter Shades of Stereotyping"

Comma (continued)

512.1 To Enclose Parenthetical Elements

Use commas to separate parenthetical elements, such as an explanatory word or phrase, within a sentence.

They stood together, away from the pile of stones in the corner, and their jokes were quiet, and they smiled rather than laughed.

—Shirley Jackson, "The Lottery"

Allison meandered into class, late as usual, and sat down.

512.2 To Set Off Appositives

A specific kind of explanatory word or phrase called an **appositive** identifies or renames a preceding noun or pronoun.

Benson, our uninhibited and enthusiastic Yorkshire terrier, joined our family on my sister's fifteenth birthday.

—Chad Hockerman, student writer

NOTE: Do not use commas with *restrictive appositives.* A restrictive appositive is essential to the basic meaning of the sentence.

Astronaut Buzz Aldrin was 29 years old when he walked on the moon.

512.3 Between Items in a Series

Use commas to separate individual words, phrases, or clauses in a series. (A series contains at least three items.)

I'd never known anything about having meat, vegetables, and a salad all at the same meal. (Three nouns in a series)

I took her for walks, read her stories, and made up games for her to play. (Three phrases in a series)

—Anne Moody, *Coming of Age in Mississippi*

NOTE: Do not use commas when all the words in a series are connected with *or, nor,* or *and.*

Her fingernails are pointed and manicured and painted a shiny red.

—Carson McCullers, "Sucker"

512.4 After Introductory Phrases

Use a comma after an introductory participial phrase.

Determined to finish the sweater by Thanksgiving, my grandmother knits night and day.

Use a comma after an introductory prepositional phrase.

In the oddest places and at the strangest times, my grandmother can be found knitting madly away.

NOTE: You may omit the comma if the introductory phrase is short.

Before breakfast my grandmother knits.

513.1 To Set Off Introductory Clauses

Use a comma after an introductory adverb (subordinate) clause.

After the practice was over, Tina walked home.

A comma is also used if an adverb clause follows the main clause and begins with *although, even though, while,* or another conjunction expressing a contrast.

Tina walked home, even though it was raining very hard.

NOTE: A comma is not used if the adverb clause following the main clause is needed to complete the meaning of the sentence.

Tina practiced hard because she feared losing.

513.2 To Set Off Nonrestrictive Phrases and Clauses

Use commas to set off **nonrestrictive** (unnecessary) clauses and participial phrases. A nonrestrictive clause or participial phrase adds information that is not necessary to the basic meaning of the sentence. For example, if the clause or phrase (in red) were left out in the two examples below, the meaning of the sentences would remain clear. Therefore, commas are used to set them off.

The Altena Fitness Center and Visker Gymnasium, which were built last year, are busy every day. (nonrestrictive clause)

Students and faculty, improving their health through exercise, use both facilities throughout the week. (nonrestrictive phrase)

Do not use commas to set off **restrictive** (necessary) clauses and participial phrases. A restrictive clause or participial phrase adds information that the reader needs to know in order to understand the sentence. For example, if the clause and phrase (in red) were dropped from the examples below, the meaning wouldn't be the same. Therefore, commas are not used.

The handball court that has a sign-up sheet by the door must be reserved.
The clause identifies which handball court must be reserved.
(restrictive clause)

Individuals wanting to use this court must sign up a day in advance.
(restrictive phrase)

A Closer Look: That and Which

Use *that* to introduce restrictive (necessary) clauses; use *which* to introduce nonrestrictive (unnecessary) clauses. When the two words are used in this way, the reader can quickly distinguish necessary information from unnecessary information.

The treadmill that monitors heart rate is the one you must use.
The reader needs the information to find the right treadmill.

This treadmill, which we got last year, is required for your program.
The reader does not need the information in the subordinate clause to find the right treadmill.

Comma (continued)

514.1 To Set Off Dates

Use commas to set off items in a date.

He began working out on December 1, 2004, but quit by May 1, 2005.

However, when only the month and year are given, no commas are needed.

He began working out in December 2004 but quit by May 2005.

514.2 To Set Off Items in Addresses

Use commas to set off items in an address. (No comma is placed between the state and ZIP code.)

Mail the box to Friends of Wildlife, Box 402, Spokane, Washington 20077.

When a city and state (or country) appear in the middle of a sentence, a comma follows the last item in the address.

Several charitable organizations in Juneau, Alaska, pool their funds.

514.3 To Set Off Dialogue

Use commas to set off the speaker's exact words from the rest of the sentence (unless the quotation is punctuated with a question mark or an exclamation point).

"It's like we have our own government," adds Tanya, a 17-year-old squatter.

—Kyung Sun Yu and Nell Bernstein, "Street Teens Forge a Home"

514.4 To Set Off Interjections and Interruptions

Use a comma to separate an interjection or a weak exclamation from the rest of the sentence.

Hey, how am I to know that a minute's passed?

—Nathan Slaughter and Jim Schweitzer, *When Time Dies*

Use commas to set off a word, a phrase, or a clause that interrupts the movement of a sentence. Such expressions usually can be identified through the following tests: (1) They may be omitted without changing the meaning of a sentence. (2) They may be placed nearly anywhere in the sentence without changing its meaning.

For me, well, it's just a good job gone!

—Langston Hughes

As a general rule, the safest way to cross this street is with the light.

514.5 In Numbers

Use commas to separate numerals in large numbers in order to distinguish hundreds, thousands, millions, and so forth.

1,101 25,000 7,642,020

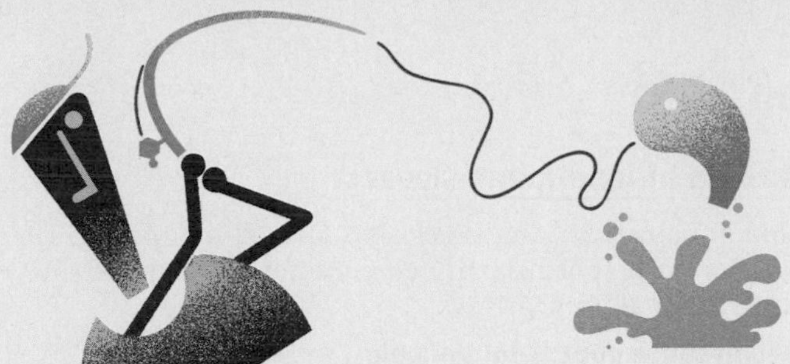

515.1 In Direct Address

Use commas to separate a noun of direct address from the rest of the sentence. A *noun of direct address* is the noun that names the person(s) spoken to.

"But, Mother Gibbs, one can go back; one can go back there again. . . . "

—Thornton Wilder, *Our Town*

515.2 To Enclose Titles or Initials

Use commas to enclose a title or initials and names that follow a surname.

Until Martin, Sr., was 15, he never had more than three months of schooling in any one year.

—Ed Clayton, *Martin Luther King: The Peaceful Warrior*

Hickok, J. B., and Cody, William F., are two popular Western heroes.

515.3 For Clarity or Emphasis

You may use a comma for clarity or for emphasis. There will be times when none of the traditional rules call for a comma, but one will be needed to prevent confusion or to emphasize an important idea.

It may be that those who do most, dream most. (emphasis)

—Stephen Leacock

What the crew does, does affect our voyage. (clarity)

515.4 Before Tags

Use a comma before a tag, which is a short statement or question at the end of a sentence.

He's the candidate who lost the election, isn't he?

You're not going to like this casserole, I know.

515.5 Following Conjunctive Adverbs and Transitional Phrases

Use a comma following conjunctive adverbs such as *however, instead,* and *nevertheless* and following transitional phrases such as *for example, in fact,* and *as a result.* (Also see 516.2.)

Jaleel is bright and studies hard; however, he suffers from test anxiety.

Pablo was born in the Andes; as a result, he loves the mountains.

Semicolon

516.1 To Join Two Independent Clauses

Use a **semicolon** to join two or more closely related independent clauses that are not connected with a coordinating conjunction. (Independent clauses can stand alone as separate sentences.)

I did not call myself a poet; I told people I wrote poems.

—Terry McMillan, "Breaking Ice"

Silence coated the room like a layer of tar; not even the breathing of the 11 Gehad made any sound.

—Gann Bierner, "The Leap"

NOTE: When independent clauses are especially long or contain commas, a semicolon may punctuate the sentence, even though a coordinating conjunction connects the clauses.

We waited all day in that wide line, tired travelers pressing in from all sides; and when we needed drinks or sandwiches, I would squeeze my way to the cafeteria and back.

516.2 With Transitional Phrases and Conjunctive Adverbs

A semicolon is used before a transitional phrase or a conjunctive adverb (with a comma after it) when the word connects two independent clauses in a compound sentence.

The layoffs weren't exactly a surprise; even so, those affected were upset at the coldness of their terminations.

We've heard that a million monkeys at a million keyboards could produce the complete works of Shakespeare; now, thanks to the Internet, we know that is not true.

— Robert Wilensky

Common Transitional Phrases

after all	at the same time	in addition	in the first place
as a matter of fact	even so	in conclusion	on the contrary
as a result	for example	in fact	on the other hand
at any rate	for instance	in other words	

Common Conjunctive Adverbs

also	however	meanwhile	nonetheless	then
besides	indeed	moreover	now	therefore
finally	instead	next	still	thus

516.3 To Separate Groups That Contain Commas

A semicolon is used to separate groups of words that already contain commas.

My favorite foods are pizza with pepperoni, onions, and olives; fried peanut butter and banana sandwiches; and liver with bacon, peppers, and onions.

Colon

517.1 After a Salutation

Use a **colon** after the salutation of a business letter.

Dear Judge Parker: **Dear Governor Whitman:**

517.2 Between Numerals Indicating Time or Ratios

Use a colon between the hours, minutes, and seconds of a number indicating time and between two numbers in a ratio.

8:30 p.m. **9:45 a.m.** **10:24:55**

The ratio of computers to students is 1:20. (one to twenty)

517.3 For Emphasis

Use a colon to emphasize a word, a phrase, a clause, or a sentence that explains or adds impact to the main clause.

His guest lecturers are local chefs who learn a lesson themselves: Homeless people are worth employing.

—Beth Brophy, "Feeding Those Who Are Hungry"

517.4 To Introduce a Quotation

Use a colon to formally introduce a quotation, a sentence, or a question.

Directly a voice in the corner rang out wild and clear: "I've got him! I've got him!"

—Mark Twain, *Roughing It*

517.5 To Introduce a List

A colon is used to introduce a list.

Be sure to pack the following items: a comb, a toothbrush, and deodorant.

A Closer Look

Do not use a colon between a verb and its object or complement, or between a preposition and its object.

Incorrect: **Min has: a snowmobile, an ATV, and a canoe.**

Correct: **Min has plenty of toys: a snowmobile, an ATV, and a canoe.**

Incorrect: **Dad watches a TV show about: vegan cooking.**

Correct: **Dad watches a TV show about a new subject: vegan cooking.**

517.6 Between a Title and a Subtitle

Use a colon to distinguish between a title and a subtitle, volume and page, and chapter and verse in literature.

Write for College*: *A Student Handbook

***Encyclopedia Americana* IV: 211** **Psalm 23:1-6**

Hyphen

518.1 In Compound Words

Use the **hyphen** to make some compound words.

jack-in-the-box (noun)

starry-eyed (adjective)

three-year-old (adjective or noun)

Writers sometimes combine words in a new and unexpected way. Such combinations are usually hyphenated.

And they pried pieces of baked-too-fast sunshine cake from the roofs of their mouths and looked once more into the boy's eyes.

—Toni Morrison, *Song of Solomon*

NOTE: Consult a dictionary for the spelling of a particular compound word. Some compound words are not hyphenated and are either open (living room) or closed (bedroom). Some are open as a noun (ice cream) but hyphenated as an adjective (ice-cream sundae); closed as a noun (tryout) but open as a verb (try out); and so on.

518.2 To Create New Words

Use a hyphen to form new words beginning with the prefixes *self-, ex-, all-,* and *half-*. Also use a hyphen to join any prefix to a proper noun, a proper adjective, or the official name of an office. Use a hyphen before the suffix *-elect.*

self-contained **ex-governor** **all-inclusive** **half-painted**
pre-Cambrian **mid-December** **president-elect**

Use a hyphen to join the prefix *great* to names of relatives, but do not use a hyphen to join *great* to other words.

great-aunt, great-grandfather (correct) **great-hall** (incorrect)

518.3 To Form an Adjective

Use the hyphen to join two or more words that serve as a single adjective (a single-thought adjective) before a noun.

In real life I am a large, big-boned woman with rough, man-working hands.

—Alice Walker, "Everyday Use"

Use common sense to determine whether a compound adjective should be hyphenated for the sake of clarity. Generally, hyphenate a compound adjective that is composed of a noun + adjective, . . .

oven-safe handles **book-smart student**

a noun + participle (*ing* or *ed* form of a verb), . . .

line-dried clothes **bone-chilling story**

or a phrase.

heat-and-serve meal **off-and-on relationship**

A Closer Look

When words forming the adjective come after the noun, do not hyphenate them.

In real life I am large and big boned.

When the first of these words is an adverb ending in *-ly,* do not use a hyphen; also, do not use a hyphen when a number or a letter is the final element in a single-thought adjective.

delicately prepared pastry (adverb ending in *-ly*)

class B movie (letter is the final element)

519.1 To Join Letters and Words

Use a hyphen to join a capital letter or lowercase letter to a noun or participle. (Check your dictionary.)

T-shirt **Y-turn** **G-rated** **x-axis**

519.2 Between Numbers and Fractions

Use a hyphen to join the words in compound numbers from *twenty-one* to *ninety-nine* when it is necessary to write them out.

twenty-five **forty-three** **seventy-nine** **sixty-two**

Use a hyphen between the numerator and denominator of a fraction, but not when one or both of those elements are already hyphenated.

four-tenths **five-sixteenths** **(7/32) seven thirty-seconds**

519.3 In a Special Series

Use hyphens when two or more words have a common element that is omitted in all but the last term.

The ship has lovely two-, four-, or six-person cabins.

519.4 To Join Numbers

Use a hyphen to join numbers indicating the life span of a person or the score in a contest or a vote.

We can thank Louis Pasteur (1822–1895) for pasteurized milk.

In the game between cross-state rivals, Stanton defeated Edgewood 28–14.

519.5 To Prevent Confusion

Use a hyphen with prefixes or suffixes to avoid confusion or awkward spelling.

re-create (not *recreate*) the image **re-cover (not *recover*) the sofa**

Hyphen (continued)

520.1 To Divide a Word

Use a hyphen to divide a word, only between its syllables, at the end of a line of print. Always place the hyphen after the syllable at the end of the line—never before a syllable at the beginning of the following line.

Guidelines for Dividing with Hyphens

1. Always leave enough of the word at the end of the line so that the word can be identified.
2. Always divide a compound word between its basic units: **sister-in-law,** not **sis-ter-in-law.**
3. Avoid dividing a word of five or fewer letters: **paper, study, July.**
4. Avoid dividing the last word in a paragraph.
5. Never divide a one-syllable word: **rained, skills, through.**
6. Never divide a one-letter syllable from the rest of the word: **omit-ted,** not **o-mitted.**
7. When a vowel is a syllable by itself, divide the word after the vowel: **epi-sode,** not **ep-isode.**
8. Never divide abbreviations or contractions: **shouldn't,** not **should-n't.**
9. Never divide the last word in more than two lines in a row.

Apostrophe

520.2 In Contractions

Use an **apostrophe** to show that one or more letters have been left out of a word group to form a contraction.

hadn't – *o* is left out **they'd – *woul* is left out** **it's – *i* is left out**

NOTE: Use an apostrophe to show that one or more numerals or letters have been left out of numbers or words in order to show special pronunciation.

class of '10 – *20* is left out **g'day – *ood* is left out**

520.3 To Form Certain Plurals

Use an apostrophe and *s* to form the plural of a letter, a number, a sign, or a word discussed as a word.

B – B's **C – C's** **8 – 8's** **+ – +'s** **and – and's**

Ms. D'Aquisto says our conversations contain too many *like*'s and *no way*'s.

NOTE: If two apostrophes are called for in the same word, omit the second one.

Follow closely the do's and don'ts (not don't's) on the checklist.

521.1 To Form Singular Possessives

Add an apostrophe and *s* to form the possessive of most singular nouns.

Spock's ears **Captain Kirk's singing** **the ship's escape plan**

NOTE: When a singular noun ends with an *s* or a *z* sound, you may form the possessive by adding just an apostrophe. When the singular noun is a one-syllable word, however, you usually add both an apostrophe and an *s* to form the possessive.

San Carlos' government (or) **San Carlos's government** (two-syllable word)

Ross's essay (one-syllable word) **The class's field trip** (one-syllable word)

521.2 To Form Plural Possessives

The possessive form of plural nouns ending in *s* is usually made by adding just an apostrophe.

students' homework **bosses' orders**

A Closer Look

It will help you punctuate correctly if you remember that the word immediately before the apostrophe is the owner.

girl's guitar (*girl* is the owner) **boss's order** (*boss* is the owner)

girls' guitar (*girls* are the owners) **bosses' order** (*bosses* are the owners)

521.3 To Form Possessives of Compound Nouns

Form the possessive of a compound noun by placing the possessive ending after the last word.

the secretary of the interior's (singular) **agenda**
her lady-in-waiting's (singular) **day off**

If forming a possessive of a plural compound noun creates an awkward construction, you may replace the possessive with an *of* phrase. (All four forms below are correct.)

their fathers-in-law's (plural) **birthdays**
or **the birthdays of their *fathers-in-law*** (plural)

the ambassadors-at-large's (plural) **plans**
or **the plans of the *ambassadors-at-large*** (plural)

521.4 To Form Possessives of Indefinite Pronouns

Form the possessive of an indefinite pronoun by placing an apostrophe and an *s* on the last word. (See 589.2.)

everyone's **anyone's** **somebody's**

In expressions using *else,* add the apostrophe and *s* after the last word.

anyone else's **everybody else's**

Apostrophe (continued)

522.1 To Show Shared Possession

When possession is shared by more than one noun, use the possessive form for the last noun in the series.

Hoshi, Linda, and Nakiva's water skis (All three own the same skis.)

Hoshi's, Linda's, and Nakiva's water skis (Each owns her own skis.)

522.2 To Express Time or Amount

Use an apostrophe and an *s* with an adjective that is part of an expression indicating time or amount.

a penny's worth	**today's business**	**this morning's meeting**
yesterday's news	**a day's wage**	**a month's pay**

Punctuation Marks

´	Accent, acute	,	Comma	( )	Parentheses
`	Accent, grave	†	Dagger	.	Period
'	Apostrophe	—	Dash	?	Question mark
*	Asterisk	/	Diagonal/Slash	" "	Quotation marks
{ }	Brace	¨ (ü)	Dieresis	§	Section
[ ]	Brackets	. . .	Ellipsis	;	Semicolon
^	Caret	!	Exclamation point	~	Tilde
(ç)	Cedilla	-	Hyphen	____	Underscore
^	Circumflex	...	Leaders		
:	Colon	¶	Paragraph		

Quotation Marks

522.3 Placement of Punctuation

Always place periods and commas inside quotation marks.

"Dr. Slaughter wants you to have liquids, Will," Mama said anxiously. "He said not to give you any solid food tonight."

—Olive Ann Burns, *Cold Sassy Tree*

Place an exclamation point or a question mark *inside* quotation marks when it punctuates the quotation and *outside* when it punctuates the main sentence.

"Am I dreaming?"

Had she heard him say, "Here's the key to your new car"?

Always place semicolons or colons outside quotation marks.

I read "Thirteen Ways of Looking at a Blackbird"; I found it enlightening.

523.1 To Punctuate Titles

Use **quotation marks** to punctuate titles of songs, poems, short stories, one-act plays, lectures, episodes of radio or television programs, chapters of books, unpublished works, electronic files, and articles found in magazines, newspapers, encyclopedias, or online sources. (For punctuation of other titles, see 525.1.)

"Santa Lucia" (song)	**"Affordable Adventures"** (magazine article)
"The Chameleon" (short story)	**"Hester at her Needle"** (chapter in a book)
"Miss Julle" (one-act play)	**"Dancing with Debra"** (television episode)

NOTE: Punctuate one title within another title as follows:

He wants to watch *Inside the "New York Times"* on PBS tonight.
(title of a newspaper within the title of a TV program)

523.2 For Special Words

You may use quotation marks (1) to distinguish a word that is being discussed, (2) to indicate that a word is unfamiliar slang, or (3) to point out that a word is being used in a special way.

(1) A commentary on the times is that the word "honesty" is now preceded by "old-fashioned." —Larry Wolters

(2) I . . . asked the bartender where I could hear "chanky-chank," as Cajuns called their music. —William Least Heat-Moon, *Blue Highways*

(3) The winner "humbly" accepted the trophy.

NOTE: You may use italics (underlining) in place of quotation marks in each of these three situations. (See 524.4.)

523.3 To Set Off Quoted Passages

Place quotation marks before and after the words in direct quotations.

"Just come to a game," he pleads. "You'll change your mind."
—Sandra Lampe, "Batter UP!"

In a quoted passage, put brackets around any word or punctuation mark that is not part of the original quotation.

(Original) **Conservation pundits point to it as the classic example of the impossibility of providing good government service.**

(Quotation) **"Conservation pundits point to it [the U.S. Postal Service] as the classic example of the impossibility of providing good government service."**
—Brad Branan, "Dead Letter Office?"

NOTE: If you quote only part of the original passage, be sure to construct a sentence that is both accurate and grammatically correct.

Restructuring the Postal Service involved "turning over much of its work to the private sector."

Quotation Marks (continued)

524.1 For Long Quotations

If you quote more than one paragraph, place quotation marks before each paragraph and at the end of the last paragraph (Example A). If a quotation takes more than four lines on a page, you may set it off from the text by indenting 10 spaces from the left margin (block form). Do not use quotation marks either before or after the quoted material, unless they appear in the original. Double-space the quotation. (Example B).

Example A	Example B
"______________	______________
______________	______________
__________.	______________
"______________	______________
______________	______________
__________.	__________.
"__________."	______________

524.2 For Quoting a Quotation

Use single quotation marks to punctuate a quotation **within** a quotation. Use double quotation marks to distinguish a quotation within a quotation that is also within a quotation.

"For tomorrow," said Mr. Botts, "read 'Unlighted Lamps.'"

Sue asked, "Did you hear Mr. Botts say, 'Read "Unlighted Lamps"'?"

Italics (Underlining)

524.3 Handwritten and Printed Material

Italics is a printer's term for a style of type that is slightly slanted. In this sentence, the word *happiness* is printed in italics. In material that is handwritten or typed on a machine that cannot print in italics, underline each word or letter that should be in italics.

My Ántonia **is the story of a strong and determined pioneer woman.** (printed)

Willa Cather's <u>My Ántonia</u> describes pioneer life in America. (handwritten)

524.4 For Special Uses

Use italics for a number, letter, or word that is being discussed or used in a special way. (Sometimes quotation marks are used for this reason. See 523.2.)

I hope that this letter *I* stands for *incredible* and not *incomplete*.

525.1 In Titles

Use italics to indicate the titles of magazines, newspapers, pamphlets, books, full-length plays, films, videos, radio and television programs, book-length poems, ballets, operas, paintings, lengthy musical compositions, cassettes, CD's, legal cases, and the names of ships and aircraft. (For punctuation of other titles, see 523.1.)

Newsweek (magazine)
Shakespeare in Love (film)
Caring for Your Kitten (pamphlet)
Chicago Tribune (newspaper)
Cold Sassy Tree (book)
Law & Order (television program)
Hedda Gabler (full-length play)

525.2 For Foreign Words

Use italics for foreign words that have not been adopted into the English language; also use italics for scientific names.

The voyageurs—tough men with natural *bonhomie*—discovered the shy *Castor canadensis*, or North American beaver.

525.3 For Emphasis

Use italics for words that require particular emphasis.

I guess it really *was* worth it to put in that extra study time.

Parentheses

525.4 With Full Sentences

When using a full "sentence" within another sentence, do not capitalize it or use a period inside the parentheses.

And, since your friend won't have the assignment (he was just thinking about calling you), you'll have to make a couple more calls to actually get it.

—Ken Taylor, "The Art and Practice of Avoiding Homework"

When the parenthetical sentence comes after the main sentence, capitalize and punctuate it the same way you would any other complete sentence.

They kiss and hug when they say "hello," and I love this. (In Korea, people are much more formal; they just shake hands and bow to each other.)

—Sue Chong, "He Said I Was Too American"

NOTE: For unavoidable parentheses within parentheses (. . . [. . .] . . .), use brackets. Avoid overuse of parentheses by using commas instead.

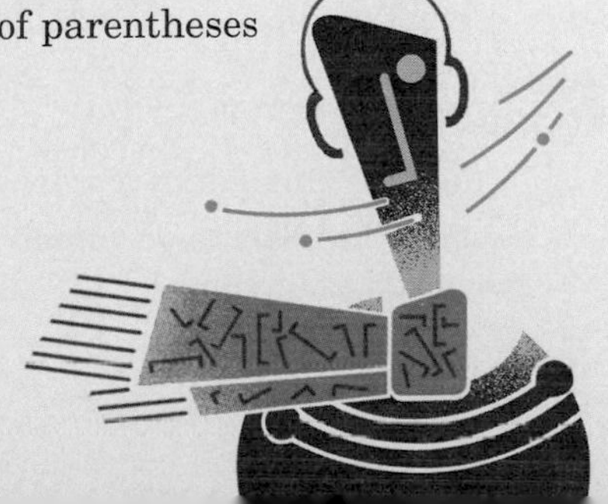

Parentheses (continued)

526.1 To Set Off Explanatory Material

You may use **parentheses** to set off explanatory or added material that interrupts the normal sentence structure.

> **Benson (our dog) sits in on our piano lessons (on the piano bench), much to the teacher's surprise and amusement.**
>
> —Chad Hockerman, student writer

NOTE: Place question marks and exclamation points within the parentheses when they mark the added material.

> **Ivan at once concluded (the rascal!) that I had a passion for dances, and . . . wanted to drag me off to a dancing class.**
>
> —Fyodor Dostoyevsky, "A Novel in Nine Letters"

Diagonal

526.2 To Show a Choice

Use a **diagonal** (also called a *slash*) between two words, as in *and/or*, to indicate that either is acceptable.

> **Press the load/eject button.**
>
> **Don't worry; this is indoor/outdoor carpet.**

526.3 When Quoting Poetry

When quoting more than one line of poetry, use a diagonal to show where each line of poetry ends. (Insert a space on each side of the diagonal.)

> **I have learned not to worry about love; / but to honor its coming / with all my heart.**
>
> —Alice Walker, "New Face"

Dash

526.4 To Indicate a Sudden Break

Use a **dash** to indicate a sudden break or change in the sentence.

> **Near the semester's end—and this is not always due to poor planning—some students may find themselves in a real crunch.**

NOTE: Dashes are often used in place of commas. Use dashes when you want to give special emphasis; use commas when there is no need for emphasis.

526.5 For Emphasis

Use a dash to emphasize a word, a series, a phrase, or a clause.

> **Some unicyclists have turned their interest into an extreme sport—mountain unicycling.**

527.1 To Set Off an Introductory Series

Use a dash to set off an introductory series from the clause that explains the series.

> **A good book, a cup of tea, a comfortable chair—these things always saved my mother's sanity.**

527.2 To Set Off Parenthetical Material

You may use a dash to set off parenthetical material—material that explains or clarifies a word or a phrase.

> **A single incident—a tornado that came without warning—changed the face of the small town forever.**

527.3 To Indicate Interrupted Speech

Use a dash to show interrupted or faltering speech in dialogue.

> **SOJOURNER:** **Mama, why are you—**
>
> **MAMA:** **Isabelle, do as I say!**
>
> —Sandy Asher, *A Woman Called Truth*

Ellipsis

527.4 To Show Omitted Words

Use an **ellipsis** (three periods with one space before and after each period) to show that one or more words have been omitted in a quotation.

(Original)

> **We the people of the United States, in order to form a more perfect Union, establish justice, insure domestic tranquility, provide for the common defense, promote the general welfare, and secure the blessings of liberty to ourselves and our posterity, do ordain and establish this Constitution for the United States of America.**
>
> —Preamble, U.S. Constitution

(Quotation)

> **"We the people . . . in order to form a more perfect Union . . . establish this Constitution for the United States of America."**

527.5 To Show a Pause

Use an ellipsis to indicate a pause.

> **I brought my trembling hand to my focusing eyes. It was oozing, it was red, it was . . . it was . . . a tomato!**
>
> —Laura Baginski, student writer

Ellipsis (continued)

528.1 At the End of a Sentence

If words from a quotation are omitted at the end of a sentence, place the ellipsis after the period that marks the conclusion of the sentence.

> **"Five score years ago, a great American, in whose symbolic shadow we stand, signed the Emancipation Proclamation. . . . But one hundred years later, we must face the tragic fact that the Negro is still not free."**
>
> —Martin Luther King, Jr., "I Have a Dream"

NOTE: If the quoted material is a complete sentence (even if it was not complete in the original), use a period, then an ellipsis.

Original: **I am tired; my heart is sick and sad. From where the sun now stands I will fight no more forever.**

—Chief Joseph of the Nez Percé

Quotation: **"I am tired. . . . From where the sun now stands I will fight no more forever."**

or **"I am tired. . . . I will fight no more. . . . "**

Brackets

528.2 To Set Off Clarifying Information

Use **brackets** before and after words that are added to clarify what another person has said or written.

> **"They'd [the sweat bees] get into your mouth, ears, eyes, nose. You'd feel them all over you."**
>
> —Marilyn Johnson and Sasha Nyary, "Roosevelts in the Amazon"

NOTE: The brackets indicate that the words *the sweat bees* are not part of the quotation but were added for clarification.

528.3 Around an Editorial Correction

Place brackets around an editorial correction inserted within quoted material.

> **"Brooklyn alone has 8 percent of lead poisoning [victims] nationwide," said Marjorie Moore.**
>
> —Donna Actie, student writer

NOTE: The brackets indicate that the word *victims* replaced the author's original word.

Place brackets around the letters *sic* (Latin for "as such"); the letters indicate that an error appearing in the material being quoted was made by the original speaker or writer.

> **"'When I'm queen,' mused Lucy, 'I'll show these blockheads whose [*sic*] got beauty and brains.'"**

"English spelling is weird . . .
or is it wierd?"
—Irwin Hill

Checking Mechanics

Capitalization

529.1 Proper Nouns and Adjectives

Capitalize proper nouns and proper adjectives (those derived from proper nouns). The chart below provides a quick overview of capitalization rules. The pages following explain some specific rules of capitalization.

Capitalization at a Glance

Names of people	**Alice Walker, Matilda, Jim, Mr. Roker**
Days of the week, months	**Sunday, Tuesday, June, August**
Holidays, holy days	**Thanksgiving, Easter, Hanukkah**
Periods, events in history	**Middle Ages, the Battle of Bunker Hill**
Official documents	**Declaration of Independence**
Special events	**Elgin Community Spring Gala**
Languages, nationalities, religions	**French, Canadian, Islam**
Political parties	**Republican Party, Socialist Party**
Trade names	**Oscar Mayer hot dogs, Pontiac Sunbird**
Official titles used with names	**Mayor John Spitzer, Senator Feinstein**
Formal epithets	**Alexander the Great**
Geographical names	
Planets, heavenly bodies	**Earth, Jupiter, the Milky Way**
Continents	**Australia, South America**
Countries	**Ireland, Grenada, Sri Lanka**
States, provinces	**Ohio, Utah, Nova Scotia**
Cities, towns, villages	**El Paso, Burlington, Wonewoc**
Streets, roads, highways	**Park Avenue, Route 66, Interstate 90**
Landforms	**the Rocky Mountains, the Sahara Desert**
Bodies of water	**Yellowstone Lake, Pumpkin Creek**
Buildings, monuments	**Elkhorn High School, Gateway Arch**
Public areas	**Times Square, Sequoia National Park**

Capitalization (continued)

530.1 First Words

Capitalize the first word of every sentence, including the first word of a full-sentence direct quotation.

The crowd was quiet. A girl whispered, "Hope it's not Nancy," and the sound of her whisper reached the edges of the crowd.

—Shirley Jackson, "The Lottery"

530.2 Sentences in Parentheses

Capitalize the first word in a sentence enclosed in parentheses, but do not capitalize the first word if the parenthetical appears within another sentence.

Shamelessly she winked at me and grinned again. (That grin! She could have taken it off her face and put it on the table.)

—Jean Stafford, *Bad Characters*

Damien's aunt (she's a wild woman) plays bingo every Saturday night.

530.3 Sentences Following Colons

Capitalize the first word in a complete sentence that follows a colon when (1) you want to emphasize the sentence or (2) the sentence is a quotation.

When we quarreled and made horrible faces at one another, Mother knew what to say: "Your faces will stay that way, and no one will marry you."

530.4 Sections of the Country

Capitalize words that indicate particular sections of the country; do not capitalize words that simply indicate direction.

Mr. Johnson is from the Southwest. (section of the country)

After moving north to Montana, he had to buy winter clothes. (direction)

530.5 Certain Religious Words

Capitalize nouns that refer to the Supreme Being, the word *Bible*, the books of the Bible, and the names for other holy books.

God **Jehovah** the **Lord** the **Savior** **Allah** **Koran** **Genesis**

530.6 Titles

Capitalize the first word of a title, the last word, and every word in between except articles (*a, an, the*), short prepositions, and coordinating conjunctions. Follow this rule for titles of books, newspapers, magazines, poems, plays, songs, articles, films, works of art, photographs, and stories.

Cold Sassy Tree ***Washington Post*** **"Nothing Gold Can Stay"**

A Midsummer Night's Dream **"The Diary of a Madman"**

531.1 Letters

Capitalize the letters used to indicate form or shape.

U-turn **I-beam** **S-curve** **T-shirt** **V-shaped**

531.2 Organizations

Capitalize the name of an organization, an association, or a team.

Democratic Party **American Indian Movement** **Lake Ontario Sailors**

531.3 Abbreviations

Capitalize abbreviations of titles and organizations. (Some other abbreviations are also capitalized. See pages 535–536.)

CEO **M.D.** **Ph.D.** **AAA** **NAACP**

531.4 Words Used as Names

Capitalize words like *father, mother, uncle,* and *senator* when they are used as titles with a personal name or when they are substituted for proper nouns (especially in direct address).

We've missed you, Aunt Lucinda! (*Aunt* is part of the name.)

I hope Mayor Bates arrives soon. (*Mayor* is part of the name.)

A Closer Look

To test whether a word is being substituted for a proper noun, simply read the sentence with a proper noun in place of the word. If the proper noun fits in the sentence, the word being tested should be capitalized; if the proper noun does not work in the sentence, the word should not be capitalized.

Did Mom (Sue) say we could go? (*Sue* works in this sentence.)

Did your mom (Sue) say you could go? (*Sue* does not work here.)

NOTE: Usually the word is not capitalized if it follows a possessive—*my, his, your*—as it does in the second sentence above.

531.5 Titles of Courses

Capitalize words like *sociology* and *history* when they are used as titles of specific courses; do not capitalize these words when they name a field of study.

Who teaches History 202? (title of a specific course)

It's the same professor who teaches my sociology course. (a field of study)

NOTE: The words *freshman, sophomore, junior,* and *senior* are not capitalized unless they are part of an official title.

Rosa is a senior this year and is in charge of the Senior Class Banquet.

Plurals

532.1 Most Nouns

Form the **plurals** of most nouns by adding *s* to the singular.

cheerleader—cheerleaders **wheel—wheels** **crate—crates**

532.2 Nouns Ending in *sh, ch, x, s,* and *z*

Form the plurals of nouns ending in *sh, ch, x, s,* and *z* by adding *es* to the singular.

dish—dishes **lunch—lunches** **fox—foxes** **mess—messes**

532.3 Nouns Ending in *y*

The plurals of common nouns that end in *y*—preceded by a consonant—are formed by changing the *y* to *i* and adding *es.*

fly—flies **jalopy—jalopies**

The plurals of nouns that end in *y* and are preceded by a vowel are formed by adding only an *s.*

holiday—holidays **buoy—buoys** **donkey—donkeys**

NOTE: Form the plurals of all proper nouns ending in *y* by adding *s.*

We have three Kathys in our English class.

532.4 Nouns Ending in *o*

The plurals of nouns ending in *o*—preceded by a vowel—are formed by adding an *s.*

radio—radios **rodeo—rodeos** **studio—studios** **duo—duos**

The plurals of most nouns ending in *o* and preceded by a consonant are formed by adding *es.*

echo—echoes **hero—heroes** **tomato—tomatoes**

Exception: Musical terms ending in *o* always form plurals by adding *s.*

alto—altos **banjo—banjos** **solo—solos** **piano—pianos**

532.5 Nouns Ending in *f* or *fe*

Form the plurals of nouns that end in *f* or *fe* in one of two ways: if the final *f* sound is still heard in the plural form of the word, simply add *s;* but if the final *f* sound becomes a *v* sound, change the *f* to *ve* and add *s.*

Plural ends with f sound: **roof—roofs; chief—chiefs**

Plural ends with v sound: **wife—wives; loaf—loaves**

NOTE: Several words are correct with either ending.

Plural ends with either sound: **hoof—hooves/hoofs**

533.1 Irregular Spelling

A number of words form a plural by taking on an irregular spelling.

crisis—crises **child—children** **radius—radii**
criterion—criteria **goose—geese** **die—dice**

NOTE: Some of these words are now acceptable with the commonly used *s* or *es* ending.

index—indices/indexes **cactus—cacti/cactuses**

Some nouns remain unchanged when used as plurals.

deer **sheep** **salmon** **aircraft** **series**

533.2 Words Discussed as Words

The plurals of symbols, letters, numbers, and words being discussed as words are formed by adding an apostrophe and an *s.*

Dad yelled a lot of *wow's* and *yippee's* when he saw my A's and B's.

NOTE: You may omit the apostrophe if it does not cause any confusion.

the three R's or **Rs** **YMCA's** or **YMCAs**

533.3 Nouns Ending in *ful*

Form the plurals of nouns that end in *ful* by adding an *s* at the end of the word.

two tankfuls **three pailfuls** **four mouthfuls**

NOTE: Do not confuse these examples with *three pails full* (when you are referring to three separate pails full of something) or *two tanks full.*

533.4 Compound Nouns

Form the plurals of most compound nouns by adding *s* or *es* to the important word in the compound.

brothers-in-law **maids of honor** **secretaries of state**

533.5 Use of Collective Nouns

A collective noun may be singular or plural depending upon how it's used. A collective noun is singular when it refers to a group considered as one unit; it is plural when it refers to the individuals in the group.

The class was on its best behavior. (group as a unit)
The class are preparing for their final exams. (individuals in the group)

If it seems awkward to use a plural verb with a collective noun, add a clearly plural noun such as *members* to the sentence.

The class members are preparing for their final exams.

You may also change the collective noun into a possessive followed by a plural noun that describes the individuals in the group.

The class's students are preparing for their final exams.

Numbers

534.1 Numerals or Words

Numbers from one to nine are usually written as words; numbers 10 and over are usually written as numerals.

two seven nine 10 25 106 1,079

Exception: Keep numbers being compared or contrasted in the same style.

8 to 11 years old eight to eleven years old

You may use a combination of numerals and words for very large numbers.

1.5 million 3 billion to 3.2 billion 6 trillion

If numbers are used infrequently in a piece of writing, you may spell out those that can be written in no more than two words.

ten twenty-five two hundred fifty thousand

534.2 Numerals Only

Use numerals for the following forms: decimals, percentages, chapters, dates, pages, addresses, phone numbers, identification numbers, and statistics.

26.2	**8 percent**	**Highway 36**	**chapter 7**
pages 287-89	**July 6, 1945**	**44 B.C.E.**	**a vote of 23 to 4**

Always use numerals with abbreviations and symbols.

8% 10 mm 3 cc 8 oz 90° C 24 mph 76.9%

534.3 Words Only

Use words to express numbers that begin a sentence.

Fourteen students "forgot" their assignments.

NOTE: Change the sentence structure if this rule creates a clumsy construction.

Clumsy: ***Six hundred thirty-nine*** **teachers attended the fall convention.**

Better: **This year, 639 teachers attended the fall convention.**

Use words for numbers that come before a compound modifier if that modifier includes a numeral.

They made twelve 10-foot sub sandwiches for the picnic.

Use words for references to particular centuries.

the twenty-first century the third century B.C.E.

534.4 Time and Money

If time is expressed with an abbreviation, use numerals; if it is expressed in words, spell out the number.

4:00 A.M. (or) four o'clock

If an amount of money is spelled out, so is the currency; if a symbol is used, use a numeral.

twenty dollars (or) $20

Abbreviations

535.1 Formal and Informal Abbreviations

An **abbreviation** is the shortened form of a word or phrase. Some abbreviations are always acceptable in both formal and informal writing:

Mr. Mrs. Jr. Ms. Dr. a.m. (A.M.) p.m. (P.M.)

NOTE: In most of your writing, you **do not abbreviate** the names of states, countries, months, days, or units of measure. Do not abbreviate the words *Street, Road, Avenue, Company,* and similar words, especially when they are part of a proper name. Also, do not use signs or symbols (%, &, #, @) in place of words. The dollar sign, however, is appropriate with numerals ($325).

535.2 Correspondence Abbreviations

United States

	Standard	Postal
Alabama	Ala.	AL
Alaska	Alaska	AK
Arizona	Ariz.	AZ
Arkansas	Ark.	AR
California	Calif.	CA
Colorado	Colo.	CO
Connecticut	Conn.	CT
Delaware	Del.	DE
District of Columbia	D.C.	DC
Florida	Fla.	FL
Georgia	Ga.	GA
Guam	Guam	GU
Hawaii	Hawaii	HI
Idaho	Idaho	ID
Illinois	Ill.	IL
Indiana	Ind.	IN
Iowa	Iowa	IA
Kansas	Kan.	KS
Kentucky	Ky.	KY
Louisiana	La.	LA
Maine	Maine	ME
Maryland	Md.	MD
Massachusetts	Mass.	MA
Michigan	Mich.	MI
Minnesota	Minn.	MN
Mississippi	Miss.	MS
Missouri	Mo.	MO
Montana	Mont.	MT
Nebraska	Neb.	NE
Nevada	Nev.	NV
New Hampshire	N.H.	NH
New Jersey	N.J.	NJ
New Mexico	N.M.	NM
New York	N.Y.	NY
North Carolina	N.C.	NC
North Dakota	N.D.	ND
Ohio	Ohio	OH
Oklahoma	Okla.	OK
Oregon	Ore.	OR
Pennsylvania	Pa.	PA
Puerto Rico	P.R.	PR
Rhode Island	R.I.	RI
South Carolina	S.C.	SC
South Dakota	S.D.	SD
Tennessee	Tenn.	TN
Texas	Texas	TX
Utah	Utah	UT
Vermont	Vt.	VT
Virginia	Va.	VA
Virgin Islands	V.I.	VI
Washington	Wash.	WA
West Virginia	W.Va.	WV
Wisconsin	Wis.	WI
Wyoming	Wyo.	WY

Canadian Provinces

	Standard	Postal
Alberta	Alta.	AB
British Columbia	B.C.	BC
Manitoba	Man.	MB
New Brunswick	N.B.	NB
Newfoundland and Labrador	N.F. Lab.	NL
Northwest Territories	N.W.T.	NT
Nova Scotia	N.S.	NS
Nunavut		NU
Ontario	Ont.	ON
Prince Edward Island	P.E.I.	PE
Quebec	Que.	QC
Saskatchewan	Sask.	SK
Yukon Territory	Y.T.	YT

Addresses

	Standard	Postal
Apartment	Apt.	APT
Avenue	Ave.	AVE
Boulevard	Blvd.	BLVD
Circle	Cir.	CIR
Court	Ct.	CT
Drive	Dr.	DR
East	E.	E
Expressway	Expy.	EXPY
Freeway	Fwy.	FWY
Heights	Hts.	HTS
Highway	Hwy.	HWY
Hospital	Hosp.	HOSP
Junction	Junc.	JCT
Lake	L.	LK
Lakes	Ls.	LKS
Lane	Ln.	LN
Meadows	Mdws.	MDWS
North	N.	N
Palms	Palms	PLMS
Park	Pk.	PK
Parkway	Pky.	PKY
Place	Pl.	PL
Plaza	Plaza	PLZ
Post Office Box	P.O. Box	PO BOX
Ridge	Rdg.	RDG
River	R.	RV
Road	Rd.	RD
Room	Rm.	RM
Rural	R.	R
Rural Route	R.R.	RR
Shore	Sh.	SH
South	S.	S
Square	Sq.	SQ
Station	Sta.	STA
Street	St.	ST
Suite	Ste.	STE
Terrace	Ter.	TER
Turnpike	Tpke.	TPKE
Union	Un.	UN
View	View	VW
Village	Vil.	VLG
West	W.	W

Abbreviations (continued)

536.1 Other Common Abbreviations

abr. abridged; abridgment
AC, ac alternating current
ACV actual cash value
A.D. in the year of the Lord (Latin *anno Domini*)
alt. altitude
AM amplitude modulation
A.M., a.m. before noon (Latin *ante meridiem*)
apt. apartment
avg., av. average
b. 1. book **2.** born
B.C. before Christ
B.C.E. before the Common Era
C 1. Celsius **2.** centigrade **3.** coulomb
c. 1. circa (about) **2.** cup
cc 1. cubic centimeter **2.** carbon copy
CDT, C.D.T. central daylight time
C.E. of the Common Era
CGI computer-generated images
chap. chapter
cm centimeter
c.o., c/o care of
co-op. cooperative
corp. corporation
CST, C.S.T. central standard time
cu., c cubic
d. 1. date **2.** died
D.A. district attorney
d.b.a. doing business as
DC, dc direct current
dec. deceased
dept. department
dist. district
DST, D.S.T. daylight saving time
dup. duplicate
ea. each
ed. edition; editor
EDT, E.D.T. eastern daylight time
e.g. for example (Latin *exempli gratia*)
est. 1. established **2.** estimated
EST, E.S.T. eastern standard time
et al. and others (Latin *et alia*)
etc. and so forth (Latin *et cetera*)
ex. example
F Fahrenheit
FM frequency modulation
F.O.B., f.o.b. free on board
ft foot (measurement)
g 1. gram **2.** gravity
gal. gallon
gloss. glossary
hdqrs, HQ headquarters
Hon. Honorable (title)
hp horsepower
Hz hertz
ibid. in the same place (Latin *ibidem*)
id. the same (Latin *idem*)
i.e. that is (Latin *id est*)
illus. illustration
inc. incorporated
Jr. junior (after surname)
K 1. kelvin (temperature unit) **2.** Kelvin (temperature scale)
kc kilocycle
kg kilogram
km kilometer
kn knot
kW kilowatt
l liter
lat. latitude
lb, lb. pound (Latin *libra*)
l.c. lowercase
lib., lbr. library
lit. literary; literature
log logarithm
long. longitude
Ltd., ltd. limited
m meter
M.A. master of arts (Latin *Magister Artium*)
Mc, mc megacycle
M.C., m.c. master of ceremonies
M.D. doctor of medicine (Latin *medicinae doctor*)
mdse. merchandise
mfg. manufacturing
mg milligram
mi. 1. mile **2.** mill
misc. miscellaneous
ml milliliter
mm millimeter
mpg, m.p.g. miles per gallon
mph, m.p.h. miles per hour
MS 1. manuscript **2.** Mississippi **3.** multiple sclerosis
Ms., Ms title of courtesy for a woman
MST, M.S.T. mountain standard time
mt. mount, mountain
neg. negative
no. number
N.S.F., n.s.f. not sufficient funds
oz, oz. ounce
PA 1. public-address system **2.** Pennsylvania
pct. percent
pd. paid
PDT, P.D.T. Pacific daylight time
PFC, Pfc. private first class
pg., p. page
P.M., p.m. after noon (Latin *post meridiem*)
P.O. 1. personnel officer **2.** purchase order **3.** postal order; post office **4.** (also **p.o.**) petty officer
pop. population
pp. pages
ppd. 1. postpaid **2.** prepaid
PR, P.R. 1. public relations **2.** Puerto Rico
P.S. postscript
psi, p.s.i. pounds per square inch
PST, P.S.T. Pacific standard time
PTA, P.T.A. Parent-Teachers Association
qt. quart
rev. revised
RF radio frequency
rpm revolutions per minute
R.S.V.P., r.s.v.p. please reply (French *répondez s'il vous plaît*)
SOS 1. international distress signal **2.** any call for help
Sr. 1. senior (after surname) **2.** sister (religious)
ST, S.T. standard time
St. 1. saint **2.** strait **3.** street
std. standard
ste. suite
syn. synonymous; synonym
tbs, tbsp tablespoon
3-D three-dimensional
TM trademark
tsp teaspoon
UHF, uhf ultra high frequency
V 1. *Physics:* velocity **2.** *Electricity:* volt **3.** volume
VHF, vhf very high frequency
vol. 1. volume **2.** volunteer
vs. versus
W 1. *Electricity:* watt **2.** *Physics:* (also **w**) work **3.** west
whse., whs. warehouse
wkly. weekly
w/o without
wt. weight
yd yard (measurement)

Acronyms and Initialisms

537.1 Acronyms

An **acronym** is a word formed from the first (or first few) letters of words in a phrase. Even though acronyms are abbreviations, they require no periods.

radar	**radio detecting and ranging**
CARE	**Cooperative for American Relief Everywhere**
NASA	**National Aeronautics and Space Administration**
VISTA	**Volunteers in Service to America**
LAN	**local area network**

537.2 Initialisms

An **initialism** is similar to an acronym except that the initials used to form this abbreviation are pronounced individually.

CIA	**Central Intelligence Agency**
FBI	**Federal Bureau of Investigation**
FHA	**Federal Housing Administration**

537.3 Common Acronyms and Initialisms

ADD attention deficit disorder
AI artificial intelligence
AIDS acquired immunodeficiency syndrome
AKA also known as
ASAP as soon as possible
ATM automatic teller machine
AWOL absent without leave
BBB Better Business Bureau
BMI body mass index
CD compact disc
COD cash on delivery
DMV Department of Motor Vehicles
DVD digital video disc
ETA expected time of arrival
FAA Federal Aviation Administration
FCC Federal Communications Commission
FDA Food and Drug Administration
FDIC Federal Deposit Insurance Corporation
FEMA Federal Emergency Management Agency
FTC Federal Trade Commission
FYI for your information
GMT Greenwich Mean Time
GNP gross national product
GPS global positioning system
HDTV high-definition television
HIV human immunodeficiency virus
HTML hypertext markup language
IQ intelligence quotient
IRS Internal Revenue Service
ISBN International Standard Book Number
IT information technology
JPEG Joint Photographic Experts Group
LCD liquid crystal display
LLC limited liability company
MADD Mothers Against Drunk Driving
MRI magnetic resonance imaging
NASA National Aeronautics and Space Administration
NATO North Atlantic Treaty Organization
OPEC Organization of Petroleum-Exporting Countries
OSHA Occupational Safety and Health Administration
PAC political action committee
PDF portable document format
PETA People for the Ethical Treatment of Animals
PIN personal identification number
POW prisoner of war
PSA public service announcement
RN registered nurse
ROTC Reserve Officers' Training Corps
SADD Students Against Destructive Decisions
SASE self-addressed stamped envelope
SCSI small computer system interface
SUV sport utility vehicle
SWAT special weapons and tactics
TBA to be announced
TDD telecommunications device for the deaf
UPC universal product code
UV ultraviolet
VA Veterans Administration
VFW Veterans of Foreign Wars
VIP *Informal:* very important person
VR virtual reality
WHO World Health Organization

Spelling Rules

QUICK GUIDE

538.1 Write *i* Before *e*

Write *i* before *e* except after *c*, or when sounded like *a* as in *neighbor* and *weigh*.

relief receive perceive reign freight beige

Exceptions: Here are several exceptions to this rule.

neither leisure seize weird species science

538.2 Words with Consonant Endings

When a one-syllable word (*bat*) ends in a consonant (*t*) preceded by one vowel (*a*), double the final consonant before adding a suffix that begins with a vowel (*batting*).

sum—summary god—goddess

NOTE: When a multisyllable word (*control*) ends in a consonant (*l*) preceded by one vowel (*o*), the accent is on the last syllable (*con trol´*), and the suffix begins with a vowel (*ing*)—the same rule holds true: double the final consonant (*controlling*).

prefer—preferred begin—beginning
forget—forgettable admit—admittance

538.3 Words with a Silent *e*

If a word ends with a silent *e*, drop the *e* before adding a suffix that begins with a vowel. Do not drop the *e* when the suffix begins with a consonant.

state—stating—statement like—liking—likeness
use—using—useful nine—ninety—nineteen

Exceptions: judgment, truly, argument, ninth

538.4 Words Ending in *y*

When *y* is the last letter in a word and the *y* is preceded by a consonant, change the *y* to *i* before adding any suffix except those beginning with *i*.

fry—fries—frying hurry—hurried—hurrying lady—ladies
ply—pliable happy—happiness beauty—beautiful

When *y* is the last letter in a word and the *y* is preceded by a vowel, do not change the *y* to *i* before adding a suffix.

play—plays—playful stay—stays—staying employ—employed

NOTE: Never trust your spelling to even the best spell-checker. Use a dictionary for words your spell-checker may not cover.

Commonly Misspelled Words

A

abbreviate
abrupt
abscess
absence
absolute (ly)
absorbent
absurd
abundance
accede
accelerate
accept (ance)
accessible
accessory
accidentally
accommodate
accompany
accomplice
accomplish
accordance
according
account
accrued
accumulate
accurate
accustom (ed)
ache
achieve (ment)
acknowledge
acquaintance
acquiesce
acquired
actual
adapt
addition (al)
address
adequate
adjourned
adjustment
admirable
admissible
admittance
advantageous
advertisement
advertising
advice (n.)
advisable
advise (v.)
aerial
affect
affidavit
again
against
aggravate
aggression
agreeable
agreement
aisle
alcohol
alignment
alley
allotted
allowance
all right
almost
already
although
altogether
aluminum
always
amateur
amendment
among
amount
analysis
analyze
ancient
anecdote
anesthetic
angle
annihilate
anniversary
announce
annoyance
annual
anoint
anonymous
answer
antarctic
anticipate
anxiety
anxious
anything
apartment
apologize
apparatus
apparent (ly)
appeal
appearance
appetite
appliance
applicable
application
appointment
appraisal
appreciate
approach
appropriate
approval
approximately
architect
arctic
argument
arithmetic
arouse
arrangement
arrival
article
artificial
ascend
ascertain
asinine
assassin
assess (ment)
assignment
assistance
associate
association
assume
assurance
asterisk
athlete
athletic
attach
attack (ed)
attempt
attendance
attention
attitude
attorney
attractive
audible
audience
authority
automobile
autumn
auxiliary
available
average
awful
awfully
awkward

B

bachelor
baggage
balance
balloon
ballot
banana
bandage
bankrupt
bargain
barrel
basement
basis
battery
beautiful
beauty
become
becoming
before
beggar
beginning
behavior
being
belief
believe
beneficial
benefit (ed)
between
bicycle
biscuit
blizzard
bookkeeper
bough
bought
bouillon
boundary
breakfast
breath (n.)
breathe (v.)
brief
brilliant
Britain
brochure
brought
bruise
budget
bulletin
buoyant
bureau
burglar
bury
business
busy

C

cafeteria
caffeine
calendar
campaign
canceled
candidate
canister
canoe
can't
capacity
capital
capitol
captain
carburetor
career
caricature
carriage
cashier
casserole
casualty
catalog
catastrophe
caught
cavalry
celebration
cemetery
census
century
certain
certificate
cessation
challenge
changeable

character (istic)
chauffeur
chief
chimney
chocolate
choice
choose
Christian
circuit
circular
circumstance
civilization
clientele
climate
climb
clothes
coach
cocoa
coercion
collar
collateral
college
colloquial
colonel
color
colossal
column
comedy
coming
commence
commercial
commission
commit
commitment
committed
committee
communicate
community
comparative
comparison
compel
competent
competition
competitively
complain
complement
completely
complexion
compliment
compromise
concede
conceive
concerning
concert
concession
conclude
concrete
concurred
concurrence
condemn
condescend
condition
conference
conferred
confidence
confidential
congratulate
conscience
conscientious
conscious
consensus
consequence
conservative
considerably
consignment
consistent
constitution
contemptible
continually
continue
continuous
control
controversy
convenience
convince
coolly
cooperate
cordial
corporation
correlate
correspond
correspondence
corroborate
cough
couldn't
council
counsel
counterfeit
country
courage
courageous
courteous
courtesy
cousin
coverage
creditor
crisis
criticism
criticize
cruel
curiosity
curious
current
curriculum
custom
customary
customer
cylinder

D

daily
dairy
dealt
debtor
deceased
deceitful
deceive
decided
decision
declaration
decorate
deductible
defendant
defense
deferred
deficit
definite (ly)
definition
delegate
delicious
dependent
depositor
depot
descend
describe
description
desert
deserve
design
desirable
desirous
despair
desperate
despise
dessert
deteriorate
determine
develop
development
device
devise
diamond
diaphragm
diarrhea
diary
dictionary
difference
different
difficulty
dilapidated
dilemma
dining
diploma
director
disagreeable
disappear
disappoint
disapprove
disastrous
discipline
discover
discrepancy
discuss
discussion
disease
dissatisfied
dissipate
distinguish
distribute
divide
divine
divisible
division
doctor
doesn't
dominant
dormitory
doubt
drudgery
dual
duplicate
dyeing
dying

E

eagerly
earnest
economical
economy
ecstasy
edition
effervescent
efficacy
efficiency
eighth
either
elaborate
electricity
elephant
eligible
eliminate
ellipse
embarrass
emergency
eminent
emphasize
employee
employment
emulsion
enclose
encourage
endeavor
endorsement
engineer
English
enormous
enough
enterprise
entertain
enthusiastic
entirely
entrance
envelop (v.)
envelope (n.)
environment
equipment
equipped
equivalent
especially
essential
establish
esteemed
etiquette
evidence

exaggerate
exceed
excellent
except
exceptionally
excessive
excite
executive
exercise
exhaust (ed)
exhibition
exhilaration
existence
exorbitant
expect
expedition
expenditure
expensive
experience
explain
explanation
expression
exquisite
extension
extinct
extraordinary
extremely

F

facilities
fallacy
familiar
famous
fascinate
fashion
fatigue (d)
faucet
favorite
feasible
feature
February
federal
feminine
fertile
fictitious
field
fierce
fiery
finally
financially
foliage
forcible
foreign
forfeit
forgo
formally
formerly
fortunate
forty
forward
fountain
fourth
fragile
frantically
freight
friend
fulfill
fundamental
furthermore
futile

G

gadget
gangrene
garage
gasoline
gauge
genealogy
generally
generous
genius
genuine
geography
ghetto
ghost
glorious
gnaw
government
governor
gracious
graduation
grammar
grateful
gratitude
grease
grief
grievous
grocery
grudge
gruesome
guarantee
guard
guardian
guerrilla
guess
guidance
guide
guilty
gymnasium
gypsy
gyroscope

H

habitat
hammer
handkerchief
handle (d)
handsome
haphazard
happen
happiness
harass
harbor
hastily
having
hazardous
height
hemorrhage
hesitate
hindrance
history
hoarse
holiday
honor
hoping
hopping
horde
horrible
hospital
humorous
hurriedly
hydraulic
hygiene
hymn
hypocrisy

I

iambic
icicle
identical
idiosyncrasy
illegible
illiterate
illustrate
imaginary
imaginative
imagine
imitation
immediately
immense
immigrant
immortal
impatient
imperative
importance
impossible
impromptu
improvement
inalienable
incidentally
inconvenience
incredible
incurred
indefinitely
indelible
independence
independent
indictment
indispensable
individual
inducement
industrial
industrious
inevitable
inferior
inferred
infinite
inflammable
influential
ingenious
ingenuous
inimitable
initial
initiation
innocence
innocent
inoculation
inquiry
installation
instance
instead
institute
insurance
intellectual
intelligence
intention
intercede
interesting
interfere
intermittent
interpret (ed)
interrupt
interview
intimate
invalid
investigate
investor
invitation
iridescent
irrelevant
irresistible
irreverent
irrigate
island
issue
itemized
itinerary
it's (it is)

J

janitor
jealous (y)
jeopardize
jewelry
journal
journey
judgment
justice
justifiable

K

kitchen
kindergarten
knowledge
knuckle

L

label
laboratory
lacquer
language
laugh
laundry
lawyer
league
lecture
legal
legible
legislature
legitimate
leisure
length
letterhead
liability
liable
liaison
library
license
lieutenant
lightning
likable
likely
lineage
liquefy
liquid
listen
literary
literature
livelihood
living
logarithm
loneliness
loose
lose
losing
lovable
lovely
luncheon
luxury

M

machine
magazine
magnificent
maintain
maintenance
majority
making
management
maneuver
manual
manufacture
manuscript
marriage
marshal
material
mathematics
maximum
mayor
meanness
meant
measure
medicine
medieval
mediocre
medium
memorandum
menus
merchandise
merit
message
mileage
millionaire
miniature
minimum
minute
mirror
miscellaneous
mischief
mischievous
miserable
misery
missile
missionary
misspell
moisture
molecule
momentous
monotonous
monument
mortgage
municipal
muscle
musician
mustache
mysterious

N

naive
naturally
necessary
necessity
negligible
negotiate
neighborhood
nevertheless
nickel
niece
nineteenth
ninety
noticeable
notoriety
nuclear
nuisance

O

obedience
obey
oblige
obstacle
occasion
occasionally
occupant
occur
occurred
occurrence
offense
official
often
omission
omitted
operate
opinion
opponent
opportunity
opposite
optimism
ordinance
ordinarily
original
outrageous

P

pageant
paid
pamphlet
paradise
paragraph
parallel
paralyze
parentheses (pl.)
parenthesis (s.)
parliament
partial
participant
participate
particularly
pastime
patience
patronage
peculiar
perceive
perhaps
peril
permanent
permissible
perpendicular
perseverance
persistent
personal (ly)
personnel
perspiration
persuade
phase
phenomenon
philosophy
physician
piece
planned
plateau
plausible
playwright
pleasant
pleasure
pneumonia
politician
possess
possession
possible
practically
prairie
precede
precedence
preceding
precious
precisely
precision
predecessor
preferable
preference
preferred
prejudice
preliminary
premium
preparation
presence
prevalent
previous
primitive
principal
principle
priority
prisoner
privilege
probably
procedure
proceed
professor
prominent
pronounce
pronunciation
propaganda
prosecute
protein
psychology
publicly
pumpkin
purchase
pursue
pursuing
pursuit

Q

qualified
quantity
quarter
questionnaire
quiet
quite
quotient

R

raise
rapport
realize

really
recede
receipt
receive
received
recipe
recipient
recognition
recognize
recommend
recurrence
reference
referred
rehearse
reign
reimburse
relevant
relieve
religious
remember
remembrance
reminisce
rendezvous
renewal
repetition
representative
requisition
reservoir
resistance
respectably
respectfully
respectively
responsibility
restaurant
rheumatism
rhyme
rhythm
ridiculous
route

S

sacrilegious
safety
salary
sandwich
satisfactory
Saturday
scarcely
scene
scenery
schedule
science
scissors
secretary
seize
sensible
sentence
sentinel
separate
sergeant
several
severely
shepherd
sheriff
shining
siege
significance
similar
simultaneous
since
sincerely
skiing
soldier
solemn
sophisticated
sophomore
sorority
source
souvenir
spaghetti
specific
specimen
speech
sphere
sponsor
spontaneous
stationary
stationery
statistic
statue
stature
statute
stomach
stopped
straight
strategy
strength
stretched
studying
subsidize
substantial
substitute
subtle
succeed
success
sufficient
summarize
superficial
superintendent
superiority
supersede
supplement
suppose
surely
surprise
surveillance
survey
susceptible
suspicious
sustenance
syllable
symmetrical
sympathy
symphony
symptom
synchronous

T

tariff
technique
telegram
temperament
temperature
temporary
tendency
tentative
terrestrial
terrible
territory
theater
their
therefore
thief
thorough (ly)
though
throughout
tired
tobacco
together
tomorrow
tongue
tonight
touch
tournament
tourniquet
toward
tragedy
traitor
tranquilizer
transferred
treasurer
tried
truly
Tuesday
tuition
typical
typing

U

unanimous
unconscious
undoubtedly
unfortunately
unique
unison
university
unnecessary
unprecedented
until
upper
urgent
usable
useful
using
usually
utensil
utilize

V

vacancies
vacation
vacuum
vague
valuable
variety
various
vegetable
vehicle
veil
velocity
vengeance
vicinity
view
vigilance
villain
violence
visibility
visible
visitor
voice
volume
voluntary
volunteer

W

wander
warrant
weather
Wednesday
weird
welcome
welfare
where
whether
which
whole
wholly
whose
width
women
worthwhile
worthy
wreckage
wrestler
writing
written
wrought

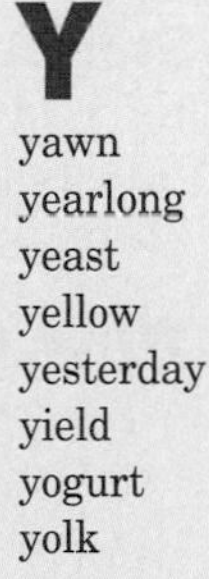

Y

yawn
yearlong
yeast
yellow
yesterday
yield
yogurt
yolk

Guidelines

Steps to Becoming a Better Speller

1. **Be patient.**

   Becoming a good speller takes time.

2. **Check the correct pronunciation of each word you are attempting to spell.**

   Knowing the correct pronunciation of a word can help you remember its spelling.

3. **Note the meaning and history of each word as you are checking the dictionary for pronunciation.**

   Knowing the meaning and history of a word provides you with a better notion of how the word is properly used, and this can help you remember its spelling.

4. **Before you close the dictionary, practice spelling the word.**

   Look away from the page and try to "see" the word in your mind. Then write it on a piece of paper. Check your spelling in the dictionary; repeat the process until you are able to spell the word correctly.

5. **Learn some spelling rules.**

   This handbook contains four of the most useful rules. (See page 538.)

6. **Make a list of the words that you often misspell.**

   Select the first 10 and practice spelling them.

   Step A: Read each word carefully; then write it on a piece of paper. Check to see that you've spelled it correctly. Repeat this step for the words that you misspelled.

   Step B: When you have finished your first 10 words, ask someone to read them to you as you write them again. Then check for misspellings. If you find none, congratulations! (Repeat both steps with your next 10 words, and so on.)

7. **Write often.**

"There is little point in learning to spell if you have little intention of writing."
—Frank Smith

"It may be said with a degree of assurance that not everything that meets the eye is as it appears."
—Rod Sterling

Understanding Idioms

Idioms are phrases that are used in a special way. You can't understand an idiom just by knowing the meaning of each word in the phrase. You must learn it as a whole. For example, the idiom *bury the hatchet* means "to settle an argument," even though the individual words in the phrase mean something much different. This section will help you learn some of the common idioms in American English.

apple of his eye	Eagle Lake is the **apple of his eye.** (something he likes very much)
as plain as day	The mistake in the ad was **as plain as day.** (very clear)
as the crow flies	New London is 200 miles from here **as the crow flies.** (in a straight line)
at a snail's pace	My last hour at work passes **at a snail's pace.** (very, very slowly)
axe to grind	The manager has an **axe to grind** with that umpire. (disagreement to settle)
bad apple	There are no **bad apples** in this class. (bad influences)
beat around the bush	Don't **beat around the bush;** answer the question. (avoid getting to the point)
benefit of the doubt	Everyone has been given the **benefit of the doubt** at least once. (another chance)
beyond the shadow of a doubt	**Beyond the shadow of a doubt,** this is my best science project. (for certain)
blew my top	When I saw the broken statue, **I blew my top.** (showed great anger)
bone to pick	Alison had a **bone to pick** with the student who copied her paper. (problem to settle)
brain drain	**Brain drain** is a serious problem in some states. (the best students moving elsewhere)

break the ice	The nervous ninth graders were afraid to **break the ice.** (start a conversation)
burn the midnight oil	Devon had to **burn the midnight oil** to finish his report. (work late into the night)
bury the hatchet	My sisters were told to **bury the hatchet** immediately. (settle an argument)
by the skin of her teeth	Sumey avoided an accident **by the skin of her teeth.** (just barely)
champing at the bit	The skiers were **champing at the bit** to get on the slopes. (eager, excited)
chicken feed	The prize was **chicken feed** to some people. (not worth much money)
chip off the old block	Jose's just like his father. He's a **chip off the old block.** (just like someone else)
clean as a whistle	My boss told me to make sure the place was as **clean as a whistle** before I left. (very clean)
cold shoulder	I wanted to fit in with that group, but they gave me the **cold shoulder.** (ignored me)
crack of dawn	Ali delivers his papers at the **crack of dawn.** (first light of day, early morning)
cry wolf	If you **cry wolf** too often, no one will believe you. (say you are in trouble when you aren't)
dead of night	Hearing a loud noise in the **dead of night** frightened Bill. (middle of the night)
dirt cheap	I got this sweater dirt cheap**.** (for very little money)
doesn't hold a candle to	That award **doesn't hold a candle to** a gold medal. (is not as good as)
drop in the bucket	The contributions were a **drop in the bucket.** (a small amount compared to what's needed)
everything from A to Z	That catalog lists **everything from A to Z.** (a lot of different things)
face the music	Todd had to **face the music** when he broke the window. (deal with the punishment)
fish out of water	He felt like a **fish out of water** in the new math class. (someone in an unfamiliar place)

fit for a king	The food at the athletic banquet was **fit for a king.** (very special)
flew off the handle	Kaili **flew off the handle** when she saw a reckless driver near the school. (became very angry)
floating on air	Celine was **floating on air** at the prom. (feeling very happy)
food for thought	The boys' foolish and dangerous prank gave us **food for thought.** (something to think about)
get down to business	After sharing several jokes, Mr. Sell said we should **get down to business.** (start working)
get the upper hand	The wrestler moved quickly on his opponent in order to **get the upper hand.** (gain the advantage)
give their all	Student volunteers **give their all** to help others. (work as hard as they can)
go fly a kite	Charlene stared at her nosy brother and said, **"Go fly a kite."** (go away)
has a green thumb	Talk to Mrs. Smith about your sick plant. She **has a green thumb.** (is good at growing plants)
has a heart of gold	Joe **has a heart of gold.** (is very kind and generous)
hit a home run	Rhonda **hit a home run** with her speech. (succeeded, or did well)
hit the ceiling	When my parents saw my grades, they **hit the ceiling.** (were very angry)
hit the hay	Exhausted from the hike, Jamal **hit the hay** without eating supper. (went to bed)
in a nutshell	Can you, **in a nutshell,** tell us your goals for this year? (in summary)
in one ear and out the other	Sharl, concerned about her pet, let the lecture go **in one ear and out the other.** (without really listening)
in the black	My aunt's gift shop is finally **in the black.** (making money)
in the nick of time	Janelle caught the falling vase **in the nick of time.** (just in time)
in the red	Many businesses start out **in the red.** (in debt)

in the same boat	The new tax bill meant everyone would be **in the same boat.** (in a similar situation)
iron out	Joe will meet with the work crew to **iron out** their complaints. (solve, work out)
it goes without saying	**It goes without saying** that saving money is a good idea. (it is clear)
it stands to reason	**It stands to reason** that your stamina will increase if you run every day. (it makes sense)
keep a stiff upper lip	**Keep a stiff upper lip** when you visit the doctor. (be brave)
keep it under your hat	**Keep it under your hat** about the pop quiz. (don't tell anyone)
knock on wood	My uncle **knocked on wood** after he said he had never had the flu. (did something for good luck)
knuckle down	After wasting half the day, we were told to **knuckle down.** (work hard)
learn the ropes	It takes every new employee a few months to **learn the ropes.** (get to know how things are done)
leave no stone unturned	The police plan to **leave no stone unturned** at the crime scene. (check everything)
lend someone a hand	You will feel good if you **lend someone a hand.** (help someone)
let's face it	**Let's face it.** You don't like rap. (let's admit it)
let the cat out of the bag	Tom **let the cat out of the bag** during lunch. (told a secret)
look high and low	We l**ooked high and low** for Jan's dog. (looked everywhere)
lose face	In some cultures, it is very bad to **lose face.** (be embarrassed)
needle in a haystack	Trying to find a person in New York is like trying to **find a needle in a haystack.** (something impossible to find)
nose to the grindstone	With all of these assignments, I have to keep my **nose to the grindstone.** (work hard)
on cloud nine	The bride is **on cloud nine.** (feeling very happy)

on pins and needles	Emiko was **on pins and needles** during the championship game. (feeling nervous)
out the window	Once the rain started, our plans were **out the window.** (ruined)
over and above	**Over and above** the required work, Will cleaned up the lab. (in addition to)
pain in the neck	Franklin knew the report would be a **pain in the neck.** (very annoying)
pull your leg	Cary was only **pulling your leg.** (telling you a little lie as a joke)
put his foot in his mouth	Lane **put his foot in his mouth** when he answered the question. (said something embarrassing)
put the cart before the horse	Tonya **put the cart before the horse** when she sealed the envelope before inserting the letter. (did something in the wrong order)
put your best foot forward	When applying for a job, you should **put your best foot forward.** (do the best that you can do)
red-letter day	Sovann had a **red-letter day** because she did so well on her math test. (very good day)
rock the boat	I was told not to **rock the boat.** (cause trouble)
rude awakening	Jake will have a **rude awakening** when he sees the bill for his computer. (sudden, unpleasant surprise)
save face	His gift was clearly an attempt to **save face.** (fix an embarrassing situation)
see eye to eye	We **see eye to eye** about the need for a new school. (are in agreement)
shake a leg	I told Mako to **shake a leg** so that we wouldn't be late. (hurry)
shift into high gear	Antoinette had to **shift into high gear** to finish the test in time. (speed up, hurry)
sight for sore eyes	My grandmother's smiling face was a **sight for sore eyes.** (good to see)
sight unseen	Liz bought the coat **sight unseen.** (without seeing it first)
sink or swim	Whether you **sink or swim** in school depends on your study habits. (fail or succeed)

spilled the beans	Suddenly, Kesia realized that she had **spilled the beans.** (revealed a secret)
spring chicken	Although Mr. Gordon isn't a **spring chicken,** he sure knows how to talk to kids. (young person)
stick to your guns	Know what you believe, and **stick to your guns.** (don't change your mind)
sweet tooth	Chocolate is often the candy of choice for those with a **sweet tooth.** (a love for sweets, like candy and cake)
take a dim view	My sister will **take a dim view** of that movie. (disapprove)
take it with a grain of salt	When you read that advertisement, **take it with a grain of salt.** (don't believe everything)
take the bull by the horns	It's time to **take the bull by the horns** so the project gets done on time. (take control)
through thick and thin	Those two girls have remained friends **through thick and thin.** (in good times and in bad times)
time flies	**Time flies** as you grow older. (time passes quickly)
time to kill	Grace had **time to kill,** so she read a book. (extra time)
toe the line	The new teacher made everyone **toe the line.** (follow the rules)
to go overboard	The class was told not **to go overboard.** A $50.00 donation was fine. (to do too much)
tongue-tied	He can talk easily with friends, but in class he is usually **tongue-tied.** (not knowing what to say)
turn over a new leaf	He decided to **turn over a new leaf** in school. (make a new start)
two peas in a pod	Ever since kindergarten, Lil and Eve have been like **two peas in a pod.** (very much alike)
under the weather	Vincente was feeling **under the weather**. (sick)
wallflower	Cho knew the other girls thought she was a **wallflower.** (a shy person)
word of mouth	Joseph learns a lot about his favorite team by **word of mouth.** (talking with other people)

"The difference between the right word and the nearly right word is the same as that between lightning and the lightning bug."

—Mark Twain

Using the Right Word

a lot ■ *A lot* (always two words) is a vague descriptive phrase that should be used sparingly.

"You can observe a lot just by watching." — Yogi Berra

accept, except ■ The verb *accept* means "to receive" or "to believe"; the preposition *except* means "other than."

The principal accepted the boy's story about the broken window, but she asked why no one except him saw the ball accidentally slip from his hand.

adapt, adopt ■ *Adapt* means "to adjust or change to fit"; *adopt* means "to choose and treat as your own" (a child, an idea).

After a lengthy period of study, Malcolm X adopted the Islamic faith and adapted to its lifestyle.

adverse, averse ■ *Adverse* means "hostile, unfavorable, or harmful." *Averse* means "to have a definite feeling of distaste—disinclined."

Groans and other adverse reactions were noted as the new students, averse to strenuous exercise, were ushered past the X-5000 pump-and-crunch machine.

advice, advise ■ *Advice* is a noun meaning "information or recommendation"; *advise* is a verb meaning "to recommend."

Successful people will often give you sound advice, so I advise you to listen.

affect, effect ■ The verb *affect* means "to influence"; the verb *effect* means "to produce, accomplish, complete."

Ming's hard work effected an A on the test, which positively affected her semester grade.

The noun *effect* means "the result."

Good grades have a calming effect on parents.

all right ■ *All right* is always two words (not *alright*).

allusion, illusion ■ *Allusion* is an indirect reference to someone or something; *illusion* is a false picture or idea.

My little sister, under the illusion that she's movie-star material, makes frequent allusions to her future fans.

already, all ready ■ *Already* is an adverb meaning "before this time" or "by this time." *All ready* is an adjective meaning "fully prepared."

NOTE: Use *all ready* if you can substitute *ready* alone in the sentence.

Although I've already had some dessert, I am all ready for some ice cream from the street vendor.

altogether, all together ■ *Altogether* means "entirely." The phrase *all together* means "in a group" or "all at once."

"There is altogether too much gridlock," complained the Democrats. All together, the Republicans yelled, "No way!"

among, between ■ *Among* is used when speaking of more than two persons or things. *Between* is used when speaking of only two.

The three of us decided among ourselves between going out or eating in.

amoral, immoral ■ *Amoral* means "neither moral (right) nor immoral (wrong)"; *immoral* means "wrong, or in a conflict with traditional values."

Carnivores are amoral in their hunt; poachers are immoral in theirs.

amount, number ■ *Amount* is used for bulk measurement. *Number* is used to count separate units. (See also **fewer, less.**)

A number of chocolate bars contain a substantial amount of caffeine.

annual, biannual, semiannual, biennial, perennial ■ An *annual* event happens once every year. A *biannual* or *semiannual* event happens twice a year. A *biennial* event happens every two years. A *perennial* event is one that is persistent or constant.

Dad's annual family reunion gets bigger every year.

We're going shopping at the department store's semiannual white sale.

Due to dwindling attendance, the county fair is now a biennial celebration.

Mom's perennial flower garden blooms beautifully year after year.

anyway ■ Do not add an *s* to anyway.

ascent, assent ■ *Ascent* is the act of rising or climbing; *assent* is "to agree to something after some consideration" (or such an agreement).

The group's ascent of the butte was completed with the assent of the landowner.

bad, badly ■ *Bad* is an adjective. *Badly* is an adverb.

This apple is bad, but one bad apple doesn't always ruin the whole bushel.

In today's game, Ross passed badly.

base, bass ■ *Base* is the foundation or the lower part of something. *Bass* is a deep sound or tone. *Bass* (when pronounced like *class*) is a fish.

beside, besides ■ *Besides* is an adverb meaning "nearby." *Besides* is a preposition meaning "other than or in addition to."

Besides the two suitcases you've already loaded into the trunk, remember the smaller one beside the van.

bring, take ■ *Bring* suggests the action is directed toward the speaker; *take* suggests the action is directed away from the speaker.

I'll bring home some garbage bags so you can take the trash outside.

can, may ■ *Can* suggests ability while *may* suggests permission.

"Can I go to the mall?" means "Am I physically able to go to the mall?"

"May I go to the mall?" asks permission to go.

capital, capitol ■ The noun *capital* refers to a city or to money. The adjective *capital* means "major or important." *Capitol* refers to a building.

The state capital is home to the capitol building for a capital reason. The state government contributed capital for its construction.

cereal, serial ■ *Cereal* is a grain, often made into breakfast food. *Serial* relates to something in a series.

Mohammed enjoys reading serial novels while he eats a bowl of cereal.

choral, coral ■ *Choral* relates to a choir (a singing group). *Coral* is the hard undersea deposit produced by polyps.

The spring choral concert is scheduled for April 2.

Many types of tropical fish make their homes in coral.

climactic, climatic ■ *Climactic* refers to the climax, or high point, of an event; *climatic* refers to the climate, or weather conditions.

If we use the open-air amphitheater, climatic conditions in these foothills will just about guarantee the wind gusts we need for the climactic third act.

coarse, course ■ *Coarse* means "rough or crude"; *course* means "a path or direction taken." *Course* also means "a class or a series of studies."

Fletcher, known for using coarse language, was barred from the golf course until he took an etiquette course.

compare with, compare to ■ Things of the same class are *compared with* each other; things of different classes are *compared to* each other.

complement, compliment ■ *Complement* refers to that which completes or fulfills. *Compliment* is an expression of admiration or praise.

Kimberly smiled, thinking she had received a compliment when Carlos said that her new Chihuahua complemented her personality.

continual, continuous ■ *Continual* refers to something that happens again and again with some breaks or pauses; *continuous* refers to something that keeps happening, uninterrupted.

Sunlight hits Iowa on a continual basis; sunlight hits Earth continuously.

counsel, council ■ When used as a noun, *counsel* means "advice"; when used as a verb, it means "to advise." *Council* refers to a group that advises.

The student council counseled all freshmen to join at least one school club. That's good counsel.

desert, dessert ■ The noun *desert* (dez´ert) refers to barren wilderness. *Dessert* (di zûrt´) is food served at the end of a meal.

The scorpion tiptoed through the moonlit desert, searching for dessert.

The verb *desert* (di zûrt´) means "to abandon"; the noun *desert* (di zûrt´) means "deserved reward or punishment."

The burglar's hiding place deserted him when the spotlight swung his way; his subsequent arrest was his just desert.

different from, different than ■ Use *different from* in a comparison of two things. *Different than* should be used only when followed by a clause.

Lateisha is quite different from her sister.

Life is different than it used to be.

discreet, discrete ■ *Discreet* means "unobtrusive" or "modest," while the adjective *discrete* means "separate."

Mr. Hobbs discreetly handed the sobbing woman a handkerchief.

Several discrete departments are housed at the company headquarters.

elicit, illicit ■ *Elicit* is a verb meaning "to bring out." *Illicit* is an adjective meaning "unlawful."

It took two quick hand signals from the lookout at the corner to elicit the illicit exchange of cash for drugs.

eminent, imminent ■ *Eminent* means "prominent, conspicuous, or famous"; *imminent* means "ready or threatening to happen."

With the island's government about to collapse, assassination attempts on several eminent officials seemed imminent.

explicit, implicit ■ *Explicit* means "expressed directly or clearly defined"; *implicit* means "implied or unstated."

The professor explicitly asked that the experiment be wrapped up on Monday, implicitly demanding that her lab assistants work on the weekend.

farther, further ■ *Farther* refers to a physical distance; *further* refers to additional time, quantity, or degree.

Alaska extends farther north than Iceland does. Further information can be obtained in an atlas.

fewer, less ■ *Fewer* refers to the number of separate units; *less* refers to bulk quantity.

> **Because we have fewer orders for cakes, we'll buy less sugar and flour.**

figuratively, literally ■ *Figuratively* means "in a metaphorical or analogous way—describing something by comparing it to something else"; *literally* means "actually or virtually."

> **The lab was literally filled with sulfurous gases—figuratively speaking, dragon's breath.**

fiscal, physical ■ *Fiscal* means "related to financial matters"; *physical* means "related to material things."

> **The school's fiscal work is handled by its accounting staff. The physical work is handled by its maintenance staff.**

good, well ■ *Good* is an adjective; *well* is nearly always an adverb. (When *well* is used to describe a state of health, it is an adjective: He was happy to be well again.)

> **The strange flying machines worked well and made our team look good.**

healthful, healthy ■ *Healthful* means "causing or improving health"; *healthy* means "possessing health."

> **Healthful foods build healthy bodies.**

hoard, horde ■ *Hoard* is a verb that means "to store up"; as a noun, it is the supply that is stored. A *horde* is a crowd.

> **A horde of people who survived the Depression hoard canned goods in preparation for the next time it happens.**

immigrate, emigrate ■ *Immigrate* means "to come into a new country or environment." *Emigrate* means "to go out of one country to live in another."

> **Martin Ulferts immigrated to this country in 1882. He was only three years old when he emigrated from Germany.**

imply, infer ■ *Imply* means "to suggest or express indirectly"; *infer* means "to draw a conclusion from facts." (A writer or speaker implies; a reader or listener infers.)

> **Dad implied by his comment that I should drive more carefully, and I inferred that he was concerned for both me and his new car.**

ingenious, ingenuous ■ *Ingenious* means "intelligent, discerning, clever"; *ingenuous* means "unassuming, natural, showing childlike innocence and candidness."

> **Many thought it an ingenious plan to put the boy-king in charge of diplomatic affairs; his ingenuous comments could sooth the sorest egos.**

insure, ensure ■ *Insure* means "to secure from financial harm or loss." *Ensure* means "to make certain of something."

To ensure that you can legally drive that new car, you'll have to insure it.

interstate, intrastate ■ *Interstate* means "existing between two or more states"; *intrastate* means "existing within a state."

it's, its ■ *It's* is the contraction of "it is." *Its* is the possessive form of "it."

It's hard to believe, but the movie *Shrek* still holds its appeal for my little sister—even after repeated viewings.

lay, lie ■ *Lay* means "to place." *Lay* is a transitive verb. (See 568.1.)

Lay your books on the big table.

Lie means "to recline," and *lay* is the past tense of *lie*. *Lie* is an intransitive verb. (See 568.1.)

In this heat, the children must lie down for a nap. Yesterday they lay down without one complaint. Sometimes they have lain in the hammocks to rest.

lead, led ■ *Lead* (lēd) is the present tense of the verb meaning "to guide." The past tense of the verb is *led* (lĕd). The noun *lead* (lĕd) is a metal.

We were led along the path that leads to an abandoned lead mine.

learn, teach ■ *Learn* means "to acquire information." *Teach* means "to give information."

I learn better when people teach with real-world examples.

lend, borrow ■ *Lend* means "to give for temporary use." *Borrow* means "to receive for temporary use."

I told Mom I needed to borrow $18 for a CD, but she said she could only lend money for school supplies.

liable, libel ■ *Liable* is an adjective meaning "responsible" or "exposed to an adverse action"; *libel* (noun) is a written defamatory statement about someone, and the verb *libel* means "to publish or make such a statement."

Supermarket tabloids, liable for ruining many a reputation, make a practice of libelling the rich and the famous.

like, as ■ When *like* is used as a preposition meaning "similar to," it can be followed only by a noun, pronoun, or noun phrase; when *as* is used as a subordinating conjunction, it introduces a subordinate clause.

If you want to be a gymnast like her, you'd better practice three hours a day as she does.

medal, meddle ■ *Medal* is an award. *Meddle* means "to interfere."

Many parents meddle in the awards process to make sure that their kids receive medals.

metal, mettle ■ *Metal* is a chemical element like iron or gold. *Mettle* is "strength of spirit."

Grandad's mettle during battle left him with some metal in his shoulder.

miner, minor ■ A *miner* digs in the ground for ore. A *minor* is a person who is not legally an adult. A *minor* problem is one of no great importance.

The use of minors as miners is no minor problem.

moral, morale ■ A *moral* is a lesson drawn from a story; as an adjective, it relates to the principles of right and wrong. *Morale* refers to someone's attitude.

Ms. Ladue considers it her moral obligation to go to church every day.

The students' morale sank after their defeat in the forensics competition.

oral, verbal ■ *Oral* means "uttered with the mouth"; *verbal* means "relating to or consisting of words and the comprehension of words."

The actor's oral abilities were outstanding, her pronunciation and intonation impeccable, but I doubted the playwright's verbal skills after trying to decipher the play's meaning.

palate, palette ■ The *palate* is the roof of the mouth; it can also refer to "taste." A *palette* is a surface for holding and mixing paint; it can also mean "the colors on the palette" or "a particular choice of colors."

Ms. Satriani declared that her son's wedding plans were too elaborate for her palate.

The decorator showed her client the proposed palette for the living room.

past, passed ■ *Passed* is a verb. *Past* can be used as a noun, an adjective, or a preposition.

That old pickup truck passed my sports car! (verb)

Many senior citizens hold dearly to the past. (noun)

Tilly's past life as a circus worker must have been . . . interesting. (adjective)

Who can walk past a bakery without looking in the window? (preposition)

peak, peek, pique ■ A *peak* is a high point. *Peek* means "brief look" (or "look briefly"). *Pique*, as a verb, means "to excite by challenging"; as a noun, it is a feeling of resentment.

The peak of Dr. Fedder's professional life was his ability to pique children's interest in his work.

"Take a peek at this slide," the doctor urged her colleague.

pedal, peddle, petal ■ A *pedal* is a foot lever; as a verb, it means "to ride a bike." *Peddle* means "to go from place to place selling something." A *petal* is part of a flower.

Don Miller paints beautiful petals on his homemade birdhouses. Then he pedals through the flea market every weekend to peddle them.

personal, personnel ■ *Personal* means "private." *Personnel* are people working at a particular job.

Choosing a major is a personal decision, but guidance personnel can help.

plain, plane ■ *Plain* means "an area of land that is flat or level"; it also means "clearly seen or understood."

It's plain to see why settlers of the Great Plains had trouble moving west.

Plane means "flat, level"; it is also a tool used to smooth the surface of wood.

I used a plane to make the board plane and smooth.

pore, pour, poor ■ A *pore* is an opening in the skin. *Pour* means "to cause to flow in a stream." *Poor* means "needy or pitiable."

Tough exams on late spring days make my poor pores pour sweat.

precede, proceed ■ To *precede* means "to go or come before," while *proceed* means "to move on or go ahead."

Our zany biology instructor often preceded his lecture with these words: "All alert sponges, proceed to soak up more fascinating facts!"

principal, principle ■ As an adjective, *principal* means "primary." As a noun, it can mean "a school administrator" or "a sum of money." *Principle* means "idea or doctrine."

His principal gripe is lack of freedom. (adjective)

The principal expressed his concern about the open-campus policy. (noun)

During the first year of a loan, you pay more interest than principal. (noun)

The principle of caveat emptor is "Let the buyer beware."

quiet, quit, quite *Quiet* is the opposite of noisy. *Quit* means "to stop." *Quite* means "completely or to a considerable extent."

The library remained quite quiet until the librarian quit watching us.

quote, quotation ■ *Quote* is a verb; *quotation* is a noun.

The quotation I used was from Woody Allen. You may quote me on that.

real, really, very ■ Do not use *real* in place of the adverbs *very* or *really.*

Mother's cake is usually very (not *real*) moist, but this one is really stale!

right, write, rite ■ *Right* means "correct or proper"; it also refers to that which a person has a legal claim to, as in *copyright. Write* means "to inscribe or record." *Rite* refers to a ritual or ceremonial act.

Write this down: It is a boat owner's right to perform the rite of christening—breaking a bottle of champagne on the stern of the ship.

ring, wring ■ *Ring* means "encircle" or "to sound by striking." *Wring* means "to squeeze or twist."

At the beach, Grandma would ring her head with a large scarf. Once, it blew into the sea, so she had me wring it out.

scene, seen ■ *Scene* refers to the setting or location where something happens; it also may mean "sight or spectacle." *Seen* is a form of the verb "see."

Serena had seen her boyfriend making a scene; she cringed.

seam, seem ■ *Seam* (noun) is a line formed by connecting two pieces. *Seem* (verb) means "to appear to exist."

The ragged seams in his old coat seem to match the creases in his face.

set, sit ■ *Set* means "to place." *Sit* means "to put the body in a seated position." *Set* is transitive; *sit* is intransitive. (See 568.1.)

How can you just sit there and watch as I set all these chairs in place?

shear, sheer ■ *Shear* means "to cut off." *Sheer* is an adjective meaning "transparent or translucent."

After the stylist sheared Marla's long hair, Marla covered her neck with a sheer red scarf.

sight, cite, site ■ *Sight* means "the act of seeing"; a *sight* is what is seen. *Cite* means "to quote" or "to summon" (as before a court). *Site* means "location."

In her report, the general contractor cited several problems at the downtown job site. For one, the loading area was a chaotic sight.

sole, soul ■ *Sole* means "single, only one"; *sole* also refers to the bottom surface of the foot. *Soul* refers to the spiritual part of a person.

As the sole inhabitant of the island, he put his heart and soul into his farming.

stake, steak ■ A *stake* is an important interest or a pointed piece of wood. A *steak* is a piece of meat.

The Herly Company has a big stake in the success of the development.

Would you like your steak grilled or broiled?

stationary, stationery ■ *Stationary* means "not movable"; *stationery* refers to the paper and envelopes used to write letters.

steal, steel ■ *Steal* means "to take something without permission"; *steel* is a metal.

than, then ■ *Than* is used in a comparison; *then* tells when.

Abigail shouted that her big brother was bigger than my big brother. Then she ran away.

their, there, they're ■ *Their* is a possessive personal pronoun. *There* is an adverb used to point out location. *They're* is the contraction for "they are."

They're a well-dressed couple. Do you see them over there, with their matching jackets?

threw, through ■ *Threw* is the past tense of "throw." *Through* means "from beginning to end."

Through seven innings, Rachel threw just seven strikes.

to, too, two ■ *To* is a preposition that can mean "in the direction of." *To* is also used to form an infinitive. (See 569.2) *Too* means "also" or "very." *Two* is the number.

vain, vane, vein ■ *Vain* means "valueless or fruitless"; it may also mean "holding a high regard for oneself." *Vane* is a flat piece of material set up to show which way the wind blows. *Vein* refers to a blood vessel or a mineral deposit.

The vain prospector, boasting about the vein of silver he'd uncovered, paused to look up at the turning weather vane.

vary, very ■ *Vary* means "to change." *Very* means "to a high degree."

Though the weather may vary from day to day, generally, it is very pleasant.

vial, vile ■ A *vial* is a small container for liquid. *Vile* is an adjective meaning "foul, despicable."

It's a vile job, but someone has to clean these lab vials.

wear, where ■ *Wear* means "to have on or to carry on one's body"; *where* asks the question *in what place?* or *in what situation?*

The designer boasted, "Where can anybody wear my pajamas? Anywhere."

weather, whether ■ *Weather* refers to the condition of the atmosphere. *Whether* refers to a possibility.

Because of the weather forecast, Coach Pennington didn't know whether or not to schedule another practice.

which, that ■ Use *which* to refer to objects or animals in a nonrestrictive clause (set off with commas). Use *that* to refer to objects or animals in a restrictive clause. (For more information about these types of clauses, see 513.2.)

The birds, which stay in the area all winter, know exactly where the feeders are located. The food that attracts the most birds is sunflower seed.

who, whom ■ Use *who* to refer to people. *Who* is used as the subject of a verb in an independent clause or in a relative clause. *Whom* is used as the object of a preposition or as a direct object.

To whom do we owe our thanks for these pizzas? And who ordered them?

who's, whose ■ *Who's* is the contraction for "who is." *Whose* is a pronoun that can show possession or ownership.

Cody, whose car is new, will drive. Who's going to read the map?

your, you're ■ *Your* is a possessive pronoun. *You're* is the contraction for "you are."

Celeste, your essay is very engaging because you're writing with such passion.

"Hold the philosophy, hold the adjectives; just give us a plain subject and verb and perhaps a wholesome, nonfattening adverb or two."

—Larry McMurtry

Parts of Speech

Noun

A **noun** is a word that names something: a person, a place, a thing, or an idea.

governor Oregon hospital Buddhism love

Classes of Nouns

The five classes of nouns are *proper, common, concrete, abstract,* and *collective.*

561.1 Proper Nouns

A **proper noun** names a particular person, place, thing, or idea. Proper nouns are always capitalized.

Jackie Robinson Brooklyn Ebbets Field World Series Christianity

561.2 Common Nouns

A **common noun** does not name a particular person, place, thing, or idea. Common nouns are not capitalized.

person woman president park baseball government

561.3 Concrete Nouns

A **concrete noun** names a thing that is tangible (can be seen, touched, heard, smelled, or tasted). Concrete nouns are either proper or common.

child Grand Canyon music aroma pizza Beck

561.4 Abstract Nouns

An **abstract noun** names an idea, a condition, or a feeling—in other words, something that cannot be touched, smelled, tasted, seen, or heard.

New Deal greed poverty progress freedom hope

561.5 Collective Nouns

A **collective noun** names a group or a unit.

United States Seattle Seahawks team crowd community

Forms of Nouns

Nouns are grouped according to their number, gender, and case.

562.1 Number of a Noun

Number indicates whether the noun is singular or plural.

A **singular noun** refers to one person, place, thing, or idea.

actor stadium Canadian bully truth child person

A **plural noun** refers to more than one person, place, thing, or idea.

actors stadiums Canadians bullies truths children people

562.2 Gender of a Noun

Gender indicates whether a noun is masculine, feminine, neuter, or indefinite.

Masculine:
uncle brother men bull rooster stallion

Feminine:
aunt sister women cow hen filly

Neuter (without gender):
tree cobweb amoeba closet

Indefinite (masculine or feminine):
president plumber doctor parent

562.3 Case of a Noun

Case tells how nouns are related to other words used with them. There are three cases: *nominative, possessive,* and *objective.*

- A **nominative case** noun can be the subject of a clause.

  Patsy's heart was beating very wildly beneath his jacket. . . . That black horse there owed something to the orphan he had made.

  —Paul Dunbar, "The Finish of Patsy Barnes"

  A nominative noun can also be a predicate noun (or predicate nominative), which follows a "be" verb (*am, is, are, was, were, be, being, been*) and renames the subject. In the sentence below, *type* renames *Mr. Cattanzara.*

  Mr. Cattanzara was a different type than those in the neighborhood.

  —Bernard Malamud, "A Summer's Reading"

- A **possessive case** noun shows possession or ownership.

  Like the spider's claw, a part of him touches a world he will never enter.

  —Loren Eiseley, "The Hidden Teacher"

- An **objective case** noun can be a direct object, an indirect object, or an object of the preposition.

  Marna always gives Mylo science-fiction books for his birthday.

  (*Mylo* is the indirect object and *books* is the direct object of the verb "gives." *Birthday* is the object of the preposition "for.")

Pronoun

A **pronoun** is a word used in place of a noun.

I, you, she, it, which, that, themselves, whoever, me, he, they, mine, ours

563.1 Types of Pronouns

There are three types of pronouns: *simple, compound,* and *phrasal.*

Simple: **I, you, he, she, it, we, they, who, what**
Compound: **myself, someone, anybody, everything, itself, whoever**
Phrasal: **one another, each other**

563.2 Antecedent

All pronouns have antecedents. An **antecedent** is the noun that the pronoun refers to or replaces.

Ambrosch was considered the important person in the family. Mrs. Shimerda and Ántonia always deferred to him, though he was often surly with them and contemptuous toward his father.

—Willa Cather, *My Ántonia*

(*Ambrosch* is the antecedent of *him, he,* and *his.*)

NOTE: Each pronoun must agree with its antecedent. (See page 590.)

563.3 Classes of Pronouns

The six classes of pronouns are *personal, reflexive* and *intensive, relative, indefinite, interrogative,* and *demonstrative.*

Personal

I, me, my, mine / we, us, our, ours
you, your, yours / they, them, their, theirs
he, him, his, she, her, hers, it, its

Reflexive and Intensive

myself, yourself, himself, herself, itself, ourselves, yourselves, themselves

Relative

what, who, whose, whom, which, that

Indefinite

all	both	everything	nobody	several
another	each	few	none	some
any	each one	many	no one	somebody
anybody	either	most	nothing	someone
anyone	everybody	much	one	something
anything	everyone	neither	other	such

Interrogative

who, whose, whom, which, what

Demonstrative

this, that, these, those

Pronoun (continued)

564.1 Personal Pronoun

A **personal pronoun** can take the place of any noun.

Our coach made her point loud and clear when she raised her voice.

- A **reflexive pronoun** is formed by adding *-self* or *-selves* to a personal pronoun. A reflexive pronoun can be a direct object, an indirect object, an object of the preposition, or a predicate nominative.

  Miss Sally Sunshine loves herself. (direct object of *loves*)

  Tomisha does not seem herself today. (predicate nominative)

- An **intensive pronoun** is a reflexive pronoun that intensifies, or emphasizes, the noun or pronoun it refers to.

  Leo himself taught his children to invest their lives in others.

  The bread the children had baked themselves tasted . . . interesting.

564.2 Relative Pronoun

A **relative pronoun** relates an adjective clause to the noun or pronoun it modifies.

Students who study regularly get the best grades. Surprise!

The dance, which we had looked forward to for weeks, was canceled.

(The relative pronoun *who* relates the adjective clause to *students*; *which* relates the adjective clause to *dance*.)

564.3 Indefinite Pronoun

An **indefinite pronoun** often refers to unnamed or unknown people or things.

Whenever I hear anyone arguing for slavery, I feel a strong impulse to see it tried on him personally. (The antecedent of *anyone* is unknown.)

—Abraham Lincoln

564.4 Interrogative Pronoun

An **interrogative pronoun** asks a question.

"Who could you be? What do you want from my husband?"

—Elie Wiesel, "The Scrolls, Too, Are Mortal"

564.5 Demonstrative Pronoun

A **demonstrative pronoun** points out people, places, or things without naming them.

This shouldn't be too hard. That looks about right.
These are the best ones. Those ought to be thrown out.

NOTE: When one of these words precedes a noun, it functions as an adjective, not a pronoun. (See 574.1.)

That movie bothers me. (*That* is an adjective.)

Forms of Personal Pronouns

The form of a personal pronoun indicates its *number* (singular or plural), its *person* (first, second, third), its *case* (nominative, possessive, or objective), and its *gender* (masculine, feminine, or neuter).

565.1 Number of a Pronoun

Personal pronouns are singular or plural. The singular personal pronouns include *my, him, he, she, it.* The plural personal pronouns include *we, you, them, our.* (*You* can be singular or plural.) Notice in the caption below that the first **you** is singular and the second **you** is plural.

Larry, you need to keep all four tires on the road when turning. Are you still with us back there?

565.2 Person of a Pronoun

The **person** of a pronoun indicates whether the person, place, thing, or idea represented by the pronoun is speaking, is spoken to, or is spoken about.

- **First person** is used in place of the name of the speaker or speakers.

  "We don't do things like that," says Pa; "we're just and honest people. . . . I don't skip debts."

  —Jesse Stuart, "Split Cherry Tree"

- **Second person** pronouns name the person or persons spoken to.

  "If you hit your duck, you want me to go in after it?" Eugie said.

  —Gina Berriault, "The Stone Boy"

- **Third person** pronouns name the person or thing spoken about.

  She had hardly realized the news, further than to understand that she had been brought . . . face to face with something unexpected and final. It did not even occur to her to ask for any explanation.

  —Joseph Conrad, "The Idiots"

Forms of Personal Pronouns (continued)

566.1 Case of a Pronoun

The **case** of each pronoun tells how it is related to the other words used with it. There are three cases: *nominative, possessive,* and *objective.*

- A **nominative case** pronoun can be the subject of a clause. The following are nominative forms: *I, you, he, she, it, we, they.*

  I like life when things go well.
  You must live life in order to love life.

  A nominative pronoun is a *predicate nominative* if it follows a "be" verb (*am, is, are, was, were, be, being, been*) or another linking verb (*appear, become, feel,* etc.) and renames the subject.

  "Oh, it's only she who scared me just now," said Mama to Papa, glancing over her shoulder.
  "Yes, it is I," said Mai in a superior tone.

- **Possessive case** pronouns show possession or ownership. Apostrophes, however, are not used with personal pronouns.

  But as I placed my hand upon his shoulder, there came a strong shudder over his whole person.

  —Edgar Allan Poe, "The Fall of the House of Usher"

- An **objective case** pronoun can be a direct object, an indirect object, or an object of the preposition.

  The kids loved it! We lit a campfire for them and told them old ghost stories. (*It* is the direct object of the verb *loved. Them* is the object of the preposition *for* and the indirect object of the verb *told.*)

NUMBER, PERSON, AND CASE OF PERSONAL PRONOUNS

	Nominative	Possessive	Objective
First Person Singular	**I**	**my, mine**	**me**
Second Person Singular	**you**	**your, yours**	**you**
Third Person Singular	**he**	**his**	**him**
	she	**her, hers**	**her**
	it	**its**	**it**
	Nominative	Possessive	Objective
First Person Plural	**we**	**our, ours**	**us**
Second Person Plural	**you**	**your, yours**	**you**
Third Person Plural	**they**	**their, theirs**	**them**

566.2 Gender of a Pronoun

Gender indicates whether a pronoun is masculine, feminine, or neuter.

Masculine: he him his **Feminine: she her hers**

Neuter (without gender): it its

Verb

A **verb** is a word that expresses action (*run, carried, declared*) or state of being (*is, are, seemed*).

Classes of Verbs

567.1 Linking Verbs

A **linking verb** links the subject to a noun or an adjective in the predicate.

On his skateboard, the boy felt confident. He was the best skater around.

Common Linking Verbs

is	are	was	were	be	been	am

Additional Linking Verbs

smell	seem	grow	become	appear	sound	
taste	feel	get	remain	stay	look	turn

NOTE: The verbs listed as "additional linking verbs" function as linking verbs when they do not show actual action. An adjective usually follows these linking verbs. (When they do show action, an adverb or direct object may follow them. In this case, they are action verbs.)

Linking: This fruit smells rotten.

Action: Maya always smells fruit carefully before eating it.

567.2 Auxiliary Verbs

Auxiliary verbs, or helping verbs, are used to form some of the **tenses** (570.1), the **mood** (573.1), and the **voice** (572.3) of the main verb. (In the example below, the auxiliary verbs are in **red**; the main verbs are in **blue**.)

The long procession was led by white-robed priests, their faces streaked with red and yellow and white ash. By this time the flames had stopped spurting, and the pit consisted of a red-hot mass of burning wood, which attendants were leveling with long branches.

—Leonard Feinberg, "Fire Walking in Ceylon"

Common Auxiliary Verbs

is	was	being	did	have	would	shall	might
am	were	been	does	had	could	can	must
are	be	do	has	should	will	may	

Verb (continued)

568.1 Action Verbs: Transitive and Intransitive

An **intransitive verb** communicates an action that is complete in itself. It does not need an object to receive the action.

He jumped and flipped and twisted. The boy flew on his skateboard.

A **transitive verb** (**red**) is an action verb that needs an object (**blue**) to complete its meaning.

The city council passed a strict noise ordinance.

The health care industry employs more than 7 million workers.

While some action verbs are only transitive or intransitive, some can be either, depending on how they are used.

He finally stopped to rest. (intransitive)

He finally stopped the show. (transitive)

Action verbs are *dynamic*, meaning that they invigorate sentences. Linking verbs, on the other hand, are *static*, meaning that they are inactive, designed to express a condition or a state of being.

568.2 Objects with Transitive Verbs

- A **direct object** receives the action of a transitive verb directly from the subject. Without it, the transitive verb's meaning is incomplete.

  The boy kicked his skateboard forward.
  (*Skateboard* is the direct object.)

- An **indirect object** also receives the action of a transitive verb, but indirectly. An indirect object names the person *to whom* or *for whom* something is done. (It can also name the thing *to what* or *for what* something is done.)

  Then he showed us his best tricks.
  (*Us* is the indirect object.)

NOTE: When the word naming the indirect receiver of the action is in a prepositional phrase, it is no longer considered an indirect object.

Then he showed his best tricks to us.
(*Us* is the object of the preposition *to*.)

NOTE: Sometimes a direct object will have an **object complement**. An object complement renames or describes the direct object.

The spectators named the boy the best performer.

(*Performer* is the object complement of the direct object *boy*.)

Verbals

A **verbal** is a word that is derived from a verb but acts as another part of speech. There are three types of verbals: *gerunds, infinitives,* and *participles.* Each is often part of a verbal phrase.

569.1 Gerunds

A **gerund** is a verb form that ends in *ing* and is used as a noun.

Swimming is my favorite pastime. (subject)

I began swimming at the age of six months. (direct object)

Swimming in chlorinated pools makes my eyes red.
(gerund phrase as subject)

569.2 Infinitives

An **infinitive** is a verb form that is usually introduced by *to*; the infinitive may be used as a noun, an adjective, or an adverb.

To swim the English Channel must be a thrill.
(infinitive phrase as noun)

The urge to swim in tropical waters is more common.
(infinitive phrase as adjective)

The children were happy to swim all day.
(infinitive phrase as adverb)

569.3 Participles

A **participle** is a verb form ending in *ing* or *ed* that acts as an adjective. Writer Scott Rice says, "participles are dynamic adjectives or, more precisely, words halfway between adjectives (qualities) and verbs (actions)."

The farmhands harvesting corn are tired and hungry.
(participial phrase modifies *farmhands*)

The cribs full of harvested cobs are evidence of their hard work.
(modifies *cobs*)

NOTE: The past participle of an irregular verb can also act as an adjective.

That rake is obviously broken.

Make sure that you use verbals correctly; look carefully at the examples below.

Verbal: **Diving is a popular Olympic sport.**
(*Diving* is a gerund used as a subject.)
Diving gracefully, the Olympian hoped to get high marks.
(*Diving* is a participle modifying *Olympian*.)

Verb: **The next competitor was diving in the practice pool.**
(Here, *diving* is a verb, not a verbal.)

Forms of Verbs

A verb has different forms depending on its *voice* (active, passive); *number* (singular, plural); *person* (first, second, third); *tense* (simple, perfect, continuous); and *mood* (indicative, imperative, subjunctive).

570.1 Tense of a Verb

Tense indicates time. Each verb has three principal parts: the *present, past,* and *past participle.* All six tenses are formed from these principal parts. The past and past participle of regular verbs are formed by adding *ed* to the present form. The past and past participle of irregular verbs are usually different words; however, a few have the same form in all three principal parts. (See page 571.)

- **Present tense** expresses action that is happening at the present time, or action that happens continually, regularly.

  In September, sophomores smirk and joke about the "little freshies."

- **Past tense** expresses action that is completed at a particular time in the past.

  They forgot that just ninety days separated them from freshman status.

- **Future tense** expresses action that will take place in the future.

  They will remember this in three years when they will be freshmen again.

- **Present perfect tense** expresses action that began in the past but continues in the present or is completed in the present.

  Our boat has weathered worse storms than this one.

- **Past perfect tense** expresses an action in the past that occurs before another past action.

  They reported, wrongly, that the hurricane had missed the island.

- **Future perfect tense** expresses action that will begin in the future and be completed by a specific time in the future.

  By this time tomorrow, the hurricane will have smashed into the coast.

- A **present continuous tense** verb expresses action that is not completed at the time of stating it. The present continuous tense is formed by adding *am, is,* or *are* to the *-ing* form of the main verb.

  Scientists are learning a great deal from their study of the sky.

- A **past continuous tense** verb expresses action that was happening at a certain time in the past. This tense is formed by adding *was* or *were* to the *-ing* form of the main verb.

  Astronomers were beginning their quest for knowledge hundreds of years ago.

- A **future continuous tense** verb expresses action that will take place at some time in the future. This tense is formed by adding *will be* to the *-ing* form of the main verb.

  Someday astronauts will be going to Mars.

  This tense can also be formed by adding a phrase noting the future (*are going to*) plus *be* to the *-ing* form of the main verb.

  They are going to be doing many experiments.

571.1 Irregular Verbs

Common Irregular Verbs and Their Principal Parts

Present Tense	Past Tense	Past Participle	Present Tense	Past Tense	Past Participle	Present Tense	Past Tense	Past Participle
am, be	was, were	been	hang	hanged	hanged	sing	sang, sung	sung
bear	bore	born,	*(execute)*			sink	sank, sunk	sunk
		borne	hang	hung	hung	sit	sat	sat
beat	beat	beaten	*(suspend)*			sleep	slept	slept
begin	began	begun	hide	hid	hidden,	slide	slid	slid
bend	bent	bent			hid	speak	spoke	spoken
bite	bit	bitten,	hold	held	held	speed	sped,	sped,
		bit	keep	kept	kept		speeded	speeded
bleed	bled	bled	know	knew	known	spend	spent	spent
blow	blew	blown	lay	laid	laid	spin	spun	spun
break	broke	broken	lead	led	led	spring	sprang,	sprung
bring	brought	brought	leave	left	left		sprung	
buy	bought	bought	lend	lent	lent	stand	stood	stood
catch	caught	caught	lie	lay	lain	steal	stole	stolen
choose	chose	chosen	*(recline)*			stride	strode	stridden
come	came	come	lie	lied	lied	swear	swore	sworn
dive	dived,	dived,	*(deceive)*			sweep	swept	swept
	dove	dove	lose	lost	lost	swell	swelled	swelled,
do	did	done	make	made	made			swollen
draw	drew	drawn	mean	meant	meant	swim	swam	swum
drink	drank	drunk	meet	met	met	swing	swung	swung
drive	drove	driven	pay	paid	paid	take	took	taken
eat	ate	eaten	ride	rode	ridden	teach	taught	taught
fall	fell	fallen	ring	rang	rung	tear	tore	torn
feed	fed	fed	rise	rose	risen	tell	told	told
feel	felt	felt	run	ran	run	think	thought	thought
fight	fought	fought	say	said	said	throw	threw	thrown
find	found	found	see	saw	seen	wake	woke,	woken,
flee	fled	fled	sell	sold	sold		waked	waked
fly	flew	flown	send	sent	sent	wear	wore	worn
forbid	forbade	forbidden	shake	shook	shaken	weave	wove,	woven
freeze	froze	frozen	shine	shone	shone	*(from cloth)*		
get	got	gotten	*(light)*			weave	weaved	weaved
give	gave	given	shine	shined	shined	*(sway)*		
go	went	gone	*(polish)*			win	won	won
grind	ground	ground	shoot	shot	shot	wind	wound	wound
grow	grew	grown	show	showed	shown	wring	wrung	wrung
			shrink	shrank	shrunk	write	wrote	written

These verbs are the same in all principal parts: *burst, cost, cut, fit, forecast, hit, hurt, let, put, quit, set, shut, split, spread, sweat, wed,* and *wet.*

Forms of Verbs (continued)

572.1 Number of a Verb

Number indicates whether a verb is singular or plural. In a clause, the verb (in **blue** below) and its subject (in **red**) must both be singular or both be plural.

- **Singular**

  One large island floats off Italy's "toe."

  Italy's northern countryside includes the spectacular Alps.

  The Po Valley stretches between the Alps and the Apennines Mountains.

- **Plural**

  Five small islands float inside Michigan's "thumb."

  The Porcupine Mountains rise above the shores of Lake Superior.

  High bluffs and sand dunes border Lake Michigan.

572.2 Person of a Verb

Person indicates whether the subject of the verb is first, second, or third person (is speaking, is spoken to, or is spoken about). Usually the form of the verb only changes when the verb is in the present tense and is used with a third-person singular subject.

	Singular	Plural
First Person	I sniff	we sniff
Second Person	you sniff	you sniff
Third Person	he/she/it sniffs	they sniff

572.3 Voice of a Verb

Voice indicates whether the subject is acting or being acted upon.

- **Active voice** indicates that the subject of the verb is, has been, or will be doing something.

  Baseball great Walter Johnson pitched 50 consecutive scoreless innings.

  For many years Lou Brock held the base-stealing record.

  Use the active voice as much as possible because it makes your writing more direct and lively. (See "Passive Voice" on page 123.)

- **Passive voice** indicates that the subject of the verb is being, has been, or will be acted upon.

  Fifty consecutive scoreless innings were pitched by baseball great Walter Johnson.

  For many years the base-stealing record was held by Lou Brock.

NOTE: With passive voice, the person creating the action is not always stated.

The ordinance was overturned. (It is not clear who did the overturning.)

573.1 Mood of a Verb

Mood of a verb indicates the tone or attitude with which a statement is made.

- **Indicative mood** is used to state a fact or to ask a question.

  Sometimes I'd yell questions at the rocks and trees, and across gorges, or yodel, "What is the meaning of the void?" The answer was perfect silence, so I knew.

  —Jack Kerouac, "Alone on a Mountain Top"

- **Imperative mood** is used to give a command.

"Whatever you do, don't fly your kite during a storm."
—Mrs. Abiah Franklin

- **Subjunctive mood** is no longer commonly used; however, careful writers may choose to use it to express the exact manner in which their statements are meant.
  - Use the subjunctive *were* to express a condition that is contrary to fact.

    If I were finished with my report, I could go to the movie.

  - Use the subjunctive *were* after *as though* or *as if* to express an unreal condition.

    Mrs. Young acted as if she were sixteen again.

  - Use the subjunctive *be* in "that" clauses to express necessity, legal decisions, or parliamentary motions.

    "It is moved and supported that no more than 6,000,000 quad be used to explore the planet Earth."

    "Ridiculous! Knowing earthlings is bound to help us understand ourselves! Therefore, I move that the sum be amended to 12,000,000 quad."

    "Stupidity! I move that all missions be postponed until we have living proof of life on Earth."

Adjective

An **adjective** describes or modifies a noun or a pronoun. The articles *a, an,* and *the* are also adjectives.

The young driver peeked through the big steering wheel.

(*The* and *young* modify *driver; the* and *big* modify *steering wheel.*)

When several adjectives are used in a row to modify a noun, arrange them in this order: Place the article, demonstrative adjective, or possessive first; place the kinds of words listed below after that.

WORDS THAT . . .

indicate time	**first, next**
tell how many	**one, few**
evaluate	**beautiful, charming**
tell what size	**big, small**
tell what shape	**round, square**
describe a condition	**messy, clean**
tell what age	**old, young**
tell what color	**white, red**
tell what nationality	**German, Vietnamese**
tell what religion	**Hindu, Protestant**
tell what material	**silky, wooden**

The toddler pointed at the three lovely white swans.

It was Mariko's last attempt to climb the tall steel tower.

574.1 Types of Adjectives

A **proper adjective** is created from a proper noun and is capitalized.

In Canada (proper noun), **you will find many cultures and climates.**

Canadian (proper adjective) **winters can be harsh.**

A **predicate adjective** follows a form of the "be" verb (or other linking verb) and describes the subject.

Late autumn seems grim to those who love summer. (*Grim* modifies *autumn.*)

NOTE: Some words can be either adjectives or pronouns (*that, these, all, each, both, many, some,* and so on). These words are adjectives when they come before the nouns they modify; they are pronouns when they stand alone.

Jiao made both goals. (*Both* modifies *goals;* it is an adjective.)

Both were scored in the final period. (*Both* stands alone; it is a pronoun.)

575.1 Forms of Adjectives

Adjectives have three forms: *positive, comparative,* and *superlative.*

- The **positive form** describes a noun or a pronoun without comparing it to anyone or anything else.

  The first game was long and tiresome.

- The **comparative form** (*-er, more,* or *less*) compares two persons, places, things, or ideas.

  The second game was longer and more tiresome than the first.

NOTE: The comparative can refer to more than two with the addition of the word *other.*

The second game was longer and more tiresome than the *other* games.

- The **superlative form** (*-est, most,* or *least*) compares three or more persons, places, things, or ideas.

  The third game was the longest and most tiresome of all.

NOTE: Use *more* and *most* (or *less* and *least*)—instead of adding a suffix—with many adjectives of two or more syllables. There are some adjectives that are considered *irregular* (*good, many, bad*) because of their comparative and superlative forms.

Positive	Comparative	Superlative
big	bigger	biggest
strong	stronger	strongest
helpful	more helpful	most helpful
comfortable	more comfortable	most comfortable
painful	less painful	least painful
critical	less critical	least critical
good	better	best
many	more	most
bad	worse	worst

Adverb

An **adverb** describes or modifies a verb, an adjective, or another adverb.

She sneezed loudly. (*Loudly* modifies the verb *sneezed.*)

Her sneezes are really dramatic. (*Really* modifies the adjective *dramatic.*)

The sneeze exploded very noisily. (*Very* modifies the adverb *noisily.*)

An adverb usually tells *when, where, how,* or *how much.*

576.1 Types of Adverbs

Adverbs can be cataloged in four basic ways: *time, place, manner,* and *degree.*

Time (These adverbs tell *when, how often,* and *how long.*)

today, yesterday **daily, weekly** **briefly, eternally**

Place (These adverbs tell *where, to where,* and *from where.*)

here, there **nearby, beyond** **backward, forward**

Manner (These adverbs often end in *ly* and tell *how* something is done.)

precisely **effectively** **regally** **smoothly** **well**

Degree (These adverbs tell *how much* or *how little.*)

substantially **greatly** **entirely** **partly** **too**

NOTE: Some adverbs can be written with or without the *ly* ending. When in doubt, use the *ly* form.

slow, slowly **loud, loudly** **fair, fairly** **tight, tightly** **quick, quickly**

576.2 Forms of Adverbs

Adverbs of manner have three forms: *positive, comparative,* and *superlative.*

- The **positive form** describes a verb, an adjective, or another adverb without comparing it to anyone or anything else.

  Model X vacuum cleans well and runs quietly.

- The **comparative form** (*-er, more,* or *less*) compares how two things are done.

  Model Y vacuum cleans better and runs more quietly than model X does.

- The **superlative form** (*-est, most,* or *least*) compares how three or more things are done.

  Model Z vacuum cleans best and runs most quietly of all.

Positive	Comparative	Superlative
well	better	best
fast	faster	fastest
remorsefully	more remorsefully	most remorsefully

Preposition

A **preposition** is the first word (or group of words) in a prepositional phrase. It shows the relationship between its object (a noun or a pronoun that follows the preposition) and another word in the sentence. The first noun or pronoun following a preposition is its object.

> **To make a mustache, Natasha placed the hairy caterpillar under her nose.** (*Under* shows the relationship between the verb, *placed,* and the object of the preposition, *nose.*)
>
> **The drowsy insect clung obediently to the girl's upper lip.** (The first noun following the preposition *to* is *lip; lip* is the object of the preposition.)

577.1 Prepositional Phrases

A **prepositional phrase** includes the preposition, the object of the preposition, and the modifiers of the object. A prepositional phrase functions as an adverb or as an adjective.

> **Some people run away from caterpillars.**
> (The phrase functions as an adverb and modifies the verb *run.)*
>
> **However, little kids with inquisitive minds enjoy their company.**
> (The phrase functions as an adjective and modifies the noun *kids.*)

NOTE: A preposition is always followed by an object; if there is no object, the word is an adverb, not a preposition.

> **Natasha never played with caterpillars before.** (The word *before* is not followed by an object; therefore, it functions as an adverb that modifies *played,* a verb.)

Common Prepositions

aboard	before	from	of	save
about	behind	from among	off	since
above	below	from between	on	subsequent to
according to	beneath	from under	on account of	through
across	beside	in	on behalf of	throughout
across from	besides	in addition to	onto	till
after	between	in back of	on top of	to
against	beyond	in behalf of	opposite	together with
along	by	in front of	out	toward
alongside	by means of	in place of	out of	under
along with	concerning	in regard to	outside of	underneath
amid	considering	inside	over	until
among	despite	inside of	over to	unto
apart from	down	in spite of	owing to	up
around	down from	instead of	past	upon
aside from	during	into	prior to	up to
at	except	like	regarding	with
away from	except for	near	round	within
because of	for	near to	round about	without

Conjunction

A **conjunction** connects individual words or groups of words. There are three kinds of conjunctions: *coordinating, correlative,* and *subordinating.*

578.1 Coordinating Conjunctions

Coordinating conjunctions usually connect a word to a word, a phrase to a phrase, or a clause to a clause. The words, phrases, or clauses joined by a coordinating conjunction are equal in importance or are of the same type.

> **I could tell by my old man's eyes that he *was nervous* and *wanted to smooth things over,* but Syl didn't give him a chance.**
>
> —Albert Halper, "Prelude"

(*And* connects the two parts of a compound predicate; *but* connects two independent clauses that could stand on their own.)

578.2 Correlative Conjunctions

Correlative conjunctions are conjunctions used in pairs.

> **They were not only exhausted by the day's journey but also sunburned.**

578.3 Subordinating Conjunctions

Subordinating conjunctions connect two clauses that are *not* equally important, thereby showing the relationship between them. A subordinating conjunction connects a dependent clause to an independent clause in order to complete the meaning of the dependent clause.

> **A brown trout will study the bait before he eats it.** (The clause *before he eats it* is dependent. It depends on the rest of the sentence to complete its meaning.)

KINDS OF CONJUNCTIONS

Coordinating: **and, but, or, nor, for, yet, so**

Correlative: **either, or; neither, nor; not only, but also; both, and; whether, or**

Subordinating: **after, although, as, as if, as long as, as though, because, before, if, in order that, provided that, since, so that, that, though, till, unless, until, when, where, whereas, while**

NOTE: Relative pronouns (564.2) and conjunctive adverbs (515.5) can also connect clauses.

Interjection

An **interjection** communicates strong emotion or surprise. Punctuation (often a comma or an exclamation point) is used to set off an interjection from the rest of the sentence.

> **Oh no! The TV broke. Good grief! I have nothing to do! Yipes, I'll go mad!**

Parts of Speech

QUICK GUIDE

Words in the English language are used in eight different ways. For this reason, there are eight parts of speech.

Noun	A word that names a person, a place, a thing, or an idea **Governor Smith-Jones Oregon hospital religion**
Pronoun	A word used in place of a noun **I you she him who everyone these neither theirs themselves which**
Verb	A word that expresses action or state of being **float sniff discover seem were was**
Adjective	A word that describes a noun or a pronoun **young big grim Canadian longer**
Adverb	A word that describes a verb, an adjective, or another adverb **briefly forward regally slowly better**
Preposition	The first word or words in a prepositional phrase (which functions as an adjective or an adverb) **away from under before with for out of**
Conjunction	A word that connects other words or groups of words **and but although because either, or so**
Interjection	A word that shows strong emotion or surprise **Oh no! Yipes! Good grief! Well, . . .**

"A sentence should read as if its author, had he held a plough instead of a pen, could have drawn a furrow deep and straight to the end."

—Henry David Thoreau

Using the Language

Constructing Sentences

A **sentence** is made up of one or more words that express a complete thought. A sentence begins with a capital letter; it ends with a period, a question mark, or an exclamation point.

What should we do for our vacation this year? We could go camping.
No, I hate bugs!

Using Subjects and Predicates

A sentence usually has a **subject** and a **predicate**. The subject is the part of the sentence about which something is said. The predicate, which contains the verb, is the part of the sentence that says something about the subject.

Like the pilot, the writer must see faster and more completely than the ordinary viewer of life.

—Paul Engle, "Salt Crystals, Spider Webs, and Words"

580.1 The Subject

The **subject** is the part of the sentence about which something is said. The subject is always a noun; a pronoun; or a word, clause, or phrase that functions as a noun (such as a gerund or a gerund phrase or an infinitive).

Wolves howl. (noun) **They howl for a variety of reasons.** (pronoun)

To establish their turf may be one reason. (infinitive phrase)

Searching for "lost" pack members may be another. (gerund phrase)

That wolves and dogs are similar animals seems obvious. (noun clause)

- A **simple subject** is the subject without its modifiers.

  Most wildlife biologists disapprove of crossbreeding wolves and dogs.

- A **complete subject** is the subject with all of its modifiers.

  Most wildlife biologists disapprove of crossbreeding wolves and dogs.

- A **compound subject** is composed of two or more simple subjects.

  Wise breeders and owners know that wolf-dog puppies can display unexpected, destructive behaviors.

581.1 Delayed Subject

The subject follows the verb in sentences beginning with *There* and a "be" verb, in questions, and sometimes in sentences beginning with *It is* or *It was*.

There was nothing in the refrigerator.
(The subject is *nothing;* the verb is *was.*)

Where is my sandwich?
(The subject is *sandwich;* the verb is *is.*)

581.2 The Predicate

The **predicate,** which contains the verb, is the part of the sentence that shows action or says something about the subject.

Giant squid do exist.

- A **simple predicate** is the verb without its modifiers.

  One giant squid measured nearly 60 feet long.

- A **complete predicate** is the simple predicate with all its modifiers.

  One giant squid measured nearly 60 feet long.
  (*Measured* is the simple predicate; *nearly 60 feet long* modifies *measured.*)

- A **compound predicate** is composed of two or more simple predicates.

  A squid grasps its prey with tentacles and bites it with its beak.

NOTE: A sentence can have a **compound subject** and a **compound predicate.**

Both sperm whales and giant squid live and occasionally clash in the deep waters off New Zealand's South Island.

- A **direct object** is part of the predicate and receives the action of the verb. (See 568.2.)

  Sperm whales sometimes eat giant squid.
  (The direct object *giant squid* receives the action of the verb *eat* by answering the question *whales eat what?*)

NOTE: The **direct object** may be compound.

In the past, whalers harvested oil, spermaceti, and ambergris from slain sperm whales.

581.3 Understood Subject and Predicate

Either the subject or the predicate may be "missing" from a sentence, but both must be clearly **understood.**

Who is making supper?
(*Who* is the subject; *is making supper* is the predicate.)

No one.
(*No one* is the subject; the predicate *is making supper* is understood.)

Put on that apron.
(The subject *you* is understood; *put on that apron* is the predicate.)

Using Phrases

A **phrase** is a group of related words that function as a single part of speech. The sentence below contains a number of phrases.

Finishing the race will require running down several steep slopes.

finishing the race (This gerund phrase functions as a subject noun.)

will require (This phrase functions as a verb.)

running down several steep slopes (This gerund phrase functions as an object noun.)

582.1 Types of Phrases

There are several types of phrases: *verb, verbal, prepositional, appositive,* and *absolute.*

- A **verb phrase** consists of a main verb preceded by one or more helping verbs.

  The snow has been falling for three straight days.
  (*Has been falling* is a verb phrase.)

- A **verbal phrase** is a phrase based on one of the three types of verbals: *gerund, infinitive,* or *participle.* (See 569.1, 569.2, and 569.3.)

  - A **gerund phrase** consists of a gerund and its modifiers. The whole phrase functions as a noun.

    Spotting the tiny mouse was easy for the hawk.
    (The gerund phrase is used as the subject of the sentence.)

    Dinner escaped by ducking under a rock.
    (The gerund phrase is the object of the preposition *by.*)

  - An **infinitive phrase** consists of an infinitive and its modifiers. The whole phrase functions as either a noun, an adjective, or an adverb.

    To shake every voter's hand was the candidate's goal.
    (The infinitive phrase functions as a noun used as the subject.)

    Your efforts to clean the chalkboard are appreciated.
    (The infinitive phrase is used as an adjective modifying *efforts.*)

    Please watch carefully to see the difference.
    (The infinitive phrase is used as an adverb modifying *watch.*)

  - A **participial phrase** consists of a past or present participle and its modifiers. The whole phrase functions as an adjective.

    Following his nose, the beagle took off like a jackrabbit.
    (The participial phrase modifies the noun *beagle.*)

    The raccoons, warned by the rustling, took cover.
    (The participial phrase modifies the noun *raccoons.*)

- A **prepositional phrase** is a group of words beginning with a preposition and ending with a noun or a pronoun. Prepositional phrases function mainly as adjectives and adverbs.

  Zach won the wheelchair race in record time. (The prepositional phrase *in record time* is used as an adverb modifying the verb *won.*)

  Reach for that catnip ball behind the couch. (The prepositional phrase *behind the couch* is used as an adjective modifying *catnip ball.*)

- An **appositive phrase,** which follows a noun or a pronoun and renames it, consists of a noun and its modifiers. An appositive adds new information about the noun or pronoun it follows.

  The Trans-Siberian Railroad, the world's longest railway, stretches from Moscow to Vladivostok. (The appositive phrase renames *Trans-Siberian Railroad* and provides new information.)

- An **absolute phrase** consists of a noun and a participle (plus the participle's object, if there is one, and any modifiers). An absolute phrase functions as an adjective that adds information to the entire sentence. Absolute phrases are always set off with commas.

  Its wheels clattering rhythmically over the rails, the train rolled into town. (The noun *wheels* is modified by the present participle *clattering.* The entire phrase modifies the rest of the sentence.)

Using Clauses

A **clause** is a group of related words that has both a subject and a predicate.

583.1 Independent and Dependent Clauses

An independent clause presents a complete thought and can stand alone as a sentence; a dependent clause (also called a subordinate clause) does not present a complete thought and cannot stand alone as a sentence.

Sparrows make nests in cattle barns (independent clause) **so that they can stay warm during the winter** (dependent clause).

583.2 Types of Dependent Clauses

There are three basic types of dependent clauses: *adverb, noun,* and *adjective.*

- An **adverb clause** begins with a subordinating conjunction and is used like an adverb to modify a verb, an adjective, or an adverb. (See 578.3.)

  If I study hard, I will pass this test.
  (The adverb clause modifies the verb *will pass.*)

- A **noun clause** is used in place of a noun.

  However, the teacher said that the essay questions are based only on the last two chapters. (The noun clause functions as a direct object.)

- An **adjective clause** modifies a noun or a pronoun.

  Tomorrow's test, which covers the entire book, is half essay and half short answers. (The adjective clause modifies the noun *test.*)

Using Sentence Variety

A **sentence** may be classified according to the type of statement it makes, the way it is constructed, and its arrangement of words.

584.1 Kinds of Sentences

Sentences can make five basic kinds of statements: *declarative, interrogative, imperative, exclamatory,* or *conditional.*

- **Declarative sentences** make statements. They tell us something about a person, a place, a thing, or an idea.

  The Statue of Liberty stands in New York Harbor.

  For over a century, it has greeted immigrants and visitors to America.

- **Interrogative sentences** ask questions.

  Did you know that the Statue of Liberty is made of copper and stands more than 150 feet tall?

- **Imperative sentences** make commands. They often contain an understood subject (*you*) as in the examples below.

  Go see the Statue of Liberty.

  After a few weeks of physical conditioning, climb its 168 stairs.

- **Exclamatory sentences** communicate strong emotion or surprise.

  Climbing 168 stairs is not a dumb idea!

  Just muster some of that old pioneering spirit, that desire to try something new, that never-say-die attitude that made America great!

- **Conditional sentences** express wishes ("if . . . then" statements) or conditions contrary to fact.

  If you were to climb to the top of the statue, then you could share in the breathtaking feeling experienced by many hopeful immigrants.

584.2 Types of Sentence Constructions

A sentence may be *simple, compound, complex,* or *compound-complex.* It all depends on the relationship between independent and dependent clauses.

- A **simple sentence** can have a single subject or a compound subject. It can have a single predicate or a compound predicate. However, a simple sentence has only one independent clause, and it has no dependent clauses.

  My back aches.
  (single subject; single predicate)

  My teeth and my eyes hurt.
  (compound subject; single predicate)

  My throat and nose feel sore and look red.
  (compound subject; compound predicate)

  I must have caught the flu from the sick kids in class.
  (independent clause with two phrases: *from the sick kids* and *in class*)

- A **compound sentence** consists of two independent clauses. The clauses must be joined by a comma and a coordinating conjunction or by a semicolon.

  I usually don't mind missing school, but this is not fun.

  I feel too sick to watch TV; I feel too sick to eat.

  NOTE: The comma can be omitted when the clauses are very short.

  I wept and I wept.

- A **complex sentence** contains one independent clause (in black) and one or more dependent clauses (in red).

  When I get back to school, I'm actually going to appreciate it.
  (dependent clause; independent clause)

  I won't even complain about math class, although I might be talking out of my head because I'm feverish.
  (independent clause; two dependent clauses)

- A **compound-complex sentence** contains two or more independent clauses (in black) and one or more dependent clauses (in red).

  Yes, I have a bad flu, and because I need to get well soon, I won't think about school just yet.
  (two independent clauses; one dependent clause)

585.1 Arrangements of Sentences

Depending on the arrangement of the words and the placement of emphasis, a sentence may also be classified as *loose, balanced, periodic,* or *cumulative.*

- A **loose sentence** expresses the main thought near the beginning and adds explanatory material as needed.

  We hauled out the boxes of food and set up the camp stove, all the time battling the hot wind that would not stop, even when we screamed into the sky.

- A **balanced sentence** is constructed so that it emphasizes a similarity or a contrast between two or more of its parts (words, phrases, or clauses).

  The wind in our ears drove us crazy and pushed us on.
  (The similar wording emphasizes the main idea in this sentence.)

- A **periodic sentence** is one that postpones the crucial or most surprising idea until the end.

  Following my mother's repeated threats to ground me for life, I decided it was time to propose a compromise.

- A **cumulative sentence** places the general idea in the middle of the sentence with modifying clauses and phrases coming before and after.

  With careful thought, and extra attention to detail, I wrote out my plan for being a model teenager, a teen who cared about neatness and reliability.

Diagramming Sentences

A **graphic diagram** of a sentence is a picture of how the words in that sentence are related and how they fit together to form a complete thought.

586.1 Simple Sentence with One Subject and One Verb

Chris fishes.

Chris | fishes

subject | verb

586.2 Simple Sentence with a Predicate Adjective

Fish are delicious.

Fish | are \ delicious

subject | verb \ predicate adjective

586.3 Simple Sentence with a Predicate Noun and Adjectives

Fishing is my favorite hobby.

NOTE: When possessive pronouns (*my, his, their,* etc.) are used as adjectives, they are placed on a diagonal line under the word they modify.

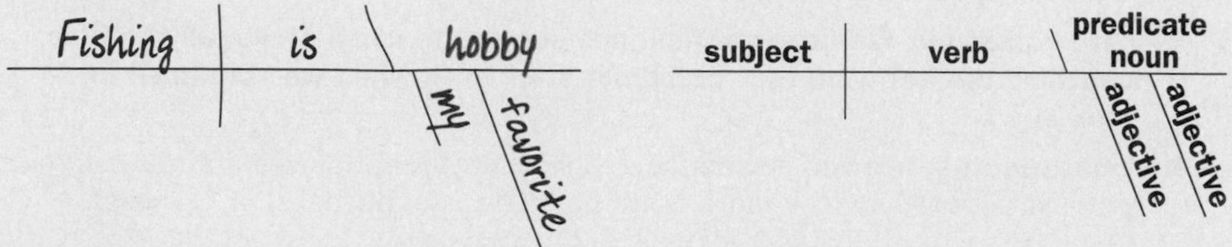

586.4 Simple Sentence with an Indirect and Direct Object

My grandpa gave us a trout.

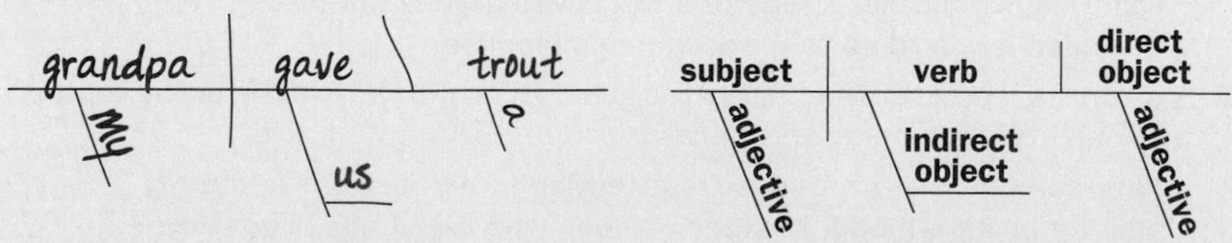

NOTE: Articles (*a, an, the*) are adjectives and are placed on a diagonal line under the word they modify.

587.1 Simple Sentence with a Prepositional Phrase

I like fishing by myself.

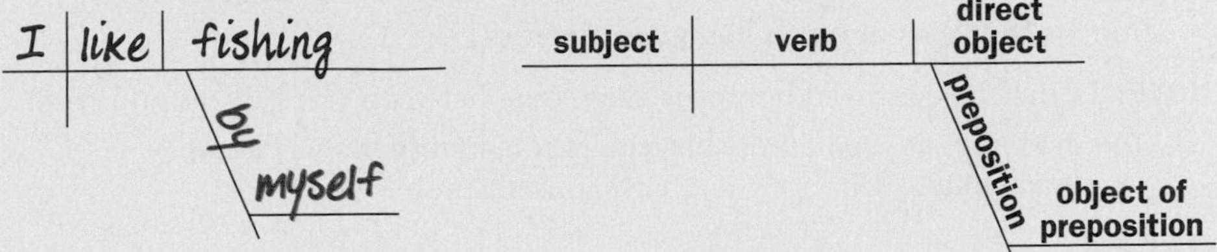

587.2 Simple Sentence with a Compound Subject and Verb

The team and fans clapped and cheered.

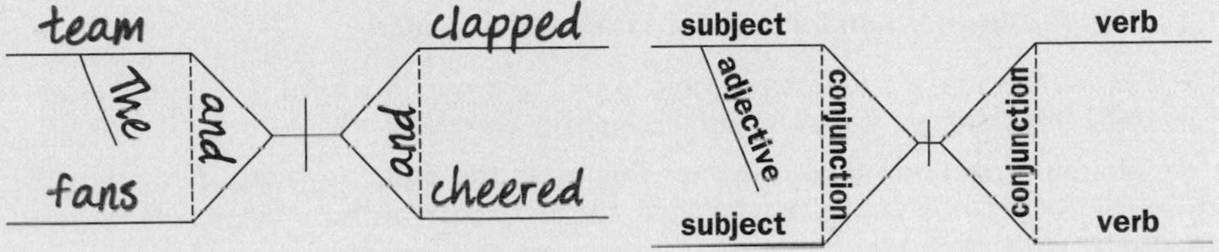

587.3 Compound Sentence

The team scored, and the crowd cheered wildly.

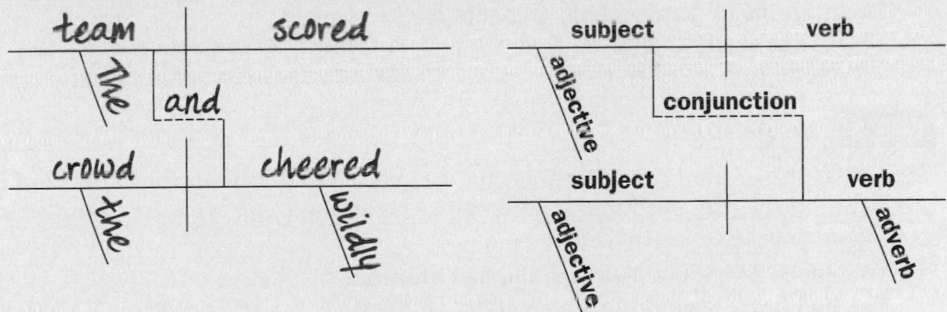

587.4 Complex Sentence with a Subordinate Clause

Before Erin scored, the crowd sat quietly.

crowd
sat
the
Before
quietly
Erin
scored
subject
verb
adjective
conjunction
adverb
subject
verb

Getting Sentence Parts to Agree

Agreement of Subject and Verb

A verb must agree in number (singular or plural) with its subject.

The student was proud of her quarter grades.

NOTE: Do not be confused by words that come between the subject and verb.

The manager, as well as the players, is required to display good sportsmanship. (*Manager,* not *players,* is the subject.)

588.1 Compound Subjects

Compound subjects connected with *and* require a plural verb.

Strength and balance are necessary for gymnastics.

Compound subjects joined by *or* or *nor* take a singular verb.

Neither Bev nor Kendra is going to the street dance.

NOTE: When one of the subjects joined by *or* or *nor* is singular and one is plural, the verb must agree with the subject nearer the verb.

Neither Yoshi nor his friends are singing in the band anymore. (The plural subject *friends* is nearer the verb, so the plural verb *are* is correct.)

588.2 Delayed Subjects

Delayed subjects occur when the verb comes before the subject in a sentence. In these inverted sentences, the delayed subject must agree with the verb.

There are many hardworking students in our schools.
There is present among many young people today a will to succeed.
(*Students* and *will* are the true subjects of these sentences, not *there.*)

588.3 "Be" Verbs

When a sentence contains a form of the "be" verb—and a noun comes before and after that verb—the verb must agree with the subject, not with the *complement* (the noun coming after the verb).

The cause of his problem was the bad brakes.
The bad brakes were the cause of his problem.

588.4 Special Cases

Some nouns that are **plural in form but singular in meaning** take a singular verb: *mumps, measles, news, mathematics, economics, gallows, shambles.*

Measles is still considered a serious disease in many parts of the world.

Some nouns that are plural in form but singular in meaning take a plural verb: *scissors, trousers, tidings.*

The scissors are missing again.

589.1 Collective Nouns

Collective nouns (*faculty, committee, team, congress, species, crowd, army, pair, squad*) take a singular verb when they refer to a group as a unit; collective nouns take a plural verb when they refer to the individuals within the group.

> **The favored team is losing, and the crowd is getting ugly.** (Both *team* and *crowd* are considered units in this sentence, requiring the singular verb *is*.)

> **The pair were finally reunited after 20 years apart.**
> (Here, *pair* refers to two individuals, so the plural verb *were* is required.)

589.2 Indefinite Pronouns

Some **indefinite pronouns** are singular: *each, either, neither, one, everybody, another, anybody, everyone, nobody, everything, somebody,* and *someone.* They require a singular verb.

> **Everybody is invited to the auditorium for the concert.**

Some **indefinite pronouns** are plural: *both, few, many,* and *several.*

> **Several like jazz medleys. Many ask for encores.**

NOTE: Do not be confused by words or phrases that come between the indefinite pronoun and the verb.

> **One of the participants is** (not *are*) **going to have to stay late to clean up.**

A Closer Look

Some **indefinite pronouns** can be either singular or plural: *all, any, most, none,* and *some.* These pronouns are singular if the number of the noun in the prepositional phrase is singular; they are plural if the noun is plural.

> **Most of the standing ovations are for the seniors.**
> (*Ovations* is plural, so *most* is plural.)

> **Most of the auditorium is standing room only.**
> (*Auditorium* is singular, so *most* is singular.)

589.3 Relative Pronouns

When a **relative pronoun** (*who, which, that*) is used as the subject of a clause, the number of the verb is determined by the antecedent of the pronoun. (The antecedent is the word to which the pronoun refers.)

> **This is one of the books that are required for geography class.**
> (The relative pronoun *that* requires the plural verb *are* because its antecedent *books* is plural.)

NOTE: To test this type of sentence for agreement, read the "of" phrase first.

> **Of the books that are required for geography class, this is one.**

Getting Sentence Parts to Agree (continued)

Agreement of Pronoun and Antecedent

A pronoun must agree in number, person, and gender with its *antecedent*. (The *antecedent* is the word to which the pronoun refers.)

Cal brought his gerbil to school. (The antecedent of *his* is *Cal*. Both the pronoun and its antecedent are singular, third person, and masculine; therefore, the pronoun is said to "agree" with its antecedent.)

590.1 Agreement in Number

Use a **singular pronoun** to refer to such antecedents as *each, either, neither, one, anyone, anybody, everyone, everybody, somebody, another, nobody,* and *a person.*

Neither of the brothers likes his (not *their*) **room.**

Two or more singular antecedents joined by *or* or *nor* are also referred to by a **singular pronoun.**

Either Connie or Sue left her headset in the library.

If one of the antecedents joined by *or* or *nor* is singular and one is plural, the pronoun should agree with the nearer antecedent.

Neither the manager nor the players were crazy about their new uniforms.

Use a **plural pronoun** to refer to plural antecedents as well as to compound subjects joined by *and.*

Jared and Carlos are finishing their assignments.

NOTE: Be careful when using pronouns that refer to collective nouns. If the collective noun refers to a group considered as one unit, it is a singular antecedent. If the collective noun refers to the individuals within a group, it is plural.

As the crowd swelled, it pushed uncomfortably toward the stage.
(The *crowd* is a singular antecedent that requires a singular pronoun, *it.*)

The cleanup crew were ready with their large, wheeled waste cans and wide push brooms. (The *crew* is a plural antecedent that requires a plural pronoun, *their.*)

590.2 Agreement in Gender

Use a **masculine** or **feminine pronoun** depending upon the gender of the antecedent.

Is either Connor or Grace bringing his or her baseball glove?

When *a person* or *everyone* is used to refer to both sexes or either sex, you will have to choose whether to offer optional pronouns or rewrite the sentence.

A person should be allowed to pursue her or his interests.
(optional pronouns)

People should be allowed to pursue their interests.
(rewritten in plural form)

Using Fair Language

When depicting individuals or groups according to their differences, you must use language that implies equal value and equal respect for all people.

591.1 Addressing Ethnicity

Acceptable General Terms	Acceptable Specific Terms
American Indians, Native Americans	**Cherokee, Inuit, Navajo**
Asian Americans (not *Orientals*)	**Chinese Americans**
Hispanic or Latino	**Mexican Americans**

African Americans, blacks
African American has come into wide acceptance, though the term *black* is preferred by some individuals.

Anglo-Americans (English ancestry), **European Americans**
Avoid the notion that *American,* used alone, means *white.* Also avoid using *Americans* to mean only *U.S. citizens.*

591.2 Addressing Age

General Age Group	Acceptable Terms
Up to age 12	**boys, girls**
Between 13 and 19	**youth, young people, adolescents**
Late teens and 20's	**young adults**
30's and older	**adults, men, women**
70 and older	**older adults, older people** (not *elderly*)

591.3 Addressing Disabilities and Impairments

Not Recommended	Preferred
handicapped	**disabled**
birth defect	**congenital disability**
an AIDS victim	**person with AIDS**
stutter, stammer, lisp	**speech impairment (impaired)**
deaf	**hearing impairment (impaired)**
blind	**visual impairment (impaired)**

591.4 Putting People First

People *with* various conditions should be referred to as such, not as though they *were* their condition.

Not Recommended	Preferred
the retarded	**people with mental retardation**
neurotics	**people with neuroses**
quadriplegics	**people who are quadriplegic**

Using Fair Language (continued)

592.1 Avoiding Sexism

- **Don't** use masculine-only pronouns (*he, his, him*) when you want to refer to a human being in general.

  A politician can kiss privacy good-bye when he runs for office.

  DO use one of the several ways to avoid sexism:

  Reword the sentence: **Running for office robs a politician of privacy.**

  Express in the plural: **Politicians can kiss privacy good-bye when they run for office.**

  Offer optional pronouns: **A politician can kiss privacy good-bye when he or she runs for office.**

- **Don't** use a male word in the salutation of a business letter to someone you do not know:

  Dear Sir: Dear Gentlemen:

  DO address both if you're not sure whether the reader is male or female . . .

  Dear Madam or Sir:
  Dear Ladies and Gentlemen:

  or address a position:

  Dear Personnel Officer:
  Dear Members of the Big Bird Fan Club:

- **Don't** give special treatment to one of the sexes:

  The men and the ladies came through in the clutch.
  Mr. Bubba Gumm, Mrs. Bubba Gumm

  DO use equal language for both sexes:

  The men and the women came through in the clutch.
  Mr. Manuel Lopez, Mrs. Elizabeth Lopez

592.2 Avoiding Gender Typecasting

- **Don't** typecast either gender.

  DO show both women and men as doctors and nurses, principals and teachers, breadwinners and housekeepers, bosses and secretaries, grocery-store owners and cashiers, pilots and plumbers, and so on.

- **Don't** associate certain qualities like courage, strength, brilliance, creativity, independence, persistence, seriousness, emotionalism, passivity, or fearfulness with only one gender.

  DO portray people of both sexes along the whole range of potential human strengths and weaknesses.

593.1 Avoiding Unfair References

- **Don't** refer to women according to their physical appearance and to men according to their mental abilities or professional status:

  The admirable Dr. William Hicks and his wife Sareena, a former model, both showed up at the party.

  DO refer to both on the same plane:

  Bill and Sareena Hicks showed up at the party.

- **Don't** take special notice when a woman does a "man's job" or vice versa:

  lady doctor   male nurse   coed   steward   policewoman   waitress

  DO treat men's or women's involvement in a profession in the same way:

  doctor   nurse   student   flight attendant   police officer   server

Not Recommended	Preferred
chairman	**chair, presiding officer, moderator**
salesman	**sales representative, salesperson**
mailman	**mail carrier, postal worker, letter carrier**
fireman	**firefighter**
businessman	**executive, manager, businessperson**
congressman	**member of Congress, representative, senator**
policeman	**police officer**

593.2 Avoiding Demeaning Portrayals

- **Don't** portray women as the possessions of men:

  Fred took his wife and kids on a vacation.

  DO portray women and men, husbands and wives, as equal partners:

  Fred and Wilma took their kids on a vacation.

- **Don't** use demeaning or sexually loaded labels:

the weaker sex	chick, fox	jock
the little woman	stud, hunk	the old man

  DO use respectful terms rather than labels; consider what the person might wish to be called:

women, females	**attractive woman**	**athletic man**
wife, spouse	**handsome man**	**father, husband, spouse**

Student Almanac

Language

This chapter provides a chart of the manual alphabet and a map showing the Indo-European languages that influenced the English language.

Manual Alphabet (Sign Language)

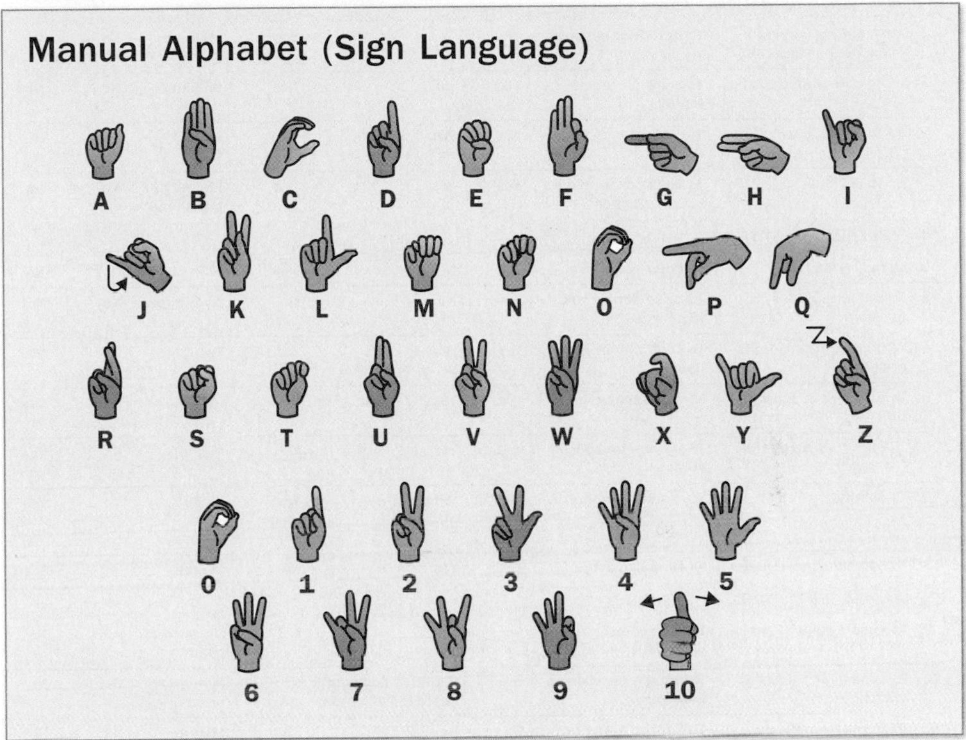

Indo-European Languages

This map identifies the Indo-European family of languages. When the ancient Indo-Europeans migrated west, they developed a number of Germanic dialects. It was the Germanic people who invaded the British Isles, bringing with them Old English, the earliest version of English.

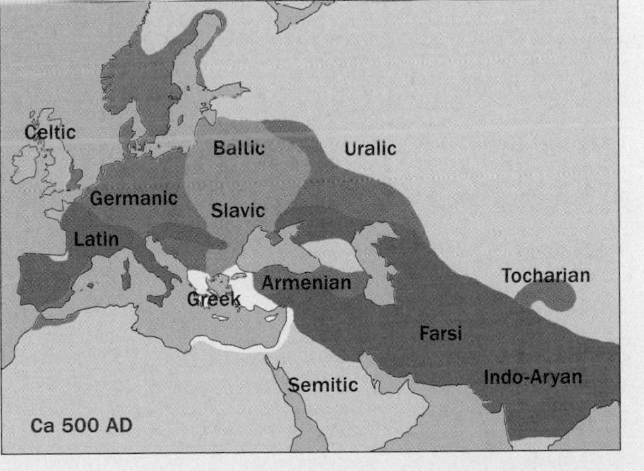

Common Parliamentary Procedures

	Motion	Purpose	Needs Second	Debatable	Amend-able	Required Vote	May Interrupt Speaker	Subsidiary Motion Applied
I.	**ORIGINAL OR PRINCIPAL MOTION**							
1.	Main Motion (general) Main Motions (specific)	To introduce business	Yes	Yes	Yes	Majority	No	Yes
	a. To take from the table	To consider tabled motion	Yes	No	No	Majority	No	No
	b. To reconsider	To reconsider previous motion	Yes	When original motion is	No	Majority	Yes	No
	c. To rescind	To nullify or wipe out previous action	Yes	Yes	Yes	Majority or two-thirds	No	No
II.	**SUBSIDIARY MOTIONS**							
2.	To lay on the table	To defer action	Yes	No	No	Majority	No	No
3.	To call for previous question	To close debate and force vote	Yes	No	No	Two-thirds	No	Yes
4.	To limit or extend limits of debate	To control time of debate	Yes	No	Yes	Two-thirds	No	Yes
5.	To postpone to a certain time	To defer action	Yes	Yes	Yes	Majority	No	Yes
6.	To refer to a committee	To provide for special study	Yes	Yes	Yes	Majority	No	Yes
7.	To amend	To modify a motion	Yes	When original motion is	Yes (once only)	Majority	No	Yes
8.	To postpone indefinitely	To suppress action	Yes	Yes	No	Majority	No	Yes
III.	**PRIVILEGED MOTIONS**							
9.	To raise a point of order	To correct error in procedure	No	No	No	Decision of chair	Yes	No
10.	To appeal for a decision of chair	To change decision on procedure	Yes	If motion does not relate to indecorum	No	Majority or tie	Yes	No
11.	To withdraw a motion	To remove a motion	No	No	No	Majority	No	No
12.	To divide a motion	To modify a motion	No	No	Yes	Majority	No	Yes
13.	To object to consideration	To suppress action	No	No	No	Two-thirds	Yes	No
14.	To call for division of house	To secure a countable vote	No	No	No	Majority if chair desires	Yes	Yes
15.	To suspend rules	To alter existing rules and order of business	Yes	No	No	Two-thirds	No	No
16.	To close nominations	To stop nomination of officers	Yes	No	Yes	Two-thirds	No	Yes
17.	To reopen nominations	To permit additional nominations	Yes	No	Yes	Majority	No	Yes
IV.	**INCIDENTAL MOTIONS**							
18.	To call for orders of the day	To keep assembly to order of business	No	No	No	None unless objection	Yes	No
19.	To raise question of privilege	To make a request concerning rights of assembly	No	No	No	Decision of chair	Yes	No
20.	To take a recess	To dismiss meeting for specific time	Yes	No, if made when another question is before the assembly	Yes	Majority	No	Yes
21.	To adjourn	To dismiss meeting	Yes	No	Yes	Majority	No	No
22.	To fix time at which to adjourn	To set time for the continuation of this meeting	Yes	No, if made when another question is before the assembly	Yes	Majority	No	Yes

Six-Year Calendar

2006

JANUARY

S	M	T	W	T	F	S
1	2	3	4	5	6	7
8	9	10	11	12	13	14
15	16	17	18	19	20	21
22	23	24	25	26	27	28
29	30	31				

FEBRUARY

S	M	T	W	T	F	S
			1	2	3	4
5	6	7	8	9	10	11
12	13	14	15	16	17	18
19	20	21	22	23	24	25
26	27	28				

MARCH

S	M	T	W	T	F	S
			1	2	3	4
5	6	7	8	9	10	11
12	13	14	15	16	17	18
19	20	21	22	23	24	25
26	27	28	29	30	31	

APRIL

S	M	T	W	T	F	S
						1
2	3	4	5	6	7	8
9	10	11	12	13	14	15
16	17	18	19	20	21	22
23	24	25	26	27	28	29
30						

MAY

S	M	T	W	T	F	S
	1	2	3	4	5	6
7	8	9	10	11	12	13
14	15	16	17	18	19	20
21	22	23	24	25	26	27
28	29	30	31			

JUNE

S	M	T	W	T	F	S
				1	2	3
4	5	6	7	8	9	10
11	12	13	14	15	16	17
18	19	20	21	22	23	24
25	26	27	28	29	30	

JULY

S	M	T	W	T	F	S
						1
2	3	4	5	6	7	8
9	10	11	12	13	14	15
16	17	18	19	20	21	22
23	24	25	26	27	28	29
30	31					

AUGUST

S	M	T	W	T	F	S
		1	2	3	4	5
6	7	8	9	10	11	12
13	14	15	16	17	18	19
20	21	22	23	24	25	26
27	28	29	30	31		

SEPTEMBER

S	M	T	W	T	F	S
					1	2
3	4	5	6	7	8	9
10	11	12	13	14	15	16
17	18	19	20	21	22	23
24	25	26	27	28	29	30

OCTOBER

S	M	T	W	T	F	S
1	2	3	4	5	6	7
8	9	10	11	12	13	14
15	16	17	18	19	20	21
22	23	24	25	26	27	28
29	30	31				

NOVEMBER

S	M	T	W	T	F	S
			1	2	3	4
5	6	7	8	9	10	11
12	13	14	15	16	17	18
19	20	21	22	23	24	25
26	27	28	29	30		

DECEMBER

S	M	T	W	T	F	S
					1	2
3	4	5	6	7	8	9
10	11	12	13	14	15	16
17	18	19	20	21	22	23
24	25	26	27	28	29	30
31						

2007

JANUARY

S	M	T	W	T	F	S
	1	2	3	4	5	6
7	8	9	10	11	12	13
14	15	16	17	18	19	20
21	22	23	24	25	26	27
28	29	30	31			

FEBRUARY

S	M	T	W	T	F	S
				1	2	3
4	5	6	7	8	9	10
11	12	13	14	15	16	17
18	19	20	21	22	23	24
25	26	27	28			

MARCH

S	M	T	W	T	F	S
				1	2	3
4	5	6	7	8	9	10
11	12	13	14	15	16	17
18	19	20	21	22	23	24
25	26	27	28	29	30	31

APRIL

S	M	T	W	T	F	S
1	2	3	4	5	6	7
8	9	10	11	12	13	14
15	16	17	18	19	20	21
22	23	24	25	26	27	28
29	30					

MAY

S	M	T	W	T	F	S
		1	2	3	4	5
6	7	8	9	10	11	12
13	14	15	16	17	18	19
20	21	22	23	24	25	26
27	28	29	30	31		

JUNE

S	M	T	W	T	F	S
					1	2
3	4	5	6	7	8	9
10	11	12	13	14	15	16
17	18	19	20	21	22	23
24	25	26	27	28	29	30

JULY

S	M	T	W	T	F	S
1	2	3	4	5	6	7
8	9	10	11	12	13	14
15	16	17	18	19	20	21
22	23	24	25	26	27	28
29	30	31				

AUGUST

S	M	T	W	T	F	S
			1	2	3	4
5	6	7	8	9	10	11
12	13	14	15	16	17	18
19	20	21	22	23	24	25
26	27	28	29	30	31	

SEPTEMBER

S	M	T	W	T	F	S
						1
2	3	4	5	6	7	8
9	10	11	12	13	14	15
16	17	18	19	20	21	22
23	24	25	26	27	28	29
30						

OCTOBER

S	M	T	W	T	F	S
	1	2	3	4	5	6
7	8	9	10	11	12	13
14	15	16	17	18	19	20
21	22	23	24	25	26	27
28	29	30	31			

NOVEMBER

S	M	T	W	T	F	S
				1	2	3
4	5	6	7	8	9	10
11	12	13	14	15	16	17
18	19	20	21	22	23	24
25	26	27	28	29	30	

DECEMBER

S	M	T	W	T	F	S
						1
2	3	4	5	6	7	8
9	10	11	12	13	14	15
16	17	18	19	20	21	22
23	24	25	26	27	28	29
30	31					

2008

JANUARY

S	M	T	W	T	F	S
		1	2	3	4	5
6	7	8	9	10	11	12
13	14	15	16	17	18	19
20	21	22	23	24	25	26
27	28	29	30	31		

FEBRUARY

S	M	T	W	T	F	S
					1	2
3	4	5	6	7	8	9
10	11	12	13	14	15	16
17	18	19	20	21	22	23
24	25	26	27	28	29	

MARCH

S	M	T	W	T	F	S
						1
2	3	4	5	6	7	8
9	10	11	12	13	14	15
16	17	18	19	20	21	22
23	24	25	26	27	28	29
30	31					

APRIL

S	M	T	W	T	F	S
		1	2	3	4	5
6	7	8	9	10	11	12
13	14	15	16	17	18	19
20	21	22	23	24	25	26
27	28	29	30			

MAY

S	M	T	W	T	F	S
				1	2	3
4	5	6	7	8	9	10
11	12	13	14	15	16	17
18	19	20	21	22	23	24
25	26	27	28	29	30	31

JUNE

S	M	T	W	T	F	S
1	2	3	4	5	6	7
8	9	10	11	12	13	14
15	16	17	18	19	20	21
22	23	24	25	26	27	28
29	30					

JULY

S	M	T	W	T	F	S
		1	2	3	4	5
6	7	8	9	10	11	12
13	14	15	16	17	18	19
20	21	22	23	24	25	26
27	28	29	30	31		

AUGUST

S	M	T	W	T	F	S
					1	2
3	4	5	6	7	8	9
10	11	12	13	14	15	16
17	18	19	20	21	22	23
24	25	26	27	28	29	30
31						

SEPTEMBER

S	M	T	W	T	F	S
	1	2	3	4	5	6
7	8	9	10	11	12	13
14	15	16	17	18	19	20
21	22	23	24	25	26	27
28	29	30				

OCTOBER

S	M	T	W	T	F	S
			1	2	3	4
5	6	7	8	9	10	11
12	13	14	15	16	17	18
19	20	21	22	23	24	25
26	27	28	29	30	31	

NOVEMBER

S	M	T	W	T	F	S
						1
2	3	4	5	6	7	8
9	10	11	12	13	14	15
16	17	18	19	20	21	22
23	24	25	26	27	28	29
30						

DECEMBER

S	M	T	W	T	F	S
	1	2	3	4	5	6
7	8	9	10	11	12	13
14	15	16	17	18	19	20
21	22	23	24	25	26	27
28	29	30	31			

2009

JANUARY

S	M	T	W	T	F	S
				1	2	3
4	5	6	7	8	9	10
11	12	13	14	15	16	17
18	19	20	21	22	23	24
25	26	27	28	29	30	31

FEBRUARY

S	M	T	W	T	F	S
1	2	3	4	5	6	7
8	9	10	11	12	13	14
15	16	17	18	19	20	21
22	23	24	25	26	27	28

MARCH

S	M	T	W	T	F	S
1	2	3	4	5	6	7
8	9	10	11	12	13	14
15	16	17	18	19	20	21
22	23	24	25	26	27	28
29	30	31				

APRIL

S	M	T	W	T	F	S
			1	2	3	4
5	6	7	8	9	10	11
12	13	14	15	16	17	18
19	20	21	22	23	24	25
26	27	28	29	30		

MAY

S	M	T	W	T	F	S
					1	2
3	4	5	6	7	8	9
10	11	12	13	14	15	16
17	18	19	20	21	22	23
24	25	26	27	28	29	30
31						

JUNE

S	M	T	W	T	F	S
	1	2	3	4	5	6
7	8	9	10	11	12	13
14	15	16	17	18	19	20
21	22	23	24	25	26	27
28	29	30				

JULY

S	M	T	W	T	F	S
			1	2	3	4
5	6	7	8	9	10	11
12	13	14	15	16	17	18
19	20	21	22	23	24	25
26	27	28	29	30	31	

AUGUST

S	M	T	W	T	F	S
						1
2	3	4	5	6	7	8
9	10	11	12	13	14	15
16	17	18	19	20	21	22
23	24	25	26	27	28	29
30	31					

SEPTEMBER

S	M	T	W	T	F	S
		1	2	3	4	5
6	7	8	9	10	11	12
13	14	15	16	17	18	19
20	21	22	23	24	25	26
27	28	29	30			

OCTOBER

S	M	T	W	T	F	S
				1	2	3
4	5	6	7	8	9	10
11	12	13	14	15	16	17
18	19	20	21	22	23	24
25	26	27	28	29	30	31

NOVEMBER

S	M	T	W	T	F	S
1	2	3	4	5	6	7
8	9	10	11	12	13	14
15	16	17	18	19	20	21
22	23	24	25	26	27	28
29	30					

DECEMBER

S	M	T	W	T	F	S
		1	2	3	4	5
6	7	8	9	10	11	12
13	14	15	16	17	18	19
20	21	22	23	24	25	26
27	28	29	30	31		

2010

JANUARY

S	M	T	W	T	F	S
					1	2
3	4	5	6	7	8	9
10	11	12	13	14	15	16
17	18	19	20	21	22	23
24	25	26	27	28	29	30
31						

FEBRUARY

S	M	T	W	T	F	S
	1	2	3	4	5	6
7	8	9	10	11	12	13
14	15	16	17	18	19	20
21	22	23	24	25	26	27
28						

MARCH

S	M	T	W	T	F	S
	1	2	3	4	5	6
7	8	9	10	11	12	13
14	15	16	17	18	19	20
21	22	23	24	25	26	27
28	29	30	31			

APRIL

S	M	T	W	T	F	S
				1	2	3
4	5	6	7	8	9	10
11	12	13	14	15	16	17
18	19	20	21	22	23	24
25	26	27	28	29	30	

MAY

S	M	T	W	T	F	S
						1
2	3	4	5	6	7	8
9	10	11	12	13	14	15
16	17	18	19	20	21	22
23	24	25	26	27	28	29
30	31					

JUNE

S	M	T	W	T	F	S
		1	2	3	4	5
6	7	8	9	10	11	12
13	14	15	16	17	18	19
20	21	22	23	24	25	26
27	28	29	30			

JULY

S	M	T	W	T	F	S
				1	2	3
4	5	6	7	8	9	10
11	12	13	14	15	16	17
18	19	20	21	22	23	24
25	26	27	28	29	30	31

AUGUST

S	M	T	W	T	F	S
1	2	3	4	5	6	7
8	9	10	11	12	13	14
15	16	17	18	19	20	21
22	23	24	25	26	27	28
29	30	31				

SEPTEMBER

S	M	T	W	T	F	S
			1	2	3	4
5	6	7	8	9	10	11
12	13	14	15	16	17	18
19	20	21	22	23	24	25
26	27	28	29	30		

OCTOBER

S	M	T	W	T	F	S
					1	2
3	4	5	6	7	8	9
10	11	12	13	14	15	16
17	18	19	20	21	22	23
24	25	26	27	28	29	30
31						

NOVEMBER

S	M	T	W	T	F	S
	1	2	3	4	5	6
7	8	9	10	11	12	13
14	15	16	17	18	19	20
21	22	23	24	25	26	27
28	29	30				

DECEMBER

S	M	T	W	T	F	S
			1	2	3	4
5	6	7	8	9	10	11
12	13	14	15	16	17	18
19	20	21	22	23	24	25
26	27	28	29	30	31	

2011

JANUARY

S	M	T	W	T	F	S
						1
2	3	4	5	6	7	8
9	10	11	12	13	14	15
16	17	18	19	20	21	22
23	24	25	26	27	28	29
30	31					

FEBRUARY

S	M	T	W	T	F	S
		1	2	3	4	5
6	7	8	9	10	11	12
13	14	15	16	17	18	19
20	21	22	23	24	25	26
27	28					

MARCH

S	M	T	W	T	F	S
		1	2	3	4	5
6	7	8	9	10	11	12
13	14	15	16	17	18	19
20	21	22	23	24	25	26
27	28	29	30	31		

APRIL

S	M	T	W	T	F	S
					1	2
3	4	5	6	7	8	9
10	11	12	13	14	15	16
17	18	19	20	21	22	23
24	25	26	27	28	29	30

MAY

S	M	T	W	T	F	S
1	2	3	4	5	6	7
8	9	10	11	12	13	14
15	16	17	18	19	20	21
22	23	24	25	26	27	28
29	30	31				

JUNE

S	M	T	W	T	F	S
			1	2	3	4
5	6	7	8	9	10	11
12	13	14	15	16	17	18
19	20	21	22	23	24	25
26	27	28	29	30		

JULY

S	M	T	W	T	F	S
					1	2
3	4	5	6	7	8	9
10	11	12	13	14	15	16
17	18	19	20	21	22	23
24	25	26	27	28	29	30
31						

AUGUST

S	M	T	W	T	F	S
	1	2	3	4	5	6
7	8	9	10	11	12	13
14	15	16	17	18	19	20
21	22	23	24	25	26	27
28	29	30	31			

SEPTEMBER

S	M	T	W	T	F	S
				1	2	3
4	5	6	7	8	9	10
11	12	13	14	15	16	17
18	19	20	21	22	23	24
25	26	27	28	29	30	

OCTOBER

S	M	T	W	T	F	S
						1
2	3	4	5	6	7	8
9	10	11	12	13	14	15
16	17	18	19	20	21	22
23	24	25	26	27	28	29
30	31					

NOVEMBER

S	M	T	W	T	F	S
		1	2	3	4	5
6	7	8	9	10	11	12
13	14	15	16	17	18	19
20	21	22	23	24	25	26
27	28	29	30			

DECEMBER

S	M	T	W	T	F	S
				1	2	3
4	5	6	7	8	9	10
11	12	13	14	15	16	17
18	19	20	21	22	23	24
25	26	27	28	29	30	31

Weights and Measures

In 1975, the United States signed the Metric Conversion Act, declaring a national policy of encouraging voluntary use of the metric system. Today, the metric system exists side by side with the U.S. customary system. The debate on whether the United States should adopt the metric system has been going on for nearly 200 years, leaving the United States the only country in the world not totally committed to adopting the system.

The metric system is a simpler form of measurement, based on the decimal system (units of 10) and eliminates the need to deal with fractions.

The Metric System of Measurement

Linear Measure

1 centimeter .... = 10 millimeters
0.3937 inch
1 decimeter .... = 10 centimeters
3.937 inches
1 meter .... = 10 decimeters
39.37 inches
3.28 feet
1 decameter .... = 10 meters
393.7 inches
1 hectometer.......... = 10 decameters
328 feet 1 inch
1 kilometer .... = 10 hectometers
0.621 mile
1 myriameter.......... = 10 kilometers
6.21 miles

Volume Measure

1 cubic centimeter ..... = 1,000 cubic millimeters
.06102 cubic inch
1 cubic decimeter ...... = 1,000 cubic centimeters
61.02 cubic inches
1 cubic meter.......... = 1,000 cubic decimeters
35.314 cubic feet

Capacity Measure

1 centiliter .... = 10 milliliters
.338 fluid ounce
1 deciliter............. = 10 centiliters
3.38 fluid ounces
1 liter .... = 10 deciliters
1.0567 liquid quarts
0.9081 dry quart
1 decaliter .... = 10 liters
2.64 gallons
0.284 bushel
1 hectoliter............ = 10 decaliters
26.418 gallons
2.838 bushels
1 kiloliter .... = 10 hectoliters
264.18 gallons
35.315 cubic feet

Square Measure

1 square centimeter .... = 100 square millimeters
0.15499 square inch
1 square decimeter..... = 100 square centimeters
15.499 square inches
1 square meter .... = 100 square decimeters
1,549.9 square inches
1.196 square yards
1 square decameter .... = 100 square meters
119.6 square yards
1 square hectometer.... = 100 square decameters
2.471 acres
1 square kilometer ..... = 100 square hectometers
0.386 square mile

Land Measure

1 centare .... = 1 square meter
1,549.9 square inches
1 are................. = 100 centares
119.6 square yards
1 hectare .... = 100 ares
2,471 acres
1 square kilometer ..... = 100 hectares
0.386 square mile

Weights

1 centigram .... = 10 milligrams
0.1543 grain
1 decigram............ = 10 centigrams
1.5432 grains
1 gram .... = 10 decigrams
15.432 grains
1 decagram .... = 10 grams
0.3527 ounce
1 hectogram .... = 10 decagrams
3.5274 ounces
1 kilogram .... = 10 hectograms
2.2046 pounds
1 myriagram .... = 10 kilograms
22.046 pounds
1 quintal.............. = 10 myriagrams
220.46 pounds
1 metric ton........... = 10 quintals
2,204.6 pounds

U.S. Customary System of Measurement

Linear Measure

1 inch	= 2.54 centimeters
1 foot	= 12 inches 0.3048 meter
1 yard	= 3 feet 0.9144 meter
1 rod (or pole or perch)	= 5.5 yards or 16.5 feet 5.029 meters
1 furlong	= 40 rods 201.17 meters
1 (statute) mile	= 8 furlongs 1,760 yards 5,280 feet 1,609.3 meters
1 (land) league	= 3 miles 4.83 kilometers

Square Measure

1 square inch	= 6.452 sq. centimeters
1 square foot	= 144 square inches 929 square centimeters
1 square yard	= 9 square feet 0.8361 square meter
1 square rod	= 30.25 square rods 25.29 square meters
1 acre	= 160 square rods 4,840 square yards 43,560 square feet 0.4047 hectare
1 square mile	= 640 acres 259 hectares 2.59 square kilometers

(Engineer's chain)

1 link	= 1 foot 0.3048 meter
1 chain	= 100 feet 30.48 meters
1 mile	= 52.8 chains 1,609.3 meters

Surveyor's (Square) Measure

1 square pole	= 625 square links 25.29 square meters
1 square chain	= 16 square poles 404.7 square meters
1 acre	= 10 square chains 0.4047 hectare
1 square mile or 1 section	= 640 acres 259 hectares 2.59 square kilometers
1 township	= 36 square miles 9,324 hectares 93.24 square kilometers

Nautical Measure

1 fathom	= 6 feet 1.829 meters
1 cable's length (ordinary)	= 100 fathoms (In the U.S. Navy 120 fathoms or 720 feet = 1 cable's length; in the British Navy 608 feet = 1 cable's length)
1 nautical mile	= 6,076.10333 feet; by international agreement in 1954 10 cables' length 1.852 kilometers 1.1508 statute miles; length of a minute of longitude at the equator
1 marine league	= 3.45 statute miles 3 nautical miles 5.56 kilometers
1 degree of a great circle of the earth	= 60 nautical miles

Cubic Measure

1 cubic inch	= 16.387 cubic centimeters
1 cubic foot	= 1,728 cubic inches 0.0283 cubic meter
1 cubic yard	= 27 cubic feet 0.7646 cubic meter
1 cord foot	= 16 cubic feet
1 cord	= 8 cord feet 3.625 cubic meters

Chain Measure (Gunter's or surveyor's chain)

1 link	= 7.92 inches 20.12 centimeters
1 chain	= 100 links or 66 feet 20.12 meters
1 furlong	= 10 chains 201.17 meters
1 mile	= 80 chains 1,609.3 meters

U.S. Customary System of Measurement

Dry Measure

1 pint	= 33.60 cubic inches 0.5505 liter
1 quart	= 2 pints 67.20 cubic inches 1.1012 liters
1 peck	= 8 quarts 537.61 cubic inches 8.8096 liters
1 bushel	= 4 pecks 2,150.42 cubic inches 35.2383 liters

Liquid Measure

4 fluid ounces	= 1 gill
(see next table)	7.219 cubic inches 0.1183 liter
1 pint	= 4 gills 28.875 cubic inches 0.4732 liter
1 quart	= 2 pints 57.75 cubic inches 0.9463 liter
1 gallon	= 4 quarts 231 cubic inches 3.7853 liters

Apothecaries' Fluid Measure

1 minim	= 0.0038 cubic inch 0.0616 milliliter
1 fluid dram	= 60 minims 0.2256 cubic inch 3.6966 milliliters
1 fluid ounce	= 8 fluid drams 1.8047 cubic inches 0.0296 liter
1 pint	= 16 fluid ounces 28.875 cubic inches 0.4732 liter

Circular (or Angular) Measure

1 minute (')	= 60 seconds (")
1 degree (°)...........	= 60 minutes
1 quadrant or 1 right angle	= 90 degrees
1 circle	= 4 quadrants 360 degrees

Avoirdupois Weight

(The grain, equal to 0.0648 gram, is the same in all three tables of weight.)

1 dram or 27.34 grains..	= 1.772 grams
1 ounce	= 16 drams 437.5 grains 28.3495 grams
1 pound	= 16 ounces 7,000 grains 453.59 grams
1 hundredweight	= 100 pounds 45.36 kilograms
1 ton	= 2,000 pounds 907.18 kilograms

Troy Weight

(The grain, equal to 0.0648 gram, is the same in all three tables of weight.)

1 carat	= 3.086 grains 200 milligrams
1 pennyweight	= 24 grains 1.5552 grams
1 ounce	= 20 pennyweights 480 grains 31.1035 grams
1 pound	= 12 ounces 5,760 grains 373.24 grams

Apothecaries' Weight

(The grain, equal to 0.0648 gram, is the same in all three tables of weight.)

1 scruple	= 20 grains 1.296 grams
1 dram	= 3 scruples 3.888 grams
1 ounce	= 8 drams 480 grains 31.1035 grams
1 pound	= 12 ounces 5,760 grains 373.24 grams

Miscellaneous

1 palm	= 3 inches
1 hand	= 4 inches
1 span	= 6 inches
1 cubit	= 18 inches
1 Biblical cubit.........	= 21.8 inches
1 military pace.........	= 2.5 feet

Handy Conversion Factors

To Change	To	Multiply By
acres	hectares	.4047
acres	square feet	43,560
acres	square miles	.001562
Celsius	Fahrenheit	1.8* *(then add 32)
centimeters	inches	.3937
centimeters	feet	.03281
cubic meters	cubic feet	35.3145
cubic meters	cubic yards	1.3079
cubic yards	cubic meters	.7646
degrees	radians	.01745
Fahrenheit	Celsius	.556* * (after subtracting 32)
feet	meters	.3048
feet	miles (nautical)	.0001645
feet	miles (statute)	.0001894
feet/sec.	miles/hr.	.6818
furlongs	feet	660.0
furlongs	miles	.125
gallons (U.S.)	liters	3.7853
grains	grams	.0648
grams	grains	15.4324
grams	ounces avdp.	.0353
grams	pounds	.002205
hectares	acres	2.4710
horsepower	watts	745.7
hours	days	.04167
inches	millimeters	25.4000
inches	centimeters	2.5400
kilograms	pounds advp. or t.	2.2046
kilometers	miles	.6214
kilowatts	horsepower	1.341
knots	nautical miles/hr.	1.0
knots	statute miles/hr.	1.151
liters	gallons (U.S.)	.2642
liters	pecks	.1135
liters	pints (dry)	1.8162
liters	pints (liquid)	2.1134
liters	quarts (dry)	.9081
liters	quarts (liquid)	1.0567
meters	feet	3.2808
meters	miles	.0006214
meters	yards	1.0936
metric tons	tons (long)	.9842
metric tons	tons (short)	1.1023
miles	kilometers	1.6093
miles	feet	5,280
miles (nautical)	miles (statute)	1.1516
miles (statute)	miles (nautical)	.8684
miles/hr.	feet/min.	88
millimeters	inches	.0394
ounces advp.	grams	28.3495
ounces	pounds	.0625
ounces (troy)	ounces (advp.)	1.09714
pecks	liters	8.8096
pints (dry)	liters	.5506
pints (liquid)	liters	1.4732
pounds ap. or t.	kilograms	.3782
pounds advp.	kilograms	.4536
pounds	ounces	16
quarts (dry)	liters	1.1012
quarts (liquid)	liters	.9463
rods	meters	5.029
rods	feet	16.5
square feet	square meters	.0929
square kilometers	square miles	.3861
square meters	square feet	10.7639
square meters	square yards	1.1960
square miles	square kilometers	2.5900
square yards	square meters	.8361
tons (long)	metric tons	1.1060
tons (short)	metric tons	.9072
tons (long)	pounds	2,240
tons (short)	pounds	2,000
watts	Btu/hr.	3.4129
watts	horsepower	.001341
yards	meters	.9144
yards	miles	.0005682

Ten Ways to Measure When You Don't Have a Ruler

1. Many floor tiles are 12-inch squares (30.48-cm squares).
2. Paper money is 6-1/8 inches by 2-5/8 inches (15.56 x 6.67 cm).
3. A quarter is approximately 1 inch wide (2.54 cm).
4. A penny is approximately 3/4 of an inch wide (1.9 cm).
5. Typing paper is 8-1/2 inches by 11 inches (21.59 cm x 27.94 cm).

Each of the following items can be used as a measuring device by multiplying its length by the number of times it is used to measure an area in question.

6. A shoelace
7. A tie
8. A belt
9. Your feet—placing one in front of the other to measure floor area
10. Your outstretched arms from fingertip to fingertip

Periodic Table of the Elements

Legend: Alkali metals; Alkaline earth metals; Transition metals; Lanthanide series; Actinide series; Other metals; Nonmetals; Noble gases

Key: Atomic Number — 2; Symbol — He; Helium; Atomic Weight (or Mass Number of most stable isotope if in parentheses) — 4.00260

1a	2a	3b	4b	5b	6b	7b	8			1b	2b	3a	4a	5a	6a	7a	0
1 H Hydrogen 1.00797																	2 He Helium 4.00260
3 Li Lithium 6.941	4 Be Beryllium 9.0128											5 B Boron 10.811	6 C Carbon 12.01115	7 N Nitrogen 14.0067	8 O Oxygen 15.9994	9 F Fluorine 18.9984	10 Ne Neon 20.179
11 Na Sodium 22.9898	12 Mg Magnesium 24.305											13 Al Aluminum 26.9815	14 Si Silicon 28.0855	15 P Phosphorus 30.9738	16 S Sulfur 32.064	17 Cl Chlorine 35.453	18 Ar Argon 39.948
19 K Potassium 39.0983	20 Ca Calcium 40.08	21 Sc Scandium 44.9559	22 Ti Titanium 47.88	23 V Vanadium 50.94	24 Cr Chromium 51.996	25 Mn Manganese 54.9380	26 Fe Iron 55.847	27 Co Cobalt 58.9332	28 Ni Nickel 58.69	29 Cu Copper 63.546	30 Zn Zinc 65.39	31 Ga Gallium 69.72	32 Ge Germanium 72.59	33 As Arsenic 74.9216	34 Se Selenium 78.96	35 Br Bromine 79.904	36 Kr Krypton 83.80
37 Rb Rubidium 85.4678	38 Sr Strontium 87.62	39 Y Yttrium 88.905	40 Zr Zirconium 91.224	41 Nb Niobium 92.906	42 Mo Molybdenum 95.94	43 Tc Technetium (98)	44 Ru Ruthenium 101.07	45 Rh Rhodium 102.906	46 Pd Palladium 106.42	47 Ag Silver 107.868	48 Cd Cadmium 112.41	49 In Indium 114.82	50 Sn Tin 118.71	51 Sb Antimony 121.75	52 Te Tellurium 127.60	53 I Iodine 126.905	54 Xe Xenon 131.29
55 Cs Cesium 132.905	56 Ba Barium 137.33	57-71* Lanthanides	72 Hf Hafnium 178.49	73 Ta Tantalum 180.948	74 W Tungsten 183.85	75 Re Rhenium 186.207	76 Os Osmium 190.2	77 Ir Iridium 192.22	78 Pt Platinum 195.08	79 Au Gold 196.967	80 Hg Mercury 200.59	81 Tl Thallium 204.383	82 Pb Lead 207.19	83 Bi Bismuth 208.980	84 Po Polonium (209)	85 At Astatine (210)	86 Rn Radon (222)
87 Fr Francium (223)	88 Ra Radium 226.025	89-103** Actinides	104 Rf Rutherfordium (261)	105 Db Dubnium (262)	106 Sg Seaborgium (263)	107 Bh Bohrium (262)	108 Hs Hassium (265)	109 Mt Meitnerium (266)	110 Ds (269)	111 Rg (272)	112 Uub (285)	113 Uut (284)	114 Uuq (289)	115 Uup (288)	116 Uuh (292)	117 Uus	118 Uuo

*Lanthanides	57 La Lanthanum 138.906	58 Ce Cerium 140.12	59 Pr Praseodymium 140.908	60 Nd Neodymium 144.24	61 Pm Promethium (145)	62 Sm Samarium 150.36	63 Eu Europium 151.96	64 Gd Gadolinium 157.25	65 Tb Terbium 158.925	66 Dy Dysprosium 162.50	67 Ho Holmium 164.930	68 Er Erbium 167.26	69 Tm Thulium 168.934	70 Yb Ytterbium 173.04	71 Lu Lutetium 174.967
**Actinides	89 Ac Actinium 227.028	90 Th Thorium 232.038	91 Pa Protactinium 231.036	92 U Uranium 238.029	93 Np Neptunium 237.048	94 Pu Plutonium (244)	95 Am Americium (243)	96 Cm Curium (247)	97 Bk Berkelium (247)	98 Cf Californium (251)	99 Es Einsteinium (252)	100 Fm Fermium (257)	101 Md Mendelevium (258)	102 No Nobelium (259)	103 Lr Lawrencium (260)

The U.S. Constitution

The U.S. Constitution is made up of three main parts: **a preamble, 7 articles,** and **27 amendments**. The *preamble* states the purpose of the Constitution, the *articles* explain how the government works, and the 10 original *amendments* list the basic rights guaranteed to all American citizens.

Together, the three parts of the Constitution contain the laws and guidelines necessary to set up and run the U.S. national government successfully. Power not given to the national government belongs to the states or the people.

The Preamble

We the people of the United States, in order to form a more perfect Union, establish justice, insure domestic tranquility, provide for the common defense, promote the general welfare, and secure the blessings of liberty to ourselves and our posterity, do ordain and establish this Constitution for the United States of America.

The Articles of the Constitution

The articles of the Constitution explain how the three branches of government work and what each can and cannot do. The articles also explain how the federal and state governments must work together, and how the Constitution can be amended or changed.

Article 1 explains the legislative branch, how laws are made, and how Congress works.

Article 2 explains the executive branch, the offices of the President and Vice President, and the powers of the executive branch.

Article 3 explains the judicial branch, the Supreme Court and other courts, and warns people about trying to overthrow the government.

Article 4 describes how the United States federal government and the individual state governments work together.

Article 5 tells how the Constitution can be amended, or changed.

Article 6 states that the United States federal government and the Constitution are the law of the land.

Article 7 outlines how the Constitution must be adopted to become official.

The Bill of Rights

To get the necessary votes to approve the Constitution, a number of changes (amendments) had to be made. These 10 original amendments are called the Bill of Rights. They guarantee all Americans some very basic rights, including the right to worship and speak freely and the right to have a jury trial. The first eight amendments grant individual rights and freedoms. The ninth and tenth amendments prevent Congress from passing laws that would deprive citizens of these rights.

Amendment 1 People have the right to worship, to speak freely, to gather together, and to question the government.

Amendment 2 People have the right to bear arms.

Amendment 3 The government cannot have soldiers stay in people's houses without their permission.

Amendment 4 People and their property cannot be searched without the written permission of a judge.

Amendment 5 People cannot be tried for a serious crime without a jury. They cannot be tried twice for the same crime or be forced to testify against themselves. Also, they cannot have property taken away while they are on trial. Any property taken for public use must receive a fair price.

Amendment 6 In criminal cases, people have a right to a speedy and public trial, to be told what they are accused of, to hear witnesses against them, to get witnesses in their favor, and to have a lawyer.

Amendment 7 In cases involving more than $20, people have the right to a jury trial.

Amendment 8 People have a right to fair bail (money given as a promise the person will return for trial) and to fair fines and punishments.

Amendment 9 People have rights that are not listed in the Constitution.

Amendment 10 Powers not given to the federal government are given to the states or to the people.

The Other Amendments

The Constitution and the Bill of Rights were ratified in 1791. Since that time, more than 7,000 amendments to the Constitution have been proposed. Because three-fourths of the states must approve an amendment before it becomes law, just 27 amendments have been passed. The first 10 are listed under the Bill of Rights; the other 17 are listed below.

Amendment 11 A person cannot sue a state in federal court. **(1795)**

Amendment 12 The President and Vice President are elected separately. **(1804)**

Amendment 13 Slavery is abolished. **(1865)**

Amendment 14 All persons born in the United States or those who have become citizens enjoy full citizenship rights. **(1868)**

Amendment 15 Voting rights are given to all [adult male] citizens regardless of race, creed, or color. **(1870)**

Amendment 16 Congress has the power to collect income taxes. **(1913)**

Amendment 17 United States Senators are elected directly by the people. **(1913)**

Amendment 18 Making, buying, and selling alcoholic beverages is no longer allowed. **(1919)**

Amendment 19 Women have the right to vote. **(1920)**

Amendment 20 The President's term begins January 20; Senators' and Representatives' terms begin January 3. **(1933)**

Amendment 21 (Repeals Amendment 18) Alcoholic beverages can be made, bought, and sold again. **(1933)**

Amendment 22 The President is limited to two elected terms. **(1951)**

Amendment 23 District of Columbia residents gain the right to vote. **(1961)**

Amendment 24 All voter poll taxes are forbidden. **(1964)**

Amendment 25 If the Presidency is vacant, the Vice President takes over. If the Vice Presidency is vacant, the President names someone and the Congress votes on the choice. **(1967)**

Amendment 26 Citizens 18 years old gain the right to vote. **(1971)**

Amendment 27 No law changing the pay for members of Congress will take effect until after an election of Representatives. **(1992)**

Historical Time Line

1500 1520 1540 1560 1580

U.S. & WORLD HISTORY

1492
Columbus reaches the West Indies.

1513
Ponce de León explores Florida; Balboa reaches Pacific.

1516
Ottoman Empire gains control of Egypt and Arabia.

1519
Great Wall of China expanded to 4,000 miles.

1522
Magellan ends three-year voyage around the world.

1547
Ivan the terrible is the first Tsar of Russia.

1565
Spain settles St. Augustine, Florida, first permanent European colony.

1570
League of the Iroquois Nations formed.

1588
English fle[et] defeats the Spanish Armada.

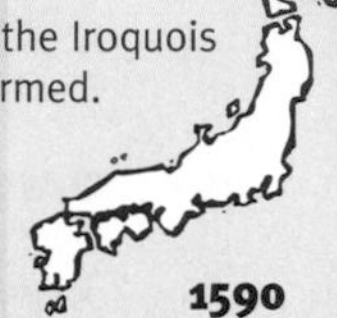

1590
Japan is united for the first time by Toyotomi Hideyoshi.

SCIENCE & INVENTIONS

1447
Gutenberg invents the moveable-type printing press.

1507
Book on surgery is developed.

1507
A new process greatly improves mirrors.

1509
Watches are invented in Germany.

1530
Bottle corks are invented.

1531
Halley's comet appears, causing panic.

1545
Garamond creates first sans serif typefaces for use on printing presses.

1558
Magnetic compass invented by John Dee.

1565
Pencils are invented in England.

1580
First water closet is designed in Bath, England.

1590
Glass lenses are developed in the Netherlands.

LITERATURE & THE ARTS

1503
Leonardo da Vinci begins painting the *Mona Lisa*.

1508-1511
Michelangelo paints the ceiling of the Sistine Chapel in Rome.

1513
Machiavelli writes *The Prince*.

1528
Durer's *The Four Books on Human Proportions* is published posthumously.

1536
The first songbook is used in Spain.

1555
Nostradamus publishes his book *Les Prophetìes* about the world's future.

1555
Andrea Amati builds the first four-string violin much like the modern instrument.

1587
Christopher Marlowe's *Timburlaine* is performed in London.

1594
Shakespeare's *Titus Andronicus* is his first published play.

1597
First edition of Francis Bacon's *Essays* is published.

U.S. POPULATION: (NATIVE AMERICAN) approximately 1,100,000

(SPANISH) 1,021

1600 **1620** **1640** **1660** **1680**

1607
First English settlement is established at Jamestown, Virginia.

1619
First African slaves are brought to Virginia.

1620
Plymouth Colony is founded by Pilgrims.

1626
New Amsterdam (the future New York City) is founded by Peter Minuit of Holland.

1629
Charter for Massachusetts Bay Colony is established.

1631
In India, Emperor Shah Jahan builds the Taj Mahal in memory of his wife.

1644
The last of the Imperial dynasties, the Qing, takes control of China and reigns until 1911.

1653
First postage stamps are used in Paris.

1666
A great fire destroys most of London.

1673
Marquette and Joliet explore the Mississippi River for France.

1682
William Penn founds Pennsylvania.

1699
French settlers move into Mississippi and Louisiana.

1600
William Gilbert coins the term *electricity* from the Greek word *elecktrais.*

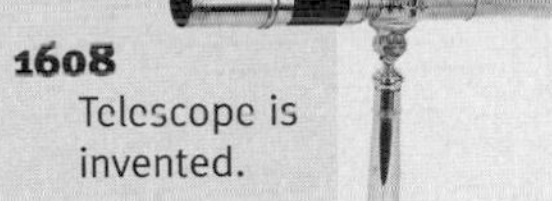

1608
Telescope is invented.

1609
Galileo makes first observations with telescope and confirms the planets circle the sun.

1641
First cotton factories open in England.

1641
Ferdinand, Duke of Tuscany, invents first thermometer.

1642
Pascal invents the first mechanical calculator.

1643
Torricelli invents the barometer.

1666
Newton demonstrates that white light is composed of colors.

1668
Reflecting telescope invented by Sir Isaac Newton.

1682
Halley's comet is studied by Edmund Halley and named for him.

1687
Newton describes gravity.

1600
Shakespeare's plays are performed at the Globe Theatre in London.

1605
Miguel de Cervantes writes the first modern novel, *Don Quixote*.

1611
The King James's version of the *Bible* is published.

1632
Dutch painter Rembrandt completes *Anatomy Lesson of Dr. Nichalas Tulp*.

1635
Through her teaching, Judith Leyster, painter of everyday life, influences many young Dutch painters including Johannes Vermeer.

1645
Musashi of Japan completes *The Book of Five Rings*.

1650
Anne Bradstreet is the first published American woman.

1658
John Comenius writes the first illustrated book for children, *World of Invisible Objects*.

1674
Milton's epic poem, *Paradise Lost*, is published in 10 books.

1675
Sir Christopher Wren begins the construction of St. Paul's Cathedral in London destroyed by the great fire of 1666.

1678
John Bunyan completes *Pilgrim's Progress*.

(ENGLISH)

350	2,302	26,634	75,058	151,507

1700	1710	1720	1730	1740

U.S. & WORLD HISTORY

1700
France builds forts at Mackinac and Detriot to control the fur trade.

1705
Virginia Act establishes public education.

Scotland
England

1707
England (English) and Scotland (Scots) unite and become Great Britain (British).

1714
The Peace of Utrecht ends the wars of Spanish succession marking the rise of the British Empire.

1718
French colonists found New Orleans.

1733
James Oglethorpe founds Georgia.

1733
British Molasses Act places taxes on sugar and molasses.

1735
Freedom of the Press upheld during the trail of John Zenger.

1747
The Ohio Company is formed to settle the Ohio River Valley.

SCIENCE & INVENTIONS

1701
Jethro Tull invents the seed drill, which plants seeds in a row.

1702
Olaus Roemer establishes fixed points to represent freezing and boiling temperatures on a thermometer.

1709
Christofori Bartolommeo invents the pianoforte (first piano).

1714
Daniel Fahrenheit makes the first mercury thermometer.

1716
First American lighthouse is built in Boston Harbor.

1728
First dental drill is used by Pierre Fauchard.

1735
Natural rubber discovered in South America.

1738
First cuckoo clock is invented in Germany.

1742
Benjamin Franklin invents efficient Franklin stove.

LITERATURE & THE ARTS

1700
The Selling of Joseph by Samuel Sewall is first protest of slavery.

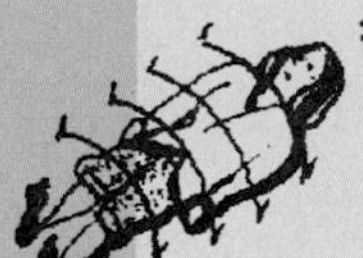

1704
Bach begins his musical career by writing his first piece, Cantata 150.

1709
Joseph Addison perfects the periodical essay in *The Tatler and the Spectator.*

1704
First successful newspaper in the American colonies, *Boston News-Letter*, is published.

1726
Joathan Swift writes *Gulliver's Travels*.

1741
Andrew Bradford publishes first American magazine *(American Magazine)*.

1746
Francisco Goya, "the Father of Modern Art," is born.

1732
Benjamin Franklin begins publishing *Poor Richard's Almanac*.

U.S. POPULATION: (ENGLISH COLONIES)

1700	1710	1720	1730	1740
250,888	331,711	466,185	629,445	905,563

1750	1760	1770	1780	1790

1750 Wooden flatboats and Conestoga wagons begin moving settlers west.

1752 First American hospital is established in Philadelphia.

1755 The U.S. postal service is started.

1760 The Industrial Revolution begins in England.

1763 Britain wins the French and Indian War.

1765 Stamp Act tax is imposed on the colonies by Great Britain.

1775 Revolutionary War begins.

1776 The Declaration of Independence is signed on July 4th.

1781 British surrender at Yorktown October 19.

1782 The American bald eagle is used as a symbol for the nation for the first time.

1787 U.S. Constitution is signed.

1789 The French Revolution begins.

1789 George Washington becomes the first U.S. president.

1791 U.S. Bill of Rights is ratified.

1794 U.S. Navy is created.

1752 Benjamin Franklin demonstrates that lightning is a form of electricity.

1762 James Hargreaves invents the "spinning jenny," a machine for spinning cotton.

1765 James Watt invents the steam engine.

1752 First American hospital is established.

1770 First steam carriage is invented by French engineer Nicholas Cugnot.

1781 Uranus is discovered.

1783 First balloon is flown by Frenchmen Joseph and Jacques Montgolfier.

1786 First ice cream company in America begins production.

1793 Eli Whitney invents the cotton gin to remove seeds from cotton.

1796 Edward Jenner develops first smallpox vaccine in England.

1799 Rosetta Stone discovered in Egypt, means hieroglyphics can be read.

1751 The first encyclopedia is published by Denis Diderot of France.

1755 Samuel Johnson publishes a dictionary of the English language.

1761 Five-year-old Mozart writes his first compositions.

1773 Phillis Wheatley publishes a book of poetry.

1775 Woodblock artist, Kitagawa Utamaro, prints his first effort (the cover of a playbook).

1775 Firsthand accounts of Revolutionary War published in Tom Paine's *Pennsylvania Magazine*.

1798 Romantic poet Samuel Coleridge completes *The Rime of the Ancient Mariner*.

1794 Thomas Paine releases his book, *The Age of Reason*.

1794 Scottish poet Robert Burns completes "A Red, Red Rose."

1,170,760	1,593,625	2,148,076	2,780,369	3,929,157

1800	1810	1820	1830	1840

U.S. & WORLD HISTORY

1800 Washington, D.C., becomes the U.S. capital.

1803 Louisiana Purchase doubles U.S. size.

1804 Lewis & Clark begin exploration of the Louisiana Territory.

1810 Mexico gains independence from Spain.

1812 Uncle Sam becomes the symbol of the U.S.

1814 U.S. defeats Britain in the War of 1812.

1815 Napoleon is defeated at Waterloo.

1819 Simon Bolivar wins independence for Colombia, Venezuela, and Ecuador.

1820 Missouri Compromise allows slavery in Missouri but bars it in the rest of the Louisiana Purchase.

1823 The Monroe Doctrine is established.

1830 The Indian Removal Act forces Native Americans west of Mississippi River.

1836 Texans defend the Alamo.

1838 Cherokee Nation is forced west on the "Trail of Tears."

1846 Harriet Tubman conducts the Underground Railroad.

1848 Gold is discovered in California.

SCIENCE & INVENTIONS

1800 Count Volta of Italy invents the first battery.

1802 Robert Fulton builds the first steamboat.

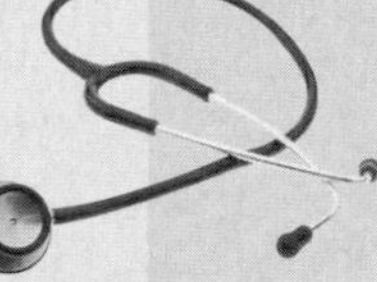

1810 Peter Durand invents the tin can.

1814 First plastic surgery is performed in England.

1816 Reneé Laënnec invents the first stethoscope.

1824 Englishman Joseph Aspdin patents Portland cement.

1824 Joseph Niépce takes the first permanent photograph.

1829 Louis Braille invents Braille printing.

1834 Louis Braille perfects a letter system for the blind.

1836 Samuel Morse invents telegraph.

1847 Joseph Fry invents the candy bar.

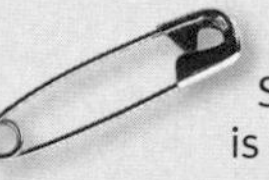

184 Safety pi is invente

LITERATURE & THE ARTS

1800 Romantic poet William Wadsworth's *Lyrical Ballads, with Other Poems* is published.

1804 The first book of children's poems is published.

1814 Francis Scott Key composes "The Star Spangled Banner."

1814 Goya paints *The Third of May* depicting the execution of Spanish citizens.

1814 Beethoven, though deaf, completes his Ninth Symphony.

1818 Percy Bysshe Shelley's "Ozmandias" is published.

1826 James Fenimore Cooper publishes *The Last of the Mohicans*.

1828 *Webster's Dictionary* is published.

1830 *Godey's Lady's Book* (periodical) begins.

1837 Ralph Waldo Emerson's "N first expresses the philoso of transcendentalism.

184 The first issue of *The Chicago Tribune* appeared.

U.S. POPULATION:

1800	1810	1820	1830	1840
5,308,080	7,240,102	9,638,453	12,860,702	17,063,353

1850 1860 1870 1880 1890

1861 Civil War begins at Fort Sumter.

1869 Transcontinental railroad is completed in Utah.

1871 Bismarck's policies make possible a united Germany.

1880 President Garfield is assassinated.

1890 The deaths of 300 Lakota and Paiute men, women, and children at Wounded Knee, South Dakota mark the end of the "Indian Wars."

1853 National Council of Colored People (NCCP) is founded.

1863 Lincoln issues the Emancipation Proclamation.

1871 Great Chicago fire destroys the downtown area.

1872 Yellowstone becomes the world's first national park.

1865 Civil War ends. The 13th amendment to the Constitution ends slavery.

1876 Custer defeated at Little Big Horn.

1876 National Baseball League formed.

1898 U.S. defeats Spain in the Spanish-American War.

1850 Levi Strauss makes the first blue jeans.

1860 Jean Lenoir builds internal combustion engine.

1873 Joseph Glidden invents barbed wire.

1893 Charles and Frank Duryea build the first successful U.S. gasoline-powered automobile.

1851 Isaac Singer begins selling the first commercially successful sewing machine.

1862 Alexander Parks invents first man-made plastic.

1876 Alexander Graham Bell patents the telephone.

1877 Emile Berliner invents the flat record player.

1896 Marconi invents wireless radio.

1866 Alfred Nobel invents dynamite.

1856 Louis Pasteur invents pasteurization.

1869 Chewing gum is patented.

1879 Thomas Edison invents the light bulb.

1898 Pierre and Marie Curie discover polonium and radium

1850 Nathaniel Hawthorne releases his novel *The Scarlet Letter*.

1859 Charles Dickens' *A Tale of Two Cities* is published.

1850 Sojourner Truth writes her memoirs entitled *The Narrative of Sojourner Truth: A Northern Slave*.

1854 Henry David Thoreau's *Walden* is published.

1855 Walt Whitman self-publishes first edition of *Leaves of Grass*.

1866 Dostoevsky's *Crime and Punishment* is published in a journal over a 12 month period.

1872-73 Impressionist painter Claude Monet completes *Impression Sunrise*.

1874 The first Impressionist painting exhibit is held in Paris.

1885 A first volume of Emily Dickinson's poems are published four years after her death

1896 John Philip Sousa writes "Stars and Stripes Forever."

1889 Postimpressionist painter Vincent Van Gogh completes *The Starry Night*.

1884 Samuel Clemens' *Adventures of Huckleberry Finn* is published.

1891 A new form of music called jazz is born.

23,191,876 31,443,321 38,558,371 50,189,209 62,979,766

1900 1905 1910 1915 1920

U.S. & WORLD HISTORY

1900-1901
Boxer Rebellion in China is defeated by European and U.S. forces.

1900
Women allowed to compete in the Olympics for the first time.

1900
American Baseball League is formed.

1906
A massive earthquake devastates much of San Francisco

1909
National Association for the Advancement of Colored People (NAACP) is founded.

1911
Chinese unite as the Republic of China.

1912
Titanic sinks.

1914
Panama Canal opens.

1914
World War I begins.

1917
U.S. enters World War I.

1918
Russian Revolution begins; World War I ends.

1920
Women receive the right to vote.

1920
Prohibition begins.

SCIENCE & INVENTIONS

1900
First mass-market camera—The Brownie

1901
Walter Reed discovers yellow fever is carried by mosquitoes.

1903
Orville and Wilbur Wright make the first successful airplane flight.

1904
The telephone answering machine is invented.

1904
New York City opens its subway system.

1905
Einstein publishes his Theory of Relativity.

1911
Marie Curie becomes first person to win two Nobel prizes.

1912
Motorized movie cameras replace hand-cranked cameras.

1913
Henry Ford establishes assembly line for automobiles.

1915
Coast-to-coast telephone system is established.

1918
Worldwide flu epidemic kills 20 million.

1920
First radio station, KDKA, is founded in Pittsburgh.

1921
Vaccine for tuberculosis is discovered.

1922
Insulin treatment for diabetes is discovered.

LITERATURE & THE ARTS

1900
Broadway becomes the centerpiece for American musical theater.

1900
An estimated 1,800 magazines are published in the U.S.

1901
Booker T. Washington's autobiography, *Up from Slavery*, is released.

1902
Anton Chekov publishes his play *Three Sisters*.

1905
Picasso's "Still Life with Chair Caning" introduces a new art form, cubism.

1906
Upton Sinclair's *The Jungle* exposes unsanitary practices in the meat-processing industry.

1908
Christian Science Monitor begins publication.

1910
The first live remote broadcasts are the operas *Cavalleria Rusticana* and *Pagliacci*.

1913
Boys Life magazine is published by the Boy Scouts.

1916
Robert Frost's collection *Mountain Interval* is published.

1916
Poet Carl Sandburg's *Chicago Poems* are published.

1917
The first African American studio, The Lincoln Motion Picture Company, is founded.

1922
T.S. Eliot's *The Waste Land* is published.

1923
Irish poet William Bulter Yeats awarded Nobel Prize in Literature.

1923
Bessie Smith, "Empress of the Blues," records her first record.

U.S. POPULATION:

1900	1910	1920
76,212,168	92,228,496	106,021,537

1925 1930 1935 1940 1945

1926
Students take the first SAT exam.

1927
Charles Lindbergh 1st to fly solo across the Atlantic to Europe.

1927
Ghandi leads revolt against Britain in India.

1929
Wall Street stock market crashes leading to the Great Depression.

1931
Dust Bowl begins forcing many to abandon their farms and move west.

1933
Franklin Roosevelt wins presidency—promises to end the Depression.

1933
Amelia Earhart 1st woman to fly solo across the Atlantic.

1933
Prohibition is repealed.

1939
World War II begins after Germany invades Poland.

1941
U.S. enters World War II after Japanese bomb Pearl Harbor.

1942
The Battle of Midway ends Japan's expansionism.

1945
World War II ends.

1945
United Nations is formed.

1947
India and Pakistan gain independence from Great Britain.

1949
Communists gain control in China.

1925
The first televised image is broadcast in London. (a dollar sign).

1926
John Baird demonstrates his television system.

1928
GE builds a 3- x 4-inch television screen.

1928
Alexander Fleming discovers penicillin.

1930
Analog computer is invented at MIT.

1931
Workers complete the Empire State Building, the tallest in the world.

1932
The 8mm movie camera is sold to the public.

1933
Albert Einstein immigrates to the U.S.

1935
Radar is invented.

1938
Modern-type ballpoint pens are developed.

1938
First photocopy machine is produced.

1939
Dr. Charles Drew sets up the first blood bank.

1940
Enrico Fermi develops nuclear reactor.

1945
The atomic bomb is invented.

1945
Percy Spencer invents the microwave oven (first one sold in 1947).

1947
Chuck Yeager flies faster than the speed of sound.

1947
The first transistor is invented in Bell Labs.

1925
F. Scott Fitzgerald releases *The Great Gatsby.*

1927
Thornton Wilder publishes *The Bridge of San Luis Rey.*

1927
First "talking movie," *The Jazz Singer*, is made.

1927
Virginia Woolf's novel *To the Lighthouse* is published.

1930
Grant Wood paints *American Gothic.*

1931
Surrealist painter Salvador Dali completes *The Persistence of Memory.*

1932
Painter Georgia O'Keeffe completes *White Trumpet Flower.*

1932
Aldous Huxley's *Brave New World* is published.

1937
Theodore Geisel begins writing "Dr. Seuss" books.

1938
Thorton Wilder produces the play *Our Town.*

1939
Steinbeck's *Grapes of Wrath* is published.

1940
Ernest Hemingway's *For Whom the Bell Tolls* is published.

1946
Dylan Thomas's "Fern Hill" is published.

1947
Anne Frank's *Diary of a Young Girl* is published.

123,202,624 **132,164,569**

1950	1955	1960	1965	1970

U.S. & WORLD HISTORY

1950 United States enters Korean War.

1953 Korean War ends.

1954 U.S. Supreme Court bars racial segregation in public schools.

1955 Rosa Parks refuses to follow segregation rules on Montgomery bus.

1959 Alaska becomes 49th state.

1959 Hawaii becomes 50th state.

1962 Cesar Chavez starts the National Farm Workers Association.

1963 Martin Luther King, Jr., delivers the "I Have a Dream" speech.

1965 U.S. combat troops sent to Vietnam.

1968 Martin Luther King, Jr., is assassinated.

1969 Neil Armstrong and Buzz Aldrin are the first men on the moon.

1971 War between India and Pakistan leads to the creation of Bangladesh.

SCIENCE & INVENTIONS

1951 Fluoridated water discovered to prevent tooth decay.

1953 David Warren invents flight recorder black box.

1953 Transistor radios are invented.

1954 Jonas Salk develops the polio vaccine.

1957 Russia launches first satellite, *Sputnik 1*.

1958 Stereo long-playing records are produced.

1960 First laser is invented.

1961 Soviet Yuri Gagarin is the first human in space, and first to orbit the earth.

1963 Cassette music tapes are developed.

1967 Cholesterol discovered as a cause of heart disease.

1968 First U.S. heart transplant is performed.

1971 Space probe *Mariner* maps surface of Mars.

1974 Public is given access to the Internet.

1973 First cell phone call is placed.

LITERATURE & THE ARTS

1951 Roger and Hanmerstein's *The King and I* debuts on Broadway.

1954 William Golding's *Lord of the Flies* is published.

1951 J.D. Salinger's *Catcher in the Rye* is published.

1952 Samuel Becket's play *Waiting for Godot* is first published.

1952 Ralph Elison's *Invisible Man* is published.

1957 Elvis Presley is the most popular rock 'n' roll musician in U.S.

1960 A revival of folk music begins.

1960 Folk artist Grandma Moses paints "Waiting for Christmas."

1960 Harper Lee's *To Kill a Mockingbird* is published.

1962 Rachel Carson's *Silent Spring* adds strength to the environmental movement.

1964 The Beatles appear on *The Ed Sullivan Show*.

1966 *Star Trek* series begins.

1968 Pop artist Andy Warhol paints his famous soup can.

1969 Kurt Vonnegut's *Slaughterhouse Five* is published.

1970 The movie *Catch-22*, based on Joseph Heller's novel, is released.

1972 *Ms.* magazine begins.

U.S. POPULATION:

151,325,798 (1950)

179,323,175 (1960)

203,302,031 (1970)

1975 1980 1985 1990 1995

1975
Vietnam War ends.

1976
Earthquake in China causes 240,000 deaths.

1976
U.S. celebrates its bicentennial.

1981
Sandra Day O'Connor becomes first female Supreme Court justice.

1981
U.S. hostages return from Iran after 444 days.

1989
Berlin Wall is torn down.

1990
East and West Germany are united.

1991
Persian Gulf War begins.

1992
Bill Clinton is elected president, the first of the Baby Boomer generation.

1991
Restructuring of Soviet Union occurs.

1994
Republicans gain control of the House for the first time in 40 years.

1994
Nelson Mandela elected president of South Africa.

1995
Truck bomb destroys a federal building in Oklahoma City.

1997
Hong Kong becomes part of China.

1998
India and Pakistan test nuclear weapons.

1976
The *Concorde* becomes the first commercial supersonic passenger plane.

1977
First personal computer is introduced.

1980
Sony introduces first camcorder.

1981
Scientists identify AIDS.

1983
Sally Ride becomes first U.S. woman in space.

1984
First digital camera is introduced.

1986
The space shuttle *Challenger* explodes.

1991
World Wide Web is launched.

1991
Concerned scientists report a hole in earth's ozone layer.

October 1990

1997
First DVD player is sold in the U.S.

1998
John Glenn, the first U.S. astronaut in space, becomes the oldest person to travel in space.

1999
First adult sheep is cloned.

1999
Scientists map the first human chromosome.

1975
Jorge Luis Borges publishes *The Book of Sand.*

1976
Alex Haley's *Roots* is published.

1977
The first *Star Wars* movie overwhelms the box office.

1982
The book *Schindler's List* is released.

1987
Tom Wolf's *Bonfire of the Vanities* is published.

1987
Toni Morrison's *Beloved* is published.

1989
Amy Tan's *Joy Luck Club* is published.

1991
Sandra Cisneros's *The House on Mango Street* is published.

1994
Zlata's Diary: A Child's Life in Sarajevo, by a Bosnian teenager, becomes a best seller in the U.S.

1997
Mitch Albon's *Tuesdays with Morrie* is published.

1997
The movie *Titanic* breaks the all-time box office sales record.

226,542,203

248,709,873

2000 **2002** **2004** **2006** **2008**

U.S. & WORLD HISTORY

2000
Colin Powell is the first African American secretary of state.

2000
More than 5 billion e-mails are sent in the U.S.

2001
George W. Bush becomes the first son of a president to take office since John Quincy Adams in 1825.

2001
The 9/11 attack destroys the World Trade Center.

2001
The U.S. invades Afghanistan, a base for the terrorists.

2003
Hispanics become the largest minority group in the U.S.

2004
Terrorists blow up a Spanish train.

2004
A tsunami in the Indian Ocean kills more than 300,000.

2005
Pope John Paul II, third longest reigning pope, dies.

2005
Condolezza Rice is the first African American woman to serve as secretary of state.

2006
Democrats regain control of the House and Senate after 12 years.

2006
U.S. population reaches 300 million people.

2007
Nancy Pelosi becomes first woman Speaker of the House.

SCIENCE & INVENTIONS

2000
The U.S. Food and Drug Administration approves a new blood-sugar monitor.

2001
Federal funding permitted for existing embryonic stem-cell lines.

2002
Steve Fossett becomes the first balloonist to fly solo around the world.

2002
Camera cell phones are offered to the U.S. public.

2003
Scientists clone a white-tailed deer.

2003
Hybrid cars are introduced.

2004
SpaceShipOne makes first privately funded suborbital flight.

2004
Number of U.S. cell phone users surpasses 171 million.

2004
Medication given by sound waves, not injected.

2005
Airbus unveils largest passenger plane (up to 840 passengers).

2005
NASA and several European space agencies land a probe on Titan, Saturn's largest moon.

2006
Scientists debate whether Pluto is a planet.

2007
More people read news on the Internet than in newspapers.

LITERATURE & THE ARTS

2002
Attack of the Clones is the first big budget film shot with digital cameras.

2002
Halle Berry is first black woman to win an Oscar for best actress.

2003
Hip-hop music becomes the most popular music among teens.

2004
Marco Evaristti paints the tip of an iceberg using 790 gallons of red paint. The work is entitled *Ice Cube*.

2005
Christo and Jeanne-Claude, artists who wrap buildings and landscapes in cloth, begin *The Gates* project in New York City.

2005
John Grisham's *The Broken* tops the best-seller list.

2006
Rembrandt 400 commemorates the 400th anniversary of the artist's birth.

2006
Donald Hall named Poet Laureate.

285,000,000 **300,000,000**

Acknowledgements

***Write for College* is a reality because of the help and advice of our team of students, educators, writers, editors, and designers:** Steven J. Augustyn, Laura Bachman, Ron Bachman, April Barrons, Gary Baughn, Colleen Belmont, Evelyn Curley, Chris Erickson, Hillary Gammons, Mariellen Hanrahan, Tammy Hintz, Judy Kerkhoff, Rob King, Lois Krenzke, Mark Lalumondier, Joyce Becker Lee, Colleen McCarthy, Michele Order Litant, Kevin Nelson, Sue Paro, Susan Rogalski, Janae Sebranek, Lester Smith, Richard Spencer, Julie Spicuzza, John Van Rys, Randy VanderMey, Jean Varley, and Claire Ziffer.

Credits

Photos

© 2007 JupiterImages Corporation: Guidelines, Inside Info icon, Reading for Better Writing icon, Tips icon, Historical Time Line photos (pp. 606–616)

istockphoto.com: Bottom Line icon

shutterstock.com: Note icon

A

B

D

E

S

U

V

W

Y